# AN
# INDEX TO
# ENGLISH

**FOURTH EDITION**

# AN
# INDEX TO
# ENGLISH

**Porter G. Perrin**

**Fourth Edition**
revised by

**Karl W. Dykema**
Youngstown University

**Wilma R. Ebbitt**
University of Chicago

SCOTT, FORESMAN AND COMPANY

I want to thank the many teachers
in the Division of Language and Literature at Youngstown University
who have helped me with their advice and suggestions, particularly
Professors Clyde T. Hankey and
Christine R. Dykema, my wife.
                                    *K.W.D.*

I am happy to acknowledge debts
to students, to colleagues—past and
present—and, most of all, to James
Sledd.
                                    *W.R.E.*

Except in a few instances where the
publishers requested credit lines
with the selections themselves, the
courtesy of author and publishers in
granting permission for quoting passages from their works is specifically
acknowledged on pages 470-471.

# Preface

*An Index to English* is the second section of *Writer's Guide and Index to English,* Fourth Edition (1965), adapted for separate publication. It combines a glossary of usage with a handbook of grammar, syntax, mechanics, and style. We believe that as a separate text the *Index* will meet the needs of a great variety of writing courses.

Because it has continued to meet with general approval, the format of the *Index* has been retained through its several editions. In this new edition entries have been brought up to date; some new ones have been added; a few old ones that seemed to have outlived their usefulness have been dropped. The book opens with "The varieties of English" (a slightly modified version of Chapter 1 of the complete *Writer's Guide and Index to English*). This discussion provides the framework and rationale for the treatment of usage in the rest of the book. In general, any shift in this edition of the *Index* has been in the direction of helping the student *as writer.*

The publishers wish to express once more their gratitude to those teachers of English whose advice and criticism contributed to the success of the fourth edition of *Writer's Guide and Index to English:* to Jayne Harder of the University of Florida and to Paul Roberts for their comprehensive critical studies; and to Dudley Bailey, University of Nebraska; George E. Jones, Bloomfield College; Robert Hall, University of South Florida; Edgar W. Lacy and Ednah S. Thomas, University of Wisconsin; T. G. McGuire, Los Angeles Valley College; Louis T. Milic, Columbia University; C. E. Nelson, Washington State University; Robert A. Peters, University of Idaho; Paul Beekman Taylor, Brown University; and Howard A. Wilson, Knox College for their criticism of the plan for revision. The comments of these teachers guided the authors in performing a difficult task. We believe—and the acceptance of the fourth edition would indicate—that the task was performed with success.

The Publishers

# Contents

The *Index,* pages 32-467, contains articles in alphabetical arrangement that fall roughly into four categories:

**a Articles on particular words and constructions** such as *continual—continuous; *fiancé, fiancée; *get, got; *like—as; *plenty; *shall—will; *so . . . that; *very

**b Articles for correction and revision of papers** indicated by longhand abbreviations before the entry word

**c Articles on English grammar** giving definitions and examples of such matters as *Case, *Conjunction, *Plurals of nouns, *Principal parts of verbs

**d Articles on various facts of language** such as *American and British usage, *Foreign words in English, *Linguistics

# Bibliography

The following works have been most useful in gathering the material for this book. They are frequently referred to, usually by author's name only. References to other sources are given in full in the separate entries.

*American Speech*, New York, Columbia University Press. A periodical, founded in 1925, containing much direct observation of current American usage, especially vocabularies of particular regions and vocations.

Baugh, Albert C., *A History of the English Language*, New York, Appleton-Century-Crofts, 1935; revised 1957. A substantial and readable history of the language.

Bloomfield, Leonard, *Language*, New York, Holt, Rinehart and Winston, 1933. A basic work on the general principles of language study.

Bryant, Margaret M., *Current American Usage*, New York, Funk & Wagnalls, 1962. The most recent reliable work on the subject.

Carroll, John B., *The Study of Language*, Cambridge, Harvard University Press, 1953. Chapter 2 is a brief and clear introduction to linguistics.

Curme, George O., *Syntax*, Boston, Heath, 1931; and *Parts of Speech and Accidence*, Boston, Heath, 1935. A very full grammar of modern English, with much historical material. (The second book is referred to as Curme, *Parts of Speech*)

Fowler, H. W., *A Dictionary of Modern English Usage*, Oxford University Press, 1926. Although based on British usage and somewhat dated, still a readable and often illuminating book. A new edition, revised by Sir Ernest Gowers, was published in 1965.

Fries, C. C., *American English Grammar*, New York, Appleton-Century-Crofts (NCTE Monograph No. 10), 1940. A number of points of grammar discussed with special reference to differences between levels of usage. (Referred to as Fries, *AEG*)

Fries, C. C., *The Structure of English*, New York, Harcourt, Brace and World, 1952. Presents a realignment of the parts of speech and a program of sentence analysis based on this realignment. (Referred to as Fries, *Structure*)

Gleason, H. A., *An Introduction to Descriptive Linguistics*, New York, Holt, Rinehart and Winston, 1955; revised 1961. Exactly what its title implies.

Hall, J. Lesslie, *English Usage*, Chicago, Scott, Foresman and Company, 1917. Historical discussion of 141 locutions on which usage has been divided or questioned.

Jespersen, Otto, *Essentials of English Grammar*, New York, Holt, Rinehart and Winston, 1933. An abridgment of Jespersen's seven-volume *Modern English Grammar*, the most complete description of English available.

Kenyon, John S., and Thomas A. Knott, *A Pronouncing Dictionary of American English*, Springfield, G. & C. Merriam Co., 1944; revised 1953. The most systematic guide to American pronunciation of individual words.

Marckwardt, Albert H., and Fred G. Walcott, *Facts About Current English Usage*, New York, Appleton-Century-Crofts (NCTE Monograph No. 7), 1938. Includes the data of the Sterling A. Leonard study (1932) of debatable and divided usage, with additional information.

Mencken, H. L., *The American Language*, 4th Edition, New York, Knopf, 1936; *Supplement I* (1945); *Supplement II* (1948). A mass of material on various varieties of American English, with commentary and references to further sources. References in this book are to the one-volume abridged edition by Raven I. McDavid, Jr., (New York, 1963).

Pooley, Robert C. *Teaching English Usage*, New York, Appleton-Century-Crofts (NCTE Monograph No. 16), 1946. Discussion of a number of debatable locutions, with evidence and recommendations for teaching.

Roberts, Paul, *Understanding Grammar*, New York, Harper and Row, 1954. A good, brief systematic English grammar.

Robertson, Stuart, *The Development of Modern English*, Englewood Cliffs, Prentice-Hall, 1934; revised 1954 by Frederic G. Cassidy. Gives the background of many points of current syntax.

Skillin, Marjorie, and Robert M. Gay, *Words into Type,* New York, Appleton-Century-Crofts, 1948; revised 1964. A detailed manual of publishers' style.

Summey, George Jr., *American Punctuation,* New York, Ronald Press Co., 1949. The most thorough and authoritative treatment of punctuation.

*United States Government Printing Office Style Manual*, Washington, Government Printing Office, revised edition, 1953. Detailed directions for preparing government publications, most of which are generally applicable. (Referred to as *GPO Manual*)

The University of Chicago Press, *A Manual of Style*, 11th edition, Chicago, The University of Chicago Press, 1949. The stylebook of a distinguished conservative publishing house.

# THE VARIETIES
# OF ENGLISH

Confidence and effectiveness in the use of English come in part from an accurate knowledge of the possibilities of language. We need to know how to choose what is most effective for us, and we need to practice until the sort of English we want to use comes easily and becomes a habit. The habit of using good English comes mainly from reading the work of good writers and listening to good speakers, giving conscious attention to how they gain their effects. But to observe language profitably and to use it effectively, we need some knowledge of how it works and some specific guidance in drawing on its resources. A composition course and a book like this can make us aware of the choices the language offers and can help us make the right ones for our purposes.

We all use English with ease and with a good deal of effectiveness in situations where we feel at home. But when we meet new people, perhaps from a different social circle or a different part of the country, or when we have to give a talk or write an important letter, a paper for a college course, or something that will be printed, we may become acutely conscious of *how* we are speaking or writing. Fortunately the greater part of our language raises no questions; it can be used at any time, under any circumstances. The ordinary names of things (*dog, dresses, politics*) and of acts (*walking, swimming, voting*) and thousands of other words are in general use; most of the forms of words are standardized (*theirs, people's, lived*); and the order of words in phrases and sentences is pretty well fixed. But some questions about usage do come up. Sometimes we have to make choices among words and forms and constructions, and because those choices contribute to the impression our talk or piece of writing makes, they are important.

These questions about English usage arise chiefly because there are different varieties of the language that do not fit equally well into every situation. The questions may be simple: Is it all right to say "It's *me*," "Go *slow*," "It's *real* interesting," or "It's *laying* on the table"? Does *phony* fit in this sentence? Is *solon* better than *congressman* here? Or the questions may be more complicated: Should this be one sentence or two? Do these words express what I mean? How can I show the connection between these ideas? What is the best order for these ideas?

The answers to some of these questions are clear-cut and definite, but the answers to others vary with the circumstances. English, like every other widely used language, is not on single set of words and constructions, everywhere and always the same; it is a variety of such sets that have much in common but are still far from uniform. This variety is stressed in this book for two reasons: to show you the immense resources our language offers and to help you form habits of easy and automatic choice in your actual usage—habits that will be appropriate to the varying situations you meet. A mature use of English means speaking and writing the sort of English that is appropriate to the situation in which you find yourself, for *English is not just "good"; it is good under certain conditions.*

## Sources of variation in English

The varieties of English that you find around you are all natural growths, and specialists in the study of language are able to describe and in some degree account for them. Understanding the reasons for the differences will give you perspective on the language and will guide you in making some choices.

*Variations due to time* • Because change has characterized every language whose history has been traced, it appears to be an inevitable trait of every living language. Ordinarily the changes are slow and barely noticeable—slightly different pronunciations, new shadings in the meaning of words, and gradual shifts in grammatical constructions. You know from reading older literature that English has changed greatly in the centuries during which it has been written.[1] A play by Shakespeare needs a good many notes to tell us what some of the words meant to the people who first heard the plays over 350

---

[1]For further discussion, see *Index* entries *Change in language and *English language; histories of the English language, especially Baugh (books cited by name of author only will be found in the Bibliography, pp. viii-1); Otto Jespersen, *Growth and Structure the English Language* (various editions); Thomas Pyles, *The Origins and Development of the English Language* (New York, 1964); *Oxford English Dictionary; Dictionary of American English.*

years ago. If we go back far enough, English looks like a foreign language, though we may recognize in the older forms the ancestors of some of our current words. Language changes as naturally and as steadily as other social habits do.

Words, forms, or constructions no longer in use are called *obsolete*. No one today refers to a *bottle* of hay, or uses *can* in the sense of *know*, or *coy* in the sense of *quiet*. Usages now disappearing from the language are called *archaic*. Fashion has just about driven out *betrothed* in favor of *fiancée*. Archaic expressions survive in some situations, such as the *thou* and *saith* of church services. A few archaic or even obsolete words are used in set phrases, such as "much *ado*" and "in good *stead*," and many are preserved in uneducated or dialect speech after they have disappeared from other varieties of English. *Learn* in the sense of *teach, you was* in the singular, *he don't,* and the *double negative[1] were all once in general and reputable use. It is often hard to tell when a word or construction is sufficiently uncommon to be called archaic; a good many words not so labeled in all dictionaries are really used very rarely (like *betimes, deem, doff*).

Because we learn our language chiefly by imitating what we hear and read, obsolete and archaic usage offers few problems, but occasionally in trying to "improve" his language a student will use an archaic expression, and sometimes a strained effort at humor produces words like *quoth* or *wight*.

We cannot know the whole history of our language, nor do we need to, but realizing that it has a history should help us adjust to reading older literature and explain many of the peculiarities of the current language (in spelling and verb forms, for instance) that we need to consider in a reference book such as this.

Words, constructions, and styles keep changing. Recent years have seen the addition of many words (*cosmonaut, drunkometer, isometrics, thalidomide*), names for scores of new chemical compounds, and so on,[2] the dropping of some from general use, and a tendency toward more concise idioms and constructions.

While new words for new things are natural additions to our vocabulary, it is wise to hesitate before adopting new words for things that have already been named. This is especially true of the abstract words (such as *recreational facilities, urban redevelopment, causal factors*) that higher education and occu-

---

[1]References to *Index* articles are indicated by an asterisk (*) .
[2]The journal *American Speech* treats many new words as they appear, and the annual supplementary volumes to the principal encyclopedias have lists of such words.

pational specialization seem to be substituting for the common words for some activities and situations.

New words have sometimes made their way into literary usage rather slowly, but most writers today use a new word whenever it is appropriate. It is important for a writer to make the fullest possible use of the current language. It is the language of his contemporaries, the language they understand best, the language they will expect to read and hear. When you write naturally, from your observation of the language and your feeling for it, you will normally write current English, and you should aim for no other kind.

*Variations due to place* • No language is spoken in exactly the same way in all parts of the country or countries in which it is used. We can easily spot an Englishman because some of his pronunciations and some of his words and constructions are different from ours. (See *American and British usage.) We can also very often tell what part of the United States a person comes from by listening to him talk. Differences in words, pronunciation, stress, phrasing, and grammatical habits that are characteristic of fairly definite regions are called *regional dialects.* Put another way, a regional dialect is speech that does not attract attention to itself in the region where it is used but does outside that area. A pronunciation, a word or meaning of a word, or an idiom that is current in one region but calls attention to itself in others is called a *provincialism* or a *localism.*

Dialects are not peculiar to backward regions, for the "Oxford accent" forms a minor dialect, and the natives of Boston and of New York speak differently from each other. Nor are dialects the result of lack of education or social standing. An educated Westerner will speak somewhat differently from a Southerner or New Englander of a similar degree and quality of education. A dialect may retain traits of the differing British dialects spoken by early settlers or may show the influence of foreign languages spoken by large numbers of people in the region, as in German sections of Pennsylvania or in the Scandinavian sections of the Middle West. It may show the influence of a neighboring language or of the language of an earlier settlement: the dialect of the Southwest, for example, contains Spanish elements, the dialect of New Orleans, French.

There are fewer differences among the dialects of the United States than would be expected in a country of such size, many fewer than exist among the dialects in much smaller Great

Britain.[1] The relative freedom of movement of the American people, transportation facilities that have prevented even the Rocky Mountains from marking a linguistic boundary, the educational system, the circulation of books and national magazines, and more recently radio and television—all these factors have helped people who are thousands of miles apart to speak substantially the same language. But words peculiar to a local terrain or to local occupations will probably survive, since they fill a real need and usually have no equivalents in other dialects. The frequent use of localisms on radio and television and in stories may help make one region more tolerant of the language of others, and it may very well introduce into general use words formerly characteristic of a particular locality.

Three major speech areas of the United States have been traditionally recognized: *Eastern* (New England and a strip of eastern New York), *Southern* (south of Pennsylvania and the Ohio River, extending west of the Mississippi into Texas), and *Northern* (extending from New Jersey on the Atlantic, through the Middle West and the whole of our Pacific Coast), also called *General American* or *Western*. Insofar as educated Americans distinguish regional varieties of pronunciation, they do it on this basis. But as a result of the work being done on *The Linguistic Atlas of the United States and Canada,* the boundaries are being more exactly drawn, subdivisions indicated, and lines of influence between areas shown. The major speech divisions are called *Northern, Midland,* and *Southern,* and their boundaries have been projected to include the entire country. Within the three main divisions there are important subdivisions; for example, the Eastern New England type of Northern differs appreciably from the North Central type, which extends from New York State—excluding New York City—west through Iowa to the Dakotas. And other regional varieties exist within each of the three main areas, as in the Ozarks or in New York City, but the differences between the speech of California and Illinois are less noticeable than the

---

[1]See Baugh, Ch. 11; Bloomfield, Ch. 19; *Dictionary of American English;* Otto Jespersen, *Mankind, Nation and Individual from a Linguistic Point of View* (Oslo, 1925); G. P. Krapp, *The English Language in America* (New York, 1925), pp. 225-273; Mencken. Many articles in *American Speech* record facts of various American dialects. Linguaphone album L-19 has recordings of twenty-four American dialects. For some results of work on the *Linguistic Atlas,* see Hans Kurath, *Handbook of the Linguistic Geography of New England* (Providence, 1939), *A Word Geography of the Eastern United States* (Ann Arbor, 1949); E. B. Atwood, *Survey of Verb Forms in the Eastern United States* (Ann Arbor, 1953); Hans Kurath and Raven I. McDavid, Jr., *The Pronunciation of English in the Atlantic States* (Ann Arbor, 1961); and Jean Malmstrom and Annabel Ashley, *Dialects—U.S.A.* (Champaign, 1963).

differences between either of these and, say, Georgia or Massachusetts. Roughly one twelfth of the population speaks what is generally called Eastern, one sixth Southern, and three fourths Northern or General American.[1]

A professional student of American English observes many differences in speech that the ordinary person might miss, but we are all aware of some of them. Some New Englanders use broad *a*, as in /äsk/, /gräss/, /päst/, where most Americans have short *a*; they usually slight *r*, as in /bän/ for *barn*.[2] A Westerner has a distinct, perhaps even a prolonged, *r* after vowels as well as before. Like most Americans he has /ä/ for the *o* in *hot, lot, cot*. Like many Americans he rounds the *o* in *hog, frog, log*. Beginning in New York State, most speakers in the Northern region do not distinguish *hoarse* and *horse*, *mourning* and *morning*, pronouncing /ōr/ (like the word *ore*) in all. A Southerner from the lowlands (as distinguished from the hill country) does not sound *r* after vowels (for example, *suh* for *sir*, /dōä/ or /dō/ for *door*). The long *i* both in the lowlands and the hills may suggest /ä/, as in the popular spelling *Ah* for *I*. Southerners from the hills usually pronounce *r* after vowels—as all fanciers of hillbilly music know. Each region—Eastern, Southern, and Northern—also has its characteristic stress and speech rhythm.

In vocabulary, different words will be found for many common objects. Which of the following is used in your locality, or is some other word used?

bag—sack—poke
gumshoe—overshoe—rubber
piazza—porch—stoop—veranda
seesaw—teeter-totter—teeterboard
cottage cheese—clabber or crud or curd or dutch or pot or smear or
    sour milk cheese—cruds—curds—smear or smier case
doughnut—fried cake—cruller—fat cake—nut cake—cookie

The map on the next page shows several words that are used within the relatively close limits of New England for the common earthworm: *angleworm, angledog, easworm* (for *eastworm*), *fish worm*. In other regions it is known by some of these names and by others as well.

Besides these different names for common objects, creatures, and things, each region has special words for local features of the landscape or for occupations that are more or less local:

---

[1]For a map showing the subdivisions, see Charles K. Thomas, *An Introduction to the Phonetics of American English,* 2nd ed. (New York, 1958).
[2]See *Pronunciation for key to phonemic transcription.

Dialect Chart for "Earthworm"

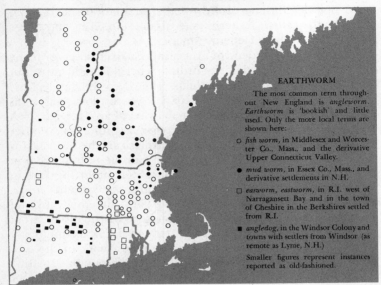

EARTHWORM

The most common term throughout New England is *angleworm*.
*Earthworm* is 'bookish' and little
used. Only the more local terms are
shown here:

○ *fish worm*, in Middlesex and Worcester Co., Mass., and the derivative
Upper Connecticut Valley.

● *mud worm*, in Essex Co., Mass., and
derivative settlements in N.H.

□ *easworm, eastworm*, in R.I. west of
Narragansett Bay and in the town
of Cheshire in the Berkshires settled
from R.I.

■ *angledog*, in the Windsor Colony and
towns with settlers from Windsor (as
remote as Lyme, N.H.)

Smaller figures represent instances
reported as old-fashioned.

After Chart 1, *Handbook of the Linguistic Geography of New England*, p.38

*coulee, hogback, sierra, mesa; mesquite, piñon; mule skinner, vara* (a surveyor's measure in the Southwest). And there are local idioms like the Southern "I'll *carry* [for *take*] you home," or like those for telling time—New Englanders generally say quarter *of* four, Southerners quarter *till* four, and Westerners quarter *to* four.

People's attitudes toward the use of localisms vary greatly. Some people feel that localisms should be weeded out; others believe that a person should retain as much as possible of the flavor of his native speech. It is a problem everyone has to settle for himself. Educated people tend to shed their more conspicuous local pronunciations, but conscious effort to change to a different pattern often results in an unhappy combination of elements from both. Natural, gradual, unconscious change is best.

***Differences between speaking and writing*** • Language is in origin speech; writing came very late in its development, no more than six thousand years ago, whereas speech, we are assured by anthropologists, archaeologists, and linguists, must go back tens of thousands, perhaps hundreds of thousands of years. And this primacy of speech remains in our own experience of language. We learn to listen and speak long before we learn to read and write, and most of us will continue to talk and listen a great deal more than we write and read. But listening and speaking, reading and writing (not to mention the even greater use of language in "thinking," about which we know so little) are related, overlapping skills. In a language like English, with vast amounts of written and printed material, the relations between speaking and writing are complex and so far have not been sufficiently studied to let us discuss them very exactly.

It is clear, however, that writing cannot be treated as merely a simplified and often inadequate transcription of speech. Spelling, especially in more logically spelled languages than English, does quite satisfactorily indicate the sequence of vowels and consonants in words spoken in isolation: c-a-t, d-o-g, b-u-l-l-y, provide pretty good instructions as to what sounds are to be uttered to make the three words. But words are never spoken out of context except in nonsense situations like the reading of spelling lists. In context they are always part of a pattern involving pitch, stress, and rhythm, for which marks of punctuation provide only the barest hints; and the sounds in the words themselves undergo alterations, usually subtle, but occasionally radical. Consider the pronunciations given in the Kenyon-Knott *Pronouncing Dictionary of American English* for the word *and;* there are eleven of them, ranging from the full, emphatic form in "John *and* Oscar" to the nonsyllabic *n* in "butter 'n' eggs." A system of transcription which attempted to indicate faithfully such normal spoken variations would be hopelessly cumbersome.

There are several nonlinguistic reasons why writing has developed some characteristics of its own. Readers are often at a distance and may be strangers, with backgrounds different from the writer's. They will probably read silently, no doubt rapidly, and they will expect to find what they read in a form easy to follow. This is one reason for stressing clearness and precision in writing. Another reason is that writing lies on the page and can be examined closely, while speech goes by rapidly. This has led to establishing standards for the written language which, though they have a fairly wide range, are much more uniform than standards for speech. Most of the details of written form have been developed by printers and publishers, who naturally enough wish for consistency in what they publish, and they enforce the details through copy editors and proofreaders, who tidy up copy to meet the standards. This standardization allows for wide circulation of printed matter, one of its greatest assets. Any writer who presents his copy for others to read is expected to approach (though not to meet in every respect) these standards by writing clearly and following the most definitely established conventions of published writing.

The written or printed word serves two rather different purposes, though too few writers are aware of the distinction. It may be intended as the basis of a spoken utterance or it may serve for silent reading only. (Usually, of course, it should lend itself to both purposes.) If it is primarily meant to be spoken, it is merely a set of cues which provide the raw material of what is to be said, cues which rely heavily on our control of the resources of speech to supply all the variations in voice which transform what is visible into natural talk. Many people can't do this and they read aloud as if reciting a list of disconnected words. They don't get their cues. Such writing makes heavy demands on the reader. Most poetry is, essentially, this kind of writing, and many people find reading poetry to themselves pretty hard going because it was written to be spoken.

Writing which is to be read silently should demand much less from the reader. "Invites Public to Tax School" (a newspaper headline) might puzzle us, at least for a moment, because we don't know whether in speech the heavier stress would come on *tax* or *school*. We wonder why the public should be invited to tax a school; but the news item makes clear that the Internal Revenue Service is inviting the public to attend a "school" on tax information.

Many people assume that what they write is a complete transcription of what they would say. Such a transcription is impossible. Linguists have devised symbols which permit a much fuller transcription of speech than does conventional writing, but even it cannot indicate such subtle things as voice quality and fine gradations of intensity. In any case such a transcription is so complex that reading would have to be relearned and even when mastered would be very slow.

A great deal of what we say is redundant. This term does not refer to the obvious repetitiousness that characterizes so much conversation. It refers to what may be called signals, often unnecessary, like *the, is, in,* etc. When we send a telegram we try to eliminate all the words that are not absolutely essential. "The picture is finished" becomes "Picture finished"; "It will arrive in Boston tomorrow" becomes "Arrive Boston tomorrow." And there are many more such signals, especially of pitch, stress, and timing, some of which have no transcription in conventional writing. Though they are often redundant, they are not always so. Occasionally the whole purpose of an utterance depends on one of them. In a detective story, for example, the narrator gives us the remarks of one of the women in the story; the last sentence reads: " 'I understand it's about a tie-up of Nero Wolfe and Dazzle Dan, having Dan start a detective agency?' " Then the narrator adds this comment: "I put the question mark there, though her inflection left it to me whether to call it a question or merely a statement." (Rex Stout, "The Squirt and the Monkey," *Triple Jeopardy,* p. 125.) The resources of conventional writing cannot transcribe all the speech signals, so the writer has to replace them with a verbal explanation, or phrase his writing to avoid the difficulty.

On the other hand, writing has certain advantages over speech, especially over unrehearsed conversation. Most important is the possibility of revision. When we talk we must get our words out at a tremendous rate, often 200 or 300 a minute. We have little chance to plan what we are to say, to choose just the right words to express our ideas. So we are uneconomical, repetitious, unorganized in our expression. This is not necessarily bad. Discursiveness and digression may lead to a wider exploration of a subject, and a repetitive discussion is easier to follow than a concentrated one. Besides, conversations are likely to be leisurely affairs, and an evening of talk will produce hundreds of thousands of words. But the person who is quite willing to sit through two or three hours of talking about a subject in a congenial social situation will probably be quite unwilling to read the same number of words if they carry the subject no further than the talking did.

When we write we set our own pace. Even our first drafts are likely to be better organized, more economically expressed than our talk would be. And we have unlimited opportunity to rearrange, excise, and rephrase. Writing can, therefore, be better organized, more economical, better worded than speech. It can be, but often it is not. After years of practice we are used to talking. Since our practice in writing is negligible in comparison, we find it hard at first to exploit the advantages of writing.

Some minor devices of writing also differentiate it from speech. In this book the special, limited sense in which certain words are defined is shown by capitalizing them. The sentence on page 24 "Most fiction is General or Informal" would make little sense if heard. But after the definitions of "General" and

"Informal" on the preceding pages, it is evident that it states that most works of fiction are written in the Informal and General varieties of English. Because these terms have been restricted by definition and their limited sense shown by capitalizing them, the statement can be made in six words instead of fourteen.

The grammar of speech differs somewhat from that of writing, at least of edited, publishable writing. The reference of pronouns is less precise; the pronunciation of prepositions is usually unstressed, so that the *of*, for example, in *a couple of birds* is so reduced that a careless transcription of it might be *a couple birds;* only a few connectives are used, especially *and* and *so;* yet we make ourselves clear. Many of the matters marked on student papers are simply such traits of spoken language transferred to paper. Spoken sentences are usually shorter than written, or if they are long, it is because one statement is added to another rather than because clauses are built together with subordinating conjunctions. Because a reader gets no help from sound as the listener does, he needs more guidance in seeing the relationship between the parts of a sentence.

But written English is not a different language from spoken. Most of the differences are in matters of grammar and style that can be tended to in revising a paper. Others stem from the difference in the situation between speaker-and-hearer and writer-and-reader. The writer often has to fill out constructions which the speaker need not. It is usually best to write nearly the same words that you would speak and then to test what you have written by reading it as a stranger might, making sure that you are telling him what you mean so exactly that he can understand it without hearing you say it, and that you are in general following the conventions of printed English.

Probably the best basis for your writing is your more careful speech, reshaped to stand scrutiny on paper. Some languages have entirely different forms for speech and writing, but in English, and especially in present-day English, the relationship is close. We sometimes say someone "talks like a book," meaning that his talk is uncomfortably elaborate or stiff; it is more often a compliment to say "he writes as he talks." Letters and accounts of personal experience are likely to be quite close to speech; most academic work, including term papers for courses, needs to meet the more exacting standards for written communication. A writer must at all times be ready to use as wide a range as possible, drawing on all the resources of spoken and written English that are effective in writing.

***Differences due to situation*** • Many words of similar meaning, though they are in current and general use, cannot be used interchangeably in all situations. Consider these groups:

indigent, impecunious, underprivileged, in want, penniless, poverty-stricken, *poor*, hard up, broke, flat

spent, fatigued, weary, exhausted, *tired*, worn-out, played out, used up, dog tired, all in, pooped

stripling, youth, lad, *boy*, youngster, kid, punk

Similarly, many idioms and constructions represent the same idea but suggest different varieties of speech:

dare not, daren't, *do not dare,* don't dare, dassent

were it not for, if it were not for, *if it was not for,* if it wasn't for, if it wan't for

*Poor, tired,* and *boy, do not dare* and *if it was not for* certainly belong to the central part of the language and might be used by anyone in any circumstance; the same is true of the words near them in these series. But as we move away from these central expressions, the words become somewhat more limited, until those at the ends would be found only in either quite formal or quite informal situations. Probably most of us would not use *indigent, spent, stripling*—they suggest old-fashioned or rather bookish usage. We all might use *broke, all in, kid* in casual company but not when talking to someone on whom we want to make a good impression. These differences are due not to any variation in the central meaning of the words but to the circumstances in which they have been generally used.

There is no well-established system of naming these varieties of English, though they have been often discussed.[1] In this book we recognize two principal varieties, Standard and Nonstandard English; and we divide the first into General, Formal and Informal English. These varieties are defined in the table on pages 30-31 and are elaborated in the next two sections of this chapter.

Although differences are easily observable between these varieties, they should not be thought of as mutually exclusive

---

[1]See, for instance, Bloomfield, pp. 52, 149 ff.; Fries, *AEG*, in which usage is treated according to social varieties; John S. Kenyon, "Cultural Levels and Functional Varieties of English," *College English*, 1948, 10:31-36; Marckwardt and Walcott; Pooley, Ch. 3.

but as relatively different, shading into each other. A passage may be considered Formal because it has a few conspicuous traits characteristic of that variety, and thus a Formal "feel" or "tone," even though the language of most of the passage is in General usage. Although individuals will differ somewhat in deciding where the dividing lines should be drawn, the principal characteristics of the varieties are pretty clear, and the illustrations in the following sections should make it possible to distinguish them.

## Standard English

**General English—unlimited use** • Most speaking and writing situations call for General English, the great central body of words and constructions of our language. In speech we find it in the conversation of educated people and in most talks to general audiences; in writing we see it in letters, in newspapers and magazines, in plays and novels, and in books of all sorts for general circulation—in most of what we read.

General written English lies close to good speech, but it is not speech exactly reproduced, partly because the resources of the written language are somewhat different. The words are likely to be from the central vocabulary, of wide currency in both speech and writing (*roomy* rather than *spacious, rainfall* rather than *precipitation*). They are likely to be concrete, close to experience, referring to things, people, actions, and events more than to abstractions, and familiar to a large number of readers. The constructions reflect those of speech (*look into, give up, take over*), and the sentences are relatively short, made up of one or two clauses without interrupting phrases or involved movement.

General English is especially appropriate to narratives of personal experience and to presentation of people and action, whether in fiction or factual accounts. In the following paragraph, a personal comment by the author of a biography of Columbus, the sentences are short, averaging nineteen words, but not monotonous. With eighteen verbs and six verbals (*shining, to spend*), two bits of conversation, and several phrases that suggest speech (*to check up on, how to get it out*), the passage is clear, fast-moving, and easy to understand.

In 1940, when we were ranging this coast to check up on Columbus, we encountered an old prospector who explained why Veragua had never been properly exploited for gold. Years before, he went up one of the rivers with a partner and an Indian guide. "Where do we find gold?" he asked, after paddling many miles. "Right here!" said the Indian, who pulled out a clasp knife, dug some clay from the river bank and panned out some ten dollars' worth of shining gold grain! The prospector and his partner began at once to plan how to spend their million dollars. They returned to the nearest town for supplies and lumber and built sluice boxes, the product of which should have made them rich. But in the next freshet all their gear was washed down into the Caribbean. That has happened again and again during the last four and a half centuries. There is still "gold in them thar hills," but only the Indians know how to get it out.—SAMUEL ELIOT MORISON, *Christopher Columbus, Mariner,* p. 136

Ideas, too, though they are by nature abstract and are often presented in Formal English for rather restricted groups of readers, may be expressed in General English. The following definition of the word *sign,* a term important in philosophical discussions of meaning, is presented concretely for general readers by Charles Morris, professor of philosophy. Professor Morris's early specific details lead to the generalization at the end. The constructions are simple, the verbs carry a good bit of the meaning (*the way we will dress*), and the sentences are simple, direct, and short, averaging 22 words. (The longest sentence in the entire paragraph, the third, is a series of clauses.)

What do all these events have in common that causes us to lump them together as signs? One core similarity: *they all influence the way we tend to react toward something other than themselves.* The alarm tells us the time, the sight of our face in the mirror informs us about our appearance, the newspaper tells us what has happened in the world, the pressure from the oranges or the odor of eggs determines which one we will select, the note to the milkman tells him how we wish him to act. The appearances of the sky or the words of the weather report influence the way we will dress, the way we will behave outdoors. We do not put on our raincoats indoors nor raise an umbrella between us and the newspaper. We eat not the menu but rather what its printed words stand for. Signs denote something other than themselves, other things or other aspects of the thing of which they are a part. The marks on the newspaper stand for happenings in China; the rate of our pulse beat stands for the condition of our heart. Signs influence our beliefs, our preferences, our feelings, our actions with respect to what they signify. They dispose us to react to something other than themselves in one way rather than another.—CHARLES MORRIS, *The Open Self,* pp. 16-17

Though General English is hard to describe by itself, partly because its characteristics are so familiar to us, it will become clearer by comparison with the other varieties that follow. Obviously it has a wide range, shading off into Formal English in one direction and Informal in the other. It is the most useful variety, without the limitations of the others, and since it has such wide currency and in fact can reach practically all readers, it is the most necessary to master, and is the proper goal of instruction.

*Formal English—limited use* • Formal English is typically found in books and articles intended for circulation in somewhat restricted groups—among teachers, ministers, doctors, lawyers, and other professional people of general or specialized intellectual interests. It is found also in addresses and other formal talks and often colors the conversation of people who do a good deal of reading, but it is more characteristic of writing than of speaking.

Although Formal English will include most of the traits of General English, it will show enough of the Formal vocabulary and constructions to give it a definite tone. The vocabulary has many words seldom used in ordinary speech, specialized words from various scientific and scholarly fields, and words of more general meaning associated with the literary tradition (*desultory, ubiquitous, redoubtable*). It uses a good many abstract nouns, which summarize rather than present experience directly (*luxury, distinction, research*). For people familiar with the words, they often carry a good deal of suggestiveness (*bosky, ominous, paradox, transcend*) and often have some appeal of sound or rhythm (*quintessence, immemorial, memorable*).

In Formal English the constructions are often elaborate and filled out; the short cuts characteristic of General and Informal English are not taken. Contractions are avoided, relative pronouns are not omitted, prepositions and conjunctions are likely to be repeated in parallel constructions, and so on. Sentences tend to be somewhat longer than in General writing, binding more ideas together, with parallel and balanced clauses; the word order may be different from the usual English pattern, and modifiers may come between the main elements of subject, verb, and object. Allusions to literature and to events of the past are common. Deliberate, *studied* choice of sentence patterns as well as words characterizes Formal writing, making its impact quite different from the more casual styles of most General and all Informal English.

This does not mean that Formal writing need be stiff or dull, though there is danger that it may; but the nature of the language of Formal writing makes its appeal somewhat limited. It often demands considerable concentration and presupposes in the reader an interest in specialized subject matter or in general ideas and some awareness of our cultural tradition. The special audience for which it is written will not only follow the material but, if it is really well expressed, will appreciate the style as well. Formal English appeals to some readers simply because it is different from everyday language.

An example will show some of the traits of Formal English. The words carry a good deal of force and suggestiveness (*high* in a special sense, *guardians of culture, time-honored, outrage*), and some are of rather restricted currency (*occupational disease, disparate, diverse*). Most of the meaning is carried by nouns and adjectives. The sentences are long, averaging 37 words, but their parts are closely and naturally related.

All such perversions of high traditions are intensified by traditionalism, the occupational disease of guardians of culture. The guardians tend to forget that tradition has always been the great enemy of the founders of great traditions: that Socrates was a radical who did corrupt the youth of Athens by impiously urging them to question the time-honored ways; or that the teachings of Christ were an outrage to precisely the most cultivated, respectable, God-fearing people of his time; or that the American Revolution was strictly a revolution, illegal, violent, and bloody. In particular, the traditionalists abuse our Western heritage by singling out some one school of thought as the "essential" or "true" tradition; whereas diversity and nonconformity are the very soul of this heritage. It is the richest tradition that man has ever known simply because it includes so many disparate elements from diverse sources, and has never been at rest.—HERBERT J. MULLER, *The Uses of the Past,* p. 58

Some highly individual styles in literature require detailed study to be understood because of the unusual use of words and the uniquely personal associations of words as well as various departures from the typical patterns of current English —the writing of Carlyle, for example. In the quite different styles characteristic of scholarly and scientific writing at its best, a precise and specialized vocabulary is employed in a compact, impersonal statement. Beyond these are abuses of

Formal English: the cumbersome, archaic, and highly repetitious language of most legal documents, and the pretentious, abstract, and equally repetitious style of some bad academic writing and of much of the official writing of government and business, popularly and appropriately known as gobbledygook.

But good Formal English may be the best way (if not the only way) to present certain ideas. The ability to read Formal English is a necessity for educated people and one of the abilities to be perfected in college. Although a good deal of writing is more Formal, or at least more difficult, than it need be, intellectual growth demands its mastery. In some college writing, as in term papers for advanced courses, the writing is appropriately Formal, though it should not be excessively so, never to the extent of seeming affected. A development toward somewhat more Formal expression will naturally come with increased experience in reading college-level material.

***Informal English—limited use*** • Informal English is at the other side of General English and grades off into Nonstandard English. When we write for our own convenience or amusement or when we talk or write to members of our family or to friends, we use the language with more freedom than when addressing strangers or people we do not know well. When Informal English is used publicly, it presupposes a regular relationship of some sort between user and receiver; it may be used in a recurring radio program or newspaper column, or for a distinctly informal situation or subject—amusing little experiences, comment on social foibles, sports reporting in a low key, humor.

Informal English has considerable range, sometimes including distinctly Formal traits for contrast or Nonstandard forms for accuracy or novelty. Most conspicuously it uses words and phrases characteristic of familiar conversation, words sometimes marked *Colloquial* in dictionaries (*snooze, in-laws, goner, arty, doohickey*); words of special currency at the moment (*in-group, overkill, escalate*); informal coinages for common things or situations (*TV, hootenanny, go steady*); clipped words (*stereo, hi-fi, psych*). It may include more *localisms than General English ordinarily would, *shoptalk (words from occupations, like *mike, strike* [to dismantle], *hypo, typo*) and *slang, words continually being formed and given a temporary currency in offhand or flashy speech: *flip, flack, flick, funky, fuzz.* Since writer and reader usually have a good deal in common, the writer can take much for granted—in material, in allusion to common experiences, and in the special current connotation of words.

Informal English has its chief use in lively conversation and in writing where the subject and situation warrant a light touch, as in this columnist's comment on the prevalence of candle heating devices for the table:

Gone are the days when a man got his coffee all saucered and blowed and at the right temperature, only to have the latter drop so rapidly that the beverage was stone cold by the time he got his handle-bar mustache parted and ready.... Now a man saucers and blows the stuff and puts it on a little iron cradle over a lighted candle, where the brew starts boiling once more in nothing flat. Then he has to begin all over again. It's going to be hard on commuters until they get the hang of the new gimmick.... The iron-monger is jubilant and the fire insurance companies will be as soon as they get hep to this situation and jack up the rates. It makes for a nice, lively business cycle, with the boys at the firehouse scarce able to get through a checker game before the siren sounds again.—INEZ ROBB, "Candle Is Remarkable Invention," *Seattle Post-Intelligencer*, Feb. 6, 1954

General, Formal, and Informal English are varieties of *Standard English*. Standard English presents, then, a wide range of usage, offering a writer many choices of words and constructions—choices which in any given paper will set its tone and define its possible audience. Some principles to guide these choices will be discussed in the last section of this chapter.

The basis of Standard English is social, the "differences due to situation" described on pages 13-14. Its basis has been well described by C. C. Fries:

On the whole, however, if we ignore the special differences that separate the speech of New England, the South, and the Middle West, we do have in the United States a set of language habits, broadly conceived, in which the major matters of the political, social, economic, educational, religious life of this country are carried on. To these language habits is attached a certain social prestige, for the use of them suggests that one has constant relations with those who are responsible for the important affairs of our communities. It is this set of language habits, derived originally from an older London English, but differentiated from it somewhat by its independent development in this country, which is the "standard" English of the United States. Enough has been said to enforce the point that it is "standard" not because it is any more correct or more beautiful or more capable than other varieties of English; it is "standard" solely because it is the particular type of English which is used in the conduct of the important affairs of our people. It is also the type of English used by the *socially acceptable* of most of our communities and insofar as that is true it has become a social or class dialect in the United States.—C. C. FRIES, *American English Grammar*, p. 13

The attention given to Standard English in schools and colleges is intended to help young people speak and write like educated people so that they will be prepared to take their part in public affairs. Writing in composition courses is practice for later work in college and after college.

## *Nonstandard English*

The everyday speech of many people, relatively untouched by school instruction or by the tradition of printed English, makes up Nonstandard or Vulgate English, the name popularized by H. L. Mencken in *The American Language*.[1] This speech variety is a very real and important part of the English language and is studied by linguists with the same seriousness with which they study other varieties. Its distinguishing traits are not lapses from any brand of reputable or Standard English. It is a different development from the same language stock, representing a selection of sounds, words, forms, and constructions made under different social conditions. It works very well in carrying on the affairs and occupations of millions of people and is consequently worthy of study and respect. It is avoided in business, government, and literature chiefly for social reasons, not because it is inadequate as a means of communication. It is not ordinarily printed, since, for various historical and social reasons, the printed language is a selection of words, forms, and constructions considered appropriate to public affairs and so to Standard English.

Nonstandard English differs most noticeably from the other chief varieties of English in the use of pronoun and verb forms and in the freer use of localisms. Many of its words have a longer history in English than the more genteel words that have replaced them in "society." Some of the forms and constructions have a continuous history back to a time when they

---

[1] See Leonard Bloomfield, "Literate and Illiterate Speech," *American Speech*, 1927, 2:432-439; Fries, *AEG*; Mencken.

were reputable: Chaucer used a double negative occasionally; *an't* or *\*ain't* and *he don't* were reputable until less than a century ago; *you was* as a singular was standard in eighteenth-century England and America. Many other features of Nonstandard English are equally natural developments of the language that by some accident of dialect or other circumstance did not become Standard English.

Nonstandard English is primarily spoken. Forms like *ain't, dassent, scairt, you was* are conspicuous when they appear in print but much less so when spoken rapidly and with appropriate (not exaggerated) emphasis. They occur in many radio and television programs, in plays, and in the conversation of stories. You will find them, often distorted, in many comic strips. Occasionally a Nonstandard form is used in humor or for special effect, as in Josh Billings' epigram: "It isn't so much the ignorance of mankind that makes them ridiculous as knowing so many things that ain't so."

The monolog of the barber in Ring Lardner's story "Haircut" is a fairly accurate representation of Nonstandard. A few traits of pronunciation are shown (though the *of* in "she'd of divorced him" is just a Nonstandard spelling of the normal contraction of *have*—"she'd've divorced him"), adverbs without the *-ly* ending, *seen* for *saw, beat her to it,* and so on.

Jim didn't work very steady after he lost his position with the Carterville people. What he did earn, doin' odd jobs round town, why he spent pretty near all of it on gin, and his family might of starved if the stores hadn't of carried them along. Jim's wife tried her hand at dressmakin', but they ain't nobody goin' to get rich makin' dresses in this town.

As I say, she'd of divorced Jim, only she seen that she couldn't support herself and the kids and she was always hopin' that some day Jim would cut out his habits and give her more than two or three dollars a week.

They was a time when she would go to whoever he was workin' for and ask them to give her his wages, but after she done this once or twice, he beat her to it by borrowin' most of his pay in advance. He told it all round town, how he had outfoxed his Missus. He certainly was a caution.—Ring Lardner, "Haircut," *Roundup,* p. 25

Since the established spellings of English words are those of Standard English, it is not easy to give an adequate representation of Nonstandard English in print. And sometimes the effort to represent it is merely a somewhat more phonetic transcription of pronunciations current in all varieties of

English, like *wuz* for *was, sez* for *says,* and *wimmin* for *women.*

Schools attempt to carry on their work in what they assume to be the language of the upper social classes, Standard English. Students who go into the professions, into many branches of business, and into most white-collar jobs continue to use Standard English more or less consistently. Those who go into manual labor and the less well-paid and less socially elevated jobs often use Nonstandard English. The differences between Standard and Nonstandard are probably decreasing as the result of influences of each on the other.

The objection to Nonstandard is not that its grammar is "bad," but that it is inappropriate to the readers for whom college students and college graduates write and to the subjects they are handling. Nonstandard English may be effective in writing the conversation of some characters in stories, and it may be used occasionally to give a note of realism to portraits of real people who naturally speak it. But ordinarily it is inappropriate in college writing.

## What is good English?

To a student of language, all varieties of English are equally a part of the language, and one variety is to be observed and studied as carefully as another. But to a *user* of English, the varieties are by no means equal. They differ in the impression they make on people and in the ideas they can communicate.

Every educated person normally wants to speak and write what may be called "good English," just as he wants to "make a good personal appearance" and to "be intelligent." But the great range and diversity of the English language raises many questions about usage. The problem of English usage is much like the other social problems which face us. In dress, to take the most convenient parallel, we gradually develop something we call taste or judgment, in part by imitating others, consciously or unconsciously, in part by consulting people who are supposed to know what is good form, in part by following our own preferences. Our usual dress lies between the extremes of work, sport, and formal clothes. It is comfortable; it reflects something of the taste of the wearer; it is appropriate to going about personal affairs, to work in stores and offices, to college classes, to informal social affairs. But a person needs to have and to be able to wear several kinds of clothes, and he needs to know when it is appropriate to wear one kind or another. In the same way, anyone who is going to take his place in public, business, social, or educational affairs needs to know the resources of the various kinds of English and when they can profitably be drawn on. For answers to questions about English usage, you can often consult books, especially dictionaries and handbooks. You can ask people who write well; you can ask teachers who have made the study of the language part of their professional training. And you can always be watching what effective writers do—how the language is handled in the better books and magazines. This observation is especially important, because, as in dress and in manners, more or less conscious imitation of those you approve of or wish to be associated with will bulk large in forming your own habits. Few will ever write with real ease unless they listen and read a good deal and so unconsciously absorb the ways of their language by direct experience.

***Basis of good English set by the purpose of communication*** • Of course, if anyone wants to talk to himself or write for his own amusement, relief, or "self-expression," or if he deliberately sets out to deceive or puzzle, then his usage need not conform to any established practice. And a writer may experiment as much as he wishes, as James Joyce and Gertrude Stein and others have done, creating for themselves a limited audience willing to study out their meaning in spite of handicaps. But the ordinary and principal function of language is immediate and effective communication, making someone understand or feel something, or getting him to do something that we want him to do.

This fundamental purpose in speaking and writing prevents the language, complicated as it is, from falling into chaos, and sets the broad limits of what is permissible. We use words in the meanings they have acquired from their past use and we make our statements in established patterns. From this point of view, Fries defines the basis of good English:

... language is a means to an end and that end is specifically to grasp, to possess, to communicate experience. Accordingly, that is good language, good English, which, on the one hand, most fully realizes one's own impressions, and, on the other, is most completely adapted to the purposes of any particular communication.—C. C. FRIES, *What Is Good English?* p. 120

In other words, so far as the writer's language furthers his intended effect, it is good; so far as it fails to further that effect, it is bad, no matter how "correct" it may be.[1]

This definition of good English may differ somewhat from other definitions you have seen. Its emphasis is on the primary purpose of language and it subordinates correctness for its own sake. Isolated details such as spelling, punctuation, capitalization, and Standard usage are important, but always in relation to their appropriateness to the immediate purpose. This appropriateness is threefold: to the subject and situation, to the expected listeners or readers, and to the writer or speaker himself. A consideration of these will yield *principles,* rather than *rules,* to guide actual practice.

*Appropriateness to subject and situation* • In conversation we automatically adjust our language as well as our topics to the situation. For our talks and papers, whether assigned or voluntary, there should be a similar adjustment. The language of a reminiscence will differ somewhat from that of an explanatory paper for a popular audience or a plea for action or a scholarly discussion of ideas.

Choosing the appropriate variety of English is one sign of a practiced, mature writer. Slang may fit in a letter or in a popular newspaper column; it is usually out of place in discussing a serious or elevated subject. Most fiction is General or Informal. Writing on a technical or professional subject is more likely to be Formal. The language of a church service and of religious and philosophical discussion is Formal.

Students—all writers, for that matter, who strive for language appropriate to subject and situation—come at last to the same resolution: *to treat simple subjects simply,* or, in terms of our varieties of English, to treat them in General English. Most subjects are relatively simple, or at least the writer is going to give only a simplified version of them. Amateur writers are often not content to be themselves but assume a dialect that is really foreign to them, too Formal to be appropriate to their subjects.

Students should also avoid writing too Informally in papers which discuss serious subjects. But the better students in a composition course often err in the direction of overly Formal writing, probably because of the emphasis on Formal correctness throughout their school careers.

---

[1] Fries, *AEG,* Ch. 1 (an unusually good statement); Fries, *The Teaching of English* (Ann Arbor, 1949), Ch. 5; Otto Jespersen, *Mankind, Nation and Individual from a Linguistic Point of View* (Oslo, 1925), Ch. 5; Pooley, Part I.

Though teachers and students will not always agree in their judgments of particular passages, they will agree on a surprising number of them. And once students fully grasp the principle of appropriateness they are not likely to return either to unnecessary pomposity or to unsuitable lightness.

The tone of a passage should be consistent unless the writer has special reason for departing from it. A conspicuous lapse from Formal to Informal or from Informal to Formal should ordinarily be avoided. These examples show obvious and awkward lapses:

Formal to Informal: If our Concert and Lecture program this year is not superior to that of any other college in the country, *I'll eat every freshman lid on the campus.*

Informal to Formal: *I was bowled over* by the speed with which the workmen assembled the parts.

Some writing—in *The New Yorker,* for example, and in many newspaper columns—successfully fuses distinctly Informal words with quite Formal ones. The expressions are unified by the vigor and smoothness with which they are brought together and are not lapses from appropriateness. Superficial consistency is not so important as the fundamental appropriateness to the situation. But for most writers one variety of English should be kept throughout a piece of writing.

Both in a composition course and out of one, keep a Formal style for complex or scholarly subjects and an Informal style for light or humorous ones; write in General English on most matters.

*Appropriateness to listener or reader* • If you are trying to reach a particular type of reader, you will adjust both your subject matter and your expression to him. To reach him, to really get your points across, you have to be more than merely intelligible: you have to meet him pretty much on his own ground. You already do this almost automatically in your letters, writing in somewhat different ways to different persons. You no doubt adjust your expression to the expectations of different teachers. Certainly in many other situations you pay some attention to the language you believe is expected of you.

Some types of writing are in theory completely adjusted to their readers, notably directions to be followed, newspaper writing, and advertising. Although we realize that they often fail, either from cheapness or from dullness and unintended formality, in a general way they do meet their readers' expectations.

Essays (or themes) are sometimes difficult to write because you lose the sense of having a reader. It is better to try to visualize a particular audience, to direct your paper to some magazine, or, more commonly, to write for the class of which you are a member. Directing your paper to the members of your class will help you select material that will interest and inform them or at least appeal to most of them, and it will help you judge what words and what kinds of sentences are appropriate. Remember that you are not writing for everyone but for a selected audience. Novels are for readers of differing tastes, and even the audiences of best sellers like *The Robe* and *Lolita* are far from identical. In most of your writing a firm General style is probably best, for many people prefer it and anyone can be reached through it.

*Clearness.* Since your aim is to convey some fact or conviction, some fancy or feeling to a person or group, appropriateness to a reader means clear expression: exact words and, for the most part, words in the vocabulary of the person you are addressing. If the subject requires words unfamiliar to him, their meaning can usually be made clear from the way they are used. If not, you can throw in a tactful explanation or in some instances resort to formal definition.

Clarity also requires careful sentence construction. Experienced readers can grasp more elaborate sentences than those who read little or hurriedly. But anyone will be pleased with direct, straightforward sentences. Clarity should be one of your main objectives in revising a paper.

*Correctness.* Avoiding what a reader might consider errors is a major task for a beginning writer. People tend to judge us by superficial traits, in language as in other matters. Spelling, for example, bulks larger in most people's judgment of writing than it reasonably should. Certainly many people take delight in finding what are (or what they consider to be) errors in language, especially in the writing or speech of those supposed to be educated or of anyone soliciting their favor. Courtesy demands that a writer should do his best in anything he is submitting to another; soiled manuscript, many interlineations, confusion of common forms like *its* and *it's,* misspelling of common words (*similiar* for *similar*) are ordinarily the result of carelessness or thoughtlessness. The chief reason for mastering the "minimum essentials" of English forms is to meet the expectations of educated readers. You need not worry about these matters as you write, but you must reserve some time for revision to bring the paper to the best state you can.

*Liveliness.* There is so much unavoidable dullness in the world that any reader will appreciate some liveliness in writing, in the expression as well as in the material. Striving for novelty is dangerous, and its results are often self-defeating. But students frequently hide behind a flat sort of language, squeezing all the life out of their writing. Your words need not be out of the ordinary; for the most part, they should be those you would use in serious conversation. Your sentences should not be formless or dragged out; they should suggest an alert interest. Refer to things people do and say, use plenty of lively detail to clarify ideas and to keep up interest, and pay special attention to the beginnings and endings of your papers.

Some professional writers have set themselves the rule "Don't write anything you couldn't read yourself." Following this principle means that you will choose your best available material, write it as interestingly as you can, and make it genuinely readable. If you promise yourself that you won't turn in a paper that you couldn't read yourself with interest and perhaps profit, you will not only be accepting responsibility for your work, but you will also be permanently improving your control of expression and laying a sure foundation for continued growth in good English.

In general, satisfy your reader's expectations insofar as you believe they are worthy of respect. But don't aim at your reader's worst, compromising yourself and insulting him. Visualize him in his better moments and write for him as he is then.

**Appropriateness to speaker or writer** • In the speaker-listener or writer-reader relationship, the speaker or writer dominates. He makes the choices; his judgment or unconscious sense of fitness finally controls. Your language in the long run represents your personality, and you are responsible for the language you use. To take this responsibility, you first need to inform yourself fully of the possibilities of the English language. Observe what is spoken and written, use dictionaries and other reference works, and consult people who have studied English as a language. You can then apply this information in your own work according to your best judgment. There is nothing mysterious about the matter; it is just a natural process of learning and applying what is learned.

The most important step in improving your language habits is to watch your own speech and writing to see what their good qualities are and what shortcomings they may have. Can you confidently pronounce the words you need in conversation or recitation? Does your language tend to be Formal, or is it predominantly Informal, or General? Do you rely too much on slang or on trite words, or do you lapse into Nonstandard expressions? When you talk or write to someone older than yourself or when you write a paper for a college course, do you choose the most appropriate part of your natural language, or do you assume an entirely different sort of English?

And, finally, is the language you use consistent with the rest of your conduct? If you are a rather casual person, informal in dress and manner, we should expect your English to be somewhat Informal; if you are conventional in dress and manner, we should expect your English to be more Formal. It is necessary for you also to realize the direction in which you are moving, for young people, especially in college, are changing, becoming either more flexible or more conventional in their ideas and manners, or making some other change. Their language should be moving similarly. In your first papers in a composition course you should write naturally so that you and your instructor can decide together on the direction your growth should take. Such growth will in part be in the direction of greater appropriateness to yourself.

The three sorts of appropriateness here suggested for arriving at good English (appropriateness to the subject and situation, to the listener or reader, and to the writer or speaker) will not always be in harmony. The subject may seem to demand words that are not appropriate to the reader. The writer can usually solve such a problem either by finding simpler words or by explaining the necessary but unfamiliar ones. The reader's expectation and the writer's natural manner of expression may be different. Such a conflict can be solved by the writer—deciding how essential to his purpose his own turns of expression are, whether he can honorably yield to the reader's expectation or whether his usage is so necessary to his sense of the subject that compromise is impossible. In the long run the writer's sense of fitness, his pride in his work, will resolve most such conflicts.

As a result of this approach to good English you should have confidence in writing. The greatest handicap in writing is fear—fear of pencil and paper, fear of making a mistake, fear of offending the reader's (teacher's) taste. The opposite attitude, cockiness, is a nuisance and is equally at odds with good writing, but fewer students suffer from that than from inhibitions about their language. As yet psychologists can't tell us much about the mental activity involved in thinking or writing, but some of them believe that the fundamental condition for effectiveness is a positive feeling of readiness—which amounts really to a sort of faith that when you prepare to write, language appropriate to the occasion will come. A wide knowledge of the possibilities of current English, backed up by sufficient practice in writing for specific readers and sufficient care in revision, should increase your confidence. With such confidence you can write your best, for good English is not primarily a matter of rules but of judgment.

NONSTANDARD ENGLISH • *Limited use*
*Chiefly spoken* • Language not much touched by school instruction; often conspicuously local; not appropriate for public affairs or for use by educated people

STANDARD ENGLISH
Informal English • *Limited use*
*More often spoken than written* • Speaking and writing of educated people in informal situations; includes shoptalk or slang and some localisms
General English • *Unlimited use*
*Both spoken and written* • Speaking and writing of educated people in their private or public affairs

Formal English • *Limited use*
*More often written than spoken* • Speaking and writing for somewhat restricted groups in formal situations

*Comments*
1. Standard English is here divided into Informal, General, and Formal English because we are mainly concerned with these variations in the English of the cultivated. The same subdivisions could be made in Nonstandard English. (See Kenyon, "Cultural Levels . . .")
2. The varieties are not to be thought of as sharply defined and mutually exclusive but as shading into each other. A passage might be regarded as Informal, for instance, if it had several conspicuous traits characteristic of that variety even though the greater part of the passage was in General English.
3. Usage is said to be *divided* when choices exist between two usages in General English, both of which are in good standing (for example, the spellings of *catalog* or *catalogue*, or a comma or no comma before the *and* of the last item in a series, or *dived* or *dove* as the past tense of *dive*).
4. *Slovenly* (impoverished speech, often including obscenity and profanity) and *Stilted* (pretentious and unnecessarily heavy speech or

*Typical uses:* Conversations of many people at home, with friends, on the job • Representations of this speech in stories, plays, movies, comic strips, on radio and television (See pp. 20-22)

*Typical uses:* Casual conversation • Letters between people who know each other well; diaries, personal writing; writing close to popular speech, as in fiction and some newspaper columns (See pp. 18-20)

*Typical uses:* Conversation; talks to general audiences • Most business letters and advertising • News and feature stories, newspaper columns • Magazine articles and books on subjects of general interest • Most fiction and other literature for general circulation • Many college papers (See pp. 14-16)

*Typical uses:* Addresses and lectures to special audiences • Some editorials and business writing • Literature of somewhat limited circulation: essays and criticisms, much poetry, some fiction • Academic writing: reference works, dissertations, most term papers, reference papers, some textbooks • Scientific and technical reports • Books and articles dealing with special subjects for professional groups and experts (See pp. 16-18)

writing—gobbledygook) may be regarded as the extremes of Nonstandard and Standard English.

5. The varieties are characterized by some differences in word forms, in pronunciation, in vocabulary, in grammatical constructions, and by the avoidance of certain locutions (as Standard English avoids double negatives). The chief differences, and the easiest to discuss, are in vocabulary.

6. Labeling a usage as belonging to any one of the varieties indicates that it is characteristically used as the description of that variety, that its connotation comes from this use, and that it is not characteristic of another variety. Such labeling does not prohibit the use of the word under other conditions but does suggest that it may be inappropriately conspicuous in another variety.

7. Though the writing situations in which Nonstandard and Informal English may appropriately be used are limited, these varieties are used much more often than General and Formal by the total number of *speakers* of the language.

# AN INDEX
# TO ENGLISH

*To make the best use of this* Index, *first read "The varieties of English" (pp. 2-31) so that you will understand the general principles involved, and then read a few consecutive pages of the* Index *articles (or a selection of them) to see those principles applied.*

*An asterisk preceding a word or phrase indicates a reference to another article within the* Index.

*A full discussion of the symbols by which pronunciation is represented appears in the article* \*Pronunciation § 1, p. 326.

*The sources most used in gathering the material for this book are usually referred to by the author's name only. The exact titles of these sources will be found in the Bibliography on pp. viii-1.*

This *Index* contains articles in alphabetical arrangement that fall roughly into four categories:

**Articles on particular words and constructions** • such as \*continual—continuous; \*fiancé, fiancée; \*get, got; \*like—as; \*plenty; \*shall—will; \*so . . . that; \*very. Information about their standing in current usage is given. The classifying labels —Nonstandard, Standard, Informal, General, and Formal—are explained in "The varieties of English." The entry words are not capitalized.

**Articles for correction and revision of papers** • indicated by longhand abbreviations before the entry word. A list of these articles is given on pp. 468-469 and on the inside front and back covers of this book. These entries are capitalized.

**Articles on English grammar** • giving definitions and examples of such matters as \*Case, \*Plurals of nouns, \*Principal parts of verbs, which are necessary for a description and understanding of the language. Entries are capitalized.

**Articles on various facts of language** • such as \*American and British usage, \*Foreign words in English, \*Linguistics, that are designed more for general information than for immediate application. Entries are capitalized.

**A •** In standard spelling the letter *a* represents several different sounds, which are also spelled by other letters. They are listed here by their traditional names because these are well-known though not phonetically accurate:

**1.** *"Short a,"* the /a/ of *hat* and *stack,* differently spelled in *plaid.*

**2.** *"Long a,"* the /ā/ of *game* and *famous*; other spellings occur in *aid, gauge, say, break, vein, weigh, they,* and *Gaelic.*

**3.** *"Broad a,"* the /ä/ of *hard, father,* and *calm,* differently spelled in *heart* and *sergeant.* Speakers of Standard British English and some speakers in the United States and Canada use this vowel in a fairly large group of words like *ask, bath, craft, demand, half,* and *laugh.* In eastern New England these words are often pronounced with a vowel between /a/ and /ä/, known as "intermediate *a.*" But the great majority of Americans and Canadians pronounce the *"ask*-group" with the /a/ of *hat.*

Some speakers try to substitute the broad *a* or intermediate *a* for their natural short *a* in these words. But this attempt to imitate a type of pronunciation not naturally acquired usually calls attention to itself, especially since the imitated vowel may be introduced into the wrong words: British *glass* /gläs/, for example, may lead to /läs/ for *lass,* which British speakers pronounce /las/. The best practice is to pronounce this group of words in the way that is natural to you.

**4.** The /ã/ of *care* and *parent,* differently spelled in *fair, pear, prayer, their,* and *where.* In these words the vowel varies regionally between the /ā/ of *gate* and the /a/ of *hat.*

**5.** The /o/ of the first syllable of *swallow* (/swol′ō/, rhyming with *follow*), more commonly spelled with *o,* as in *rock* and *novel.* Many speakers have /ä/ in these words.

**6.** *"Open o,"* the /ô/ of *tall* and *warm,* differently spelled in *broad, maul, draw, soft, taught,* and *thought.* Here, too, pronunciation varies in different regions; many use this vowel only before *r,* pronouncing the other words so that *stalk* and *stock, caller* and *collar* are identical.

**7.** The *"schwa"* /ə/ of *soda* and *about.* This *neutral vowel sound occurs only in unstressed syllables and is also spelled with the other vowel letters, as in *society, pencil, lemon, circus.*

(Reference: *Webster's Third New International Dictionary,* "A Guide to Pronunciation," p. 34a.)

**a •** The prefix *a-* (from Greek meaning *not*) forms many words in the Formal and scientific vocabularies (*amoral, asexual, asymmetrical, atypical, achromatic*). It is usually pronounced /ā/.

An Old English prepositional prefix *a-* is found in many words (*abed, aloud, asleep, alert, afraid*), and survives in such regional and Nonstandard phrases as *going a-fishing, a-hunting.*

**a, an** •
1. The choice between *a* and *an* depends on the initial sound, not on the initial letter, of the word that follows:

*A* is used before all words beginning with *a consonant sound* —that is, before all words spelled with initial consonant letters except silent *h*, as in *hour*—and before words spelled with initial vowel letters that represent combined consonant and vowel sounds, as in *eulogy* /ū′lə jē/, *unit* /ū′nit/: *a business, a European trip, a D, a usage.*

*An* is used before all words beginning with *a vowel sound,* including words spelled with initial silent *h* (see *H): *an apple, an F, an hour apart, an honor.*

In words beginning with *h* but not accented on the first syllable, as in *histo′rian, hyste′rical, h* was formerly not pronounced, so that *an* was used. Although the *h* is now often pronounced, some people continue to say and write *an histor′ical* event (but *a his′tory*). In contemporary usage *a* is the more common in such locutions, but an individual may use whichever comes more easily.

2. Repeating *a* or *an* before each noun of a series tends to keep the various words distinct and make the expression emphatic: *a pen, a sheet of paper, and an envelope* (*a pen, sheet of paper, and envelope* would be less emphatic).

3. *Awhile, a while.* The adverb *awhile* is written as one word (He came *awhile* ago) but not the noun (He came for *a while*). The *a* is also separate in *a lot, a bit, a little.* (See *half for *a half hour, half an hour,* etc. For *kind of a, sort of a* see *kind of a, sort of a.)

**Abbreviations** •
*Revision: Write in full the abbreviation marked.*

Ab

1. *Appropriateness.* Abbreviations are appropriate in manuals, reference books, business and legal documents, scholarly footnotes, and other works in which saving space is important. They also fit in Informal writing—notes for one's own use, letters to friends. In college papers and most Formal writing, abbreviations are held to a minimum.

*Shoptalk, familiar conversation, and *slang use many abbreviations for the names of things frequently mentioned: *d.t.'s—delirium tremens, VIP—very important person.*

**2.** *Standard abbreviations. Dr., \*Mr., \*Mrs., \*Messrs.* are always abbreviated when used with names. A number of abbreviations, such as *St.* (see \*Saint), *\*a.m.* and *p.m.*, and abbreviations for government agencies such as *TVA* and *SEC,* are commonly used. In Formal writing, titles like *\*Reverend, \*Professor, President,* and *Senator* would not be abbreviated at all, but in most other writing they are found abbreviated *when initials or given names are used:* not *Prof. Hylander,* but *Professor Hylander* or *Prof. G. W. Hylander.*

English still has many abbreviations of Latin words:

| | |
|---|---|
| A.D. | *Anno Domini*—in the year of our Lord (see \*Centuries) |
| cf. | *confer*—compare (for which *see* may be used) |
| e.g. | *exempli gratia*—for example |
| \*etc. | *et cetera*—and so forth |
| ibid. | *ibidem*—the same (used in footnotes) |
| i.e. | *id est*—that is |

Such abbreviations are not italicized, unless there is a special reason for italics (as when *ibid.* represents the title of a book), since they are regarded as English words. Less commonly used abbreviations from Latin are usually italicized: *c.* or *ca.* (*circa,* "about," used with uncertain dates), *seq.* (*sequentes* or *sequentia,* "following").

Dictionaries give frequently used abbreviations in the main alphabetical list of words or in a special list. (See \*References § 2 for abbreviations used in footnotes of reference papers.)

**3.** *Period with abbreviations.* Most abbreviations are still normally followed by a period; where standard practice requires the period, its omission is a careless slip. Only one period is used after an abbreviation at the end of a sentence.

The omission of the period after an abbreviation that ends with the last letter of the word abbreviated is chiefly British: *Dr, Mr, Mrs, vs, Wm.*

Periods are increasingly omitted with the abbreviations of names of government agencies (*SEC, TVA, FBI*) and of other terms if the abbreviation is generally used instead of the name (*AFL-CIO, UNESCO, NATO, CBS*), and of phrases like *mph, hp, kwh, rpm* in scientific contexts or when used with figures (*780 rpm*).

Abbreviations that are pronounced as words (*Wac, Nazi, UNESCO*) are called *acronyms.* The number of these has been increasing; over 12,000 of them are listed in *Acronyms Dictionary: A Guide to Alphabetical Designations, Contractions and Initialisms* [of nonprofit organizations] (Detroit, Gale Research Co., 1960).

(For information on abbreviation of dates, see \*Months; of names, see \*Given names; of references in scientific papers, see *References in scientific papers § 1c. Compare *Contractions, *Origin of words § 3c.)

**ability to** • The idiom with *ability* is *to* and an infinitive (ability *to do*, not *of doing*): *He has the ability to design beautiful buildings.* The idea is often better expressed by an adjective or verb: *He is able to [He can] design beautiful buildings. He designs [is designing] beautiful buildings.*

**able to** • *Able to* is rarely followed by a passive infinitive (like *to be done* or *to be ended*) because the construction sounds awkward.

*Awkward*:   This was not able to be done because of lack of time.
*Improved*:   This could not be done because of lack of time. [Or] They were not able to do this because of lack of time.

Though *able to* may sometimes be replaced by *can* or *could*, it is mandatory to express some time relationships: *will be able, might be able.* (See *Tenses of verbs § 1.)

**-able, -ible** • These two suffixes, alike in meaning, cause trouble in spelling because we pronounce them alike. In earlier English they were pronounced differently, as they are in Latin and French, but the English tendency to obscure the vowels in unstressed syllables has obliterated the distinction. Since pronunciation is of no help, we must learn the spelling of each word. The suffix *-able* is by far the more common form and should be used in coining occasional words like *jumpable* or *come-at-able.*

**1.** *-able.* This list contains a few of the many words ending in *-able*:

| | | | |
|---|---|---|---|
| advisable | imaginable | movable | teachable |
| applicable | incurable | noticeable | tolerable |
| changeable | indispensable | perishable | unbearable |
| comfortable | inseparable | presentable | unbelievable |
| desirable | intolerable | receivable | unmistakable |
| detestable | justifiable | serviceable | unpronounceable |
| eatable | laughable | sizable | unspeakable |
| excusable | lovable | suitable | usable |

**2.** *-ible.* The following rather common words have *-ible*:

| | | | |
|---|---|---|---|
| accessible | convertible | edible | impossible |
| audible | corruptible | eligible | incredible |
| combustible | credible | feasible | indefensible |
| compatible | digestible | flexible | indelible |
| comprehensible | discernible | gullible | inexhaustible |
| contemptible | divisible | horrible | intelligible |

| invisible | permissible | responsible | susceptible |
|---|---|---|---|
| irresistible | plausible | reversible | tangible |
| legible | possible | sensible | terrible |
| negligible | reducible | suggestible | visible |

3. *-able* or *-ible.* Several words are found with either *-able* or *-ible.* The more common form is put first: *collapsible—collaps-able, collectable—collectible, preventable—preventible.*

**about** • Like most English preposition-adverbs, *about* has a variety of uses, a few of which have raised questions.
1. *about—around.* In describing physical position these are nearly interchangeable, though *around* is the more common (about the barn—around the barn). In the sense of *nearly* or *approximately, about* is more common; both are Standard.
2. *about—almost.* In the sense of *almost* (about finished), *about* is Standard but slightly Informal.
3. *at about.* Strictly speaking, something would be either *at* or *about,* but the two words are frequently used together (At about four o'clock we crossed the line), with the *about* then best regarded as an adverb, emphasizing the indefiniteness. (See *at about, at around.)
4. *About* followed by an infinitive is a convenient idiom for *on the point of* with the added advantage of allowing a future or anticipated act to be put into past time: *He was about to make a third try.*

**above** • *Above* is primarily used as a preposition (above the clouds) or adverb (dark above and light below). Its adverbial use in such phrases as "the evidence cited above" is common in contemporary prose; but many writers prefer "the evidence already cited" or some such expression. The use of *above* as an adjective (the above prices, the prices above) or as a noun (the above is confirmed) is often found in commercial and journalistic writing, the adjective use the more frequent, but it is usually avoided elsewhere. (Reference: Bryant, pp. 3-4.)

**Abridged clauses** • See *Clauses § 3b.

**Absolute constructions** • Absolute constructions like *The narrows passed* in "The narrows passed, we went along at a fairly good speed," modify the sentence as a whole. They are "absolute" not because they are independent but because they lack connectives defining their relationship to other sentence elements, being joined to the rest of the sentence only by their position, by contact. When absolute phrases follow the main clause, they are a convenient way of adding details:

She walked slowly, big flakes falling on her lamb coat and cling-
ing to hair over her ears, the lazily falling snow giving her, in her
thick warm coat, a fine feeling of self-indulgence.—MORLEY CAL-
LAGHAN, *A Native Argosy*, p. 135

Here everything except the main clause, *She walked slowly*,
is in what are usually known as absolute phrases.

(See *Participles § 3, *Infinitives § 5. References: Francis
Christensen, *College English*, 1950, 11:401-403; Jespersen,
*Modern English Grammar*, V:6; Bryant, pp. 145-146.)

**Absolutes, comparison of** • See *Comparison of adjectives and
adverbs § 4.

**Abstract and concrete words** •

*Abst*   *Revision: Replace the abstract word or words with a
concrete word or words.*

Nouns that name qualities, conditions, actions, or sum-
maries of particular facts are abstract: *love, civilization, danger, naturalism*. They contrast with concrete nouns, which
name persons and things that can be seen and touched: *bus,
schoolhouse, tree*. Abstract nouns are necessary in discussing
ideas but in many kinds of writing they are less exact and
forceful than concrete words. When the topic of your paper
calls for the use of abstract terms, define them in more concrete
language and illustrate them with specific examples.

**Academic writing** • One conspicuous trait of academic writing—that is, the publications of teachers and scholars and
others engaged in research and in originating ideas—is its
documentation, the devices of bibliography and footnote reference that give the sources of material used in preparing the
paper. Scrupulousness in giving exact references to those
materials sets scholarly writing off from popular books and articles. (See *References.)

Another trait of academic writing is its Formal style. When
scholarly articles and monographs deal with the results of
experiments, of historical research, or of special investigation
in any field, they naturally show the specialized vocabulary,
compactness, and impersonality of *scientific and technical
writing.

Partly because many works by scholars and research workers
are written more impersonally than they need be, "academic"
is often used to describe writing that is unpleasantly abstract,
distant, and dry, and to describe the style of many books supposedly for general reading that do not show sufficient adapta-

tion to the desired readers. But such partial failures in communication should not hide the importance of academic
writing. Very often the men engaged in discovering new facts,
in originating interpretations of facts, are not particularly
interested in popularizing them and leave that task to others.
This passage, itself in the Formal style of academic writing,
discusses the language of specialists:

The truth is that the language of science and scholarship and that
of ordinary literature are different engines of communication, though
they have something in common. It is essential for academics to write
as far as possible in normal language, and desirable for them to write
well. It is essential for them to explain what they are doing to non-
specialists and this task, if it is to be carried out adequately, requires
them to write well. But they will not themselves judge the value of
academic writing by literary standards. When a mathematician or
nuclear physicist speaks of beauty and elegance—and he speaks of
both as often as the composer or chessplayer, and may strive for both
as hard as the poet—he has not in mind the proper ordering of words,
but of ideas. And for him, as for Spinoza, their beauty may be so
great that it altogether dwarfs the lesser beauties of the word. But
those of us who do not share his aesthetics, and perhaps cannot
understand them, are ill at ease.—"The Language of Scholarship,"
*The Times Literary Supplement*, Aug. 17, 1956, p. viii

**Accent** • In this *Index* the term *stress* rather than *accent* is
used for the prominence given certain syllables in speech; in
English it results from greater force of exhalation. (See \*Pronunciation § 2a, and b.)

**Accent marks** • French words in English sometimes keep the
accent marks of their original spelling:

*Acute*: café    outré    attaché    fiancée
*Circumflex*: crêpe    tête
*Grave*: frère    suède

Though the accent marks are regularly used in Formal
writing and Formal publications, in General writing they are
usually dropped, though both forms of some words are found
—for instance, *fete* and *fête*, *role* and *rôle*. Newspapers rarely
use accent marks. (See \*Foreign words in English, and for
particular words consult a recent dictionary.)

An accent mark is sometimes used in English to show that
a syllable is pronounced, especially in verse. The grave (')
is best used for this, though sometimes an acute is found
(belovéd).

**accept, except** • See \*except, accept.

**Accusative case** • In English six distinctive pronoun forms have survived which are often called accusative (or objective) forms and usually occur in the object function (but see *It's me): *me, her, his, us, them, whom. You* and *it* do not have such distinctive forms. English nouns have no distinctive form to show the object function; noun objects of verbs and prepositions are in the common case form. (See *Case; *Objects; *Infinitives § 5; *Gerund § 2; *who, whom.)

**Acronyms** • See *Abbreviations § 3.

**Active voice** • See *Voice.

**actually** • *Actually* has been a convenient word of spoken emphasis (Did you actually see him?) usually better omitted in writing. Its usefulness even in speech has been damaged for the present, however, by repetition as a filler in television interview responses: *"Well, uh, actually, Jack . . . ."*

**ad** • *Ad,* the clipped form of *advertisement,* is spelled with one *d* and no period. Like other clipped words it belongs to General and Informal speech and writing.

**adapt, adopt, adept** • The first two are verbs; the third is an adjective: They *adopted* a boy who proved *adept* at *adapting* himself to his new home. *Adept* is used with both *at* and *in,* the latter probably more common except with *-ing* words: *adept in architecture, adept at designing.* Either is Standard idiom.

**addresses** • When the various parts of a person's address are written on the same line, they are separated by commas:

Miss Louise Finney, 48 Adirondack View, Middlebury, Vermont, is a native of Carroll County, Virginia, and a graduate of Smith College.

(See *Letters § 1b, 2 for addresses in and on letters.)

**Adjective clauses** • See *Clauses § 2b, *Relative clauses, *Restrictive and nonrestrictive.

**Adjectives, definitions** • See *Parts of speech.

**Adjectives in use** • Adjectives should add something to the exactness of a writer's statement or to the definiteness of his picture. As Herbert Read puts it, "appropriate epithets may be either exact or happy." Final judgment about the effectiveness of a particular adjective can only be made by considering the context in which it appears, but some general criteria for appropriateness can be suggested. In *briny* ocean, the *briny* does not add, because all oceans are briny; *stark* does not add much to the meaning of *tragedy,* or of *madness* either. Very general adjectives like *good* or *bad* or *nice* or *beautiful* or *wonderful* do not as a rule add; the reader wants more specific detail, a particular sort of *good* (*generous, affable, efficient*). Many adjectives that are exact enough have been used too often with certain nouns (*fond* farewell, *beady black* eyes) and are merely trite. Because most people do not use exact adjectives in conversation, they often fall back on these flat and stale modifiers in writing—and professional writers sometimes fall back on them too. (See *Trite.)

A writer may try too hard to make a picture exact. Most of the adjectives in the following paragraph from a student theme are exact—that is, they add to the meaning. But there are too many of them; the writer has been too conscientious. The passage would be more readable if those in brackets, and probably others, were taken out.

In a hotel dining room there is not the [*clamorous, raucous*] bedlam of its *immediate* surroundings, but a *refined, subdued* atmosphere, pervaded by *distinct,* faintly *audible* sounds. The orchestra, with a barely *perceptible* diminuendo, concludes the [*melodic,*] *slow-tempo* arrangement, climaxed by the [*beautiful*] strains of the "Merry Widow" waltz—*rising, falling, fading* with *plaintive* supplication. Then later, while a *modern, rhythmic* melody is being played, the *hushed* clash of cymbals, the [*musical*] tinkle of the chimes, and the *muted* blare of brass blend harmoniously with the [*pulsing,*] *vibrant* voice of the *featured* soloist, only to be anticlimaxed by the *perfunctory* applause of the diners. The [*constant,*] *relentless* shuffle, shuffle, shuffle of *dancing* feet becomes *monotonous* with its [*endless*] repetition and *imperceptible* variation, while *trite* conversation is often interrupted by the *affected* voice of the *solicitous* waiter. The whispers and [*gay*] laughter, the *discordant* clatter of dishes upon trays, and the [*careless*] scraping of chairs blend into the room's *distinctive* personality.

But a sensible and sensitive use of adjectives is necessary. In most factual writing the first requirement of adjectives is exactness; they must answer the needs of the material, like the italicized words in the next paragraph:

*Many* counselors on *public* relations had *one* foot in commerce and the other in politics—even *international* politics. The most *eminent* figure in *this* class was the *late* Ivy Lee. It seems a pity that he died silently, leaving behind, so far as anyone knows, no *real* record of *his* activities. The *candid* reminiscences of Ivy Lee would be as *useful* to a *future* historian as Pepys' Diary—and perhaps as *interest-*

*ing* to the student of *human* souls. He began *his larger* career as counselor for *certain* Rockefeller interests. He was *careful*, nevertheless, not to identify himself with the Rockefellers or *any other* group, so leaving himself *free* to serve *all* clients. He had a hand in an agitation for recognition of Russia as a means of increasing our *export* market. Indeed, he may have directed *this* campaign. So, too, when an element among the bankers decided that cancellation of *European war* debts would benefit *American* finance, they used Lee's talent for sweetening *unpopular* causes. And in the *last* year of his life he was advising the *new German* government on ways and means for making *Nazi* principles and methods less *hateful* to the *average American* citizen.—WILL IRWIN, *Propaganda and the News,* pp. 267-268

In writing that makes a definite attempt to capture the feelings and sensations of the reader, the adjectives must be exact (as they are in the following paragraph) but they must also deserve the epithet "happy"; that is, they must seem to fit and at the same time lead the reader to the writer's feeling, perhaps by making an imaginative appeal. In describing an actual experience Ernest Hemingway presents a picture rather than merely a series of facts:

In the *five* days I saw a *dozen* or *more kudu* cows and *one young* bull with a string of cows. The cows were *big, gray, striped-flanked* antelope with ridiculously *small* heads, *big* ears, and a *soft, fast-rushing* gait that moved them in *big-bellied* panic through the trees. The *young* bull had the start of a spiral on *his* horns but they were *short* and *dumpy* and as he ran past us at the end of a glade in the dusk, *third* in a string of *six* cows, he was no more like a *real* bull than a *spike* elk is like a *big, old, thick-necked, dark-maned, wonder-horned, tawny-hided, beer-horse-built* bugler of a bull-elk.—*Green Hills of Africa,* p. 138

Notice that the relatively insignificant *glade, dusk,* and *trees* are not modified but that the *gait* is *soft, fast-rushing.* The gait needed to be described; the dusk and the trees are merely part of the background.

Adjectives sometimes tend to make a slow movement in writing partly because many of them have a falling rhythm—that is, the stressed syllable is followed by one or more unstressed syllables. They may contribute to a leisurely, relaxed effect:

The sheltering trees only emphasized the ashen deadness of the wrinkled clapboards.

Too many of them result in an excessively slow movement.

Carl Sandburg has been credited with advising a writer, "Think twice before you use an adjective." This is probably sound advice for anyone who is writing a good deal and who automatically attaches an adjective to every noun. And according to E. B. White, "The adjective hasn't been built that can pull a weak or inaccurate noun out of a tight place." But it is also important for a writer to fix his eye on his subject and write about it as he really sees it. Without stuffing in adjectives he should fill in the qualities that are needed for the reader to re-create the picture or idea for himself. The adjectives then should be at least exact, and some of them may be happy.

(Compare *Adverbs in use.)

## Adjectives, types and forms •

**1.** *Forms.* Many adjectives can be identified by the fact that they are compared by adding -er or -est to the positive (or base) form or by preceding the positive form with *more* or *most*:

| Positive | Comparative | Superlative |
|---|---|---|
| warm | warmer, more warm | warmest, most warm |
| talkative | more talkative | most talkative |

(See *Comparison of adjectives and adverbs for further examples and discussion of use; see also *unique.)

Many adjectives have come down from an early period of the language (*high, handsome, civil*) without a distinctive adjective form, but many have been made and are still being made by adding a derivational ending or *suffix to a noun or verb. Some suffixes that are still active are:

| | |
|---|---|
| *-able* (*-ible*) —translatable, edible | *-ish*—darkish, womanish |
| *-al*—critical, hypothetical | *-less*—harmless, fearless |
| *-ed*—sugared, four-footed | *-ous*—callous, ferrous |
| *-ful*—playful, soulful | *-y*—cranky, dreamy, corny |

**2.** *Position of adjectives.* We recognize adjectives in sentences chiefly by their position in relation to the nouns that they modify, especially by the fact that they can stand between an article (*a/an, the*) or words like *our, this, some* and a noun: an *old* parka, our *youngest* son, this *characteristic* gesture, some more *favorable* opportunity.

According to its position in a sentence, an adjective is either *attributive* or *predicate*:

*a—Attributive* adjectives are placed next to their nouns, usually preceding, as in *tiny* brook, *horseless* carriages. Sometimes there is good reason for placing an adjective after its noun:

a woman *sweet, simple, home-loving* (Two or more adjectives sometimes follow the noun.)

the outfit *complete* (For emphasis)

court *martial,* attorney *general* (Following French patterns)

a good plan *gone* wrong (Participle modified by adverb)

a plan so *complicated* no one could follow it (The adjective modified by other words)

a *white* cap, *small* and beautifully *made* (Avoiding an awkward piling up of adjectives before the noun)

*b–Predicate* adjectives, also called *predicatives,* come after some form of the verb *be* or some other linking verb, stated or implied (*taste, feel, turn*), except in inverted sentence order (*Silent* was the night).

| | |
|---|---|
| The day is *warm.* | That pie smells *good.* |
| The train was *crowded.* | For a while I felt *bad.* |
| The dog was *old.* | They found the man *dead.* |

(See *Linking verbs, *Predicate adjective.)

3. *Types of adjectives.* Adjectives are conventionally regarded as of three types according to their meaning or the character of their modification:

*a–Descriptive* adjectives, the most common type, are said to modify the noun by naming a quality or condition of the object named: a *gray* shutter, *vivid* colors, *difficult* words. They are ordinarily compared and may themselves be modified by intensive and qualifying adverbs, words like *almost, very, quite.* Participles (*laughing, wrecked*) function like them but usually are not compared or modified by qualifying or intensive adverbs. Because this class of words has no definable limits and new members are constantly being added, it is called an *open class.*

*b–Proper* adjectives, derived from proper nouns, originally are limiting: *French* possessions, the *Puritan* colonies—but often become descriptive: *French* culture, *Puritan* manners. Sometimes they mingle both functions, as *Elizabethan* in the *Elizabethan drama* both limits drama to a period and brings to mind qualities of a group of plays.

Often a proper adjective is used so frequently in a merely descriptive sense that it loses its relation to the proper noun from which it came and becomes a simple descriptive adjective, written without a capital: *bacchanalian, pasteurized, diesel, india* ink, *paris* green. They are, like descriptive adjectives, an *open class,* and may even be compared: *He is Frencher than the French.*

*c–Limiting* adjectives, a loose and not very numerous group of words, placed in a separate category by some recent grammarians, point out in some way the object named (*this, that, his, other, former*) or indicate quantity or number (*two, second, both*). Several of the first group are pronouns regularly used in the function of adjectives. The articles *a, an,* and *the* are often included in this group. Limiting adjectives cannot ordinarily be compared or modified by other words. They also differ from *a* and *b* in being a *closed class*; new ones are not added. (See *Possessive adjectives.)

**4.** *Adjective function.* The function of an adjective is to modify a subject, object, or indirect object, that is, to restrict or limit it. Since phrases, clauses, and words which are usually other parts of speech also perform this function, we can speak of adjectival functions performed by them.

*a*–Phrases and clauses used in adjectival function:

The man *with his hat on* is Harry.
I like the one *on the end* best.
a bird *with a long bill* (=a *long-billed* bird, a descriptive adjective)
a bird *in the hand*
Everyone *who approves of this* will please raise his right hand.
That was the summer *we went to Yellowstone.*
He asked the first man *he met.*

(See *Clauses § 2, *Restrictive and nonrestrictive for further examples and discussion.)

*b*–*Other parts of speech in adjectival function.* One of the outstanding traits of English is the use of nouns in the adjective function: a *glass* jar, the *Churchill* government, a *hurry* call, *store* bread, *ski* pants, *adjective* modifier, the *high school* course, a *stretcher* case, the *horse and buggy* days. (See *Parts of speech.)

Participles are *verbals which function like adjectives: a *coming* man, a *deserved* tribute.

**5.** *Adjectives as subjects and objects.* Preceded by an article, words that are ordinarily adjectives occur in the functions of nouns: the *just,* the *rich,* the *unemployed,* a *high* (of weather), an all-time *high,* ∴ new *low.* As a rule such words do not have genitive or plural forms.

(References: Curme, *Parts of Speech,* Chs. 3, 11; *Syntax,* Chs. 5, 13, 14, 25; Roberts, Chs. 4, 14.)

**Adverbial clauses** • See *Clauses § 2c, *Purpose, *Result.

**Adverbs, definitions** • See *Parts of speech.

**Adverbs in use** • Adverbs, like adjectives, should be either exact or happy or both. They should add something to the definiteness of the writer's expression (*Adjectives in use). In portraying rapid or violent action, amateur writers are likely to use adverbs too freely. In this paragraph we could picture the scene more clearly if the adverbs were deleted:

Shrill horns scream *threateningly*. Automobiles careen *wildly*. Giant buses lumber *dominantly* along. Policemen shout *warningly* and then *desperately*. Pedestrians scurry across the broad avenue.

Some writers tend to qualify too much, to make a statement and then draw part of it back with such words as *probably*, *apparently*. It is better to choose the most accurate word available and use that.

I shall [probably] try to read your paper tonight.

Many of the longer adverbs are unemphatic because they are unstressed toward the end, and when two or more of them come close together they make a clumsy or unpleasant sounding phrase. The repetition of the *-ly* calls attention to itself.

She sang *resonantly*, if *slightly nasally*, between the towering walls of the adjacent buildings.

They respond to recurrent temperamental differences, and to analogous though *chronologically distantly* separated social conditions.

Many of the adverbs we regularly use in conversation are superfluous and are better omitted in writing:

The college student meets [up with] a different type of instructor in English than he had in high school.

Sometimes writers use an adverb plus an adjective or a verb when an accurate adjective or exact verb would be neater and just as expressive.

Scholarships should be kept for those who are *studiously inclined*. [That is, for those who are studious.]

When no one was looking I took the goggles and *swiftly made my way* out of the store. [The simpler *hurried* would say as much.]

(See *Prepositions § 3b; *very)

**Adverbs, types and forms** •

*Adv*     *Revision: Revise the form of the adverb marked (§ 1).*

Traditionally the parts of speech category of adverbs has been a sort of rag bag, including a variety of words that modify verbs, adjectives, other adverbs, and whole clauses and sentences. (Some words in the category, like *almost, very, quite, yes, no,* obviously differ in certain respects from typical adverbs—they cannot be compared—and could be set off as different parts of speech; but because some of their functions resemble those of adverbs, they have also been regarded as a group of adverbs.) Grammarians are formulating other categories for some of these words, but since there is as yet no widely accepted grouping, this article follows the traditional grouping. (See *Parts of speech, *Particles.)

1. *Forms of adverbs.* Most adverbs are adjectives or participles plus the ending *-ly: badly, deservedly, laughingly, surely.* Some adverbs have developed from Old English forms without a special adverbial sign: *now, quite, since, then, there, where.*

There are a number of adverbs with the same forms as adjectives, most of them in use for hundreds of years. For example:

| | | | | |
|---|---|---|---|---|
| bad | doubtless | hard | much | slow |
| better | early | high | near | smooth |
| bright | even | late | new | straight |
| cheap | fair | loose | right | tight |
| close | fast | loud | rough | well |
| deep | first | low | sharp | wrong |

Most of these also have forms in *-ly,* so that we can write "He sang *loud*" or "He sang *loudly.*" The *-ly* forms are likely to be preferred in Formal English and the shorter forms in speech and Informal writing. The choice between the two is chiefly a matter of style. The shorter forms are often more vigorous than the longer:

Go *slow.* Don't talk so *loud.* It was so windy that I had to hold on *tight* to the iron stand to keep from being blown away.

In speech and Informal writing some other short forms of adverbs are used: Take it *easy.* It came *easy.* He talked *big.*

In Nonstandard usage the adverb sometimes occurs without the *-ly* which characterizes it in Standard, such as *real, special, considerable* for *really, specially, considerably.* This practice should be avoided in writing. When in doubt consult a good dictionary.

Most adverbs are compared, either by adding *-er* and *-est* or by preceding them by *more* and *most.* (See *Comparison of adjectives and adverbs.)

2. *Functions of adverbs.* Adverbs are used typically in four functions:

*a*–Modifying a single word or sentence element:

He will come *today.* (Modifying verb *come*)
She was *rather* shy. (Modifying adjective *shy*)
*Almost* immediately we saw them. (Modifying adverb *immediately*)

*b*–Modifying whole sentences:

*Perhaps* he will come today. *Unfortunately* there were no more left. *Later* I was sorry. *That evening* I was sorry. *As soon as I said it,* I was sorry.

*c*–Connecting clauses and also modifying their meaning (see *Conjunctive adverbs):

We agreed to call the matter closed; *however,* they were by no means convinced.

The museum, we discovered, was closed on Fridays; *consequently,* we drove on to the next city.

*d*–Introducing questions:

*When* did you begin to feel this way?
*Where* was the car when you first saw it?

**3.** *Adverbs grouped by meaning.* Adverbs have been traditionally identified by considering their meaning, according to what question they answer (a classification which tells little about their grammatical function):

*a*–How? (Adverbs of manner)

alike   so   worse   keenly   openly   painstakingly

*b*–When? In what order? (Adverbs of time and succession)

afterwards   when   finally   late   lately   never   soon

*c*–Where? (Adverbs of place and direction)

below   far   north   there   upstairs

*d*–How much? To what extent? (Adverbs of degree and measure)

all   almost   less   little   much   quite   completely   equally

*e*–Why? (Adverbs of cause and purpose)

consequently   therefore

*f*–Yes or no. (Adverbs of assertion, condition, and concession)

yes   no   certainly   doubtless   not   perhaps   possibly   surely
*Informal*: O.K.   nix   absolutely

**4.** *Other constructions in adverbial function.* Nouns may be used in the function of adverbs (see *Genitive § 2):

He came *mornings.* He plans to stay a *month.*

Phrases may have the functions of adverbs (see *Phrases):

He came *in the morning. After the examinations* he quit.

Clauses may have the functions of adverbs:

*When it came time to go,* he didn't know what to do. He stayed on and on *because he didn't know how to leave.*

**5.** *Position of adverbial modifiers.* Unlike the position of adjectival modifiers, the position of adverbial modifiers in a sentence is variable and cannot be used as a way of identifying them with certainty. They should be placed in a position that is natural for a native user of the language and that will represent his desired emphasis.

Single word adverbs modifying single words tend to be placed next to the word modified: the *almost* perfect state, the *most disagreeably* certain result, they *certainly* tried, they all worked *hard*. Adverbial phrases and clauses precede or follow the main construction. These versions of the same sentence show some typical variations in the position of adverbials:

1. *When the tide turned,* all the boats *hurriedly* headed *for the channel.*
2. All the boats *hurriedly* headed *for the channel when the tide turned.*
3. All the boats headed *for the channel hurriedly when the tide turned.*
4. *Hurriedly* all the boats headed *for the channel when the tide turned.*
5. All the boats, *when the tide turned, hurriedly* headed *for the channel.*
6. All the boats headed *for the channel when the tide turned hurriedly.*

All of the first five would be possible, though four and five only if special emphasis was wanted on *hurriedly* or *when the tide turned.* In the sixth the position of *hurriedly* relates it to *turned,* and thus conveys a different meaning.

(Reference: Curme, *Parts of Speech,* pp. 73-86; all grammars give some information.)

**advice—advise** • The first is the noun—*to give advice*—the second, the verb. The General idiom with the verb is an infinitive: *He advised me to forget it.* Possible, but more Formal, is: *I advised his forgetting it.* The business use of *advise* meaning *inform*—erected into a monumental cliché in *beg to advise*—continues an older use of the word and is often, in addition, *deadwood: "We beg to advise that your chair is done" means no more than "Your chair is done." But it remains in good General use for information rather formally given: *The President was also advised that* . . . .

**-ae-, -oe-** • Words of Greek and Latin origin that contain the digraphs *-ae-* and *-oe-* have been for a long time variously spelled in English. (Most printers do not now use the ligatures —*æ, œ*—except in works dealing with the ancient languages.) Both *-ae-* and *-oe-* are pronounced as though written *e* (either long or short). Many spellings have simplified in the past: *economics, pedagogy, penal* were formerly *oeconomics, paedagogy, poenal.* Medicine has adopted many of the simpler forms like *anesthetic* (for *anaesthetic*). The long series of words beginning with *haem-* (meaning "blood") now preferably begin with *hem- (hematic, hemoglobin, hemorrhage,* and so on). The American Historical Association long ago adopted *medieval*. Dictionaries now give such words as *ameba, cesura, dieresis, esthetic, subpena* as alternate spellings. For a particular word consult a good recent dictionary. Formal style tends to keep the older two-letter forms, General to use the simple *e*.

Latin plurals in *ae* still keep the two letters: *alumnae, antennae, formulae* (see *Plurals of nouns § 4); and in Greek and Latin proper names the two letters are kept: *Boeotia, Caesar, Oedipus*.

**affect—effect** • Since a distinction is seldom made in pronouncing these words /ə fekt′/, it is easy to confuse their spellings.

*Affect* is usually a verb, meaning "influence" or "put on" (compare *Affectation) or "pretend": *This will affect thousands. He affected a stern manner. He affects boredom.*

The noun *affect* is a technical term in psychology.

*Effect* is usually a noun, meaning "result": *The effects of this will be felt by thousands. What is the effect of doubling the amount?*

*Effect* is also a verb in Formal English, meaning "bring about": *The change was effected peaceably.*

**Affectation** • We learn our language as children by imitating the speech of people around us, and we expand our language later in life by imitating what we hear others say or what we find in reading. So long as these changes furnish us with more varied and more exact ways of expressing ourselves, they are proper and necessary and represent a healthy growth. But sometimes we are led to adopt different pronunciations or different words or different constructions not so much to make our speech more effective as to make it seem more elegant, or even for the effect of the language itself rather than for what it is conveying. Such changes are affectations and are unpleasant because they are not part of our variety of English. Writing is usually more precise than speech, but writing in a style quite different from one's speech is affectation.

Affectation is most easily spotted in pronunciations. In some parts of the United States /bēn/ for *been*, /rä′ᴛHer/ for *rather*, and /ī ᴛHer/ for *either* are common pronunciations, but consciously adopting them is affectation in regions where /bin/, /ra ᴛHer/, or /ē ᴛHer/ are usual. For many people *one should* or *shouldn't one* is an affectation, and so are Briticisms like *early on* and *that which* for *what*. Using slang except for humorous effect is an affectation in someone who knows little slang and seldom uses it in natural speech.

The line between natural and affected speech is hard to draw, since it depends chiefly on motive. In general, picking up expressions not commonly heard from the educated people of a community is risky. Increasing the expressiveness of one's speech is praiseworthy but just trying to be "different" will usually result in bad English. The way to avoid affectation is to consider the appropriateness and expressiveness of language and to shun the *big words that smack of pedantry and pretentiousness. In speech as well as in writing, keep your language simple, clear, and direct. (See "What is good English?" p. 22, *Pronunciation § 3.)

**after** • *After* is an element in numerous verb-adverb combinations: *look after the children, takes after his father, go after the largest one, came after a cup of sugar.* Its basic prepositional meanings of "behind" (in space) and "later" (in time) have allowed a number of extensions, especially in common idioms: *after all, after dark.* In crediting illustrations it means "redrawn from another's work": *after Rubens.*

**aggravate** • In Informal usage *aggravate* means to "annoy" or "irritate": *I was never so aggravated in my life.* In Formal and usually in General English *aggravate* means "to intensify or increase something unpleasant," as to *aggravate suffering* or *a wound* or *a crime.* The same distinction is made with the noun *aggravation.*

**Agreement** •
*Revision: Make the pronoun or verb marked agree in form with the word to which it is related: its antecedent if it is a pronoun, its subject if it is a verb.*

*Agr*

Certain parts of speech which vary in form for gender, person, or number agree in Standard English when they stand in relationship to each other:
**1.** *Subject* and *verb* agree in number (The *man is* old; The *men are* old) and person (*I go* tomorrow; *He goes* tomorrow). (See *Subject and verb, *Collective nouns.)
**2.** When a *pronoun* has an antecedent, it agrees with the antecedent in number (The *boy* had lost *his* way; The *hikers* had lost *their* way), in gender (The *girl* found *her* keys; Every *question* has *its* answer), and when conveniently possible in person. (See *Reference of pronouns, *each, *every and its compounds.)
**3.** A *demonstrative adjective* usually agrees in number with the noun it modifies (*That coat* is expensive; *These shoes* cost

more than my old black suede pair did). (See *Demonstrative adjectives, *this, *kind, sort.)

The chief cause of lack of agreement is that since formal agreement in English is not vital for intelligibility, we tend to ignore the form of what we started with. This is especially true if the subject is a collective noun or pronoun or if several words, some of them plural, come between a singular subject and its verb, so that we are tempted to use a plural verb. Another cause is that there may be a conflict between agreement by form and agreement by meaning. (See *Collective nouns, *every and its compounds.)

In Formal English, agreement by form is quite strictly followed, but there are many locutions in which variations have become acceptable in General and Informal English. (See, for example, *either, *one of those who, *who, whom.)

**agree to, agree with** • One agrees *to* a plan and agrees *with* a person. One thing agrees *with* another. Other idioms are: I agree *in* principle; we agreed *on* a plan of attack.

**ain't** • *Ain't* is one of the commonest and most easily identifiable Nonstandard words, and prejudice against it among educated people has been almost unanimous for the last half century or so, though it is directly descended from formerly accepted contractions. In conversation it could be an economical single form for *am not, is not, are not, has not, have not,* but the schools' condemnation of it over the past century has been very effective because it is learned as one word and like an oath can be easily identified.

Used in the first person, especially in question form (*ain't I*) where there is no easy natural contraction—*amn't* is hard to pronounce—*ain't* is occasionally heard among educated speakers and was marked "disputable" and "almost established" in the Leonard study of 1932. *Aren't* is often used in this construction, especially in England: *I'm making real progress, aren't I?* Though in the first person, both *ain't* and *aren't* may perhaps be regarded as Informal, other uses of *ain't* are Nonstandard. Except in dialog, *ain't* is Nonstandard in General and Formal writing.

(See *Divided usage. References: Curme, *Parts of Speech,* p. 248; Marckwardt and Walcott, pp. 48, 95-96; the entry *ain't* in *Webster's Third New International Dictionary.*)

**a la** • *A la* is regarded as an English preposition, meaning "in the manner of": *a la Whistler, a la The New Yorker.* In Formal writing and modish advertising (as of cosmetics and fashionable clothes), the accent mark is usually kept (*à la*); elsewhere it is written *a la*. The other French forms, *à l'* and *au,* occur only in borrowed phrases: *au gratin. Alamode* (whether meaning "in the fashion" or referring to ice cream on pie) is usually written as one word without the accent mark. The French form *à la mode* is now rare.

**albeit •** *Albeit* is archaic as a conjunction and heavy as a preposition: *It has a kind of structure, albeit a kind of structure that almost defies description. Even though* (or *although*) is more appropriate to General English.

**all and its compounds •** Watch the following words and phrases:

> *all ready* (adjective phrase) : At last they were all ready to begin.
> *already* (adverb of time) : They had already begun.
> \**all right* (adjective phrase) : The seats seemed all right to me.
> \**all the farther* (adverb, equivalent to *as far as*) is a localism: That's all the farther I'll go.
> *all together* (adjective phrase) : We found them all together in an old trunk. There were six all together.
> *altogether* (adverb, equivalent to *wholly*): That's altogether another matter.

**all of •** In General and Informal usage *all* is followed by *of* in many constructions where the *of* is less likely in Formal writing:

> All of the milk was spilled.
> They passed all of the candidates.
> You can't fool all of the people all of the time.

*All of* is required with a pronoun in Standard English.

> All of them went home.
> They wanted all of it but got only half.
> He gave all of us some candy.

**all right—alright •** *All right* is the usual Standard spelling of both the adjective phrase (He is all right) and the sentence adverb, meaning "yes, certainly" (All right, I'll come).

*Alright* is a natural analogy with *altogether* and *already* but at present is found mainly in advertising, comic strips, in unedited writing, and, rarely, in fiction. Though it is gaining respectability, the prejudice against it is still strong.

**all-round •** *All-round* is usually hyphened: *an all-round athlete, an all-round education.* Many readers still object to *all-around.* In either version, the word has been so overused that it has become trite.

**all the farther** • Although *all the farther* is often heard in Informal and General speech, it is Nonstandard in writing. (Reference: Bryant, pp. 19-20.)

**Alliteration** • *Alliteration* is the repetition of the same sound usually at the beginnings of several words in a series or at the beginnings of stressed syllables within several words close together. Besides contributing to the pleasure that a reader may find in the similar sounds, alliteration serves to bind the phrase, or sometimes a whole series of phrases, into a unit:

... the *c*rowded, *c*loistered *c*olleges of Oxford.—PAUL ELMER MORE
... ran over the *s*tarry *s*moothness of the lagoon, and the water between the piles lapped the *s*limy timber once with a *s*udden *s*plash.
—JOSEPH CONRAD

Alliteration is one of the figures of sound that contribute to the musical effect of poetry, though not one of the most important:

> Here I a*m*, an old *m*an in a dry *m*onth,
> *B*eing *r*ead to *b*y a *b*oy, waiting for *r*ain.
> T. S. ELIOT
> The *s*ilken, *s*ad, un*c*ertain, ru*s*tling...
> EDGAR ALLAN POE

In ordinary expository prose conspicuous alliteration is usually out of place because it tends to attract attention to the expression at the expense of the idea. Its use in Formal prose, especially in prose with an oratorical or poetic background, is more appropriate.

Alliteration is one of the chief weapons of advertising sloganeers and makers of flashy titles, who simply push to a conspicuous point the natural binding power of the figure:

*F*ilter, *f*lavor, *f*lip-top box      *M*ealtime *M*agic with *M*ilk

Alliteration is also characteristic of humorous verse and prose of any mannered writing on the light side:

> Tell me, what is a man to do
> When the *l*ady his *l*ife is based upon
> *L*ikes to be *w*ooed but *w*on't be *w*on?
> OGDEN NASH, *Hard Lines*, p. 58

**Allusion** • See *Echo phrases.

**-al ly** • English has a number of adjectives with the (Latin) endings *-al* and *-ical*: *fatal, final, medical, historical, political.* Usually an adverb is made by adding *-ly* to this. This ending should be remembered in spelling these words, especially since the unstressed final sounds give the impression that there are fewer syllables than must be spelled.

| | | | |
|---|---|---|---|
| accidental | accidentally | mental | mentally |
| fundamental | fundamentally | political | politically |
| incidental | incidentally | practical | practically |

Several adjectives ending in *-ical* show a tendency to drop the *-al*: *alphabetic, biographic, geographic, philosophic* following the course of *academic, frantic, emphatic, poetic,* and others that have already shed the final syllable. But the two forms may vary somewhat in meaning: Compare *historical fact* (a fact of history) and *historic fact* (a memorable fact in history). Although *public* and a few others have adverbs without the *-al-* (*publicly*), most reinstate that ending before *-ly*:

| | | |
|---|---|---|
| academically | dramatically | prolifically |
| athletically | heroically | specifically |
| automatically | idiotically | terrifically |

**alma mater** • An anglicized Latin term ("fostering mother") meaning one's school or college; rather pretentious in General writing. Pronounced /al′mə mä′tər/, /äl′mə mä′tər/, /al mə ma′ter/.

**almost** • See *most, almost.

**already** • See *all and its compounds.

**alright** • This is not yet an accepted spelling. (See *all right.)

**also** • *Also* is weak as a connective; ordinarily *and* works better:

He came with tents, cooking things, *and* [better than *also*] about fifty pounds of photographic equipment.

(See *Conjunctive adverbs.)

**alternative** • *Alternative* comes from the Latin *alter,* "the second of two." Some Formal writers, in deference to the word's origin, confine its meaning to "one of two possibilities," but it is regularly used to mean one of several possibilities, and is so defined in dictionaries.

**although, though** • *Although* and *though* connect with the main clause an adverbial clause of concession—that is, a statement that qualifies the main statement but does not contradict it. *Although* is more likely to introduce a clause that precedes the main clause, *though* one that follows:

Although [Though] the rain kept up for almost three weeks, we managed to have a pretty good time.

We managed to have a pretty good time, though [although] the rain kept up for almost three weeks.

Here there is no distinction in meaning; the choice between the two may be based on sentence rhythm. *Although* is a heavier and slightly more Formal word and hence occurs less frequently. (Reference: Bryant, pp. 216-218.) As a conjunctive adverb only *though* is used: *He did it, though.*

Often one of two clauses connected by *but* can be thrown into an *although* clause to vary the sentence pattern:

We had rehearsed that act time and time again, but we all missed our cues the first night.

Although we had rehearsed that act time and time again, we all missed our cues that first night.

The spelling *altho* has made more headway than *tho* and *thru* and is appropriate in Informal writing and in some General writing (if editorial or course policy approves), but would not be used in Formal writing. (See *but. Reference: Curme, *Syntax,* pp. 332-340.)

**alumnus** • Four Latin forms of this word exist in English:

| | |
|---|---|
| One male graduate is an | alumnus /ə lum′nəs/ |
| Two or more male graduates are | alumni /ə lum′nī/ |
| One female graduate is an | alumna /ə lum′nə/ |
| Two or more female graduates are | alumnae /ə lum′nē/ |

By common practice *alumnus* and *alumni* are used for graduates of coeducational institutions. Because of this clumsy complication of forms, *graduate* and *graduates* are increasingly used. *Alum* /ə lum′/ is used in some institutions.

**a.m. and p.m., also A.M. and P.M.** • These abbreviations (for *ante meridiem,* "before noon," and *post meridiem,* "after noon") are most useful in tables and lists of times. In General writing they are used only with figures for specific hours: *from 2 to 4 p.m.* (Not: *I'll see you this p.m.*)

Though *M.* is the abbreviation for noon (*12 m.*), *12 noon* is more common; midnight is *12 p.m.*

**Ambiguity** •
*Revision: Make the meaning you intend unmistakable.*

*Amb*

Although inexact writing is common enough, actually ambiguous writing, in which there is possibility of confusing two meanings, is relatively rare. The context usually shows which of two possible meanings must be taken. The most common sources of actual ambiguity are:

1. *Inexact reference of pronoun,* especially in \*indirect discourse:

He told his father he had been talking too much.

Such a sentence usually needs re-forming, perhaps as:

He admitted to his father that he had been talking too much.
He criticized his father for talking too much.

(See \*Reference of pronouns.)

2. *Modifiers*

*a—Squinting modifiers* that may refer to either of two words or constructions:

The governor penalized those office holders who had opposed him *for good reason.* (The governor had good reason for penalizing those who had opposed him. Or: The governor penalized those who had had good reason to oppose him.)

Some people *I know* would go there anyway. (Some people whom I know.... Or: Some people would go there anyway, I know.)

*b—Modifiers temporarily misleading,* as in headlines:

Police repair man killed by car
Horse bites off ear of owner—Man says he will keep biting mare

Such sentences are usually clear in spoken English, and even in writing the intended meaning can be wrung out by rereading. But the writer should not require his reader to be a detective. (See \*Hyphen § 2.)

3. *Incomplete idioms,* especially in comparison:

"I like Alice as well as Will" might mean "I like Alice as well as Will does," "I like Alice as well as I do Will," or "I like both Alice and Will."

4. *"Yes" or "no" after negatives. Yes* or *no,* in response to a negative question or in commenting on a negative statement, often needs a clause to make the meaning clear.

You haven't any more red ink, have you? (*Answer:* "Yes, I have" or "No, I haven't.")

Let's not use such a long quotation. (No, let's not.)

5. *Changing meanings.* Many words in English are undergoing changes in meaning. Sometimes the transition can be completed without risk of ambiguous communication because the context makes the intention clear. As *car* came to apply primarily to an automobile rather than a railroad or street car, such restricting words as *motor, railroad,* or *street* prevented misunderstanding. But when such safeguards are not present, serious ambiguity may occur. Examples: \*disinterested—unin-

terested, *imply—infer, *transpire, *grammar, inflammable—
flammable, *incredible—incredulous, *censor—censure.

**6.** *Intentional ambiguity.* Incomplete or ambiguous statements are sometimes intentional, like the sign in an airport
limousine, "Tipping for this service not required," which drew
tips from most passengers.

(See *Comma § 7 for information on using a comma to
avoid ambiguity.)

**American** • Since there is no word to describe the United
States (as *Italian,* for example, describes Italy), *American* is
ordinarily used. It is obviously inexact, since Canadians and
Mexicans are also American. But it is no more inexact than
many other words and is generally used in this sense. Perhaps
we can take an Englishman's judgment:

> The use of *America* for *the United States* & *American* for *(citi-
> zen) of the U.S.* is open to as much & as little objection as that of
> *England* & *English(man)* for *Great Britain (& Ireland), British* &
> *Briton.* It will continue to be protested against by purists & patriots,
> & will doubtless survive the protests.—H. W. FOWLER, *A Dictionary
> of Modern English Usage,* p. 18

It is more exact to use *the United States* as the name of our
country, but the use of *America* is common. Use *American* as
the adjective and the name of an inhabitant. (Reference:
H. L. Mencken, "Names for Americans," *American Speech,*
1947, 22:241-256.)

**American and British usage** • For several reasons the spoken
and written English of the United States differs from that of
England. Since the seventeenth and eighteenth centuries, when
the English language was brought to North America, the language used on both sides of the Atlantic has changed in somewhat different ways.

The people in the United States and England live under
different governments; they are educated in different school
systems. Social stratification, affecting the ideals and habits of
large classes of people, is considerably different. In spite of the
mutual circulation of publications, visits of lecturers, professors, and government officials, and interchange by way of
movies, radio, and television, many of the factors that tend to
keep the speech within the British Commonwealth more like
that of England cannot operate as effectively between England
and the United States. Finally, dialectal varieties which were
brought from England in the seventeenth and eighteenth centuries have sometimes remained influential in this country
while losing ground in England.

The differences in language have led to interesting emotional attitudes on both sides. In the past Britishers have scorned "vulgar Americanisms." The maker of the glossary to the London edition of Sinclair Lewis' *Babbitt* went beyond simple definition when he wrote for *ice cream soda,* "Ice cream in soda water. A ghastly American summer time drink." Fowler says that the realization that Americans had dropped the *u* from words ending in *-our* stopped the British from making the same change. Some Americans used to look upon British accent and vocabulary as ludicrous or at best snobbish, but these attitudes are becoming less prevalent.

In the written language some spelling differences stand out. The British tend still to prefer *-re* to *-er* in words like *center* and *\*theater,* though they use both forms; they still keep *-our* in a number of words (see *\*-or, -our*), though they are gradually simplifying; they use *x* in a few words like *inflexion*; they tend to double more consonants, as in *traveller, waggon*; and there are various individual words that differ, such as *tyre* (automobile *tire*). But these distinctions affect only a small number of words, and actually for most of them usage is divided in both countries. They are just pervasive enough to show that a book is of British or American origin, but they do not interfere with reading. Such differences can be used to make a good argument for allowing more individual freedom in spelling, but they continue to offer a problem to a publisher who wishes to circulate a book in both countries.

For a number of years scholars in the United States have been at work discovering and describing our speech. The magazine *American Speech,* which was founded in 1925, has published specific observations of usage and more general articles. George Philip Krapp's *The English Language in America* (New York, 1925) and John S. Kenyon's *American Pronunciation* (Ann Arbor, 1950) are scholarly works. The four editions of H. L. Mencken's *The American Language* (New York, 1919-1936) have given a good defense of American as against British usage. Mencken is not quite fair in that he usually pits American Nonstandard against formal British, but his main point, the existence of a distinctive popular speech in the United States, is well proved (though not his implication that there is a distinct American language); Raven I. McDavid's large abridgment of Mencken's work (1963, with the assistance of David W. Maurer) includes many additions and presents a more balanced approach. *The Dictionary of American English* and *The Dictionary of Americanisms* present the record of many words as they have been used in the United States.

There are of course several varieties of English in use on both sides of the Atlantic; and Great Britain presents a greater variety than the United States, in part because of sturdy remains of older dialects in the various counties, in Scotland, and in Wales. Among Englishmen and Americans of average education and social position, differences in pronunciation are likely to be particularly striking. There are different intonations, different values for the vowels, differences in particular words like the British /trā/ *trait*, /prō cess/, /con tents′/, /lef ten′ ənt/ *lieutenant*, /ral′ i/ for the American /rô′ lē/ *Raleigh*, and in general a more rapid speech and a tendency to drop the secondary stress (such as an *-ar* in *dictionary*). The slower, fuller pronunciation of most Americans seems wasteful and provincial to some Britishers.

Everyone knows some of the differences in vocabulary in certain common words: In England an *elevator* is a *lift, radio* is *wireless, crackers* are *biscuits* (*cakes* and *muffins* are also different from those in America), a *sit-down* strike is a *stay-in* strike, a *run* in a stocking is a *ladder, daylight saving time* is *summer time, installment buying* is the *hire-purchase system, white-collar* workers are *black-coat* workers. From the group word *tin can* the British have taken *tin*, Americans *can*. A *truck* is a *lorry,* an *automobile* is a *motor car* (though both are compromising on *car*), *gasoline* is *petrol,* sold in a *gallon* much larger than the American measure. A *billion* is a thousand million in America (and France) and a million million in England (and Germany). But recent innovations are more likely to get the same names in both countries.

There is a Nonstandard speech in both England and America, an array of slang that baffles readers on the opposite side of the Atlantic, and many colloquialisms unique to each. In a book or play *no end* and /rä тНėr′/ are supposed to identify an Englishman as clearly as *guess* or *reckon* is supposed to identify an American. But it is not easy for a writer to catch the distinctive differences, as a reading of a modern detective story by a British writer will show; if Americans are introduced, their speech doesn't ring true. One reason for careful study of the differences between the spoken language in England and in this country has been the vogue of realistic fiction, which necessarily made use of more colloquial English and more colloquial American. In fact, the increased informality of modern prose in both England and the United States has tended to emphasize the distinctions between the two.

The grammar of the popular levels of English and of American differs somewhat—contrast the speech of ordinary people in novels of the two countries. But in the General writing of the two there is less difference in grammar than in vocabulary.

Collective nouns are more likely to be plural in British usage (*the government intend*); British writers differ in small matters like the position of *only,* the proper preposition with *different,* the use of *shall,* and various idioms. (See Stuart Robertson, "British-American Differentiations in Syntax and Idiom," *American Speech,* 1939, 14:243-254.)

A fairly long catalog of such minor differences between these two branches of English could be drawn up, but their importance should not be exaggerated or allowed to obscure the fundamental fact that the resemblances far outnumber the differences and that the speech of the two countries represents two different strands of the English language.

For an American there is no virtue in consciously cultivating British pronunciations or adopting British words and idioms (Briticisms). If he uses generally accepted American English, he will reach his proper public, and if what he writes is interesting or important enough, he can reach British readers too. (Many particular entries in this *Index* note differences between British and American usage.)

**among, between** • See *between, among.

**amount, number** • The distinction between these words is that *amount* is used of things viewed in bulk, weight, or sums; *number* is used of things that can be counted in individual units:

> a large *amount* of milk (but a large *number* of cans of milk)
> a small *amount* of time, an *amount* of money
> a large *number* of seats, a *number* of people, a *number* of mistakes

No native speaker substitutes *number* where *amount* is conventionally used, but *amount* sometimes replaces *number: the amount of people, an amount of books.* This usage is better avoided.

**Ampersand** • *Ampersand* is the name for the & sign (originally a linking of the letters of *et*), called also *short and.* Its primary use, obviously, is to save space; therefore it belongs only where abbreviations are appropriate. In addressing firms, use the form they habitually use (*. . . and Company* or *. . . & Company*), and in quoting, follow your original carefully. Use *and* in college papers.

**Analogy in language** • *Analogy* is the name for the natural tendency in users of a language to make their speech more regular by forming new words like some existing ones, bringing old words closer together in form, or bringing constructions in line with familiar patterns. It results from the fact that, in general, language is a complex of consistent patterns (noun plurals end in -s, past tenses in -ed, etc.). It is easiest to watch analogy in the attempts of children to master their language. Before they learn the irregular conventional forms used by grownups, they regularize on the basis of the patterns they are familiar with: Most children for a time say *mans* before they learn to say *men, singed* for *sang* or *sung, digged* for *dug,* or they may say *dag* instead of *dug.*

Analogy is the force that has disposed of many irregularities in the main body of language. Out of various plural forms used in Old English, -s has won in all but a few words, and analogy is still bringing more words to that form, like *\*formula, formulas.* Words occasionally are changed in spelling by analogy, as the -b was rather recently added to *crumb* and *thumb* from analogy with *dumb*; and *humble* suggested *crumble*; and so on. *Cole slaw* is often replaced by *cold slaw* by folk etymology, *cole* (from Dutch *kool,* cabbage) being unfamiliar. *Adviser* is now changing to *advisor* from analogy with *advisory* and words like *inspector, distributor. Alright* is slowly making its way from analogy with *already* (see \*all right). New words are formed on analogy with old ones, like *avigation, aerobatics.*

The extension of *was* to the plural—a common form in Nonstandard English, based on the analogy of most English verbs in the past tense (*I did—we did, he went—they went*)—illustrates not only the force of analogy but the fact that the result, however logical and consistent, is not necessarily acceptable. The *was-were* distinction is the sole survival from a considerable group of verbs in Old English which had different forms for the preterit singular and plural—*sing, drive, choose,* for example. To be accepted the analogical form must be frequently used by educated writers and speakers—and *we was* is not. (See \*Change in language, \*due to, the words starred in this article, and various other examples of analogy treated in particular *Index* articles. Reference: E. H. Sturtevant, *Linguistic Change,* Chicago, 1917, p. 38 ff., Ch. 6. See also the indexes of most works on language for their treatment of analogy.)

**-ance, -ence (-ant, -ent)** • Two of the most troublesome groups of words in English spelling are those ending in *-ance (-ant)* and *-ence (-ent)*. Most of them are nouns and adjectives descended from verbs of different Latin conjugations whose stem vowels are generally represented in these endings. There is no difference in our pronunciation of the endings—both get the neutral vowel ə: /di fen′dənt/, /di pen′dənt/. There is a slight tendency for printers to adopt the ending with *e*, but for the present all we can do is learn the individual forms by memory or consult a dictionary.

Here are some of the commoner words of these types:

### -ANCE, -ANT

| | |
|---|---|
| appearance | reluctance, reluctant |
| attendance, attendant | repentance, repentant |
| balance | resemblance |
| defendant | resistance, resistant |
| descendant (or descendent) | significance, significant |
| extravagance, extravagant | tolerance, tolerant |
| intolerance, intolerant | vigilance, vigilant |

### -ENCE, -ENT

| | |
|---|---|
| competence, competent | innocence, innocent |
| confidence, confident | insistence, insistent |
| consistency, consistent | obedience, obedient |
| dependence, dependent | persistence, persistent |
| existence, existent | reverence, reverent |
| independence, independent | turbulence, turbulent |

A group of similar nouns end in *-ense*:

defense   dispense   expense   offense   pretense   suspense

## and •

1. *Appropriate uses of "and." And* is the most used connective, joining two or more elements in a series, usually of equal grammatical rank:

> *Adjectives*: a *pink* and *white* apron; a *blue, green,* and *white* flag
> *Adverbs*: He drove *very fast* and *rather carelessly.*
> *Nouns*: *trees* and *shrubs*; *trees, shrubs,* and *plants*
> *Verbs*: I *found* the book and *opened* it at the exact place.
> *Phrases*: *in one ear* and *out the other*
> *Dependent clauses*: *While the boys were swimming* and [*while*] *the older folks were resting,* I was reading.
> *Independent clauses*: *The first generation makes the money* and *the second spends it.*

2. *Inappropriate uses of "and."* In careless writing, elements of unequal grammatical value are sometimes connected by an unnecessary *and*:

> Main verbs and participles: Three or four men *sat* on the edge of the lake with their backs to the road, [and] apparently *watching* the ducks.

> Independent and dependent clauses: *A contract has been let to install new copper work on the Post Office* [and] *which will require 4500 pounds of lead-coated copper.* (See *which § 4.)

*And* is often used in amateur writing where no connective is needed or where some other connective would show more clearly the logical relation:

All the passages inside the muskrats' house tended to head upward and we pushed the traps far enough in to reach dry ground. (Since all the passages . . . , we pushed . . . .)

The freshmen have a number of required courses and [but] the upperclassmen almost none.

**3.** *At beginning of sentences.* In current writing of all varieties, *and* sometimes stands at the beginning of sentences. If this usage becomes conspicuous, some of the *and*'s should be dropped or two sentences put together as a compound sentence.

**4.** *Omission of "and."* In some compact writing *and* is omitted between series of items. Judiciously used, this omission makes for economy, but overused contributes to a *"telegraphic" style, which is usually inappropriate for General writing.

(These *Index* articles involve *and*: *Compound predicate, *Compound sentences, *Compound subject, *Conjunctive adverbs, *Coordinating conjunctions, *between you and me, *which, *Series.)

**and etc.** • See *etc., et cetera.

**and/or** • Though *and/or* was originally a legal and business locution, it is useful when three alternatives exist (*both* circumstances mentioned or *either one* of the two): *fruit and/or vegetables* means "fruit" or "vegetables" or "fruit and vegetables."

*And/or* is increasingly found in General writing, but many readers object to it because of its business connotation and odd appearance. Before you use it, consider its probable effect on your reader.

**angle** • *Angle* is often *deadwood and suggests a colloquial or business phrase that is rather out of place in General writing:

In a preparatory school the masters go at the matter from a different angle [that is, *differently*] and make the same kind of literature more enjoyable.

**Antecedent** • *Antecedent* is the grammatical term for the word or statement to which a pronoun or *pronominal adjective refers. It may stand before or after the pronoun:

We did not hear their call again and when we found the Thompsons they were almost exhausted. (*The Thompsons* is the antecedent of the pronominal adjective *their* and the pronoun *they*.)

(For relations between antecedents and their pronouns see *Agreement, *Reference of pronouns.)

**anti-, anti** • The prefix *anti-,* meaning "against" in its various senses, is hyphened only before root words beginning with *i* and before proper nouns:

| | | | |
|---|---|---|---|
| antibiotic | antifreeze | anti-intellectual | anti-Semitic |
| anti-British | anti-imperialistic | antimonarchic | antisocial |

*Anti-* is pronounced /an′ti/, an′tə/, or often /an′tī/. *Anti* is an Informal noun, meaning "a person opposed to something"; plural *antis*: *The pros spoke amid boos from the antis* (/an′tīz/ or /an′tēz/).

**Anticipatory subject** • See *it, *there is, there are.

**Anticlimax** • An *anticlimax* is an arrangement of a series in order of descending importance of the elements. It may be intentional, as a form of humor (as in Pope's "Men, monkeys, lap-dogs, parrots, perish all"), or unintentional because of a lapse of judgment on the writer's part ("She had a warm and sympathetic personality, a quick and perceptive intelligence, beautiful features and a lovely figure, and she could play Scrabble"). Such lapses should be corrected.

**Antonym** • An *antonym* is a word that means approximately the opposite of another word: *hot, stingy, boring* are antonyms of *cold, generous, entertaining.* Most books of synonyms also give antonyms, as do the synonym entries in dictionaries.

**any, and compounds with any** •
1. *Any,* deriving from the same source as *one, a, an,* is used primarily as an adjective (any member of the family, Any dog is a good dog) but also as a pronoun (Any will do).

In comparisons of things of the same class, *idiom calls for *any other: This book is better than any other on the subject.* But: *I like a movie better than any book* (different class of things).
2. *Compounds with "any."* Anybody, anyhow, anything, and *anywhere* are always written as single words. *Any rate* is always two words: *at any rate. Anyone* is written as one word when the stress is on the *any* (Anyone /en′ ē wun/ would know that), and as two when the stress is on the *one* (I'd like any one /en ē wun′/ of them.)

*Anyway* is one word when the *any* is stressed (I can't do it anyway /en′ ē wā/), and two when the stress is about equal (Any way /en′ ē wā′/ I try, it comes out wrong). If the word

*whatever* can be substituted for the *any* (Whatever way I try, it comes out wrong), *any way* should be written as two words.
3. *Pronouns referring to "anybody," "anyone."* *Anybody* and *anyone* are singular in form and take singular verbs (Anybody [Anyone] feels bad at times). They are referred to by *he, his, him* (*Anybody* knows what *he* deserves), or, since they are often felt to be collective, Informally by a plural pronoun:

... and a top that goes up and down without *anybody* losing *their* temper.—Thornton Wilder (letter), *Theatre Arts*, Nov. 1940

(See *Divided usage. Compare *every and its compounds; Fries, *AEG,* p. 50.)
4. *Informal forms* (not appropriate in college writing). *Any place* is Informal for *anywhere* (He wasn't any place I looked). *Anyways* is regional for the generally used *anyway,* and *anywheres* is Nonstandard for *anywhere.* *Any more = now* is a Standard idiom in a negative context (You don't see that any more). Its regional use in an affirmative context (*Any more I do that*) is Nonstandard outside quotation marks.

**Aphorisms** • See *Epigrams.

**Apostrophe (')** •

*Apos*

*Revision: Insert an apostrophe where it belongs in the word marked; or take out a wrongly used apostrophe.*

The apostrophe is one of the most useless anachronisms in our traditional system of spelling, as Bernard Shaw demonstrated in his printed works; but you must know the conventions governing its use and follow them.
1. *In genitives.* The most common use of the apostrophe is in spelling the *genitive (possessive) case of nouns and of the indefinite pronouns (*anyone, nobody, someone*—See *Pronouns § 8): *Dorothy's* first picture, The *companies'* original charters, *Everybody's* business is *nobody's* business, The *boys'* dogs.

It should be kept in singular genitives of time even though they carry no idea of possession: a *day's* hike, this *month's* quota.

It is often omitted from plurals that can be regarded as nouns used in the function of an adjective especially when used as proper names: *teachers* college, a *girls* school. (See *Genitive case for discussion of special examples of possessive form.)
2. *In contractions.* The apostrophe is used to show the omission of one or more letters in contractions: *can't, I'm, I'll, it's* [*it is*]. (See *Contractions.)

**3.** *In plurals.* An apostrophe is ordinarily used in plurals of figures, letters of the alphabet, and words being discussed as words: *three e's, the 1920's, the first of the two that's.* There is some tendency to omit this apostrophe:

> The legendary Miss Millay, the feminine Byron of the *1920s....*
> —Louis Untermeyer

**4.** *In representing speech.* An apostrophe may be used to show that certain sounds represented in the usual spelling were not spoken:

> "An' one o' them is the new schoolmaster," he said.

This is a legitimate use, but too many apostrophes make a spotted page and confuse the reader. It is better to suggest occasional pronunciations of this sort than to try to represent them conscientiously. In the example the indicated pronunciations are in fact Standard.

**5.** *Personal pronouns.* Apostrophes are not used in the genitive of the personal pronouns: *his, hers, its, ours, theirs, yours.*

**6.** *Simplified spellings.* No apology is needed for simplified spellings that are entered in the dictionary: (*altho,* not *altho';* *thru,* not *thro'.*) *Till* is a word, equivalent to *until,* not *'til.* In some college classrooms, simplified spellings are acceptable; in some they are not.

**appearing** • *Appearing* is an inflated (or unnecessarily Formal) substitute for *looking: a comfortable looking* [better than *appearing*] *street, a fine looking* [better than *appearing*] *moraine locust.*

**appendix** • The English plural *appendixes* is now commoner than the Latin *appendices* and is the better form except in quite Formal usage; it is the only plural form used in referring to the appendix of appendicitis.

**Apposition, appositives** • *Apposition* is the placing of a construction next to another so that the second either complements or supplements the first. The complementary relationship is called close or restrictive apposition because the second element completes the first; it is not set off by commas. The supplementary relationship is loose or nonrestrictive; it is usually set off by commas.

| *Close (restrictive, complementary)* | *Loose (nonrestrictive, supplementary)* |
|---|---|
| Coach Bradley | Our coach, Bradley, |
| William the Conqueror | William I, conqueror of England, |

| | |
|---|---|
| My aunts Mary and Agnes (He had more aunts.) | My aunts, Mary and Agnes, (He had only two.) |
| Fletcher the grocer | Fletcher, our grocer, |
| The fact *that he had been over the road before* gave him an advantage. | This fact, *that he had been over the road before,* gave him an advantage. |

An appositive pronoun agrees with its headword in number and case:

> He called the two of us, *John and me* [object].
> The two of us, *John and I* [subject], were going together.

(References: Curme, *Syntax,* pp. 82-92; Jespersen, pp. 93-95; articles in *American Speech,* 1952-1956.)

**apt—likely—liable** • See *likely—apt—liable.

**Arabic numerals** • See *Numbers § 3.

**arise** • See *rise.

**around—round** • See *round—around.

**Articles** • Traditionally *a* and *an* are known as *indefinite articles* and *the* as the *definite article.* They belong principally with nouns and as a part of speech are regarded as a class of adjectives, being modifiers of a sort, or in other systems as *function words. They are usually omitted in *telegraphic style. (For some details of usage see *a, an, *the.) Many languages do not have corresponding words and even those that have them use them differently from English.

**as** • *As* is one of the most common and versatile words in English. Some of its more important uses can be conveniently listed under traditional part-of-speech categories:
**1.** *Conjunction. As* occurs most commonly as a conjunction, introducing several kinds of clauses.

> Degree or manner: . . . *as* far *as* I could.
> Time (=while) : *As* I was coming in he was going out.
> Cause: *As* it was getting dark, we made for home.

Such a handy word is of course much used in speech, which often prefers *counter words to more exact ones. But the very variety of possible uses makes *as* a problem in written English. It is necessary in comparisons (We went *as* far *as* he did) and for attendant circumstances (*As* we walked along he told us stories) though *while* is preferable if the emphasis is on the time or the action (*While* we were walking along he told us stories).

*As* may be used as a weaker *because*. But usually *since* or *because* fits better in writing and certainly better in Formal English:

*Informal*: *As* it was almost time to go, we were getting more and more exasperated.

*More exact and emphatic*: *Since* it was almost time to go, we were getting more and more exasperated. Or: *Because* it was almost time to go, we were getting more and more exasperated.

(Reference: Bryant, pp. 27-28.)

2. *Preposition. As* occurs as a preposition with the meaning "in the position of" (She had a job *as* stenographer); "in the role of" (He was in the cast *as* Mercutio). In the Informal construction "I don't like him *as well as her*" (meaning "I don't like him *as well as I like her*"), *as her* may be construed as a prepositional phrase: Who would want to go with such a poor skater *as me*? (Formal usage would often have ". . . with such a poor skater *as I* [*am*].")

There is a growing tendency to use *as* as a preposition where *like* or *such as* would be preferred by many: Some writers, *as* Faulkner, take their material from a particular region. This probably results from uncertainty about the distinction between *like* and *as* and a conviction that *as* is the lesser risk.

3. *Adverb. As* occurs as an adverb of degree: I came *as* soon as I could. It also introduces appositives: There were several kinds of shellfish, *as* scallops, oysters, crabs, lobsters.

4. *Pronoun*. In Formal English *as* occurs as a pronoun usually with *same* or *such* as antecedent: It was such a day *as* one rarely sees.

As a common Nonstandard relative pronoun, it takes the place of *who* and *that*: Everyone *as* has his ticket can go in.

(Compare *like—as. References: Curme, *Syntax,* pp. 269-271; *Parts of Speech,* pp. 78-82, and index references in both books.)

## as . . . as •

1. *In double comparisons* we sometimes do not complete the first construction with a second *as*: He is fully *as* tall if not taller than his older brother. The pattern is completed if we add the second *as*: He is fully *as* tall *as,* if not taller than, his older brother. But since the interrupted sentence movement is somewhat artificial in General English, it may be better to complete the first comparison and then add the second: He is fully *as* tall *as* his older brother, if not taller.

2. *In negative comparisons* Formal English slightly prefers *not so . . . as*: The winters are *not so* long *nor so* cold *as* they used to be. The winters are *neither so* cold *nor so* long *as* they

used to be. General English does not as a rule make this distinction: The winters are *not as* long *or as* cold *as* they used to be. Which idiom is to be used depends on the formality of the context and the taste of the writer.

**as if, as though** • In Formal English the *subjunctive is used after *as if* or *as though*: He acted *as if [as though] he were* losing his temper. In General English the subjunctive is often replaced by the indicative: He acted *as if [as though] he was* losing his temper. Often in Informal English and sometimes in General, *like* is used instead of *as if*: He acted *like he was* losing his temper. The subjunctive is never used with *like*. Many readers are irritated by these General constructions. (See *like—as.)

**as it were** • This set expression now seems old-fashioned and is better avoided.

**as—like** • See *like—as.

**as though** • See *as if.

**as to** • *As to* is often a clumsy substitute for a single preposition, usually *of* or *about*:

Practice is the best teacher as to [in, for, of] the use of organ stops.

If the question contains words as to the exact meaning of which [of whose exact meaning] you are uncertain, by all means get out your dictionary.

But it is fairly common in all varieties of written English.

*As to* as a sentence opener emphasizes a word by pulling it out of normal position: *As to my father, everyone likes him.*

**as, when, if** • See *when, as, and if.

**Asides, apologetic** • See *Parentheses.

**asset** • Something of value, currently overused for *advantage, aid, benefit, property,* and so on.

**Assonance** • *Assonance* refers to the like sound of vowels in syllables having different consonants (*brave—vain, lone—show*). It is a common and effective sound element in verse and is also common in prose, especially in an emotional or heightened style:

that id*ea*l country, of gr*ee*n, d*ee*p lanes and high gr*ee*n banks.
—Osbert Sitwell

**Asterisk (*)** • Except in reference works, the asterisk or star is not used so much now as formerly, because it is a conspicuous mark and attracts more attention than is necessary.
1. In works which have very few footnotes, an asterisk may be used as a reference mark, placed after the statement calling for the note and again at the beginning of the footnote; but numbers are more common; for example [31]. (See *References.)
2. Asterisks sometimes indicate a rather long omission in a quotation, a stanza or more from a poem, or a paragraph or more from prose, though spaced periods are now more common. (See *Ellipsis.)
3. In fiction a group of asterisks has been used to suggest that action is omitted or to indicate passage of time between movements of a story, but here again a line of spaced periods or extra space between the movements is more common. (See *Ellipsis.)
4. In this book the asterisk is used to refer to *Index* articles.

**at about, at around** • It can be argued that since an arrival is either "at seven" or "about seven," "at about seven" is redundant. But in informal speech and writing the construction is common. Since *at* or *about* alone seems more precise, the single word is preferred in General and Formal writing. (See *about § 3. Reference: Bryant, pp. 31-32.)

**athlete, athletic, athletics** • Watch your spelling and pronunciation of these: /ath′lēt/, /ath let′ik/, /ath let′iks/.
When *athletics* refers to sports and games it usually takes a plural verb and pronoun: Our athletics *include* football, basketball, and baseball. When *athletics* refers to skill or activity it usually takes a singular verb and pronoun: Athletics *is* recommended for every student.

**at last, at long last** • See *last, at long last.

**Attributive** • An adjective that stands next to its noun is attributive (a *blue* shirt; a shirt, *blue* and *clean*), as contrasted with a predicate adjective that is related to its noun by a *linking verb (The shirt is *blue*). A noun modifying another noun (*horse* race, *football* field) is used *attributively*. (See *Adjectives, types and forms § 2a.)

**atom—atomic** • We have the choice of *atomic* (adjective) *bomb* or *atom* (attributive noun) *bomb* and usage favors the latter. More debatable is *atomic age* or *atom age*. The former is more widely used, but the latter occurs.

**-augh** • See *-ough, -augh.

**Auxiliary verb** • A verb used with another verb to form a phrasal tense or voice is called an *auxiliary verb* or *helping verb*:

I *am* going.   He *will* go.   They *were* lost.   He *should* watch out.

*Be, do, have* are the commonest auxiliaries; *can, may, shall, will, must, ought, should, would, might* are primarily used as auxiliaries; *get, let, need,* and *used* sometimes. (See *Index* articles for these verbs, the general article *Verbs, *Modal auxiliaries. Compare *Function words.)

**awake** • See *wake.

**awful** • In Formal English *awful* means "inspiring with awe." In Informal English it is a convenient utility word of disapproval—"ugly, shocking, ludicrous" (*awful* manners). As a result of this contamination the word is seldom used in General writing. *Awfully* is common in speech as an intensive, but in writing it is an example of *schoolgirl style.

**awhile, a while** • *Awhile* is an adverb (They talked awhile). Strictly, a prepositional phrase in which *while* is a noun should be in three words (for a while, in a while), but *awhile* is sometimes found. (See *a, an § 3, *while.)

**Awkward** •
Awk (K)    *Revision: Rewrite the passage marked to make the phrasing smoother and more effective.*

A rather general word of disapproval sometimes used in correcting themes. It may refer to clumsy phrases, unnatural word order, unnecessary repetition of a word or phrase, or other phrasing that attracts unpleasant attention or handicaps a reader. The remedy is to recast the sentence or passage.

**aye** • Used for *yes* in voting: pronounced /ī/.

**B** • The letter *b* occurs frequently in English spelling as a *silent letter and therefore is a possible snare in spelling and sometimes in pronunciation. Many silent *b*'s, especially after *m*, represent *b*'s that were pronounced in Old English but perhaps have not been generally sounded for hundreds of years: *climb* /klīm/, *comb* /kōm/, *dumb* /dum/, though the *b* is pronounced in the Formal or archaic *clamber,* in *limber,* and in a few other words. A *b* not in Old English has been added in *crumb* and *thumb.* Other silent *b*'s represent sounds that had been in the Latin ancestor words but that were dropped as the sound disappeared in Old French, from which the words came into English: *debt* (from *debitum*), *doubt* (from *dubitare*), *subtle* (from *subtilis*). Some of these *b*'s were inserted by Renaissance scholars because they wished to tie English closer to Latin: Chaucer wrote *det* but we do not.

When *b* comes next to *p* the two sounds sometimes are assimilated to one: *cupboard* /kub′ ərd/, *subpoena* /sə pē′ nə/.

**Back formations** • See *Origin of words § 3e.

**bad—badly** • *Bad* is an adjective of varied application: *a bad man, a bad cold, a bad night, a bad accident, bad weather, bad news, a bad light, a bad taste.*

In "I feel bad about it," "She looks bad," *bad* functions as a predicate adjective. In "I feel badly," *badly* is in the position normally filled by a predicate adjective. Perhaps the form in *-ly* was introduced under the misapprehension that the modifier had an adverbial function. Whatever the reason, the *-ly* form is now about as common as the other in Standard speech and not uncommon in Formal writing. The analogous "He looks badly" is objected to by many authorities. (See *Linking verbs.)

Both *badly* and *bad* are also used as adverbs, the latter only in very Informal usage.

He draws *badly.* The starter has always worked *badly* [Informal: *bad*].

(References: Lillian M. Feinsilver, "How Bad(ly) Do You Feel?" *American Speech,* 1949, 24:161-170; Bryant, pp. 35-36.)

*Badly,* meaning "very much" (He wanted it *badly*) is in Standard use.

*Worse, worst,* the comparative and superlative of *bad,* of course come from a quite different root. They were earlier used in comparing *evil* and *ill,* and when *bad* acquired the meaning of those words, *worse* and *worst* were used for it too.

**Bad grammar** • *Bad grammar* is used as a term of reproach and is applied to all sorts of locutions from "I ain't got none" to imaginary confusions in the use of *shall* and *will.* It is too vague and emotional a term to be useful. (See "Nonstandard English," p. 20, *Grammar.)

**Basic English** • *Basic English* is a simplified form of English devised by C. K. Ogden and intended to facilitate international communication. It has a vocabulary of only 850 words. (Reference: C. K. Ogden, *The System of Basic English,* New York, 1934.)

**be** • Some grammarians prefer not to call *be* a verb, restricting that term to words that conform more consistently to one established pattern. Here we shall classify its principal uses according to traditional categories.

1. *Forms. Be* has forms from three originally separate verbs (as in *are, was, been*). Though the forms are irregular, we use them so much that they give little trouble:

*Present:* I am, you are, he is; we, you, they are
*Present subjunctive:* I, you, he, we, you, they be
*Past:* I was, you were, he was; we, you, they were
*Past subjunctive:* I, you, he, we, you, they were
*Infinitive:* be
*Present participle:* being
*Past participle:* been

Some old forms survive in stock phrases ("the powers that be") and in the Nonstandard "You ain't (sometimes be'n't) going, be you?" Nonstandard also uses *was* in the plural ("Was the Adamses there?"), leveling the past tense to one form (*was*), like the past of other English verbs.

2. *As a linking verb. Be* is the most common *linking verb, joining, without adding specifically a meaning of its own, a subject and a predicative:

*Predicate nominative:* Jerome was the secretary.
*Predicate adjective:* She is sick.

With the *finite parts of *be* the predicate noun or pronoun is usually in the nominative form in written English; such constructions are rare in writing, and their variation from the spoken ones makes them uncomfortably artificial:

It was *he*. (Informal: It was *him*.)

"It's I" is Formal for the General "It's me." (See *It's me.)
When the infinitive has a subject and complement, both are in the accusative form: I wanted *him* to be *me*.
When the infinitive has no subject, Formal usage has a nominative as the complement (I wanted to be *he*), but General usage would more often have an accusative (I wanted to be *him*).

3. *As auxiliary verb.* Forms of *be* are used with the present participles of other verbs to form the progressive tense form:

I *am* asking    he *was* asking    you *will be* asking

Forms of *be* with past participles form the passive voice:

I *am* asked      you *will* be asked      he *was* asked

**4.** *As verb of complete predication. Be* is a verb of complete predication when indicating states or positions:

He *was* at home anywhere.      The fire *was* just across the street.

In the sense of "exist," "live" (Hamlet's "To be, or not to be," "Can such things be?"), *be* is now rather rare. (See *Subjunctives, *Subject and verb, *ain't.)

**because** • *Because* introduces a subordinate clause giving the reason for the statement in the independent clause:

*Because* we were hungry, we began to look for a restaurant.

*Since* and *as* can be used in such clauses, but they are less definite, more casual, and more characteristic of easy speech than of writing:

In a small rural school these young children have to stay for the rest of the day's session, *because* [more definite than *as* or *since*] there is no one to take them home.

*For,* which also introduces reasons, is a slightly more Formal word, rather rare in conversation and General writing. It also often has the sense of giving evidence for the statement, for the writer's knowledge of the fact stated:

*General:* I know he is reliable, *because* I have traded with him for years.

*More Formal:* I know he is reliable, *for* I have traded with him for years. ("He is reliable *because* [or *for*] I have traded with him for years" would not be exact.)

(See *reason is because, *for, *as. See also *due to.)

**Beginning paragraphs** •
*Revision: Revise the opening paragraph to make it lead more directly into your subject and to arouse your reader's interest.*            *Beg*

The first few sentences of a paper should get the subject under way and should interest the reader enough to make him want to read on. From the start, he should be convinced that the writer has something to say. Apologies, aimless anecdotes, and large generalizations about life often create just the opposite impression.

**beside—besides** • *Beside* is a preposition referring to place, "by the side of," as in "beside the road," "beside her," and is used figuratively in a few rather Formal idioms like "beside the point," "beside himself with rage." (*Beside* is less commonly used as an adverb, with the meaning of *besides*.)

*Besides* as adverb or preposition means "in addition to" or "except":

We tried two other ways *besides*. (adverb)

*Besides* our own members, . . . (preposition)

It is also used as a conjunctive adverb: *He didn't think that he ought to get into the quarrel; besides, he had come to enjoy himself.* (Notice the punctuation.)

**between, among** • *Among* implies more than two objects: *They distributed the provisions among the survivors.*

*Between* is most strictly used of only two: *They divided the prize between Kincaid and Thomas.* But the attempt to limit *between* to use with only two items has failed. As the *Oxford English Dictionary* shows, it has from the first been used of several: *Between sobs and groans and tears. He showed the relationship between peoples, races, and cultures.* When a group is treated as a collective unit, only *among* is used: *Divide the books among the poor.* (Reference: Pooley, pp. 135-137; Bryant, pp. 38-40.)

**between you and me** • Since the accusative form of the personal pronoun ordinarily follows a preposition, the expected form is *between you and me, for you and me, to you and me* (or when the pronouns are objects of a verb, "He will take *you and me*").

But *between you and I* is frequently heard, perhaps because the speakers remember the prejudice against *It's me* and carry over the taboo to a different construction; or because *you and I, he and I,* etc., are felt as unalterable units; or because *I* is felt to be more genteel than *me*. Such constructions should be avoided.

**Bible, bible** • When referring to the Christian Scriptures, the word is capitalized but not italicized: "You will find all that in the Bible, and more too." In the sense of an authoritative book or a book much consulted or quoted, the word is not capitalized: "Gray's *Manual*, the botanist's bible, . . ."

The usual form of particular references to parts of the Bible is:

the Old Testament and the New Testament [capitalized but not italicized]

The Ten Commandments are in Exodus xx [or: in Exodus 20].

The Ten Commandments are in Exodus 20:3-17.

I Corinthians 4:6

The adjective *biblical* ordinarily is not capitalized.

**Bibliography** • See *References, *References in scientific papers.

**Big words** •
*Revision: Use a simpler, more natural word instead of
the Formal or heavy one marked.*

A word is "big" if it is too heavy or pretentious for the subject. Words of many syllables may be essential and appropriate, particularly in technical writing, while such short words as *deem, doff,* and *dwell* can spoil a paper by suggesting that its author is a stuffy show-off. Continued use of big words alienates readers and may leave the writer uncertain of his own meaning. (See also *Gobbledygook.)

**biography** • Pronounced /bī og′ rə fē/ or /bi-/. A biography is the life of a person written by someone else; an autobiography is the life of a person written by himself.

**Blend** • A *blend* is a word made by fusing two words, often with a syllable in common: *paratroops, cinemactress, imagineering, smog, motel, beautility, snoopervise.* (See *Origin of words § 3c.)

Until a blend has established itself in the language, as *electrocute* (from *electric* and *execute*) has, it is usually more appropriate to Informal than to General or Formal writing. (See *New words.)

**blond, blonde** • Following the French gender distinction, *blond* would be used of a man, *blonde* of a woman:

He is a *blond.*   She is a *blonde.*   a peroxide *blonde* (or *blond*)

But in both the noun and adjective use, the *-e* is gradually disappearing. Some write *blonde* when it refers specifically to a woman (a *blonde* Helen) and *blond* elsewhere, including *blond* hair.

*Brunet, brunette* are in the same situation: masculine *brunet,* feminine *brunette.*

**Boners** • Confusion of two similar words, mistaken constructions, combinations of ideas that don't belong together have always been a source of fun for everyone except the persons who made them. Volumes of these boners have been gathered and several periodicals run specimens that they find in other publications. Here are a few that have cropped up in themes:

My papers have a decided tendency toward longevity.

He is descended from one of the most virulent [really *poisonous?* or merely *virile?*] families in the U.S.A.

Jean is no plastic saint.

For the lowly freshmen are moved by sediment rather than by intellect in their voting.

The arduous loves of movie stars are not always convincing.

Many times I started for the library to do some research on Gestalt's psychology.

Keep your eye out for boners in manuscript and in print and get what fun you can from them—but most of all scan your own writing to catch them before they come to anybody else's attention.

**born—borne** •

**1.** A useless distinction in the spelling of the past participle of *bear* was introduced in the eighteenth century; in most of its senses it is now spelled *borne*:

They had *borne* this poverty without complaining.
The ship, *borne* along by the breeze, was soon out of sight.

*Bear* in most of these senses is somewhat Formal; *carry* or *endure* would be more common. But in "It was more than I could *bear*," *bear* is less Formal than *endure* would be.

In the sense of "give birth to," the past participle of *bear* is spelled *borne* except in the (very common) passive when not followed by *by*:

Of the four children *borne* by his wife.... (but ... *born* to his first wife)
He was *born* in 1891. A *born* liar.
The children, *born* in Chicago....
Passion *born* of hatred....

**2.** In autobiographical papers students often become self-conscious or humorous in giving the facts of their birth: "I saw the light of day first on June 28, 1948," "No planets blazed on the night of June 28, 1948, when a squally infant appeared in the home of Mr. and Mrs...." None of these is as satisfactory as the simple and natural statement "I was born June 28, 1948."

**Borrowed words** • See *English language, *Foreign words in English, *Origin of words § 2b.

**both** • *Both* is a favorite way of emphasizing two-ness:

The twins were both there. They are both alike. Both Harry and his brother went.

Though none of these *both*'s is necessary, each gives a legitimate emphasis.

"The both women got along well enough together" is a localism for "The two women got along well enough together." But "The both of them" is a fairly common spoken idiom.

**both ... and** • See *Correlative conjunctions.

**Brace { or }** • A brace is the mark used to group two or more lines of writing. Its use is chiefly in technical writing, especially in tables and formulas. Examples will be found in the article *English language.

**Brackets [ ]** • Brackets are rarely used in General writing and are not in the standard typewriter keyboard, but in much academic and professional writing they have specific and convenient uses. If they are needed in typing, you can make them by using a diagonal and two underscores ( $\diagup \diagup$ ), or you can put them in by hand.

Brackets are primarily editorial marks, in these examples used to show where some explanation or comment has been added to the text, especially to quoted matter:

The preposition *due to* is not more incorrect than the preposition *owing to,* which is approved by the same dictionary [the *Concise Oxford Dictionary*], but it is not yet so thoroughly established in the language.—G. O. CURME, *Syntax,* p. 561

In quoting material, *sic in brackets is sometimes used to indicate that an error in the original is being reproduced exactly: "New Haven, Conneticut [sic] ..."; or a correction may be inserted in brackets: "When he was thirty-eight [Actually he was forty-three] he published his first novel."

Brackets function as parentheses within parentheses, particularly in legal documents or in footnotes to theses, etc.

In this *Index,* brackets are used in examples of faulty writing to enclose words that might better be left out or to suggest an improved expression:

Throughout [the course of] the year I read such books as *Oliver Twist* and *Boots and Saddles.*

The continuously moving belt makes a noise *similar to* [*like*] a concrete mixer.

**bring up** • *Bring up* is the General idiom (that's the way I was *brought up*) for the more Formal *rear* or *nurture*; it also means "to introduce" (a subject). (See *raise—rear.)

**British usage** • See *American and British usage.

**Broad reference** • A pronoun referring to a preceding idea rather than to a particular antecedent is said to have a broad reference. (See *Reference of pronouns § 1.)

**brunet, brunette** • See *blond, blonde.

**bunch** • In Formal English *bunch* is limited to objects that grow together or can be fastened together (a bunch of carrots, roses, keys). The Informal "bunch of kids" is the Formal or General "group of children."

**burst, bust** • The principal parts of *burst* are *burst, burst, burst*:

One *bursts* almost every day. Two tanks *burst* yesterday. One tank had *burst*.

*Bust,* in origin a variant pronunciation of *burst,* has the principal parts *bust, busted, busted.* It is used in Nonstandard English in the sense of *burst.* But it also occurs in Informal English in the sense of "being broke" or "being demoted," and in General English in the sense of "busting a broncho" or "busting a trust."

**bus** • The plural is spelled *buses* or *busses,* the first much more common American usage.

**Business English** • The writing of business English has attained a very high standard of mechanical form. The layout, spacing, and mechanics of most business letters and reports are excellent, reflecting the skill of professional typists; and the skill of layout men and printers is available for printed matter.

But the usage and style of business communications vary considerably. Most firms at present pay a good deal of attention to the style of their written and printed matter. The old clichés—*in re, the above, Yrs. of 23d inst. rec'd and contents noted, and oblige*—have practically disappeared. Naturally all degrees of Formality and Informality are found. The prime virtues of good business writing are *directness* and *adaptation to reader.* Adapting the style to the reader is especially difficult in writing advertising and business letters, since usually the writer is not acquainted with his reader and in spite of elaborate market analyses may not size him up correctly. If the letter is sent to many people, there is the difficulty of making it *seem* personal when it really cannot be. For most purposes "business English" is merely good English applied to the specific needs of industry and trade.

Business people have adopted a General style and have handled English with the freedom a living language deserves.

They have pioneered in the much needed simplifying of our spelling. Business writers have used all the native resources of the language in making new names and in brightening style— outright coinages like *kodak, vaseline, fabrikoid,* blends like *servicenter, unisteel, sunoco,* compounds and respellings like *cutex, denticuring* (preventive dentistry), *tudor* (cars), *lubritory.* Though many such words are ludicrous or overcute or in poor taste, some are expressive and are normal language developments. They are much better than attempts at false dignity (*client* for *customer, favor* for *letter,* *business world* for *business, cheque* for *check*).

The question of fitness arises when certain words with obvious business connotation are used in other contexts. Some are frequently borrowed and are useful: *deal,* *asset, feature, bank on,* and *take stock in* are in General usage. But many people, for various reasons, are offended by *beg to advise,* *angle,* *and/or,* *contact,* *realtor.* Such words are out of place in Formal writing and in discussions of ideal rather than practical affairs, but in General writing, business locutions are often useful. H. S. Canby used ordinary business terms to point up a comment on current literature:

No; public taste, ease of publication, variety of interest, even editorial capability, have all arisen with the intellectual development of the country; only the professional writers, as a class, have not progressed. They have become astonishingly clever, as clever as the mechanism of a Ford; but as a class they have not moved ten feet towards literature. *They have standardized their product without improving the model.—Saturday Papers,* p. 56

(See *Euphemisms, *Gobbledygook, *Letters, *man, woman, *Reports, *Shoptalk.)

**business world** • *Business world* is a pretentious term for *business* or *businessmen: I expect to enter the business world* (I expect to go into business).

**but** • *But* is the natural *coordinating conjunction to connect two contrasted statements of equal grammatical rank. It is more natural than the Formal *however* or *yet,* and more emphatic than *although.*
1. *Connects equals.* The locutions connected by *but* should be of equal grammatical rank:

*Adjectives:* not blue *but* green.

*Adverbs:* He worked fast *but* accurately.

*Phrases:* He didn't come in the forenoon *but* in the early evening.

*Clauses:* The first day we rested, *but* the second we got down to work.

*Sentences:* Enigma of the semitropics, the Rio Grande defied the best engineering minds of two countries for a century. *But* $10,000,000 in flood control work has harnessed the treacherous stream.

(See *which § 4 for comments on *but which.*)

**2.** *Connects statements in opposition.* The statements connected by *but* should be actually in opposition. Contrast the first example with the second and third:

He knows vaguely that the nation is not much good any more; he has read that the crust of the earth is shrinking alarmingly and that the universe is growing steadily colder; *but* he does not believe that any of the three is in half as bad shape as he is.—JAMES THURBER, *My Life and Hard Times,* Preface

He supported a wife and three children on this pittance *and* [not *but*] he seemed very proud that he wasn't on relief.

Our view was limited to about twenty yards down Tuckerman Ravine; [not *but*] beyond that everything was in clouds.

**3.** *"But" with "however."* But should be used efficiently, carrying its real meaning. It should not be doubled by a *however,* which can add nothing (see *however):

The students wanted to extend the Christmas vacation a day beyond New Year's, *but* [*however* not needed] the Administration couldn't see their point of view.

**4.** *At beginning of sentences.* But, like *and,* often stands at the beginning of sentences, especially if the sentences are short; neither *and* nor *but* should be overused as a sentence opener.

**5.** *Punctuation.* Two clauses connected by *but* should ordinarily be separated by a comma. The contrast in idea suggests the use of punctuation even when the clauses are relatively short.

I couldn't get the whole license number, *but* it began with A30.

*But* is part of the clause in which it stands and should not be separated from it by a comma. A parenthetical phrase following the *but* may be set off by commas, especially in Formal English.

His speech was supposed to be extemporaneous, *but* he had really been practicing it for a week.

His speech was supposed to be extemporaneous, *but,* to be quite truthful, we must add that he had practiced it for a week.

**6.** *Minor uses of "but."*

*a*–As subordinating conjunction, after *no doubt,* in questions with *know,* and in a few other constructions:

There is no doubt *but* [or *but that,* or more Formally, *that*] he had. Who knows *but* everything will come out right?
Nothing would do *but* I must spend the night with them.

*b*–As a preposition, equivalent to *except* (no comma preceding):

We didn't get anything *but* a couple of shad.

No one could have done it *but* me.

*c*–As a rather Formal adverb, equivalent to *only*:

If he *but* stops to think, he can interpret his own reactions.

*d*–With "not." *But* is sometimes used after *not* in Standard usage, especially in speech: *There aren't but three eggs left.* This construction develops from "There are *but* three eggs left"; evidently *but* was felt as not strong enough and *not* was added.

(See also *Correlative conjunctions. References: Fowler, article "but"; Curme, *Parts of Speech,* index; Bryant p. 147.)

**but that—but what** • *But that* is the more usual conjunction in written English; *but what* is Informal and General:

He didn't know *but that* [Informal: *but what*] the other car could still turn out.

*Informal and General:* I don't doubt *but that* he will come. [Or: I don't doubt *but what* he'll come.]

*Formal:* I do not doubt *that* he will come.

(Reference: Bryant, pp. 46-47.)

**but which** • See *which § 4.

**C** • In Old English *c* represented two related /k/ sounds: One remained /k/—*cruma,* "crumb," *celan,* "to cool," *cyning,* "king"; but before *e* or *i* the other soon became /ch/ (*ceosan, ciepan, cild*) and is spelled *ch* in Modern English: *choose, cheap, child.* The Norman Conquest complicated *c* spellings, for it brought in many French words in which *c* spelled the /s/ sound. Today *c* is an unnecessary letter, doing work that could more clearly be done by *k* and *s.* Many words spelled with *c* must be respelled with *k* or *s* to show pronunciation: /sit'ē/ (*city*), /sel/ (*cell*), /fôrs/ (*force*), /kōld/ (*cold*), /kum/ (*come*), /ärk/ (*arc*).

Before *e, i,* or *y, c* regularly represents /s/: *cent, civil, cynic;* before *a, o, u,* and any consonant but *h, c* is regularly /k/: *can't, coffee, cute, fact.* Marked with a *cedilla, as in *façade, c* has the /s/ sound before *a, o,* or *u.*

*C* may represent /sh/: *ocean* /o'shən/, *conscience* /kon'shəns/, *special* /spesh'əl/; and /ch/: *cello* /chel'ō/.

*C* is silent in *czar, indict, muscle,* and a few other words.

Before *e* or *i*, *cc* spells /ks/: *accident, occident, success, vaccine*; otherwise it is /k/: *acclaim, accommodate*. The pronunciation of *cc* as /s/ in some words like *accessory* and *flaccid*, though widespread, is objected to by many speakers. (See *ch.)

**c., ca.** • See *Abbreviations § 2.

**calculate, guess, reckon** • *Calculate* (cut in Nonstandard to /kalk′lāt/ or even to /kal′āt/) and *reckon* are localisms for the *think, suppose, expect* of General English. They should be avoided in writing unless the audience addressed uses them habitually in writing as well as in speaking. *Guess* has moved into General English in the United States.

**can—may (could—might)** •
**1.** In General English *may* occurs rather rarely except in the sense of possibility:

It may be all right for her, but not for me.

*Can* is generally used for both permission and ability:

Can I go now? You can if you want to.
I can do 80 miles an hour with mine.

This is in such widespread usage that it should be regarded as Standard English in speaking and in writing and is so described in modern dictionaries.

*Can't* almost always takes the place of *mayn't* in the United States:

Can't I go now? We can't have lights after twelve o'clock.

**2.** In Formal English a distinction is sometimes made between the auxiliary *can*, with the meaning of ability, "being able to," and *may*, with the meaning of permission:

You may go now. He can walk with crutches. You may if you can.

*May* also indicates possibility: *He may have the right one.*
**3.** *Might* and *could*. *Might*, originally the past of *may*, and *could*, the past of *can*, are now used chiefly to convey a shade of doubt, or a smaller degree of possibility. And in General English *could* often replaces *might*.

It might be all right for her, but it isn't for me.
It might have been all right for her, but not for me.

Adverbs are likely to be used instead of *may* or *might* in such constructions, especially for the past tense:

*Perhaps* it was all right for her, but not for me.

*Can* and *could*, *may* and *might* are often interchangeable, except that *could* and *might* are perhaps more deferential or tentative; compare:

May I help you?               Can you help me?
Might I help you?             Could you help me?

*Could* also suggests doubt or qualified possibility:

Perhaps I could write a poem, but I doubt it.

*Be able to* tends to replace *can* and *could* when the idea of
ability needs emphasis:

I am able to live on my income.

(See *Divided usage. Reference: Gladys D. Haase, *College
English*, 1950, 11:215-216.)

**cannot, can not** • Usage is divided; *cannot* is more common.

**can't help but, can't seem to** • There are three possible idioms:

*Formal:* I cannot but feel sorry for him.
*General:* I can't help feeling sorry for him.
*General:* I can't help but feel sorry for him.

The last is an established idiom, though avoided by many
writers. *Can't seem to* appears to be restricted to Informal
speech and writing. At the same time, a locution like "I *can't
seem to* get started" makes excellent sense—"I'm not sure just
why, but I can't get started"—and is more natural than "I
seem to be unable to . . . ." (See *seem.)

**Capital letters** •
*Revision: Capitalize the word marked, for one of the
reasons shown in this article; or, if the word marked
is written with a capital, make it a small letter.*      *Cap*

*Proofreading marks can be used for correcting themes.
Three lines under a small letter means: make this a capital.
A slanting line drawn through a capital means: make this a
small letter (see *Lower case).

march 15   He came from West of Buffalo.

Certain uses of capitals, as at the beginning of sentences or
for proper names, are conventions followed by everyone; certain others show divided usage or are matters of taste. Formal
English tends to use more capitals than General English, and
newspaper usage tends to cut them to a minimum.

This article summarizes the principal uses of capitals in current writing. Further discussion and examples will be found
in the articles marked by asterisks.
1. *Sentence capitals.* The first word of a sentence is capitalized. In quotations, the first word of a quoted sentence or part

of sentence is capitalized, but when the quotation is broken, the second part is not capitalized unless it is a complete sentence:

He said, "The first time I came this way almost none of the roads were hard surfaced."

He said, "Perhaps," and went on.

"The first time I came this way," he said, "almost none of the roads were hard surfaced."

"That was your last chance," she said. "Don't ever ask again."

Complete sentences that stand in *parentheses are capitalized always if they stand between other sentences, but if they stand within sentences they usually are not.

A complete sentence standing after a *colon is not capitalized if it is short and closely connected to the preceding words, but may be if it is long or if for some reason the writer wants to emphasize it or keep it distinct:

Charles Sumner wanted to know his opinion on European law journals: what should he say?—H. S. COMMAGER, *Theodore Parker*

He promised this: The company will make good all the losses.—*New York Times Style Book* (1962), p. 30

**2.** *Proper names.* Proper names and abbreviations of proper names are capitalized: names of people, places, races (Indian, *Negro, Caucasian), languages (French, Latin), days of the week, months, companies, *ships, institutions, fraternities, religious bodies, historical events (the Revolutionary War), documents (the Constitution), *course names.

The names of the *seasons (summer, fall, midwinter) are not capitalized except for stylistic reasons.

The points of the compass (north, southwest) are not capitalized when they indicate direction, but are usually capitalized when they denote a region (though this practice is now declining):

He started west in 1849.

He was much more popular in the West than in the East.

*Army, Navy,* and so on, are not capitalized unless they refer to the organized forces of a particular nation: United States *Army,* the British *Navy,* and even *the Army* when referring to that of a particular nation. Also:

He went to college.

He went to Beloit College.

He went to the College (if a particular college is clearly understood in the context).

Proper nouns that have become common nouns (*tweed, sandwich, burnsides, plaster of paris, silhouette, guillotine*) are not capitalized nor are proper adjectives in senses that no longer suggest their origin: *Paris fashions* (fashions originating in Paris), but *paris green*.

**3.** *Lines of verse.* The first letter of a line of verse is capitalized unless originally published without a capital, as in the second example below:

> Burly, dozing humble-bee,
> Where thou art is clime for me.
>
> RALPH WALDO EMERSON, "The Humble-Bee"

> the Cambridge ladies who live in furnished souls
> are unbeautiful and have comfortable minds
>
> E. E. CUMMINGS, "the Cambridge ladies"

**4.** *\*Titles of articles, books, etc.* The usual convention is to capitalize the first word, all nouns, pronouns, verbs, adjectives, and adverbs as well as prepositions that stand last or contain more than four (sometimes more than five) letters:

| | |
|---|---|
| *With Malice Toward Some* | *The Book of a Naturalist* |
| *You Can't Take It with You* | *Pity Is Not Enough* |

**5.** *"I," "O."* The pronoun *\*I* is always capitalized. The exclamation *\*O* is capitalized, but *oh* is not unless it begins a sentence or is especially emphatic.

**6.** *Names of relatives, individuals.* In personal and Informal writing, as a matter of courtesy, and in General writing, when they are used as proper nouns, names for members of one's family are often capitalized:

> She talked it over with Father, however, just to see what he'd say.
> —CLARENCE DAY, *Life with Mother,* p. 117

They are not usually capitalized when used as common nouns: *My sister and two brothers are older than I.*

*President* referring to the President of the United States is always capitalized, and ordinarily titles of people in high office when referring to an individual (the Senator). Other titles may be capitalized when referring to individuals (The Colonel was there). (See *\*Titles of persons.*)

**7.** *References to Deity.* God, Jesus, nouns such as *Savior,* and pronouns referring directly to them are capitalized—though practice is divided on the pronouns:

> Webster for the first time in an English Bible rendered Jesus's saying as He said it.—HARRY R. WARFEL, *Noah Webster,* p. 411

> As we think of him [God], do we think of what he has done or what he can do for us? Do we love him so much that we would keep him for ourselves?—S. K. YEAPLE, *Your Money and Your Life,* p. 30

Pronouns referring to pagan deities (Zeus, Jove, Venus) are not capitalized.

**8.** *Street, river, park,* etc. Usage is divided over capitalizing such words as *\*street, river, park, hotel, church* when they follow a proper name. Typically, books and conservative magazines would use capitals; General writing, as in many magazines and most newspapers, would not:

| | | |
|---|---|---|
| Formal: | the Mississippi River | Thirty-second Street |
| General: | the Mississippi river | Thirty-second street |

An organization is likely to capitalize more words pertaining to its functions than an outsider would, as the Government Printing Office capitalizes many words having to do with government.

**9.** *Abstract nouns.* Abstract nouns are likely to be capitalized, more often in Formal writing than in General, when the concept they refer to is personified or when they refer to ideals or institutions: *The State has nothing to do with the Church, nor the Church with the State.*

**10.** *Stylistic capitals.* Some writers, usually in a rather Formal style, use capitals as a form of *\*emphasis, to lead the reader to stress certain words a little or give them more attention:

And a woman is only a woman, but a good Cigar is a Smoke.— RUDYARD KIPLING, "The Betrothed"

Such unconventional use of capitals is now rare and is usually better avoided. Sometimes, however, the device works:

They will learn, like the boy who cried wolf, that people who mock the Last Laugh are incinerated by it when it finally sounds.— *The New Yorker,* "Talk of the Town," Sept. 21, 1963, p. 33

(For additional information on capitals, see \*Foreign words in English § 3, \*Proper adjectives, \*References in scientific papers. Also consult the stylebooks of periodicals and publishers, such as the GPO *Style Manual.*)

**Cardinal numbers** • See \*Numbers § 5.

**Carelessness** •
  *Revision: Correct the obvious and apparently careless mistake marked.*

X

Conferences with students on their themes show that well over half the mistakes and slips that an instructor has to mark result from carelessness, not ignorance. Everyone is liable to careless lapses in hasty work. But a course paper is not supposed to be hasty work. Slips like *it's* for *its* (or the other way around), *detract* for *distract,* most \*comma faults and \*fragmentary sentences, and scores of others are due to lack of attention in the final stages of preparing a paper. An instructor can sympathize with lack of knowledge but not with lack of care; in fact, he has every right to refuse to read an obviously careless paper.

Sometimes carelessness will show itself in your writing because you do not know what is expected by your readers or because you have not paid enough attention to your reading or to previous English teaching, and sometimes simply because of inattention at the time of writing; sometimes it will show itself in the use of Nonstandard forms or constructions, either because of social background or laziness. If you make elementary, careless mistakes, take steps to eliminate them. In some cases you may need to review systematically such grammatical matters as the forms of verbs or pronouns.

Because the most obvious and elementary mistakes are usually the result of carelessness, not ignorance, they can easily be eliminated by attentive proofreading.

In hasty writing it is easy to leave out an occasional letter—the *n* in *an,* a final *-y* or *-ed*. Watch especially *used to,* because even though "use to" seems a more accurate spelling of what we *say,* we must write "used to": He had a hard time getting *used to* college; we *used to* do it the other way. (See *-ed.)

Be sure to put in end punctuation marks, especially the question mark (not a period) at the end of a question and the closing quotation mark after something quoted.

Do not run small words together. Watch especially for those that frequently seem to form units: *a / lot; in / turn; any / more; on the other / hand; in a / while.*

Sometimes small words, usually connectives, are carelessly repeated:

*On* this one point I have already commented *on.* [Either *on* could be kept; probably the first is preferable in writing.]

Some words are commonly confused, and it may take a moment's thought to see which one fits. See *a, an, *to, *too, and *then—than. In addition to these three common confusions, the following word pairs often cause trouble: affect—effect, lose—loose, whether—weather (or wether), quite—quiet, principal—principle. Others are listed in *Homonyms. Some of these troublesome pairs are discussed in separate articles.

A careful reading of your final manuscript is a most useful educational discipline. It will make the paper more presentable (and worth a better grade), as well as give you the satisfaction that comes from seeing a job through to the best of your ability. Reading with a pencil point just below the line slows the eye and helps you catch careless errors. And sometimes the ear will hear what the eye does not see. Reading a paper aloud may bring to your attention *dangling modifiers and *fragmentary sentences as well as the unintentional *repetition of a word or sound.

**Caret ( ∧ )** • This inverted v-shaped mark put in or under a line of manuscript shows that something between the lines or in the margin should be inserted at that point:

```
      Yes, they were smart, but there wasn't any reason
                           because
   why they shouldn't be,∧all they did was study.
```

This is an acceptable way to revise papers (it was used in the original copy of our Constitution) and should be used to improve a paper to be handed in or to make a correction suggested by an instructor. Too frequent use shows lack of care in the preliminary writing and revision.

A caret may be used by an instructor as a correction mark to show where something should be inserted.

**Case** • One of the relationships between a noun or pronoun and another element in a sentence is called *case*. In languages like Latin and German, whose nouns, pronouns, adjectives, or articles are elaborately declined, the case endings of the nominative, genitive, dative, and accusative (and ablative in Latin) are important clues to the relations of the words in the sentence. In English, the few forms which survive are much less useful as clues. Our adjectives have no case endings; regular nouns have only two forms, the common form (*soldier*) and the form ending in *s* for genitive and plural, distinguished only in writing (*soldier's—soldiers*); and the personal pronouns are reduced to three, a nominative, genitive, and, except for *it* and *you*, accusative (*I—my—me*), or two (*you—your—you*).

We signal the relation of nouns and pronouns to other sentence elements through *word order* (an object following its verb or preposition, for example) and by means of *prepositions* (*to Fred* instead of a dative ending). The few problems that we have come chiefly from the surviving dative-accusative form of pronouns (*It's me; *who, whom).

This *Index* has articles on four cases to call attention to the few functions in which the case forms are significant, to note problems in usage that are due to case forms, and to make possible some comparison between English and the languages which rely more definitely on case forms to signal relationship between words:

*Nominative (or subjective)—the subject of a verb, complement of a linking verb

*Genitive (or possessive)—indicating not only possession but various adjectival and adverbial relations

*Dative—principally notions of interest or location or "indirect objects"

*Accusative (or objective)—the object of a verb or preposition

Fuller accounts of the grammatical points involved will be found in the articles on the various functions indicated: *Subject and verb, *Objects, *Infinitives § 5, *Linking verbs, *Gerund § 2, *Nouns, *Pronouns, types and forms; *Word order. For more complex treatments of problems of English cases, see Jespersen, Ch. 14 (the two-case system); Curme, *Parts of Speech,* pp. 127-136 (the four-case system).

**case** • Some of the commonest bits of *deadwood in writing are various locutions with the word *case*. *Case* has a number of specific meanings known to everybody. As a general filler for prose, it is unnecessary and annoying. "In some cases," "in the case of," and "in that case" are pat phrases which do no harm if used sparingly; often they can be replaced with a more meaningful word or phrase.

The delegates drank very moderately except in a few scattered cases. [Most of the delegates drank very moderately.]

**catalog, catalogue** • Spelling usage is divided, with the shorter form gaining. More than half the colleges in the United States now use *catalog* as the name of their annual bulletin of announcements.

**Cause** • Cause-effect connections are made regularly in all kinds of writing, and in some essays the analysis of causes and effects is the main task of the writer. For such papers to succeed, the causal relationships must be convincing. Following (with very simple examples) are the "canons" formulated by John Stuart Mill for testing causal relationships:

1. *The method of agreement.* If two or more instances of the phenomenon under investigation have only one circumstance in common, the circumstance in which alone all the instances agree is the cause (or effect) of the given phenomenon. (If several people have an attack of food poisoning after eating lunch in the same cafeteria, and if it is learned that the one item their meals had in common is smoked fish, it is probable—but not certain—that the smoked fish caused the food poisoning.)

2. *The method of difference.* If an instance in which the phenomenon under investigation occurs, and an instance in which it does not occur, have every circumstance in common save one, that one occurring only in the former; the circumstance in which alone the two instances differ, is the effect, or the cause, or an indispensable part of the cause, of the phenomenon. (If two people had exactly the same menu except

that one added smoked fish and if he became sick while his companion did not, the fish probably—but not certainly—was the cause of his illness.)

**3.** *The joint method of agreement and difference.* If two or more instances in which the phenomenon occurs have only one circumstance in common, while two or more instances in which it does not occur have nothing in common save the absence of that circumstance, the circumstance in which alone the two sets of instances differ is the effect, or the cause, or an indispensable part of the cause of the phenomenon. (This method combines the first two; it suggests the process of testing over an extended period of time used by doctors to isolate, through elimination of various possibilities, the cause of an allergy.)

**4.** *The method of residues.* Subduct from any phenomenon such part as is known by previous inductions to be the effect of certain antecedents, and the residue of the phenomenon is the effect of the remaining antecedents. (If only four people could have committed a crime and three can be proved not to have done it, then the fourth is presumed guilty.)

**5.** *The method of concomitant variation.* Whatever phenomenon varies in any manner, whenever another phenomenon varies in some particular manner, is either a cause or an effect of that phenomenon, or is connected with it through some fact of causation. (If a field which is heavily fertilized yields a better crop than one which has received half as much fertilizer and a much better crop than one which has received none at all, the farmer concludes that there is probably a connection between the amount of fertilizer he uses and the yield of the crop.)

For discussion and criticism of Mill's canons, see textbooks in logic. Detailed treatments are in Irving M. Copi, *Introduction to Logic,* 2nd ed., 1961, pp. 363-407, and Philip Wheelwright, *Valid Thinking,* 1962, pp. 228-238.

**-ce, -ge** • A few special spelling problems arise from the use of *c* for the sound of *s,* and of *g* for the sound of *j.*

A word ending in *-ce* (pronounced /s/) or *-ge* (pronounced /j/) normally keeps the final *e* before suffixes beginning with *a, o* or *u* to indicate the pronunciation: *courageous, noticeable, peaceable, vengeance* (but *mortgage, mortgagor* or *mortgager*). Before a suffix beginning with *e* or *i,* the final *e* is dropped: *diced, noticing, encouraging.*

Usually a word ending in *-c* (pronounced /k/) adds a *k* before an ending beginning with *e* or *i* or *y* so that it will still be pronounced /k/: *colic, colicky; mimic, mimicking; picnic, picnicked, picnicking.* (See also \*-ei-, -ie-.)

**Cedilla** • The cedilla is a mark under the letter *c* (ç) to show that before *a* or *o* it is pronounced /s/. In English spelling the cedilla persists in words originally French: *façade, Français, Provençal, garçon, aperçu, soupçon.* It is also used as a phonetic alphabet symbol.

**censor—censure** • When we *censure,* we condemn or blame or disapprove. When we *censor,* we delete or suppress. But the adjective *censorious* refers to *censuring.*

**center around** • *Center around* (The story *centers around* the theft of a necklace) is the General idiom. The Formal idiom is *center on* or *upon.*

**Centuries** • Remember that the fifth century A.D. ran from the beginning of the year 401 to the end of the year 500, the nineteenth century from January 1, 1801, through December 31, 1900. Thus to name the century correctly, add one to the number of its hundred. It will help to remember that you live in the *twentieth* century.

Popularly the distinction is not closely kept, since people feel that the century changes when the figure for the hundreds changes: there were celebrations for the beginning of the twentieth century on January 1 of both 1900 and 1901, and there was debate over whether the second half of our century began with 1950 or 1951.

Because of errors made in this scheme of indicating centuries, the practice of naming the hundred can be used, even in Formal writing (the seventeen hundreds).

The abbreviation A.D. once regularly stood before a date. It was not used with centuries, since it stands for *anno Domini,* "in the year of our Lord." But like B.C. (before Christ) it commonly follows the year (431 B.C., 1681 A.D.), and even historians use it to designate centuries (the fifth century A.D.).

**cf.** • See *Abbreviations § 2.

**ch** • *Ch* usually spells the sounds *tsh* (pronunciation symbol /ch/), as in *arch, bachelor, chatter, check, cheese, child, church.* When the sound is not at the beginning of a word, it is often spelled *tch* (*batch, watch*) and *ti* in such words as *question, Sebastian.* Compare also *righteous* /rī′chəs/ and *literature.* It is spelled *c* in *cello, cemballo.*

In some words from French, *ch* has the French sound /sh/: *champagne, chagrin, mustache, machine.*

In a number of words from Greek, *ch* is sounded /k/: *chemist, chimera, chorus, echo.*

**chairman, chairwoman** • Although *chairwoman* is entered in some dictionaries, it is no more necessary to indicate the sex of a presiding officer than of a beginning college student (*freshman*). *Chairlady* is not in good use.

**Change in constructions** • See *Shifted constructions.

**Change in language (oral and written)** • The inevitability of change in language is attested by the records of all languages whose histories have been traced. Sometimes changes appear to be relatively sudden and far-reaching, as after an invasion, but ordinarily they are slow—the accumulation of slightly different pronunciations and gradual shifts in grammatical forms and constructions. Vocabulary varies much more rapidly and less consistently than the basic structure of a language.

English shows many changes during the centuries in which it has been recorded. (See *English language.) When we think of the millions of people using our language and of the wide territory over which it is spread, the wonder is that change is not more rapid. Although schools, radio and television, books, periodicals, and newspapers may tend to stabilize the language somewhat, English continues to change. One of the fundamental principles of linguistics is that this change in language is natural and inevitable.

Attempts to direct the course of English have not been very successful. Beginning in the eighteenth century the speech and writing (or at least the writing) of a small and influential group were modified by the application of a formal grammar, but the language of most users of English was unaffected.

Even the transcription of the language—which, it must be remembered, is not the language itself, though most people think of it as such—has been little affected by so sensible and needed a movement as that for simplified spelling. At present, advertising is the chief source of spelling change, though some teachers and nearly all linguists believe that our spelling should be modified.

Conservative influences like schools and publishing houses have taken a pretty firm stand against change, some of them even now presenting usage of the middle nineteenth century. It is to be hoped that this will not always be true.

A person interested in writing needs to be aware of the naturalness and necessity of change in his language and should cultivate the habit of watching the small signs of change that he hears and sees in speech and writing. He needs also to decide whether he is going to oppose change, to welcome it in all its forms, or to try to discriminate, adopting in his own work those new words and forms and constructions that seem to be more convenient and more expressive than older ones. Following cautiously the direction in which English has already been moving (as the increase in nouns making their *plural with -s) is a good general principle to follow.

In addition to the general discussion of change and the sources of change in language in "The varieties of English," pp. 2-31, the *Index* includes several articles which treat points of change and suggest what the language-watcher should pay attention to: *Analogy in language, *Divided usage, *Origin of words.

The study of the changes that have taken place in English is fascinating, and ample materials exist for carrying it on. The *Oxford English Dictionary* gives the history of individual words from their first appearance in the language, recording their changes in form and in meaning. Histories of the language, like those by Albert C. Baugh and Stuart Robertson, tell the story in detail. The general and orderly process of change is described in Otto Jespersen, *Language,* Part IV, and in E. H. Sturtevant, *Linguistic Change* (Chicago, 1917). See also Bloomfield, Ch. 20 ff.

**Chapters** • Chapters are numbered in Roman (I, II, III) or Arabic (1, 2, 3) numerals, the latter increasingly used. In bibliographies lower case Roman numerals (i, ii, x) are now more common than capitals (I, II, X), and Arabic are also common.

In Formal book style, references to titles of chapters are usually in quotation marks. In General writing they may simply be capitalized.

*Formal:* Kennedy, Chapter XIV, "Improvement of the English Language."

*General:* Kennedy, Chapter 14, Improvement of the English Language.

**Charts** • See *Diagrams, graphs, etc.

**check, cheque** • *Cheque* is the regular British spelling, but its use in the United States is pretentious.

**Chinese** • Preferable to *Chinaman, Chinamen,* because of an offensive connotation sometimes carried by those words. Use *a Chinese, the Chinese.* In Formal compounds *Sino-* /sī'nō/ or /sin'ō/ is used: the *Sino-Japanese War.*

**Christian names** • See *Given names.

**Circumlocution** • See *Wordiness § 1.

**Cities** • The name of the country or state need not be given with the name of a well-known city: Athens, Berlin, Chicago, Hollywood, London, New York, Rome, San Francisco. But many American cities and towns bearing the same names need identification if there is a possibility of confusion: Athens, Georgia; Berlin, New Hampshire; Roanoke, Illinois. (See *Proper names, *Comma § 9b.)

**Clarity** • See *Ambiguity, *Clearness, *Comma § 7.

**Clauses** •
1. *Definition.* A clause is an element of a compound or complex sentence that ordinarily has a subject and a finite verb. (But see § 3 and § 4.) By means of a conjunction or of an implied connection the clause construction is related to the rest of the sentence. A simple statement, like "The bird flew higher and higher in slow, easy circles," is usually called a sentence, not a clause.

Compound sentences have two or more independent clauses of grammatically equal value (coordinate), connected usually by *and, but, or, for,* or another *coordinating conjunction. (See *Coordination.) Complex sentences have at least one independent (also called *principal* and *main,* though this does not mean they are of chief importance in meaning) clause, grammatically capable of standing alone, and one or more dependent (because not grammatically independent—also called *subordinate* or *relative*) clauses, joined to the independent clause or clauses by *as, because, since, when,* or some other *subordinating conjunction, or by a *relative pronoun, such as *that, who, which*:

[Compound sentence, first independent clause:] A government as totalitarian as the Chinese has to maintain a vast army of officials, [second independent clause, coordinate with the preceding one:] and it is far in excess of the number of educated men available. [Complex sentence, dependent clause:] Although all have nominally some knowledge of the basic principles of Communism, [independent clause:] their acquaintance with them is often hazy or perverted.—GUY WINT, *Spotlight on Asia,* p. 87

2. *Functions of dependent clauses.* These clauses are classified according to the grammatical function they serve in the sentence:

*a—*\*Noun clauses are subjects and objects of verbs or objects of prepositions:

[Subject, usually Formal:] *That herons fed at night* was not news to him.

No one knew [Object:] *which way they had gone.*

*b*–Adjective clauses modify nouns:

The man *whom they met* [or: The man *they met*] did not return.
The cement road turned into a macadam road, *which in time turned into a clayey unsurfaced road.*

*c*–Adverbial clauses are used for notions of time, place, cause, effect, concession, etc.:

*When they finally got that straightened out,* it was too late.
They were discouraged *because they had tried very hard.*

Here is a passage of nineteen sentences in which four (6, 7, 9, 18) are simple, two are compound-complex (11, 16), and the others complex. The dependent clauses are in italics, and at the end of the passage are the conventional grammatical interpretations of them.

(1) Without question a young man *who is not a radical about something* is a pretty poor risk for education. (2) The relevant question to ask is, *What does this young man's radicalism express?* (3) In general, *if it is doctrinaire,/if he has learned all the answers to the world's problems out of a book or from a wise guy outside,* the worth of his beliefs is slight, both to him and to society. (4) The cut-and-dried patter must first be got out of him *before his mind will give a clear tone.* (5) It is true *that the reasons for the early adoption of ready-made beliefs often deserve sympathy.* (6) Poverty, injustice, a sense of wrong connected with a physical or other defect, are predisposing causes. (7) In other instances it may be great intellectual curiosity coupled with a yearning for absolute truth. (8) This is *why students—though the Trustees do not trust it—can go easily from the doctrine of Karl Marx to the doctrine of Saint Thomas.* (9) By means of these systems, converts can act out their dissent from the regular way and secure the comforts of a vast intellectual edifice.

(10) But dissent of a different type remains the really fruitful element in undergraduate thought; *though here again quality is important.* (11) Dissent from teacher *because he is an authority* is meaningless, but the defiant conviction *that it is no atrocious crime to be a young man, born later, with a different world impressed on the mind, with the consciousness of untried powers and unlimited courage—*that form of dissent is without doubt the one quality to nurture when found and to shield *if need be* against all literal conformity. (12) For *what it fulfills* is the solitary truth rattling through the empty periods of the Commencement orator *when he says:* "Young man, the future is in your hands."

(13) Imagine a generation of young men *who did not think/ they could govern better than their fathers,/ who did not want to revolutionize the world with new inventions or make T. S. Eliot's laurels fade.* (14) *If they do not believe/ they can do this,* who will

tell them? (15) Certainly not the institutions *that rightfully nurse a Tradition.* (16) But a tradition lives by being added to, and it is the young men *who must make the effort of creation.* (17) It is irrelevant to suggest *that this ambition moves thousands of hearts every year and ends in workaday routine and indolence.* (18) That is to look only at the husks. (19) *As long as we cannot prophesy/ who will turn out a winner,* we have no right to question initiative and self-dedication—JACQUES BARZUN, *Teacher In America,* pp. 238-239

1. Adjective clause modifying *young man*
2. Noun clause, predicative after *is*
3. Two adverbial clauses (condition), modifying the independent clause
4. Adverbial clause (time), modifying the independent clause
5. Noun clause, postponed subject of *is.* (Obviously here the "main" idea is in the "subordinate" clause.)
8. Noun clause (*why* . . .), predicative after *is*; adverbial clause (*though* . . .), modifying the *why* clause
10. Adverbial clause modifying the independent clause (though it has the value of a coordinate clause, as is borne out by the punctuation)
11. Adverbial clause of reason (*because* . . .) on the face of it (but what does it "modify"?); noun clause (*that* . . .), in apposition with *conviction*; adverbial clause of condition (*if* . . .), modifying *to shield. When found* could be regarded as a subjectless clause of time.
12. Noun clause (*what* . . .), subject of *is*; adverbial clause of time (*when* . . .), modifying the independent clause, or it could be regarded as modifying the quotation. A quotation is conventionally regarded as a noun clause, object of the verb of saying.
13. Two adjective clauses modifying *young men*; noun clause (*they could* . . .), object of *think*
14. Adverbial clause (condition), modifying the independent clause; noun clause, object of *do believe*
15. Adjective clause, modifying *institutions*
16. Adjective clause, modifying *young men*
17. Noun clause, object of *to suggest*
19. Adverbial clause of time, modifying independent clause; noun clause, object of *prophesy*

**3.** *Verbless clauses.* The typical clause has a subject and verb, but some items without finite verbs can be analyzed as clauses:

*a—Elliptical clauses,* in which a verb can be supplied from another part of the sentence or can be added with some certainty because of the frame of the sentence:

I don't believe it any more than you [Supply: *do,* or *believe it*].
When [Supply: *he was*] sixteen, he had gone to work.

*b*-"Abridged clauses" in which no verb element stands. These should not be construed as elliptical clauses, since no verb ever enters the speaker's or listener's mind. They are better interpreted as idiomatic formulas. Some familiar sayings illustrate the abridged clause:

So far[,] so good.

The more[,] the merrier.

The better the day, the better the deed.

4. *Clause and phrase.* Dictionaries define *clause* approximately as in § 1 above and *phrase* as in the *Index* article for that term. But since phrases centered on verbal elements function much like clauses, it has been argued that they should be classified as a kind of clause. (See *Phrases and *Verbals.)

(See *Adjectives, types and forms § 4, *Adverbs, types and forms § 5, *Conditions, *Contact clauses, *Coordination, *Noun clauses, *Purpose, *Relative clauses, *Restrictive and nonrestrictive, *Result, *Subordination, *that, *when, *where. References: Curme, *Syntax,* Ch. 10; Roberts, pp. 343-345.)

**Clearness** • Clearness, or clarity, is one of the fundamental virtues of writing, perhaps the fundamental virtue, but it is hard to discuss helpfully. No accumulation of small virtues or banning of particular faults will guarantee clarity. Pronouns should match their antecedents, verbs and subjects should agree, constructions should not be wantonly shifted. These traits, somewhat ignored in speech, and usually with little or no consequent loss of communication, require closer attention in writing.

Determination to convey to the reader your ideas and feelings will increase the clarity of your writing. But though clearness is a major virtue of prose—it enables the author to carry out his fundamental purpose, communication—writing has other purposes too: influencing people, entertaining them. And expressiveness also has other virtues. Preoccupation with clarity for its own sake may produce clear writing that is also cold and dry. If a paper is not clear, it will certainly be bad, but clearness alone may not make it good. Certain situations demand suggestion; the sensibilities of readers must be considered, as well as the writer's own feeling for the material. All of these elements may reduce in some small way the immediate clearness yet add to a complete understanding of the whole and so be essential to good writing. If the writer has thought his subject and its implications through, has decided on the relation of the parts to the whole, and thought of his reader as "looking over his shoulder," his writing is likely to be clear. (See *Comma § 7.)

**Cliché** • See *Trite.

**Clipped words** • See *Origin of words § 3d.

**Close modifiers** • See *Restrictive and nonrestrictive.

**Cognate** • *Cognate* means "related, of the same family." It is applied to languages that are from the same stock, as Spanish and French are both descended from Latin. *Cognate* is often used of words in different languages which are modern forms of some one word in an older ancestral language: German *Wasser,* English *water*; also for borrowed words: English *literature* from French *littérature.*

**Coherence** •

*Coh*

> *Revision: Make the relation between the parts of this sentence or between these sentences or paragraphs exact and clear to a reader.*

Coherence—the traditional name for *relationship, connection, consecutiveness*—is a difficult but essential virtue in writing. It is essential because the reader's mind differs from the writer's; the reader does not see the relationships, and must be led through the writer's thought, guided from one stage, from one sentence, to another. It is difficult because in a coherent presentation the writer has triumphed over his natural human casualness and has arranged his thought so that it can be grasped by others.

Coherence is a quality of finished writing to be checked in the final revision. A writer cannot be always worrying about the connection between his statements while he is at work. There is, of course, always some relation between his consecutive "thoughts," but the relation may be apparent only to him. Careful consideration of material before starting to write should help the coherence of a paper, especially if some sort of plan is drawn up, arranging the different stages in a natural and sensible order. But coherence must be tested after writing. The writer should try to go over his copy impersonally to see if what he has written hangs together not only for him but for those who will read it. He should ask, "Is the relation between these statements clear? Can a reader pass from this sentence or from this paragraph to the next without feeling a break?"

A natural arrangement of material is not enough for this; there must often be signs of the relationship between sentences and paragraphs. These signs, various suggestions pointing toward coherence, and examples of successful and unsuccessful attempts at coherence are discussed in this *Index,* especially in *Conjunctions, *Prepositions, *Reference of pronouns, *Transition.

**Coinage of words** • See *Origin of words § 2a.

**Collective nouns** •
*Revision: Change, according to the conventions out-
lined in this article, the verb and/or the pronoun to
agree with the collective noun marked.*

*Coll*

1. A collective noun is one whose singular form names a group of objects, persons, or acts. Common collective nouns are:

| | | | |
|---|---|---|---|
| army | company | gang | *number |
| *athletics | contents | group | offspring |
| audience | *couple | herd | politics |
| band | crowd | jury | *public |
| class | dozen | *majority | remainder |
| *committee | flock | mankind | team |

When the group as a whole is intended, the collective noun takes a singular verb and singular pronoun; when the individuals of the group are intended, the noun takes a plural verb and plural pronoun:

The *crowd* that *has* been noisily engaged in finding *its* seats *settles* down and the incessant murmur of voices slowly quiets.

The *crowd* that *have* been noisily engaged in finding *their* seats *settle* down and the incessant murmur of voices slowly quiets.

The first *couple* on the floor *was* Tom and Janet.

One day when we were near where the old *couple were* living, we dropped in to see *them*.

The rule is simple enough. Its application is more compli-
cated because (1) some collectives have regular plural forms (*army, armies*), others do not (*athletics, offspring*); (2) even in the same sentence the sense may shift from singular to plural (see § 2 and § 3 below); (3) words which are not ordinarily collectives may be so used (the baseball *nine* were . . .); (4) some collectives more commonly take singular verbs (*herd, man-
kind*); others, plural verbs (*people*).

British and American practices differ somewhat; for ex-
ample, *government* and *party* referring to political groups are plural in England, singular here.

2. In speech we often make casual shifts in number. In writ-
ing, especially Formal writing, a collective should not be treated as both singular and plural in the same context:

The *company was* organized and immediately sent out *its* [not *their*] representatives.

Mess is over and the guard *have* [not *has*] a busy morning ahead of *them* [not *it*].

In using a collective noun there is often a temptation to try to keep it singular when the meaning really calls for a plural construction. Often the writer slips unconsciously from singular to plural in such a passage:

Into the church *troops* the entire *town, seats itself* on the uncomfortable wooden benches and there *remains* for a good two hours, while an aged curé preaches to *them* [consistency demands *it*] of *their* [*its*] wicked lives and awful sins. [This might better have started "All the people of the town troop into the church, seat themselves. . . ."]

In making constructions consistent you will often find, as in the sentence above, that it is the first member, the collective subject, that needs to be changed, rather than its pronouns. **3.** In speech (and consequently in some Informal and in much unedited writing) our tendency not to continue constructions across intervening words usually operates: The verb, which comes close to the noun, is singular, but a pronoun at some distance tends to refer to the individuals, in the plural.

*Spoken:* The team *was* called together for last minute instructions and sent out to *their* positions.

*Written:* The team *were* called together for last minute instructions and sent out to *their* positions.

*Spoken:* The election committee *has* from the beginning misused *their* rights in issuing false instructions for absentee ballots.

*Written:* The election committee *has* from the beginnin misused *its* rights in issuing false instructions for absentee ballots.

**4.** The plural of a collective noun signifies different groups:

The audiences of New York and Chicago differed in their receptions of the play.

**5.** In measurements and amounts a plural noun is often followed by a singular verb:

About 80 pounds of carbon disulfide *is* [or *are*] added.

(See *Subject and verb § 2; *Reference of pronouns § 2, *every and its compounds § 1. References: Curme, *Syntax,* pp. 539-540, 50-51; Fries, *AEG,* pp. 48-50, 54, 57-59; Jespersen, pp. 210-212; Pooley, pp. 85-88.)

**Colloquial English** • Usage that is characteristic of speech is *colloquial.* In modern writing there is not so sharp a division as formerly between what is spoken and what is written, but some spoken usages may be inappropriate in writing, just as some features of written English are inappropriate in speech.

(For discussion of the traits of colloquial English see *Spoken and written English § 2, *Vernacular, and "Informal English," p. 18.)

**Colon (:)** •
*Revision: Use a colon here.*

*Colon*

The colon is a mark of anticipation, indicating that what follows the mark will supplement what preceded it. Its function differs from that of the semicolon, which is a stop, almost a period. Most students could profitably use more colons than they do; often they mistakenly use a semicolon instead:

Yesterday I received a clipping from home, the essence of which is as follows: [not ;] . . . .

The principal uses of the colon are:
1. *Anticipatory use.* A colon is used after an introductory expression, as in the second line above, and after the salutation of formal letters:

Dear Sir: [*Contrast the comma in informal letters:* Dear Fritz,]

It is generally used to anticipate quotations in factual writing (not in fiction), especially if the quotation is a complete grammatical unit and runs to more than one sentence. Whether or not a colon is appropriate with shorter quotations depends in part upon the formula with which they are introduced. If the quotation is closely built into the sentence, a comma is usual (*says,* in the quotation below); if the introduction is more formal, a colon is usual (below, *was added:*).

A card made out at 10:45 P.M. on Nov. 4, 1928, says, "Arnold Rothstein, Male, 46 years, 912 Fifth Avenue, gunshot wound in abdomen, found in employee's entrance, Park Central Hotel, 200 West Fifty-sixth Street. Attended by Dr. McGovern, of City Hospital. Removed to Polyclinic Hospital. Reported by Patrolman William M. Davis, Shield 2943, Ninth Precinct." Two days later the word "fatal," in parentheses, was written in after the word "abdomen," and a second report, with more detail, was added: "Rothstein apparently had been engaged in card game with others in Room 349 on third floor of Park Central Hotel when an unknown man shot him and threw revolver out of window to street. Body found by Lawrence Fallon of 3164 Thirty-fourth Street, Astoria, employed as house detective for the hotel."—MEYER BERGER, *The New Yorker,* Nov. 26, 1938

2. *Between clauses.* A colon is used between clauses when the following one is either an illustration, a restatement in different terms, or an amplification of the first:

If a gunnery officer can't explain what he wants done, one of two things is going to happen: either the gun won't be fired or he'll have to do it himself.

Lazy minds give up in despair: "I can't write anyhow," say students to me year after year; they mean they won't think.—BARRETT WENDELL, *English Composition*, p. 136

The supposition that words are used principally to convey thoughts is one of the most elementary of possible errors: they are used mainly to proclaim emotional effects on the hearers or attitudes that will lead to practical results.—H. R. HUSE, *The Illiteracy of the Literate*, p. 21

**3.** *Conventional uses.* There are a few conventional uses of the colon, though they vary among publishers:

*a*—Between hours and minutes expressed in figures:

11:42 a.m.  3:28 p.m.
(or, especially British: 11.42 a.m., 3.28 p.m.)

*b*—In formal bibliographies and formal citations of books:

*Between volume and page*—*The Mt. Adams Review*, 160:129-140
*Between chapter and verse in citing the Bible*—Genesis 9:3-5
*Between author and title*—Stuart Chase: *Men and Machines*
*Between place of publication and publisher*—New York: Holt, 1958

In the last two of these a comma would often be found.

*c*—In proportions when the numbers are written as numerals:

Concrete mixed 5:3:1.

**4.** *Stylistic use.* Some writers prefer colons where most would use commas or semicolons:

It [a castle] is a shut place that commands by its shutness the open place about it. A castle is builded of the stone of its world: it rises from the stone of its world: it *is* the stone of its world. A castle is austere toward the world which it defends. It is invariable, forbidding: its strength is that of a perpetual shutting-out of all which lies outside it. Sun beats on the castle wall: inside it is dark. Moon melts its bastion and bathes its county blue: it is harsh and rigid. Water and wind make song of the green hills: the castle is silent. It is the lord of its county because it is apart from it. A castle is hot in a cold land: a castle is cold in a hot land: a castle is high in a low land: a castle is full in a land of dearth: a castle is dry in a land of verdure.—WALDO FRANK, *Virgin Spain*, p. 108

This is a matter of taste rather than of correctness and is usually (as here) Formal. The mark ordinarily attracts some slight attention to itself when used this way.

**5.** *Capitals following.* After a colon either a capital or a small letter may be used. The capital is more usual when the matter following the colon is in the form of a complete sentence, a small letter when it is a subordinate element. (See *Capital letters § 1.) That the deciding factor is largely the closeness of thought relation between the two parts of the sentence is suggested by the following quotations from a single article:

Thus the task of democracy has always been a twofold one: to prevent political privilege from reëstablishing itself, and to make peaceful settlement of disputes possible in a society without privilege.

Those who believe that fascism is simply a tool which Big Business created as soon as it found democracy dangerous overlook one important fact: the opposition of Big Business to democracy is much older than fascism.

The ways in which the kings settled social disputes were very different, in spirit as well as in technic: The kings of France, after having subdued the rebellious nobles, protected the social privileges of the nobility to the point of subjecting both citizens and peasants to cruel oppression; the kings of Prussia, who occasionally liked to be called "kings of beggars," without fully living up to the implications of that title, tried to restrict exploitation of the masses; so, much earlier, did Elizabeth of England.—CARL LANDAUER, in *The American Way,* ed. D. C. Coyle et al.

(For other uses of the colon see the *GPO Manual* and other style books.)

## Comma (,) •
*Revision: Insert or remove a comma at the place marked, in accordance with one of the sections in this article.*   Comma

### 1. *Between coordinate clauses.*   C₁

*a*–A comma is used before the conjunction when the independent clauses are rather long and when it is desirable to emphasize their distinctness, especially if the clauses have different subjects:

The frozen steel edges shrieked as they bit into the ice-covered turns, and the driving sleet slashed against their goggles and jackets with such force that it was impossible to keep clear vision.

A comma is not used when the coordinate clauses are short and closely related in meaning, especially in easy narrative:

There was a knock at the front door [  ] and Mary ran to open it.

*b*–A comma is generally used between two coordinate locutions joined by *but* or *not* to emphasize the contrast:

I can remember Mother telling me that a book was one's best friend, but I couldn't understand how anyone could feel that way.
Those who hold these ideas are to be pitied, not blamed.

## Uses of the Comma

The following list of uses of the comma outlines the treatment in this article. The numbers and letters refer to sections and subsections. Brackets mean that a comma should be avoided.

1. *Between coordinate clauses*
   *a*–Between rather long coordinate clauses
   *b*–Between clauses connected by *but, not*
   *c*–Between clauses connected by the conjunction *for*
2. *With dependent clauses*
   *a*–After a dependent clause or long phrase preceding the independent clause
   *b*–Before a dependent clause following the independent clause and not closely related to it
3. *With nonrestrictive modifiers*
4. *With interrupting and parenthetical elements*
   *a*–Around interrupting constructions
   *b*–Around conjunctive adverbs not standing first in their constructions
5. *In lists and series*
   *a*–Between units of a list or series
   *b*–Between coordinate adjectives in the same relation to their noun
   *c*–[Not between two words or phrases joined by *and*]
6. *For emphasis and contrast*
7. *For clearness*
   *a*–Before words of two possible functions *(for, but)*
   *b*–To prevent a noun being mistaken for an object
   *c*–To prevent wrong interpretation
   *d*–To separate consecutive uses of the same word
8. *With main sentence elements (S-V-O)*
   *a*–[Not between a short subject and its verb]
   *b*–Sometimes after a long or heavily modified subject
   *c*–[Not between verb and its object]
   *d*–[Very rarely between compound predicates]
9. *In conventional uses*
   *a*–In dates       *b*–In addresses
   *c*–After salutations of informal letters
   *d*–After names in direct address       *e*–In figures
   *f*–With degrees and titles       *g*–With weak exclamations
   *h*–[Not to show omission of a word]
10. *With other marks of punctuation*
    *a*–[Not with a dash] (*Dash § 6)
    *b*–With parentheses (*Parentheses § 4)
    *c*–With quotation marks (*Quotation marks § 4, b and c)

*c*–A comma is generally used between clauses connected by the conjunction *for,* to avoid confusion with the preposition *for*:

*Conjunction:* They are obviously mistaken, *for* all intercollegiate sports are competitive.

*Preposition:* Our English instructor had assigned us *Lord of the Flies for* a book report.

(For the use of commas between complete clauses that could stand as separate sentences, see *Contact clauses. See also *Comma fault.)

**2. *With dependent clauses.***  $C_2$

*a*–A comma is used after a dependent clause (or a long phrase) that precedes the independent clause or is not closely connected to it:

If that lake wasn't frowning at something or other that night, I'll drink it down to the last drop.

Although willing to use his athletic ability, he wouldn't study hard enough to become eligible.

When the preceding clause or phrase is short and closely related in thought to the main clause (especially when the subjects of the two clauses are the same), there is usually no comma following it:

Without a doubt [ ] Jack is the best linesman our school has.

When we had all gathered near the fence [ ] we could see that they were bums. (Subjects the same)

When appropriations are before the House [ ] he continually checks the Democrats' expenditures. (A close relationship)

*b*–A comma usually stands before a dependent clause (or long phrase) that follows the main clause if the relationship in thought is not close:

Kemal Ataturk's death had come as a blow to a nation of 14,000,000 people, though he reformed their social customs, their religion, and their economics with dictatorial zeal and speed.

They had tried four times to start it, the starter every time giving just a short whine.

**3. *With nonrestrictive modifiers.*** Modifiers which do not limit  $C_3$ the meaning of a noun or verb but add a descriptive detail are nonrestrictive and are set off by a comma or commas. The expressions in italics are nonrestrictive:

From where I was standing, *almost directly above the treasure,* I could see many articles that had been lost. [The clause *that had been lost* is restrictive and so is not set off by a comma.]

Pigeons breed in the spring and the hen lays two eggs, *one of which usually hatches into a cock and one into a hen.*

A restrictive modifier, one that is essential to a correct understanding of the word it modifies, is not set off by punctuation. The expressions in italics are restrictive:

Wouldn't it be as just to remove from his suffering a person *who has committed no crime* as to make suffer one *who has committed a crime?*

Great tracts were left, eaten bare of the grass *which had kept the soil in place.*

Intonation helps distinguish nonrestrictive from restrictive clauses. If you read a sentence aloud, you will be conscious of a slight pause and drop in voice before a nonrestrictive clause; before a restrictive clause there is no such change of voice.

Many modifiers may be considered either restrictive or nonrestrictive, and their punctuation should follow the writer's sense of the closeness with which they limit the word they modify; this can be shown by the way he reads the sentence aloud. The expressions in italics might or might not be set off by commas, depending on the writer's intention:

A winding road *that seemed to lead nowhere in particular* passed through the village.

It was quite a satisfaction *after working a difficult logarithm problem* to know that something had been accomplished.

(Further examples of restrictive and nonrestrictive expressions will be found in *Restrictive and nonrestrictive.)

C₄ **4.** *With interrupting and parenthetical elements.*

*a*–A phrase or clause that interrupts the direct movement of the sentence should be set off by commas—*two* commas:

Next summer, no matter what comes up, we will go to Europe.
The prank, I dare say, seemed amusing to you then.
Mr. Devant, as was customary with him, stopped at the tavern on his way home.

Usage is divided over setting off short parenthetical words and phrases like *incidentally, of course.* Setting them off with commas is more characteristic of Formal than of General writing, though there is often a difference in emphasis according to whether or not commas are used:

Mr. and Mrs. Crayton, of course, were late.
Mr. and Mrs. Crayton of course were late.
The speaker, naturally enough, was irritated by the interruption.
The speaker naturally enough was irritated by the interruption.

Adverbs that modify the verb or the statement closely should not be set off when they are in their natural position:

Undoubtedly [ ] this package was intended for Smith.
This package was intended for Smith, undoubtedly.

*b*–When a *conjunctive adverb stands after the first phrase
of its clause, it is usually set off by commas, and often it is set
off when it stands first in the clause:

His ridiculous proposal, nevertheless, was the one adopted.

Furthermore, all leaves are canceled until February 15.

*But* and other lighter conjunctions are a part of the clauses
in which they appear and should not be set off:

Hart had received permission to finish his experiment after class.
But [  ] he filed out with the others when the bell sounded.

**5.** *In lists and series.*                                        C₅

*a*–The comma is the natural mark to use between the units
of enumerations, lists, series (unless the units are long or contain commas within them, when semicolons would be used—
see *Semicolon § 1).

There are, among others, an actor out of a job, a murderer, a
Mexican dipsomaniac, a man obsessed with a philosophical concept
of time, an Indian oil millionaire who prefers waffles to any other
food, and assorted females, mostly tough.—*The New Yorker,* Nov.
26, 1938

Commas ordinarily are not used when conjunctions stand
between the units of the series.

A bit of tarnish on the brass work [  ] or untidy life preservers [  ]
or matches on the decks seem to be of little concern to him.

Sometimes a comma is needed to make the meaning clear;
otherwise usage is divided on the comma before the last item
in a series: *celery, onions, and olives,* or *celery, onions and
olives.* (See *Series.)

*b*–Adjectives in series. In the sentence

Although it was a hot, sticky, miserable day, Mrs. Marston looked
cool in her fresh gingham dress.

there are commas between *hot—sticky—miserable* because each
stands in the same relation to the noun *day.* There is no
comma between *fresh* and *gingham* because *fresh* modifies
*gingham dress* rather than just *dress.* A comma following *fresh*
would throw more emphasis upon gingham and might sometimes be wanted. Compare these two versions:

The bright, red draperies showed to advantage against the dark,
gray walls.

The bright red draperies showed to advantage against the dark
gray walls.

Either version is satisfactory, but in the first, *red* and *gray*
stand out as separate modifiers of their nouns.

*c*–Two items connected by *and* are not usually punctuated:

Old Mrs. Clayton was always ready to watch over the young children in her neighborhood [ ] and to help their mothers with light housework.

C₆ **6.** *For emphasis and contrast.* The pause indicated by a comma tends to keep distinct the constructions it separates and to emphasize slightly the construction that follows the mark:

The office manager was delighted with the prestige of his new position, and with the increase in pay.

This is especially true when a connective is omitted:

He repeated the story many times, repeated it when it no longer had any meaning.

In idioms like *the more . . . the greater,* Formal usage tends to have a comma, General does not:

. . . And the more meaning the Grammarian finds crowded into the verb [,] the happier he is.—P. B. BALLARD, *Thought and Language,* p. 87

C₇ **7.** *For clearness.* Often a comma can guide a reader in interpreting a sentence and make it unnecessary for him to go back over it for meaning. Two such constructions are especially helped by commas:

*a*–When a word has two possible functions. *For* or *but* may be either a conjunction or a preposition, and confusion may be avoided by using a comma before either when it is used as a conjunction:

The crowd hurried, for the river was rising swiftly. [*Not:* The crowd hurried for the river. . . .]

*b*–When a noun might be mistaken for the object of a verb:

When the boll weevil struck, the credit system collapsed and ruined a great part of the landowners and tenants. [*Not:* When the boll weevil struck the credit system. . . .]

Soon after the inspector left, the room was crowded with curious onlookers. [*Not:* Soon after the inspector left the room. . . .]

*c*–Sometimes a faulty interpretation of word grouping can be prevented:

A great crowd of early shoppers milled around inside, and outside hundreds more were storming the doors.

*d*–Ordinarily when the same word occurs twice consecutively a comma should be used:

What Janice does, does not concern me.

C₈ **8.** *With main sentence elements.*

*a*–Short subjects. Care should be taken not to separate short subjects from their verbs:

The first family to come [ ] sends word back to those left in the Old Country.

The six boys [ ] all came on the run.

*b*–Long subjects. When the subject of a sentence is a long phrase or a noun followed by modifiers—that is, when it is a locution of five or six words or more—Formal usage often puts a comma between it and the verb, but General usage does not:

Whether a program is appealing or not [*Formal* (,)] is quickly reflected in the sale of the sponsor's product.

*c*–Verb and object. There is some temptation to put a comma after a verb, separating it from its object or complement. This is especially true after verbs which in speech would be followed by a slight pause. Punctuation does not exactly represent speech, and such commas should be taken out in revision:

Since they know nothing whatsoever about their future occupation, they must start what might be termed [ ] a second schooling.

She always thought [ ] that I would never be a success.

*d*–Compound predicates. Except very rarely (and then only if the verbs are separated by several words), no comma is used between the verbs of a compound predicate:

We watched television until seven [ ] and then hurried over to the auditorium for the first of the lecture series.

After the supervisor's lecture, the girls returned sullenly to their tasks [ ] and whispered furtively the rest of the morning.

**9.** *In conventional uses.*                                     C₉

*a*–In dates, to separate the day of the month from the year: *May 26, 1965.* When the day of the month is not given, a comma may or may not be used: *In September, 1965* or *In September 1965.* The neater use is without the comma. In *26 May 1965* no comma is used.

*b*–In addresses, to separate town from state or country when they are written on the same line:

Washington, D.C., is too hot and humid to be a nation's capital.
Chicago, Illinois          Berne, Switzerland
Hamilton, Madison County, New York

*c*–After salutations in informal letters: *Dear Dot, Dear Len,*
*d*–After names in direct address: *Jim, try that one again.*
*e*–In figures, to separate thousands, millions, etc: *4,672,342.*
*f*–To separate degrees and titles from names:

Elihu Root, Esq.               Charles Evans Hughes, Jr.
Wallace W. Emmett, A.B.        Wallace W. Emmett, A.B. '36

But not in *J. W. Smith III* or *King George III.*

*g*–After a weak exclamation like *well, why, oh.*

*h*–A comma is not now commonly used to show the omission of a word that is required to fill out a grammatical construction:

He must have taken the right-hand turn and I [,] the left.

C₁₀ **10.** *With other marks of punctuation.*

*a*–A comma is now rarely used with a dash. (See *Dash § 6.)

*b*–When a parenthesis comes within a construction that would be followed by a comma, the comma stands after the parenthesis. (See *Parentheses § 4.)

*c*–For use with quotation marks see *Quotation marks § 4, b and c. (Reference: Summey, index entries under *Comma*.)

## Comma fault •

CF

*Revision: Revise the sentence marked by changing the comma to a semicolon or a period, or by inserting an appropriate conjunction, or by rephrasing to make it a more effective sentence.*

You should do more than merely remove the comma fault; you should make certain that you have written an effective sentence.

A comma fault (comma blunder, comma splice, *fused sentence) is two or more statements (independent clauses) that are punctuated as a single sentence—that is, with a comma between them (or even run together with no mark at all). Occasionally sentences of this sort may be effective (see *Contact clauses), but here we are considering only those that are unjustified either because of their form or the thought relation between the clauses or both.

There are various remedies for a comma fault:

1) The most obvious remedy is to put a semicolon or a period in place of the comma, but often a period inserted makes two weak sentences instead of one.

2) If the constructions really belong together in one sentence, they may be joined by a conjunction that shows the relationship, and ordinarily the comma is retained.

3) Often the sentence needs to be rephrased—perhaps a relative pronoun used instead of a *this* or *these*—or to be completely rewritten. Remember that the aim is to make an effective sentence.

The following examples show some common types:

| *Comma fault* | *Suggested revision* |
|---|---|
| He took a couple of steps, stopped, reached out and turned a valve, as he did that he told us | He took a couple of steps, stopped, reached out and turned a valve. As he did that he told us |

| | |
|---|---|
| that all the valves were right-hand valves. | that all the valves were right-hand valves. |
| Charley then crossed the room and threw a switch which started a motor, returning he wiped the perspiration from his forehead with the back of his hand. | Charley then crossed the room and threw a switch which started a motor. Returning he wiped the perspiration. . . . |
| They still produce aluminum tips for broken skis, these are very successful as a device for temporary repair. | They still produce aluminum tips for broken skis, which are very successful as a device for temporary repair. |

If you can make a sure distinction between an independent clause and a dependent clause, you should find it easy to spot the comma faults in your sentences. Look first to see how many independent subject-verb combinations you have in a group of words punctuated as a single sentence. If there are two independent clauses, look to see if you have a connective between them. If there is no connective but only a comma, you have probably produced a comma fault. (For exceptions, see *Contact clauses. See also *Conjunctions.)

**Commands and requests** • Direct commands (also called *imperatives*) are expressed by the simple (infinitive) form of the verb:

> *Hurry up!*    *Shut* the door, please.
> *Fill out* the coupon and *mail* it today.

In speech the force of the command or request is shown by the stress and tone of voice, which are hard to represent on paper. Emphatic commands are punctuated with an exclamation mark, less emphatic with a period. The form with *do* is often emphatic (*Do* come!). Negative commands are expressed with *not* and the *do* form of the verb: *Don't go yet.*

Softened or more polite commands and requests depend on phrasing and usually involve auxiliaries or adverbs of courtesy. Often they are in the pattern of a question, written either with a period or a question mark, depending on the intonation intended.

> Try to get them in on time.
> You will write at least six pages.
> Please think no more of it.
> Would you be willing to take part in this program?
> Would [or *Will*] you please close the window.
> Let's go around and see what we can do with him.
> Suppose we say nothing more about it.

In indirect discourse a command becomes an infinitive with *to* or a clause with *should*:

He told us to write a 5000-word paper. [*Or*] He said that we should write a 5000-word paper. [*Direct form:* Write a 5000-word paper.]

He wired me to come at once. [*Direct:* "Come at once."]

(For further discussion of forms of commands see Curme, *Syntax,* pp. 419, 430-436; Ralph H. Long, *The Sentence and Its Parts,* pp. 76-79.)

**Commercial English** • See *Business English.

**committee** • *Committee* is a *collective noun, usually construed as singular but sometimes as plural when the writer is thinking of the several individuals who compose it. In the latter situation we are more likely to write *the members of the committee.* The singular would usually be the desired form:

The committee meets today at four.

The committee [*or:* the members of the committee] get together once a month.

**Common case form** • See *Accusative case, *Case.

**comparative, comparatively, comparison, comparable** • These words are so spelled in our inconsistent practice. *Comparable* is pronounced /kom'pə rə bļ/.

**compare—contrast** • *Compare* is used: (1) to point out likenesses (used with *to*); (2) to find likenesses or differences (used with *with*). *Contrast* always points out *differences.*

He compared my stories *to* Maupassant's [*said they were like his*].
He compared my stories *with* Maupassant's [*pointed out like and unlike traits*].

When the things compared are of different classes, *to* is used:

He compared my stories *to* a sack of beans.

In the common construction with the past participle, either *to* or *with* is used:

Compared *with* [or *to*] Maupassant's, mine are pretty feeble.
In comparison *with* [not *to*] Maupassant's, mine are pretty feeble.

Idioms with *contrast*:

He contrasted my work *with* [sometimes *to*] Maupassant's.
In contrast *to* [rarely *with*] Maupassant's, my stories are feeble.

Note the difference in stress between *contrast* /kon'trast/ the noun and *contrast* /kən trast', kən tras'təd, kən trast'ing/ the verb.

## Comparison of adjectives and adverbs •

*Revision: Change the form or construction of the adjective or adverb marked, in accordance with the section below that applies.*

*Comp*

Adjectives and adverbs change their forms (see § 5) to show a greater degree of what is named in the simple word (*long, longer, longest*). The forms are easy enough to remember, but some questions arise in using them.

1. *Uses of the comparative.* The comparative degree expresses a greater degree (It is *warmer* now) or makes specific comparison between two units (He was *kinder* [*more kind*] than his wife).

The terms of a comparison should be actually comparable:

*Comparable:* His salary was lower than a shoe clerk's [Or: *than that of a shoe clerk*. Not: *His salary was lower than a shoe clerk.*]

*Comparable:* His face was round and healthy looking, like a recent college graduate's. [Not: *His face was round and healthy looking, like a recent college graduate.*]

With a comparative, idiom calls for *other* when the comparison is with something in the same class of things but not when the comparison is with things of a different class:

She is a better dancer than the other girls.
She is a better dancer than the boys [*than any of the boys*].

The comparative is frequently used absolutely, with no actual comparison involved (*higher education, the lower depths, older people*), or the reader is left to supply a comparison (*Look younger—Live longer*). (Reference: Esther K. Sheldon, "The Rise of the Incomplete Comparative," *American Speech,* 1945, 20:161-167.)

2. *Uses of the superlative.*

*a*–The superlative is used to indicate the greatest degree of a quality among three or more people or things (He was the *jolliest* of the whole group; This is the *brightest* tie in the showcase). The form with *most* is also used as an intensive to indicate an extreme degree. (You are *most kind*; She is *most clever*) in which no specific comparison is intended. Such genteel expressions of emotion are now pretty much restricted to social occasions and social correspondence.

Superlatives are not completed by *other*:

The Egyptians had obtained the highest degree of cultivation in medicine that had up to that time been obtained by any [not *other*] nation.

She is the best dancer of all the [not *other*] girls.

*b*–In many instances the same idea may be expressed by the comparative and the superlative: *He was taller than the other boys. He was the tallest of the boys.*

*c*–In Informal English a superlative is often a form of emphasis: *We saw the loveliest flowers when we visited her garden. Hasn't she the sweetest voice?*

*d*–It is also used in comparing two items: *His new novel is the best of the two.* Fries says (p. 101): "The use of the superlative rather than the comparative for two, thus ignoring a dual as distinct from a plural, is a fact of Standard English usage and not a characteristic limited to Vulgar English." (Reference: Russell Thomas, "The Use of the Superlative for the Comparative," *English Journal* (College Edition), 1935, 24:821-829; Bryant, pp. 201-202.)

3. *Idioms with comparatives.*

*a*–*as much as if not more than.* In "The styles vary as much as if not more than the colors," two constructions have been telescoped into one: "The styles vary as much as the colors; perhaps the styles vary even more than the colors." The telescoped form is more economical and therefore occurs in Standard speech and even in Standard writing. Prescriptive textbooks have condemned it since the eighteenth century, but the more legitimate objection is to its stylistic awkwardness. Possible solutions are:

The styles vary as much *as* if not more *than* the colors.

The lobby is as strong *as* if not stronger *than* it was in 1955. [Or: *The lobby is as strong as it was in 1955, if not stronger.*]

(Reference: Bryant, pp. 57-58.)

*b*–*as . . . as.* In the sentence below the use of *than* instead of the second *as* is not Standard:

I paid ten times as much for it *as* [not *than*] for the bigger bus ticket.

(See *as . . . as.)

4. *Comparison of absolutes.* Purists raise objections to the comparison of *black, dead, excellent, fatal, final, impossible, perfect, *unique,* since their meaning is thought to be absolute so that there are no degrees of *deadness* or *blackness* or *impossibility.* But in common use these words are frequently compared: "This was even *more impossible*"; and the Constitution has ". . . to form a more perfect union. . . ." Many are used figuratively with less absolute meanings (This is the *deadest* town I was ever in), which naturally admit comparison. (See *Divided usage. Reference: Bryant, pp. 58-59.)

5. *Choice of forms.* English adjectives and adverbs are compared in two ways:

*a*–By adding *-er, -est.*

|  | Positive | Comparative | Superlative |
|---|---|---|---|
| Adjective: | early | earlier | earliest |
|  | hoarse | hoarser | hoarsest |
|  | unhappy | unhappier | unhappiest |
| Adverb: | fast | faster | fastest |
|  | soon | sooner | soonest |

*b*–By using *more, most.* The change in degree may be shown by prefixing *more* and *most* to the positive form. This form is generally used for adjectives and adverbs of three syllables or more, and for many of two syllables. But no absolute rule can be formulated. It may also be used with those of one syllable, so that for many comparatives and superlatives there are two forms.

|  | Positive | Comparative | Superlative |
|---|---|---|---|
| Adjective: | exquisite | more exquisite | most exquisite |
|  | empty | emptier, more empty | emptiest, most empty |
|  | able | abler, more able | ablest, most able |
| Adverb: | comfortably | more comfortably | most comfortably |
|  | often | oftener, more often | oftenest, most often |
|  | hotly | more hotly | most hotly |

Words with a short vowel followed by a single consonant double the consonant to indicate the short sound (*thin, thinner, thinnest*). Words ending in *y* change the *y* to *i* before the endings: *dry, drier, driest; shy, shier, shiest* (sometimes *shyer, shyest*).

The meanings of the two forms (*-er* or *more*; *-est* or *most*) are essentially the same, so that whichever seems better can be used. But the *-er* or *-est* form necessarily places the stress on the root part of the word and so tends to emphasize the quality (kind′er), whereas the *more* or *most* form allows the stress to fall on the sign of the degree (more′ kind; you are most′ kind) so that there could be some difference in the suggestion value of the two. This stress pattern is, however, exceptional.

(References: Curme, *Parts of Speech,* Chs. 11, 13; *Syntax,* Ch. 25; Fries, *AEG,* pp. 96-101.)

**Complement** • *Complement* (also *predicative*) often refers to the noun or adjective completing the meaning of a linking verb and modifying the subject:

He was *busy.* He became *the real head* of the concern.

In some grammars *complement* is used to include direct and indirect objects. (See *Linking verbs, *Predicate adjective.)

**complement—compliment** • *Compliment* has to do with praise:

His progress deserved a *compliment.*

*Complement* means a number or amount that makes a whole, or an allotment (related to *complete*):

The regiment was brought up to its full *complement.*

**Complex sentences** • See *Clauses.

**Compound-complex sentences** • See *Compound sentence.

**Compound predicate** • Two or more verbs with their modifiers having the same subject are known as a compound predicate: Ruth *wrote* and *mailed* three letters.

Compound predicates are one of the chief devices of economy in writing. Note how far removed these sentences are from the one-small-idea-to-a-sentence type so often used by immature writers:

They (1) accepted the quinine and, in their gratitude, often (2) kissed the hygienists' hands. Heeding their advice, they (1) graveled the village roads, (2) began to drain their lands, (3) enlarged the windows of their dwellings, (4) built sidewalks, sanitary backhouses, and concrete platforms for manure, and so on.—Louis Adamic, *The Native's Return,* p. 318

(For further discussion see *Subject and verb.)

**Compound sentence** • *Compound sentence* is the term usually applied to two or more potentially independent syntactical units each with a subject and complete verb but linked to form a single grammatical unit. In speech the voice inflection at the end of the clause links the units. (See *Clauses.)
**1.** *With coordinating conjunction.* Usually the clauses of a compound sentence are connected by one of the coordinating conjunctions, most commonly by *and, but, for, or,* and the combinations *either . . . or, neither . . . nor*:

What a fool he was to be thus startled *but* always he had hated cats from childhood.—Walter Duranty, *Babies Without Tails,* p. 11

*Either* you learned these simple things in high school *or* you will have to learn them in college.

**2.** *Without connective.* A compound sentence may stand without a connective (see *Contact clauses). Such sentences are usually punctuated with a semicolon:

They are generous-minded; they hate shams and enjoy being indignant about them; they are valuable social reformers; they have no notion of confining books to a library shelf.—E. M. Forster, *Aspects of the Novel,* p. 33

Since each of these clauses could be written as a separate sentence, it is apparent that the traditional definition of sentence is somewhat arbitrary.

3. *With conjunctive adverb.* The clauses of a compound sentence may be connected by a conjunctive adverb (*however, moreover, whereas, consequently, therefore...*):

The F.B.I. had proved themselves expert in publicizing their solution of crimes; consequently some local police gave them only grudging support.

4. *Compound-complex.* Since one or more of the coordinate clauses of a sentence can be modified by dependent clauses, we have the category of *compound-complex sentences*:

He was an old man with a long beard, whose clothes were rags; but Mr. Kiddle had all the way wished to tell some one how proud he was of Ada, who did all the running, so he was glad to have even a tinker to talk to.—T. F. Powys, *Mr. Weston's Good Wine*, p. 66

This sentence has three independent clauses (making it compound): *He was an old man ... but Mr. Kiddle had all the way wished ... so he was glad to have ...*; and three dependent clauses (making it compound-complex): *whose clothes were rags, how proud he was of Ada, who did all the running.*

In current style compound-complex sentences occur more frequently than compound ones.

**Compound subject** • Two or more elements standing as the subject of one verb are called a *compound subject*:

*Capitalists, militarists, and ecclesiastics* co-operate in education, because all depend for their power upon the prevalence of emotionalism and the rarity of critical judgment.—Bertrand Russell, *What I Believe*, p. 53

The verb following a compound subject is usually plural:

*Christianity and humanity* *have* gone hand in hand throughout history.

(Some special cases are described under *Subject and verb § 2.)

**Compound words** • Compound words in written English are combinations of two or more words which are written as one word or hyphened: *doorknob, notwithstanding, quarter-hour, father-in-law, drugstore.* But the conventions of writing ignore a large number of compounds which though written as separate words express more than the sum of the parts: the *White House, high school, post office.* In speech these are usually distinguished by the stronger stress on the first words: compare *a white house* and *the White House.*

(See *Hyphen, *Plurals of nouns § 5. See also *Group words and check your dictionary.)

**Compounding or combining elements of words** • See *Origin of words § 3.

**Concluding paragraphs** •
*Concl*     *Revision: Revise the end of your paper to round out the discussion of your subject or to make the paper end more strongly.*

The last paragraph of a paper should round out the subject and give the final emphasis. Apologies, afterthoughts, and added minor details can only weaken the effect. If rightly done, the last paragraph will sound like a genuine conclusion, giving the reader a satisfying sense of completion.

**Concrete words** • See *Abstract and concrete words.

**Conditions** • A conditional clause states a condition or action necessary for the truth or occurrence of the statement made in the independent clause that the conditional clause modifies. *If* is by far the most common conjunction for conditional clauses, with its negatives *if not* and *unless* (=*if not*), and *whether* (=*if . . . if, if . . . or if*). Somewhat more Formal words and phrases introducing conditions are *in case, provided, provided that, on condition that, in the event that.*
1. *Simple conditions.* Simple (or practical) conditions are statements of actual or reasonable conditions under which the main statement will hold. The indicative (ordinary) verb forms are used:

*If the red light is on,* you know a train is in that block of track.
He will be there *unless something happens to his car.*
*Whether he comes or not,* I shall go just the same.

An older type of condition survives in some proverbs:

Spare the rod and spoil the child. [*If you spare the rod,* you will spoil the child.]

In speech, we often express condition by a compound sentence:

You just try that and you'll be sorry.

2. *Less vivid conditions.* Less vivid (theoretical or hypothetical but still possible) conditions are usually made with *should. . . would* or with the past tense:

*If he should raise his offer another $100,* I would take it. [Or: *If he raised his offer,* I would take it.]

*If you revised your papers carefully,* your writing would improve and would receive a higher grade.

**3.** *Contrary to fact conditions.* Conditions that cannot be met, or that are untrue, contrary to fact, are indicated by the past tense of the verb used in a present or future sense (If he *was* here [now], we would have seen him). In some Formal English, especially in writing, the plural form of the past tense is not unusual in the third person singular, usually called a subjunctive (If he were here . . .); and *If I were you* is a firmly established petrified construction. Formal English also sometimes uses a rather archaic inversion (*Were* he here . . .). The whole situation in cultivated practice has become almost hopelessly confused as the result of prescriptive teaching. Enforcing the subjunctive in one location may lead to its misuse in others.

*General:* If I was going to be there, I'd be glad to help.

*Formal:* If I were President, I would change that.

*General:* If I had known what I do [or *know*] now, I would [*I'd*] never have let him go.

*Formal:* Had I known what I now know, I should never have let him go. [Inversion with no conjunction]

*General:* If he was only here, he. . . .

*Formal:* If he were only here, he. . . .

(See also *if, *Subjunctives. References: Curme, *Syntax,* pp. 317-332, 421-429; Fries, *AEG,* pp. 104-107; Jespersen, p. 254 ff.)

**Conjugation •** *Conjugation* of a verb is the set of inflected and phrasal forms in which it may occur to show person, number, voice, and tense. (See *Verbs, *Tenses of verbs, *Principal parts of verbs.)

**Conjunction •** *Conjunction* is the traditional term for a limited group of words which lack distinctive formal traits and which introduce clauses, tie clauses together, and join series of words and phrases. Conjunctions are discussed here as:

*Coordinating (*and, but, for,* etc.)
*Correlative (*either . . . or, not only . . . but,* etc.)
*Conjunctive adverbs (*however, therefore, consequently,* etc.)
*Subordinating (*as, because, since, so that, when,* etc.)

There are also articles on many of the particular conjunctions: *although, *and, *as, *because, *but, and so on. See *Comma fault and *Contact clauses for punctuation between independent clauses not joined by a conjunction.

Since many words which function as conjunctions also have other functions, especially adverbial ones, identifying them as a part of speech is not always possible, nor is the distinction between coordinating and subordinating conjunctions always apparent.

(See *Particles. References: Fries, *AEG,* pp. 206-240; Roberts, pp. 231-242; Harold Whitehall, *Structural Essentials of English,* New York, 1956, pp. 65-77; all grammars have discussions.)

**Conjunctions, use** •

Conj
    *Revision: Make the conjunction marked more accurate (§ 1) or more appropriate to the style of the passage (§ 2).*

1. *Accurate conjunctions.* An exact use of conjunctions in fitting together clauses is a sign of mature, practiced writing. In everyday speech we get along with a relatively small number—*and, as, but, so, when,* and a few others—because we can emphasize shades of meaning and exact relationships by pauses, tones of voice, gestures. In writing, careful choice of connectives goes a long way toward making up for the absence of these oral means of holding ideas together.

Accurate use of conjunctions needs to be stressed. There are some easy temptations, like using *but* when there is no contrast between the statements (see *but § 2). Some conjunctions vary in definiteness of meaning: *As* means *because,* but means it very weakly (*as § 1); *while* may mean *although* or *whereas,* but the core of its meaning relates to *time. For examples of such refinements in the use of these words see the discussions in the articles on the particular conjunctions.

2. *Weight.* Conjunctions should be appropriate to other traits of style. Their weight should fit with the weight of other words and with the formality or informality of constructions.

A common fault is the use of the *conjunctive adverbs (*however, therefore, consequently . . .*) in General writing. These words fit best in rather Formal style. Although *but* and *however,* for example, both connect statements in opposition, one cannot always be substituted for the other. Whereas *but* fits in all varieties, *however* is often too heavy for General writing:

The entrance and registration desk didn't strike me as beautiful. From here, *however,* I went upstairs and then I could see what they meant. (*But* from here. . . .)

The English language has a number of long connecting phrases that will weaken a written style when used in place of shorter, more compact conjunctions:

At that time going to the movies was the usual evening pastime *in the same manner in which* [better: *as*] watching television is today.

(See *Conjunctive adverbs and *Function words.)

**3.** *Repetition of conjunctions.* Repeating a conjunction at the beginning of each element of a series gives distinctness to each element, avoids possible confusion, and achieves the advantage of clear-cut parallelism. This is more characteristic of Formal writing and often gives a definite rhythm:

... designs of spears *and* shields *and* bastions *and* all the pomp of heraldry.—NORMAN DOUGLAS, *Siren Land,* p. 152

For these five days *and* nights the Australians lived *and* ate *and* slept in that gallery of the mine of death, ... —JOHN MASEFIELD, *Gallipoli,* p. 165

On the other hand, omitting *and* before the last member of a short series results in a crisp emphasis:

Last week multimillion-dollar expansion programs were announced by Lockheed in Georgia, International Paper in Alabama, Reynolds Metals in Florida, Allied Chemical in South Carolina. —*Time,* June 19, 1964, p. 84

(See *Series, *Telegraphic style.)

**4.** *Coordination versus subordination.* For discussion of this phase of the use of conjunctions see *Coordination and *Subordination.

(References: Curme, *Parts of Speech,* Ch. 7, and *Syntax,* §§ 19 and 21, and index references.)

**Conjunctive adverbs •**

**1.** A number of words primarily adverbs are used also as connectives. They are called *conjunctive adverbs* (or *transitional adverbs* or *adverbial conjunctions* or *sentence connectors* or *sentence adverbials*). They are essential to the construction in which they occur as adverbs, but they do not occur unless there is a preceding utterance to which they are related; hence their conjunctive or transitional traits (as *hence* in this sentence). Ordinarily, they join the independent clauses of compound sentences. The most common are:

| | | |
|---|---|---|
| accordingly | furthermore | *namely |
| *also (See *too) | hence | nevertheless |
| anyhow | *however | *so (See § 4) |
| anyway (colloquial) | indeed | still |
| *besides | likewise | *then |
| consequently | moreover | *therefore |

*Adverb:* No campaign, *however* violent, could make him vote.
*Conjunction:* The results were poor; *however* we were not surprised.

**2.** *Weight and use.* Because most of the conjunctive adverbs are relatively heavy connectives, they are most appropriate in

Formal writing and in sentences of some length and complexity; they are less appropriate in General writing. They are now more likely to occur in constructions written as separate sentences than as elements within the same sentence.

Note these appropriate and inappropriate uses:

It is, *therefore,* unfortunate that at a time like the present, which plainly calls for a Socrates, we should instead have got a Mencken. [Appropriate, as is suggested by the Formal sentence structure; connects with thought of preceding sentence]—IRVING BABBITT, *On Being Creative,* p. 205

When morning came, *however,* I was still sick; *nevertheless,* when the bugle blew, I got up. *Consequently,* I looked very white at breakfast. [*However* could be omitted; *consequently* replaced by *but.*]

3. *Position.* Conjunctive adverbs are often placed within their clauses instead of at the beginning. This helps take the initial stress from them and gives it to more important words. When they are so placed, they are usually set off by commas as in the sentences in § 2 above.

4. *Punctuation.* A clause introduced by a conjunctive adverb is preceded by a semicolon; however, with *so* a comma is sufficient:

The whole forenoon had been a complete bore, *so* we wanted to make sure that we had a good time after lunch.

The advice sometimes given to strengthen *so* and *then* by adding *and* ("*and so* we wanted to make sure...") is usually wrong, since *and* adds nothing to the meaning of the connective. A better way to improve the illustrative sentence above would be to rephrase it:

The whole forenoon had been such a complete bore that we wanted to make sure we had a good time after lunch.

**connected with, in connection with** • These are wordy locutions, usually for *in* or *with:*

The social life *in connection with* a fraternity [in a fraternity] will be something you have never experienced before.

**Connectives** • See *Conjunctions, *Conjunctive adverbs, *Function words, *Relative pronouns.

**Consistency in constructions** • See *Parallel constructions, *Shifted constructions.

**Construction** • A construction is a group of words which stand in some grammatical relationship to each other, as that of modifier and head-word (*black cat*), preposition and object (*to* the *roof*), or subject and predicate (*They walked slowly*).

A grammatical pattern may be spoken of as a construction, as in the phrases *sentence constructions,* *parallel constructions.*

**contact** • The objections to certain recent uses of *contact* ("Will you contact Mr. Hubble?") rest on the fact that the uses came out of salesmanship—and many people have unpleasant associations with being "contacted" or with brokers' "contact men." Others object to using business terms in nonbusiness contexts. But the usage seems to serve a purpose in many fields besides business and, with the qualifications just mentioned, must now be considered established in Standard English. (See *Divided usage. Reference: College English, 1955, 16:247.)

**Contact clauses** • Two or more clauses of a sentence written together without a connective between them are known as *contact clauses.* Many compound sentences are in the form of contact clauses, as in the famous, "I came, I saw, I conquered" or in "But in him the pretence is justified: he has enjoyed thinking out his subject, he will delight in his work when it is done" (MAX BEERBOHM, *Yet Again,* p. 77). In these two examples the clauses joined by commas are parallel in form and the semantic relationship is very close. Occasionally, too, clauses which in meaning seem subordinate are set beside the main clause without a connective:

Give your decision, it will probably be right. But do not give your reasons, they will most certainly be wrong.—BERNARD HART, *The Psychology of Insanity*

This very old type of sentence punctuation has largely disappeared in print, though never quite abandoned by writers. In recent years it has re-emerged as a more convincing transcription of a natural and common form of speech.

On land, the Florida scenery is mostly man-made, concocted; it is not a terrain, it is just real estate.—STEPHEN BIRMINGHAM, "The Florida Dream," *Holiday,* Dec., 1963, p. 65

Contact clauses have a definite bearing upon one of the perennial problems of writing, the "comma fault," since many sentences containing clauses put together without expressed connectives are really effective as they stand and need no expressed connective. They are especially common and appropriate in rapid narrative where specific labeling of causes and results would slow up the movement. They are less common in straight exposition but occasionally occur. Many, of course, are the result of carelessness, but, as these examples suggest, they may produce the effect of a rapid and natural style. Deciding on the justification for contact clause punctuation is one of the more difficult problems of students and teachers.

They can usually agree that contact clause punctuation is most appropriate in easy narrative, almost always inappropriate in Formal writing. (See *Comma fault. References: Curme, *Syntax,* pp. 170-173; Jespersen, pp. 360-361.)

A more common type of contact clause, which is always restrictive and therefore never set off by punctuation, is the relative clause not introduced by a pronoun. Usually it is one in which the absent pronoun would be the object of the clause; but other constructions also occur: *He has found the key you lost yesterday. This is the boy we spoke of. There is a man below wants to speak to you. I am not the man I was.* The construction is an old one in English and firmly established in all varieties of the language. (References: Jespersen, *Modern English Grammar,* III: 7; Bryant, pp. 174-176.)

**content, contents** • *Adjectives*: The stress is on the second syllable both for the rather Formal *content* (He would be content with less) and the more common *contented* (He would be contented with less): /kən tent'/, /kən ten'təd/.

*Nouns*: In American English the stress is on the first syllable; *content* is used more as an abstract term (the content of the course) and in amounts (the moisture content); *contents* is rather more concrete (the contents of the box, the contents of the book): /kon'tent/, /kon'tents/.

**Context** • In writing, the *context* is the discourse that surrounds and limits a word or passage that is being separately discussed: "By itself the word might seem insulting, but in its *context* it could not possibly give offense."
**1.** The context is tremendously important in revealing the particular meanings of words. What, for instance, does the word *check* mean? By itself no one can tell which of the forty dictionary senses of the word is meant. Yet in actual use, in definite contexts, it gives no trouble:

They were able to *check* the fire at the highway.
The treasurer's books *check* with the vouchers.
He drew a *check* for the entire amount.
The tablecloth had a red and white *check.*
He moved his bishop and shouted *"Check!"*
With difficulty he held his temper in *check.*
He had the *check* list on the desk in front of him.

And so on. *Check* has more senses than most English words, but a very large proportion of our words have more than one sense so that their particular meaning must be gathered from the context—and ordinarily it can be. Context is important not only in indicating the particular denotative sense of a

word, as illustrated with *check,* but also in indicating the connotative value of the word, as suggested in the quotation in
the first paragraph of this article.

2. Statements of ideas depend for full understanding upon
the context in which they stand, and in quoting or alluding
to a writer's thought we should be careful to take the context
into account. Cardinal Newman's definition of a gentleman
as a man who never inflicts pain is often referred to as though
it represented Newman's ideal, but in its context (*The Idea
of a University,* Discourse viii) he was showing that this gentle-
man is all very well but without religious conviction he falls
far short of being an ideal type. Taking care that allusions and
quotations are true to the context in which they occur, that
they really represent the ideas of their authors, is a basic requirement of an honest writer. In speech there is also the *situ-
ational context,* the whole set of conditions in which words
are uttered.

**continual—continuous** • Dictionaries define *continual* as "frequently or closely repeated," with little or no time between:

Dancing requires continual practice.
He continually interrupted the lecture with foolish questions.

*Continuous* they define as "without interruption, unbroken":

A continuous procession of cars passed during the hour.
He has been continuously in debt for ten years.
*But:* He is continually running into debt.

Sometimes the context rather blurs the distinction: *The roar
of the planes overhead continually disturbed us* (or: *was continuously disturbing*).

**Contractions** • This term is applied to the written forms of
words in which an effort is made to indicate the colloquial
pronunciation, usually by substituting an apostrophe for one
or more letters of the standard spelling. They are appropriate
in Informal English and usually in General English but are
ordinarily out of place in treatments of dignified subjects and
in a Formal style, whether in routine exposition (as in
academic papers) or in more literary compositions. You could
probably read through a chemistry textbook without finding
a single contraction, but you would find a story with the dialog
printed without any contractions excessively stilted.

A more Formal style is not achieved merely by writing out
the contractions of Informal speech. "I have not time" is not
good Formal English for the Informal "I haven't time." For
Formal writing another idiom is often needed: "I have no
time."

In General English the fitness of a contraction is usually determined in part by the naturalness with which it falls into place, in part by the rhythm:

It wasn't that way to start with, when the Air Force first contracted for the plane in 1957.—*Newsweek*, May 18, 1964, p. 90

Contractions are necessary in reporting most conversation and in writing dialog for plays and stories:

"That's right. She's had a chance to think it over and realize how foolishly she was behaving. I'd even go so far as to make a guess that she's laughing over it by now. They're very changeable, you know."

"They're just like chameleons.... Why you wouldn't believe it."
—Evan S. Connell, Jr., "The Suicide," *Saturday Evening Post*, May 2, 1964, p. 49

An apostrophe ordinarily stands in the place of the omitted letter or letters (*doesn't, can't, shouldn't, he's*), though only one apostrophe is used in *shan't, won't,* and *ain't.*
(See \*have, \*shall—will.)

**Contrary to fact conditions** • See \*Conditions.

**contrast—compare** • See \*compare—contrast.

**Conversion** • A word most commonly used in one part-of-speech function when used in another part-of-speech function is said to have undergone *conversion* or *functional shift*: a *must* book; a *commercial* (adjective used in the function of a noun, meaning the advertising part of a television program); in the *know*; and (less well established) I wouldn't *fault* him. Sometimes a writer will use the noun form in preference to the adjective form:

...affected by the *monster* growth of London....—Sir Charles Grant Robertson, *England Under the Hanoverians,* p. 337

The principle of functional shift is well established, but a writer should be cautious in experimenting with new conversions. The student who wrote the following sentence was experimenting—unsuccessfully:

She stooped as if *to negative* her height.

Although conversion is not peculiar to the English language, it is facilitated by the absence of those distinctive forms for the parts of speech so characteristic of Latin, for example. *Round* is identified in dictionaries as *adj., n., v., adv.,* and *prep.,* but there is nothing in the form of the word itself to identify it as any of those. (For further discussion see \*Parts of speech.)

**Coordinate clauses** • See *Clauses, *Compound sentence.

**Coordinating conjunctions** •
**1.** The principal coordinating conjunctions are: *and, *but, *for, nor (=and not), *or, *yet. Only (I'd come, only I have a class) and *while (He's an expert, while I know nothing about the game) and other connectives are also occasionally used informally as coordinating conjunctions. The *conjunctive adverbs (therefore, however, and so on) are coordinating connectives, as are the *correlative conjunctions (either . . . or, not only . . .but, and so on).
**2.** Coordinating conjunctions are used between words, phrases, clauses, or sentences to connect elements of equal grammatical rank and substantially equivalent in thought:

> *Words:* books and papers; books, pamphlets, or magazines
> *Phrases:* in one ear and out the other
> *Clauses:* I would venture to say *that his description is perfect,* but *that there are some who would not agree with that verdict.*— BONAMY DOBRÉE, *Modern Prose Style,* p. 69
> *Independent clauses:* What they talk of was in the books, but there was the stimulus of personality.—ARTHUR E. HERTZLER, *The Horse and Buggy Doctor,* p. 181

**3.** For different effects of repeating or omitting conjunctions in a series see *Conjunctions § 3 and *Series.
**4.** For coordination versus subordination see *Coordination and *Subordination. For various uses of coordinating conjunctions see *Conjunctions, *Clauses § 1, and articles on individual conjunctions.

**Coordination** •
*Revision: Correct the faulty coordination.*

*Coord*

Two or more grammatically equivalent words, phrases, or clauses joined by a coordinating conjunction are said to be coordinate. (See *Coordinating conjunctions § 2.) Many *shifted constructions result from the writer's failure to put grammatically equivalent elements into matching structures. As used here, the term "faulty coordination" refers not to all such weaknesses but only to those relating to independent clauses. Faulty coordination is not a lapse in grammar or usage but a failure to make clear the logical relationships of the material. Often, therefore, it can be discussed satisfactorily only in the context in which it appears. A combination of independent clauses that is perfectly appropriate in one context might be puzzling or ineffective in another. Faulty coordination means that in the particular context the material calls for a relationship or emphasis different from the one reflected in the writer's use or arrangement of independent clauses.

1. Sometimes faulty coordination can be corrected by turning one of the independent clauses into a dependent clause. "He went to France for the summer, and his novel was published" suggests that there is an obvious causal relationship between his going to France and the publication of his novel. In some contexts, this might make sense. But if the only relationship that can be established is a temporal one—two events happening at about the same time but not otherwise related—the sentence needs to be revised: "When he was spending the summer in France, his novel was published" or "At the time his novel was published, he was spending the summer in France," or in some other way.

2. In the example above, coordination might be confusing or misleading. Sometimes it is simply ineffective: "When I reached the intersection, I found a group of people gathered around the body of a man. The left front tire had had a blowout, and the car had gone out of control and rolled over, and the driver was obviously dead." The independent clause "the driver was obviously dead" needs to be taken out of the coordinate relationship it is in; to gain its proper effect, it should be made a separate sentence—unless, of course, the writer is deliberately establishing a relationship in which the death of the driver has no more importance than the blow-out and the crash.

(See *Subordination. Reference: James Sledd, "Coordination (Faulty) and Subordination (Upside-Down)," *College Composition and Communication,* 1956, 7:181-187.)

**Copula** • See *Linking verbs.

**Copy** • Manuscript before printing is *copy.* (For points of form see *Typewritten copy.)

**Corrections in copy** • See *Proofreading.

**Correlative conjunctions** •
1. Some coordinating conjunctions are used in pairs:

both ... and     either ... or     neither ... nor
not so ... as     not only ... but [but also]     whether ... or

2. Except *either ... or* and *both ... and,* these correlative conjunctions are slightly Formal, showing a more conscious planning than is common in Informal or General English:

Not only was the water muddy, *but* it had tadpoles swimming in it.

3. Since these correlatives are coordinating conjunctions, they provide the skeleton for two parallel constructions. In practice, especially in speech, the parallelism is not always complete (I wondered whether *I should go* or *to beg off*). It is sometimes said that in writing, the more complete the parallelism, the more satisfying the result is likely to be. This means not only that the elements connected by the conjunctions should be of equal value but also that the constructions linked by the conjunctions should have the same word order, as in the first part of this sentence. But too strict adherence to this principle may make for artificiality, and variations, such as the shift from active to passive in the last example below, are common:

*Nouns:* He said that both *the novel* and *the play* were badly written.

*Adjectives:* He must have been either *drunk* or *crazy*.

*Phrases:* They can be had not only *in the usual sizes* but also *in the outsizes*.

*Clauses:* Whether *the sale was for cash* or *a mortgage was given*, it seemed too much to pay.

(See also *Parallel constructions. Reference: Lillian Mermin, "On the Placement of Correlatives in Modern English," *American Speech*, 1943, 18:171-191, and 19:66-68. For number of verb in constructions with *either . . . or*, see *Subject and verb § 2b, and as references, Dorothy J. Hughes, *College English*, 1941, 2:697-699; Bryant, pp. 62-64.)

**could—might** • See *can—may.

**Counter words** • Words which also have more restricted precise senses but are used frequently as general terms of approval or disapproval have been called *counter words*. Their popularity is a matter of fashion and is related to slang, except that they are ordinary English words and lack the element of surprise that good slang has. In Elizabethan times *fair* was such a word; recently *fabulous, definitely, mixed-up* have had such currency. In ordinary speech *colossal, cute, fine, fix, grand, lousy, lovely, nice, gorgeous, poor* are samples, and in more educated circles words like *adjusted, creative, dynamic, structure, vital, challenge, charismatic,* and often epithets like *red, radical, conservative, reactionary* are used as vague expressions of like or dislike without regard to more exact meaning.

In advertising and other more or less forced writing, *super-, -conscious* (we are *air-conscious, flower-conscious, defense-conscious* by turns), *-conditioned, -type, -wise* all enter into counter words. They are appropriate in Informal English (in which *certainly* has the sense of *yes*) but seem out of place in serious writing because their vagueness makes them inexact.

**couple** •
1. The primary meaning of *couple* is two persons or things associated in some way, typically as in "a married couple." In speech it is equivalent to the numeral *two*: *a couple of pencils*; or equivalent to *a few*: *a couple of minutes*.
2. Since in speech *of* is usually reduced to /ə/ before a consonant and assimilated to the preceding unstressed syllable, we may interpret what we hear as the omission of *of* and write:

He'd had a couple drinks.     I'll be gone only a couple days.

This transcription occasionally finds its way into print in General writing:

Mr. Freeman's statement left unanswered a couple [  ] pertinent questions: . . . —*The New Republic,* June 16, 1952, p. 15

**Course names** • In general discussions, only the names of college subjects that are proper adjectives (the languages) are capitalized. In writing a list of courses including one or more of these proper adjectives, it is possible to capitalize them all for consistency (and courtesy), though the distinction would usually be kept, as in the first example:

My program is biology, chemistry, European history, English composition, and French.

My program is Biology, Chemistry, European History, English Composition, and French.

In referring to the various departments of an institution, all names would be capitalized, as they would also when preceding the number of a course:

the Department of Applied Psychology     Psychology 201
the English Department     English 101
the Department of History     History 347
the School of Biological Sciences     Biology 413

In newspaper style *department* and *school* would probably not be capitalized when they follow the proper name.

**criterion, criteria** • *Criterion* and *criteria* are respectively the singular and plural forms; dictionaries also list *criterions* as a plural.

**curriculum** • *Curriculum* has the Latin plural *curricula,* and the English *curriculums.* The adjective is *curricular,* and the compound adjective with *extra* is ordinarily written as one word: *extracurricular. Curriculum* is also used as a modifier:

. . . the guidance of college students, curriculum and instructional problems at the college level. . . .—*Current Issues in Higher Education*, 1955, p. 220

**D** • In our spelling this letter usually represents the first sound in *die, do,* the second in *addict, addle,* and the last in *pod; d* represents the /t/ sound when it follows the sound of /f, k, p, s, ch, sh, *or* th/ in the same syllable: *walked* /wôkt/, *blessed* /blest/ (but /bles′id/), *kicked* /kikt/, *raced* /rāst/, *telegraphed* /tel′ə graft/, *fished* /fisht/, *matched* /macht/, *toothed* /tütht/. The /t/ sound is produced exactly like the /d/ sound except that in its production the vocal chords are not vibrated; it is voiceless, /d/ is voiced. With the loss in Early Modern English of the vowel of the suffix spelled -*ed,* the /d/ was next to a voiceless sound and lost its voiced quality.

In Standard English in the seventeenth and eighteenth centuries /d/ before an unstressed /y/ sound usually became /j/: *grandeur* /gran′jər/, *soldier* /sōl′jər/. Spelling pronunciation has now restored the /iə/ pronunciation in some of these words and the older /j/ sound is heard only in the speech of some older or Nonstandard speakers: *Indian* /in′jən/. British and American practice also differ: British English often has /i mē′jit/ for *immediate* but /kôrdiəl/ for *cordial.* There are local extensions of the sound to stressed *u* syllables: /jü′ti/, *duty.*

**Dangling modifiers** •
*Revision: Revise the sentence so that the expression marked is clearly related to the word it is intended to modify.*    DM

A construction is said to "dangle" ( or to be "misrelated") if its position makes it seem to relate to a word which can only make nonsense of the meaning, or if, in a context which demands an explicit relationship, the phrase has no clear relation to any word in the sentence.

A participle which is used in the function of an adjective should modify accurately either a noun or pronoun:

Looking further to the left, we saw the spire of a church. [*Looking* clearly modifies *we.*]

Defined in psychological terms, a fanatic is a man who consciously overcompensates a secret doubt. [*Defined* clearly modifies *fanatic.*]
—ALDOUS HUXLEY, *Proper Studies,* p. 220

A verbal that precedes the main clause and does not relate to the subject of that clause is dangling.

Upon telling my story to the advisor, he stopped and thought. [For: *When I told....*]

Motoring down Route 17 toward New York City, numerous signs read "Visit Our Snake Farm." [For *Motoring down Route 17 toward New York City, we saw numerous signs that read....*]

What if, forced to climb over this solid cloud bank, ice should form on the wings and force them down into the wild country? [The ice isn't forced to climb.]

Born in England in 1853, John MacDowell's seafaring activities began after he had emigrated to this country [His seafaring activities were not born in England.]

Dangling participles are to be avoided simply because educated readers do not expect to find them. As a rule there is no real question of the intended meaning of the sentence, though sometimes the faulty reference of a participle is ludicrous as it is in Arthur G. Kennedy's gem: *Having swelled because of the rains, the workman was unable to remove the timber.* In Informal use, some constructions of this sort are common: *If possible, I'll call before five.* (Reference: Robert M. Browne, *College English,* 1959, 21:100-101.)

Such dangling constructions should not be confused with *absolute phrases, in which the participial phrase is equivalent to a subordinate clause and is effectively used, especially for adding details: *He had worked for four hours, copy piling up quite satisfactorily.* (See *Gerund § 3 and *Participles for further examples. References: Curme, *Syntax,* pp. 158-160; Reuben Steinbach, "The Misrelated Constructions," *American Speech,* 1930, 5:181-197; Bryant, pp. 64-65.)

Infinitive phrases may be dangling:

*Imprecise:* To get the most out of a sport, the equipment must be in perfect condition. [The equipment does not profit from the sport.]

*Improved:* To get the most out of a sport, you must have your equipment in perfect condition.

This construction should not be confused with an absolute infinitive phrase which is well established in Standard English:

To judge from his looks, he can't be more than forty-five.

(See *Infinitives § 5.)

Prepositional phrases sometimes dangle:

At eleven, our family moved to Kansas City. [Clearer: *When I was eleven, our family moved to Kansas City.*]

**Dash** • Three dashes of varying lengths are used in printing: – (en dash), — (em dash, the usual mark), and —— (2-em or long or double dash). On the typewriter use a hyphen for the first, two hyphens not spaced away from the neighboring words for the usual dash, and four hyphens for the long dash.

The em dash, the one we have in mind when we say just *dash,* has aroused more discussion and more violent feeling than a mark of punctuation seems to deserve. Some textbooks and some publishers forbid its use generally, while others specify minute shades of meaning which they believe it indicates. Some writers rarely use it. Others, especially in matter not intended for publication, use it at the expense of other marks.

Most dashes are roughly equivalent to commas—that is, they separate units within a sentence—but the separation is sharper and the dashes suggest a definite tone, usually a note of surprise, an emotional emphasis. Some other mark could always be substituted for the dash, but there would be a difference in movement and suggestiveness in the sentence. At its best it is an abrupt, emphatic, and effective mark of punctuation.

**1.** *To mark a sharp turn in thought.* Most typical is its use to indicate a sharp turn in thought or syntax:

The old nations still live in the hearts of men, and love of the European nation is not yet born—assuming that it ever will be.— RAYMOND ARON, "Old Nations, New Europe," *Daedalus,* Winter 1964, p. 66

**2.** *Before a final summarizing statement.* It is often used before an inserted or added phrase, usually one that summarizes what has just been said or that gives contrasting or emphasizing details of what has been said, or often a striking apposition. This dash has the force of a vigorous comma:

The waiting, the watching, the hundreds of small necessary acts about the sickroom—all this was past.

The elements of every story are these five: character, incident, nature, fate, and milieu—the social, historical, vital background.—D. H. PARKER, *Principles of Aesthetics,* p. 236

He [the Englishman of the 1870's and 80's] was strongly in favor of peace—that is to say, he liked his wars to be fought at a distance and, if possible, in the name of God.—GEORGE DANGERFIELD, *The Death of Liberal England,* p. 7

**3.** *Between compound clauses.* A dash is sometimes used between two compound clauses for abrupt separation:

The "womanly" woman became as obsolete as the buggy. The nurse must tend the children, the cook must order the meals—life must be spectacular, not frittered away in little household dullnesses.—IRENE AND ALLEN CLEATON, *Books and Battles,* p. 92

**4.** *To enclose parenthetical statements.* Dashes may be used for parenthetical statements that are more closely related than parentheses would indicate, separating the expression from the context more than commas but less definitely than parentheses would:

The general effect upon readers—most of them quite uneducated —is quite different from what the serious messiah intends.—T. S. ELIOT, *After Strange Gods*, p. 36

**5.** *Overuse.* The overuse of dashes detracts from their special quality and proves that they are, as Bonamy Dobrée says, "a sandy joint." (See also *Schoolgirl style.)

She [Marlene Dietrich] was turned into a static image of lorelei charm, frozen in a lovely pose—and to bring that image to life, there seems to be no proposal except to point again to its overpublicized legs, and its—by this time—rubber-stamp "allure."

**6.** *With other marks.* Formerly a dash was often combined with other marks, especially with a comma or a colon, but this use has declined. The dash adds nothing in the salutation of a letter (*Dear Sir:*— means no more than *Dear Sir:*) and adds a displeasing mark to the page. Within sentences the old comma-dash combination has very generally disappeared also, so that now we find either a comma or, if a desire for emphasis makes it useful, a dash alone.

**7.** *Other uses.*

*a*–In the place of a colon when the statement ends with a question mark: *How do you explain this?—"English 23, F."*

*b*–To precede a credit line, as at the end of the quoted passages in this book. (See §§ 1-4 above for examples.)

*c*–After introductory words which are to be repeated before each of the lines that follow:

We recommend—
    That a constitution be drawn up.
    That it be presented to the student council.

*d*–To separate run-in questions and answers in testimony: *Q. Did you see him?—A. No.*

**8.** *Double dash.* Besides some arbitrary uses prescribed by particular publishing houses and in incomplete names (Mr. S——), the 2-em dash is chiefly an *end-stop in dialog when a speech is interrupted:

"... I can't say, of course, whether or not my layman's logic adds lustre to the gladsome light of jurisprudence——"

"Your reasoning is consistent as far as it goes," cut in Markham tartly.—S. S. VAN DINE, *The Greene Murder Case*, p. 220

**9.** *En dash.* A writer does not need to worry about the en dash, slightly longer than a hyphen, but printers use it between inclusive figures (*1837–1901*) and instead of a hyphen when one or both elements of an expression ordinarily requiring a hyphen are made up of two words: *the New York—Bar Harbor express.* (Reference: Summey, pp. 101-104.)

**data** • Pronounced /dā′tə/ or sometimes /dat′ə/ or (affecting Latin) /dä′tə/. (See *Latin and English.)

*Data* is the plural form of the Latin noun whose singular, *datum,* is little used in English; *data* is the usual English form for both singular and plural. Its meaning is actually collective and may sometimes stress a group of facts as a unit and so be used with a singular verb. When it refers to the individual facts, *data* is used with a plural:

*Singular idea*: The actual data of history *consists* of contemporary facts in the form of remains and documents.—MORRIS R. COHEN, *Reason and Nature,* p. 381

*Singular idea*: Data concerning measurement of social attitudes *has* been included in the next chapter. . . .—LUELLA COLE, *Psychology of Adolescence,* p. 102

*Plural idea*: When the data *have* been secured the task is to analyze, to sift, to select and to arrange those data which *bear* upon each particular phase of the object or event examined until at the end the scientist has what one might call a logical construct.—G. D. HIGGINSON, *Fields of Psychology,* p. 10

*Either possible*: These data *are* [This data *is*] unpublished.

The singular verb can be safely used in any but the most Formal writing. (See *Plurals of nouns § 4. Reference: A. Bartlett in "Current English Forum," *College English,* 1954, 15:417.)

**date** • *Date* is Informal for "appointment, engagement" (I had a date for the evening) and for "a person with whom one has an engagement" (After all, she was his date); as a verb, "to have or make an appointment with." *Blind date* is a useful and economical Informal expression, saying in two syllables something that would take several words in Formal English. (Reference: Bryant, pp. 67-68.)

**Dates** • The commoner form for writing dates is: *August 19, 1965.* The form *19 August 1965* is increasingly popular (partly as a result of its use by the armed services) and has a small advantage in that it makes a comma unnecessary.

Never write the year out in words except in formal social announcements, invitations, etc. Expressions like "January in the year 1885" are wasteful. *January 1885* is enough. If saving space is important, or in business or reference writing, months having more than four letters should be abbreviated:

Jan. Feb. Mar. Apr. Aug. Sept. Oct. Nov. Dec.

In Informal writing, figures are convenient: 8/19/65, 11/27/65. (In England and other European countries the day usually comes first: 27-11-65, sometimes with a Roman numeral for the month: 27 XI 65.)

Better style now usually omits the *st, nd, rd, th* from the day of the month: May 1 rather than May 1st.

In Formal style the day of the month may be written in words when the year is not given (September seventeen or September seventeenth).

Roman numerals are rarely used for the year except for decoration, as on the title page of a book.

(See *Letters, *Months, *Numbers § 1a, *Social correspondence.)

**Dative case** • English has no distinctive form for the dative function, which in some inflected languages indicates the indirect object of a verb, and can hardly be said to have a dative case in any sense. A noun in a construction that in another language might have a dative is in the common case form and a pronoun is in the accusative case form. Usually we have a phrase made with *to, for,* or *on.* (See *Case, *Objects § 2.)

**Deadwood** •

*Dead*    *Revision: Remove the unnecessary word or words, revising the sentence if necessary.*

*Deadwood* is a convenient label for a type of *wordiness in which a word or phrase adds nothing at all to the meaning of the statement.

[In] many [cases] students have profited by this.

He was a handsome [looking] man.

The book is divided into various sections, all dealing with [the matter of] unemployment.

He was quite conscious [of the fact] that he had failed.

Many phrases of this sort make writing flabby and are a mark of amateur or careless writing. (See *case, *Wordiness. See also *Jargon.)

**Declension** • *Declension* is the change of form of nouns and pronouns (and in many languages the form of adjectives and participles also) to show number (singular or plural), gender (masculine, feminine, neuter), and case (nominative, genitive, accusative, etc.). The English noun has only two regular forms (the genitive form and the common form, which is used for all other relationships), and the variations in pronoun forms are not regular; English has no declension in the sense that Latin has. (See *Case, the articles on the various cases, *Plurals, and the articles referred to there.)

**definitely** • *Definitely* is one of the most frequently misspelled words. Remember there is no *a* in it, and associate def i *ni* tion with def i *nite* and def i *nite* ly.

At present *definitely* is overused as a *counter word to give emphasis or in the sense of "certainly, quite" (I will not do it, definitely; He was definitely worse than usual; She definitely disapproves of those methods; But definitely!) instead of in its more limited sense of "clear-cut, in a definite manner."

**Definition** • Whenever a word has several meanings and the context of your paper does not make readily apparent the meaning you intend, you should specify the sense in which you are using the word. You should also define technical terms that your audience cannot fairly be expected to know. Definitions are of different kinds to suit different purposes. Sometimes an illustration or a synonym does an adequate job of defining. At other times you may need to supply a *logical* (or formal) definition. The logical definition falls into the pattern of

$$term = genus \text{ or } class + differentia(e)$$

as illustrated in "Man (term) is a rational (differentia) animal (genus)." The following are traditional rules for testing the soundness of a logical definition:

1. The definition must be neither too broad nor too narrow. In "A bachelor is a person who is unmarried," the genus *person* is too broad; it should be limited to *man*. In "A shoe is a leather covering for the human foot," the definition is too narrow; the differentia *leather* excludes shoes made of other materials.

2. Unless privation or negation is the distinguishing characteristic (as in bachelor, *not* married; orphan, *without* parents) the definition should be positive, not negative. "Liberty is the state of not being restrained" violates this rule for a logical definition.

3. The definition should not be circular, as in "Hostility is the state of being hostile."

4. The definition should not be expressed in figurative language. This rule excludes the famous definition of Karl Marx, "Religion is the opiate of the people."

Constructing logical definitions and testing them by these rules gives training in precise, literal statement. It should be

remembered, however, that many excellent definitions are not
—and are not intended to be—logical definitions.

**Degree** • See *Comparison of adjectives and adverbs.

**Degrees** • Ordinarily a person's academic degrees are not
given with his name except in college publications, reference
works, and articles and letters where the degrees indicate competence in a particular field, as in a doctor's comment on a
medical matter. When used, they are separated from the name
by a comma and in alumni publications are often followed by
the year in which they were granted:

Harvey J. Preble, A.B.    Harvey J. Preble, A.B. '08
James T. Thomson, M.A.    James T. Thomson, A.B. '21, M.A. '24
Robert Bernath, M.D., gave the principal address.
Royce Walton, B. Arch., discussed Wright's mile-high building.

As a rule, except in reference lists, only a person's highest
degree in an academic professional field need be mentioned.

If the institution granting the degree is named, the following forms are usual:

George H. Cook, A.B. (Grinnell), A.M. (Indiana), Ph.D. (Chi-
cago)
D. C. Browning, B.A. (Oxon. [= Oxford])
J. H. Plumb, Ph.D. (Cantab. [= Cambridge])

Two kinds of degrees are granted by American colleges and
universities. *Earned* ("in course") degrees are given at the completion of a required course of study. Some of the ones commonly granted are:

A.B. (*or* B.A.)—Bachelor of Arts
B.S.—Bachelor of Science
B.E.—Bachelor of Engineering
B.D.—Bachelor of Divinity
B. Mus.—Bachelor of Music
B. Arch.—Bachelor of Architec-
ture
Ph.B.—Bachelor of Philosophy
LL.B.—Bachelor of Laws
A.M. (*or* M.A.)—Master of Arts
M.S.—Master of Science
M.E.—Master of Engineering
M.Ed. (*or* Ed.M.)—Master of
Education

M.B.A.—Master of Business
Administration
M.F.A.—Master of Fine Arts
M.Ped.—Master of Pedagogy
(*or* M.Ed., Ed.M.—Master of
Education)
Ed.D.—Doctor of Education
Ph.D.—Doctor of Philosophy
S.T.D.—Doctor of Sacred
Theology
M.D.—Doctor of Medicine
D.D.S.—Doctor of Dental
Surgery

*Honorary* ("honoris causa") degrees are granted by institutions as a token of respect. Of the following, the first four are
the most common:

LL.D.—Doctor of Laws

D.D.—Doctor of Divinity

Lit(t).D.—Doctor of Literature
   *or* Letters

Sc.D.—Doctor of Science

D.C.L.—Doctor of Civil Law

L.H.D.—Doctor of Humanities

Eng.D.—Doctor of Engineering

British and other European degrees are similar but less numerous.

**Delete** • *Delete* means "take out, erase, remove." It is a direction to printers made by putting a Greek small *d* ( δ-delta) in the margin and drawing a line through the matter to be removed. (See *Proofreading.)

To delete material in your manuscripts, simply draw a line through it (don't use parentheses or black it out completely).

**Demonstrative adjectives and pronouns** • *This, that, these, those* are called demonstrative adjectives or demonstrative pronouns, according to their use in a sentence:

Adjectives:                       Pronouns:

*This* car we bought in May.    *This* cost a good bit more than *those*.

*Those* fellows never think of anyone else.       *That*'s a good idea.

(See *Agreement, *that, *this, *kind, sort.)

**Dependent clauses** • See *Relative clauses, *Clauses.

**Derivation of words** • See *Origin of words.

**descendant** • *Descendant* spells both adjective and noun, as does *descendent*. The adjective has an added sense. Consult a good dictionary.

**Description** • See *Adjectives in use, *Adverbs in use.

**detail** • Pronunciation usage of *detail* is divided: /di tāl′/, /dē′tāl/, the first older, the second especially common in situations where the word is used a great deal (army life, architecture, composition, etc.).

**Details** •

*Revision: Develop this topic more fully by giving pertinent details.*

*Det*

Adequate development of a topic in writing usually comes from the use of details—images, facts, evidence, bits of observation, and so on. They not only make the reader understand what you are discussing but to a large extent it is details that make a paper interesting and convincing. In description and narration, details can be so arranged that the reader is led to shape for himself a clear impression of what the writer has observed or experienced. In explanation and persuasion, details are essential to support or prove the generalizations.

**develop** • *Develop* is the usual Standard spelling for the verb and *development* for the noun; *develope* and *developement* are now extremely rare.

**Development** • See *Outline form.

**devil** • *Devil* (and *hell*) seldom receive the courtesy of a capital except for stylistic emphasis.

**Diacritic marks** • See *Pronunciation § 1.

**Diagramming sentences** • Diagramming sentences by placing sentence elements in an arbitrary graphic organization in an effort to show their function in the sentence is of questionable value for any purpose other than learning the rules of a game. This exercise, however, seems to have appealed to a good many teachers and even some students. The futility of diagramming has been demonstrated repeatedly; two studies are: Harry A. Greene, "Direct versus Formal Methods in Elementary English," *Elementary English,* 1947, 24:273-285; Anthony L. Tovatt, "Diagramming, A Sterile Skill," *English Journal,* 1952, 41:91-93.

**Diagrams, graphs, etc.** • The function of diagrams, charts, graphs, and illustrations is to make a writer's meaning more clear and more concrete than his words alone could. They cannot be a substitute for a discussion in words, but they can make it easier for readers to grasp figures, to understand relationships, and especially to make comparisons between facts that can be graphically portrayed. The making of graphs, charts, maps, and so on is discussed in technical and specialized manuals. (References: Herbert Arkin and Raymond R. Colter, *Graphs—How to Make and Use Them,* New York, 1940; Frederick E. Croxton and Dudley J. Cowden, *Applied General Statistics,* 2nd ed., New York, 1955, Chs. 4 and 6; and W. O. Sypherd, Alvin M. Fountain, and V. E. Gibbens, *Manual of Technical Writing,* Chicago, 1957, Ch. 7; chapters on graphic methods in other introductions to statistics.)

**Dialects** • A dialect is the speech (words, sounds, stress, phrasing, grammatical habits) characteristic of a fairly definite region or group, or more accurately, it is speech that does not attract attention to itself among the residents of a region (*re-*

*gional dialect*) or among members of a group (*group* or *class dialect*), but that would be recognizably different to an outsider. In linguistics a dialect is any development from a parent language: French and Italian are dialects of Vulgar Latin.

*Localism* is used in this book for a regional dialectal usage. Conspicuous dialectal words are usually out of place in General and Formal writing except to give a local flavor. They are more effective in speech, in fiction, and in Informal writing. (For a brief description of dialects in the United States, see "Variations due to place," p. 5.)

**Diction** •
*Revision: Replace the word marked with one that is more exact, more appropriate, or more effective.*

D

*Diction* here means primarily the choice of words in speaking or writing. Good diction means that the words seem to the reader or listener well chosen to convey the meanings or attitudes of the writer or speaker; faulty diction, that the words either fail to convey the meaning fully or accurately or do not satisfy the reader's expectation in some other way. Many specific words have articles of their own (*contact, *drunk, *hope, *however, *notorious, *ye = the). Often—but not always— the solution to a question of diction can be found in a dictionary. (See also *Big words, *Slang, *Usage, *Words, *Wrong words.)

**Dictionaries** • Not every dictionary is reliable and no dictionary can be depended on entirely. A good dictionary is one with a recent copyright date and a clear indication that a scholarly staff was responsible for the editing of the book. Even an unabridged dictionary is not complete, and all smaller ones are necessarily even less complete. The information in the entries varies in reliability according to the difficulties involved in getting and presenting it: spellings are most reliable, pronunciations least. Definitions are abbreviated and often overcompressed because of lack of space.

**Dieresis** • Two dots placed over the second of two consecutive vowels to show they are to be pronounced separately are referred to as a *dieresis* /dī er'ə sis/: *reëxamine, coöperation*. A hyphen is often used to indicate that the vowels are to be kept separate, especially in words with *re-* (*re-enlist*). There is a tendency not to use either dieresis or hyphen in the more commonly used words, so that *cooperation* and *zoology*, for example, are now the more usual forms. Do not confuse this mark with *umlaut in German words, which when placed over *a, u,* or *e* makes separate alphabetical entities.

**different** • In American writing the commonest preposition after *different* is *from*:

> His second book was entirely different from his first.
>
> Sharon was so different from what we expected that we were all surprised.

But General usage is divided, with *than* sometimes and *to* rarely replacing *from* (*different to* is a common British idiom). *Different than* is common when the object is a clause:

> The house was a good deal different than he remembered it. [This idiom is neater than "different from what he remembered."]

Since many people still object to *different than*, students should avoid it in their Formal writing. (References: D. L. Bolinger, *English Journal*, 1939, 28:480; Gladys D. Haase, *College English*, 1949, 10:345-347; Bryant, pp. 69-70; Bergen and Cornelia Evans, *A Dictionary of Contemporary American Usage*, New York, 1957, pp. 135-136.)

**Digraph** • Two letters used together to spell a single sound are known as a *digraph*. English spelling has many digraphs:

| | |
|---|---|
| *ea* as in *head* or *heat* | *ee* as in *seed* |
| *ei* as in *either* or *neighbor* | *oa* as in *coat* |
| *oo* as in *book* or *food* | *ph* as in *physics* |
| *sh* as in *shall* | *th* as in *then* or *thin* |

**dining** • *Dine, dined, dining, dining room* all have to do with eating—as does *dinner* with two *n*'s and a short *i*; *dinning* (short *i*) has to do with *din*, "noise."

*Dine* and *dining* are Formal words. *Dinner* is used in all varieties.

**Diphthong** • A *diphthong* is a vowel-like sound made by moving the tongue, jaw, and lips from the position for one vowel to that of another while vibrating the vocal cords. (The term has also been used as equivalent to *digraph*.) The standard method of transcribing these glide sounds is to use two vowel symbols, which are to be interpreted as indicating where the diphthong begins and where it ends. The common distinctive diphthongs of American English are: /ī/, /ä to i/; /oi/, /ô to i/; /ou/, /ä to ü/; and /ū/, /i [y] to ü/.

Most English vowels have some diphthongal quality. (For further details about American diphthongs, see J. S. Kenyon, *American Pronunciation*, § 327 ff, and the discussions of pronunciation in good modern dictionaries.)

**Direct address** • *Direct address* is the term used to describe the construction in which persons (or objects) are addressed in speaking, reading, or writing:

*My friends,* I wish you would forget this night.
What do you think, *Doctor,* about his going home now?
*Rain, rain,* go away.

Words in direct address are separated from the rest of the sentence by a comma or, if in mid-sentence, by two.

**Direct objects** • See *Objects § 1.

**disinterested—uninterested** • From its first recorded uses in the seventeenth century, *disinterested* has had two senses: (1) impartial, not influenced by personal interest; (2) indifferent, inattentive, uninterested. (See *Oxford English Dictionary* and the 1933 *Supplement.*) The context usually indicates the sense:

The rules [for criticism] may be given in one word: by being disinterested. And how is it to be disinterested? By keeping aloof from practice; by resolutely following the law of its own nature, which is to be a free play of the mind on all subjects which it touches; . . .— MATTHEW ARNOLD, "The Function of Criticism at the Present Time"
Next was the question: Are modern students actually disinterested in reading?—RUTH DAVIES, "We Join the March of the Moderns," *English Journal* (College Edition), 1939, 28:203

Recently there have been a number of attacks on the use of *disinterested* in the sense of *uninterested.* Usage records the word in both senses, but stylistically (in part because of the honorific connotation of *disinterested,* which *impartial* and *objective* have not acquired) sensitive readers prefer the first sense. A writer should take their preference into account.

The noun *disinterest* means "lack of interest" (and is probably one reason for the increased use of the adjective to mean "uninterested"):

He instances religious corruption, political corruption, and disinterest of the well-to-do.

(Reference: Robert J. Geist, "Usage and Meaning," *College Composition and Communication,* 1955, 6:88-91.)

**disremember** • See *remember.

**Ditto marks (")** • Ditto marks are used with lists and tabulations in reference works instead of repeating words that fall directly below. In typewritten manuscript, use quotation marks for ditto marks:

```
m, as in man, men, mine, hum, hammer
n, "  " no, man, manner
```

Ditto marks are not used in consecutive writings nor in footnotes or bibliographies. In general they are much less used than formerly.

**Divided usage** • Usage is said to be *divided* when two or more forms exist in the language, both in reputable use in the same dialect or variety. *Divided usage* is not applied, for example, to *localisms, like *poke* for *sack* or *bag,* or to differences like *ain't* and *isn't* which belong to separate varieties of the language. It applies to spellings, pronunciations, or constructions on which those of similar education might differ.

There are many more of these divided usages within Standard English than most people are aware of. For instance, most dictionaries record these and hundreds of other instances of divided usage:

*In pronunciation:*

/ab′də mən/—/ab dō′mən/
/ad′vər tīz′mənt/—/ad vėr′tis mənt/—/ad vėr′tiz mənt/
/lev′ər/—/lē′vər/
/ī′sə lāt/—/is′ə lāt/

*In spelling:*

| | |
|---|---|
| buses—busses | millionaire—millionnaire |
| catalog—catalogue | although—altho |

*In verb forms:*

Past tense—*sing*: *sang* or *sung*; *ring*: *rang* or *rung*
Past participle—*show*: *shown* or *showed*; *prove*: *proved* or *proven*

It is hard for some careful users of the language to realize that others may speak or write somewhat differently from themselves and still be following Standard practice. Before calling a person to account, either seriously or playfully, for a usage, we should make sure that his is not a variant that is as reputable as the one we may prefer; that is, we should avoid emotional attitudes and useless disputes whenever possible. This is not always easy. Words (usage) can acquire powerful associations. For instance: The past tense of *eat* pronounced /et/ is for many Americans associated with lack of education, though it is used by many educated Southerners. In England both /et/ and /āt/ are in widespread Standard usage, yet Fowler (in the entry for *eat*) is quite dogmatic: "The past is spelt *ate* (rarely *eat*) and pronounced /ĕt/ (wrongly /āt/)." British dictionaries show that "wrongly" is not accurate; but Fowler evidently felt strongly about it. If he, a distinguished and competent lexicographer, could object so violently to a

Standard pronunciation, other people, lacking his linguistic background, will have similar prejudices even less well-founded.

The point about divided usages is that both are acceptable. A person who has learned to say /rash'ən/ for *ration* need not change to /rāsh'ən/ nor the other way around. When you may choose between variants of equal standing, choose the one that you use naturally, that is appropriate to your style, or, if you are taking pains to be tactful, the one that is customary among the audience you are to reach.

The entries in this *Index* include a number of divided usages. When one or the other of two acceptable usages is likely to disturb many readers or listeners and arouse emotional attitudes, evidence is usually presented: there is security in knowing what is dangerous ground. For examples, see:

*Words*: \*can—may, \*drought—drouth, \*enthuse, \*farther—further
*Forms*: \*-ed, \*It's me, \*slow, slowly, \*Principal parts of verbs
*Pronunciations*: \*either
*Constructions*: \*different from, \*due to, \*like—as, \*reason is because

## Division of words •

*Revision: Break the word at the end of this line between syllables.*

Div

Whenever it is necessary in manuscript or in print, a word is divided at the end of a line by a hyphen ("division hyphen"). But in preparing manuscript you will not be forced to divide many words if you will leave a reasonable right hand margin. A good habit is to divide words only when the lines will be conspicuously uneven if the last word is completely written or completely carried over to the next line. In manuscript for publication most publishers prefer an uneven right margin to divided words.

When you are not sure how to divide a word, consult a dictionary. Both the divided parts should be pronounceable, though this does not necessarily mean that the established printing practice records the actual spoken division of syllables; words of one syllable, like *matched, said, thought,* should not be divided at all. English syllables are difficult to determine, but in general they follow pronunciation groups: *auto-cratic* would be divided into syllables *au to crat ic,* but *autoc-racy* is *au toc ra cy.*

The following words are divided to show typical syllables:

| | | | | |
|---|---|---|---|---|
| mar gin | ca ter | hy phen | chil dren | long ing |
| hi lar i ous | cat ty | ac com plished | ad min is trate | |

Double consonants are usually separable:

ef fi cient      com mit tee      daz zling      bat ted

A single letter is never allowed to stand by itself: do not divide at the end of lines words like *enough* (which would leave a lone *e* at the end of a line) or *many* (which would put a lone *y* at the beginning of a line).

Words spelled with a hyphen (*half-brother, well-disposed*) should be divided only at the point of the hyphen to avoid the awkwardness of two hyphens in the same word.

Division of words is primarily a printing and editing problem and fuller directions will be found in the stylebooks of publishing houses (like the *Manual of Style* of the University of Chicago Press).

**do** • *Do* is one of the most important auxiliary verbs in English. Its conjugation follows the regular strong verb pattern (the past tense and past participle are formed by a change in vowel) except for the pronunciation of the third person singular *does* /duz/ and of the contracted *don't* /dōnt/.

**1.** *"Do" in verb phrases.*

**a**–*Do* is used to form what are called emphatic verb phrases with all verbs except the modal auxiliaries (*can, may, shall* . . .) and usually *be*:

| *Present* | *Past* |
|---|---|
| I, you do wish | I, you he, she did wish |
| he, she does wish | we, you, they did wish |
| we, you, they do wish | |

**b**–With *not* (in speech contracted to *don't, doesn't, didn't). This is the Standard way of negating all English verbs except the modal auxiliaries and usually *be*:

He did not feel well enough to go out. I don't expect to go.

**c**–In questions:

Do you think I was right?
Did you like the show as well as you expected to?

**2.** *"Do" as a pro-verb. Do* is used to avoid repetition of a simple verb that has just been used:

I like him better than you do [than you like him].

**3.** *"Do" in idioms. Do* has many idiomatic meanings and is part of many idiomatic phrases: A girl *does* her hair; a steak is well *done*; we *do away* with things; *do for* (which may mean "be enough"—That will *do* for you—or "put the finishing touches on"—That *did* for him—or, in some localities, "work for, serve"—She *does* for Mrs. Lawrence); *done for*; *do in*; *do over* ("redecorate"); *do up* ("wrap up, launder").

(References: Fries, *AEG*, pp. 146-149; Fries, *Structure*, pp. 96-97, 149-151.)

**don't** • *Don't* is the contraction of *do not*, universally used in conversation and often in writing when *do not* would seem too emphatic or when the rhythm seems more comfortable with the shorter form.

Until about 1900 *don't* was the usual third person singular in Informal speech, and the usage still often finds its way into familiar speech and even into casual writing: "He don't look as well as he used to." Educated people now avoid it, though Atwood found that *Linguistic Atlas* evidence for the Eastern states showed nearly half of the cultured informants using the construction. In another study of *Atlas* material, Malmstrom found *he don't* unevenly distributed in the speech of the culti-vated: Middle Atlantic, 75 percent; South Atlantic, 50 percent. But in the New England, North Central, and Upper Midwest areas *he doesn't* predominated. (References: Karl W. Dykema, "An Example of Prescriptive Linguistic Change: 'Don't' to 'Doesn't,'" *English Journal*, 1947, 36:370-376; E. B. Atwood, *A Survey of Verb Forms in the Eastern United States*, Ann Arbor, 1953, p. 28; Jean Malmstrom, "Linguistic Atlas Find-ings versus Textbook Pronouncements on Current English Usage," *English Journal*, 1959, 48:191-198; Bryant, pp. 73-74.)

**Dots** • See \*Ellipsis, \*Leaders.

**Double comparison** • See \*as . . . as.

**Double genitive** • See \*Genitive § 1c.

**Double negative** •
1. *In Standard English.* Two negative words in the same state-ment are not used in Standard English to express a single negation (Not: "He could*n't* find it *no*where," but "He could*n't* find it *any*where" or "He *could* find it *no*where").

There are, however, occasional constructions in which one negative statement modifies another negative statement to give a qualified meaning or a meaning with some special emphasis. In Informal and General English, mostly in speech: "He is not sure he won't slip in at the last minute" does not mean "He will slip in at the last minute" but "He may possibly slip in. . . ." "And don't you think he isn't clever" stands for some-thing more complex than "He is clever"—for "I've found out he's clever" or "You'd better believe he's clever (though I know you don't yet)." Other examples are: "I couldn't not in-vite her, could I?" "I couldn't just say nothing." In Formal

English: "A not unattractive young woman." "Not for nothing did he sacrifice himself."

**2.** *In Nonstandard English.* Although double negatives are probably not so common in Nonstandard English as comic writers suggest in their cartoons and stories, two or more negatives are very often used to make an emphatic negative in this variety. "I don't have nothing to lose" makes negative two parts of the idea and emphasizes the negative; if the *nothing* isn't stressed, it is a simple negative in two parts, as French uses *ne ... pas.* Such a double negative is not a backsliding from the idiom of more Formal English but the survival of a desire for emphasis. In earlier English two negatives were used in all varieties of the language. Chaucer wrote:

> In al this world *ne* was ther *noon* him lyk
> A bettre preest, I trowe that *nowher noon* is.

The objection to a double negative is not that "two negatives make an affirmative," for they do not. The objection is simply that the construction is not now in fashion among educated people.

**3.** *Hardly, scarcely.* Students sometimes fall into a concealed double negative when using *hardly* or *scarcely. Hardly* means "not probably" and *scarcely* means the same a little more emphatically. Consequently in Standard English a sentence like "For the most part our college paper contains *hardly nothing*" should read "For the most part our college paper contains *hardly anything*," and "For a while we *couldn't scarcely* see a thing" should read "For a while we *could scarcely* see a thing." (Reference: Bryant, pp. 75-76, 106-107.)

**Double prepositions** • See *Prepositions § 3b.

**Doubling final consonants** •
**1.** Words of one syllable ending in a single consonant following a single vowel (*brag, fat, win*) double the consonant before adding a syllable beginning with a vowel (*-able, -ed, -er, -ing, -y*):

| | |
|---|---|
| brag: bragged, bragging | fat: fatted, fatter, fatty |
| win: winner, winning | *Exception*—gas: gassed, |
| scrap: scrapper, scrapping, | gassing; *but* gaseous |
| scrappy | gasify |

The consonant is not doubled in words with two vowel letters before the final consonant (*daub, daubed; seed, seeded*) or in words ending with two consonants (*help, helped; hold, holding*).

**2.** In words of more than one syllable ending in one vowel plus one consonant, the final consonant is traditionally doubled if the word is accented on the last syllable. A few words so accented are very common:

con trol': controlled, controller, controlling
re fer': referred, referring
*Also:* confer'   equip'   excel'   infer'   occur'   prefer'

If the accent of the lengthened word shifts to an earlier syllable, the consonant is not doubled:

infer'—in'ference      prefer'—pref'erence      refer'—ref'erence

If the word is not accented on the last syllable, the consonant need not be doubled, and in American usage preferably is not doubled, though usage is divided on many words:

com'bat [or com bat']: combated or combatted, combating or combatting, *but always* com'ba tant

A few are never doubled:

ben'e fit: benefited, benefiting
o'pen: opened, opening
par'allel: paralleled, paralleling

Usage on *bias, diagram, kidnap, quarrel, travel, worship* is divided, but usually one consonant is preferred.

3. The part of the rule for doubling final consonants that applies to words of one syllable is useful, because it keeps distinct a number of pairs of words similar in appearance:

bat: batted, batting—bate: bated, bating
din: dinned, dinning—dine: dined, dining (*but* dinner)
grip: gripped, gripping—gripe: griped, griping
plan: planned, planning—plane: planed, planing
scrap: scrapped, scrapping—scrape: scraped, scraping

The boy who wrote "The scene in which she almost kills her husband is griping" did not convey the meaning that he intended.

4. Words already ending in a doubled consonant keep both consonants before suffixes beginning with a vowel but may lose one consonant before suffixes beginning with another consonant:

enroll: enrolled, enrolling; *but* enrolment or enrollment
install: installed, installing, installation; *but* instalment or installment
fulfill: fulfilled, fulfilling; *but* fulfillment or fulfilment
skill: skilled; *but* skillful or skilful

These rules are of some help, but they also suggest that the safest way to be sure of the established spelling of any word is to check it in a good dictionary.

**doubt** • Idioms with *doubt*:

1. *Negative* (when there is no real doubt), *doubt that*:

*Formal:* I do not doubt that he meant well.

*General:* I don't doubt but that [sometimes: but what] he will come.

2. *Positive* (when doubt exists), *that, whether, if*:

*Formal:* I doubt whether he meant it that way.

I doubt that he meant it that way. [indicating unbelief really more than doubt]

*General:* I doubt if he meant it that way.

**draft, draught** • The second spelling is now chiefly British.

**drought—drouth** • Both forms are in good use, *drought* probably more common in Formal English, *drouth* in General. Two pronunciations also occur, /drout/ and /drouth/, which do not always correspond to the spellings.

It is true the longest drouth will end in rain.—ROBERT FROST

**drunk** • It seems to take courage to use this General word. We either go Formal—*intoxicated*; or grasp at respectability through euphemisms—*under the influence of liquor* or *indulged to excess*; or make a weak attempt at humor with one of the dozens of Informal phrases like *looped, bombed, stoned*. But *drunk* is the word.

**due to** • The preposition *due to* is especially interesting as an illustration of the difficulties a new locution has in getting textbook recognition.

*Due* was originally an adjective and is still most strictly used as one: "The epidemic was *due* to the brown rat," in which *due* modifies *epidemic*. But *due to* as it is used in "The Mediterranean has its share of minority problems and they have become more prominent *due to* Italo-British tension in that area" (*Kaltenborn Edits the News*, p. 99) has long been popular, in magazine writing as well as in literature by writers of undisputed respectability. Advocates of strict usage have set themselves sternly against it, forgetting perhaps that *owing to,* which they have suggested should be substituted for it, has come from a participle to a preposition in exactly the same way.

An excellent example of a linguist's approach to a matter of divided and debatable usage is John S. Kenyon's treatment of *due to* in *American Speech,* 1930, 6:61-70. He presents an imposing number of quotations from current writers, discusses the history of the phrase, and concludes:

Strong as is my own prejudice against the prepositional use of *due to,* I greatly fear it has staked its claim and squatted in our midst alongside of and in exact imitation of *owing to,* its aristocratic neighbor and respected fellow citizen.

A study reported by Bryant shows that in some thousands of pages of books, periodicals, and newspapers, *due to* as a preposition occurred in 56 percent of the instances, *because of* in 25 percent and *owing to* in 19 percent ("Current English Forum," *College English,* 1954, 15:478). And in her *Current American Usage* (1962), Margaret Bryant presents further evidence to confirm the established status of the practice (p. 81). A person may not care to use *due to* as a preposition, but in view of actual usage today he hardly has the right to deny it to others.

# E •

1. The "long *e*" sound /ē/ is found variously spelled in stressed syllables: b*e*, s*ee*d, rec*ei*ve, sh*ie*ld, m*ea*t, p*eo*ple, k*ey*, qu*ay*, *ae*gis, Ph*oe*be, mach*i*ne.

An unstressed or lightly stressed *e* may vary in pronunciation from long /ē/ in platform delivery of a word such as *descend* /dē send′/ to a short /i/ or /ə/ in ordinary speech /di send′/; *hero* and *zero* may be /hir′ō/ or /hē′rō/, /zir′ō/ or /zē′rō/.

2. The "short *e*" sound /e/ is also variously spelled, as in f*e*d, l*ea*ther, b*u*ry, m*a*ny, s*ai*d, l*eo*pard, fr*ie*nd, s*ay*s.

Before final *r* or *r* plus a consonant, short *e* represents the sound in *learn, fern, err* marked /ėr/—/lėrn/, /fėrn/, /ėr/.

3. "unstressed *e*" (as in *kindness, difference*) represents a slight and rather obscure sound in speech. It may represent short /i/ /kīnd′nis/, or the neutral vowel sound represented in this book by /ə/ /kīnd′nəs/.

Before *l, m, n,* and *r* unstressed *e* is often a part of the consonant ("syllabic" *l, m, n, r*). In this book such syllables are represented by ə or by ḷ ṃ ṇ ṛ: *settle* /set′əl/ or /set′ḷ/, *wooden* /wood′ən/ or /wood′ṇ/.

4. Miscellaneous sounds represented by *e*: *e* may represent /ã/ before *r,* as in *there* /ᴛʜãr/; /ä/ as in *sergeant* /sär′jənt/ and many words in British usage which in the United States have /ėr/ as in *derby* /dėr′bē/ and *clerk* /klėrk/.

5. Silent or mute *e*: In general, words spelled with a final silent *e* drop the *-e* before additions beginning with a vowel and keep it before additions beginning with a consonant:

change: changed, changing; changeless (*but* changeable)
grease: greased, greaser; greasewood
like: likable, liking; likeness

pursue: pursuant, pursued, pursuing
use: usable, used, using; useful, useless
*Exceptions:* argument, awful, duly, ninth; judgment (*sometimes* judgement)

A few other exceptions keep -*e* to indicate pronunciation, chiefly after *c* and *g* before suffixes beginning with *a* or *o*:

change: changeable   courage: courageous   notice: noticeable

(See \*-ce, -ge.)

In a few words the -*e* is retained to avoid confusion with other words or to keep the connection with the root word obvious:

lineage /lin′e ij/ vs. linage /līn′ij/
singeing /sin′jing/, dyeing /dī′ing/

**each •**

**1.** *Each,* though singular in form, never occurs without an expressed or implied reference to more than one. Since the idea of plurality is always present when *each* is used, it inevitably attracts plural forms. In speech and increasingly in writing, *each* is regarded as a collective when the plural idea is uppermost (compare \*every):

*Each* of these people undoubtedly modified Latin in accordance with *their* own speech habits.—ALBERT C. BAUGH, *A History of the English Language,* p. 32

**2.** In Formal usage *each* is singular:

Each of the three *has* a different instructor.
Each ran as fast as *his* legs could carry *him.*

**3.** As an adjective, *each* does not affect the number of the verb; when the subject modified by *each* is plural, the verb is also plural:

Each *applicant has* to fill out the blank in full.
Three *students,* also from this county, each *receive* a scholarship.
*They* each *feel* keenly about it.

(Reference: Russell Thomas, "Concord Based on *Meaning* versus Concord Based on *Form,*" *College English,* 1939, 1:38-45.)

**each and every •** *Each and every* may have its place, but the phrase has been greatly overused.

**each other •** *Each other,* basically used of two, is also in good use for more than two, though Formal usage more often has *one another.*

*General:* The men were shouting to each other.

*Formal:* The men from farms on both sides of the river were shouting to one another.

(See *Reciprocal pronouns. References: Russell Thomas, " 'Each Other' or 'One Another'?" *College English,* 1957, 18: 422-424; Bryant, pp. 82-83.)

**Early Modern English** • See *English language § 4.

**Echo phrases** • Sometimes it is convenient to form a phrase on the pattern of one well known or to echo one less known but apt. This is a type of allusion. The echo phrase may be either serious or light:

I have seen American textbooks in which lesson after lesson is devoted to the lofty purpose of eliminating *got.* As though the fear of *got* were the beginning of wisdom. ["The fear of God is the beginning of wisdom."]—P. B. BALLARD, *Thought and Language,* p. 205

...but democracy means simply the bludgeoning of the people by the people for the people.—OSCAR WILDE, *The Soul of Man Under Socialism*

Ask not what broadcasting can do for you. Ask what you can do for broadcasting.—NEWTON N. MINOW, an address to the National Association of Broadcasters, May 9, 1961

In General writing, echoes of common phrases usually fit, and in more Formal writing there is certainly no harm in a writer showing that he has done some reading, but a parade of echo phrases may seem pretentious.

**-ed** • A conspicuous spelling problem is the omission of *-ed* in past verb forms (§ 1) and in modifiers made from verbs (§ 2) and from nouns (§ 3). Students often raise questions about these forms, and teachers are much concerned about them. They must also be a problem for editors, who have to insert many *-ed*'s in copy. The *-ed* is rarely omitted in published works, but it is frequently missing in unedited copy—in menus, in signs, and in letters.

To understand the situation it will help to consider the processes that have already led to many accepted forms without *-ed.* In the development of Modern English a final /d/ sound has become a /t/ sound before voiceless consonants /f, p, s, t .../: *watched* /wocht/, *pot* /pot/. Often the words in *-ed* come before *to* or other words beginning with *t* so that the two sounds are assimilated to one: *relieved to hear* /ri lēv tə hir/, *released time* /ri lēs tīm/.

1. *In verb forms.* This trait of pronunciation has led to the complete loss of the /d/ sound in the past tense and past participle of a few verbs, or to an optional form without the end-

ing: *bet, burst, cast, knit, quit, wed.* (Compare the verbs in § 4 that are regularly spelled with a final *t.*)

But carrying this practice into the spelling of past forms of regular verbs irritates educated readers. In these verbs it is well to remember that in spite of omission or assimilation of the *-ed* in speech, *the written form of the past tense and of the past participle should have -ed.* In proofreading go by your eye rather than your ear.

He was *unprejudiced* toward all.
I am forced to admit I *liked* the show.

(See \*used to—the most common offender in this group.)

**2.** *In modifiers from verbs.* The past participle is commonly used as a modifier: *abandoned farms, dressed chickens.* The same features of pronunciation are at work here, and many fixed phrases without *-ed* are Standard usage: *butter pecan, frame house, grade school, ice cream, oil cloth, salt pork, skim milk.* (Many of these were opposed when they first appeared.) Others of the same type are sometimes found in print but are debatable: *advance headquarters, bottle beer, whip cream.* In all of these except *whip cream* the resulting form could be regarded as a noun in the function of an adjective so that these expressions seem natural to English speakers.

A routine solution would be to go by a dictionary, but dictionaries will be found to vary, and many of the terms have not attracted the attention of dictionary makers. Two principles may help: (1) For a word group that is well established in speech, the oral form is likely to be appropriate in a written context reflecting its common use; (2) for others, appropriateness to other traits of style will be a useful guide. In Formal writing only those that have been generally accepted, as in the first group of the preceding paragraph, should be used. In Informal writing, especially if it suggests speech, more could stand. In General writing the more conventional form of *-ed* is advisable.

**3.** *In modifiers from nouns.* Frequently *-ed* is added to nouns to form adjectival modifiers: *barbed wire* (wire with barbs), *long-haired, moneyed, one-armed.* No verb is involved in the derivation of these terms. Consequently when the *-ed* is dropped the result is a noun used in the function of an adjective, a construction that is increasing in current English. In many group words the form without the *-ed* is well established: *one-arm bandit* and *barbwire* occur, and there are *blue-back speller, high-heel shoes, seven-room house, king-size cigaret, hard-surface road, wing chair.* (See \*size.)

Forms like these are appropriate in writing and similar forms are also, if they can be taken as nouns used as modifiers.

When a noun is not suggested or if the modifier is not conventionally bound to the headword, the *-ed* should be kept: *advanced courses, middle-aged, old-fashioned, one-sided.* (References: Curme, *Parts of Speech,* pp. 260-296; W. Nelson Francis, "More of the Lost *-ed,*" *Word Study,* Oct. 1954, pp. 6-7; Ralph H. Lane, "Passing Participles," *Word Study,* Feb. 1955, pp. 1-3.)

**4. *-ed or -t.*** In the past tense and past participles of verbs in which the *-ed* is (or may be) pronounced as /t/, simpler spelling has *-t.* A few words have been rather generally adopted with sound and spelling and with alteration of the root vowel: *crept, dreamt* /dremt/, *leapt* /lept/, *slept*; also *spelt.*

**5. *-ed or 'd.*** When *-ed* is added to words that are formed unusually, *'d* is sometimes used instead, as in *shanghai'd, ok'd.*

**Editorial we** • See \*we § 2.

**-ee** • This is an ending derived from French denoting the one who receives or is directly affected by an act or grant of power, the opposite of nouns ending in *-er* (*payer,* one who pays; *payee,* one who is paid): *employee, draftee, grantee.*

It takes two people to say a thing—a sayee as well as a sayer. The one is as essential to any true saying as the other.—SAMUEL BUTLER, "Thought and Language"

In French one *e* would indicate masculine, two feminine, which distinction sometimes leads to the spelling *employe* in English.

**effect—affect** • See \*affect—effect.

**e.g.** • See \*Abbreviations, \*namely and other introductory words.

**-ei-, -ie-** • Words with *-ie-* are much more common than words with *-ei-* and on the whole give less spelling trouble. The most common sound represented by *-ie-* is /ē/.

Some words with *-ie-* are:

| | | | |
|---|---|---|---|
| achieve | field | hygiene | priest |
| belief | fiend | mischief | shriek |
| believe | financier | niece | siege |
| cashier | friend | piece | sieve |
| chief | grieve | pier | view |

Plural of nouns ending in *-y*: *academies companies lotteries*

Third person singular present of verbs in *-y*: *cries fortifies fries*

After *c*, -*ie*- is seldom used, but it does occur: *ancient, species.*
There are fewer words with -*ei*-, but their spelling needs
careful watching. The most common sound spelled -*ei*- is /ā/:

| | | | |
|---|---|---|---|
| deign | freight | neighbor | skein |
| eight | heinous | reign | sleigh |
| feign | inveigle [or /ē/] | rein | veil |
| feint | neigh | seine | weigh |

A number of words spell the sound /ē/ with -*ei*-, especially
after *c*:

| | | |
|---|---|---|
| ceiling | leisure | receive |
| conceive | neither | seize |
| either | perceive | weird |

And a few words spell other sounds with -*ei*-:

| | | | | |
|---|---|---|---|---|
| counterfeit | forfeit | height | heir | their |

Again pronunciation is not a reliable guide.

In some words *i* and *e* stand together but are parts of different syllables:

fi ery    headi er    si esta

(Reference: Donald W. Lee, *College English,* 1944, 6:156-
159.)

**either** •

1. *Either* means primarily "one or the other of two," as an
adjective (either way you look at it) or as a pronoun (bring
me either). For emphasis the pronoun is usually supported by
*one* (bring me either one). Used of three or more objects (either
of the corners), it is loose and rare; "any of the corners" is the
more usual idiom.

*Either* is usually construed as singular, though its use as a
plural is increasing (Fries, *AEG*, p. 56):

Either Grace or Phyllis is [*or:* are] expected.

2. *Either* with the meaning "each" is rare in present English
and definitely Formal: *broil the fish on either side, with one
turning—on either side of the river. Each* or *both* (*both sides*)
would be more common in such expressions.

3. The pronunciation /ī'тнər/ or /ī'тнə/ has not made so
much progress in the United States as in England, and outside
some communities in New England and a few families or
circles that radiate from New England it is usually an affectation. Say /ē'тнər/, unless your family or social group generally
says /ī'тнə(r)/. Similarly, *neither* is usually /nē'тнər/, occasionally /nī'тнə(r)/.

4. *Either* is also used as an adverb of emphasis: He didn't
*come either.* (For its use with *or* see \*Correlative conjunctions.)

**elder, eldest** • These archaic forms of *old,* which survive in Formal English, are used only for members of the same family —"the elder brother," "our eldest daughter"—and in some phrases like "the elder statesmen."

**Ellipsis ( . . . )** •

1. A punctuation mark of three or sometimes four spaced periods to indicate that something is omitted is called an *ellipsis* (plural *ellipses*). Formerly asterisks (***) were used, but they have been generally discontinued because they are too conspicuous. When an ellipsis comes at the end of a statement marked with a period, that period is added, as in the first and third instances in this passage:

> As Beret drank in these words the tenseness all left her; the weapon she had seized dropped from her hand; her body straightened up; she looked about in wide-eyed wonder. . . . Were those church bells she heard? . . . But the voices were beginning again on the other side of the wall. . . . Hush! Hush!—O. E. RÖLVAAG, *Giants in the Earth*

2. *a*—The ellipsis is an editorial mark showing where a word or more, which is not needed for the purpose of the writer using the quotation, has been left out. The preceding sentence might be quoted with the *which* clause omitted: "The ellipsis is an editorial mark showing where a word or more . . . has been left out." Every such omission in quoted matter should be indicated by an ellipsis. If the omission is a line or more in a verse quotation, the periods should be extended to the full length of the line.

*b*—An ellipsis is also used to show a series or enumeration continued beyond the units named; it is equivalent to *et cetera*:

> the coordinating conjunctions (and, but, for . . .)

3. In narrative an ellipsis is used to mark hesitation in the action, suggesting passage of time, as in the quotation above from *Giants in the Earth,* and in the quotation below from Conrad Aiken:

> "Well—I can see this much. You *are* in love with her. Or you couldn't possibly be such a fool. But it's precisely when you're in love that you need to keep your wits about you. Or the wits of your friends. . . . You *mustn't* marry her, Harry."
>
> "Well—I don't know."
>
> "No! . . . It would be ruinous."—CONRAD AIKEN, "Spider! Spider!"

It is also used as an *end-stop to mark a statement that is unfinished or is let die away:

> I go away to a town, a big strange town, and try to hammer out a good book. The days come, the days go, and big ships sail into the harbor. . . . —ALBERT HALPER, "Young Writer Remembering Chicago"

**4.** An ellipsis is sometimes used in advertising copy or in instructions to separate statements for emphasis:

RINSE BY HAND ... Rinse thoroughly to remove all soap ... DO NOT WRING ... as wringing will tend to add wrinkles.

**5.** For the use of the word as a grammatical term, see the next entry.

**Elliptical constructions** • *Ellipsis* and *elliptical* refer to a construction in which an element that can be supplied from a neighboring construction is not expressed:

I work a good deal harder than you [*Supply*: work].

The notion of ellipsis has often been misused to apply to the shorter way of expressing a notion. A person may write either:

We went through the same experience that you did. [*or*]
We went through the same experience you did.
"Are you going?" "No, I can't (go) ."

It can of course be argued with considerable cogency that in the first two constructions above there is an ellipsis following *did*. But for ordinary purposes of grammatical analysis it is safer to deal only with the words actually expressed. The second construction is not necessarily elliptical but an alternative one; a *that* is not "omitted," it just isn't thought or spoken or written. The choice between the longer and shorter constructions is a matter of style rather than grammar. Formal English uses the longer ones, tends to fill out all constructions (the professor whom I saw). General and Informal English use the shorter constructions freely (the professor I saw). (See *Clauses § 3a. References: Curme, *Syntax,* p. 2 and index references; Jespersen, *The Philosophy of Grammar,* p. 306 and index references.)

**else** •
**1.** Because *else* follows the word it modifies (usually a pronoun), as the last word in a noun phrase, it takes the sign of the possessive:

I hated wearing somebody else's clothes.
At first he thought the book was his, but he finally decided it was somebody else's.

**2.** *Else* is sometimes used in speech as an *intensive, but in writing it is likely to be *deadwood and should be removed:

Finally I started talking, just to hear something [else] besides the roar of the motor.

**3.** *Nothing else but* is sometimes used for emphasis in speech, but the *else* would not ordinarily be used in writing:

*Written*: There was nothing but wheat as far as you could see.
*Spoken*: There was nothing else but wheat as far as you could see.

**emigrate—immigrate** • *Emigrate* means to move out of a country or region, *immigrate* to move into a country. An *emigrant* from Norway would be an *immigrant* to the United States.

**Emphasis** •
*Revision: Strengthen the emphasis of this passage by one or more of the methods suggested below.*   *Emph*

The purpose of emphasis is to get your reader to accept your ideas with the same degree of importance as you do—the most important as most important, the less important as less important, the incidental as incidental.

Ways in which emphasis can be conveyed are discussed more fully in other sections of the *Index*, referred to in this summary.

**1.** *Position.* In most types of writing, except news stories and reference works, the most emphatic position is the end and the second most emphatic position is the beginning. Emphasis by position applies to the order of words in sentences (see *Word order), to the order of sentences in paragraphs, and to the order of paragraphs in whole papers (see *Beginning paragraphs, *Concluding paragraphs).

**2.** *Mass or proportion.* Position is supported by the amount of space given to a particular point. Roughly speaking, the more important an idea the more space it deserves. Watch the last topics in a paper, which are likely to be so hurried over and hence underdeveloped that they do not seem as important as their writer intends.

**3.** *Distinction of expression.* In general, *big words and long *function words and phrases weaken a statement, as do abstract and indefinite words. Fresh, concrete words in direct and economical constructions make for a clear-cut emphasis.

**4.** *Separation, distinctness.* Careful paragraphing clarifies and emphasizes the relationship between main blocks of material. A short simple sentence following a sequence of fairly long or elaborately constructed sentences can be an excellent means of emphasizing an idea.

**5.** *Repetition.* Repetition of significant words drives them home, and repetition of statements either in similar or different words, perhaps figurative expressions, is a useful form of emphasis if it is not overdone. Repeating a structural pattern (especially in a series that builds to a climax) is a device for emphasizing as well as clarifying.

**6.** *Intensives.* Words added to intensify meaning are generally used in speaking but they are less useful in writing. (See *very.)

Labeling a statement "It is interesting to note," "This is an important phase of the subject" is seldom effective. Such phrases can be eliminated in revision by making the fact or opinion stand out in other ways.

**7.** *Mechanical devices.* Writing and printing have various mechanical means—*underlining (italics), *capitals, emphatic punctuation—for stressing words and passages. These devices are often used by amateur writers in an attempt to make up for deficiencies in style or content.

(Compare *Exclamations, *Negatives § 1.)

**employee** • This spelling is much more common than *employe*. (See *-ee.)

**en-, in-** • *In-* is either a native English prefix or a prefix of Latin origin; *en-* is the same Latin prefix modified in French. (*Em-* and *im-* are variant forms.) For several common words usage is divided, though usually one form is more prevalent. Fowler and other British sources are not safe guides to American usage on this matter because Americans tend to use *in-* more than the English do. The safest way is to consult a recent American dictionary, but even American dictionaries do not always agree, so that the choice is often a matter of style.

Here are a few samples with the dictionaries' preference first where there seems to be one:

encase—incase
enclose—inclose
encumber—incumber
endorse—indorse
engulf, rarely ingulf
entrust—intrust

encrust—incrust
infold or enfold
inquire—enquire
insure—ensure (Always *insure* in the financial sense, *insurance,* etc.)

**-ence, -ance (-ent, -ant)** • See *-ance, -ence.

**End-stop** • *End-stop* is a mark of punctuation—usually a period, exclamation mark, or question mark—used at the end of a sentence. In writing conversation, the double or two-em dash (——*Dash § 8) is used as an end-stop when a speech is interrupted. The *ellipsis (. . .) is often written as an end-stop for a sentence that is intentionally left unfinished or that is let die away.

When two end-stops would fall together at the end of a sentence, as when a question stands within a sentence, only one mark, the more emphatic or more necessary for meaning, is used:

When we say, for example, that Miss A. *plays* well, only an irredeemable outsider would reply, "Plays what?" So, too, ...—C. ALPHONSO SMITH, *Studies in English Syntax*, p. 8

(For further comment on end-stops see the articles on the individual marks. See also *Verse form.)

## English language •

1. *Indo-European.* English is one of a group of languages deriving from what is called Indo-European, a parent tongue for which no written records exist. The family includes most of the languages of Europe, a number of languages of India, the languages of Persia and of certain adjoining regions. It is usually classified into nine branches, English belonging to the group known as Germanic. (On the next page is a diagram showing the relations in greatly simplified form.)

A brief selection of facts about the different periods of our language will show some of the roots of the richness—and complexity—of Modern English.

2. *Old English, 450-1050.* The Angles, Saxons, and Jutes brought to England from their old homes in northwestern Europe somewhat differing Lowland West Germanic dialects. They pushed back the native Celts from the part of the island they conquered, so that Celtic speech contributed almost nothing to English but survived as Welsh, Cornish, and Highland Scotch. The conquerors' languages developed into several main dialects—Northumbrian, Mercian, Kentish, West Saxon—which together are known as Old English (or Anglo-Saxon). These dialectal variations still leave their marks in the regional speech of various parts of England. Most of these dialects made some contribution to the Standard language, but it was principally from the East Midland dialect, a descendant of Mercian, that Modern English developed.

Perhaps a quarter—no precise figures are possible—of the total present English vocabulary goes back to the words of Old English. The modern descendants of Old English words are often changed in meaning and almost always in pronunciation, according to regular processes: Old English *stan* /stän/ becomes Modern English *stone, ban* /bän/ becomes *bone*, etc. Our common verbs (*go, sit, eat, fight, whistle*), many of our most common nouns (*meat, house, breakfast, land, water*) and adjectives (*fast, slow, high*) go back to Old English words, so that though less than a fourth of the words in an unabridged dic-

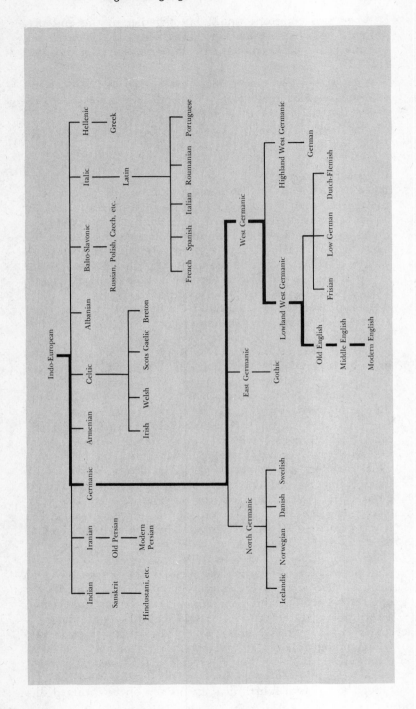

tionary are of this "native" origin, they play a part in our speech out of all proportion to their number.

Furthermore, most of the machinery of our language is from Old English: the articles *a, an, the*; most of the pronouns (*I, we, us,* . . .); the inflectional endings of nouns: house—house*s*, boy—boy*s*, boy'*s*; of adjectives and adverbs: merry—merri*er*—merri*est* or *more* merry—*most* merry; harsh*ly*, kind*ly*; the forms of verbs: pass, pass*es*, pass*ed*, pass*ing*. These endings are applied to words taken from other languages (*indict-ed, politi-cal-ly*), so that although three quarters of the vocabulary may come from Romance or other languages, the borrowed words are built into an English pattern. And when we consider word order, we see that the texture of English is Germanic too. For all these reasons, English must be regarded as a Germanic language. Furthermore, our habits of pronunciation have remained Germanic. Unlike most other Indo-European languages, we show heavy accent by greater loudness and lack of accent by absence of loudness, and we like the accent to stay put, usually on the first syllable of a word.

Within the Old English period the practice of absorbing words from other languages was already strong. A number of Latin words, some of them originally Greek, were taken in, most of them pertaining to the church (*abbot, priest, school*), though there was still a tendency to translate the elements of the Latin words into Old English elements, so that we have *gospel* from the Old English *god spell*, meaning "good news," which is a translation of the Greek-Latin *evangelium*.

In the ninth century the east and north of England was conquered by the Danes, whose language left a large number of words and forms, both because it was closely related to the language then spoken in England, and because of the contact between the two peoples. The *sk* words are likely to date from this mixture—*sky, skin, scream, skirt* (a cousin of the Old English *shirt*, both related to *short*), place names ending in *-by* and *-thorp,* and a number of common words like *odd, anger, egg.*

A number of the most conspicuous irregularities of Modern English existed in Old English: *be, is, are, was, were, been* as forms of the verb "to be"; *may, might, shall, should, ought,* and the other auxiliaries; pronouns—*I, my, me, we, our, us, he, it.* . . . These words are in such common use that they retain patterns of inflection which have otherwise disappeared. Here and there we have remnants of Old English forms that lost out in the development of the language, like the plurals *children, oxen, men, geese,* instead of the regular plural in *-s.*

A considerable body of writing from the Old English period survives. It includes poems, sermons, riddles, history, translations from Latin, and most conspicuously the *Anglo-Saxon Chronicles, Beowulf,* and the large group of writings and translations in West Saxon made by or at the court of Alfred the Great, King of the West Saxons, 871-901. Some 30,000 different words are found in this literature.

**3.** *Middle English, 1050-1450.* The conquest of England by the Norman French in 1066 coincided with the beginning of Early Middle English. The speakers of Old English in the main became serfs, servants, everything but leaders in affairs. Their language was seldom used in official proceedings and rarely written. One result was the loss of the more elevated and abstract Old English words that had been used in poetry.

As a result of the Old English habit of pronouncing unaccented words and syllables lightly, the endings of most words were obscured and could no longer be distinguished. A far-reaching development of this period was therefore the further decline and in some instances complete loss of the inflectional endings of Old English. The definite article no longer had distinctive forms (our *the* is the sole descendant of ten grammatically significant forms in Old English); -*n* disappeared from the infinitive of most verbs; and other unstressed endings also dropped away. This process went far to make English one of the least inflected of Indo-European languages and far more dependent on word order to show the relations of words in sentences than Old English had been.

On the other hand the vocabulary of the invaders made headway. The words for the acts of the ruling class—*war, government, law, social activity*—were Norman French and they have generally come down to Modern English: *siege, soldier, judge, jury, suit, dinner, servant, obey.* The majority of the Norman French words were ultimately from Latin, though considerably changed in form. For many notions Modern English has two roughly synonymous words, one Latin or French, one Old English: *dress—clothes, aid—help, cottage—hut, solitary—lonely.* Some French spellings made their way into English, like *gu* for hard *g—guest, guess; qu* for *cw—queen* for Old English *cwen.*

In 1362 English was restored as the language of the law courts, an official recognition that it had established itself once more in higher circles. The speech of the region around London was now the basis for future development not only of the spoken language but of the literary language. How far English had incorporated French resources can be seen from a few lines by Chaucer, written in the 1380's, French in italics:

> "What folk ben ye, that at myn hoomcominge
> *Perturben* so my *feste* with *cryinge*?"

Quod Theseus, "have ye so greet *envye*
Of myn *honour,* that thus *compleyne* and *crye*?
Or who hath yow misboden, or *offended*?
And telleth me if it may been *amended*;
And why that ye ben clothed thus in blak?"
—GEOFFREY CHAUCER, "The Knightes Tale"

Except for the Old English *misboden* ("insulted"), all of these words, both native and French, are in use today, though *quod* (quoth) is archaic, and *feste* is *fête*; in spite of some differences in spelling, the passage can be read by anyone. Many of the words show inflectional endings that have since been dropped or changed: *ben* (for *are* or *be*), perturb*en*, tell*eth*, and the final *e* of nouns.

4. *Early Modern English, 1450-1700.* In this period we have the beginnings of conscious concern for the language and actual or attempted "improvement" by manipulation of words and constructions—"schoolmastering the speech." The early printers, from 1476 on, felt the need for uniformity, especially in spelling and choice of word forms, and began the domination in these matters that has been exercised by publishers ever since. Translators and writers sometimes considered the language rough, unpolished, incapable of doing what Latin and Greek had done and what Italian could do. They set about enlarging the vocabulary, chiefly by transliterating words from Greek and Latin. A substantial portion of Modern English words are pretty directly from classical languages, and very often we have two words that go back to the same Latin original, one brought in by the Norman French and one taken in directly later: *paint—picture, certainty—certitude.* Latin was the language of the Church at the beginning of this period, though after the Reformation the Book of Common Prayer, and after 1611 the King James translation of the Bible, became tremendous forces for elevated English. Most books of the learned world were in Latin, and college classes were conducted in Latin, even in America, until two centuries ago.

The spoken language was vigorous and was written down in some popular literature, but most literature that has survived was from the hands of educated men and conscious stylists. Shakespeare shows the complete range, from formal, Latinized lines to rough-and-tumble lines, often combining the elevated and the simple in a single speech:

No, this my hand will rather
The multitudinous seas incarnadine
Making the green one red.

Prose style lagged behind poetic, especially in sentence sense, producing "sentence heaps" running to hundreds of words. In the sixteen hundreds the wealth of experiment of the preceding century was analyzed and many words and phrases were disposed of. The less useful and more ponderous of the Latin importations were dropped, and interest in native words increased the proportion of native words in use. Prose style especially developed in directness and sureness until in Dryden Modern English prose is usually said to be established. In spite of small differences in idiom and word order, the following two paragraphs do not seem 300 years old:

To begin, then, with Shakespeare. He was the man who of all modern, and perhaps ancient poets, had the largest and most comprehensive soul. All the images of Nature were still present to him, and he drew them, not laboriously, but luckily; when he describes anything, you more than see it, you feel it too. Those who accuse him to have wanted learning, give him the greater commendation: he was naturally learned; he needed not the spectacles of books to read Nature; he looked inwards, and found her there. I cannot say he is everywhere alike; were he so, I should do him injury to compare him with the greatest of mankind. He is many times flat, insipid; his comic wit degenerating into clenches, his serious swelling into bombast. But he is always great, when some great occasion is presented to him; no man can say he ever had a fit subject for his wit, and did not then raise himself as high above the rest of the poets,

*Quantum lenta solent inter viburna cupressi.*

[As the cypresses tower among the humbler trees.]

The consideration of this made Mr. Hales of Eaton say, that there was no subject of which any poet ever writ, but he would produce it much better done in Shakespeare; and however others are now generally preferred before him, yet the age wherein he lived, which had contemporaries with him Fletcher and Jonson, never equalled them to him in their esteem: and in the last king's court, when Ben's reputation was at highest, Sir John Suckling, and with him the greater part of the courtiers, set our Shakespeare far above him.—JOHN DRYDEN, *An Essay of Dramatic Poesy* (1668)

**5.** *Modern English, 1700-*     This *Index* gives a partial picture of current English, especially as it appears in print, and suggests in some of its specific articles changes that have taken place in the last few generations. Such articles may be taken as continuations of this brief historical sketch, for by 1700 English had become substantially the language we now know and use. The vocabulary has been enlarged in the last two centuries chiefly from two sources: borrowings from India and America and from peoples touched by British and American traders; and through scientific coinages, chiefly from Greek and Latin roots. There has been, especially in recent years, a tendency toward shorter and more direct sentences. The paragraph has become a more distinct unit in written expression. One important development has been the study of the different varieties of usage, and different traditions of style, especially Formal, General, and Informal styles.

Today English as the native language of England, the British Commonwealth, and the United States is spoken by about 300,000,000 people—certainly the largest group of people who can easily understand each other in their native language. In addition English is probably the most important second language in the world today.

The result of this varied history is a language full of anomalies, but of unusual range and flexibility, capable of great subtlety and force of expression.

(See also *American and British usage, *Analogy in language, *Basic English, *Business English, *Change in language (oral and written), *Experiment in written English, *Foreign words in English, *Latin and English, *Linguistics, *Newspaper English, *Origin of words, *Parts of speech, *Pronunciation, *Reading and writing, *Shoptalk, *Spoken and written English, *Style, *Usage. References: Baugh; Robertson; Otto Jespersen, *Growth and Structure of the English Language* (various editions), which describes the accumulation of the English vocabulary, and his *Language,* New York, 1923, Part iv, which discusses language change especially apropos of English; Morton W. Bloomfield and Leonard Newmark, *A Linguistic Introduction to the History of English,* New York, 1963; Thomas Pyles, *The Origins and Development of the English Language,* New York, 1964.)

**enormity—enormousness** • Because *enormity* looks like a more compact way of expressing the idea of *enormousness,* it is sometimes used in that sense. But it usually means "enormously evil," "great wickedness"—as in "the enormity of the crime."

**en route** • Pronounced /on/ *or* /en/ *or* /in rüt′/; or imitating French, /än rüt′/. "On the way" or "going to" often fits a sentence more naturally:

They were en route [on the way] to Philadelphia.

**enthuse** • *Enthuse* is a back formation (see *Origin of words § 3d) from *enthusiasm.* Many people object to it, and some dictionaries label it "colloquial" or "informal." But *enthuse* seems to be an improvement over the only locution we have for the idea, the clumsy *be enthusiastic over* or *about.*

**Epigrams** • An *epigram* is a short, pithy statement, in verse or prose, usually with a touch of wit. In prose this means really a detached or detachable and "quotable" sentence. In consecutive prose, epigrams sometimes become too prominent, attract too much attention to themselves, or suggest straining for effect. But they can focus attention or put a fact or opinion so that a reader can remember (and perhaps repeat) it:

Conscience is the inner voice which warns us that someone may be looking.—H. L. MENCKEN, *The Vintage Mencken*, p. 231

It's no disgrace to be poor, but it might as well be.

Bees are not as busy as we think they are. They jest can't buzz any slower.—KIN HUBBARD, *The Sayings of Abe Martin*

Closely related to epigrams are *aphorisms*—pithy statements but more likely to be abstract and not necessarily witty. The essays of Francis Bacon are packed with aphorisms, and some modern essayists use them too:

To spend too much time in studies is sloth; to use them too much for ornament, is affectation; to make judgment wholly by their rules, is the humour of a scholar. . . . Read not to contradict and confute; nor to believe and take for granted; nor to find talk and discourse; but to weigh and consider. . . . Reading maketh a full man; conference a ready man; and writing an exact man.—FRANCIS BACON, "Of Studies"

*Proverbs* are often-quoted, concrete expressions of popular wisdom. They are likely to make observations on character or conduct. As a rule their authors are unknown:

It never rains but it pours.

Still waters run deep.

It's hard for an empty sack to stand upright.

A special type of epigram is the *paradox*, which makes a statement that as it stands contradicts fact or common sense or itself and yet suggests a truth or at least a half truth:

All generalizations are false, including this one.

Dr. Richards is no mystic; he is a behaviourist, a behaviourist being a psychologist who does not believe in psychology.—P. B. BALLARD, *Thought and Language*, p. 265

(Reference: *Oxford Dictionary of Proverbs*, Oxford, 1936, compiled by William G. Smith.)

**-er, -or** • Names of persons or things performing an act (nouns of agent) and some other nouns are formed in English by adding *-er* to a verb (*doer, killer, painter, thinker*), but many end in *-or*, chiefly nouns taken from Latin or French (*assessor, prevaricator*).

Since the two endings are pronounced the same /ər/, it is hard to tell whether *-er* or *-or* should be written. Here are a few as samples; a dictionary will have to settle most questions.

### With -er:

| | | |
|---|---|---|
| advertiser | consumer | peddler (or pedlar) |
| better (or bettor) | debater | promoter |
| condenser | manufacturer | propeller |

### With -or:

| | | |
|---|---|---|
| accelerator | conductor | motor |
| administrator | distributor | objector |
| author | editor | proprietor |
| bachelor | governor | spectator |
| carburetor | inventor | sponsor |
| chiropractor | (or inventer) | supervisor |
| competitor | legislator | ventilator |

There are a few nouns of agent ending in -ar: *beggar, burglar, liar.*

**-er, -re** • Many words formerly ending in -re are now spelled -er in American usage. This group includes the following:

| | | | |
|---|---|---|---|
| caliber | luster | meter | somber |
| center | maneuver | scepter | specter |
| fiber | meager | sepulcher | theater |

British usage tends to -re in most of these words, though Fowler says they are being changed to -er one by one, because "we prefer in England to break with our illogicalities slowly."

An American writer who wishes a slightly Formal flavor will tend to use the -re forms; most will naturally use the -er forms.

*Theater* is divided in spelling, partly because it is found in a good many proper names of buildings and companies which were set up when *theatre* was the more common spelling, partly because of prestige associations of *theatre.* Keep the form actually used in proper names and whichever you prefer elsewhere.

*Acre, lucre, massacre, mediocre* keep the -re to represent a *c* pronounced /k/, and *ogre* is the current form, though some words with g, like *meager,* have changed. We also keep -re in *macabre, cadre.*

**err** • Standard pronunciation of *err* was /ėr/; but as it occurred infrequently in speech, the tendency to pronounce it /ãr/, by \*analogy with error /ãr'ər/, has established /ãr/ as an alternative pronunciation.

**Esq., Esquire** • Written following a man's name in the inside and outside address of a letter, *Esq.* or *Esquire* is Formal, with archaic or British suggestion, and in the United States is not often used except occasionally to professional men, chiefly to lawyers. If used, no other title (*Mr., Dr., Hon.,*) should precede the word: *Harry A. Kinne, Esq.*

**etc., et cetera** • *Etc.,* spoken as *et cetera* or *and so forth,* has been appropriated so extensively for communication in business that it is not conventionally used in serious writing. When it is used, *etc.* is preferred to *et cetera.*

The case is suitable for prints, maps, blueprints, etc.

In consecutive writing most people prefer the English "and so forth" (or "and so on," "and the like"). But it is better to avoid these end tags (which really take away from emphasis by putting a catchall at the end of a clause or sentence) by rephrasing the list, preceding it by *such as* or some other warning that the list you are giving is not exhaustive:

The case is suitable for large sheets *such as* prints, maps, and blueprints.

Using *and etc.* shows the writer doesn't realize that the *et* of *etc.* means *and;* in effect, he is writing *and and so forth.*

(See also *Abbreviations § 2, *Ellipsis § 2b.)

**Etymology** • See *Origin of words.

**Euphemisms** • A euphemism is a softened word used in place of one that names more vigorously something unpleasant, or something regarded as not quite nice: *natural son* for *illegitimate son* or *bastard, separate from the college* for *expel* or *flunk out, perspire* for *sweat, intoxicated* for *drunk, senior citizens* for *old people.*

Occasionally euphemisms are warranted to avoid embarrassment or hurting someone's feelings. But in general it is safer—and better style—to call things by their right names, even if they are somewhat unpleasant. (See *Obscenity, *Profanity.)

**Euphony** • See *Alliteration, *Assonance, *Style § 2b, *Repetition §3.

**every and its compounds** •
1. *Every, everybody, everyone* in the early development of the language were treated as singulars and are often so used today:

Every man on the team did his best.
Everybody likes the new minister.
Everyone took his purchases home with him.

But these words are very often treated as collectives in all varieties of English. A verb immediately following *everyone* or *everybody* is usually singular, but a pronoun referring back to it from a little distance is likely to be plural:

Everybody in the room is taking off their hats.

This construction, especially common in British printed practice, is reasonable, since the reference is to a number of people. To make these expressions conform to Formal American written usage, it is often better to change the *everybody* to a more accurate plural or collective than to change the later pronoun:

They all did their best.
The crowd are taking off their hats.

(Reference: Fries, *AEG,* p. 50.)

**2.** *Everybody* is always written as one word; *everyone* is usually written as one word, but when the *one* is stressed, as two:

Everybody knew what the end would be.
Everyone knew what the end would be.
Every one of the family knew what the end would be.

**3.** *Every so often, every bit as* are useful General idioms:

Every so often someone in the crowd would give a terrific shout.
They are every bit as happy as they expected to be.

**4.** *Every place* is an adverbial phrase, more widely used than *any place* (See *any § 4):

Every place I looked the people said the same thing.

**Examples** • See *Details.

**except, accept** • *Except,* verb, means to "leave out, exclude": *He excepted those who had done the assignment from the extra reading.* It is decidedly Formal, and *excused* would be more natural.

*Accept* means to "receive" or to "answer affirmatively" and is slightly Formal: *I accept with pleasure. He accepted the position.*

**Exclamation mark (!)** • An *exclamation mark* (or *point*) is used after an emphatic interjection, after a phrase, clause, or sentence that is genuinely exclamatory, and after forceful commands. Clear-cut exclamations offer no problem:

Oh! Ouch! No, no, no!
"But," he protested, "it's the chance of a lifetime!"

But many interjections are weak and deserve no more than a comma:

Well, well, so you're in college now.

Often sentences cast in exclamatory pattern are really statements put that way for variety (See *Exclamations) and the exclamation mark is optional. Its use would depend chiefly on appropriateness.

Exclamation marks are more characteristic of imaginative writing, especially of fiction, than of factual writing. In factual writing it is well to remember that in some newspaper offices the exclamation mark is known as a screamer—and that its overuse is a mark of nervousness or of *schoolgirl style.

In typing, the mark can be made with a period below an apostrophe.

**Exclamations** • *Exclamations* are expressions of strong feeling or emphatic statements of fact or opinion. They range from the simple and often involuntary *Oh!* or *Ouch!* to fully developed sentences.

One word exclamations may be punctuated as full sentences if they deserve that much emphasis: *Oh! You nearly upset my plate.* They may be punctuated as parts of sentences if they seem to belong with other sentence elements: *Oh! you're here at last!* or *Oh, you're here at last!*

Many exclamations begin with *what* or *how*: *What a view! How could you! How lucky you are!*

An exclamation expressing an emphatic opinion gives not only emphasis but variety in a passage:

But the methods chosen for the transition must always bear those human values in mind, for a whole new social order must inevitably result from a new kind of economic system, and in the process of slow nurture and growth initial trends may be all-important. Compulsion is a bad way to make men free!—ALFRED M. BINGHAM, *Insurgent America,* p. 6

Used just for variety or to give emphasis to what are really commonplaces, exclamations are ordinarily ineffective and give the effect of a strained or *schoolgirl style:

Think how often you have judged a person by the way in which he speaks! Think of a salesman who is a poor talker! It sounds like the height of unreality, but what a situation in this highly competitive world! Think of a college professor who could not intelligently lecture to his classes because he had not learned the art of elocution!

(For a summary of characteristics of exclamations, or interjections, see *Parts of speech.)

**excuse—pardon** • Small slips are *excused*; more considerable faults (and crimes) are *pardoned*. "Pardon me" is sometimes considered more elegant than "Excuse me" in upper-class social situations. Either is appropriate for the numerous perfunctory apologies we make in everyday life. *Excuse* also has the special meaning of "giving permission to leave."

**expect** • *Expect* means "to look forward to" and also "to look for with confidence." In Formal English it is usually kept close to some meaning involving anticipation, but in Informal usage its meaning is extended and weakened to "suppose"—"I expect you'd better be going."

**Experiment in written English** • Language and literary style tend to become stereotyped; as the same kinds of words are used over and over in the same kinds of constructions, their effectiveness in conveying individual impressions decreases. The more skillful writers escape monotony by the force of their message or the individuality of their expression, and most of them more or less consciously either ignore some conventions of language or experiment with words or constructions.

We might call any departure from the commonly written and printed English an experiment—if it is not just the result of carelessness or ignorance. Almost anyone with an interest in writing will experiment in his own private and Informal writing, trying unusual words or combinations of words, unorthodox sentence patterns, even variations in spelling. Some writers in their published work experiment also. Strikingly "experimental" writing is more characteristic of fiction than of non-fiction. Most of us have quite enough to do learning to exploit the tremendous resources of the language within accepted, conventional patterns.

**Expository writing, exposition** • Most of the writing required in college courses is explanatory—writing that is intended primarily to inform and enlighten the reader. Writing of this kind is called *expository writing* or *exposition*. Competence in expository writing—that is, in presenting information accurately, objectively, and clearly—is the most useful writing skill the student can acquire, both for course papers and examinations in college and for his later career.

**extracurricular** • *Extracurricular* means "outside the course of study" (extracurricular activities); it is sometimes hyphened but usually not.

**F** • The sound /f/ occurs spelled *f, ff, ph,* and *gh* (see *-ough, -augh*). The words with *ph* go back to Greek words with *phi* (Φ): *philosophy, telephone*; a few have been simplified to *f*: *fantasy, sulfur*.

Nouns ending in -*f* often have the corresponding voiced sound /v/ in the plural: *leaf—leaves, loaf—loaves, wife—wives*; *beef* has either *beeves* or *beefs*. But not *golf, gulf, oaf, safe, tiff, whiff*.

**Factual and imaginative writing** • The fundamental distinction between factual and imaginative writing is that in the first the writer's primary responsibility is to present, analyze, and reason about material that can be made available for others to observe, study, and discuss; in the second he has the liberty of shaping any action or picture or idea that may serve his purpose.

The principal types of factual writing are news stories, interviews, characterizations of people, biography, history, explanatory articles of all kinds, reviews, editorials, critical articles on all sorts of subjects, personal essays, and discussions of more general ideas such as demonstration of hypotheses, theories, ideals, philosophical concepts. Whatever other qualities these articles may have, whatever their virtues or faults, they are fundamentally good or bad according as they approach the truth and correspond to some strand of human observation or experience.

The imaginative types, in which the writer's conception is the controlling factor, are poems, plays, short stories, novels. These are also referred to as creative writing.

**famed** • When *famed* is used for *famous* or *well-known*, it usually suggests a journalese style, or a \*staccato one:

famed eating place          famed Nobel prize winner
At seven-thirty we anchored off the famed yachting center.

It is often a sign of amateur writing to label as *famed* (or as *famous*, for that matter) merely well-known people.

**farther—further** • In Informal English little distinction is made between *farther* and *further* in their adverbial and adjectival functions. As a verb, however, *further* is now the only one in use.

In Formal English a distinction is often made between *farther* and *further*, confining the first to expressions of physical distance and the second to abstract relationships of degree or quantity:

We went on twenty miles *farther*. He went *farther* than I, but neither of us reached the town.

He carries that sort of thing *further* than I would.

He went *further* into his family history. He got *further* and *further* into debt.

In General English, *farther* is usually used of distance, *further* for both distance and degree. In the superlative *farthest* is commoner than *furthest*. (Reference: Bryant, pp. 209-210.)

**faze** • *Faze* has worked its way from dialect (*feeze*, to disturb) into General usage. It means "to daunt or disconcert" and is almost always used negatively (The bawling out didn't faze him). Do not confuse this word with *phase*, meaning "state" or "stage of development."

**fellow** • *Fellow* is General and Informal when used to mean "person" but Formal in sense of "associate." It is most commonly used in writing in the function of an adjective: *his fellow sufferers, a fellow feeling* ("a similar feeling," or "sympathy"). Especially among young people it means a young man as contrasted with a young woman (girl).

**female** • Usage now restricts *female* to designations of sex, usually in scientific contexts. This leaves English without a single comfortable word for female-human-being-regardless-of-age; somewhat the same comment applies to *male*.

**fewer—less** • See *less—fewer.

**fiancé, fiancée** • A century ago the English *betrothed* was replaced by the French word (probably by "society" journalists), and now we are cursed not only with accent marks but with separate forms for the man (*fiancé*) and the woman (*fiancée*). Pronunciation for both is /fē'ɔn sā'/, with a tendency to /fē-än'sā/. The plurals are *fiancés, fiancées*. In newspapers and much General writing the accent is dropped, and it will probably soon disappear.

**Figures** • See *Numbers.

**Figures of speech** •
*Revision: This figure of speech is inappropriate, inconsistent, or threadbare. Revise the passage.*     *Fig*

When we talk of music in terms of color or moral problems in terms of a game, we are using figures of speech. Appropriate, fresh figures render meaning more vividly than literal expression does. But careless, tasteless figures detract. They may be threadbare (a ribbon of concrete, old man Winter). They may be strained and unnatural (Over yonder hill Apollo thrust the blade of his golden sword, severing the filmy mist that blanketed the paths of old Onondaga). Or they may be inconsistent or "mixed" (But then the molehill of annoyance grew into a mountain of hate and chased love out of the home).

The most common figures make comparisons or establish relationships. A *simile* asserts likeness, using *as* or *like* (the mist was like a blanket). A *metaphor* asserts identity (the mist was a blanket). An *analogy* shows or implies several points of similarity between things that are unlike—between education and mass production, for instance. *Synecdoche* substitutes the part for the whole (many mouths to feed) or the whole for a part (the army adopts a policy). *Metonymy* uses one word for another that it suggests: *grandstand* for the audience in the grandstand; *Java,* a source of coffee, for coffee.

*Overstatement* or *hyperbole* is exaggeration used to dramatize or make laughable. *Understatement* or *litotes* achieves the same ends by the opposite method (Joe Louis was not a bad fighter).

(For the effective use of figures of speech, see *Style § 2h. For ineffective figures, see *Trite. See also *Alliteration, *Epigram, *Imitative words and phrases, *Imagery, *Irony, *Negatives, *Personification, *Puns.)

**fine** • *Fine* is widely used as a *counter word of general approval, slightly more vigorous than *nice,* but is of little value in writing and better omitted:

Spring football practice has one aim, to weld eleven men into a [fine,] coordinated team.

It may, of course, be used in any of its more restricted senses. (Reference: Bryant, pp. 87-88.)

**Fine writing** • *Fine writing* is generally a term of dispraise, applied to writing that is too pretentious for the material or the purpose. Fine writing betrays itself chiefly in the use of *big words and in strained, artificial *figures of speech.

**Finite verbs** • *Finite verb* is a grammatical term indicating that the verb form is limited (Latin *finis,* "end, limit") in *person* (by one of the pronouns or by a subject), in *time* (by a tense form: *goes, went*), or in *number* (singular or plural). By contrast, the "nonfinite" parts—the infinitives (*go, to go, to have gone*), participles (*going, gone*), and verbal nouns (*going*)—are not limited in person or number. These are combined with auxiliaries to form verb phrases which function like simple finite forms (he *is* going, he *will* go, he *has* gone).

Finite verbs can be main verbs in clauses and sentences (I *had gone* before he *came*); nonfinite parts are ordinarily in subordinate constructions: Before *coming*; *Gone* with the wind. (But see *Infinitives § 5 and *Participles § 4.)

**first—former, last—latter** • See *former—first, latter—last.

**fish** • The plural is also *fish* (We got only six fish after fishing all day), except in speaking of various species of fish, as in "Most of the income of the island is from these fishes: cod, halibut, and sword." This distinction is not always made in speech.

**fix** • In Formal usage *fix* means to "fasten in place"; in General usage it means to "repair" or to "put in shape." *Fix* as a noun meaning "predicament" (to be in a fix) is Informal, as is its sense of "a bribed arrangement."

**flaunt—flout** • *Flaunt* /flônt/, to "wave, display boastfully," and *flout* /flout/, to "insult, treat with contempt," are sometimes confused.

**folk—folks** • Formal English and some local speech use *folk* as the plural; General usage has *folks,* especially in the sense of "members of a family." (Reference: Bryant, pp. 91-92.)
*Folklore* and *folkway* are written as one word, *folk dance, folk music, folk tale* usually as two; *folk song* and *folksong* are both used.

**Footnotes** • See *Asterisk § 1, *References, *References in scientific papers.

**for** • For distinction between *because* and *for,* see *because.
A comma is usually needed between two coordinate clauses joined by *for;* without it the *for* might be read as a preposition:
He was glad to go, for Mrs. Crane had been especially good to him. [*Not:* He was glad to go for Mrs. Crane. . . .]
Since *for* almost always comes between the clauses it joins, it is usually classified as a coordinating conjunction, but the clause it introduces is often actually subordinate: *He was exhausted, for he had gone two nights without sleep.* (Reference: Henry L. Wilson, "The Classification of the Conjunction 'For,'" *American Speech,* 1952, 27:257-260.)

**Foreign words in English** •
1. *Anglicizing foreign words.* English has always borrowed words and roots freely from other languages and is still borrowing, especially from Greek and French. Most borrowed words that have been used for a long time cannot be told from

native English words, but those taken in recently often raise questions. They usually cross the threshold of English with their foreign spelling, perhaps with un-English plurals or other forms, and no established English pronunciation. The process of anglicizing brings them more or less in line with English usage, but they may keep some of their foreign quality, like the *i* of *machine,* the silent *s* in *debris,* the *t* where English is tempted to put a *d* in *kindergarten.*

Many loan words are in a transition stage, showing two or more spellings (*naif, naïf, naive, naïve; naïveté, naiveté, naivety, naïvety; role, rôle*); with others we are experimenting with pronunciations, the winner not yet clearly seen (*melee*: /mā lā′/, /mā′lā/, /mel′ā/, and /mē lē/; *zwieback*: /tsvē′bäk/, /tswē′bäk/, /swī′bak/, /zwī′bak/; *menu*: /men′ yo͞o/, /män′yo͞o/). Some words that have been in English a considerable time are still changing, especially in stress (*debris*: /də brē′/—/deb′rē/) and in consonant sounds (*massage*: /mə säzh′/—/mə säj′/). These words show how a rough compromise is worked out between English practice and the original form.

The speed and degree of anglicizing depends on how frequently the word is used, the circumstances in which it is used, and the people who use it. The attitude of linguists is that if a word proves useful it will assume a natural English form. *Hors d'oeuvre* is a useful word, but it looks conspicuously un-English. If menu makers would spell it *orderve,* we could all be happy with it. The solution with *maître d'hôtel* has been to clip it to *maitre d'* /mātər dē/.

Formal writers and conservative editors tend to keep the foreign spellings longer than General writers and editors. If the words come in through the spoken language, like those of the automobile vocabulary, they usually become English or near-English sooner than if they come in by way of literature: we have *chassis* (/shas′ē/ or /shas′is/, sometimes /chas′is/), *chauffeur* (/shō′fər/—the spelling lagging), *garage* (/gə räzh′/ or /gə räj′/—in England /gar′ij/, *detour* (/dē′tür/. Words that come in through and remain in literary, scholarly, or "polite" circles change more slowly, in both spelling and pronunciation: *tête-à-tête, faux pas, nouveau riche, laissez faire.*

2. *Use of borrowed words.* The best reason for using an unnaturalized or partly naturalized word is that it supplies a real lack in English—perhaps says in one word what English would have to use a phrase or sentence to express. *Entrepreneur,* "one who undertakes business, especially assumes commercial risk," is useful since the English *undertaker* has a special meaning of its own. *Beige,* "the color of unbleached wool or cotton," *suede, tableau, protégé* are useful. We have also taken in a

number of words and phrases of doubtful usefulness: *entre nous,* when we have *between ourselves,* or *in confidence; affaire du coeur* for *love affair, raison d'être* for *reason for being,* and so on.

Sometimes the gain is in force or tone or suggestion, as *ersatz* is stronger than *substitute,* and *liaison* brings either a connotation of social unconventionality or of military activity, depending on the context. *Nouveau riche* brings its suggestion of dispraise, replacing an earlier borrowing, *parvenu,* which in turn displaced the more blunt *upstart.* French words are often used for tone, especially in discussing (and more especially in advertising) women's fashions: *chic, svelte, lapin (rabbit* in other places)—and even *sacque,* which doesn't exist in French. A couple of generations ago French was used a good deal for polite social euphemisms, to avoid plain English: *demi-monde, fille de joie, femme de chambre, enceinte, accouchement.* Now these have generally gone out of use, their place once more taken by straight English, except with the falsely modest. Parading foreign words, a temptation to some who are learning a language or have just returned from abroad, is usually in bad taste, and their use even by people wholly at home with the languages is likely to be inappropriate. Fitness to material, to readers, and to the writer himself will usually determine whether a foreign word should be used.

3. *Handling borrowed words in copy.*

*a*–Italics. Words which have not been completely anglicized are printed in italics in magazines and books and should be underlined in copy. Newspapers do not use italics for such purposes, and their practice of course has tended to lessen the use of italics by others. There are always many words on the borderline which will be found sometimes in italics, sometimes not. Formal writers tend to use more italics; General, fewer. Consult a recent dictionary for doubtful words—remembering that it can never quite represent present usage.

*b*–Accent and other marks. Words recently taken in from French are usually written with accent marks if they were so written in French. Newspapers do not use accent marks except sometimes in departments like the editorial, art, music, and fashion pages. After they have been used for a time in English, the accents are usually dropped unless they are necessary to indicate pronunciation. *Matinee, melee, role* do not need marks; *blasé* does. Similarly *cañon* is now usually spelled *canyon,* but: *piñon.* A *cedilla shows that a *c* before *a* or *o* is pronounced /s/: *façade, soupçon.*

In German all nouns are capitalized, and recent or infrequent borrowings from German are capitalized in English, particularly if they are still printed in italics (*Anschluss, Real-*

*politik, Weltanschauung,* but hinterland, kindergarten, blitz-krieg). The *umlaut can be replaced by an *e* after the vowel: *Mädchen* or *Maedchen.*

*c*–Plurals. English usually brings borrowed words into its own system of conjugation and declension, though some words change slowly, especially words used mainly in Formal writing (*formulae*). *Beaus* is now as common as *beaux,* and *tableaus* is gaining on *tableaux.* (See *Plurals of nouns § 4.)

A few French adjectives may keep both masculine and feminine forms: *blond, blonde; naïf, naïve.*

**4. Pronunciation.** For pronunciation of borrowed words, see the examples given in § 5 or consult a dictionary. Because the speech sounds of one language differ somewhat from those of another, it is almost impossible to say a foreign word the way it is spoken in its original language unless you are thoroughly familiar with that language. If there is an established English pronunciation, you should use it, especially since you are more likely to be understood.

**5. *List of borrowed words.*** This list contains a small selection of loan words in fairly common use. Those in italics would ordinarily be italicized in print. When two forms are separated by a dash, they are both common. A form in brackets is less common than the other. Pronunciations are indicated for words which might offer difficulty. For words not given here consult a recent dictionary. (See *Pronunciation § 1 for key to symbols.)

aide-de-camp—aid-de-camp
  /ād' də kamp'/
*a la
à la carte
a la mode
bourgeois /bùr'zhwä—
  bùr zhwä'/
brassiere /brə zir'/
buffet /bu fā'—bù fā'/
bushido /bü'shē dō'/
café—cafe /ka fā'—kə fā'/
chic /shēk—shik/
cliché /klē shā'/
coiffure /kwä fyoor'/
communiqué /kə mū'nə kā'—
  kə mū'nə kā/
corps; plu. corps /kôr; plu. kōrz/
coup; plu. coups /kü; plu. küz/
coup d'état /kü dā tä'—
  kü də tä'/
coupé—coupe /kü pā'—küp/

crèche—creche /kresh—krāsh/
crepe—crêpe—crape /krāp/
crescendo /krə shen'dō—
  krə sen'dō/
debut /di bū'—dā'bū—dā bū'/
debutante /deb'yù tänt—
  deb'yə tant/
dirndl /dèrn'dl/
Don Juan /don jü'ən—
  don hwän'/
Don Quixote /don kwik'sət—
  don kē hō'tē/
dramatis personae
  /dram'ə tis pər sō'nē/
éclair—eclair /ā klār'—i klār'/
entrée—entree /än'trā/
fete—fête /fāt/
hara-kiri—hari-kari /har'ə kir'ē—
  hä'rə kir'ē/
lingerie /lan'zhə rē'—län'zhə rā'/
matériel—materiel

matinee /mat ə nā'—mat'ə nā—mat'nā'/
mayonnaise
menu /men'ū—mā'nū; French pronunciation not current/
milieu /mē lyœ'—mēl yü'/
monsieur /mə syœ'/; plu. messieurs—messrs. /mā syœ'/
muzhik—moujik /mü zhik'—mü'zhik/
negligee—négligé /neg'lə zhā'—neg'lə zhā'/
obbligato—obligato /ob'lə gä'tō/
papier-mâché /pā'pər mə shā'/
passé /pa sā'—pas'ā/
précis /prā'sē—prā sē'/
premiere—première /pri mir'—prə myer'/

protégé (masc.), protégée (fem.) /prō'tə zhā/
quasi /kwā'sī—kwā'zī [kwä'sē]/
questionnaire [questionary] /kwes'chən ãr'/
rendezvous /rän'də vü/; plu. rendezvous /rän'də vüz/
repertoire /rep'ər twär [rep'ər twôr]/—repertory
résumé /rez'ù mā'/
ricochet /rik ə shā'—rik ə shet'/
salon /sə lon'—sä lôn'/
slalom /slä'lōm [slä'ləm]/
status quo /stā'təs kwō—stat'əs kwō/
stein /stīn/
suede—suède /swād/
vs.—vs /vėr'səs/
Weltschmerz /velt'shmerts'/

(See *English language, *Latin and English, *Origin of words. References: Kenyon and Knott, § 122; Brander Matthews, "The Englishing of French Words," *Society for Pure English Tracts,* Tract V, 1921, 3-20; T. R. Palfrey, "The Contribution of Foreign Language Study to Mastery of the Vernacular," *Modern Language Journal,* 1941, 25:550-557.)

**Form classes** • See *Parts of speech.

**Formal correspondence** • See *Social correspondence.

**Formal English** •
*Revision*: *The word or passage marked is too Formal for the subject or for the style of the rest of the paper. Revise, making it more General.*   Form

Formal English is the usage characteristic of people who work a good deal with books, particularly members of the various professions. It is the appropriate variety for discussions of ideas, for scientific and scholarly writing, for addresses to audiences of considerable education, for literary works that are intended for a somewhat restricted reading public. Formal English is not so appropriate for day to day speaking and writing, for accounts of personal experience, casual comment, and other sorts of writing intended for the general reading public. (For discussion and examples, see "Formal English," p. 16. See also *Academic writing, *Gobbledygook, *Legal language. Other articles treating details of Formal usage include *Abbreviations, *Agreement, *Alliteration, *Collective nouns, *Contractions, *Dates, *Gender.)

**former—first, latter—last** • *Former* and *latter* refer only to two units:

> The mountain and the squirrel
> Had a quarrel,
> And the former called the latter, "little prig";
> —RALPH WALDO EMERSON, *Fable*

*First* and *last* refer to items in a series, usually of more than two:

> The first president had set up a very informal organization.
> His last act was to advise his family on their future.

*Latest* refers to a series that is still continuing (the latest fashions). *Last* refers either to the final item of a completed series (their last attempt was successful) or to the most recent item of a continuing series (the last election). *Latest* for *last* is archaic: His *latest* breath. Note the spelling of *latter,* sometimes confused with *later.* (See *last, latest.)

**Forms of discourse** • For the last hundred years or so it has been conventional to divide writing into "four forms of discourse"—narration, description, exposition, and argument. The chief value of this classification is that it emphasizes purpose as the controlling element in a piece of writing. Studying the forms one by one allows concentration on certain traits of material, organization, and style peculiar to each type. The categories are not, however, sharply distinct—description contributes to all, notably to narration; many essays which are primarily argumentative include long stretches of exposition, and so on.

**formula** • The plural is *formulas* or *formulae,* the former the more common.

**Formulas** • Every language has some constructions that have become fixed by long usage in certain situations and whose total meaning is largely independent of the words in it: *Once upon a time, Ladies and gentlemen, Good morning, How are you? How do you do? Best wishes, Dear Sir, Yours truly.* Occasionally fresh substitutes can be found for these, but more often the attempt merely calls attention to itself. Such phrases, though stereotyped, are too useful to be called *trite, and they are not, as most trite expressions are, substitutes for some simpler locution. They should be used without apology and without embarrassment whenever they are needed. (See *Idiom and idioms, *Subjunctives § 2a.)

**Fractions** • Fractions are written in figures when they are attached to other figures (72¾), or are in a series that is being written in figures (½, ⅔, 1, 2, 4), or are in tables or reference matter. In consecutive writing they are usually written in words (In the local newspaper three fourths of the space was given to advertising, one eighth to news, and one eighth to miscellaneous matters). Hyphens may be used between the numerator and denominator if neither part itself contains a hyphen, but they are less used than formerly and are not used at all when the numerator has the value of an adjective (as in "He sold one half and kept the other").

> seven tenths [seven-tenths]      eight twenty-sevenths
> twenty-nine fortieths—twenty nine fortieths

Decimals are increasingly used in place of fractions in factual writing, since they are more flexible and may be more accurate. They are always written in figures: .7   .42   3.14159 (See *Numbers.)

**Fragmentary sentence** •
*Revision: The construction marked is not a satisfactory sentence. Revise by completing its form, by joining to a neighboring sentence, or by rewriting the passage.*

**Frag**

A fragmentary sentence (sentence fragment) is a part of a sentence—usually a phrase or dependent clause—carelessly or ineffectively punctuated as a whole sentence. By its form, it suggests dependence on another construction, and editors usually make sure it does not stand as a sentence. Ordinarily one should be joined to the preceding or following sentence or made into an independent sentence. In college writing, fragmentary sentences are usually the result of carelessness; they are one of the most obvious blunders and should be eliminated in revision.

Three common types with suggested revision follow:

| *Fragmentary sentence* | *Revised* |
|---|---|
| Since 1939 we had been walking slowly in the direction of war. [Phrase:] Step by step until finally there was no other alternative but to declare war. | Since 1939 we had been walking slowly in the direction of war, step by step, until finally there was no other alternative but to declare war. |
| He talked for fifty minutes without taking his eyes off his | He talked for fifty minutes without taking his eyes off his |

notes. [Participial phrase:] Apparently not noticing that half the class was asleep.

notes. Apparently he did not notice that half the class was asleep.

The first six books I looked for couldn't be taken out of the library. [Dependent clause:] Because they were on reserve for an advanced history course.

The first six books I looked for couldn't be taken out of the library because they were on reserve for an advanced history course.

(For help in identifying fragments, see *Clauses, *Finite verbs, *Gerund, *Participles, *Phrases.)

**freshman, freshmen** • Since these words are pronounced alike /fresh′mən/, their spelling is sometimes confused, not so often when they are used as nouns (a freshman, forty freshmen) as when *freshman* is used as a modifier (freshman class, freshman spirit). *Freshmen* should never stand before a noun in this construction.

It is not necessary to capitalize *freshman* (or *sophomore, junior, senior*), but courtesy or emphasis sometimes makes a capital appropriate, and often one is used when speaking of an entire class—the Freshman Class, the Junior Class.

**-ful, full** • When the adjective *full* is used as a suffix to nouns of measure (*basketful, spoonful*) or of feeling or quality (*peaceful, sorrowful, soulful*) it has only one *l*.

The plural of nouns ending in -*ful* is usually made with -*s*: *spoonfuls, basketfuls* (also *basketsful*). (See *spoonful, spoonfuls.)

**Function words** •
1. Some words carry relatively little independent meaning in themselves, serving rather to indicate relationships, to point out grammatical functions. They are also called *form-words, structure-words, empty-words.* Since they are limited in number—new ones are rarely added to a class—they belong to *closed classes.* Some such words are:

*Prepositions,* which join nouns to other words in a construction; the *of* in the phrase form of the genitive (of the man) is conspicuously a function word.

*Conjunctions,* which show the relation between sentence elements.

*Auxiliary verbs* when they indicate time, person, number, of a verb (*is* asking, *has* asked, *did* he ask) without otherwise modifying meaning. (See *have § 1, 2.)

*Some of what are traditionally called *adverbs and *adjectives,* for example, *more* and *most* in comparisons of adjectives and adverbs (more handsome, most handsome), or *the, a, an.*

**2.** *Stylistic qualities of function words.* Different varieties of usage have some characteristic habits in the use of function words. In the more elaborate sentences of Formal English, heavier connectives, such as *conjunctive adverbs (however, accordingly . . .),* are more appropriate; General style tends to rely more on coordinating conjunctions *(but, for, and . . .)* and subordinating conjunctions *(although, because, since . . .).*

Informal English shows a good many compound or group prepositions, for many of which Formal English would use a single preposition: *in back of (behind); in regard to (about).* Too many of these long connectives tend to give a sentence a rather weak movement and a rhythm without many strong stresses. In rapid speech they are passed over easily, but they sometimes become conspicuous in writing.

(See *Parts of speech, *Conjunctions, *Prepositions. See also *Wordiness, *Newspaper English § 3, *Telegraphic style. Linguists vary in their definitions of function words. A full treatment is in Fries, *Structure,* Ch. 6.)

**Fundamentals •** The selection of what can be regarded as fundamentals in estimating a piece of writing depends on judgment, and judgments vary. Suggestions follow for one approach to fundamentals:

**1.** *The content* of the paper (always considered in relation to the writer's purpose) deserves most weight in evaluating a piece of writing. Nothing can take the place of important and interesting material.

**2.** *The treatment* of the material by the writer is of next importance. He may use too few details or too many; he may select them according to an intelligent or an unwise or biased principle; he may have an exaggerated idea of the importance of his subject, or approach it with too much or too little sentiment, reverence, humor, or realism; he may or may not direct his statements to readers.

**3.** *The plan* of an essay is important, since in part through it the writer guides the reader to see his sense of the matter. Too slow a beginning and too trivial an end are serious faults, as is failure to show relation between parts.

**4.** Finally, a piece of writing is affected by the *mechanics and style* of the writer, which may either hinder the reader or increase his satisfaction. Poor material presentably written has no future, but worthwhile material even if poorly written can with sufficient work be made presentable.

We consciously or unconsciously make some such balancing of qualities in deciding what we think of what we read. Realizing the relative worth of these qualities makes it easier for student and teacher to understand each other's judgments.

**funny** • In Formal English *funny* means only "comical," "laughable," but in Informal English it means also "odd": *"That's funny. I thought he did."* See that the meaning intended is appropriate to the variety of English being used.

**further—farther** • See *farther—further.

**Fused sentence** • A *fused sentence* is the name sometimes given to two grammatically complete sentences written with no mark of punctuation between them (The dress shop was sponsoring a style show they asked Jeanine to model since she was a steady customer). It usually results simply from exceptional carelessness in writing, one step worse than the typical comma fault. (See *Comma fault.)

**Future tense** • See *Tenses of verbs, *shall—will.

**G** • *G*, like *c*, spells a "hard" and a "soft" sound. The hard sound is more common than the soft.
1. *"Hard g"* /g/. *G* is hard before *a, o,* and *u* (except in *margarine* and the British *gaol* [*jail*]): *garrulous, gong, gutter*; when doubled: *doggerel, noggin, toboggan*; at the ends of words: *beg, dig, fig*; before another consonant in the same syllable: *togs, glen*; frequently before *h, l,* and *r*: *gherkin, glow, great*; and sometimes before *i* and *e*: *begin, gig, girl, eager, gear, get.*
  *Gu,* taken from French, spells hard *g*: *guard, guess, guide, guernsey.*
2. *"Soft g"* /j/ is found typically before *e, i,* and *y*: *gem, gentle, genus, giblet, gin, gym, gyrate.* It is often spelled *ge* or *dge*: *age* /āj/, *edge* /ej/, *fudge* /fuj/; other spellings of the sound are *joy, exaggerate, verdure, grandeur, soldier.*
3. *G* is sometimes pronounced /zh/, chiefly in partly anglicized words from French: *garage, massage, mirage.* These words tend to have a soft *g* after they have been in English a long time (*carriage, marriage*): *garage* is often /gə räj′/ (in England, /gar′ij/); *massage* is tending toward /mə säj′/.
4. *"Silent g."* Initial *g* is silent in such words as *gnaw, gnat, gnome, gnu,* and within a word *g* is often silent before *m* or *n*: *diaphragm, sign.* It is sounded in some derivatives of this latter type of word: *signal.*
5. *"Dropping g's."* In Formal and much General speech the present participle ends in the single nasal consonant sound

spelled *ng*; in Informal speech this /ng/ sound is often replaced by the /n/ sound, written *n'*: *singin', laughin'*. Because of the spelling, this is usually referred to as "dropping *g's*," though none of the sounds spelled by *g* alone are involved. Of the participle forms ending in these two different nasal consonants —/ng/ and /n/—the form ending in *-n* is the older. Originally the present participle ended in *-and* and later in *-en* or *-in*, and this has always been the form for the majority of speakers of English. In the speech of London and vicinity, which became the basis of written English, the present participle was confused with the verbal noun, ending in *-ung*. Now everyone *writes* the participle with *-ing*, but many continue the old pronunciation with *-in*. (See Milton Ellis, *English Journal*, 1937, 26:753. Compare *ng. Reference: Kenyon and Knott, *-ing*; *Webster's Third New International Dictionary, -ing*.)

**-ge, -ce** • See *-ce, -ge.

**Gender** • *Gender* as applied to English is the indication of sex or sexlessness, literally or figuratively. In the many languages which have special endings for masculine, feminine, and neuter nouns and for articles and adjectives modifying them, gender is primarily a grammatical concept, but English had lost this system six centuries ago. Now, except in the pronouns *he, she, it* and a few nouns with endings such as (feminine) *-e, -ess, -a, -ix, -euse*, and (masculine) *-or, -us, -er, -eur* (blonde, blond; actress, actor; alumna, alumnus; aviatrix, aviator; masseuse, masseur), gender can be determined only from the meaning of a word: *man—woman, nephew—niece, rooster—hen*. And even in the pronouns and suffixes, gender is rather a matter of meaning than of grammar. Compounds, partly to show gender, partly for emphasis, are common and expressive: *she-witch, he-bear, boy friend, girl friend*. Nouns referring to inanimate objects are neuter. For most English words gender is identifiable only by the choice of the meaningfully appropriate pronoun (*he, she, it*) and is consequently hardly a grammatical category:

> The speaker hesitated, choosing *his* next words deliberately.
> The novelist has presented *her* chief character effectively.

In Formal, literary English there is a weak sort of personification (or animation) in which the sun or moon or a ship or almost any object may be referred to as *he* (The sun sent forth his cheering beams) or more often *she* (The moon has cast her gentle light). In Informal English *she* frequently replaces *it*, especially if intimacy or affection is involved. A car or a college or a country or any object may be a *she*.

We lack a singular pronoun to represent either-he-or-she; in the plural English is noncommittal: *they* refers indifferently to male, female, inanimate in any combination. Referring to a baby or an animal of unknown sex, *it* is the usual solution; otherwise *he*. (See *he-or-she, *blond, blonde, *naive-naïve.)

**General English** • *General English* is a variety of Standard English—the central body of words and constructions of our language. (For discussion and examples, see "General English," p. 14. Articles that treat details of General usage include *Abbreviations, *Business English, *Contractions.)

**Genitive •**

**1.** The genitive (or possessive) function in English is shown in four ways:

*a*—The *s*-genitive. *'s* is the spelling of the genitive of all singular and a few plural nouns and noun phrases in which the word is pronounced with an added /s/ or /z/ sound and of the indefinite pronouns (*anyone, everybody* . . .):

| | | | |
|---|---|---|---|
| boy's | horse's | one's | King of England's |
| men's | brother-in-law's | somebody's | anyone's |

An apostrophe alone may be added to words that already end in an /s/, /sh/, or /z/ sound, as in regularly made plurals in -*s*; the last three could also add an *s* after the apostrophe:

| | | |
|---|---|---|
| horses' | coaches' | *Jones' (singular) |
| Joneses' (plural) | Moses' | conscience' (for |
| | | conscience' sake) |

Words of one syllable ending in these sounds have either the apostrophe alone or *'s*, pronounced as an added syllable:

Charles' /chärlz/—Charles's /chärl'zəz/    coach's /kōch'əz/
fish's /fish'əz/    Zeus' /züs/—Zeus's /züs'əz/

The apostrophe is a visual mark which signals the genitive only in writing; in speech the genitive is distinguished from the plural by its position before a noun (the doctor's first case) or as a predicate where the context would make a plural impossible (The criticism is Gamble's). In writing, the genitive plural is distinguished from the singular by the position of the apostrophe, but in speech the number is not always clear: *I saw the boy's(boys') books.* (See *Jones—plural and possessive forms.)

When two coordinate nouns are in the genitive, the apostrophe is often added only to the last one:

Fred and Bert's first attempt. [*Formal:* Fred's and Bert's].
He had never thought of his wife and children's future.
[*But:*] Mary's and Tom's bicycles. (Separate objects possessed)

*b*–The *of*-genitive. The term *genitive* derives from the Greco-Roman grammarians, who used it only to describe inflections. In English the function of the genitive can often be performed by an *of*-phrase, and the term *of*-genitive is used to describe the construction: *He had never known the love of a child* (= *a child's love*); *the plays of Shakespeare.*

The *of*-genitive always stands after the noun it limits: *the leaves of the tree* (= *the tree's leaves*).

The *of*-genitive is rather more common with names of inanimate objects than the *s*-genitive is, but both are used; the *s*-genitive is the more common form with names of people, though both are used:

| | |
|---|---|
| the car's rattles | the rattles of the car |
| the field's flowers | the flowers of the field |
| a day's work | the work of a day |
| Doctor Clark's house | the house of Doctor Clark |

(References: "Current English Forum," *College English,* 1953, 14:236-239; 1954, 16:55-56; Bryant, pp. 93-94.)

In most instances sound—euphony and rhythm—decides whether the *s*- or *of*-genitive is used. Since the *of*-form is longer, it often fits into sonorous and emotional phrases (at the home of Doctor Clark) and allows a more characteristic English rhythm than the compact *s*-genitive.

There is also a possible difference of meaning between the two forms. "Jane's picture" would usually mean a picture belonging to Jane, though it might mean a picture of Jane. "A picture of Jane" can only mean that Jane is represented in the picture.

*c*–Double genitive. Using both the *s*- and *of*-genitives together is an English idiom of long and respectable standing. It is especially common in locutions beginning with *that* or *this* and usually has an informal flavor:

that boy of Henry's      friends of my father's      hobbies of Jack's

It is useful in avoiding the ambiguity mentioned at the end of § b above: "Jane's picture" is resolved either as "the picture of Jane" or "the picture of Jane's."

*d*–Genitive of the personal pronouns. The personal and relative pronouns have genitive forms without an apostrophe:

my      your      his      her      its      our      their      whose

It is as important *not* to put apostrophes in these pronouns (and in the forms used without nouns: *ours, yours, theirs, hers*) as it is to put one in a noun in the genitive. (See *Possessive adjectives, *Pronouns § 1, *its, *which, *who, whom.)

**2.** *Uses of the genitive.* The most common function of the genitive is to indicate possession:

the professor's house     my son     Bert's wife

The genitive also indicates a number of other relationships:

*Description:* a man's job     children's toys     suit of wool

*Doer of an act* ("Subjective genitive") : the wind's force     the force of the wind     Sinclair Lewis' second novel     with the dean's permission     with the permission of the dean (The subjective genitive usual with gerunds) : the doctor's coming relieved the strain. (See *Gerund.)

*Recipient of an act* ("Objective genitive") : the policeman's murderer     the murderer of the policeman     the bill's defeat

*Adverb:* He drops in of an evening.

(More details of these and other genitive relations will be found in the large grammars. References: Curme, *Parts of Speech,* pp. 133-136, *Syntax,* pp. 70-88; Fries, *AEG,* pp. 72-88.)

## Gerund •

1. *Form and use.* A *gerund*—also called a verbal noun—is the form of the verb ending in *-ing* used in the function of a noun. It has the same form as the present participle but differs in use:

*Gerund: Running* a hotel appealed to him. (*Running* is the subject.)

*Participle:* He was busy *running* a hotel. (*Running* modifies *he.*)

A gerund may take an object (as in *running a hotel*) or a complement (*being a hero*), and it may serve in any noun function:

*Subject: Looking* for an apartment always fascinated her.

*Object:* He taught *dancing.*

*Predicate noun:* Seeing is *believing.*

*Used as modifier:* a *fishing* boat (a boat for fishing, not a boat that fishes) , *boiling* point, a *living* wage.

When not in one of these constructions, a gerund is related to the rest of the sentence by a preposition (§ 3).

Gerunds may show tense:

| | Active | Passive |
|---|---|---|
| *Present:* | Just *seeing* the fire was enough. | *Being seen* was bad enough. |
| *Perfect:* | Just *having seen* the fire was enough. | *Having been seen* was bad enough. |

Gerunds may be modified by adjectives when the noun function is uppermost or by adverbs when the verb function is emphasized:

*Modified by adjective: Good boxing* is first-rate entertainment.

*Modified by adverb: Playing well* was his great pride.

**2.** *Subject of a gerund.* The subject of a gerund sometimes has the genitive and sometimes the accusative (or common) case. In Formal writing the genitive is more usual; in General writing, both occur. Use whichever seems more natural.

*a*–When the subject is a personal pronoun or a word standing for a person, it is usually in the genitive:

*His coming* was all that she looked forward to.
She looked forward to *Bob's coming*.

*b*–If the subject is a plural noun, it is likely to be in the common form. Note that in speech it is impossible to decide whether *students* is genitive, but in writing, a decision must be made:

I don't approve of *men drinking*.
I don't approve of *students coming and going* as they like.
*With a pronoun:* I don't approve of *them drinking.* [*Or:*] I don't approve of *their drinking*.

*c*–If the subject is abstract or the name of an inanimate object, it is usually in the common form:

It was a case of *imagination getting* out of control.
The *roof* [or *roof's*] *falling in* was only the first disaster.

*d*–When the subject is modified by other words, it is in the common form:

In spite of the *plan* of the committee *being voted down* no one could offer a better one.
The principal's *contract running out* gave an excuse for letting him go.

*e*–When the subject is stressed, it is usually in the accusative, even if it is a pronoun:

Who would have thought of *him* [stressed] *getting* the prize?
Have you heard about *Gertrude* [stressed] *getting* a job?

*f*–If the subject has no genitive form (*this, many,* etc.) the common form is inescapable:

We disapproved of so *many being taken*.
He could not conceive of *this being done*.

**3.** *Phrases with gerunds.* Gerunds are often used in phrases that have the value and function of dependent clauses (see *Verbals):

*In coming to an agreement,* they had compromised on all points.
It's the best thing *for coughing at night*.

The relation of the gerund phrase to the word it modifies should be immediately apparent. In the first two examples below, though there is no real ambiguity since only one interpretation is possible, there is likely to be some interruption of the flow of communication as the reader pauses to make sure just what it is that the writer intended:

*Dangling: In coming to an agreement,* a compromise had to be voted. [The compromise did not come to the agreement; *they* or some other word meaning the voters should be made the subject.]

*Dangling: After reading sixteen books,* the subject is still a blank to me.

*Immediately clear: After reading sixteen books,* I am still blank about the subject.

(See *Dangling modifiers.)

**4.** *Without "the."* In current style there is a tendency to use gerunds without *the* and with a direct object rather than an *of* phrase. This exploits the verbal force of the word and makes for economy and emphasis:

His chief amusement is *telling jokes* on the President. [Rather than: His chief amusement is *the telling of jokes* on the President.]

In *revising the first draft,* a writer can check all the spellings. (Rather than: In *the revising of the first draft.* . . .)

**5.** *Idioms with gerunds.* Some words are characteristically followed by gerunds, others by infinitives. For example:

| *Gerunds* | *Infinitives* |
|---|---|
| cannot help *doing* | compelled *to do* |
| capable *of painting* | able *to paint* |
| the habit *of giving* | the tendency *to give* |
| an idea *of selling* | a wish *to sell* |
| his object *in doing* | obligation *to pay* |

With many words, especially common ones, either idiom is used: the way *of doing* something, the way *to do* something. (Compare *Participles, *Infinitives. Reference: Curme, *Syntax,* Ch. 24.)

**get, got** •

**1.** *Forms.* Principal parts: *get, got, got* and *gotten*:

I am getting a new racket. I got six inside an hour.

I had already got [gotten] mine.

Rebel though I was, I had got the religion of scholarship and science.—LINCOLN STEFFENS, *Autobiography,* p. 127

*Gotten* was brought to America by the colonists of the seventeenth century, when it was the usual English form, and has remained in general American usage ever since, while in England (less so in Scotland) the form has largely given way to *got* except in compounds (*beget, forget*). Today both forms are used by Americans as the past participle (except in "have got," as in § 2 below), the choice between them depending largely on the emphasis and rhythm of the particular sentence and on the user's speech habits. *Gotten* is probably the more common.

He could have [*gotten* or *got*] here by now.

In the past I have [*gotten* or *got*] a good meal here.

**2.** *Have got.* *Got* (not *gotten*) is used as an informal way of intensifying *have* in the sense of possess or of being obligated (Have you got a pencil?—I've got to study now). The *have* alone could carry the meaning, but it is unemphatic, especially when contracted, because it is so frequently used as a mere auxiliary of tense that we are not accustomed to feeling it as a verb of full meaning. Consequently *got* has a considerable advantage in speech. Some Formal writers avoid it, but the idiom is in General use and is appropriate in any but the most Formal situation. (References: Albert H. Marckwardt, " 'Have Got' in Expressions of Possession and Obligation," *College English,* 1955, 16:309-310; Thomas L. Crowell, *"Have Got,* a Pattern Preserver," *American Speech,* 1959, 34:280-286.)

**3.** *"Get" in idioms.* *Get* is one of the most popular verbs in idiomatic phrases, in most of which it doesn't have its original meaning shown in the sentences under § 1 but is a relatively colorless linking verb. Most of these idioms are Informal:

| | | | |
|---|---|---|---|
| get cold | get sick | get tired | get scared |
| get going | get to go | get in touch with | get supper |
| get left | get on my nerves | get away with | get along with |
| get me? | get it across | get together | get with it |

"But I got to," she cried. "I just have to talk to somebody. I didn't go home. I got worried, awful scared."—ARTHUR SOMERS ROCHE, *Shadow of Doubt,* p. 63

The first *got* in this passage would be preceded by *I've* in Standard Informal writing. Transcribing the locution as *I got* makes it look worse than it often sounds; in speech *I've* is often spoken with such reduced stress and so rapidly that the /v/ sound is virtually inaudible.

**4.** *"Get" as a passive auxiliary.* *Get* is increasingly used as an Informal emphatic passive auxiliary:

He got thrown out inside of an hour. Our house is getting painted.

(See Adelaide C. Bartlett, *College English,* 1949, 10:280-282; Curme, *Parts of Speech,* p. 218; Pooley, pp. 148-151.)

**get up, arise, rise** • See *rise.

**Given names** • Ordinarily either spell out or use the initial of *given names* (also called Christian names) rather than such abbreviations as *Chas., Thos., Wm.*:

| C. T. Graves | or | Charles T. Graves |
|---|---|---|
| T. W. Lane | or | Thomas W. Lane |

**glamor—glamour** • The first would be the normal American spelling (see *-or, -our), but in the fashion and entertainment "worlds" *glamour* is more common (glamour girl). The adjective is generally *glamorous*.

**go** •
1. *Go* is a useful little word, especially as a *linking verb in a number of idioms, most of which are Informal:

| | | |
|---|---|---|
| go blind | go mad | go dry |
| go steady | go hard | go wrong |

2. *Go and* is a spoken form of emphasis: *Go and try it yourself* [no actual movement meant]. *She went and shot the bear herself.* These are primarily oral expressions, but they are appropriate in some Informal and General writing.

**Gobbledygook** • A suggestive label for an abuse of Formal English, characteristic of some government and business communications, marked by overheavy (abstract) words and confusing, pseudo-legal or pseudo-scientific sentences. What relatively simple statement is being made in this sample?

By encouraging and maintaining a reciprocal interest between the prime contractor and his subcontractors in the business matter of fulfilling the obligations of the prime contract, contractual requirements, particularly inspection, can be greatly assisted in furnishing the consignee with the required information that material has received inspection in accordance with the contract.

(See *Big words, *Jargon.)

**good—well** • *Good* is usually an adjective in Standard English; *well* is either an adjective or an adverb: "I feel *good*" and "I feel *well*" (adjectives) are both usual but have different meanings (*good* implying actual bodily sensation, *well* referring merely to a state, "not ill").

In Nonstandard usage *well* is rarely used, *good* taking its place ("He rowed good" for "He rowed well"). In Informal speech *good* is occasionally heard when the subject is an inanimate object: *The motor runs pretty good.* Perhaps this is because *good* is felt as modifying *motor*. But this usage is not yet appropriate in writing. (Reference: Bryant, pp. 100-101.)

**good and** • *Good and* is a common spoken equivalent of *very* (I'm good and mad) but is seldom appropriate in writing. (Reference: Bryant, pp. 99-100.)

**good-by—good-bye** • Both are in use, often without the hyphen.

**got, get, gotten** • See *get, got.

**grade school—graded school** • *Graded school* is the older word but *grade school* is much more common, and always appropriate.

**graduate** • The idiom *to be graduated* from an institution has generally gone out of use except in Formal and somewhat archaic writing and has been replaced by *graduated from: He graduated from Yale in 1902.* Omitting the *from* is Nonstandard: *He graduated high school in 1957,* perhaps a confusion with the acceptable *finished.* (Reference: Bryant, pp. 102-103.)

**Grammar** • *Grammar* derives from the Greek *gramma,* meaning a written symbol; the first grammarians were teachers of writing and reading. In the Middle Ages, to know grammar meant not only to know how to read and write Latin but to possess the powers of a literate man in a largely illiterate society. In modern English, *grammar* is used in several senses:
1. *The basic structure of a language.* Every language is a complex of patterns developed over a long period of time by the people using it. In the English sentence *You see it,* we know *you* is the subject (here the actor) and *it* is the object (the thing seen), because *you* precedes the verb and *it* follows it. In French, however, the sentence would be written, *Tu le vois,* with the subject first, object second and verb last. The order of the elements, as well as their form, depends on the conventions of the particular language. Every native speaker learns these and a host of other patterns in his language as a child and can understand and use them automatically. These patterns may be called the complete or total grammar of the language; in this sense English grammar is "the English way of saying things."
2. *Descriptive grammar.* This is an attempt to describe as systematically and objectively as possible the total system of a language. In his method, the descriptive grammarian attempts to be scientific: he observes the language as it is in an effort to discover its underlying system but without trying to guide the language habits of speakers and writers. Since a language is extensive, complex, varied, and elusive, a particular grammar will never be complete but will depend on the limitations the grammarian has set himself and those imposed on him; he will usually limit himself to one variety of the language (ordinarily that used by the educated because the material is most readily available), and he will be limited by his training (the

linguistic philosophy he embraces), the information available to him, and, of course, his individual competence.

When the description of a language covers a considerable period of time, describing the evolution of words and forms and constructions, perhaps explaining present usage in the light of the past, it is called *historical* (or *diachronic*) *grammar*. When several related languages are compared, as English might be with Latin or German, it is called *comparative grammar*. When one stage of a language is described, it is called *synchronic grammar*.

For one variety of the language there will be one basic structure, one underlying system, one grammar in the sense of § 1 above. Every attempt to describe this grammar will be a grammar; in this second sense there may therefore be several grammars. A brief account of the three principal types of these follows:

*a*–Classical. This is a rather arbitrary and somewhat misleading name, chosen because *descriptive* has already been applied to all three types. It has the justification, however, that the grammarians who developed it attempted to work within the Greco-Roman grammatical tradition, and that they are the earliest modern grammarians—Jacob Grimm, for example, first published his *German Grammar* in 1819—to attempt a systematic description of a language on the basis of a careful examination of it. Though fully aware of the primacy of speech as language, they were able to break away only gradually from the habit of depending on written records for their evidence, especially as they were much concerned—Grimm again, for example—with the history of the language. Nevertheless their achievements have been enormous, and they established the firm foundations of modern linguistics.

Among the more important grammars in this tradition are Henry Sweet, *A New English Grammar,* 2 vols., 1892, 1898; H. Poutsma, *A Grammar of Late Modern English,* 4 vols., 1904-1926; Otto Jespersen, *A Modern English Grammar,* 7 vols., 1909-1949 (a convenient brief example is Jespersen's *Essentials of English Grammar,* 1934); and in this country, George O. Curme, *Syntax,* 1931, and *Parts of Speech and Accidence,* 1935.

*b*–Structural. This approach, to which Americans have been major contributors, carries through much more rigorously two principles of the classical descriptive grammars: the primacy of speech and the importance of the structural patterns of the language in conveying grammatical meaning (see *Lexical meaning). Structural descriptive grammars therefore begin with the *phoneme, go on to the *morpheme, and attempt to identify the syntactical devices by which grammatical relations are signalled.

Among the more important grammars in this tradition are Charles C. Fries, *The Structure of English,* 1952; W. Nelson Francis, *The Structure of American English,* 1958; James Sledd, *A Short Introduction to English Grammar,* 1959; H. A. Gleason, *An Introduction to Descriptive Linguistics,* 1961.

*c*–Transformational and generative. This most recent approach—again American—assumes that the very large total of sentence patterns which can be described for a language is based on a relatively small number of kernel sentences. As we learn our language we unconsciously acquire the rules by which these kernel sentences can be transformed into others. We gradually master the capacity to generate an increasing proportion of the total possible sentences. The task of this kind of grammarian is to discover the basic sentence patterns and the rules by which these can be transformed.

An account of the various transformational grammars will be found in Emmon W. Bach, *An Introduction to Transformational Grammars,* 1964. An elementary presentation is given in Paul Roberts, *English Sentences,* 1962, Ch. 10.

3. *Prescriptive grammar.* Besides these uses of the term *grammar* we also speak of *prescriptive* or *normative grammar.* A prescriptive grammar is a body of rules presented as guides to expression, statements of how, in the belief of the writer, people should speak and write. Many English grammars of this type, represented principally by textbooks prepared for the use of students, are now in disrepute because they are out of touch with descriptive grammar and with actual usage. Too many school grammars represent either older usage or traditional rules that are not consistently followed and some that have never been followed by users of English. To the extent that they are describing a variety of English actually used, they present Formal English as the only (or best) English and discourage General and Informal usage.

One unfortunate result of prescriptive grammar is that the teaching of Formal English has seemed so unreal to students that, unable to separate the useful from the useless advice, they have paid almost no attention at all to it. If they talked as their textbooks said they should, they would be laughed at; consequently they have usually continued their old habits.

Although the usage recommended in schools will probably always be a little more Formal than that being practiced by actual writers, school grammar is now gradually getting away from traditional prescriptive grammar and is coming closer to the actual usage of the educated as presented in the descriptive grammars.

4. *Grammar as remedy.* Many people are occasionally oppressed by a feeling of inadequacy in their use of English.

They believe that all their deficiencies, real or imagined, in vocabulary, effective expression, spelling, usage, and punctuation would be removed if they studied "grammar" conscientiously. This is back of the demand for "More grammar!" in the schools. This demand is really based on a desire for more varied and more acceptable *usage,* "good English" as discussed on pp. 22-31. The best remedy is wide listening and reading and regular practice in using language effectively. Grammatical terms play a useful but subordinate part in summarizing and describing the facts of the current language, but they are not themselves the remedy.

When you use *grammar* in speaking or writing, you should be aware of its various meanings and varied uses, and if necessary indicate the sense in which you are using it. In this book the term is restricted to the first two senses described in this article, the exact meaning being shown by the context.

The terms used in grammar deserve a comment also. The analysis of language is a discipline more than two thousand years old, going back in Western culture to the philosophers and rhetoricians of ancient Greece. The terminology devised by the Greeks was used with little modification until modern linguistics made its inadequacy for the description of other languages apparent. Some of the old terms have been kept and given more restricted or more precise definition and new terms have been introduced. Some grammatical and linguistic terms are still not standardized, but by making their reference clear we can and must use them in discussing language.

Many people steadfastly refuse to learn the technical terms of grammar. Students who gaily toss about *schizophrenic, marginal utility, Hanseatic League, dicotyledonous,* or *trinitrotoluene* will not learn the pronunciation and meaning of *predicative, metonymy,* or even *apostrophe* or *agreement,* and some teachers of the subject try to work without naming exactly what they are talking about. Many of the words are a bit difficult—Greek or Latin names that have been taken into the language—but they are not nearly so difficult as the vocabulary of psychology or chemistry. This book uses a good many of these terms, without apology, though when there is a choice of name the simpler and more suggestive has usually been taken. It is only good sense to gain control of the words that name common facts of usage and style, words which are an essential part of the English vocabulary of educated people.

(See *Linguistics, *Latin and English § 3. References: The works in the bibliography at the beginning of this *Index,* specifically Fries and Pooley, discuss many of the particular rules of prescriptive grammar besides offering their own observation of usage; see especially Fries, *AEG,* Chs. 1, 2, 11, and Robert C. Pooley, *Teaching English Grammar,* New York, 1957; also the descriptive grammars mentioned in § 2 above.)

**grammatical, ungrammatical •** These adjectives will have senses derived from definitions § 1 and § 3 of the article *Grammar: for § 1, *grammatical* means fitting into the system of the language, *ungrammatical* means not fitting in (**It's me* would be grammatical; the Frenchman's literal translation *She [the table] is large* would be ungrammatical); for § 3, *grammatical* means fitting into arbitrarily prescribed rules, *ungrammatical* means not fitting those rules (*It's I* would be grammatical, *It's me* ungrammatical). *Bad grammar* is approximately synonomous with the § 3 sense of *ungrammatical.* Obviously these terms should be used with great caution.

**Group words •** In English many groups of two or more words (that is, phrases) function like single words. Often the division of the elements into separate words in print is quite arbitrary. *High school* is not the noun *school* modified by the adjective *high* so much as a noun in its own right just as *highway* is. But established practice is to spell the first as two words, the second as one. Many of our verbs are made up of a verb plus an adverb: *close up, hold off, look into* (see *Verb-adverb combinations); many prepositions are phrases: *according to, in opposition to.*

Other typical group words are:

*Nouns:* hay fever     back door     holding company     home run
safety razor     baby blue     school year     sacrifice hit
*Verbs:* dig in     back water     back step (military)     flare up
follow through     follow up     show up     blow up
*Prepositions:* in spite of     in consequence of     previous to
due to

"In such cases," George P. Krapp wrote, "it is contrary to the idiom of the language to try to analyze the groups into their constituent parts so as to give every word, standing alone, a clearly defined structural value." Consequently in this book we ignore the superficial difference between a part of speech written as a single word and one that is written as a group of words. "Noun" or "verb" or "preposition" refers both to single words and to *group words* functioning as noun or verb or preposition. (References: Curme, *Syntax,* Ch. 30; George P. Krapp, *The Knowledge of English,* New York, 1927, pp. 313-316 where such phrases are called "function groups.")

**guess, calculate, reckon •** See *calculate, guess, reckon.

**H** •
**1.** As a distinctive sound, *h* /h/ always occurs at the beginning of syllables: *harsh, heel, high, horrible, ahead.*
**2.** *H* is likely to be silent at the beginning of unstressed syllables: *forehead* /fôr′id/, *behind* (when spoken rapidly in unstressed part of phrase), /bi īnd′/, *he, his, her,* etc., when lightly spoken (*Give it to him′* versus *Give′* it to [h]im).
*H* is silent in *rh* words—*rhetoric, rhyme, rhythm.*
In many words from French the *h* was formerly not pronounced: *habit, history, hotel* ... but now is except in *heir, honest, honor, hour,* and sometimes in *herb, hostler, huge, humble, humor.* So long as the *h* was not pronounced, *an* was used before these words, and it is still by some people in the forms in which the stress is not on the first syllable: *an historical work, an habitual error,* though *a* is now more common. (See *\*a, an, \*wh.*)

**Habitual action** • *Habitual action* is expressed in English in a variety of ways, of which the following are samples:

> He would always go by the longer way.
> I get up every morning at six.
> He came here every week.
> He used to go by the longer way.
> He usually went by the longer way.

**Hackneyed** • See *\*Trite.

**had better, had rather** • *Had better* is the usual idiom for giving advice or making an indirect command:

> You had better take care of that cold.
> You'd better go.

The assimilation of the *d* of *you'd* by the *b* of *better* has given rise to the Informal construction without *had*:

> If he asks you to do it, you better do it.

*Had rather* and *would rather* are both used to express preference, the latter the more Formal:

> He would rather ski than eat.
> He had [He'd] rather ski than eat.

Since the *had* or *would* is unstressed in speech (and the contraction *he'd* is frequently used), it is impossible to tell which is being said.

**half** • The more Formal idiom is *a half*; the General, *half a*:

> *Formal:* He ran a half mile; a half hour.
> *General:* He ran half a mile; half an hour.

*A half a* (a half an hour) is a redundancy sometimes found in Informal and Nonstandard speech but not in Standard written English.

**hanged—hung** • In Formal English the principal parts of *hang* when referring to the death penalty are *hang, hanged, hanged*, the archaic forms kept alive by legal phrases such as "hanged by the neck until dead"; in other senses they are *hang, hung, hung*: Murderers are *hanged*, pictures are *hung*.

General and Informal usage does not keep this distinction, often using *hang, hung, hung* in all senses:

> They hung the Turk that invented work
> In the Big Rock Candy Mountain.

**Hanging indention** • See *Indention.

**hardly** • See *Double negative.

**have** •
1. *Auxiliary. Have* occurs most frequently in the perfect tenses, for which it is now the sole auxiliary in English (in earlier English *be* was also used). *Have* plus a past participle makes the perfect tense (They have come); *shall have* or *will have* plus a past participle makes the future perfect tense (They will have gone by then); *had* plus a past participle makes the past perfect (They had gone to the beach before we arrived). In this use it is a *function word—a signal of tense. (See *Tenses of verbs.)
2. *Independent meaning.* As a verb of independent meaning *have* means to "own, possess" in a literal (have a car) or transferred sense (have the measles). There are many idioms with *have* such as:

to have a look      the book (or gossip) has it that
have it your own way      to have it out
*Informal:* He had his arm broken.
*General:* He had a broken arm.
*Formal:* He suffered a broken arm.

Because *have* occurs so frequently as an "empty" auxiliary word, its meaning as an independent word is often reinforced by *got*. (See *get, got § 2.)
3. *Contractions.* In speech, *he, she, it* and unstressed *has* are contracted to *he's, she's, it's* (He's not tried to in years; It's rained for over a week). This contraction is indistinguishable from that of *is; He's gone* may be *He has gone* or *He is gone. I, you, we, they have* are contracted to *I've, you've, we've, they've.*

*Would have, wouldn't have* are sometimes written *would of, wouldn't of,* an unacceptable transcription of what is spoken as *would've, wouldn't't've.*

**4.** *Had ought* and *hadn't ought* are idioms with *have* that occur frequently in speech. *Hadn't ought* (He hadn't ought to lie like that) is regional and Informal. *Had ought,* on the other hand, is a common Nonstandard idiom, although it, too, is sometimes heard in Informal speech.

*Nonstandard*: He had ought to take better care of himself.

*Standard*: He ought to take better care of himself.

**5.** *Have to* and *must* are nearly synonymous in the affirmative (*I have to* or *must go now*), but in the negative there is a difference (*I don't have to go, I mustn't go*). *Have to* has the advantage that it can be conjugated in all tenses. In present tense forms the last consonant is unvoiced: /haf'tə, has'tə/.

**6.** *Other idioms.* For *have got* see *\*get, got* § 2. See also *\*had better, had rather.*

**he-or-she •** Since English has no third person singular pronoun to refer to individuals of either or both sexes, English speakers are faced with a problem unique in Indo-European languages; in all the others the third person singular pronouns have grammatical reference, not sexual (see *\*Gender*). As we must often refer to nouns that name either or both male and female, the language has developed three ways of making up for the lack of an accurate pronoun:

**1.** The prescribed way is to use *he* or *his* alone even when some of the persons are female:

There is considerable discussion whether a man or a woman will be appointed to the vacant cabinet post. Whoever receives the appointment will find *his* task a difficult one.

Mr. Brown and Miss Trevor led the discussion, each giving *his* opinion of the poem.

Sometimes when the typical individuals or the majority of the group referred to are women, *her* is used in the same way:

Each of the teachers in this school is required to submit *her* report to the principal in person.

**2.** A common way in General usage is to resort to a plural pronoun because it evades the question of sex:

Neither [a man and a woman] tasted what *they* ate.—KATHERINE ANNE PORTER, *Flowering Judas*, p. 26

**3.** Sometimes both *he* and *she* are used:

A teacher gives *his* or *her* own opinions on matters of politics and religion and often influences a pupil to think as *he* or *she* does.

(Either of the two pronouns would be better in this sentence than both of them).

Every student wishes to participate in some activity authorized by *his* or *her* college. (*His* or *her* sounds pedantic here; *his* alone would be better.)

The two pronouns are almost always clumsy and really no more accurate, since the meaning is determined by the antecedent. (Reference: Bergen and Cornelia Evans, *A Dictionary of Contemporary American Usage*, New York, 1957, entries for *his* and *they*.)

**Headword—head** • A *headword* or *head* is a word modified by another word, especially by one or more adjectives (his first long *sleep*) or a verb modified by one or more adverbs (*run* slowly around the rim). The term is used variously by different linguists, but always to mean a word that is regarded as primary in a word group. (See Harold Whitehall, *Structural Essentials of English*, New York, 1956, Ch. 2; Paul Roberts, *Patterns of English*, New York, 1956, pp. 77-105; Ralph B. Long, *The Sentence and Its Parts*, Chicago, 1961, p. 490.)

**healthful, healthy** • *Healthful* meant "giving health"; places and food were healthful. *Healthy* meant "having good health"; persons and animals were healthy. This distinction is still attempted by some writers and speakers, but many simply use *healthy* in both senses.

**Heightened style** • See *Style.

**hell** • See *devil.

**help but** • See *can't help but, can't seem to.

**hence** • See *Conjunctive adverbs.

**high school** • Capitalize only when referring to a particular school (some newspaper styles do not use capitals even then):

I graduated from high school at seventeen.
I graduated from Bismarck High School in 1964.

**highbrow** • After a period of slang overuse, *highbrow* (and *lowbrow* too) has settled down as a useful General word.

There is a widespread belief that chamber-music makers are long-haired musical intellectuals, bloodless esoterics, highbrows with a G string.—JOSEPH WECHSBERG, "The Music of Friends," *Horizon*, Nov. 1962, p. 45

*Middlebrow,* a more recent coinage, has also established itself.

**himself, herself** • *Himself* and *herself* are used in two ways:
1. As reflexive pronouns, referring to the subject of the sentence:

George has always taken himself pretty seriously.
She looked at herself in the window and gave her hat a little pull.

2. As *intensives for emphasis:

He told me so himself.
I looked up and there was Mrs. Goodenow herself.

(Compare *myself, *self.)

**home, homely** •
1. *Home* is used in the function of a noun, verb, adjective, or adverb—an example of the English habit of making one form serve several functions (see *Parts of speech):

*Noun:* His home was now in Cleveland.
*Verb:* They homed the missiles in by radar.
*Adverbial modifier:* He came home unexpectedly. His remark went home.
*Adjectival modifier:* He reports to the home office.

In "They are home," *home* is a General expression for *at home. To home* is Nonstandard and regional.
2. *Home—house.* For a realtor a *home* is any house; in sentimental (and some Formal) use a *home* is only the "place of one's domestic affections." But in General use *home* is a lived-in house (or any extension needed for animal, plant, or object).
3. *Homely.* In some contexts, particularly in British usage, *homely* has the sense of "informal, unassuming, characteristic of home life." In the United States, however, *homely* usually means "ugly in appearance." In this country it is therefore safer to use the word only in the second sense.

**Homonyms, homophones** • Two words of different meanings that are pronounced alike (*bear, bare; plain, plane*) are called *homonyms* or *homophones.*

English has a great many such pairs of words, most of them in common use. They have developed for various reasons. Some Old English words once different in sound have come to be pronounced alike because of changes in form through the centuries: *bear* (the animal) from *bera, bear* (the verb) from *beran; plain* and *plane* both go back to Latin *planus,* but the spelling of the first was altered in coming through Old

French. Many words are from different languages, having fallen into similar forms by accident: *rest* meaning "peace" is from Old English, *rest* meaning "remainder" is from French; *bark* of a tree is from Scandinavian, *bark* of a dog from Old English, and *bark,* the vessel, a more recent borrowing from French-Italian.

There is little chance of misunderstanding such words because their context will tell which is which—though their similarity is often exploited in *puns. Where real conflict exists, the resolution has usually been by one or both words going out of use. The verb *halve* hardly exists in speech anymore because of almost certain confusion with *have:* "We'll halve (have) the pie." But homophones like *plain—plane* make a good deal of trouble in spelling. Much of this confusion is really carelessness, for the words are common. Try to visualize the troublesome ones in phrases that show their meaning, something like these:

priest at the *altar*—who can *alter* human nature?
Father gave his *assent* to the marriage—the *ascent* of Mount Everest
*bearing* pain—*baring* his arm
a lower *berth*—his tenth *birth*day
*born* in June 1947—*borne* by the wind
the *bridal* party, *bridal* suite—a horse's *bridle,* the *bridle* path
the *capital* of Illinois is Springfield—the *capitol* has a gilded dome
a *coarse* oath—on the golf *course*
every woman likes *compliments*—the *complement* of the angle
the *core* of meaning—a *corps* of volunteers
there are five members of the *council*—*counsel* is advice—*counsel* for the defense
a *dual* personality—a pistol *duel*
a *mantle* covered her—the trophy cups on the *mantel*
a *piece* of paper—*peace* or war
air*plane, plane* geometry—the Great *Plains,* a *plain* statement
*pore* over a book—*pour* coffee
the *principal* charge—the *principle* of justice
he *rode* horseback—the *road* was macadam—he *rowed* a dory
a box of *stationery*—a *stationary* engine—*stationary* desks
*tea* to drink—*tee* on a golf course

(See *Spoken and written English. Reference: Arthur G. Kennedy, *Current English,* Boston, 1935, § 82.)

**Honorable •** As a title of respect, for persons in political office of some prestige, this word is capitalized and is usually preceded by *the*; it may be abbreviated in addresses when initials or first names are used:

the Honorable Ernest Gruening    The Hon. Ernest Gruening
the Honorable Member from Alaska

**hope** • Both *in hope of* and *in hopes of* are in General usage, with the former perhaps preferred because of sound:

After leaving Montreal we drove on *in hope of* [or: *in hopes of*] reaching Quebec as soon as possible. [Or: *in the hope of* reaching]

The participle *hoping* is probably more usual:

After leaving Montreal we drove on, *hoping* to reach Quebec as soon as possible.

**Hours** • In consecutive writing, especially if it is Formal, hours are written in words: *at four o'clock.*

In newspapers and in much General writing, figures are used, especially if several times are mentioned:

at 4 p.m.      just after 9 a.m.      from 10 to 12

(See *a.m. and p.m., *Numbers § 1b. See also *Period § 2d.)

**house—home** • See *home, homely.

**however** • As a connective, *however* is more appropriate to the fully developed sentences of Formal style and is especially useful as a connective between sentences:

Occasionally the beat man writes his own story in the press room of the public building in which he is stationed, and sends it to the office by messenger. This, however, is unusual as it involves loss of time.—C. D. MacDougall, *Reporting for Beginners,* p. 65

Amateur writers are likely to overuse *however; but* is usually more appropriate, especially in simple, direct writing:

During the eight weeks I was in the hospital, Al visited me twice, assuring me that as soon as I was able, I could have my old job. But [better than *however*] after four weeks of convalescing at home, it was time for me to go to college.

Clauses in one sentence connected by *however* are conventionally separated by a semicolon. (See *Conjunctive adverbs, *but.)

When two contrasts must be stated in sequence, *however* is useful to avoid repetition: *I got there on time, but he came late; however, he had a good excuse.*

**Humor** • See *Epigrams, *Malapropism, *Puns, *Spoonerism.

**hung—hanged** • See *hanged—hung.

**Hyphen (-)** • The hyphen is a mark of punctuation, rather than of spelling, that is used sometimes to join and sometimes to keep distinct two or more printed units. Its commonest use is to mark the division of a word at the end of a line of manuscript or type (see *Division of words). Other uses of the hyphen are somewhat variable: dictionaries and publishers' stylebooks do not always agree on specific practices. Consequently they are in part a matter of style, with Formal writers tending to use more hyphens than General writers. The following uses are fairly well standardized and may be taken as a guide for General writing.

1. *In compound words.* Many compound words will be found written in three ways: as two words, or hyphened, or as one word (*prize fighter, prize-fighter, prizefighter*); as a rule the form does not affect meaning. In the past, words that were becoming fused into compounds passed through a probationary period with hyphens before being written as single words. *Baseball,* for instance, was hyphened for a time, and so were *football* and *basketball.* There is less tendency now, except in quite Formal writing, to use such hyphens, and compounds are made immediately without hyphens if the words are needed.

Two words of one syllable are most often written solid (*bedroom, kickback, lineman, skylight*), especially when the first element is more heavily stressed in speech; but a hyphen is likely if the first is not a simple modifier of the second: *by-pass, close-up, cure-all, hair-do.* A hyphen is more likely to be used when one of the elements, especially the first, has two or more syllables, though two words is always an option:

... and we have even seen their guilty simulacra in tenement-house and shopfronts.—LEWIS MUMFORD, *Sticks and Stones,* p. 180

*Schoolbook* is usually written solid; *reference book* is two words.

A hyphen is conventional in three groups of words:

*a*–In the compound numerals from twenty-one to ninety-nine, and in fractions, though this use is not universal:

| | | |
|---|---|---|
| forty-seven | ninety-ninth | one hundred sixty-two |
| three-sixteenths | one thirty-second | |

*b*–In names of family relationships:

*Hyphened:* father-in-law, daughter-in-law
*One word:* stepson, stepdaughter, stepmother
*Two words:* half brother, half sister (sometimes hyphened)

*c*–In compounds with *self-,* which are usually hyphened in dictionaries but are often found in print as two words:

| | | |
|---|---|---|
| self-contained | self-government—self government | |
| self-help—self help | self-importance | self-pity—self pity |

*Selfhood* and *selfless* are written as one word. (Compare *-wise.)

A hyphen or a separation is used if the first member of the compound ends in the same vowel that the second begins with (*fire-eater, fire-escape* or *fire escape*) or if a misleading or awkward combination of consonants would result from joining the words (*mess hall* or *mess-hall, bell-like*).

If a compound word raises a question, consult a reliable recent dictionary both under the entry for the word and in the discussion of hyphens and compounds. If no information is forthcoming, use a hyphen or not as your taste dictates.

**2.** *In modifiers.*

*a*–A number of adjectives composed of two words are conventionally hyphened when they precede a noun:

| | | |
|---|---|---|
| clear-cut | easy-going | up-to-date |
| clear-eyed | first-class | would-be |
| clear-headed | narrow-minded | |

The more commonly used ones are given in dictionaries. Most of them are an adverb plus a verbal; and other phrases formed on this pattern are hyphened when the adverb does not end in *-ly*:

a late-flowering iris  slow-moving goods
a well-marked trail   [but] a plainly marked trail

Usually such modifiers are not hyphened in predicate position:

a clear-eyed boy  [but]  The boy was clear eyed.

Such phrases should not be hyphened in a verb construction:

a well-matched pair  They were well matched.
They were well suited to each other.

Short, frequently used combinations are generally hyphened:

a two-year term  a small-town sheriff  a no-hit, no-run game

Longer phrase modifiers are usually hyphened:

on a pay-as-you-go basis
a 5-cent-an-hour wage increase
a detailed question-and-answer sheet
two-hundred-pound, six-foot-two halfbacks

*b*–Usage is divided on hyphening noun phrases when used as modifiers, as in *seventeenth century philosophy.* Formal writers would usually write *seventeenth-century*; General, *seventeenth century.* This distinction applies to such expressions as the following:

a Seventh Avenue shop  summer vacation freedom

*c*–Occasionally some pairs of modifiers might be ambiguous without a hyphen: *a light yellow scarf* might be either a light scarf that was yellow or a scarf that was light yellow, so that *light-yellow* is safest for the latter meaning, and *light, yellow scarf* for the first. There is a possible distinction between a *great-grandfather* (indicating relationship only) and a *great grandfather* (indicating quality of a grandfather), and between a new car-owner and a new-car owner. In speech the distinction might be achieved through intonation, but in both speech and writing a re-ordering of the sentence elements would prevent possible ambiguity.

*d*–A numeral as part of a modifier (5-cent, 27 9-inch boards) and a letter linked to a noun (H-bomb, T-square, X-ray) are hyphened.

*e*–A hyphen may be used to carry the force of a modifier over to a later noun ("suspension hyphen"):

The third-, fourth-, and fifth-grade rooms have been redecorated.

In both thirteenth- and fourteenth-century texts

3. *With prefixes.* In certain types of compounds of a prefix and a root word a hyphen may be used to avoid confusion, or for emphasis or for appearance:

*a*–Between a prefix ending with a vowel and a root word beginning with the same vowel (though a *dieresis is used by some publishers) :

re-elected      re-enter      pre-eminent      pre-existent

(See *pre-, *re-.)

Usage is divided on words made with *co-,* the more common ones now generally being written solid:

cooperate or co-operate      coordinate or co-ordinate

*b*–To avoid confusion with another word:

re-collect—recollect      re-cover—recover

*c*–Between a prefix and a proper name:

pre-Sputnik      ex-President Truman      pro-Eisenhower

*d*–When the prefix is stressed:

ex-husband      ex-wife      anti-vivisection (or antivivisection)

4. *Miscellaneous uses.*

*a*–Between the letters showing how a word is spelled:

The loser spelled *receive* r-e-c-i-e-v-e.

*b*–Often to show syllabication:

hy-pos-ta-ti-za-tion

Hyphening is more an editor's worry than a writer's. A publisher may wish for uniformity in principle and may struggle to get it in printing particular words, though absolute consistency is impossible. The manual of the Government Printing Office devotes over fifty pages to rules for hyphening, and stylebooks of newspaper and other publications have numerous rules, many of them arbitrary choices of form made simply to insure consistency. In a person's ordinary writing, he does not need to be so particular. For words in common use he can consult a dictionary or do as he finds reputable publications doing.

The conclusion one comes to after a serious consideration of current habits in the use of hyphens is well put by John Benbow in *Manuscript & Proof,* the stylebook of the Oxford University Press of New York: "If you take hyphens seriously you will surely go mad."

(References: *GPO Manual,* pp. 63-120; Summey, Ch. 10; and discussions in recent dictionaries.)

## I •

1. *"Long i"* /ī/. The sound of long *i* is a diphthong, gliding from /a/ or /ä/ to short /i/ or short /e/: *ice, wild, find, guide, night, tiny.* It is also spelled as in *aisle, ay, aye, height, eye, by, buy, bye, lie, choir.*

In unstressed syllables /ī/ has a similar sound but is somewhat shorter: /dī am′ə tər/.

2. *"Short i"* /i/ as in *bit, city.* This sound is spelled in a number of other ways: s*ie*ve, dut*y,* forf*ei*t, all*ey,* mess*a*ge, Sund*ay,* marri*a*ge, foreh*ea*d, mount*ai*n, min*u*te, bisc*ui*t.

3. *"Continental i"* /ē/. In a few words the Continental (European) value of *i* is preserved: *machine* /mə shēn′/, *police* /pə-lēs′/, *visa* /vē′zə/, and in recent unanglicized borrowings.

4. *As a consonant* /y/. *I* may represent a /y/ sound before a vowel, especially in rapid pronunciation: *opinion* /ə pin′yən/. (For the plural *-ies* see *Plurals § 1b and *Y. See also *-ile and *J.)

5. *Before* r. *I* may spell the sound represented by /ė/: *bird* /bėrd/, *third* /thėrd/.

## I •

1. *Capital.* The pronoun *I* is written as a capital simply because in the old manuscripts a small *i* might be lost or get attached to a neighboring word, and the capital helped keep it distinct. No conceit is implied.

2. *As first word.* The notion that *I* should not be the first word in a letter (sometimes even that it should not be the first word of a sentence) is not justified by prevailing cultivated practice. *I* should be used wherever it is needed, though if it opens several consecutive sentences the repetition becomes irksome. People with only average concern for themselves need not worry; the conceited will give themselves away anyway.

Circumlocutions to get around the natural use of *I* are usually awkward and likely to attract attention to themselves:

> There is a feeling in me [I feel] that relief projects are unsound.

The best way to avoid conspicuous use of *I* (or of any other word) is to keep it out of emphatic sentence positions, especially from the stressed beginning of a sentence. A dependent clause or longish phrase put first will throw the stress off the *I*:

> After a long struggle I decided to go. [*Instead of*: I decided to go, after a long struggle.]

**3.** *Omission of I.* In clipped personal writing—diaries, casual and Informal letters—*I* is often appropriately omitted if the style is also clipped in other respects:

> Talked to John. Very informative. He doesn't think it can be done.

(See *It's me, *myself, *we § 2.)

**ibid.** • See *Abbreviations § 2.

**-ible, -able** • See *-able, -ible.

**idea** • The word *idea* is frequently used as a substitute for *intention, impression,* and similar words in constructions that are usually wordy:

> I got the idea [I thought] that every policeman was my enemy.
> *Wordy:* We started out with the idea in mind of going to a dance.
> *Improved:* We started out intending to go to a dance.

**Idiolect** • An *idiolect* is the set of speech habits of an individual. A dialect or a language is the speech patterns of people with similar idiolects, the similarities being closer in the former.

**Idiom and idioms** •
*Revision: The expression marked is not idiomatic. Revise it, referring to an article in this* Index *or to a dictionary if you are not sure what it should be.*

Id

The word *idiom* is used in two different, almost opposed, senses:

**1.** It may mean *the usual forms of expression of a particular language,* as we may compare German idiom with English idiom, meaning the ways in which words are characteristically put together in the two languages. German, for example, has suspended constructions (*Ich habe den alten Mann schon gesehen*—I have the old man already seen), separable prefixes, and participial constructions, whereas English tends to complete its constructions immediately. In French, adjectives usually come after the nouns they modify (*une maison blanche*), in English they usually come before (*a white house*). "Idiomatic English" connotes natural English. It ordinarily is contrasted with stilted usage and suggests a mastery of the basic constructions of General English.

**2.** The word *idiom* may also mean *an accepted phrase that differs from the usual construction of the language,* either in not submitting to the typical grammatical analysis (like *somebody else's,* in which the sign of the possessive is added to the adjective rather than to the noun) or in having a total meaning not obviously suggested by the meanings of the parts (like *to center around,* or *in respect to,* which are ridiculous when analyzed). These idioms are usually particular phrases which we learn as separate items—easily in our own language, with difficulty in another—differing from the idioms discussed in the preceding section, which are patterns for large numbers of locutions.

Collecting English idioms is good sport and so is trying to analyze them. Considering them grammatically and literally, what can you make of these?

| | |
|---|---|
| to come in handy | be your age |
| how do you do | strike a bargain |
| to catch fire | to be taken in (deceived) |
| catch his eye | takes after her mother |
| a hot cup of coffee | look up an old friend |

These expressions are thoroughly respectable members of the language. No one need apologize for using them, for they are part of the stock in trade of the language and most of them are appropriate in all varieties. If they defy conventional analysis, it is because of the inadequacy of the analytical procedure.

The dictionaries give a great many idioms, usually listed under the most important word in the phrase. The *Oxford English Dictionary* is especially rich in idioms.

(See *Comparison of adjectives and adverbs § 3, *Gerund § 5, *Phrases, *Prepositions; see also *Ambiguity § 3; for idioms with verbs see *do § 3, *doubt, *get, got § 3, *go § 1, *have § 4, 5. References: *Oxford English Dictionary*; Logan Pearsall Smith, *English Idioms,* Oxford, 1927; V. H. Collins, *A Book of English Idioms, A Second Book of English Idioms, A Third Book of English Idioms,* London, 1956, 1958, 1960.)

**-ie-, -ei-** • See *-ei-, -ie-.

**i.e.** • See *Abbreviations § 2, *namely and other introductory words.

**if** •

1. *Subordinating conjunction. If* is a subordinating conjunction introducing a condition:

If the weather holds good, we shall stay another week.

If they had known the beacon was out, they would have come in before sunset.

(See *Conditions. Reference: Fries, *AEG*, pp. 224-225.)

2. *"If" and "whether."* In Formal and General usage, *if* is used for conditions, and *whether*, usually with *or*, is used, though not consistently, in indirect questions and in expressions of doubt:

*Simple condition:* If the weather holds, we will come.

*Indirect question:* He asked whether the mail had come in. He asked whether they were all going or only some of them.

*Doubt:* They had all been wondering whether the doctor would get there in time.

From the first returns they could not be sure whether the state was Republican or Democratic.

In Formal English *if* is not used with *or*:

No matter whether [not *if*] the boy goes to preparatory school or high school, his father has to pay local school taxes.

In Informal English *whether* is rarely used:

He asked if they were all going or only some of them.

He asked if the mail had come in.

He was so old, and so shrunken, that it was difficult to tell, at first, if he was a man or woman.—WILLIAM MARCH, *The Little Wife*

3. *For "although" or "but."* In some idioms *if* or *even if* is used for *although* or *but*:

She was a good dog, if she did bark at strangers.

4. The use of *would have* after *if* rather than *had*, though increasing, is not established in Standard written English:

If he had [not *would have*] been there...

(See *as if, *like—as, *when, as, and if.)

**-ile** • Usage is divided on the pronunciation of words ending in *-ile*. Some of the more common are:

agile /aj′əl [aj′īl]/

fertile /fėr′tḷ [fėr′tīl]/

futile /fū′tḷ [fū′tīl]/

gentile /jen′tīl/

hostile /hos′tḷ [hos′tīl]/

infantile /in′fən tīl/, /in′fən tḷ/

juvenile /jü′və nḷ/, /jü′və nīl/

reptile /rep′tḷ—rep′tīl/

senile /sē′nīl/, /sē′nil/

textile /teks′tḷ/, /teks′tīl/

British pronunciation more commonly has -īl: /fėr′tīl/, /hos′tīl/, /rep′tīl/.

**ill, sick** • See \*sick, ill.

**illiterate** • Both *illiterate* and *literate* are used in a narrower and a wider sense: "(in)capable of reading and writing"; "(un)acquainted with what is written, hence (un)educated." Usage that is often loosely referred to as *illiterate* is called Nonstandard in this book. (For discussion and examples, see "Nonstandard English," p. 20.)

**illusion** • *Illusion*—"a deceptive appearance," as *an optical illusion, an illusion of wealth*—is, because of similarity in pronunciation, sometimes confused with *allusion*, "a reference to something": *He opened his talk with an allusion to recent events*. A *delusion* is a self-deception.

They all saw the oasis, but it turned out to be a mirage, an optical *illusion*.

In *Paradise Lost* Milton makes many *allusions* to the Bible.

He suffered from *delusions* of grandeur.

**Illustration (Pictorial)** • *Pictorial illustration* may greatly help the interest and understandability of an article—though it cannot (in spite of the picture magazines) take the place of text. Illustrations for articles and books are often arranged for by the publisher, but the writer can suggest possibilities or he can submit drawings or photographs. Many feature articles are accepted by newspapers and magazines largely because of their illustrations.

A student can often add considerably to the value of a paper by drawings or by snapshots. These can be inserted by tucking the corners into slits cut in the manuscript pages, so that they can be taken off after they have served their purpose; or gummed corners available in stationery shops may be used. Travel papers, narratives of experience, and explanations of processes profit especially from illustration. (Compare \*Diagrams, graphs, etc.)

**Imagery** • An image is a word or group of words that may make an appeal to one of the "senses": sight (*bright, yellow, thick brown hair*), hearing (*rumble, faraway shouts, three loud booms*), taste (*sweet, sour, a pickled pear*), smell (*jasmine, a blown-out candle*), touch (*smooth, glassy, a tweed coat*), and the muscular tension known as the kinesthetic sense (*squirm, jogging heavily along*). Obviously a word may appeal to more than one sense (*tweed, glassy, jasmine*), though in a specific context one would usually be dominant. Whether a reader's senses are actually "aroused" depends chiefly on his suggestibility. Some people are easily stimulated by words; some are more sensitive to one sense than to another. For the use of imagery in writing, it is enough that words *capable* of suggesting sensory images are present; we cannot be sure of the response of anyone but ourselves. But images—actually sensed or potential—are the foundation of much writing, of all in fact that does not deal principally with ideas.

Imagery is especially characteristic of poetry, in which ideas, states of mind, and feelings are often represented by images:

> Jack Ellyat felt that turning of the year
> Stir in his blood like drowsy fiddle-music
> And knew he was glad to be Connecticut-born
> And young enough to find Connecticut winter
> Was a black pond to cut with silver skates
> And not a scalping-knife against the throat.
> —STEPHEN VINCENT BENÉT, *John Brown's Body*, p. 22

Fiction, too, since it must present pictures of people and places and actions, has much imagery:

> The sun came in warm in long streaks across the floor, and the giant geranium plants made a pattern across its gold. When we touched our glasses, white circles of light would move on the walls and ceiling, and the cut-glass dish with the peaches in it made a rainbow-bar on the cloth.—JOSEPHINE JOHNSON, *Now in November*, p. 83

In explanatory prose, images are the basis of discussions of people, of experience and situations, of things and processes. Even in expressions of opinion and discussions of ideas, most writers keep in close touch with the visible and touchable world. Current writing is conspicuously concrete and imagistic.

Studying the images in a writer's work will usually show what has impressed him in his experience, what appeals to him—colors, lines, odors, what not—and your writing also should show images drawn from your experience. Images that come from your own experience and that definitely appeal to you will carry over clearly to a reader and are infinitely better than the trite roses and violets of accumulated literature. Don't take out of your writing an image that appeals to you unless you realize that in the context it is misleading. (See *Figures of speech, *Style § 2g.)

**Imaginative and factual writing** • See *Factual and imaginative writing.

**Imitative words and phrases** • A number of words seem to imitate, or at least suggest in their pronunciation, particular sounds: *bang, buzz, clank, swish, splash, whirr, pop, clatter, cuckoo, ping pong.* These words are established in the English vocabulary and will be found in dictionaries. It is possible to make new ones to fit specific sounds, and they are often necessary, especially in fiction. Sometimes it is better to use the conventional forms even when they are not very exact (*humph, uh huh*) rather than make new ones, which may do nothing except puzzle a reader.

When such words are used for special effect in writing they form a trait of style known as *onomatopoeia* /on′ə mat′ə pē′ə/. Imitative words or sounds in a series that suggest the action or idea or tone of the subject matter are a useful form of intensification of meaning, as in these justly famous lines from Pope's *An Essay on Criticism*:

> 'Tis not enough no harshness gives offense,
> The sound must seem an Echo to the sense:
> Soft is the strain when Zephyr gently blows,
> And the smooth stream in smoother numbers flows;
> But when loud surges lash the sounding shore,
> The hoarse, rough verse should like the torrent roar:
> When Ajax strives some rock's vast weight to throw,
> The line too labours, and the words move slow;
> ALEXANDER POPE, *An Essay on Criticism,* lines 364-371

Often a picture or a narrative can be sharpened by using an imitative word instead of a general or colorless word like *said* or *walked*: *barked, droned, snarled, whined*; *clattered, stamped, strutted.* Conspicuous striving for such words will make a passage seem melodramatic, but accurate words that come naturally will add to its effectiveness.

In *The Red Badge of Courage* Stephen Crane frequently uses imitative words to good effect:

> The regiment snorted and blew.... The song of the bullets was in the air and shells snarled among the tree-tops.... Near where they stood shells were flip-flapping and hooting.... Occasional bullets buzzed in the air and spanged into tree trunks....

**Immediate constituent** • Linguists use *immediate constituent,* usually abbreviated to *IC,* to indicate one of the elements into which a specific expression can be analyzed. The *IC*'s of a typical English sentence are the complete subject and the complete predicate, each of which may be made up of *IC*'s, which in turn may be analyzable into smaller elements. The analysis can be carried down to the elements of words (morphemes) and to the sounds (phonemes) of which they are composed. (For a phonemic analysis the sentence would have to be phonemically transcribed.)

| The | o l d | e s t | b o y | s |
|---|---|---|---|---|
| | Base form | Super-lative suffix | Base form | Plural suffix |
| Article (determiner) | Adjective | | Noun | |
| | Noun phrase | | | |
| Complete subject | | | | |

Shown at left and below is a diagram analysis of the immediate constituents and smaller elements of the sentence: *The oldest boys walked the greatest distances.*

| w a l k | e d | t h e | g r e a t | e s t | d i s t a n c e | s |
|---|---|---|---|---|---|---|
| Base form | Past tense suffix | Article (deter-miner) | Base form | Super-lative suffix | Base form | Plural suffix |
| | | | Adjective | | Noun | |
| | | | Noun phrase | | | |
| Verb | | Object | | | | |
| Complete predicate | | | | | | |

Like other diagrams, this is a device for analysis and exposition, useful to a specialist, a student of the language. Analyzing a sentence of average complexity requires a considerable amount of linguistic knowledge, especially if the suprasegmental *phonemes of pitch and juncture are included. The concept of immediate constituents, however, is basic to any analysis of language, especially for syntax, which examines the relations between elements in utterances. This approach makes visually clear the patterns of sentence structure and helps us to see how sentences are built. (References: Fries, *Structure,* pp. 256-273, and most recent books on linguistics.)

**immigrate—emigrate** • See *emigrate—immigrate.

**Imperative** • A verbal construction used in commands and requests is called an *imperative*; in such constructions usually no word occurs as a separate subject. (See *Commands and requests.)

**imply—infer** • A distinction is made by most careful educated users of English, and in college papers it is wise to keep the distinction. A writer or speaker *implies* something in his words or manner; a reader or listener *infers* something from what he reads or hears.

The dean implied, by the way he tilted his head and half closed his eyes, that he doubted my story.

One might infer from his opening words that the speaker was hostile to all social change.

But *infer* has been used so much in the sense of suggesting, expressing indirectly, that it is also given as a definition of *imply* in dictionaries.

**in •**
**1.** *Uses.*

*Preposition:* in the box in town in the rain
in a circle in training in words in bronze
*Adverb:* mix in They are not in. Put in the butter.
[Local: She wants in.]
*Adjective:* the in box
*Noun:* the ins and the outs
*Verb:* [local] to in the beets, to in the car

**2.** *In combinations.* In speech *in* is often used in combination with another preposition: *in back of, in behind, in between.*

In most writing these would be simply: *back of, behind, between.* (See *Prepositions § 3b.)

**in-, en- •** See *en-, in-.

**in—into—in to •** *In* generally shows location (literal or figurative); *into* generally shows direction:

He was in the house. He came into the house.
He was in a stupor. He fell into a deep sleep.

Informally *in* is often used for *into*:

He fell in the brook.

*In to* is the adverb *in* followed by the preposition *to*:

They went into the dining room. They went in to dinner.

**in-, un- •** *In-* or *un-* (variants *im-, il-*) prefixed to many words gives them a negative meaning: *inconsiderate, incapable, uneven, unlovable, unlovely, unloved.* If you are not sure whether a word takes *in-* or *un-*, you will have to consult a dictionary—an American dictionary, since British usage differs in many words. *Un-* is likely to be used with words from Old English and *in-* with words from Latin, but this is not a safe guide (witness *indigestible, undigested, inequality, unequal, inadvisable, unadvised*). A sample list follows:

| | | | |
|---|---|---|---|
| inadequate | †indistinguishable | immoral | uncontrollable |
| inadvisable | inept | impractical | uncontrolled |
| inartistic | †inescapable | unacceptable | undistinguished |
| inaudible | inexperienced | unadvised | unessential |
| incommunicable | infallible | unalterable | unnamed |
| incompatible | †infrequent | unbelievable | unnatural |
| incomplete | †insubstantial | uncertain | unnecessary |
| incomprehensible | †insupportable | uncollected | unrecognizable |
| inconclusive | illiberal | uncommu- | unresponsive |
| inconsequential | illiterate | nicative | unsustained |
| †indecipherable | immoderate | uncompleted | unversed |

Those marked † are also found with *un-*.

Not all words beginning with *in-* are negatives (*innate, insure, intoxicate*), and *invaluable* means having a value so great it cannot be determined; *inflammable* has apparently come to be considered so ambiguous as a warning that *flammable* has displaced it on tank trucks (see *Ambiguity § 5); *un-* is also tricky (see *unbend, unbending* in a dictionary).

**in connection with, connected with** • See *connected with, in connection with.

**in hope of, in hopes of** • See *hope.

**Incoherence** • Writing is incoherent when it lacks connection within itself or when the relationship between parts ( of a sentence, of a paragraph, of a whole paper) is not evident. (Various examples of incoherence are discussed in *Dangling modifiers, *Gerund § 3, *Participles. See also *Coherence.)

**Incomplete sentence** • See *Fragmentary sentence.

**incredible—incredulous** • A story or situation is *incredible* ("unbelievable"); a person is *incredulous* ("unbelieving"). (See *Ambiguity § 5.)

**Indefinite article** • See *a, an.

**Indefinite pronouns** • See *Reference of pronouns, *you.

**Indention or indentation** • *Indenting* in manuscript or printed copy is beginning the first line of a paragraph in from the left-hand margin. In longhand copy, paragraphs are indented about an inch, in typewritten copy from five to eight spaces.

*Hanging indention* is setting in all lines below the first line, as in many newspaper headlines, outlines (see *Outline form), headings, and addresses of *letters. If a line of verse is too long to stand on one line, the part brought over to the second line should be indented (see *Poetry):

> A line in long array where they wind betwixt green islands,
> They take a serpentine course, their arms flash in the sun—
>     hark to the musical clank,
>                     —WALT WHITMAN, "Cavalry Crossing a Ford"

Aside from these uses, indention is mainly a publisher's problem, treated in detail by the stylebooks (For information about indenting quotations, see *Quotation marks § 1d.)

**Independent clause** • See *Clauses.

**Indicative mood** • *Indicative mood* is a term from Latin grammar for the set of verb forms which express fact; in English it is applied to the usual form of the verb in sentences and clauses:

> They *sat* on the porch even though it *was* late October.
> *Will* you *come* if you *are invited?*

(See *Verbs; compare *Subjunctives, *Mood.)

**Indirect discourse (Indirect quotation)** • Quotations that are paraphrased or summarized in the writer's words instead of being quoted exactly as originally spoken or written are in indirect discourse:

> *Indirect:* He said he wouldn't take it if they gave it to him.
> *Direct:* He said, "I won't take it if they give it to me."

Notice that the tense of the verb changes in indirect discourse. (See *Quotation marks § 2b, *Tenses of verbs § 4, *Mood; see also *Commands and requests.)

**Indirect object** • See *Objects § 2.

**Indirect question** • An *indirect question* is a question restated at second hand:

> *Indirect:* He asked if everyone was all right.
> *Direct:* He asked, "Is everyone all right?"

(See *Questions § 2, *Tenses of verbs § 4, *whether.)

**Indo-European languages** • See *English language.

**infer—imply** • See *imply—infer.

**Infinitives** • *Infinitive* is a Latin grammatical term for a verb form expressing the general sense of the verb without restriction as to person or number. In English, there is no longer a distinctive infinitive form; instead, the bare form of the verb is used in the infinitive function. Usually *to* precedes the bare form, but after certain auxiliaries *to* does not occur. So-called infinitive constructions cause great difficulty to foreign learners of English, but native speakers generally need be concerned only with the divided usage discussed in the last part of § 5 and in § 6.

**1.** *Tenses.* What are traditionally called the infinitive forms are:

|  | Active | | Passive |
|---|---|---|---|
| | *simple* | *progressive* | |
| *Present:* | (to) ask | (to) be asking | (to) be asked |
| *Perfect:* | (to) have asked | (to) have been asking | (to) have been asked |

The present infinitive indicates a time the same as or future to that of the main verb: He is here now *to ask* you. . . . They had come *to ask* you. . . . He is coming (future) *to ask* you. . . .

The perfect infinitive primarily indicates action previous to the time of the main verb: I am glad *to have been* one of his boys. (See *Tenses of verbs § 3c, 4.)

**2.** *The "to" infinitive. To* is the "sign of the infinitive" used in most infinitive constructions—that is, it connects the infinitive to the *finite verb—but it is not part of the infinitive.

> They all tried *to get* in first.    He set out *to get* it.

**3.** *The "bare" infinitive.* After a few verbs (*can, may, must, shall, will, do, dare, need,* etc.) *to* is never or seldom used:

> I can *see.*    He must *carry* it.    We might *be seeing* him
> He does *care.*    It does me good *to see* him.

With some other verbs usage is divided:

> I helped him *to learn* to drive.    I helped him *learn* driving.
> You had better not *go.*    You had *to go.*
> He *dared* to go.    He *dared* go.

In short, clear, unemphatic series of infinitives in parallel constructions, the *to* is not repeated; in more Formal series, when the actions are not part of one general process, or when the separate verbs deserve emphasis, the *to* is repeated (see examples under § 4 [Subject] below).

**4.** *Other uses of infinitives.*
Subject:

> *To sit* and *smoke* and *think* and *dream* was his idea of pleasure.

> *To walk* around among these exhibits, *to see* the horse races where runners, trotters, and pacers with Kentucky and Tennessee pedigrees compete on a mile track, and then *to listen* to the political speakers discussing "purr-ins-a-pulls" and "the Const-ti-too-shun"—this made a

holiday for the farmers and city people who came.—CARL SANDBURG, *Abraham Lincoln: The Prairie Years,* 2:6

Object:

He wanted *to go* fishing.     He tries *to do* it every day.

Adjectival modifier:

wool *to spin,* money *to burn.*     They have plenty of fish *to eat.*

Adverbial modifier (to show purpose, result, etc.):

He bought *to sell* again.

Reporters are constantly on the move *to cover* important events.

Television tends *to become* a nuisance.

With auxiliaries:

He will *pass* this time. He didn't *dare* go along.

**5.** *Subject of infinitive.* Infinitives are increasingly used in subordinate constructions as alternatives to finite verbs:

It would be better *for you and me to discuss the matter* before calling in the others.

as the alternative to:

It would be better *if you and I discussed the matter* before calling in the others.

If the subject of the infinitive is a pronoun, it is in the accusative:

Supposing *them to be new men,* we all shouted, "Get off the grass."

Often these constructions are \*absolute constructions:

*To judge by the appearances,* the party must have been pretty rough.

*To make a long story short,* they didn't go.

For the pronoun after the infinitive of a linking verb that has no expressed subject, General English usually has the accusative pronoun; Formal would probably have a nominative, but the locution makes the pronoun prominent and might better be phrased differently.

*General:* I always wanted to be *him.*

*Formal:* I always wanted to be *he.* [*Or:* He was the one I always wanted to be.]

(Compare \*Participles § 3, 4, \*Gerund; see Jespersen, *Modern English Grammar,* VII:6.)

**6.** *Split infinitive.* See \*Split infinitive, \*Latin and English § 3.

(References: Curme, *Syntax,* Ch. 23; Jespersen, *Essentials of English Grammar,* Ch. 32; Roberts, pp. 359-367.)

**Inflection** • In grammar *inflection* refers to the change of

form by which some words indicate certain grammatical re-
lationships, as the plural of nouns or the past tense of verbs.
It includes *Declension, *Conjugation, and *Comparison. (For
English inflections see *Case and the articles referred to there,
*Plurals of nouns, *Pronouns, types and forms, *Verbs, *Com-
parison of adjectives and adverbs. Reference: Curme, *Parts of
Speech*.)

**Informal English** •
*Revision: The word or passage marked is too Informal
for the subject or for the style of the rest of the paper.* **Inf**
*Revise, making it more appropriate.*

*Informal English,* as described on pp. 18-20, is appropriate
in writing for some personal narratives and light topics, but
its words and constructions in General or Formal papers, except for an occasional intended effect, violate the tone. A conspicuously Informal expression marked on a paper should be
changed to one more characteristic of General English. (Articles dealing with Informal usage include *Collective nouns,
*Dates, *Function words.)

**institutions of higher learning** • This is a clumsy phrase, and
more abstract than *colleges and universities.* It would be convenient if we had one word for the notion, or a group word
as economical even as *secondary schools* for "high and preparatory schools." Either *colleges* or *universities* is often used to
apply to both.

**Intensive (reflexive) pronouns** • See *myself, *Pronouns, types
and forms § 4.

**Intensives** • Adverbs like *very, too, much,* and some constructions, like the superlative of adjectives and adverbs, are used
to emphasize meaning. If overused, they bore the reader, and
the intended emphasis is lost. (See *very, *Comparison of
adjectives and adverbs § 5, *himself, *myself. References:
Fries, *AEG,* pp. 200-206; Curme, *Parts of Speech,* pp. 48-50.)

**Interjections** • See *Exclamations, *Parts of speech.

**Interrogation point** • See *Question mark.

**Interrogative pronouns** • See *Pronouns, types and forms § 3.

**Interrogative sentences** • See *Questions.

**Interrupted sentence movement** • See *Commas § 4.

**into—in to—in** • See *in—into—in to.

**Intonation** • *Intonation* is a general term for the "melody" of a language, used by linguists to include somewhat varying groups of sound qualities but primarily patterns of pitch variation. Since these variations in pitch are closely bound up with stress and other related features of speech, the total phenomenon is difficult to analyze; some account of it is given under *Phonemes § 2. We acquire the intonation of our own language by unconscious imitation and rarely make a mistake in it, but it is usually the last quality attained in learning a second language—witness the odd melody of someone who has learned English as a second language in his later years. And you may assume that your intonation of the modern foreign language you have studied sounds just as odd to a native speaker of that language. Intonation is one of the most conspicuous differences between British and American English, especially obvious in questions.

**intramural** • *Intramural* has no hyphen. It means etymologically "within the walls," specifically college activities carried on by groups of the same college.

**Intransitive verbs** • See *Transitive and intransitive verbs.

**Introductions** • See *Beginning paragraphs.

**Introductory words** • See *namely and other introductory words.

**Inversion** • *Inversion* means placing the verb before its subject—a rather uncommon order in English except in questions. It also occurs, however, in a few established constructions: *What a fool is he! Long may it wave. Out gushed the water. Among the callers was Mrs. Brown.*
  In questions inversion is the regular syntactical pattern, with the auxiliary before the subject and the infinitive or participle after it: *Is he coming? Will she go? Did he like it?*

**invite** • The word *invite* is ordinarily a verb. Its use as a noun /in'vīt/ is hardly even Informal except facetiously in speech: *Did you get an invite?* (Reference: Bryant, p. 116.)

**Irony** • *Irony* implies something markedly different, at times even the opposite, from what is said. Light irony is humorous —as in the greeting "Lovely day!" when the weather is wretched. Severe irony is usually a form of sarcasm or satire.

**irregardless** • *Irregardless* is not used in reputable writing and better avoided in speech. The second negative, the prefix *ir-*, is perhaps an effort to reinforce the *-less* suffix, perhaps the result of analogy with *irregular, irresistible, irresponsible.*

**Irregular verbs** • See *Principal parts of verbs.

**-ise, -ize** • See *-ize, -ise.

**it** • *It* is the neuter third person singular pronoun, used to refer to an object, a situation, or an idea. *It* is also used to refer to a baby or an animal whose sex is unknown or unimportant for the statement (The dog wagged *its* tail) and in certain impersonal statements about the weather and events in general (impersonal *it*):

> It rained all night.    It's the way things go.

*It* is also used to refer to the idea of a preceding statement:

> We changed two tires in record time. It is not easy to do on a dark and rainy night.

Sentences beginning "It is . . ." or "It was . . ." (anticipatory subject) are often wordy and weakening, since they have put a colorless locution in the emphatic beginning of the sentence:

> [It was] then [that] his wife had taken to going with other men.

But this *preparatory it* may be useful when what it represents could not conveniently be placed in the usual position:

> It is no use trying to evade the question asked you.

*It* may also stand in the object position:

> He always made it a rule to check every one of his quotations.

*It* is also used in a number of idiomatic constructions:

> There would have been no party if it hadn't been for your help.
> You'll catch it if you don't hurry home.
> We'll make a night of it.

(See *there is, there are, *its, *It's me. References: Emerson Beauchamp, Jr., "A Study of 'It': Handbook Treatment and Magazine Use," *American Speech*, 1951, 26:173-180; for history see Jespersen, *Modern English Grammar*, VII:6.)

**its—it's** • The possessive pronoun does not have an apostrophe:

> The dog wagged its tail.    A car is judged by its performance.

Associate *its* with *his* and *hers*.
*It's* is the contraction of *it is* or *it has*:

> It's going to rain.    It's rained for over a week now.

**It's me** • The argument over "It's me" is a case of narrow theory versus established practice. The theory is that after the verb *be* the subject form should always be used, but this theory is consistently contradicted by the actual usage of good speakers (see \*be § 2).

We tend to use the nominative form of a pronoun when it is the subject and stands close to the verb—usually before it— and to use the accusative in most other positions, especially when it comes after the verb—in "object territory," as Charles C. Fries has called it. For this reason it is natural to say *it's me, it's us, it's him, it's her.* (Compare \*who, whom.)

All the large grammars of English regard *it's me* as acceptable colloquial usage—and since the expression is not likely to occur except in speech, that gives it full standing. Fowler approves it, and one of the "judges" in Marckwardt and Walcott's *Facts about Current English Usage* (p. 108) wrote:

> *I* sounds quite mad in certain cases; e.g., pointing to a photo: "Which is I?"!!! "Oh, I see, that's I"!!! Absolutely non-English, hang all the grammarians on earth.

*Us* and *him* after *be* are less common, but usage is divided. *Current English Usage* found "If it had been *us,* we would admit it" uncertainly established and "I'll swear that was *him*" and "I suppose that's *him*" disputable. Very often speakers who try to be correct resort to some circumlocution, saying instead of "It was *she* (or *her*)" "That's who it was."

The upshot of the discussion is that in their natural settings "It's me," "It was him all right," "Something was wrong—was it him or the crowd?" are appropriate. (See \*Case. References: Marckwardt and Walcott, pp. 77-78; Wallace Rice, "Who's there? Me," *American Speech,* 1933, 8:58-63; Robertson, pp. 492-503; Fries, *AEG,* p. 91; Bryant, pp. 120-121.)

**Italics** • In manuscript, both longhand and typewritten, italics are shown by underlining. (Specific uses of italics are listed in \*Underlining. See also \*Foreign words in English § 3, \*Ships' names, \*Titles of articles, books, etc.)

**-ize, -ise** • English has many verbs ending in the sound of /īz/, some of which are spelled *-ise* and some *-ize*; in many, usage is divided. American usage, differing somewhat from British, prefers *-ize,* as in the following common verbs of this class:

| | | | |
|---|---|---|---|
| anesthetize | dramatize | revolutionize | sympathize |
| apologize | memorize | sensitize | visualize |
| characterize | realize | standardize | |

In the following, *-ise* is the usual spelling:

| | | | |
|---|---|---|---|
| advise | despise | exercise | surmise |
| arise | devise | revise | surprise |
| chastise | disguise | supervise | |

Both *-ize* and *-ise* are commonly found in:

advertise—advertize     analyze—analyse     criticize—criticise

In general, follow American usage. When in doubt, consult a good dictionary.

Some readers object to recent extension of the verbs in *-ize,* such as *concertize, finalize, picturize,* but aside from the fact that any new word is a bit disconcerting, there seems little reason for the objection unless the new verb duplicates in meaning one already in common use. Sometimes the form expresses something the already existing word cannot do: *Moisturize* the air in the house (*moisten* would hardly do).


**J** • *J* is a common spelling for the "soft *g*" sound at the beginning of syllables: *jam, jet, jibe, journey, jury.* At the end of a syllable the sound is variously spelled, often by *-dge: edge* /ej/, *judge* /juj/. (For other spellings of the sound see *G § 2.)

An approximation of some foreign sounds of *j* is attempted in particular words: Latin /y/, *Hallelujah*; French /zh/, *bijou* /bē′zhü/, *jabot* /zha-bō′/; Spanish /h/ *marijuana* /mä′ri-hwä′nə/, German /y/, *jaeger* /yā′gər/.

In the alphabet of the Romans, *i* and *j* were merely different forms of the same letter; though the letter had both a vowel and a consonant function in Latin, no attempt was made to distinguish those functions in writing. Only in recent times have the two forms gained a separate place in Western alphabets and come to represent different sounds.

**Jabberwocky** • Linguists have found the *Jabberwocky* opening stanza from Lewis Carroll's *Alice Through the Looking Glass* ('Twas brillig, and the slithy toves/ Did gyre and gimble in the wabe. . . .) a convenient device to show that it is possible to recognize the forms and grammatical functions of English words without reference to meaning. Similarly you have no difficulty in identifying four parts of speech and four inflectional forms in: *The harbiger ligs′ sollips drave brustrily in the stroks.*

**Jargon** •
1. *Applied to style.* Sir Arthur Quiller-Couch popularized *jargon* as the name for verbal fuzziness of various sorts—wordi-

ness, a heavy reliance on abstract words, and unnecessarily complicated sentence structure. We also apply the term to the special vocabulary developed by experts: art criticism has its jargon and so does anthropology. (See *Big words, *Deadwood, *Gobbledygook, *Legal language, *Wordiness. References: Sir Arthur Quiller-Couch, *On the Art of Writing,* New York, 1916, pp. 100-126; Richard M. Weaver, *The Ethics of Rhetoric,* Chicago, 1953, pp. 186-210.)

**2.** *Linguistic sense.* *Jargon* (also *pidgin* and *creole*) is a word used among linguists to mean a dialect composed of the mixture of two or more languages. Jargons involving English are used by non-English-speaking peoples in doing business with the English. The best known of these are the Chinook jargon of the Pacific Northwest, beach-la-Mar (or *bêche-de-mer*) of the Pacific Islands, and the Chinese-English jargon, pidgin English. (References: Otto Jespersen, *Language,* New York, 1922, pp. 216-236; R. B. LePage (ed.), *Proceedings of the Conference on Creole Language Studies,* London and New York, 1961.)

**job, position** • *Job* is General for the Formal *position*: *He got a job at an oil refinery.* The word *position* has more dignity and what it refers to is usually thought of as better paid. *Job* is Informal for *something made,* such as an automobile or refrigerator ("a nice little job there").

**Jones—plural and possessive forms** • The plural of *Jones* and of most nouns ending in an /s/ or /z/ sound is formed by adding *-es,* pronounced as a separate syllable: *Joneses* /jōn′zəz/, *consciences* /kon′shən səz/, *Jameses.* When two syllables ending in an /s/ or /z/ sound are in the root word, usage is divided: *the Moses* or *the Moseses.*

In the possessive, usage is divided. We may write (and, less frequently, say) *Dr. Jones'* /jōnz/ *office*; or write and say *Dr. Jones's* /jōn′zəz/ *office.* Probably the first form is the more common in writing. Also: For *goodness'* sake, *Charles'* collection, though *Charles's* /chärl′zəz/ is equally reputable.

The possessive plural is pronounced the same as the plural and is written by adding (') to the plural form: *Joneses',* *Moses'* or *Moseses'.*

**Journalese** • See *Newspaper English.

**judgment—judgement** • *Judgment* is the more common American spelling.

**Juncture** • See *Phonemes § 2c.

**just** • Most readers find *just* redundant in expressions like *just exactly* and *just perfect*.

**K** • The /k/ sound, as in *keep,* is spelled *c* (*call, actual, cute*), *cc* (*accord*), *ck* (*back, track*), and also with other letters (*queen, chord, ox, strength, cheque*). *K* before *n* is now silent in a number of words (*knave, kneel, knife*) from Anglo-Saxon, where it was pronounced.

Business sometimes changes *c* to *k* and *qu* to *kw* (*Kwick Kleaners*), either to make the alliteration more obvious or to make a trademark. (See Louise Pound, "The Kraze for 'K,' " *American Speech,* 1925, 1:43-44.) Such substitution is not acceptable in ordinary writing.

**kid** • As a noun *kid* is Informal for "child," "youngster"; *kids* is the plural (*kidders* is a local plural). As a verb it is Informal for "joke," "tease"; from this verb comes the Informal noun *kidder.*

**kind, sort** • *Kind* and *sort* are both singular nouns in form:

This kind of person is a menace at any party.
This sort of thing shouldn't be allowed.

As singular nouns, they are expected to take singular demonstrative adjectives in General and Formal writing:

That kind of story doesn't interest me.
Problems of this sort bother him.

But *kind* and *sort* are so closely associated with the noun they stand before that they seem like modifiers and in speech and Informal writing the demonstrative adjectives used with them agree with the principal noun of the construction:

Those sort of ideas in his head and that sort of life with his wife. ...—A. S. M. HUTCHINSON, *If Winter Comes,* p. 324

You next reach the conclusion that, as these kind of marks have not been left by any other animal than man....—T. H. HUXLEY, "The Method of Scientific Investigation"

The *Oxford English Dictionary* has examples of *these kind of* and *these sort of* from the fourteenth century to the present, many of them from the "best authors." Fries found the plural regularly used with *kind* and *sort* by his Group I (Standard English) writers (*AEG,* p. 58). Only the unnodding vigilance of editorial copy readers keeps the construction from being as common in writing as in speech. Jespersen, p. 202, even suggests that *kind* and *sort* be regarded as unchanged plurals and therefore correct. But the construction is still felt by many to be Nonstandard. (References: Curme, *Syntax,* pp. 544-546; Bryant, pp. 215-216.)

**kind of, sort of** • *Kind of* and *sort of* are used as Informal adverbs, equivalent to *rather* or *somewhat* in more Formal usage:

I feel kind of logy today.     It was sort of dull, but he said a lot.

Especially in writing, these would be:

I was rather [somewhat, a little, very, pretty] tired.
It was pretty [very, rather] dull, but he said a good deal.

**kind of a, sort of a** • Though there is objection to *kind of a* and *sort of a,* they are very common in General English and fairly common among respected writers:

I want to find someone on the earth so intelligent that he welcomes opinions which he condemns—I want to be this kind of a man and I want to have known this kind of a man.—JOHN JAY CHAPMAN, *Letters,* p. 124

Now, suppose the battle of Salamis had been fought, not in the full light of Greek history, but in the misty dawn of the Epos, what sort of a story should we have had?—GILBERT MURRAY, *The Rise of the Greek Epic,* p. 200

These two sentences from the same short story show the two idioms in differing degrees of Formality, in considerably different tempos:

...he had never once brought her a comical, stuffed animal or any sort of an object with a picture of a Scottie on it.

Bob McEwen wasn't the sort of man to do a sentimental thing like that unless he meant it.—SALLY BENSON, *People Are Fascinating,* pp. 30-31

In educated speech, *sort of* and especially *kind of* are preferred to *rather* or *somewhat.* But in writing one of the last two would be usual. (Reference: Jean Malmstrom, "*Kind of* and Its Congeners," *English Journal,* 1960, 49:498-499.)

In Formal writing *kind of a* and *sort of a* should be avoided, but they are accepted General idioms.


**L** • *L* is a "liquid" consonant that varies considerably in quality in the speech of individuals and groups and with its position in a word: *land, leaf, almost, silly, fill;* it is the only letter to represent this group of related sounds (*phoneme) in English.

*L* is silent in a few common words: *almond* (usually), *folk, half, salmon, talk, walk, would, yolk.* It is often not sounded in other words as in *golf course* /gôf′kôrs′/. Despite its frequency in spelling, the doubled *l* sounds just like the single one; compare *collar—color, llama—lamb, fell—fail.*

In many syllables no specific vowel is sounded before an *l*, and the pronunciation can be indicated by "syllabic *l*" /l̞/: *marble* /mär′bl̞/, *tickle* /tik′l̞/.

**lady** • See *man, woman; compare *female.

**laissez faire, laisser faire** • The spelling is still French, and the pronunciation /les′ā fār′/ still an attempt at French, but the word is not italicized except in conspicuously Formal writing.

**Language** • See *English language.

**Language study** • See *Linguistics, *Usage.

**last, at long last** • A recently revived archaic idiom, *at long last* is slightly more emphatic than *at last,* at least when it is spoken, but the phrase may have a British or Formal connotation, as in this:

> An economic power born of the travail of men at long last asserts its title to political dominance.—HAROLD J. LASKI, *The Rise of Liberalism*

**last, latest** • In Formal usage *last* refers to the final item of a series; *latest,* the most recent in time of a series which may or may not be continued:

> His latest (we hope it won't be his last) biography is of Peter Cooper.

This distinction is not strictly kept, so that both words are used as superlatives of *late.*

**last—latter, former—first** • See *former—first, latter—last.

**later, latter** • See *latter, later.

**Latin and English** •
1. *Latin words.* Many Latin words came into English in early periods of the language, either directly or through French, and are no longer felt to be foreign words: *patience, candle, receive, wine* (see *English language). Most borrowings from Latin are subject to the same process of anglicizing as other *foreign words in English, and in general they are pronounced

as English words—*agenda* /ə jen′də/, *erratum* /i rā′təm/ or /i rä′təm/—instead of according to the system of pronunciation now taught in Latin classes.

Since Latin is dead as a first language and rare as a second language, new borrowings come in through written rather than spoken use and belong to the Formal dialects, used chiefly in science, law, religion, medicine, and academic work. Since practically all college work was carried on in Latin until about 1750, and a good deal of it later than that, considerable Latin is preserved in college use. Many diplomas are in Latin, and at some institutions the commencement formulas are in Latin. At a more routine level, several Latin words and abbreviations are used in the footnotes of academic research (*ibid., passim, supra, infra, loc. cit.*), though there is a tendency to use English words for many of these. Prefixes of Latin origin (*ante-, ex-, in-, pre-, re-, sub-*) and other compounding elements, such as *uni-* (*unilateral*), *bi-* (*biweekly*), are active in forming new English words. At present scientific words are being formed more from Greek than from Latin elements.

**2.** *Latin forms.* English continues to use the Latin forms for some words that are used principally in the Formal dialects (\**alumnus—alumna, bacillus—bacilli*), but those commonly used have either English plurals or both (*formula, formulas* or *formulae*; *focus, focuses* or *foci*; *stadium, stadiums* or *stadia*). (See \*Plurals of nouns § 4, \*data.)

**3.** *Latin and English grammar.* The first and most later English grammars were composed by men thoroughly familiar with Latin, many of whom believed that English should be a language like Latin. As a result, English, which was a Germanic language in structure, was described in terms of Latin grammar, and rules were devised for making the language fit the picture.

The fact that English was first described in terms of Latin grammar may be one reason for the old taboo of the \*split infinitive (which would be impossible in Latin because the infinitive is one word, as in *laborare,* where English has *to work*) and of putting a preposition at the end of a sentence (\*Prepositions § 3d), which almost never occurs in Latin but is a characteristic English idiom.

Only recently has English grammar begun to be based squarely on a careful examination of the English language itself and freed from some of the categories and rules of Latin grammar. (See \*Linguistics. Reference: K. W. Dykema, "Where Our Grammar Came From," *College English,* 1961, 22:455-461.)

**latter—last, former—first** • See \*former—first, latter—last.

**latter, later** • *Latter* /lat'ər/ and *later* /lā'tər/ are often carelessly confused in spelling. The habit of reading your copy aloud to yourself should catch this type of error. (See *former —first, latter—last.)

**lay—lie** • In much spoken English the work of these two verbs is done by one (*lay*; *lay* or *laid*; *laid*). In writing they are regularly distinguished:

lie ("to recline," intransitive), lay, lain
lay ("to place," transitive) , laid, laid

In Standard English the distinctions are these: You *lie* down for a rest or *lie* down on the job; a farm *lies* in a valley. You *lay* a floor, *lay* a book on the table, *lay* a bet, *lay* out clothes. Yesterday you *lay* down to rest (in speech often indistinguishable from *laid*); you *laid* a book on the table. Egg laying is *lay, laid, laid.*

**-le words** • A large and interesting group of English verbs ends in *-le—fiddle, giggle, meddle, tickle, waddle, whistle, whittle*—in which the ending usually suggests an action continued or habitually repeated. In spelling, lab*el*, mant*el* (the shelf), mod*el*, and nick*el* give some trouble because they are exceptions to the usual English spelling of this final syllable.

**lead, led** • *Lead* and *led* show the confusion we suffer because English spelling represents one sound by different symbols. *Lead* /lēd/, the present tense of the verb, gives no trouble; but *led,* the past tense, is often incorrectly spelled with *ea* by analogy with *read* /rēd/, *read* /red/, and the noun *lead.*

Please *lead* the horse away.
*Lead* poisoning *led* to his death.

**Leaders** • *Leaders,* or *period leaders,* are a line of spaced periods used to guide the reader's eye across a page. They are often used in statistical tables and the table of contents of a book:

In typed copy, hyphens are often used instead of periods.

**Leading question** • See *Questions § 3.

**learn—teach** • Nonstandard English often uses *learn* in the sense of *teach*: *He learned me how to tie six kinds of knots.*

Standard usage makes the distinction: *He taught me how to tie six kinds of knots. I learned how to tie knots from him.*

**leave—let** • See *let—leave.

**led, lead** • See *lead, led.

**-ledge, -lege** • Two common words are spelled with the ending *-ledge*: *acknowledge* (*acknowledging, acknowledgment*), *knowledge*. Do not confuse them with words spelled with *-lege*: *allege* (*alleged, alleging*), *college, sacrilege* (*sacrilegious*); also *ledge* but *legend*.

**Legal language** • Most legal matters are carried on in a style bristling with long series of synonyms ("do hereby give, grant, bargain, sell and convey"), archaic or foreign (French, Latin) words for everyday things and situations, abbreviations and stereotyped phrases that puzzle laymen and sometimes lawyers themselves. The need for certain technical words is great, but the reason for much of the jargon is unconsidered tradition. Perhaps it must be tolerated in legal business, but lawyers and others who have much to do with law should realize that it is a trade dialect (*shoptalk).

Many lawyers and judges write with distinction, using only the technical terms demanded by the subject. Although they use an appropriately Formal style and must allude to cases that give precedents, they still find room for allusion to general experience, without any loss of exactness.

A brief dissenting opinion of Mr. Justice Holmes illustrates a compact but readable judicial style. A majority of the Supreme Court had decided that the State of Ohio could tax a membership in the New York Stock Exchange owned by a resident of Ohio, on the ground that it was personal property, not like real estate, which would be taxed by the state in which it lay.

The question whether a seat in the New York Stock Exchange is taxable in Ohio consistently with the principles established by this Court seems to me more difficult than it does to my brethren. All rights are intangible personal relations between the subject and the object of them created by law. But it is established that it is not enough that the subject, the owner of the right, is within the power of the taxing State. He cannot be taxed for land situated elsewhere, and the same is true of personal property permanently out of the jurisdiction. It does not matter, I take it, whether the interest is legal or equitable, or what the machinery by which it is reached, but the question is whether the object of the right is so local in its foundation and prime meaning that it should stand like an interest in land.

If left to myself I should have thought that the foundation and substance of the plaintiff's right was the right of himself and his associates personally to enter the New York Stock Exchange building and to do business there. I should have thought that all the rest was incidental to that and that that on its face was localized in New York. If so, it does not matter whether it is real or personal property or that it adds to the owner's credit and facilities in Ohio. The same would be true of a great estate in New York land.—*Representative Opinions of Mr. Justice Holmes,* edited by Alfred Lief, pp. 265-266

(References: Benjamin N. Cardozo, *Law and Literature,* New York, 1931, pp. 3-40; F. A. Philbrick, *Language and the Law,* New York, 1949.)

**lend** • See *loan as a verb.

**less—fewer** • *Fewer* refers only to number and things that are counted:

Fewer cars were on the road.      Fewer than sixty came.

In Formal usage *less* refers only to amount or quantity and things measured:

There was a good deal less tardiness in the second term [amount].
There was even less hay than the summer before.

*Fewer* seems to be declining in use and *less* often takes its place:

Less hands were required for this work....—KENNETH BURKE, *Attitudes Toward History,* p. 175

...but polled only a sliver of additional votes and won three less seats.—*Foreign Policy Bulletin,* Mar. 3, 1950, p. 2

Many readers find this usage stylistically objectionable.

**less, lesser** • Both are used as comparatives (of *little*)—*less* more usually referring to size or quantity (less time, less food); *lesser,* a Formal word, referring to value or importance (the lesser of two evils, a lesser writer).

**let—leave** • A common Nonstandard idiom is the use of *leave* where Standard English has *let.* Both uses are shown in this sentence by a student obviously making a transition between the two varieties:

In high school I was cured of the practice of leaving [Nonstandard] notebooks go, but I fell into the habit of letting [Standard] homework slide.

*Let*: let it go, let it lie where it is.
*Leave*: And so we leave him going happily away. Leave it where it is.

The meanings of *leave* and *let* are so close—dictionary definitions use one in defining the other—in all varieties of English that it is hardly surprising to find the semantic function of *let* in one variety being performed by *leave* in another and the other way around. The history of the two words also shows this fluctuation, even in Standard English. But recent dictionaries in their description of Standard practice indicate substitution only in *Leave* (or *let*) *me* (*him, her*) *alone.* (Reference: Bryant, pp. 127-129.)

**let's** • *Let's,* the *imperative contraction of *let us,* needs an apostrophe. Though *let's us go, let's you and me go* are common in speech, they have no place in writing.

**Letters** •
1. *General observations on correspondence.*

*a*—Materials. A good quality of stationery is worth its cost in the good impression it helps make on the reader. The stationery stores are full of novelties, which may appeal to one's taste, but the standard sizes and styles of paper are never outmoded and are usually cheaper and of better quality:

Note paper—A four-page sheet to be folded once across the middle for the envelope.

Club paper—A sheet about 7¼ by 11 inches, with two folds fitting an envelope 3¾ by 7½.

Business letter paper—8½ by 11 inches, to be folded twice across for a long envelope or folded across the middle and then twice more for the ordinary envelope about six inches long.

*b*—Styles. The pages should appeal to the reader's eye: good margins, centering the body of the letter on the page so that the whole presents a neatly proportioned appearance, spacing the parts of the letter so that they are distinct but still form a unit, and so on. The paragraphs are usually short, three or four sentences or less, and spaced distinctly.

Ingenuity can usually find a way of subduing even long addresses that must sometimes be used in headings. Find an arrangement of the lines that looks well in your typing or longhand.

Style in indenting at the end of display lines is divided. In typed letters a straight lining at the left of the heading and inside address is more usual now than *indention:

| | |
|---|---|
| *Straight form—more common* | *Indented form—less common* |
| Graham, Sutton and Company | Graham, Sutton and Company |
| 1007 E. Newgate Street | 1007 E. Newgate Street |
| Chicago, Illinois 60603 | Chicago, Illinois 60603 |

In longhand letters the indented form is perhaps more common.

The form of the address on the envelope should be consistent with that used for the heading and the address on the first page of the letter; either the straight or the indented form should be used throughout. Commas are not now used at the ends of the lines of address or heading:

|  *Indented form* | *Straight form* |
|---|---|
| Graham, Sutton and Company | Graham, Sutton and Company |
| 1007 E. Newgate Street | 1007 E. Newgate Street |
| Chicago, Illinois 60603 | Chicago, Illinois 60603 |

*c*–Envelopes. The first requirements of the address on the envelope are completeness and clearness, for the sake of the post office. Address your mail to street and number. Always include the ZIP codes of both the mailing address and the return address.

**2.** *Business letters.* Since business letters usually pass between people who are not acquainted or at least for whom the immediate occasion for writing is not friendship, certain matters of form are important in handling routine information.

The writer's complete address is necessary, either in a printed letterhead or in a written heading, to serve as an address for the reply. An inside address is conventional (and useful when the letter is dictated or when several are being written at the same time or when a carbon is to be filed). In addressing a firm, *Messrs.* is not often used in the United States. The salutations are:

Dear Sir:          Gentlemen:          Dear Sirs:
Dear Madam:          Ladies: [Formal or showy, *Mesdames:*]

When a letter is intended for a particular member of a firm, this form is sometimes used:

>Graham, Sutton and Company
>1007 E. Newgate Street
>Chicago, Illinois 60603
>
>Attention Mr. Stephen Lange
>
>Gentlemen:

A less Formal and more direct form of address is more common.

>Mr. Stephen Lange
>Graham, Sutton and Company
>1007 E. Newgate Street
>Chicago, Illinois 60603
>
>Dear Mr. Lange:

The body of a business letter should be clear, direct, and as brief as is consistent with clearness. A separate paragraph is used for each item or for each subdivision of the message. The tone may be curt in routine matters—amateurs are apt to indulge in unnecessary explanation—or it may be full and persuasive. All relevant information should be given, especially in letters asking questions or outlining plans.

The desire for brevity should not lead to a telegraphic style or shortcuts in expression. The old tags like "Yours received and contents noted," "In reply to your favor of the 12th inst.," and "Would say" have disappeared entirely from the correspondence of careful business houses.

The best way to become informed on business letters is to study the practice of reputable companies. If you are specially interested in business correspondence, start a collection of the best examples that come your way. The close of a business letter is:

Yours truly,        Sincerely yours,        Very truly yours,

or some such formula. Only the first word is capitalized and the phrase is followed by a comma.

Although in Formal correspondence a woman does not use *Mrs.* or *Miss* with her name in her signature, in Informal and business correspondence it is frequently used and is a courtesy to the receiver of the letter, who may otherwise not know whether to reply to *Mrs.* or *Miss.* The title should be restricted to the typed signature, which should always be included as well as the written one.

(Mrs.) Dorothy Olson        (Miss) Dorothy Olson
Dorothy Olson        (Mrs. Henry Olson)

(See *Business English. Recent manuals of business writing will give further details of form and suggestions for content.)
**3.** *Personal letters.*

*a*–Form. The form of personal letters varies with the intimacy between the writer and recipient. No heading except the date is needed between regular correspondents, but the writer's address in the heading is often a convenience and is a necessity in letters to occasional correspondents.

The salutation varies:

Dear Bob,        Dear Miss Breckenridge,
Dear Miss Breckenridge: (The colon is more Formal.)
*Formal*: My dear Miss Breckenridge:

Formal personal letters, especially between professional men who are not intimate, may have the salutation "Dear Sir:" and the recipient's name and address at the bottom, flush with the left margin.

The complimentary close ranges from "Yours" or any other expression of sentiment to "Yours sincerely," "Cordially yours,"

"Yours very truly," between people little acquainted.

*b*–Tone and style. Letters to relatives and friends are like conversation, and the style will ordinarily be Informal or whatever you would use when face to face with the recipient. But, as in so much conversation, we often sink to our laziest in letters to the people we write the oftenest. It is worth while occasionally to read over a letter to see if *we* would enjoy receiving it, to see if we have told enough to make the incidents interesting, to see if we have written with reasonable care and are paying our readers the courtesy they deserve in neatness and appropriate expression.

(For Formal invitations and so on, see *Social correspondence.)

**Levels of usage** • In earlier editions of this book the varieties of usage in English were called *levels*. But since *levels* suggests a value judgment, *varieties* (a more accurate term) is now used. (See "The varieties of English," pp. 2-31.)

**Lexical meaning** • In linguistics a distinction is often made between grammatical or structural meaning and lexical meaning. In *Birds were killed,* the information which *bird* and *kill* give us is of the sort regularly provided by a dictionary or lexicon—hence lexical meaning; the information given by the *s* of *birds* (plural), *were* (past tense, passive voice), and the *ed* of *killed* (past participle in this position) is of the sort provided by our awareness of the structure or grammar of the language— hence grammatical or structural meaning. When we fully understand the sentence we have grasped its total meaning.

**Lexicography** • See *Dictionary.

**liable—likely—apt** • See *likely—apt—liable.

**lie** • See *lay—lie.

**lighted—lit** • Both forms are in good use as the past tense and past participle of *light*. *Lighted* is more common as the adjective and past participle:

a lighted lamp      He had lighted a fire.

*Lit* is perhaps more common as the past tense.

He lit a cigaret. [Or: He lighted a cigaret.]

**lightning, lightening** • The flash before the thunder is *lightning*; *lightening* comes from the verb *lighten, to make lighter,* meaning either "to reduce weight or darkness."

**like—as** •

**1.** *As prepositions.* In all varieties of English *like* is used as a preposition introducing a comparison:

> The description fits him like a glove.
> Habit grips a person like an octopus.
> She took to selling like a duck to water.

*As* seems to be increasing in use in this position:

> He was built as a sword fish.... —ERNEST HEMINGWAY, *The Old Man and the Sea*

**2.** *As conjunctions.*

*a*–In all varieties of English *as, as if,* and *as though* are used as conjunctions introducing clauses of comparison:

> People try to get to college as they used to try to get to heaven.
> Habit grips a person as an octopus does.
> It looked as if he would land flat, but he entered the water perfectly.
> He walked as though he was hurt.

*b*–*Like* appears in both educated and uneducated usage as a conjunction introducing clauses of comparison. Probably the most widely known recent example is:

> Winston tastes good like a cigarette should.—*Advertising slogan*

*c*–In the last few years the use of *like* as a conjunction has greatly increased, and it is certainly now within the range of Standard English:

> She looked now like she had looked the last times he had seen her. —MORLEY CALLAGHAN, *Now That April's Here*, p. 22
> "Suddenly everybody wanted to look like he came from Harvard, or like he thought everyone looked at Harvard," says Grossman. —*Time,* Feb. 28, 1964, p. 83

Historically both forms have a respectable ancestry, since both are parts of the older *like as* ("Like as a father pitieth his children ..."). The speakers of some regions have taken *as,* of others *like.* A case might be made for *like* as preferable from the standpoint of meaning, because *as* has more meanings and so is relatively less exact in a comparison. But many people are prejudiced against the use of *like* as a conjunction, perhaps because they associate it with advertising and radio comedy programs, and consequently writers should avoid it except in distinctly Informal papers. It is a good instance of change in usage, and of resistance to it. *Like for* rather than *like* alone is common in speech, especially in the South, but is rarely found in print. (References: Curme, *Syntax,* pp. 281-282; Pooley, pp. 153-155; "Current English Forum," *College English,* 1952, 13:463-464; Bryant, pp. 133-135.)

**3.** *Like* also functions as a noun, verb, adjective, and adverb; *as* also functions as an adverb and pronoun.

**like, similar to** • See *similar to.

**likely—apt—liable** • The principal meanings of these words are:

*likely*: expected, probably
*apt*: tending toward, naturally fit
*liable*: possible (of an unpleasant event); responsible (as for damages)

*Likely* is the most commonly needed of the three. *Apt* is widely used in the sense of *likely*, as well as in its own narrower meaning, and is so recorded in dictionaries. The use of *liable* in the sense of *likely* is common, but because of the prejudice against the usage it should be confined to Informal speech:

It's *likely* [or, *apt*; or, Informally, *liable*] to rain when the wind is southwest.

**Limiting adjectives** • See *Adjectives, types and forms § 3c.

**line** • *Line* is business English (What's your line?—a line of goods) or Informal (He handed her a line). As a *counter word it is usually *deadwood and could better be left out:

My own experience along business lines [that is, *in business*] has been slight.

Another book along the same lines as *Microbe Hunters* [similar to *Microbe Hunters*], but with a fine story, is *Arrowsmith*.

**Linguistics** • Linguistics has been defined as the scientific study of language. A more modest definition would be the systematic study of human languages. Scientific study is today commonly associated with such natural sciences as physics, chemistry, and biology, whose conclusions lend themselves to objective verification more readily than those arrived at by investigators of human behavior. Since speech is a uniquely human phenomenon, the systematic study of it remains, despite the assistance received from other disciplines, a humanistic study, a study whose ultimate objectives are based on humane values. Linguistics is scientific, nevertheless, both in the rigor and objectivity of its methods and in the technical help it has received from the natural and social sciences.

Any language—in this book our examples are drawn mainly from English—is an extraordinarily complex phenomenon. The more thoroughly languages are analyzed, the more astonishing their complexity becomes. This complexity suggests a structure, and even the earliest ancient Greek investigators of language recognized the existence of a structure.

Since language is sequences of sound, and sound is invisible, we cannot see its structure as we can, for example, see the bony structure of a body—its skeleton. As we recognize the basic elements of the linguistic structure we invent names for them and attempt to describe the total structure part by part. It is one of the great beauties of plane geometry that its structures can be seen in their entirety. Though the native speaker seems to have a full grasp of the total grammatical structure of his language, we have no way of describing that structure so that it can all be seen at once. Instead we must break it up into what seem to be its most significant or at least its most conveniently describable parts and present them one after another. This is a most exasperating approach. All the parts are interrelated and necessary to the functioning of the whole, and a native speaker controls them all, utilizes them simultaneously, and never gives a conscious thought as to how he is using the structure to communicate his ideas. We know our English but we seldom know how it works. So we find it irritatingly hard to learn a lot of names for what we do so easily and unconsciously. It is the function of linguistics to discover the structure, to find names for its parts, and to use those names to explain how the system operates. Some of the basic areas of linguistic investigation are briefly defined below:

1. *Phonology* studies and attempts to describe the primary sound units of speech. Two related approaches are made in phonetics and phonemics. (See *Phonemes.)

2. *Morphology* studies and attempts to describe the primary meaningful units of speech; these are called *morphemes.

3. *Syntax* studies and attempts to describe the arrangement of morphemes in meaningful utterances, usually called *sentences.

4. *Grammar* is a term with a number of senses. Linguistics is concerned with the first two which are defined in the article *grammar.

5. *Semantics* studies and attempts to describe meaning. In this definition "meaning" is not used in the same sense as in § 2 above. Morphological meaning is restricted to the linguistic unit itself; the *s* on *cats* means "plural" and is recognized as such even though we don't know what a cat is. For example, if the sentence "I saw a *dat*" is changed to "I saw some *dats*," we know that *dats* is plural though we have no notion of what a *dat* is. Semantics studies the relationship between the word and what it stands for; the relationship between *cat* and the concept of a feline which it represents for us is its meaning.

Semantics gets us into what is called metalinguistics—studies that go beyond linguistics—matters that involve more than the language itself. Most of the concern of this book is metalinguistic because it deals with such matters as *spelling, *dictionaries, *rhetoric, *dialect, *jargon, as well as the *lexical meanings of words. The structures of meaning, in so far as they exist, are certainly far less apparent than the structures examined in phonology, morphology, and syntax. The modern linguist has therefore given most of his attention to these more obvious aspects of language. There is an irony in this because the layman is far more interested in what an utterance means than in how it is structured. And his attitude is right to this extent: Language does have as its primary purpose the communication of meaning. But the educated layman tries to have some understanding of all the more significant aspects of his environment. Language is the most important of these and he should therefore have some understanding of it. This linguistics tries to provide.

A language is a human phenomenon, which will differ somewhat even from person to person; it will differ far more from one place to another and from one time to another. These variations in persons, times, and places give rise to such studies as *dialectology, linguistic geography, historical* and *comparative linguistics*; and, collaborating even more with other disciplines, *lexicography,* the making of dictionaries, *orthography,* the study of spelling, and *paleography,* the study of ancient texts.

1. *The analysis of languages.* In the last few decades linguists have developed a rigorous technique for the analysis of languages, in part in reaction against previous methods of study, particularly philology, which was concerned chiefly with the Indo-European languages and based largely on the study of literature, especially of written literature. A basic principle of linguistics is that language is primarily speech; the methods of analyzing speech (such as establishing categories by comparing "minimal pairs," two locutions alike in all but one linguistic feature—*cat, rat*) have become relatively standardized and have been applied to other aspects of language. Perhaps the most difficult aspect of linguistics has been the separating (for the purposes of analysis) of linguistic activities from the current of life in which they appear. The words *structure* and *structural,* often applied to linguistic study (sometimes almost with a mystical or magical overtone), emphasize this separation. Structural linguistics isolates the linguistic activity and stresses that despite the variety in a language there is a system or a series of patterns which can be

discovered and described by linguistic methods and which alone are the proper subject of linguistics.

Because of the tremendous importance of language in life, there have been numerous pressures for practical applications of the methods and findings of the new science. To date, the notable successes have been in recording and analyzing languages not previously written, recording many that were on the point of extinction, and in teaching the spoken form of a second language through more detailed and accurate analysis.

**2. *The reanalysis of English*.** Considerable progress has been made in describing English in newer and more precise terms. Features like word order and intonation patterns have been more systematically explored. Real advances have been made in abandoning or at least minimizing some categories inherited from Latin grammar but not significant for English, such as forms for case in nouns and mood in verbs; in defining various categories more objectively, such as the parts of speech (or form classes)—defining them by reference to form and function rather than to meaning; in giving more definite recognition to the phrase patterns basic to syntax; and in providing a syntax grounded in observation of speech.

**3. *Linguistics in a composition course*.** The purpose of a composition or communication course is to further the communicative skills of the students. Its organization and general direction should aim toward this end, based on the principles of composition—rhetoric. The current language is the medium, and consequently the rhetoric must be presented on the basis of this language. (In the last few generations "grammar" has often triumphed over "rhetoric," partly because of the uncertain control of Standard English by many students and partly because the elementary facts of language have seemed more definite and consequently easier to present and test.)

The description of English should be as accurate as possible, and gradually linguistics is furnishing a more complete and consistent description. Even now there are gains in using some of the terms and categories of linguistics: a few topics such as sentence boundaries and restrictive punctuation can be more accurately presented than formerly, even though the precise definitions of the terminals (see *Phoneme § 2d) involved are uncertain.

But a composition course is not an introduction to linguistics and can hardly spare time for a very secure grounding in such a technical field—though some teachers with specialized training in the field report considerable success in using linguistics as the basic material of the course.

The language part of a composition course, beyond a few pretty elementary topics, is certainly in the area of metalinguistics, involving social habits and attitudes. Most of the questions are of the order of "Shall I say or write this in this situation?" Linguistic generalizations, whether in traditional or more scientific form, can help in presenting general patterns, in summarizing general practices, but they do not go far in guiding choices between similar expressions when both are in the range of Standard English. To make these decisions students need not only the paradigms but a wide knowledge of the varieties of current usage, what educated people say and write. Since this knowledge by itself will not answer the questions, principles are also needed, especially principles of appropriateness. These involve value judgments, the cultivation of taste and some sensitivity to styles.

(See *Style, *Usage, "The varieties of English," pp. 2-31. References: Bloomfield, Carroll, Fries—*Structure,* Gleason, and works listed under *Grammar; also Archibald A. Hill, *Introduction to Linguistic Structures,* New York, 1958; Charles F. Hockett, *A Course in Modern Linguistics,* New York, 1958; Barbara M. H. Strang, *Modern English Structure,* London and New York, 1962; W. Nelson Francis, *The English Language: An Introduction,* New York, 1965.)

**Linking verbs** • When a verb is used so that it has little *lexical meaning but functions chiefly in connecting a subject with a modifier, it is called a *linking verb* or *copula.*

The most commonly used linking verb is *be,* followed by modifiers which function as adjectives or nouns (single words, phrases, or clauses), traditionally known as *predicate adjectives* and *predicate nominatives,* respectively. (In this book *predicative* designates both.)

This bottle *was* full.          The man *is* a carpenter.

Many other verbs are used as linking verbs—Curme counts about sixty in current English. Instead of having a verb of full meaning like *colden,* English uses the nearly meaningless verb *turn* or *get* and the adjective *cold* (which carries the chief part of the meaning) in such a sentence as "The weather turned cold." Many verbs are used both with full meaning of their own (as *fell* in "The tree fell into the water") and as linking verbs (*fell* in "She fell silent" or "He fell ill"). Some typical linking verbs are:

He *became* a doctor. The butter *tastes* rancid. She *felt* sad. He *acts* old. The ground *sounds* hollow. He *grew* moody. He *appeared* to be gaining ground. This *looks* first rate. His story *seemed* credible.

The construction "He felt badly" is puzzling. The tendency in English is for the adjective form to supplant the adverb form, as is apparent in Nonstandard "He worked bad," where the limiting word *bad* obviously restricts *worked,* not *he.* But in "He felt badly," the connection of *badly* is with *he,* a relationship which might be expected to reinforce the use of *bad* from earlier stages of the language when *bad* was the regular form. The plausible explanation is that the proscription of *bad* after such verbs as *played, worked, ran,* etc., and the prescription of *badly* in this position has led speakers to distrust *bad* in any postverbal position and to play safe by using *badly* in all positions. The same thing has happened with *sad, sadly.* When the adjective and adverb have the same form, such ambiguities as "The cat looked longer than the dog" can occur. (See *look.)

(See *be § 2, *Predicate adjective. References: Curme, *Parts of Speech,* pp. 66-69, *Syntax,* pp. 26-28.)

**Lists and series** • See *Series.

**literary** • *Literary,* as applied to style, usually means possessing traits that are characteristic of an older tradition of English literature. Its connotation may be "distinguished" or it may be "bookish." (See "Formal English," p. 16.)

**literate** • See *illiterate.

**Litotes** • See *Negatives § 1.

**little** • *Little* can be overused to the point of sentimentality ("little dear" and so on); but such English diminutive suffixes as those in "lamb*kin,* ring*let,* duck*ling*" don't have as much vitality as those in some other languages (French *-ette,* German *-chen* and *-lein*), and *little* in part supplies the need.

**loan as a verb** • In spite of attempts to restrict *loan* to a noun function and to make *lend* the corresponding verb, *loan* is regularly a verb, at least in American usage:

*Verb:* I loaned [or *lent*] him two dollars.
*Noun:* He got a loan of two dollars.

**Loan words** • See *Foreign words in English, *Origin of words § 2b.

**Localisms** •

Local     *Revision: The expression marked is in local use only. Replace it by a word or construction in General American use.*

A *localism,* or *provincialism,* is a word or other expression in regular use by many speakers in a limited region but not in the entire area. Localisms are appropriate to conversation and to Informal writing but are usually out of place in General and Formal writing. (See "Variations due to place," p. 5, *Dialects.)

**locate** • *Locate* is used for *settle* (The family located near the present town of Nashua) and for *find* (I can't locate the letter now) where *settle* and *find* would be preferable. It is *deadwood in defining the location of specific places or people:

He is now [located] with the Ford Motor Company in Detroit.

**Locution** • *Locution* is a handy term for referring to a word or a unified group of words; that is, it may be applied to a single word or to a phrase or clause considered as a meaning group. *Phrase, a meaning group, that is* are three locutions.

**Logic** •
*Revision: Reexamine and revise the logical relationship that is expressed or implied.*

Logic is a complex and difficult subject covering a broad range of topics, from vagueness and ambiguity in statements to the methods of scientific investigation. But "logic" is also a necessary part of our daily lives, whether we are making a judgment, deciding on what action to take, or simply trying to understand what goes on around us. It is equally important in our attempts—spoken or written—to communicate with each other. Everyone (whether he's ever heard the term *logic* or not) has at some time or other protested, "That doesn't make sense" or "That doesn't follow from what you just said." Everyone, that is, has some notion of the difference between logical and illogical reasoning.

Logic has a place in a composition course, if only because what is written should "make sense"—should reflect clear and responsible thinking about the material. Clear thinking in itself by no means guarantees good writing, but no paper is good unless the thinking that has gone into it is clear. A mechanically perfect paper that presents a nonsensical argument is unacceptable by college standards. Unclear thinking may reflect itself in all aspects of a paper—irrelevant material, faulty organization, sentences that don't "hang together," and imprecise choice of words. More narrowly, it shows up in errors in reasoning, in faulty relationships between one idea and another, one statement and another.

Logic will not help you learn the "truth" about your subject; it does not give you information or ideas or insights. But it does furnish techniques for testing the relationships that you have set forth in a paper. Being aware of the possible fallacies or errors in reasoning doesn't guarantee that you won't fall into them, but it should make you more alert to detecting and correcting them once you have set them down on paper.

Logic is a special subject matter with a special vocabulary. The following check list of possible sources of error in reasoning is intended as a review for those students who are already acquainted with the basic concepts and terminology.

The chief fallacies in *inductive* reasoning are: hasty generalizing, *post hoc propter hoc* (faulty causal reasoning—see also *Cause), faulty comparisons and analogies.

In *deductive* inference, fallacies are of various kinds, depending on the type of syllogism.

In the hypothetical syllogism (If P, then Q; P; therefore Q), the conclusion is invalid if the minor premise denies the antecedent or affirms the consequent.

In the alternative syllogism (Either A or B; not A; therefore B), the conclusion is invalid if the enumeration of alternatives is incomplete or if, in an inclusive relationship, the minor premise is affirmative.

In the categorical syllogism (M is P; S is M; therefore S is P), the conclusion is invalid if the meaning of one of the three terms shifts, if the middle term is undistributed in both premises, if a term that is distributed in the conclusion was not distributed in the premises, if both premises are particular, or if both premises are negative.

Other common fallacies, which have to do with the material rather than the inferences drawn, are *begging the question, ignoring the question,* and *argumentum ad hominem.*

(References: Three of the many excellent textbooks on logic are Morris R. Cohen and Ernest Nagel, *An Introduction to Logic and Scientific Method,* New York, 1934; Irving M. Copi, *Introduction to Logic,* 2nd ed., New York, 1961; Philip Wheelwright, *Valid Thinking,* New York, 1962.)

**Logic and language** • Sometimes items of usage are objected to as being "illogical," as *he don't, the *reason is because.* The former is a matter of history and of language variety, *he doesn't* being Standard English and *he don't* now generally Nonstandard. When the objection to the second is elaborated, it is usually "that an adverbial clause (because . . .) is equated with a noun (reason)"; these terms are from grammar rather than from logic. Logic proper is not involved in either objection.

A great many *idioms are not the cumulation of the meaning of their separate words: *get sick, hard to come by, a little water, many is the time, out of order.* These show, more clearly than the equally arbitrary general habits of the language, that language is a human development, the result of millions of speech situations, not a preplanned system; it is not illogical but simply nonlogical. The wonder is that it is as systematic as it is.

Probably arguments from logic had an influence in establishing the *double negative as Nonstandard English, since in language ordinarily the more negatives there are, the more definitely negative the statement is. But arguments from logic have had few such successes, and the term *logical* cannot be applied to language in its technical sense but only in its most general popular sense of "more or less systematic."

**Long function word** • See *Wordiness § 2.

**Long variants** • Some amateur writers are tempted to add an extra prefix or suffix to a word that already carries the meaning they intend. They write *irregardless, though *regardless* already means "without regard to," or doubtless*ly* for *doubtless.* Some like to use sonorous suffixes that add nothing to the meaning, like the *-ation* in *origination.* Some other long variants usually to be avoided are:

*analyzation* for *analysis*
*certificated* for *certified*
*confliction* for *conflict*
*emotionality* when only *emotion* is meant
*commercialistic* for *commercial*
*ruination* for *ruin* [*ruination* is an older emphatic form of *ruin*]
*hotness* for *heat*
*intermingle* for *mingle*
*orientate* for *orient*
*repay* when simple *pay* is meant, as in paying dividends
Unnecessary *-al* endings, as *transportation*[*al*] system, *government*[*al*] policy
*utilize* when only *use* is meant

Some of these words are not in good use at all (*analyzation*) and show lack of observation of language by anyone who uses them. Others are respectable but should be used sparingly. They can occasionally produce an effect, but the more compact form is usually preferable. (Occasionally the longer form acquires a special sense: A *certificated* teacher is one who has a certificate from the state licensing him to teach.) If a number of long variants are used they will weigh down a piece of writing and make it flabby. There is some merit in George Orwell's rule: "Never use a long word where a short one will do." (See *Origin of words § 3. Reference: Fowler, "Long variants.")

**look** • When used as a verb of complete meaning (to use the eyes, gaze), *look* is modified by an adverb: *look searchingly, look longingly.*

As a linking verb, equivalent to *appear, look* is followed by an adjective which modifies the subject: He looks *well,* or *healthy,* or *tired....* (See *Linking verbs.)

**lose, loose** • Associate the spelling of these words with the pronunciation and meaning:

lose /lüz/—lose a bet, lose sleep, lose money
loose /lüs/—loose a knot, a loose screw
loosed /lüst/—He loosed the boat from its moorings
lost /lôst/—a lost road, a lost soul, lost his way, have lost

**lot, lots of** • Both *a lot of* and *lots of* are in General use. But they tend to be avoided in Formal writing, particularly *lots:* *We tried a lot of different kinds. He has lots of friends ... a lot of money.* (Formal: *He has many friends ... a good deal of money.*) Do not spell the article and the noun as one word: *a lot,* not *alot.*

**lousy** • Except when meaning "infested with lice" (a sense in which it is rarely needed any more), *lousy* is a strong Informal word of abuse, now weakened to a *counter word of disapproval, expressive if not used too often, but offensive to most ears.

**lovely** • *Lovely* is a *counter word of approval, popular perhaps because its pronunciation can (by some people) be drawn out indefinitely and practically sung: *We had a love-ly time.*

**Lower case** •
*Revision: Use a lower case (small) letter instead of a capital in this word.*

ℓc

(See *Capital letters.)

**-ly forms** • See *-al ly, *Adverbs, types and forms § 1.

**M** • The sound represented by the letter *m* is a nasal consonant made with the lips closed: *man, music, diamond, drum-*

*mer, sum, lamp*; *m* is the only regular spelling for this sound, but it often occurs with other letters which are not sounded: so*me*, sole*mn*, co*mb*.

*M* may represent a syllable by itself ("syllabic *m*"): *stop 'em* /stop'm̩/. Some people tend to make a syllable with *m* in words like *elm, film* (/el'əm/, /fil'əm/) instead of using the more standard pronunciations: /elm/, /film/.

**m.** • See *a.m., p.m.

**madam** • As a formula of address *Madam* or *Dear Madam* is used for both married and unmarried women. The French spelling *madame*, better pronounced /mad'əm/, is sometimes used as the title for a foreign married woman, often for a woman musician, and sometimes in social and commercial contexts. In speech *madam* is usually *ma'am*: *Yes, Ma'am,* /mam/ or /mäm/. As a word of address or in social use (journalistic or Formal) the plural of *madam* is *mesdames* /mā däm'/. (See *Titles of persons.)

**Magazine references** • See *References.

**Main clauses** • See *Clauses. See also *Absolute constructions; *Adverbs, types and forms § 5; *Comma § 2; *Subordination § 3.

**maintain, service, repair** • See *service.

**majority—plurality** • Strictly *majority* means "more than half of" a certain number; *plurality* means "more than the next highest." *Plurality* is not much used now in the United States, the meaning *majority* being extended to "an excess of votes over all others cast"—and even often used in the exact sense of *plurality*, simply the excess of votes over the next highest. In an election with three candidates and 12,000 votes cast, one received 7000, one 3000, and one 2000; the winner would have a *plurality* of 4000 (in common usage, a majority of 4000); strictly speaking, he would have a *majority* of 1000.

Informally *majority* is often used of amounts or quantities as well as of numbers:

*Informal*: We spent the majority of the day there.
*General*: We spent most [or: the greater part] of the day there.
*Wordy*: The majority of students are interested in football.
*Better*: Most students are interested in football.

**Malapropism** • A *malapropism* is a confusion of two words somewhat similar in sound but different in meaning, with a consequent ludicrous kind of sense, as *arduous* love for *ardent* love. Malapropisms are the cause of many *boners but are often intentionally used for humorous effect, as they were by Richard Brinsley Sheridan in creating the part of Mrs. Malaprop in *The Rivals*. It is, of course, the speeches of Mrs. Malaprop that have given the name to these confusions in language:

"I would by no means wish a daughter of mine to be a progeny of learning.... Then, sir, she should have a supercilious knowledge in accounts;—and as she grew up, I would have her instructed in geometry, that she might know something of the contagious countries...."
—Richard Brinsley Sheridan, *The Rivals*, Act I, Scene ii

**man, woman** • These are preferred to the more pretentious *gentleman* or *lady*, except when *man* or *woman* would sound conspicuously blunt.

*Ladies and gentlemen* is a *formula in addressing an audience.

The singular forms alone are used as modifiers:

| | | | |
|---|---|---|---|
| manpower | manholes | woman hater | woman suffrage |

**Manuscript form** •

MS
> *Revision: Your manuscript does not have the proper form. Revise or rewrite as directed.*

Instructors usually establish their own specifications for manuscript form at the beginning of the course. Whatever the details, the goal is a clean, legible copy that can be easily read. Use regulation paper, leave adequate margins, number the pages, make corrections neatly, and observe your instructor's directions for endorsing the paper. In brief, put your best foot forward. (See *Carelessness, *Division of words, *Proofreading, *Submitting manuscript, *Typewritten copy.)

**may—can** • See *can—may.

**may be, maybe** • *Maybe* is an adverb meaning "perhaps," a reduction of *it may be*; *may be* is a verb form:

Maybe you'll have better luck next time.     He may be the next mayor.

In speech *maybe* often becomes /me′bi/, with the /ā/ sound becoming /e/ as it has in the *break* of *breakfast*.

**me** • See *Pronouns, types and forms § 1, *between you and me, *It's me.

**Meaning** •
*Revision*: *The word, phrase, or sentence does not make
sense in this context. Replace it with one that conveys
the meaning you intend.*

Mng

When the reader questions the meaning of what you have
written, it indicates a rather drastic failure in communication.
Ordinarily the problem is not simply the use of one word for
another that is reasonably close to it in sound or meaning—
*comprehension* for *comprehensibility,* for instance. This would
be marked *WW* ("wrong word"); the reader knows the word
is "wrong" because he knows what the "right" one is. But
*Mng* suggests that the reader cannot make an intelligent guess
at what you were trying to say. Rethinking and rewriting are
in order. (See *Ambiguity, *Wrong word.)

**media—medium(s)** • The plural of *medium* is usually *medi-
ums*—always in the spiritualistic sense, practically always in the
general sense. *Media* is most used in scientific contexts and in
the phrase *mass media* (of communication) and usually now
as applied to the different advertising *media* (newspapers,
magazines, television, billboards, etc.).

**medieval** • Some years ago the American Historical Association decided to change their spelling of this word from *mediae-
val* to *medieval,* now the commoner form. Pronunciation is
/mē′di ē′vl̩/, or /med′i ē′vl̩/, rarely /mid ē′vl̩/. (See *-ae-, -oe-.)

**messrs.** • *Messrs.* is the abbreviation of French *messieurs*
which in English is pronounced /mes′ərz/. It is used as the
plural of *Mr.* (*Messrs. Ives and Johnson*) and sometimes,
though rarely now in American usage, used in addressing firms
(*Messrs. Brown, Hubbell and Company*). The occasions for its
use are Formal. (See *Abbreviations § 2.)

**meter** • *Meter* is now a more common spelling than *metre.*
The second *e* drops out in derivatives: *metrical, metrics, metric
system.* (For a description of English meters see *Verse form;
see also *-er, -re.)

**Middle English** • See *English language § 3.

**might—could** • See *can—may.

**Misrelated modifiers** • See *Dangling modifiers.

**mix, mixer** • *Mix* is Informal for "associate with," *mixer* for "sociable person" or for "the person who develops new acquaintances readily." Though slang in their origin, they seem excusable because of the colorlessness of the more reputable words. *Mixer* is also used as a noun to mean "social gathering."

**Mixed usage** • Experienced writers sometimes deliberately shift from one variety of English to another to achieve special effects, but many weaknesses in expression spring from the *unintentional* mixture of different varieties of usage. Conspicuously Informal words or *idioms may stray into Formal writing; Nonstandard locutions or words usually confined to law or business may appear in General writing. Distinctly Formal words and idioms are equally inappropriate in General writing. (They often appear because the writer is trying to substitute for a natural expression one that will dazzle his reader.) The principal way to develop in language is to cultivate feeling for different styles and their fitness for a given job. (See "The varieties of English," pp. 2-31.)

**Modal auxiliaries** • *Can, could, may, might, must, ought, *shall, should, will, would* are called *modal auxiliaries* (though they have nothing to do with grammatical "mood"). They differ from other verbs in having no *s* in the third person singular, no participles, and therefore no compound forms, and they always occur as part of verb phrases, complete or elliptical. *Dare* and *need* are also sometimes used as modal auxiliaries. (See *Elliptical constructions.)

**Modern English** • See *English language § 5.

**Modifiers** • *Modifiers* are words or word groups that stand in a sentence in a secondary relationship to other words or word groups (*Headwords). Typically they limit and make more exact the meaning of the headword. In these examples the words in italics modify the words in small capitals:

a *cold, windy* DAY     He FAILED *miserably*.     a *truly* GREAT—a *truly great* MAN     *Coming around the corner,* WE met him head on. *As we came around the corner,* WE SAW HIM BOARDING A TROLLEY.

(See *Absolute constructions, *Adjectives in use, *Adverbs in use, *Ambiguity § 2, *Apposition, appositives, *Clauses § 2b, c, *Dangling modifiers, *Gerund § 1, *Hyphen § 2, *Infinitives § 4, *Nouns § 2, *Participles § 2, *Phrases, *Restrictive and nonrestrictive, *Verbals.)

**Money** •
1. Exact sums of money are usually written in figures:

72¢        $4.98        $5        $168.75        $42,810

Round sums are more likely to be written in words: *two hundred dollars, a million and a half dollars.*

In factual books or articles involving frequent references to sums of money, however, figures are often used throughout.

**2.** In consecutive writing, amounts are usually written out when they are used as modifiers: *a million dollar* project. Informally, figures are often used: *an 85¢ seat.*

**3.** Commas and periods, $ and ¢ signs are used as in the examples in § 1 above. (For an example of writing sums of money in text, see the paragraphs of illustration in *Numbers § 2.)

**Monosyllables** • A *monosyllable* is a word of one syllable:

asked        bright        feel        fill        longed        word

Monosyllables should not be divided at the end of lines, not even words like *asked, longed.* (See *Division of words.)

A *polysyllable* strictly has three or more syllables, but since we use *dissyllable* (having two syllables) rather rarely, *polysyllable* usually means a word having two or more syllables.

**Months** • In reference matter and Informal writing, the names of months with more than four letters are often abbreviated in dates:

Jan. 21, 1965        16 Aug. 1966        Dec. 25, 1966
[But:] May 1, 1967        June 30, 1967        4 July 1968

When only the month or month and year are given, abbreviation would be rare:

Every January he tries again        January 1959

In Formal writing, the names of the months would not be abbreviated at all. (See *Numbers § 1a, *Dates.)

**Mood** • By the forms of *mood* (occasionally, *mode*), verbs in many languages may distinguish the way in which a statement is regarded by the writer. Modern English verbs hardly have moods in the Latin grammar sense, but the terms are still conventionally used:

*Indicative:*        [as a fact, a statement]        I am
*Subjunctive:*        [as a wish, possibility, doubt]        If I were
*Imperative:*        [as a command]        Stop!

(See *Indicative mood, *Subjunctives, *Commands and requests, *Verbs.)

**moral, morale** • Although the *e* is not in the French noun we borrowed as /mə ral′/ ("a confident mental state"), it is a convenient and natural English way of showing there is something peculiar in the pronunciation. It also distinguishes this *morale* from *moral* ("concerning right conduct").

**more, most** • See *Comparison of adjectives and adverbs § 5b.

**Morpheme** • *Morpheme* is a term in linguistics for what is most briefly described as the smallest grammatically meaningful unit in a language. It may be a word—"free form"—(*boy, tall, Massachusetts*) or a part of a word that can combine with other elements—"bound form"—(*-s, -ing, anti-, -ness*). (For a sentence analyzed into morphemes see *Immediate constituents. See also *Linguistics, *Parts of speech, *Origin of words. Reference: Gleason, especially Chs. 5-8.)

**Morphology** • See *Linguistics, *Morpheme.

**most, almost** • In speech *almost* is often reduced to *most*: *A drop in prices will appeal to most anybody. Most,* used thus, is Informal and ordinarily out of place in written English. If you can substitute *almost* for *most* in a sentence (*almost* always, *almost* anywhere), *almost* is the word you need.

**Mr.** • Usually abbreviated, this title is written out only when it represents spoken usage and when it is used without a name:

They're only two for five, mister. [But:] Mr. Schlesser

(See *Abbreviations § 2, *Titles of persons.)

**Mrs.** • This title is usually written out only to represent Nonstandard usage and is then spelled *missis* or *missus*:

Standard: Mrs. Dorothy M. Adams    Mrs. Adams
Nonstandard: Where's the missis?

*Mrs.* is not combined with a husband's title except in small town journalese. Write *Mrs. Dodd,* not *Mrs. Prof. Dodd.* (See *Abbreviations § 2, *Titles of persons. For suggestions on the use of this title with a signature see *Letters § 2.)

**MS.** • *MS.,* usually in caps, is the conventional abbreviation for *manuscript*; plural *MSS*. The shoptalk word for manuscript intended for publication is *copy*.

**must** • *Must* has recently become an adjective modifier in General use:

the President's must legislation
This is a must article for every intelligent American.

It has long been a noun in newspaper shoptalk, a *B.O.M.* being a *Business Office Must,* a story that has to be run because of some advertising tieup. (See *Auxiliary verb.)

**myself** • *Myself* is a reflexive or intensive pronoun, referring back to *I* when used as an object or as an intensive:

*Object*: I shave myself.
*Intensive*: I saw the whole thing myself.

*Myself* and the other *-self* pronouns are used as the second part of compound subjects or objects commonly in speech but rarely in writing. They are seldom appropriate in good written style:

*Informal*: Another fellow and myself saw the whole thing.
*General*: Another fellow and I saw the whole thing.
*Informal*: Sam invited John and myself to dinner.
*General*: Sam invited John and me to dinner.

(See *Pronouns, types and forms § 4; *self; *himself, herself. References: Josephine M. Burnham, "The -Self Forms as Personal Pronouns," *American Speech,* 1950, 25:264-267; Bryant, pp. 141-143.)

**N** • /n/, as in *now, gnaw, inning, been. N* may be a syllable by itself ("syllabic *n*"), as in *cotton, hidden, couldn't* (/ˈkotˈn̩/, /ˈhidˈn̩/, /ˈkudˈn̩t/), where the intrusion of a vowel sound between the consonants is often considered Nonstandard (see Kenyon and Knott, ¶ 114); *n* is the only regular spelling for this sound, but it often occurs with other letters which are not sounded: *k*nife, *p*neumonia, *g*naw.

*N* is generally silent in *kiln* and in a number of words after *m*: *autumn, damn, hymn, solemn.* The sounding of *n* in derivatives of such words varies with each word. It is not sounded in *hymned* /himd/ and in *damned* only in archaic or ultra poetic contexts /ˈdamˈned/. It is sounded in *autumnal, damnation, hymnal, solemnity,* and in general before a suffix when the suffix begins with a vowel.

An *ñ* (the wavy line is called a *tilde*) is found in some words from Spanish (*señor*). If the word is commonly used, the spelling is usually changed to *ny* (*canyon* instead of *cañon*). (See *ng.)

**naive—naïve** • The form without the dieresis (*naive*) is gaining over *naïve.* It is unnecessary to keep the French masculine form *naïf* in English because we do not have the grammatical *gender which requires it. *Naive* can do all the work. Pronounced /nä ēv′/.

### namely and other introductory words •

**1.** The beginning of wisdom with "introductory words" like *namely, that is, for example, such as* is to use them as seldom as possible. *Namely, viz., i.e., e.g.,* and some others are often found in Formal scholarly prose, but *for example, for instance, such as* are more appropriate to most writing. Very often such words can be omitted altogether in compact, General writing:

> He instructed us in the mysteries of punctuation: [such as] semicolons between clauses of a compound sentence, position of quotation marks with other marks, commas with nonrestrictive clauses.

**2.** In Formal style or in a long, rather complicated sentence, an introductory word is usually preceded by a semicolon:

> The interview is of value, then, because it aids in discovering certain traits; e.g., emotional and temperamental attitudes—which do not submit so readily to other modes of attack.—G. D. Higginson, *Fields of Psychology*, p. 395

When one of these words introduces a series of short items, it is often followed by a comma rather than by a colon:

> The boys in training are thoroughly grounded in the fundamental processes of the work, for example, planning, building, and launching.

No comma should follow *such as*:

> Large animals, such as bears, moose, and elk, are often found here.

### Names •

In factual writing all names used should be complete and accurate. In current writing, made-up names and other dodges are not used much except in humor. In the following they stamp the paper as amateur:

> Across the table sat Cornelius Van Stuck-up between two feminine admirers whose names I will not mention but will call Miss X and Miss Y. Miss X said to Miss Y. . . .

Use the real names of people and places unless there are cogent reasons for avoiding them; if there are, invent convincing names or use pronouns or *a man* or a less conspicuous device. The use of actual names makes a style seem concrete, immediate, and current.

(Articles providing information on points of usage include: *Capital letters, *Esquire, *Given names, *Nicknames, *Professor, *Proper names, *Reverend, *Ships' names.)

**necessary** • *Necessary* is spelled with one *c* and two *s*'s. Very often a verb is more direct and emphatic but less polite than a construction with *necessary*:

You *must* [or *have to,* rather than *It is necessary that you*] pay.

**necessity** • The idiom is *necessity of* or *for* doing something (not *to* do something):

I don't see *the necessity of* [or: *for*] *reading* so many pages to get so few facts. [Or, more concise: I don't see *the need of reading* so many pages. . . .]

**need—needs** • Both are third person singular of the verb *need,* but used in different idioms. *Needs* is the form in affirmative statements, *need not* or *does not need* in negative statements, *need* or *does . . . need* in questions:

He needs a haircut.
He needs to have a haircut. [Infinitive with *to*]
Does he need a haircut?
*Formal:*     He need not come. [Infinitive without *to*]
*General:*   He doesn't need to come. [Also:] He needn't come.
*Formal:*     Need she come?
*General:*   Does she need to come?

*Need* followed by the past participle rather than the present infinitive is a localism:

*General:* It needs to be covered.
*Local:* It needs be covered.

**Negatives** • The meaning of a negative in language is not always equivalent to its meaning in mathematics, where —3 is as much less than 0 as +3 is more than 0 and — (—3) = +3 because the only mathematical alternative of — is +. In language a contrary is likely to be stated by another positive (*good—evil, white—black*); the negative usually means "less than" or "different from"; *not good* is *less than good* but not necessarily *evil,* and *not white* is *different from white* but not necessarily *black.* This quality of negation provides the weakened positive which results from a negated negative: in *not uncommon,* we get a reduced reduction; *uncommon* is *less than common, not uncommon* is *less than less than common* or *not quite common.*

On the other hand, when two (or more) negatives in a sentence affect different words (In *He can't never do no work,* *n't* affects *can* and *never,* and *no* affects *do* and *work*), they actually reinforce the negation. But this cumulative effect is no longer used in Standard English. (See *Double negative.*)

Sometimes the negative form shows unexpected variation from the affirmative: *must go* and *have to go* are nearly synonymous; *mustn't go* and *don't have to go* are not. (Reference: Otto Jespersen, *Philosophy of Grammar*, New York, 1924, Ch. 24.)

1. *Emphasis.* A statement may sometimes be made more emphatic or striking by being put negatively (in a figure of speech known as *litotes* or *understatement*):

He carried not only his own burden but hers too.

He made not just one great discovery but several.

The assimilating power of the English language is not less remarkable than the complexity of its sources.—J. B. GREENOUGH and G. L. KITTREDGE, *Words and Their Ways in English Speech*, p. 147

2. *Separation from positive.* Within a single sentence words of positive and negative import usually need to be separated because the constructions in which they occur will not be parallel:

I have learned through this practice to overcome stage fright, and I have gained in vividness of speech. [Not: *I have learned ... to overcome stage fright and vividness of speech.*]

3. *Double negative.* See *Double negative.

(For a discussion of negative comparisons see *as ... as.)

**Negro** • Capitalize, like *Caucasian, Indian*. Plural, *Negroes*.

**neither** • See *either, *Correlative conjunctions.

**Neutral vowel** • A good many words give spelling trouble because they contain various spellings for the vowel sound represented in this book by /ə/ (*schwa): /ə kad'ə mē/ (*academy*). This is Standard pronunciation, so that no drill in sounding the syllable can help. A number of these words are related to others in which this syllable has a stress, making the vowel stand out. Such pairs as the following may help you spell accurately the vowel italicized in the first word:

| | |
|---|---|
| academy—academic | despair—desperation, desperado |
| affirmative—affirmation | extravagance, extravagant— |
| angel—angelic | extravaganza |
| comparable—compare | hypocrisy—hypocritical |
| competition—compete | medicine—medicinal |
| definitely—definition | preparation—prepare |
| degradation—degrade | repetition—repeat |
| democracy—democratic | ridicule—ridiculous |

But for the great majority of words with the neutral vowel either a good memory or a good dictionary is essential.

**New words** • New words are coming into English more rapidly than ever. They originate in various ways (see *Origin of words § 2, *Conversion). Many of them stand for new concepts and provide the means of communicating those concepts. Others are novelties and irritate the many readers and listeners who dislike mere innovation. When you use a new word, always consider the effect it may have on your audience. This does not mean that you necessarily avoid all new words which might disturb. Shock effect may be an appropriate device. But be aware of what you are doing.

**Newspaper English** • Joseph Pulitzer's famous motto for workers on the old *New York World* still stands as the ideal for the material and style of newswriting—*Accuracy, Terseness, Accuracy.* Complete accuracy is not easy for a reporter who has perhaps only a few minutes to get the facts of a complicated event, and terseness is not easy either for a man who writes habitually, often of very similar happenings, with little personal interest in his material. The result is that newspapers contain some of the worst writing that gets into print and some of the best.

There is no special dialect for newswriting, though the organization of a newspaper story is, of course, likely to be different from a historical account of the same event. Papers have some conventions for giving ages, names, places of residence, and other routine matters, but good newspaper English is simply General English applied to the daily recording of affairs. It is a style written to be read rapidly and grasped by the eye; except in headlines, tricks of sound—*alliteration, rhyme, *assonance—are out of place. The sentences are typically short and direct; the words are concrete and from the General vocabulary.

1. *Journalese.* The two most common sins of newswriting are inflation (*big words) and triteness, which we can lump as symptoms of *journalese.* Granting that *our fair city, ample outlet for her histrionic ability,* and scores of such trite phrases belonging to paleo-journalism are not found now outside small town papers, there is still a vast amount of wordy and lazy writing in newspapers. Every *stylebook contains a list of journalese expressions to be avoided. Triteness (see *Trite) is the next worst offense in journalese.

2. *Headlines and headlinese.* While writers of news stories have to write with an eye on inches of space, headline writers have to watch every letter. A given style of head has a "count" of so many letters, and, as the compositor says, "there ain't no rubber type." This necessity for compression and a desire to

"sell the papers" give rise to the punch of headlines. As the Waterbury, Conn., *Republican* style sheet puts it:

> PUT PUNCH IN HEADS
> SAYS OLD SLOT MAN
> Wants Accurate, Terse, Positive
> and Pungent Guides to
> News
> BEGS FOR ACTIVE VERBS
> Bald-Domed Editor Wants Blue
> Pencil Novices to Lay Off
> Fuzzy Words

This leads to the omission of *function words (*a, an, the,* connectives) and to the use of short words and clipped forms:

> Fly ocean; tell fight with gale 3 miles in air—12 Navy planes battered

To save space, short words are used, nouns are used as verbs, verbs as nouns, and any words or even long phrases as adjectives:

> Senate Set for Votes on Trade Bill Curbs
>
> Superintendent and Supervisor Refute
> Charge of Spying on *Traction Company
> Bus Drivers' Union Enrollment* Meeting

Worrying that headline style will ruin our language is silly; nobody ever talks headlinese—it's too concentrated. The feeble circumlocution of the stories that often stand below the heads is a greater menace to our language than the clipped heads.

(References: There are many textbooks on newspaper writing. Two of the most useful are: Curtis D. MacDougall, *Interpretative Reporting,* New York, 1948, and George C. Bastian and Leland D. Case, *Editing the Day's News,* New York, 1943. The stylebooks of newspapers are important. Some, like those of *The Detroit News* and *The New York Times,* 1962, are for sale. The magazine *Editor & Publisher* is the best source on current American journalism.)

**Newspaper titles** • See *Titles of articles, books, etc.

**ng** • /ng/ is the pronunciation symbol for the sound produced with the back of the tongue against the soft palate and the air coming through the nose with the vocal cords vibrating, most frequently spelled *ng* (*long, bringing*) but also spelled *n: anchor* /ang′kər/, *angry* /ang′grē/, *sink* /singk/, *uncle* /ung′kļ/.

Pronunciation is divided when a syllable ending in *n* is followed by one beginning with *g* or *k*: *congress* /kong'gris/ but *congressional* /kən gresh'ən ļ/ or /kən gresh'nəl/.

**nice** • *Nice* is a *counter word indicating mild approval, useful in speech but so general in meaning that it is of little use in writing. One of the word's former meanings, "exact, precise," is seen in *a nice distinction*. (Reference: C. C. Fries, "The Meanings of Words," *English Journal*, 1927, 16:602-606.)

**Nicknames** • *Nicknames* are rarely appropriate in Formal writing. In other writing they are often appropriate and should be used naturally, without apology. Some writers will put a nickname in quotes the first time it is used but not when it is repeated.

**no** • See *yes.

**No.** • The abbreviation *No.* for *number* (from the Latin *numero,* "by number") is written with a capital. It is appropriate chiefly in business and technical English. In the United States *No.* is not written with street numbers.

**nobody, nothing, nowhere** • All are written as single words. *Nobody* and *nothing* are singular in form and are usually treated grammatically as such, though *nobody* is Informally treated as a collective (see *every and its compounds):

*Formal*: Nobody thinks that his own dog is a nuisance.
*Informal*: Nobody thinks their own dog is a nuisance. Nothing is further from the truth. The dog could be found nowhere.

**nohow** • Nonstandard: *We couldn't get there nohow*; Standard: . . . *by any means* [or] . . . *any way we tried*.

**Nominative case** • A noun or pronoun that is the subject of a finite verb is sometimes said to be in the *nominative* (or *subjective*) *case*. The form of the nominative singular is the common form of the noun, the form to which, typically, the endings for the genitive and for the plural are added. *I, you, he, she, it, we, you, they* are the nominative forms of the personal pronouns; *who, which,* and *that* are the nominative forms of the relative pronouns. These forms are the usual ones for the nominative function; but see *It's me and *Pronouns. (See also *Case, *Subject and verb.)

**Nonce words** • Strictly, a *nonce word* is a word used but once as far as existing writing shows; a word coined for the occasion and not attaining a general use, as *thrillier* in a theater sign: "Thrillier than *Diabolique*."

**none, no one** • *None* is a single word, but *no one* is often used instead of *none,* for emphasis. *None* may be either singular or plural but is now more common with the plural:

As only ten jurors have been chosen so far, none of the witnesses were called [or: *was called*].

She tried on ten hats, but none of them were attractive.

I read three books on the subject, no one of which was helpful.

(Reference: Fries, *AEG*, pp. 50, 56.)

**Nonrestrictive and restrictive** • See *Restrictive and nonrestrictive.

**Nonstandard English** •

**NS** *Revision: Change the Nonstandard word, form, or idiom to one appropriate to Standard usage.*

For discussion and examples, see "Nonstandard English," p. 20. Among the articles that treat Nonstandard words or forms are *Adverbs, types and forms § 1, *Double negative, *lay-lie, *learn-teach, *nowheres, *Principal parts of verbs, *without.

**nor** • See *Correlative conjunctions.

**not hardly, not scarcely** • See *Double negative § 3.

**not to exceed** • *Not to exceed* is a business and legal locution; in other contexts *not more than* is usual:

The undersigned will be liable for property damages, not to exceed $500 for one accident.

The enrollment in the course was to be not more than fifty.

Not more than two people could live on that pay.

**nothing** • See *nobody, nothing, nowhere.

**notorious** • *Notorious* means "well known for unsavory reasons": *a notorious cheat. Notable* is "worthy of note, remarkable." *Famous* is "well known for accomplishment or excellence": *a famous writer, aviator. Infamous* means "odious, detestable": *an infamous deed. Noted* is journalistic for "famous, well known."

**Noun and verb stress** • Though identical in spelling, some nouns and verbs, mostly from French, are differentiated in speaking by stressing the first syllable in the noun and the last in the verb. When this shift occurs, the verb often has an altered vowel sound. Some of these are listed below:

| Noun | Verb |
|---|---|
| com'press | com press' |
| con'duct | con duct' |
| con'flict | con flict' [often con'flict] |
| con'trast | con trast' [often con'trast] |
| con'vict | con vict' |
| de'crease [and de crease'] | de crease' |
| di'gest | di gest' |
| es'cort | es cort' |
| ex'tract | ex tract' |
| in'cline | in cline' |
| in'crease | in crease' [often in'crease] |
| in'sult | in sult' |
| ob'ject | ob ject' |
| prod'uce, pro'duce | pro duce' |
| rec'ord | re cord' |

Several of these verbs in common use show the natural English tendency to put the stress on the first syllable. The following words are both nouns and verbs with the same stress:

ac'cent    cos'tume    dis'count    im'port

**Noun clauses** • A *noun clause* is a construction having a subject and *finite verb and functioning typically in a sentence as a subject or object. Many noun clauses are introduced by *that,* some by *what, who, whoever, whatever, why, when,* and other connectives.

*Subject*: *That anyone could raise his grades by studying* had never occurred to him. *Whether or not he should go* had bothered him.

*Object*: He knew *that it would never happen again.* [Or:] He knew *it would never happen again.*

*Predicate noun*: His favorites were *whoever flattered him.*

*Object of preposition*: Sam is always sure of *what he does.*

*Appositive*: The doctrine *that we must avoid entangling alliances* was first stated by Washington.

*That* and *whether* clauses as subjects are, as the examples above show, distinctly Formal constructions. (See *Clauses § 2a, *reason is because.*)

**Nouns** •

1. *Forms.* In English an important way in which we identify nouns is by their forms.

Most nouns have two forms: a plural form in an /s/, /əz/, or /z/ sound, spelled s or es: *hats, kindnesses, lecturers* (minor types are described in *Plurals of nouns); and a genitive form with the same sound but written with an apostrophe: *boy's, boys', cat's, church's.* (See *Genitive.)

There are a few distinctive endings found in groups of nouns, such as *-er* or *-or, -ness, -th, -tion.*

A very few nouns in English have different forms for masculine and feminine: *actor—actress, confidant—confidante, executor—executrix.* (See *Gender.)

Nouns may be single words or compound words written solid, as two words, or hyphened: *bathroom, bookcase, hub cap, go-getter, stick-up.* (See *Group words, *Hyphen.)

**2.** *Position and functions.* Nouns are also identified by their typical positions in sentences: standing before a verb as subject or after it as object, being preceded by an article (*a, an, the*) or demonstrative (*this, that,* and so on), or being the *headword in a prepositional phrase.

The principal functions of nouns in sentences are listed below:

*Subject of a sentence*: The *wind* blew for three days. (See *Subject and verb.)

*Object of a verb*: The wind blew the *silo* over. (See *Objects.)

*Object of a preposition*: in the *night,* behind the *house,* after *breakfast,* of the *president* (See *Prepositions.)

*Predicative*: He had become *president* of the firm. (See *Predicate adjective.)

*Possession*: the *woman's* first dress for two years (See *Genitive case § 2.)

*Apposition*: The first settler, *Thomas Sanborn,* came in 1780. (See *Apposition, appositives.)

*Modifiers of other nouns*: a *baby* hippopotamus; the best *high school basketball* team in years (See *Genitive, *Parts of speech, *Adjectives, types and forms § 4.)

*Modifiers of verbs or statements*: He came two *months* ago. *Mornings* he would work a little. (See *Adverbs, types and forms § 4.)

**3.** *Classes of nouns.* Nouns are conventionally classified by their meaning, as follows:

*a*–Proper nouns, names of particular people and places, written with capitals and usually without *the* or *a*: *Anne, George W. Loomis, London, Georgia, France, the Bay of Naples.* (See *Proper names.)

In contrast with these proper nouns, all the other groups are *common nouns.*

*b*–Concrete nouns, names of objects: *leaf, leaves, road, panda, manufacturer.*

*c*–Mass nouns, names of materials in general rather than materials in particular forms: *water, coffee, cement, steel, corn.*

*d*–Collective nouns, names of a group of things regarded as a unit: *fleet, army, company, committee, trio, bevy.* (See \*Collective nouns.)

*e*–Abstract nouns, names of qualities, actions, ideas: *kindness, hate, manufacture, idealism, fantasy, concept.* Many of these are \*gerunds: *fishing, drinking, manufacturing.*

(For additional information see \*Capital letters, \*Case, \*Infinitives § 4. References: Curme, *Parts of Speech,* Chs. 1, 9, *Syntax,* Chs. 2, 4, 26, and other references; Fries, *Structure,* pp. 65-79.)

**nowhere •** See \*nobody, nothing, nowhere.

**nowhere near •** Though occurring in print, the usage has an Informal tone: *It was a good score but nowhere near as large as we'd hoped for.* (Preferable in writing: *not nearly so large as.*)

(Reference: Bryant, pp. 148-149.)

**nowheres •** *Nowheres* is Nonstandard for *nowhere.*

**Number •** *Number* in English grammar is the singular and plural aspect of nouns and pronouns and verbs. The indication of number is of great importance in nouns and pronouns (though *you* is ambiguous), of little importance in verbs, which in most forms cannot show number. (See \*Plurals of nouns, \*Subject and verb, \*Reference of pronouns.)

**number •** *Number* is a collective noun, taking a singular or plural verb according as the total or the individual units are meant; *a number* takes plural:

A number of tickets have already been sold.
A number of pages were torn.

*The number* takes singular:

The number of tickets sold is astonishing.
The number of pages assigned for translation was gradually increased.

(See also \*amount, number.)

**Numbers •**
*Revision: Revise the figure or figures in this passage according to conventional usage.*

Num

1. *Uses.* Formal and General English show only minor differences in the conventions they follow. Figures are used for:

*a*–Dates. Only in Formal *social correspondence are dates written out in words; *1st, 2nd (2d)*, and so on may be used when a date is given without the year, but not ordinarily with the year:

Oct. 4, 1960    October 4, 1960    October 4    October 4th

Years are always written in figures.

*b*–Hours when *a.m. or p.m. is used:

5 p.m. [But:] five o'clock

*c*–Street numbers (with no comma between thousands):

2841 Washington Avenue    Apartment 3C, 781 Grand Street

*d*–Pages and other references:

page 642    pp. 431-482    Chapter 14 [Or:] Chapter XIV
Act III, scene iv, line 28

*e*–Sums of money, except sums in round numbers or, in Formal style, sums that can be written in two or three words:

$4.98    75¢    a million dollars [Or:] $1,000,000

*f*–Statistics and series of more than one or two numbers within a sentence:

In the political science class mock election the Republicans gained 50 seats in the House, 6 seats in the Senate, and 13 new governorships.

**2.** *Figures or words.* Usage varies in writing numbers that are parts of consecutive sentences. In general, newspapers and Informal writing have figures for numbers over ten, words for smaller numbers; magazine and book styles (most General writing) have figures for numbers over 100 except when the numbers can be written in two words:

*Informal (newspaper)* : four, ten, 15, 92, 114
*General (book)* : four, ten, fifteen, ninety-two, 114. [But practice is not uniform.]

This passage illustrates a typical book style in use of figures and sums of money:

With a well-integrated, rapidly growing organization, Swedish coöperators were ready to go forward to new triumphs—over galoshes this time. It sounds funny but it is not at all; the victory over the galosh cartel—really the rubber cartel—was a very tangible achievement. Galoshes are a necessity in the Swedish winter, to say nothing of the Swedish spring and the Swedish fall. And four manufacturing firms, formed into an air-tight trust, exploited this necessity for years. Annual profits of 60 per cent, 62 per cent and even, in one exceptional year, 77 per cent were recorded. On a capital of less than a million dollars the four factories realized in fourteen years more than twelve and a half million dollars and voted many stock dividends besides. As in the case of the milling cartel, the public yelled long and loud but with no visible results.

... Within a few weeks, merely on the basis of this announcement, the cartel reduced the price of a pair of men's galoshes more than fifty cents, with corresponding reductions all down the line. ... The result, within a year, was another seventy cents sliced off the price of a pair of galoshes. Having achieved this, K. F. began the manufacture of automobile tires at the Gislaved plant and by 1932 was producing 50,000 tires a year.—MARQUIS W. CHILDS, *Sweden—The Middle Way*, pp. 12-13

When most writing was longhand it was conventional to express numbers in words and then repeat them in figures in parenthesis. In clear copy, especially in typewritten copy, this is not done except in legal or important business documents.

Except in dates and street numbers, a comma is used to separate thousands, millions, etc., though it may be omitted in four-digit numbers:

1952 [the year]     1,952 [Or:] 1952 bushels     $4,682,921

Numbers in two words between 21 and 99 are usually hyphened, though the practice is declining: *forty-two* or *forty two*.

In consecutive writing a number at the very beginning of a sentence is written in words rather than in figures:

Two to 3% of loading and up to 10% is common and 20 to 30% in specially surfaced papers. ... —"Paper Manufacture," *Encyclopaedia Britannica*, p. 234

3. *Arabic and Roman numerals.* Arabic numerals (*1, 2, 146* ...) are used in almost all places where numbers are not expressed in words. Roman numerals, either lower case or capitals (i, ii, cxlvi ...; I, II, CXLVI ...), are occasionally used to number units in rather short series, as in outlines, chapters of a book, acts of a play, though now less often than formerly. The preliminary pages of books are almost always numbered with Roman numerals, because a new pagination is begun with the body of the book. Sometimes they are used on title pages for the date and on formal inscriptions.

In Roman numerals a small number preceding a larger is to be subtracted from the larger (ix = 9, xc = 90). The following table shows the common Roman numerals (lower case):

| | | | | | | | |
|---|---|---|---|---|---|---|---|
| 1 | i | 7 | vii | 13 | xiii | 25 | xxv |
| 2 | ii | 8 | viii | 14 | xiv | 27 | xxvii |
| 3 | iii | 9 | ix | 15 | xv | 29 | xxix |
| 4 | iv | 10 | x | 19 | xix | 30 | xxx |
| 5 | v | 11 | xi | 20 | xx | 40 | xl |
| 6 | vi | 12 | xii | 21 | xxi | 41 | xli |

| 49 | xlix | 80 | lxxx | 110 | cx | 600 | dc |
| 50 | l | 90 | xc | 199 | cxcix | 900 | cm |
| 51 | li | 99 | xcix | 200 | cc | 1000 | m |
| 60 | lx | 100 | c | 400 | cd | 1500 | md |
| 70 | lxx | 101 | ci | 500 | d | 1968 | mcmlxviii |

**4.** *Plurals of figures.* The plural of a figure is written either with *'s* or *s*:

> *Six fives:* six 5's, six 5s    *By tens:* by 10's, by 10s

**5.** *Cardinal and ordinal numbers.* The numbers in simple counting, indicating number only, are *cardinal numbers: 1, 2, 3, 68, 129.* . . . The numbers indicating order, *first, second, third* . . . are *ordinal numbers.* Except in numbering items in a rather routine enumeration, ordinals should be spelled out rather than abbreviated to *1st, 2nd, 3rd.* . . .

Since the simple forms *first, second,* and so on can be either adjective or adverb, the forms in *-ly* (*firstly*) are unnecessary and now are rarely used.

(See also *Fractions, *Money, *No., *Comma § 9e, *Hyphen § 1a, 2d, *References in scientific papers § 1c, 2.)

**O** • Speakers of English vary in their pronunciation of the *o* spellings as they do of the *a* spellings. Because of this widespread variation, pronunciation of particular words, especially with short *o*, can be indicated only roughly.

**1.** *"Long o"* /ō/, the sound in *go, hoe, oh, oats, note, shoulder, soldier, sew, slow, beau.*

Before spelled *r* the sound of long *o* is somewhat modified, as in *door* /dōr/, and may approach "open *o*" /ô/, as in some pronunciations of *horse, born,* and so on. (See *R.)

In unstressed and rapidly spoken words the sound of long *o* is shorter and may differ in quality: *obey* /ō bā′/ or /ə bā′/, *hotel* /hō tel′/.

**2.** *"Short o"* /o/. A rounded short *o* is not very frequent and is more characteristic of New England than of other parts of the country, where it is best illustrated in the first vowel of *gonna* (going to). The more common American sound is the unrounded or "open *o*" /ô/ or especially in Northern English, broad *a* /ä/: *soft* /sôft/, /säft/, /soft/; *pond* /pônd/, /pänd/, /pond/. Since there is no single pronunciation of these words throughout the United States, the symbol /o/ is used for them without indicating the regional variants.

**3.** *"Open o"* /ô/, most clearly identified in its spelling *aw* (*law, lawn, spawn*) but also the vowel sound in *lord, all, fault, fought, taught, cloth, broad, talk* /lôrd/, /ôl/, /fôlt/, /fôt/,

/tôt/, /klôth/, /brôd/, /tôk/. In some areas this sound is distinguished from the /ä/ sound only before *r*: *for* and *far* are different, but *taught* and *tot* are the same.

In unstressed syllables *o* may spell the *neutral vowel (*schwa) /ə/: *actor* /ak'tər/, *nation* /nā'shən/, or it may entirely disappear as in most people's pronunciation of *chocolate* /chôk'lit/ or sophomore /sof'môr/.

*O* represents several other vowel sounds—/ü/ as in *move*, /ů/ as in *wolf*, /u/ as in *son, money*, /ė/ as in *work*. (See also *ou.)

**O, oh** • *O* is always capitalized, and usually it is so closely related to some other word, often a name in direct address, that it is not followed by a mark of punctuation:

O dear, I suppose so. O yes. O God, unseen, but ever near.

*Oh* is an exclamation, followed by a comma if the force is weak, by an exclamation mark if the stress is strong. It is capitalized at the beginning of a sentence but not in the middle of a sentence:

Oh! Don't do that! Oh, I wish he would.

In Informal writing the distinction between *O* and *oh* is not always kept, and *O* is often found where traditional usage would have *oh*.

**Objects •**
1. *Direct objects*
   *a*–An *object of a verb* is the noun element (noun, pronoun, noun clause) *following* a verb and intimately related to it, though less so than is the *subject (see also *Adjectives, types and forms § 5, *Infinitives § 4). In meaning it ordinarily names what is affected or effected by the action of the verb. In those pronouns with an accusative case form (*me, him, her, us, them, whom*), that form is used as object after verbs and prepositions:

They made the *boat* themselves.
Terry chased the *cat* up a tree.
He took *her* to the three formals of the year.
I don't believe *that he told the truth*.

Occasionally, for emphasis, the object precedes both the subject and the verb:

This boat [object] the boys [subject] built themselves.

*b*–It has been conventional to call the object in certain passive constructions a "retained object" and even to forbid the construction on the ground that a passive verb by definition is incapable of taking an object. But since the position and the relation to the verb are no different from the typical object's, it is simpler to say that a passive verb may take an object:

He was given a *subscription* to a book club.

**2.** *Indirect objects.* With verbs of asking, telling, giving, and so on there is often a second or "indirect" object that names the receiver of the message, gift, etc.:

He gave the *church* a memorial window.
In desperation she showed *him* the snapshot album.

In American usage the indirect object usually comes before the direct object, as in the sentences just given. A prepositional phrase is common for the indirect object when it follows the direct object:

He gave a memorial window *to the church.*
In desperation she showed the snapshot album *to him.*

**3.** *Objects of prepositions.* The object of a preposition is the noun element whose relation to some other part of the sentence is shown by the preposition, as *some other part of the sentence* is the object of *to* and *the preposition* is the object of *by* in this sentence. The *what* clause in *Your grade will depend chiefly on what you do on the examination* is the object of *on.* (See *Prepositions.)

**4.** *Objects of adjectives.* A few adjectives take objects:

It was worth *a fortune.*
Are you sure *that she will come?*
He is like *his father.*

**Obscenity •** Certain words have acquired connotations offensive to prevailing notions of morality and decency and, especially when written or printed, are considered disgusting or repulsive. To the extent that such words are entered in dictionaries at all, they will be labeled *vulgar* or *obscene.* They obviously can have a powerful shock value, and they are more precise than the *euphemisms and circumlocutions which ordinarily replace them in most cultivated speech and writing. They appear in print, but they very rarely have any place in the writing of college students. (See *Profanity.)

**occasion, occasional, occasionally •** All three of these words are spelled with two *c*'s and one *s.*

**-oe-, -ae- •** See *-ae-, -oe-.

**of, off •** Besides its use as a preposition of numerous meanings, *of* is used to make the phrasal genitive: *of a man = man's,* and so on. (See *Genitive case.)

*Of* is frequently used in speech in the doubling of prepositions—*inside of, off of, outside of. Inside of* and *outside of* are sometimes used in Informal writing, *off of* less so and should usually be reduced to *off*: *He stepped off* [of] *the sidewalk.*

*Of* is occasionally used by fiction writers to give a Nonstandard tone to dialog by spelling the contraction of *have* as it usually sounds, but this spelling should not be used in General writing:

He *should have* [possible but awkward: *should've*; not *should of*] known better.

(Reference: Bryant, pp. 115-116, 150-151.)

**often** • The usual Standard pronunciation is /of'ən/. The *t* is sometimes sounded, but the pronunciation /of'tən/ is regarded as an affectation by most people.

**OK, O.K.** • *OK* or *O.K.* is Business and Informal English for "correct, all right, approved": *The foreman put his OK on the shipment.* Occasionally it is spelled *okay.* As a verb the forms are *OK*; *OK'ed,* or *OK'd*; *OK'ing*; *Oke* and *okeydoke* are slang.

(Reference: For the most extensive treatment of the history of *OK,* see the series of studies by Allen Walker Read in *American Speech,* 1963-1964.)

**Old English** • See *English language § 2.

**Omissions** • See *Apostrophe § 2, *Ellipsis, *Elliptical constructions.

**on the part of** • See *part, on the part of.

**one** •
1. The use of the impersonal pronoun *one* is characteristically Formal, especially if it must be repeated:

*Formal:* One can't be too careful, can one?
*General:* You can't be too careful, can you? [Where *you* is really impersonal.]

Repetition of *one,* to avoid *I* or when *you* would be more natural, is deadly.

American usage normally follows older English practice in referring back to *one* by pronouns of the third person—*he, his, him* (or *she, her*):

One is warned to be cautious if he would avoid offending his friends and bringing their displeasure down upon his head.

(See *they, *you.)
2. *One* may be used to avoid repeating a noun in the second of two compound elements:

Fred took the new copy and I took the old one.

The plural *ones* is often used; the apparent lack of logic need not concern us because *one* is not only a number but an indefinite pronoun.

She has two velvet dresses and three silk ones.

3. *One* is very often *deadwood, reducing the emphasis on the adjective which carries the real meaning:

The plan was certainly [an] original [one].

(Reference: Fries, *AEG,* pp. 245-246.)

**-one** • *One* is written solid with *any-, every-, some-* in making an indefinite pronoun; but when the *one* is stressed it is written as a separate word:

Anyone can do that. Any one of the four will be all right.
Everyone may study late. Every one of us was surprised.
Someone ought to tell her. Some one of the plans will work.

(See *any § 2, *every and its compounds, *some.)

**one another** • See *Pronouns, types and forms § 5.

**one of those who** • In written English the clause following *one of those who* and similar locutions is usually plural:

He is one of those people who believe in the perfectibility of man. [*Who* refers to *people.*]
That's one of the books that make you change your ideas. [*That* refers to *books.*]

In Informal speech and writing and sometimes in General writing the second verb is attracted to the singular by the emphatic main subject:

He is one of those people who believes in the perfectibility of man.

(See also *Subject and verb § 2d. References: John S. Kenyon, "'One of Those Who Is,'" *American Speech,* 1951, 26:161-165; Bryant, pp. 11-13.)

**only** •
1. The importance of the position of *only* has been greatly exaggerated. "Logically," perhaps, it should stand immediately before the element modified:

I need only six more to have a full hundred.

But usage in this construction is conspicuously in favor of placing the *only* before the verb of the statement. There is no possible misunderstanding in the meaning of:

I only need six more to have a full hundred.

There are instances in which the placing of *only* can produce a rather ludicrous statement ("with only a face that a mother could love"). But placing *only* with the verb is a characteristic and reputable English idiom:

In reality we only have succession and coexistence, and the "force" is something that we imagine.—HAVELOCK ELLIS, *The Dance of Life,* p. 91

They only opened one bag and took the passports in and looked at them.—ERNEST HEMINGWAY, *The Sun Also Rises,* p. 94

(References: Gladys Haase, "Current English Forum," *College English,* 1950, 12:400-402; J. S. Kenyon, "Current English Forum," *College English,* 1951, 13:116-117; Bryant, pp. 155-156.) **2.** In this respect *even, ever, nearly, just, exactly,* and other such limiting adverbs are similar to *only.* But since they are used much less than *only,* and some of them only in Formal English, the idiom is not so common. Like *only* they can be placed so that they spoil the emphasis:

The way I can stand in front of a store window and persuade myself that I need some novel article even surprises me [surprises even me].

**Onomatopoeia** • See *Imitative words and phrases.

**onto, on to** • When *on* is an adverb and *to* a preposition in a separate locution, they should be written as two words:

The rest of us drove on to the city.

Used as a preposition, they are written solid:

The team trotted onto the floor. They looked out onto the park.

*Onto* is frequently used as a double preposition in speech where *on* or *to* by itself would be more common in writing:

They finally got *on* [Spoken: *onto*] the bus.
The crowd got *to* [Spoken: *onto*] James Street.

(Reference: Bryant, p. 152.)

**or** • *Or* is a coordinating conjunction and, like *and, but,* and *for,* should connect words, phrases, or clauses of equal value. (See *Coordinating conjunctions, *Compound sentences, *Series.)

*Words*: He must be drunk or crazy.
*Phrases*: We could go by car or by train.
*Clauses*: We could go by car or we could go by train.

Two subjects joined by *or* take a singular verb if each is singular, a plural verb if both are plural or if the one nearer the verb is plural:

Cod liver oil or halibut oil is often prescribed.

Cod liver oil or cod liver oil capsules have the same effect.

Cod liver oil capsules or cod liver oil has the same effect.

The second construction is more usual than the third. (See also *Subject and verb § 2b.)

*Or* correlates with *either* and sometimes with *neither*:

*General*: Either /ē'ᵗʜ ər/ or /ī'ᵗʜ ər/ is correct.

*Less common*: Neither /ā'ᵗʜ ər/ or /ī'ᵗʜ ər/ is widely used in America.

*General*: Neither /ā'ᵗʜ ər/ nor /ī'ᵗʜ ər/ is widely used in America.

(See *Correlative conjunctions.)

**-or, -er •** See *-er, -or.

**-or, -our •** American spelling prefers *-or* in such words as *color, governor, honor*. When referring to Jesus Christ, *Saviour* is frequently spelled with the *u* but in other senses without it. *Glamour* is used in advertising and social contexts to elevate the tone.

British usage is divided on this point, though of course to an American reader the words in *-our* are conspicuous. Fowler said that the American change to *-or* has actually hindered the simplification that was going on in England:

Those who are willing to put national prejudice aside & examine the facts quickly realize, first, that the British *-our* words are much fewer in proportion to the *-or* words than they supposed, &, secondly, that there seems to be no discoverable line between the two sets so based on principle as to serve any useful purpose. By the side of *favour* there is *horror*, beside *ardour pallor*, beside *odour tremor*, & so forth. Of agent-nouns *saviour* (with its echo *paviour*) is perhaps the only one that now retains *-our*, *governor* being the latest to shed its *-u-*.—H. W. FOWLER, *A Dictionary of Modern English Usage*, p. 415

In quoting directly from British writings and in referring to British institutions, like the Labour Party, their spelling should be exactly followed; otherwise use *-or*. (References: Fowler, "-our & -or"; *Oxford English Dictionary*, "-or"; John Benbow, *Manuscript & Proof*, New York, 1937, pp. 75-77, discusses spelling in American books that are to be circulated in England.)

**oral, verbal •** Etymologically, *oral* means "spoken," and *verbal* means "in words"; but *verbal* has been so long used in the sense of *oral* that the sense is recognized in dictionaries:

He delivered an oral message.    He had only a verbal agreement.

**Organization** •
*Revision: Improve the organization of your paper and/or correct the form of your outline.*          Org

Organization is faulty when related material is scattered rather than grouped, when irrelevant material is included, or when there is no logical progression in the order in which the material is presented. Sometimes the weakness has its origin in the outline. (See *Coherence, *Logic, *Outline form, *Transition, *Unity.)

**Origin of words** •
1. *The study of word origins.* Every word has a history. Some, like *chauffeur, mores, television, parapsychology,* are relatively new in English; some have been in the language for centuries, like *home, candle, go, kitchen;* others have recently acquired new meanings, like *satellite* (from a Latin word for "attendant," a term in astronomy which probably now means for most people a man-made object which orbits the earth, moon, or other celestial body). *Etymology,* the study of word origins, traces the changes of forms and combinations of word elements (as in *dis/service, wild/ness, bath/room, room/mate*) and pursues the word or its component parts to Old English and beyond or to the foreign language from which it came into English, and so on back to the earliest discoverable forms. Of some words, especially Informal words like *dude, stooge, rumpus,* earlier forms are unknown; of others, like *OK* or *blizzard,* the sources are debated. But the efforts of generations of scholars have discovered pretty full histories for most words. These are given briefly in most dictionaries and more fully in the *Oxford English Dictionary* and in special works.

Most people working with words have some curiosity about where they came from and about how new ones can be made. They find that many of our everyday words come down directly from Old English (*brother, go, house, tell*) or, if they are of foreign origin, that they were borrowed many centuries ago (*candle, debt, pay, travel*). The vocabulary of high society has many French words, of both early and recent borrowings (*debutante, gallant, fiancée*). The vocabulary of philosophy and abstract thought has a large Latin element (*concept, fallacy, rational, idealism*), and the vocabulary of science has many Greek elements (*atom, hemoglobin, seismograph*).

The sources of words will often reveal something about our history, as the many Norman French and Latin words in law (*fine, tort, certiorari, subpoena*) remind us of the time, following 1066, when the government of England was in the hands of the Norman French. But it is more interesting to discover what meanings the words have had in their earlier career in English and in the foreign languages from which they have come. *Supercilium* in Latin meant "eyebrow"; *rehearse* is from a French word meaning to "harrow again"; *sarcophagus* is, according to its Greek originals, "a flesh eater," referring to the limestone coffins that hastened the disintegration of bodies; *profane* (Latin) meant "outside the temple" and gathered the meaning of "against religion, the opposite of sacred"; *alcohol* goes back to an Arabic word for a finely ground powder, used for painting eyelids, and from its fineness the word became applied, in Spanish, to specially distilled spirits, and so to our alcohol.

Following up the biographies of words makes a good hobby —and it may sharpen a writer's sense for the exact meaning and for the suggestion carried by a given word, even though he must use it in its present sense. This article chiefly presents the various ways in which words have arrived and are still arriving in English. There are two general processes—making new words, either created or borrowed, and compounding or clipping words and parts of words that are already in the language. Then this stock of words is increased in usefulness by changes in the meanings of the forms which are established. **2. *New words*.**

*a*–Creation of words. Outright creation, "coinage," of words is rare. Even *gas,* first used by Van Helmont (1578-1644), a Belgian scientist, probably had the Greek *chaos* as well as a Dutch or Flemish word behind it. *Kodak* is probably an actual creation, as are a good many other trade names, some of which are quite familiar so long as the advertising of them is kept up. Informal words like *dud, burble* were also creations, good sounding words someone made up. F. Gelett Burgess (1866-1951) invented *blurb,* defining it as "self-praise; to make a noise like a publisher." *Imitative words like *buzz, honk, swish, whiz* are attempts to translate the sounds of nature into the sounds of language. Various exclamations of surprise, pain, scorn, may have started as unconsciously emotional noises— *ow, ouch, fie, phooey*—and then became regular words, used by anyone. Of course in the first stages of a language the words were created somehow, but just how is guesswork.

Occasionally a person coins a word for a particular statement, known as a *nonce word (used but once). One might write that a certain person "was the acme of hasbeenivity" and *hasbeenivity* would be a nonce word, and would probably remain one. As a rule arbitrary coinages do not stick. Outright creation is a very minor source of new words.

*b*–Borrowed words. English has always borrowed words freely, from Latin, German, French and from other languages with which English-speaking people have come in contact. It has assimilated words of quite un-English form: *khaki* (Hindustani), *seersucker* (Persian, Hindustani), *tycoon* (Japanese), *ski* (Norwegian), *hors d'oeuvres* (French), *intelligentsia* (Russian). The various words for *porch,* itself Norman French but the oldest and the most English-seeming of the group, come from various languages: *piazza* (Italian), *portico* (Italian), *stoop* (Dutch), *veranda* (Anglo-Indian).

Borrowing is still going on, though perhaps more slowly than at some periods. Some words come into Formal English and remain Formal words: *intelligentsia, bourgeois, chef-d'oeuvre, objet d'art, Zeitgeist, Anschluss,* and many others of political, philosophical, scientific, or literary bearing. *Sphygmograph* and many other scientific words are recent compoundings of Latin and especially of Greek words which are not otherwise in English usage, so that they may be regarded as borrowings as well as compounds. Others come in as General words, especially when large numbers of people go abroad, as during a war (*blitzkrieg, camouflage, ersatz*) or when a foreign invention becomes suddenly popular, as in *chauffeur, garage, chassis* of the automobile vocabulary. Some words brought by immigrants have stuck: *sauerkraut, kohlrabi, pronto, pizza, kosher, goulash.*

Many are dropped before they gain any general currency. The useful words are more or less adapted to English spelling and pronunciation and become true English words. (See *English language, and for suggestions about the use of recently borrowed words, *Foreign words in English.)

3. *Changes in form of words.*

*a*–Word composition. Most new words are made by putting together two or more elements to make a new word of different meaning or function, as *un-* added to *interesting* gives a word of the opposite meaning, *uninteresting,* or *-ize* added to the noun *canal* gives a verb, *canalize.* The fact that dictionaries separate words formed with prefixes into two groups, those to be defined and those which are self-explanatory, shows how deceptive affixes can be. The elements may be a prefix placed before the root word (*mis-related*), or a suffix added (*foolishness*), or a combining element like *mono-* (*mono-syllable, mono-rail*), or two independent words built together (*book-case, basket-ball, gentle-man*). *Group words like *high school, out of town,* though not written as single words, could be included as a type of word composition.

A list of prefixes and suffixes that are still active in English would take several pages. Here are a few of the more common:

*a- (not) : asymmetrical, amoral, atypical
ante- (before) : anteprohibition era

anti- (against) : antiprohibition
bi- (two) : bivalve, biplane, bicycle
dis- (not) : disinterested, dispraise
in- (in): income, impart, instill
in- (not) : inelegant, impractical
mis- (wrong): mistake, misnomer
*pre- (before): preview, prenatal, preempt
*re- (again) : revise, redecorate
up- (up) : upend (verb) , upswirl (noun)

A few suffixes are:

-en (to form a verb) : heighten, lighten, weaken
-ful (full) : playful, spoonful
-fy (to make) : electrify, horrify
-ish (to form an adjective) : dryish, foolish, smallish
-ize (to form a verb) : circularize

(See also *-er, *-ous, -us.)

Combining elements include a number of words or roots, many of them Greek:

-graph- (writing) : biography, photograph
micro- (small) : microcosm, micrometer, microphone, microbiology
mono- (one) : monotone, monorail
-phil- (loving) : philanthropy, philately, Anglophile
-side-: sidewall, sideswipe, ringside
-smith: locksmith, silversmith, gunsmith
tele- (distant) : television, telemeter
-trop- (turning) : geotropic, heliotropic

At first a compound has no more than the meaning to be expected by putting its elements together: *unable = not able*. But often a compound will develop an independent sense which can hardly be guessed at from the meanings of its elements: *cupboard, loudspeaker*.

Several pairs of prefixes and suffixes have the same meaning, so that often two words of the same meaning but somewhat different in form exist side by side, especially words with *in-* (not) and *un-* and nouns with *-ness, -ity,* or *-tion*:

aridness, aridity
completeness, completion
corruption, corruptness
ferociousness, ferocity

indistinguishable,
undistinguishable
torridness, torridity
unobliging, disobliging

When such a pair exists, take the one that is more familiar to you or that fits best in the rhythm of the sentence. But don't make your style conspicuous by coining a form when there is already a similar word in good use. The only sure way to know whether there is one available or not is to consult a good dictionary.

*b*–Phonetic alterations. For a variety of reasons, one word may have two or more developments in its pronunciation, each form emphasizing a different shade of the older word's meaning. Here are four Anglo-Saxon words which have had such double developments: from *ān* we get *one* and *a, an*; from *of* come *off* and *of*; from *thurh, through* and *thorough*; and from *ūtera, utter* and *outer*. There are, of course, many more, especially if we go further back. Many such doublets are not so obvious because the spellings do not differ, though the pronunciations, functions, and meanings do: *con'duct*, noun; *con duct'*, verb, etc.

*c*–Blends. Informal English has a number of words that show the liberties that the users of language have always taken with their words and always will take. Some of their experiments have proved useful and have become a part of the main English vocabulary.

One common type is *blends*, or portmanteau words, made by telescoping two words into one, often making a letter or syllable do double duty. *Squish* is probably a blend of *squirt* and *swish, electrocute*, of *electro-* and *execute; smog*, of *smoke* and *fog*. They are common in business: *servicenter, corrasable* (a paper—*correct* plus *erasable*), the names of many firms and products. In humor they abound: *posilutely, absotively, solemncholy, absogoshdarnlutely*, and also in more serious conversation, often presenting two ideas at once: *snoopervize* (*snoop—supervise*), *politricks, happenstance, anecdotage, slanguage*. They may be useful in a humorous context or to suggest derogation.

*d*–Clipped words. One of the commonest types of word change is clipping, dropping one or more syllables to make a briefer form: *ad* from *advertisement, bus* from *omnibus, taxi* from *taxicab* (earlier from *taximeter cab*), *quote* from *quotation, mob* (an eighteenth-century clip from *mobile vulgus*), *auto, movie, plane, phone*, and so on. *Shoptalk has many clips—*mike* for *microphone* or *micrometer*. The speech of any closely related group is full of clips; campus vocabulary shows a full line: *econ, home ec, phys ed, grad, prom, dorm, ad building, varsity, lab, exam, gym, prof, pre-med*, and scores more. Clipped words are written (when they are appropriate to the context) without apostrophe or period.

*e*–Back formations. A back formation differs from clips like *exam* and *auto* chiefly in that it is formed on *analogy with other words and is usually needed to serve as a different part of speech. *Beg* was formed from *beggar*, corresponding to *hunt, hunter*. A number of back formations have made their way, like *diagnose* from *diagnosis, edit* from *editor;* some, like *enthuse*, are slowly making their way; but most are formed in

fun, like *burgle,* and are used either in humor or in a deroga-
tory sense, like *orate. Donate* seemed unnecessary, since we had
*give,* though it has acquired the specialized sense of a publi-
cized giving to charity; *enthuse* is more justifiable, since it
takes the place of the clumsy *be enthusiastic over.*

*f*–Common nouns from proper names. A number of words
have come into general use because of some association with a
person or place: *boycott,* from the name of an Irish land agent,
Captain Boycott, who was so treated; *macadam,* from the inven-
tor of the road surface, John L. MacAdam; *sandwich* from an
Earl of Sandwich; *jersey,* from the island of Jersey; *pasteurize,*
from Louis Pasteur, who developed the process.

*g*–Playful formations. Blends and back formations are likely
to have a playful note and so do some other word shifts that
can't be classified. Some, like *hire education,* are convenient
puns. Some become quite generally used: *dingus, doodad,
beanery. Jalopy* seems a perfect word for its meaning.

Watching these recent and familiar formations may lead to
a study of the earlier and less obvious origins of words in the
General English vocabulary.

(References: The great authority on the origin of English
words is the *Oxford English Dictionary,* and now the *Diction-
ary of American English* and the *Dictionary of Americanisms*
are supplementing it for words peculiar to the United States.
Besides general books on English, the following pay special
attention to origin of words: Otto Jespersen, *Growth and
Structure of the English Language,* various editions; George
H. McKnight, *English Words and Their Backgrounds,* New
York, 1923; J. B. Greenough and G. L. Kittredge, *Words and
Their Ways in English Speech,* New York, 1901.)


**Originality** • *Originality* is applied to writing in two somewhat different senses:

1. The first sense refers to material. Material is "original"
when it is gathered by the writer from his experience, from his
observation of people, events, or places, or from documents
like letters and newspapers. Secondary or second-hand material
has been worked over by someone else, as in textbooks, encyclopedias, most magazine articles and books. This material has
been organized and given form in words. Original material has
to be sorted, selected, and laid out by the writer. Obviously
one can learn more and find more profitable practice in handling significant original material than in handling most secondary material.

Most student papers should contain some original material.
The content may come entirely from the writer's experience.

At least the central idea, the purpose can come from his present desires, some of the examples, details, or applications can come from his observation, and the opinions and the point of view can represent the way he thinks. Merely rewriting a magazine article is not a very profitable exercise in composition. Putting together material from several such secondary sources is more useful, since it requires selection and comparison of material. But the most useful work for growth in writing is composing papers in which a good deal of the material is original. The writing is a little harder, but it is more fun, and the gain is much greater than in simply working over what others have done. (Compare *Plagiarism.)

2. Originality in expression, in style, is a different matter. The English language has been used a long time, and absolutely new words and phrases are rare. The most threadbare figures and phrases can be avoided, and an honest attempt to tell exactly what the writer sees and believes will ordinarily result in straightforward, readable writing, which is more valuable than mere novelty. The one sure fact is that striving too hard for originality is almost certain to result in strained writing, uncomfortable to writer and reader alike. When a style deserving the label *original* appears, it is usually the by-product of an active and independent mind, not the result of trying to be different.

**Orthography** • See *Spelling.

**other** • See *any, and compounds with any § 1.

**ou** • In the *Pronunciation key (§ 1) /ou/ represents the sound in *bout, out, house*; the sound is also spelled *ow* in *cow* /kou/, *ough* in *bough* /bou/.

Words spelled with *ou* are variously pronounced: *trouble* /trub'l/, *soul* /sōl/, *soup* /süp/, *trousseau* /trü'sō/.

**-ough, -augh** • A handful of words containing -*ough* and -*augh* are one of the many scandals of English spelling. They are common words, so that we learn to spell most of them well enough—but it is hard to believe we should be asked to do so.

The objection to these forms is not so much that they are cumbersome, as that they "spell" such different sounds—*although, bough, cough, thorough, through, bought, taught, laugh.* This can be explained by the history of the pronunciation of the individual words chiefly by the fact that the pronunciations now generally current have come from different localities of early English speech—but that does not justify them.

For a while *altho* and *tho* and to a less extent *thru* and *thoro* were used somewhat in personal writing and in business writing, especially in advertising, and even in a few periodicals and in some books—though most publishers went by traditional stylebooks. They are still given as permissible spellings in the recent dictionaries, but their use seems to be declining. They are out of place in Formal writing, and their use in General writing should depend chiefly on their appropriateness to other traits of style and to the expectations of readers. (The *Chicago Tribune,* which once championed their use, has abandoned them.)

**ought** • See \*should—would § 2, \*want.

**-our, -or** • See \*-or, -our.

**-ous, -us** • *-ous* is an adjective ending: *fictitious, ominous*; *-us* is a noun ending: *cactus, campus, impetus.*

**out** • Though *out* has adjective, adverb, noun, preposition, and verb functions, it gives little trouble except in the Nonstandard locution *want out* for "want to go" or "come out."

**out of date** • *Out of date, out of doors, out of town* are usually hyphened when they stand before a noun but otherwise are written without hyphens:

He has an out-of-date model.     His model is out of date.

**Outline form** •
1. *The title.* The title of the paper should stand over the outline, but it is not a part of the outline and should not be numbered. The heads should carry their full meaning and not refer back to the title by pronouns. (See \*Titles of papers.)
2. *Sentence statement.* It is a good idea to put a sentence stating the subject and scope of the whole paper between the title and the first main head. If a sentence statement is used, it should be a full, meaningful sentence, not a mere announcement of the topic.
3. *Numbering systems.* The most widely used numbering system alternates letters and figures, as shown in § 7 on page 288. Avoid intricate or confusing schemes of numbering.
4. *Indention.* Write the main heads flush with the left margin and indent subheads two or three spaces from the left—enough to place them clearly in a different column. Heads that run over a single line should be further indented.
5. *Punctuation and capitalizing.* No punctuation is needed at the end of lines in a topic outline. In a sentence outline the

punctuation should follow regular sentence practice. Only the first word of a head and proper names are capitalized; an outline head is not a title.

**6.** *Heads*

*a–*Meaningful heads. Each head should be understandable by itself. It is especially important that heads convey clear, full meaning if the outline is to be shown to someone for criticism. The following would do as a scratch outline but would not be satisfactory for other purposes:

My Vocation
  I. The work I am interested in
 II. Why I prefer this type of work
III. What my responsibilities would be
 IV. The chances for success

Subheads, too, should carry full meaning. In this section from an outline for a paper on "The House of Morgan," the subheads are far too general to indicate what the actual content of the subdivisions will be:

A. Started by Junius Spencer Morgan
   1. What he did
B. Succeeded by J. P. Morgan I
   1. What he did
C. Succeeded by J. P. Morgan II
   1. What he did

*b–*Heads of equal importance. The main heads of an outline, those usually marked by Roman numerals, should show the several main divisions of the material. Similarly, the immediate subdivisions of these heads, those usually marked by capital letters, should designate logical divisions of one phase of the subject. The same principle applies to further divisions under any subhead.

| *Unequal headings:* | *Equal headings:* |
|---|---|
| Books I Have Enjoyed | Books I Have Enjoyed |
| I. Adventure stories | I. Adventure Stories |
| II. Historical novels | II. Historical novels |
| III. *The Old Man and the Sea* | III. Character studies |
| IV. Autobiographies | IV. Autobiographies |
| V. What I like most | V. Books on ethics and religion |

*c–*Headings in parallel form. Parallel heads or subheads are expressed in parallel grammatical form. A sentence outline should use complete sentences throughout; a topic outline should use phrase heads only. Such heads or subheads should use parallel phrasing for all heads of the same rank; that is, the heads in one series should be all nouns or all adjectives or all phrases, or whatever is the most appropriate form.

|   *Heads not parallel:*   |   *Parallel heads:*   |
|---|---|
| The Art of Putting | The Art of Putting |
| I. The stance is fundamental | I. The stance |
| II. The grip | II. The grip |
| III. Importance of the backswing | III. The backswing |
| IV. Stroking the ball | IV. The contact with the ball |
| V. Follow through with care | V. The follow-through |

**7.** *Division of main points.* Since a topic is not "divided" unless there are at least two parts, an outline should have at least two subheads under any main head—or none at all. For every heading marked *I* there should be as least a *II,* for every *A* there should be a *B,* and so on.

|   *Illogical single heads*   |   *Proper subdivision*   |
|---|---|
| The Tripartite System of Government | The Tripartite System of Government |
| I. The executive branch | I. The executive branch |
|   A. President and Cabinet |   A. President |
| |   B. Cabinet |
| II. The Legislative branch | II. The Legislative branch |
|   A. The House |   A. The House of Representatives |
|   B. The Senate |   B. The Senate |
|     1. Functions |     1. Special functions |
| |     2. Special privileges |
| III. The judicial branch | III. The judicial branch |
|   A. The Supreme Court |   A. The Supreme Court |
| |   B. Lower courts |

If there is a single detail, it may be included in the heading. For example, for an organization in which the whole executive power lay in the president the head might be:

    I.  The executive branch (The President)

Sometimes an exception is made for an outstanding illustrative example, which may be put in an outline as a single subhead:

    B. Injustice of grades in figures
        1. Example: My almost-Phi Beta roommate

**8.** *Introductions and conclusions.* Ordinarily a paper does have a beginning, a middle, and an ending (or an introduction, a body, and a conclusion), but you should not use labels such as these in the outline. For one thing, they are too general to reflect the specific content of your paper. For another, the beginning and ending can rarely be represented by heads that are coordinate with the others. The first and last topics in the outline are from the main body of material, chosen with a special view to their fitness for meeting and for taking leave of a reader.

**over-** • Compounds with *over-* are not usually hyphened:

overanxious       overalls       overdraft       overseas

**P** • *P* spells the sound as in *purr, tip, puppy*. It is silent in a few common words (*corps, cupboard, raspberry, receipt*) and in a number of words from Greek (*pneumonia, psalm, pseudo-, psychology*).

After *m, p* is often silent in such words as *empty* /em′tē/, and a /p/ is generally sounded after /m/ in words such as *dreamt* /drempt/ and *warmth* /wôrmpth/. In *pumpkin* two pronunciations are recognized, /pump′kin/ and /pung′kin/, and the variant spelling *punkin*.

**paid—payed** • *Paid* is the spelling of the past tense and past participle of *pay* (He paid his bills) in all senses except *payed out a line, rope,* etc., and occasionally in that sense also.

**pair** • In General usage the plural of *pair* is ordinarily *pair* when it comes after a number: *six pair of socks.* In other positions *pairs* is the usual plural.

**pants, trousers** • The Formal word is always *trousers*; the General and Informal, *pants* (clipped from *pantaloons*) or *trousers* —but always *ski pants.*

**Paradox** • See *Epigram.

**Paragraph indention, No paragraph indention** •
*Revision: Indent here for new paragraph; or join this paragraph to the preceding one.*          ¶, No¶

**Paragraphs** •
*Revision: This paragraph is unsatisfactory. Revise or rewrite it.*          Par

A paragraph is a group of related statements that a writer presents as a unit in the development of his subject. It strikes the eye as a unit because it is physically set off by indention or spacing. It should also strike the mind as a unit because the statements it contains are closely related, representing a stage in the flow of the writer's thought.

The most common faults in paragraphs are:
1. *Lack of development.* The writer fails to provide the particulars that will lead the reader to understand and accept his general statement about the subject.
2. *Lack of unity.* The writer fails to make every sentence contribute to the core of meaning that is the focus of the paragraph and that justifies its inclusion in the paper.
3. *Lack of continuity.* The writer fails to make clear the relation between the statements that make up the paragraph.
4. *Lack of transition.* The writer fails to fit the paragraph into the paper by tying it to what precedes and what follows.

## Parallel constructions •

*Paral*

> *Revision: Make the two or more elements in this series parallel in form.*

Typical shifted (unparallel) constructions are these:

| *Shifted:* | *Made parallel:* |
|---|---|
| To me orientation week seems both [noun:] a necessity and [adjective:] worth while. | To me orientation week seems both [two adjectives:] necessary and worth while. |
| Jack has received offers from Hollywood not only [phrase:] for his fishing experiences but [clause:] because he resembles the late Will Rogers. | Jack has received offers from Hollywood not only [two phrases:] for his fishing experiences but for his resemblance to the late Will Rogers. |

(For other examples see *Shifted constructions.)

**pardon—excuse** • See *excuse—pardon.

## Parentheses ( ) •

1. *For additions.* Parentheses (also called *curves* and by printers called *parens*) are sometimes used in writing, chiefly to enclose words, phrases, or whole sentences that add to the clearness of a statement without altering its meaning and that are allowed to stand outside the construction of the sentence. These additions are likely to be (1) illustrations, (2) definitions, or (3) added information thrown in for good measure, as in the first sentence of this paragraph.

He has a scholarship at Cornell (Iowa) .

This bill, commonly called the Lockport plan, has been the basis of all later city-manager charters (there are now 438) .

Can we historians of this present day and age, let alone those yet to come (who will have been nurtured and educated exclusively in artificial surroundings), succeed in recovering imaginatively what

that old milieu of thousands of years ago was like?—CARL BRIDEN-
BAUGH, "The Great Mutation," *American Historical Review,* Jan.
1963, p. 317

His concerts were well received in most cities (in Chicago the
reviews were so enthusiastic that he was given a return engagement),
but he was still dissatisfied with his performance.

These uses are slightly stiff, belonging most appropriately to
rather Formal exposition, and should be used sparingly.

**2.** *For apologetic asides.* Sometimes parentheses are used to
mark an apologetic aside, as much as to say "You know this,
but let me remind you"—though this use is less common today
than formerly:

Madison (the fourth president) enunciated the doctrine in 1823.

**3.** *To enclose numbers in an enumeration.* Parentheses are
often used to enclose the letters or figures used to mark items
in an enumeration, as in § 1 of this article, though this tends
to make the numbers or letters more conspicuous than they
deserve to be.

**4.** *With other marks.* When the parenthetical unit is a complete sentence, the period comes *inside* the curves, but it is
usually omitted if the expression falls within a sentence. Punctuation marks belonging to the sentence including the parenthesis come *after* the second curve.

Some words have various meanings with different prepositions, as
agree *with* (a person), agree *to* (a suggestion), agree *in* (principles,
qualities).

(See \*Capital letters § 1 for a discussion of capitalizing sentences in parentheses. Do not confuse parentheses and brackets;
see \*Brackets.)

**part, on the part of** • *Part* or *on the part of* is often a rather
clumsy way of saying *by, among, for,* and the like:

It resulted in less wild driving on the part of [*by*] young people.

In the past ten years there has been a definite move on the part
of [*by* or *among*] our religious leaders to unite all Protestants in one
church.

**Participles •**

1. Forms of participles.

|  | *Active* | *Passive* |
|---|---|---|
| *Present*: | asking; singing | being asked; being sung |
| *Past*: | having asked; having sung | asked, having been asked; sung, having been sung |

The simple participle forms (*asking, asked*) are used in
various verb phrases:

I am asking    I am being asked    I have asked    I have been asked

Because the participles do not indicate definite time themselves but time in relation to the context in which they are used, the terms *first participle* and *second participle* have been suggested, as well as others. But *present* and *past* are firmly established as names for them and work well enough if we remember that they are grammatical terms, not descriptions of meaning. (See *Tenses of verbs.)

**2.** *As modifiers.* When not a part of a phrasal verb form, the participles are most commonly used like adjectives. They have qualities of adjectives in that they modify nouns and pronouns (the pen *used* in signing the treaty; a *coming* era; the leaves *falling* in the street). They have qualities of verbs in that they may take an object (*Following these clues,* he soon found her) and be modified by adverbs (The car, *rolling crazily* . . .). (See *Adjectives, types and forms § 3a, 5.)

Sometimes in analyzing a sentence it is difficult to tell a participle used like an adjective from a participle which is a part of a passive verb form. Since grammatically the constructions are indistinguishable, the decision rests on whether the meaning requires the participle to modify the subject as a predicate adjective with a linking verb, or whether it describes an action.

*Passive voice*: The candidate of the Republican party *was defeated.*

*Predicate adjective*: The candidate was *defeated* but happy.

When used as a modifier, a participle should refer clearly to some particular noun or pronoun:

Opening his shirt at the neck, he went back to his chopping. [*Opening* modifies *he.*]

A college education, looked at from this point of view, may be a liability. [*Looked* modifies *college education.*]

There should be no reasonable doubt of what is modified. A modifying participle "dangles" or is "misrelated" when it seems to refer to a word the writer does not mean it to refer to:

*Dangling*: Walking on the campus, several of the newer buildings will catch the visitor's eye.

*Clearer*: Walking on the campus, the visitor will notice . . . .

*Dangling*: Combined with his scientific understanding, Dr. Hertzler is a man who would have made his name for wisdom in any profession.

*Clearer*: Dr. Hertzler's scientific understanding would have made him a name in any profession.

(See *Dangling modifiers.)

**3.** *In absolute constructions.* The participle-as-adjective should not be confused with the participle in a phrase which relates to the whole sentence (to the situation) rather than to a particular word. Some such phrases are very common, even *formulas:

> Judging from her looks, she isn't under fifty.
> Beginning with the class of 1965, the tuition was raised $50.

(See *Verbals.)

**4.** *Stylistically objectionable participles.* Amateur writers often use participles in constructions in which a subordinate clause would sound better:

> Uncle Joe was prompt, *necessitating our hurrying* [so that we had to hurry].
> The sea was running heavily, *being boosted* by a strong southeast wind. [Omit the *being*.]

Especially conspicuous are clumsy "nominative absolutes," made like Latin ablative absolutes:

> Then, *the feature being ended,* everyone began to file out of the theater. (Then, after the feature was over . . .; or, *perhaps:* The feature over, everyone. . . .)

(For *very* with participles see *very § 2. Compare *Gerunds. References: Curme, *Syntax,* pp. 158-160; C. A. Smith, *Interpretative Syntax,* Boston, 1906, pp. 55-59; Reuben Steinbach, "The Misrelated Constructions," *American Speech,* 1930, 5:181-197; H. C. Wyld, *A Short History of English,* pp. 237-258.)

**Particles** • Of the eight traditional parts of speech, four have no inflected forms in English—*adverbs, *prepositions, *conjunctions, interjections—and appear never to have been inflected in the Indo-European languages. They are sometimes lumped together under the term *particles.* To the grammarian they cause some discomfort. In the classical languages, nouns, adjectives, and pronouns have elaborate declensions, and verbs have elaborate conjugations, so a grammarian can always start with a detailed description of all those forms. And even in English there are at least remnants of inflection for all these words. But for the particles, descriptive comment—aside from listing them—must be entirely about their syntax, their use in utterances. And since syntax is the most elusive part of descriptive grammar, discussion of the use of particles is especially difficult. (See *Idiom and idioms.)

**Parts of speech** • Certain sentence functions are regularly filled by certain kinds of words which are not ordinarily used

## Parts of Speech in English: Summary of Characteristics

| Formal characteristics (as spelled) | Some derivational endings | Central syntactical functions | Common secondary functions |
|---|---|---|---|
| **Nouns:** Plural -s, -es or equivalents; Genitive 's, s' | -ance, -ee, -er (-or), -ism, -ment, -th | Subject or object of verb; object of preposition | Modifier of another noun; apposition; adverbial modifier |
| **Pronouns:** See *Pronouns, types and forms | (A closed class— no alterations possible) | Subject or object of verb; object of preposition | In altered (possessive) form, modifier of noun; apposition |
| **Verbs:** -s, -ing, -ed, or equivalents; in phrases after auxiliaries | -ate, -ize, -en, -fy | Predicate | As a gerund or infinitive, a subject or object; as an infinitive or participle, a modifier of noun |
| **Adjectives:** Comparison with -er, -est or more, most | -able, -al, -ant, -ary, -ic, -ish, -ous | Modifier of noun | Subject or object when preceded by a/an, the |
| **Adverbs:** Comparison with -er, -est or more, most (Except almost, very, etc.) | -ly, -wise | Modifier of verb, adverb, adjective, clause, or sentence | Connective; occasional modifier of noun; rarely subject or object |
| **Prepositions:** (Invariable) | (A closed class— no alterations possible) | Forming phrase with noun or noun equivalent as headword | Joining phrase to a word or sentence |
| **Conjunctions:** (Invariable) | (A closed class— no alterations possible) | Coordinating: joining words, phrases, clauses  Subordinating: introducing, forming a clause and joining it to another clause or to some other sentence element | |

**Interjections, or exclamations,** may be regarded as a subtype of Adverbs

| Typical position in sentences | Principal subtypes | Word groups with same function | Traditional definition |
|---|---|---|---|
| Before and after verb; after *a/an*, *the*, *our*, *this*, *some*, etc.; followed by *of*-phrase | Common, proper; abstract, concrete; mass, collective, etc. | Clauses with *that*, *whoever*, etc. Gerund and infinitive phrases | The name of a person, place, thing, relationship, etc. |
| Before and after verb; after preposition | See *Pronouns, types and forms | Often a noun or noun equivalent | A word used in place of a noun |
| Following subject in statements; often first in commands and questions | Open class: most verbs Closed class: linking verbs; auxiliaries (See *Verbs § 1.) | Verb-adverb combination | A word indicating action, state, or being |
| Between *a/an*, *the*, etc., and noun; after linking verb | Descriptive, limiting, proper | Clauses with *who*, *that*, etc.; wide variety of phrases | A word qualifying, making more exact, the meaning of a noun |
| Variable; after verb plus object | See *Adverbs, types and forms | Clauses with *when*, *since*, *although*, etc.; wide variety of prepositional phrases | A word modifying a verb, adjective, or another adverb |
| Before a noun or noun and its modifiers; often at end of construction | (None) | (None) | A word relating a noun to another word |
| At beginning of clause or sentence | Coordinating, subordinating, correlative, conjuctive adverbs | (None) | A word joining two words, phrases, clauses, or sentences |

in other functions. In *The teacher who realized it has died,*
the words cannot be rearranged to replace each other. *The
realizes who teacher it has died* is as impossible as *It teacher realizes the who has died* or any other rearrangement. Some words
in English play more than one part (*round* the corner, *round*
shape, *round* of ammunition, etc.) but the functions of most
words are so sharply restricted that it is apparent that speakers
of the language have them classified into categories. Hence the
traditional name, *parts of speech.* In some highly inflected languages like Latin, *form* (declensions, conjugations, derivational
endings) is a reliable basis for assigning words to the parts of
speech, though there is always a residue of *particles with only
one form. In English, change of form works moderately well in
identifying nouns, verbs, adjectives, and adverbs, which are
consequently often referred to as *form classes.* Even in these
classes, however, there are exceptions and minor variations, like
our nouns with plural in *-en* instead of the usual *-s,* or with a
foreign language plural, or with only a singular or a plural
form; and there are adverbs that are not compared (such as
*almost, quite, very*) and verbs with only one form (such as
*must* and *ought*). Many languages have derivational endings
that indicate the part of speech; English has a few, like *-ize*
to make a verb from a noun (*dramatize*) and *-ed* to make an
adjective from a noun (*fair-minded*), but such endings indicate
the part of speech of a very small number of words.

Since form is not always a reliable way of classifying words
in English, their *typical function in sentences* is used as supporting data or as the main data. Typically, English uses the
same word form in the function of more than one part of speech.

Sometimes a word develops the forms characteristic of more
than one part, as *radio* has the forms of verbs (*radios, radioing,
radioed*) and of a noun (*radios* as the plural and the same
form spelled *radio's* or *radios'* as a genitive), or *yellow* has the
forms of an adjective (*yellower, yellowest*), of a noun (*yellows,
yellow's*), and of a verb (*yellows, yellowing, yellowed*). In a dictionary or other general discussion of words, such words have
to be given as "belonging to" (that is, having the basic characteristics of) more than one part of speech. In a specific sentence,
the syntactical function, the way the word is used, is the final
clue, as *walk* is a noun in *Let's go for a walk* and a verb in
*They would rather walk than ride.*

Often, however, a word is used in the function of another
part of speech without acquiring the characteristic changes of
form; *bomb* has the forms and functions of a noun as well as
those of a verb but is used as a modifier (as in *bomb shelter*)
without acquiring the comparative forms of an adjective. In
the past there has been much loose description of this trait.

*Stone* in *stone cabin,* for instance, has been called "an adjective" or, somewhat more accurately, has been said to be "used *as* an adjective." Actually it is used *like* an adjective, in the function of an adjective—that is, as the modifier of a noun. Some linguists use separate terms for the parts of speech and for these functional shifts or for phrases and clauses used in the function of a part of speech. Most commonly they add the suffix -*al* to the name of the corresponding part of speech. An adjective used in the function of a noun (The *poor* are always with us) or a clause used in a typical function of a noun (*What she said* didn't matter to him) is called *nominal* or *nounal*; nouns used like adjectives (the *house* mother) are sometimes called *adjectivals*; nouns used like adverbs (Then we went *home*) are sometimes called *adverbials*; and so on. In this book, words used in such functional shifts are labeled by their function in a sentence, as subject or verb or modifier: *the light headed* might be a subject or object; in *Whoever was in that car saw it,* the clause is the subject. Referring to clauses as noun, adjective, or adverb clauses or to phrases as adjective or adverb phrases is a convenient way of saying that they are used *like* the part of speech indicated.

Linguists have not yet agreed upon a system for describing the parts of speech in English, though they are quite sure that such categories exist unconsciously in the minds of native speakers of a language and that those speakers have devices for using the words only in their appropriate functions. This book therefore uses basically the traditional categories with somewhat more precise criteria in their definitions. The table on pp. 294-295 lists the principal points regarding the parts of speech; some further details will be found in the *Index* article for each.

(References: Sumner Ives, "Defining Parts of Speech in English," *College English,* 1957, 18:341-348, is a good introduction to the problem. All books intended for use in the study of English treat the parts of speech.)

**party** • See *person.

**passed, past** • The past tense and the past participle of *pass* are *passed* (He passed the first post; He had passed), though *past* is fairly common as the participle. *Past* is the adjective (past favors), preposition (past the crisis), and adverb (past due; They went past). Pronunciation: /past/ or (Eastern) /päst/. (See *A § 3.)

**passer-by** • Usually hyphened: plural *passers-by.*

**Passive verbs •**
Pass
    *Revision: Change the passive verb or verbs to active.*

Amateur writers tend to use passive statements when active verbs would sound more natural ("The music *was enjoyed* by us" instead of "We *enjoyed* the music"). Awkward passives are sometimes used to avoid *I*:

*Passive*: The situation was taken in by me with great amusement.
*Active*: I took in the situation with great amusement.

This passage shows both effective and ineffective passives:

The year 1965 is here. With it comes a host of '65 model automobiles. Most of these cars *were heralded in* during the closing months of 1964. They *were awaited* in anxious curiosity by the buying public. In many instances, they *were looked forward to* with too much anticipation.

Although an awkward phrase, *were heralded in* is a legitimate passive, because the "heralders" need not be named; the passive *were awaited* places *the buying public* at the end of the sentence for emphasis and would not be noticeable if it was not followed by *were looked forward to,* which clearly shows that the writer was not paying attention to his work. Those two sentences might better stand:

The buyers awaited them in anxious curiosity, often with too much anticipation.

The use of passive verbs is often objectionable because it involves a thoughtless shift from the active voice and adds to the wordiness of what is usually already wordy and fuzzy writing. (For the formation of the passive voice and its profitable use see *Voice.)

**Past tense •** See *Tenses of verbs.

**peeve •** Informal for *annoy* and *annoyance, peeve* is a back formation from *peevish* (see *Origin of words § 3e). It is used most commonly as a modifier: *peeved.*

**per •** *Per* (Latin, "through, by, by the, among," etc.) is most appropriate when used in phrases that are still close to their Latin originals—*per capita, per cent,* or in a definitely commercial setting—*$18 per week, $2.60 per yard, forty-four hours per week,* or in certain standardized technical phrases—*revolutions per minute.*

Because of its commercial and technical connotation, *per* is less appropriate in General writing, where the English equivalent usually fits more naturally: *$18 a week, 20¢ a quart, four times a year.*

**per-, pre-** • Do not spell the *per-* words with *pre-*: write *per-*form, *per*spire, *per*fect, and so on. Remember that *pre-* means "before" (*pre*war, *pre*school, *pre*eminent).

**percent** • *Percent* is not followed by a period, and is sometimes written as two words. In Informal and General writing it is often used instead of *percentage* or even of *proportion*: *Only a small percent of the class was* [or *were*—collective agreement] *there.*

With figures the percent sign (%) is ordinarily used: 97.6%.

**Perfect tense** • See *Tenses of verbs.

**Period ( . )** •

1. *At the end of statements.* The principal function of the period is to mark the end of a statement—that is, the end of every completed sentence not definitely a question or exclamation.

Sometimes sentences in the form of exclamations or questions are really to be regarded as statements. After such a sentence a writer may use the exclamation mark or question mark, but he will usually have a period if the tone is lacking in emphasis or if he wishes to minimize the emphasis of the sentence form he has chosen. (See *Rhetorical questions.)

2. *Miscellaneous conventional uses.*

   *a*–After *abbreviations:    Oct.    n.b.    Mr. Wm. Fraser

   *b*–In sums of money, between dollars and cents: $5.66. The period is not used unless the dollar sign is used: 66 cents or 66¢; $0.66.

   *c*–Before decimals, or between the whole number and the decimal: .6, 3.14159, 44.6%.

   *d*–A period is sometimes used between hours and minutes represented in figures (2.36 p.m.), though a colon is usual in the United States (2:36 p.m.).

   *e*–Three spaced periods (. . .) are used as *ellipses, to mark the omission of words; several are often used to guide a reader's eye across the page. (See *Leaders.)

   *f*–After a letter or number denoting a series. The dash after *f* at the beginning of the preceding line, for example, could be a period.

3. *Period with quotation marks.* Most American publishers place a period coming at the end of a quotation inside the quotation marks: "The longer you put it off," he said, "the harder it's going to be." (See *Quotation marks § 4b.)

The period is also called a *full stop,* especially in British usage. For other uses see a stylebook.

**Periphrastic verbs** • See *Phrasal verb.

**Person** • Pronouns are classified according to *person* (first, second, and third) and *number* (singular and plural):

*First person,* the one speaking: [Singular] *I, my, me*; [Plural] *we, our, us*

*Second person,* the one spoken to: [Singular and plural] *you, your* [Archaic: *thou, thy, thee*]

*Third person,* the one spoken of: [This singular also shows masculine, feminine, and neuter; more accurately, male, female, and inanimate] *he, him, his*; *she, her*; *it, its*; [Plural] *they, them, their*

Nouns go with the third person form of the verb.

Except in the verb *be* (I am, you are, he is . . .), English verbs have only one form to distinguish person and number—the third singular of the present tense: I have, you have, he *has*; we, you, they have; and the *auxiliary verbs don't have even that.

**person** • *Person* is the ordinary word for referring to a human being. *Individual* has the same meaning (though it is applied also to single objects and animals as well) but emphasizes the person's singleness, aloneness, and is slightly heavy or pretentious unless that emphasis is needed. *Party* is legal or light. In British usage *person* sometimes has an unfavorable connotation. Often *people* is used rather than *persons*:

There was one person waiting.

There were several people [not *persons*] waiting.

*Personally* is sometimes used as a conversational *intensive ("I personally think") but is usually inappropriate in writing.

**Personal letters** • See *Letters.

**Personal pronouns** • See *Person, *Possessive adjectives, *Pronouns, types and forms § 1. See also *Apostrophe § 5.

**Personification** • *Personification* is a *figure of speech in which an object or animal or quality or ideal is given some attributes of a human being:

> Deal gently, *Love,* with him and her
> who live together now!
> REX WARNER, *Poems,* p. 71

It is less common today than formerly, and less common in prose than in verse. Flat and unnecessary personification is likely to have an amateur sound: *No steam engine can brag of such efficiency.*

**ph** • *Ph* is a *digraph for the /f/ sound in words of Greek origin: *phlox, photography, photograph....* In *Stephen* (and formerly in *nephew*), *ph* represents /v/.

Most words with *ph* belong to the Formal vocabulary, so that the simplification to *f* is very slow. In a few, like *fantasy* and *sulfur* the *f* form is now the commoner.

In *diphtheria* and *naphtha* the *ph* is pronounced /f/ and also /p/.

**phenomenon, phenomena** • *Phenomenon* is the singular and *phenomena* the plural (phenomena of the mind).

Originally *phenomenon* meant "any observable event," but now it also means "something remarkable," and *phenomenal* is almost always used in this sense. Often a shorter or more exact word is preferable.

**phone** • *Phone* is a clip for *telephone,* in General use as noun, verb, and modifier (on the phone; phone me later; the phone book). It is written without an apostrophe.

**Phonemes** • In linguistics *phoneme* is the term for the smallest distinctive unit, hence the smallest contrastive unit in speech. It may more easily be understood as what speakers of a variety of a language hear as "the same speech sound." "The same sound" actually is a range of sounds similarly produced. We make the /p/ at the beginning of *pit* by closing our lips, building up a pressure of air in the mouth, then opening the lips suddenly with a consequent audible explosion. The /p/ at the end of *stop,* on the other hand, can be clearly recognized merely from the abrupt cutting off of the vowel sound resulting from closing our lips; we don't have to open them again. In these words beginning and ending with /p/, the initial and final sounds are evidently different. Yet we call them "the same sound" because we interpret what we hear as the same thing. Each one of these phonetically different but similar sounds is called an *allophone*; they are actual noises; our interpreting them as "the same sound" results from our experience of learning our native language. Our capacity to do this permits us to classify the thousands of slightly different sounds of speech into a manageable number of categories (between 40 and 50) which exist, of course, only in our minds and are called phonemes.

Phonemes are of two kinds: those called *segmental* are more or less accurately represented by the letters of the conventional alphabet; those called *suprasegmental* may for the moment be described negatively as those devices of speech which are not represented by letters.

1. *Segmental phonemes.* The distinctive and contrastive function of the phoneme is most easily shown through the segmentals. The word *cat* is a sequence of three speech units, *c-a-t*, and forms a segment of speech; *rat* is another. The two are distinguished solely by the differing initial units. *I saw the cat* and *I saw the rat* are different statements because *c* contrasts with *r*. There are other differences in the sounds of *cat* and *rat*; getting from *c* to *a* involves movements in the mouth which differ from those in getting from *r* to *a*. But in learning English we have unconsciously trained ourselves to disregard these (subphonemic) differences. Therefore the smallest significant contrastive units are the *c* and the *r*.

In English the correspondence between the letters of the alphabet and the segmental phonemes is at best approximate (for the consonants), at worst quite bad (for the vowels and diphthongs). Accurate indication of the phonemes requires a phonemic transcription; the one most widely used is based on the International Phonetic Alphabet (IPA), which can be found in any book on linguistics and in some dictionaries. The phonemes of one language or even of one variety of a language may differ from those of another.

2. *Suprasegmental phonemes.* An alphabet is itself a recognition of segmental phonemes; therefore the inventors of an alphabet must have analyzed their language to determine the segmental phonemes, though of course they didn't use that term. The history of our system of writing shows no comparable analysis of stress, pitch, juncture, terminals, and rhythm. One is tempted, therefore, to assert that though they are a characteristic part of the language, they are not an essential part. But such an assertion assumes that conventional writing tries to represent all aspects of speech; it obviously does not. Since the systematic analysis of the suprasegmental features is much more recent than the analysis of the segmental ones, it is hardly surprising that there is disagreement about what they are, how many there are, and even whether they should be called phonemes. The following discussion is therefore tentative and, since this is primarily a book for writers, necessarily brief and incomplete.

In English speech we can observe that some syllables seem more prominent than others, the pitch of the speaker's voice varies, there are variations in the time and manner of getting from one word to the next, the speaker's voice in some way marks the ends of clauses and phrases, and there is a perceptible rhythmical pattern in the succession of syllables.

These features are more difficult to isolate than the segmental phonemes, partly because they are interdependent, partly because as their name suprasegmentals—above, beyond, in addition to the segmentals—suggests, they complement the vowels and consonants. What follows is only the sketchiest account of the suprasegmentals.

*a*–Stress. This is the most obvious. The greater prominence of the first syllable of *daily* and of the last syllable of *today* is evident to anyone. This light and heavy stress distinguishes words with the same segmental phonemes from each other: *impórt* (verb), *ímport* (noun). Often a third degree of stress is apparent, as in *óratòry*, where the prominence of the third syllable is greater than that of the second and fourth but not so great as that of the first. Occasionally a fourth degree becomes significant. (Symbols: ′ primary, ^ secondary, ` tertiary, ˇ least—usually not shown). The stress patterns of *irritàting* and *óratòry* are the same; but to emphasize one or the other of the words in a phrase, we make the first syllable of one word a bit more prominent than the first syllable of the other: *irritàting óratòry* or *ìrritàting óratòry*.

*b*–Pitch. It is also obvious that speakers of English vary the pitch of their voices as they speak. But the significance of that variation is much harder to discover than for stress. Linguists usually identify four distinctions in relative pitch, marked by superior figures from 1 to 4, 1 now usually indicating low pitch and 4 high, with 2 representing the common pitch of utterance. Frequently, especially in terminal syllables, the pitch glides within the syllable, as *here* in *Look here* might start on 3 and end on 1. In *He's never late, oh no* if the emphasis is on *he,* the pitches might go: [3]*He's* [2]*never late, oh* [3]*no*[1]. Pitch is closely associated with stress, and it takes a good deal of training to be able to distinguish it with accuracy.

*c*–Juncture or transition. In English, syllables and words usually follow each other without any breaks. *This is a board* or *This is aboard* would be indistinguishable in sound. The name given to this usual kind of transition is *close,* and in a transcription it is not ordinarily shown. But sometimes we get from one syllable to the next in such a way as to mark clearly the end of the first and the beginning of the second. In the old rhyme *I scream, you scream, we all scream for ice cream,* we can distinguish *I scream* from *ice cream* by putting the open transition (symbol $+$) in different places: *I+scream* and *ice+cream.* Context usually makes the distinction provided by this juncture superfluous, and the history of some English words suggests that speakers have not been much concerned about it (*a newt* for Anglo-Saxon *an ewt; an apron* from Middle English *a napron*). But it is a resource which is available, and occasionally speakers may use it to make significant contrasts.

*d*–Terminals. These are the combination of pitch changes and pauses that occur at the ends of phrases. They are far more significant than junctures, and three are usually recognized: sustained, symbolized by $\longrightarrow$ or | ; rising, symbolized by ↑ or || ; and falling, symbolized by ↓ or #. For example: *John here? No, he's not.*

↑   $\longrightarrow$   ↓

*e*–Rhythm. Rhythmical patterns occur in English speech because there are two major contrasts in stress—primary and least—plus two lesser ones—secondary and tertiary—and the weak and strong stresses tend to alternate. The gradations in intensity are actually far greater than the two or four significant ones just mentioned. It is these finer gradations—repetition with variation—which provide the pleasure we find in both verse and prose rhythm. And since the inherent rhythm of English comes through to some extent even in silent reading, the latent rhythmical patterns are important to the writer.

This account of the suprasegmentals does not give an adequate indication of how integral a part they are of English speech. They obviously convey a good deal of the meaning of speech. A native speaker learns them unconsciously and rarely "makes a mistake" in them, except perhaps from nervousness or inattention, as when a radio announcer reads a commercial mechanically, without sensing what he is reading. Neglect or misuse of them reveals the speaker as a foreigner or as one who is speaking artificially. The proper formation of the segmentals is essential to intelligibility, and of the suprasegmentals for effective oral communication. But the suprasegmentals are rarely essential to mere intelligibility, as is evident from their virtual elimination in song and their general omission in writing.

An understanding of the suprasegmentals is helpful in learning a second language (see *Intonation) and in describing scientifically the sounds of English, especially in finding the boundaries of constructions. In resolving occasional ambiguities in printed sentences, we supply the suprasegmentals; a man and a woman speaking the sentence *"I can be just as stubborn as any man"* would use different suprasegmental patterns with *any man*. Understanding of these features—with or without a knowledge of the term—is also helpful in revising one's writing where they have some bearing on punctuation; but since the written language has had a somewhat independent development they cannot be accepted as infallible guides.

(References: Gleason, Chs. 4 and 16.)

**Phonology** • See *Linguistics.

**Phrasal verb** • A verb formed by an auxiliary and an infinitive or past participle is called a *phrasal verb*: *will go, must go, has gone, had gone, should have gone.* Even in the tenses which have simple forms (goes, went), we get different shades of meaning by using phrasal forms (went, did go, was going, etc.). Phrasal verbs are also called *periphrastic* verbs. (See *Verbs.)

**Phrases** • A *phrase* is a group of two or more grammatically related words without a subject and finite verb that functions as a unit in a clause or sentence. Phrases are conventionally classified in terms of their elements:

*Prepositional*: in the room    before the war    because of that
*Participial*: coming into the room    pasted on the wall
*Gerund*: learning French
*Infinitive*: to live peacefully    to have seen him

Though the elements in a phrase usually stand together, they need not do so. In *He puts it off,* we have a verb phrase, *puts off,* interrupted by its object, *it.*

Other word groups that function as syntactical units are also referred to as phrases (have gone, a large house) in this article. Phrases function like single sentence elements:

*Nouns*: [Subject] *The first four games* were lost. [Object] He lost *the first four games.* [Genitive] the work *of the masters*
*Adjectives*: a heart *of gold*    *Crossing the street,* he nearly was hit by a car.
*Adverbs*: *beyond the town*    *in the morning*    He did it *in the Dutch manner.*
*Prepositions*: *Because of* John we were late.

(See *Absolute constructions, *Adjectives, types and forms § 4, *Adverbs, types and forms § 4, 5, *Dangling modifiers, *Gerund § 3, *Idiom and idioms, *Immediate constituents, *Participles, *Prepositional phrase, *Prepositions.)

**picnic** • When an ending that begins with a vowel is added to a word with final *c, k* is added before the ending to make sure the /k/ sound is retained:

picnicker, picnicked, picnicking
trafficked, panicked

**Pitch** • See *Phonemes § 2b.

**Plagiarism** • *Plagiarize* is defined in *Webster's Seventh New Collegiate Dictionary* as "to steal and pass off as one's own (the ideas or words of another)." *Steal* is an ugly word, but plagiarism is an ugly thing. If anything can be said in extenuation of it, that something is to be found in the explanations of why students do it.

First in importance, perhaps, is the fuzziness of their awareness of what plagiarism is. And for this there are justifications. Most of our ideas and some of our phrasings come from others. We can hardly talk or write without to some extent parroting the ideas of others, occasionally even in their exact words, though quite unconsciously and unintentionally.

The second explanation is to be found in the student's earlier educational experience. He may have been called upon to provide reports or criticisms, the material for which he could not possibly have obtained except from printed sources. Often he has simply copied the material without bothering to indicate his source. Since his teacher knew he had done this and he knew his teacher knew it, no deception was intended or achieved. But a careless habit was established.

As a third explanation there is the possibility of panic. Sometimes in college a combination of assignments put off and of tasks utterly overwhelming puts a student into such a state of terror that his sense of values is confused and he stoops to devices which in a normal state he would shrink from.

Finally, of course, there is the dishonest person. For him, no doubt, there is also an explanation but no justification.

A large part of the problem can be solved by careful self-examination of one's ideas and by an awareness of the procedures to be followed in writing so as to give credit where credit is due.

If a student copies from dishonest motives, he must take the consequences, which are likely to be severe. If he copies from fear or ignorance of proper practices, he deserves consideration and help. Whatever the motive, the penalty—failing the paper or perhaps, if it is an important one, failing the course—does not represent the vengeance of the instructor but the failure of the student, failure in the fundamental purpose of a composition course, which is to increase students' skill in communicating their information and ideas to others. Copying from the work of another is the most complete failure possible.

The student who is scared or puzzled should go at once to his instructor and discuss his situation frankly, the reasons for his difficulties, the present faults in his work, and ways to overcome them. Serious effort intelligently directed should bring improvement. A student who feels he is moving in the right direction, even if he is moving slowly, is doing something valuable, and in the long run work is more satisfying and less wearing than worry.

The student who has not learned how to handle material obtained from reading and study needs guidance in the fundamentals of study and scholarship. A writer expects that what he has published will be read and will be used; but he has a right to expect that his exact words will not be used without his receiving credit and that his facts and ideas will not be used in print without his permission. His rights in these matters are legal, covered by copyright, and violation of them through plagiarism exposes the plagiarist to prosecution.

Anyone using published material, then, has a twofold responsibility: first, of absorbing the ideas into his own thought and, second, of giving credit to important sources. A student—or anyone else—is not *composing* when he is merely copying. He should read and digest the material, get it into his own words (except for brief, important quotations that are shown to be quotations). He should be able to *talk* about the subject before he *writes* about it. Then he should refer to any sources he has used. This is not only courtesy but a sign of good workmanship, part of the morality of writing. In an informal paper the credit can be given informally, perhaps a note on the cover saying "This paper is based on. . ."; or it may be in the body of the paper: "Professor Keane said in a lecture. . .," "Walter Lippmann wrote recently. . .," or "So-and-so said. . . ." Or credit may be given more formally in footnotes at the bottom of the page (as described in *References). Footnotes must be used in a research paper and are in order in any paper for which a student has found material in print. The greatest temptation to plagiarize is in a research paper, in which the material is ordinarily based on reading various sources. But a research paper offers also the best opportunity for learning how to gather, digest, and give credit for material from published sources. At any rate it is necessary for college students to learn how to use such material—by getting much of it into their own words and then giving appropriate credit to sources used. (See *Originality.)

**play** • See *show.

**plenty** • As an adverb (I was plenty worried; The car is plenty large) *plenty* is marked colloquial by some dictionaries and is in Informal use; it is not found in Formal writing and is usually inappropriate in college writing.

The omission of *of* after *plenty* in speech (*plenty* [ ] *time*) results in an adjectival use. The idiom is rarely found in print.

**Pleonasm** • *Pleonasm* is using two words for the same grammatical function (My *Uncle Fred, he* said he would give me twenty-five cents for every bird I could find and name). It is quite common in speech and for emphasis occasionally appears in writing; but it should not be used in writing except for very good reason.

**plurality—majority** • See *majority—plurality.

**Plurals of nouns** • The plural of the great majority of English nouns is made by adding an /s/ or /z/ sound, spelled -s, to the singular form of the noun. This -s is pronounced as part of the syllable to which it is added:

> buckets   rats   days   rooms   trees
> There are ten *Romes* in the United States.

Since this is the usual way of forming the plural, dictionaries list only the exceptional plurals under the entry for each irregular noun. But several groups of words form their plurals in other ways. The discussion which follows deals only with the spelling of plurals. Pronunciations of plurals are sometimes exceptional: The plural of *edge* has two syllables, though only an *s* is added in the spelling; the *s* of *house* becomes a /z/ in *houses*; etc.

1. *Special groups in "-s" or "-es":*

*a*–Nouns ending in -*ch*, -*s*, -*sh*, -*x*, or -*z* add the spelling -*es*:

> birches   churches   bridges   ledges   *buses [or *busses*]
> kisses   bushes   *Joneses   axes   fixes   buzzes   quizzes

*b*–Common nouns ending in -*y* preceded by a consonant change *y* to *i* and add -*es*:

> beauties   bodies   caddies   cherries   cities   cries   enemies

Exceptions to this rule are proper nouns (*Henrys*) and a few common nouns: *stand-bys, emptys* (bottles).

Words ending in -*y* preceded by a vowel (except -*quy*) add -*s*:

> bays   boys   moneys [sometimes *monies*]   monkeys   toys

These plural forms should not be confused in writing with the genitive singular in '*s*: *beauty's, body's, caddy's,* and so on.

Nouns ending in -*quy* replace *y* with *ies*: *soliloquies.*

*c*–Words ending in -*o* preceded by a vowel make regular plural with -*s*: *cameos, folios, radios, studios.*

Words ending in -*o* preceded by a consonant vary and have to be remembered or looked up in a dictionary. Some of the commoner of these are:

> With -*s* only: banjos   cantos   dynamos   Eskimos   Filipinos
> pianos   silos   solos   sopranos
> With -*es*: echoes   heroes   Negroes   noes   potatoes   tomatoes
> torpedoes   vetoes

Several words ending in -*o* are used with either -*s* or -*es*. The -*es* form is usually the more common, but the increasing number of -*os* forms suggests that English is gradually reducing these irregular words to the regular plural form:

cargoes, cargos            desperadoes, desperados
zeros, zeroes              hoboes, hobos

*d*–Nouns ending in -*i* usually add -*s*:

skis [but] taxis, taxies

*e*–Nouns ending in -*oo* add -*s*:

cuckoos

*f*–Some common nouns ending in -*f* or -*fe* use -*ves*:

calf, calves   half, halves   knife, knives   leaf, leaves   loaf, loaves
self, selves   shelf, shelves   thief, thieves   wife, wives   wolf, wolves

But proper nouns do not: *Wolf, Wolfs*
Many words ending in /f/ sounds are regular:

beliefs   chiefs   dwarfs   fifes   gulfs   proofs   roofs

Some have two forms:

elf, elfs–elves   hoof, hoofs–hooves   scarf, scarfs–scarves
staff, staffs–staves   wharf, wharfs–wharves

2. *Same form for both singular and plural*:

*Names of some animals, especially as game*: fowl, sheep, fish [*fishes* for varieties of fish]
*All words in* -ics: athletics, civics, mathematics, politics
*Common measurements*: foot, pair, ton
A number of words rarely, if ever, used in the singular:

| | | | |
|---|---|---|---|
| bellows | headquarters | odds [in betting] | smallpox |
| billiards | means | pants | species |
| gallows | measles | pincers | tactics |
| goods | morals | scissors | trousers |

3. *Survivals of older English plural forms*:

*In* -en: child, children   ox, oxen   brother, brethren [Church use]
*Change of vowel*: foot, feet   goose, geese   louse, lice   man, men
mouse, mice   tooth, teeth   woman, women

4. *Foreign language plurals.* English keeps the foreign form of many words that have been borrowed from other languages. As they become more commonly used, the plural is usually formed regularly in -*s*; words used chiefly in scientific or Formal writing tend to keep the foreign form longer. *Antenna*, for instance, makes *antennae* in biology but *antennas* in electronics. When the word is in transition, both forms will be found.

A few borrowed words that now regularly have plurals in -*s* or -*es* will suggest the extent of the change to English forms:

| | | | |
|---|---|---|---|
| area | campus | encyclopedia | museum |
| arena | circus | era | panacea |
| asylum | dilemma | ignoramus | panorama |
| bonus | diploma | metropolis | plateau |
| bureau | dogma | minus | quota |

Some common words that still have the foreign form or sometimes are found with the foreign plural (as in Formal, academic, or scientific writing) are:

| | | |
|---|---|---|
| addendum -da | diagnosis -ses | nebula -las, -lae |
| alumna -nae | erratum -ta | neurosis -ses |
| *alumnus -ni | focus -ci (scientific), | nucleus -clei, -cleuses |
| ameba -bae, -bas | -cuses (General) | oasis oases |
| analysis -ses | *formula -las, -lae | opus opera |
| apparatus -tus, | fungus -gi, -guses | ovum ova |
| -tuses | gladiolus -luses, -li | parenthesis -ses |
| appendix -dixes, | hiatus -tuses, hiatus | psychosis -ses |
| -dices | hypothesis -ses | radius radii, radiuses |
| automaton -ta, | index indexes, | rostrum -trums, -tra |
| -tons | indices | species species |
| axis axes | larva -vae | stadium -diums, -dia |
| bacillus -li | libretto -tos, -ti | stimulus -li |
| basis bases | locus loci | stratum -ta, -tums |
| beau beaus, beaux | madame mesdames | syllabus -bi, buses |
| cactus -ti, -tuses | matrix -trixes, | synopsis -ses |
| chateau -teaus, | -trices | synthesis -ses |
| -teaux | *medium -dia, | tableau -bleaus, |
| cherub cherubs, | -diums | -bleaux |
| cherubim | memorandum -da, | terminus -nuses, -ni |
| (scriptural) | -dums | thesis -ses |
| crisis crises | momentum -tums, | trousseau -seaus, |
| criterion -teria | -ta | -seaux |
| curriculum | monsieur messieurs | vertebra -brae, -bras |
| -lums, -la | moratorium -iums, | vortex -tices, -texes |
| datum *data | -ia | |

Because the languages English has borrowed from form plurals in so many different ways, speakers of English are sometimes confused by the variety and produce some odd forms. *Data* is a Latin plural, but because it is sometimes used with a singular verb we get the Nonstandard *datas*. *Bus* is a shortened form of the Latin *omnibus,* already a plural, from which those with a smattering of Latin formed *omnibii* which has not survived. (See *Foreign words in English § 3c.)

5. *Compound and group words.* Most compound words and group words add -s to the end of the group, whether written as one word or several:

bookcases     high schools     cross-examinations

In a few the plural sign is added to the first element:

daughters-in-law    courts-martial    mothers-in-law    *passers-by
attorneys general    postmasters general    poets laureate [also *poet laureates*]    sons-in-law

**6.** *Plurals of figures, words, letters.* Usually the plural of a letter of the alphabet, of a word discussed as a word, or of a figure is written with -'s:

There are two *c*'s and two *m*'s in *accommodate.*
Three 2's    six 8's
Don't use several *that*'s in a row.

(See *Numbers § 4.)

**7.** *Plural substitutes.* A plural notion is expressed often by a phrase that remains grammatically singular:

College after college has gone in for intramural sports.
The coach, with the captain and manager, makes up the schedule.
The coach, together with the captain and manager, makes [often *make*] up the schedule.

(Other *Index* articles dealing with the formation of plurals include *Apostrophe § 1, *Genitive § 1, *-ful, full. Singular and plural constructions are treated in *Subject and verb, *Reference of pronouns. References: Curme, *Parts of Speech,* pp. 112-127, *Syntax,* pp. 539-548; Fries, *AEG,* p. 40 ff.)

**p.m., a.m.** • See *a.m. and p.m.

**Poetry** • When verse is quoted, it should be lined off as written. If possible, the quoted lines should be approximately centered on the page, indented according to the scheme of the original. When so spaced, quotation marks are not needed around lines of verse quoted and inserted in a prose passage. The first word of each line should be capitalized if it was capitalized in the original. (See *Verse form, *Capital letters § 3.)

**politics** • *Politics* is construed as either a singular or plural word but should not be both in the same passage:

In almost any group, politics is a controversial subject.
Republican politics were offensive to the Federalists.

**Polysyllables** • See *Monosyllables.

**position, job** • See *job, position.

**Positive degree** • The *positive degree* of adjectives and adverbs is the simple adjective form (*poor, high, golden*) or adverb form (*slow, slowly, bitterly*). (See *Comparison of adjectives and adverbs.)

**Possessive adjectives** • *My, your, his, her, its, our, your, their* (the genitive case forms of the personal pronouns) are often called *possessive adjectives* when they modify a noun:

> my car    his first lecture    their experiences

**Possessive case** • See *Genitive.

**practical** • *Practical* and its derivatives give some trouble in spelling:

> *practical,* adjective: a practical scheme, He has a practical mind.
> *practically,* adverb: They were practically inclined [Informal in phrases like *practically all there*]
> *practicable,* adjective: a practicable method
> *practicability,* noun: They questioned the practicability of the idea.

**pre-** • The prefix *pre-* means *before* in time (*preexist, pre-Victorian*), or in place (*precerebral*), or rank (*preeminent*). For the spelling of words beginning with *pre*—written solid or hyphened—consult your dictionary.

**pre-, per-** • See *per-, pre-.

**Precious, preciosity** • Applied to style, *precious* and *preciosity* (or *preciousness*) mean "excessive fastidiousness in the use of language." The terms were borrowed from French and, though sometimes useful, have limited currency.

**Précis** • A *précis* /prā'sē/ is a concise summary of facts or, more often, of an article or other written document, giving in a brief space the essential content, the attitudes, and the emphasis of the original. Writing a précis can be an excellent device for testing your comprehension of a chapter, an article, or even a book.

**Predicate** • The *predicate* of a clause or sentence is the verb with its modifiers—object, complement, etc.—and predication is the function of a full verb in a clause or sentence. The subject and predicate are the two main elements of a sentence. The predicate may be a simple verb of complete meaning (The big bell *tolled*), a verb and adverbial modifier (The sun *went behind the cloud*), a transitive verb and its object (He *finally landed the big fish*), a *linking verb and complement (The oldest member of a family *is usually the first to go*).

Two verbs depending upon one subject are known as a
*compound predicate:

The three of them *washed* and *wiped* the whole lot in fifteen
minutes.

(See *Subject and verb, *Compound sentence, *Objects,
*Verbs.)

**Predicate adjective** •
*Revision: Use an adjective here, since the verb is a
linking verb.*                                              *P Adj*

Adjectives and nouns that follow linking verbs are called
*predicate adjectives* and *predicate nouns* (or *nominatives*), or
*predicatives.*

Predicate adjective: The horse is *fast.* I feel *bad.* It is going to
turn *warm.* It got *colder.* That one is *best.* The coffee tastes *sweet.*
The hedge grows *thick* around the deserted house.

Predicate noun: Gibbon was a *historian.* Jackson became a *doctor.*

(See *Adjectives, types and forms § 2b, *bad—badly, *Linking
verbs, *Nouns § 2.)

**Predicative** • *Predicative* is an inclusive term for *predicate
adjective* and *predicate noun.*

**predominant** • *Predominant* is the adjective: *a predominant
sentiment, a sentiment predominant in the village. Predominate*
is the verb: *This sentiment predominated in the village.* The
present participle *predominating* is often used adjectivally.

**prefer** • *To* is ordinarily used with *prefer:*

I prefer *Babbitt* to *Main Street.*
He preferred going by train to going in their car.

*Would* (or *had*) *rather. . .than* is less Formal and more
used:

He would [or *had* or *He'd*] rather go by train than in their car.

**Prefix** • A *prefix* is an element that can be placed before a
word or root to make another word with a different meaning
or function: *anti- (antiprohibition), bi- (biweekly), mis- (misfit).*
(See *Origin of words § 3a. See also *Latin and English,
*Hyphen §3, *Long variants.)

**Prepositional phrase** • A *prepositional phrase* is a phrase
made up of a preposition and its object: *without hope, in a
hurry, toward a more abundant life.*

Prepositional phrases are modifiers, used in the functions of adverbs or adjectives:

*Adverbial modifier*: They came *at just the right time*.
*Adverbial modifier*: He lives *in the white house*.
*Adjective modifier*: The woman *in the black dress* has left.

To suggest the importance of prepositional phrases in English, here is a sentence of 42 words in which 27 stand in prepositional phrases (in italics), 15 in other constructions:

The settings *of the novels* ranged *from the fiords of Norway to the coasts of Tasmania,* and every page betrayed that intimate knowledge *of a foreign country* which can only be acquired *by a thorough study of the chattier sort of guide-books.*—STEPHEN VINCENT BENÉT, *Thirteen O'Clock,* p. 71

## Prepositions •

Prep

*Revision: Change the preposition, making it more exact or idiomatic (§ 3a), less conspicuous (§ 3b), or making the construction less Informal (§3d).*

1. *Definitions.* Prepositions are \*particles with no distinctive form which belong to a closed class; therefore they are identified by us partly by our having learned them all, partly by the way they are used. Many words function as prepositions, adverbs, or conjunctions; recognition of them as belonging to the preposition class is therefore not enough. Their prepositional function becomes clear to us through a combination of our awareness that they may function as prepositions plus our recognition of their standing in a characteristic prepositional position in relation to other words:

*Preposition*: The wettest summer *since* the Flood.
*Conjunction*: *Since* the price was so low, we took three.
*Adverb*: He hasn't been around *since*.

The principal function of a preposition is to signal the unity of the phrase it introduces: *in turn, after the first try, for a long time.* The phrase then takes its place in a sentence as a unit, and the preposition, partly through its meaning, helps relate it to some other sentence element: to a verb (He showed her *to* her room), to a noun (the click *of* flying wheels), or to an adjective (old *in* experience). A noun following a preposition is called its object (*room, wheels, experience* in the examples just given). Prepositions may be word groups as well as single words: *in regard to, according to.*

There has lately been a tendency to minimize the \*lexical meaning of prepositions. In concrete senses they carry as much meaning as other words: being *under* a bed is quite different

from being *on* a bed. Even in more abstract contexts, prepositions have meaning, though it may seem more arbitrary:
*beneath* contempt, *for* love, *in* or *with* haste, agree *to* a proposal or *with* a person. These meanings, like those of abstract
nouns, are learned in a context of language rather than of
physical experience, but none the less learned.
**2.** *List of prepositions.* The following list shows characteristic
uses of the commoner prepositions. Many of them show both
a concrete and an abstract meaning (*at* home, *at* odds). Fries
estimates that nine of them (*at, by, for, from, in, of, on, to,
with*) account for over 92% of prepositions used.

*aboard*   aboard the airliner [Formal: *on board*]
*\*about*   about the town, about her, about his work
*\*above*   above the clouds, above the average, above suspicion
*according to*   according to the reports, according to Hoyle
*across*   across the bow, across the street
*\*after*   after supper, we all ran after him [Technical: for a drawing based on another's drawing—*after Newcourt*]
*against*   against the door, against the grain
*ahead of*   ahead of his generation, ahead of time
*along*   along the shore, along the route
*alongside*   alongside the dock [Informal: *alongside of*]
*amid (amidst)*   [Formal] amid the smoke, amidst the ruins
*among*   among the lucky ones [used of three or more]
*apart from*   apart from the others, apart from his own earnings
[rather Formal]
*apropos*   [Formal] apropos our discussion; *or,* apropos of our discussion
*around*   around the edge, around the town
*as*   as judge, as chairman
*as far as*   as far as the door, as far as New Orleans
*\*as to*   as to the objection, as to your interest
*at*   at home, at Johnstown, at his suggestion, at midnight
*back of*   back of the screen, back of the house, back of the proposal. *Back of, in back of* are less likely to occur in Formal writing
than *behind.*
*because of*   because of the war, because of his need
*before*   before the flood, before an audience, before replying
*behind*   behind the door, behind the pretense
*below*   below the surface, below our level
*beneath*   beneath the surface, beneath contempt [more Formal
than *below*]
*\*beside*   beside the sea, beside the point, beside oneself
*besides*   besides those named, no other besides this
*\*between*   between New York and Philadelphia, between life and
death
*beyond*   beyond the river, beyond reach

*by*   by the house, by an inch, by force, by himself, by night
*concerning*   concerning my friend, concerning our interest
*considering*   considering the difficulty
*contrary to*   contrary to orders, contrary to our expectation
*despite*   [Formal] despite hostile criticism
*down*   down the chute, down the slope, down the list
\**due to*   due to an error, due to carelessness
*during*   during the last ten years, during the services
*except*   except the children
*following*   following the rule
*for*   for you, for profit, for the community
*from*   from the attic, from the Far East, from fear
*in*   in the country, in the house, in the Bible, in trouble
*in back of*   (see *back of, behind*)
*in place of*   in place of the old regulations
*inside*   inside the house, inside ten minutes [Often, somewhat
Informally, *inside of*]   inside of ten minutes
*in spite of*   in spite of the law, in spite of his prejudices
*in view of*   in view of these concessions
*into*   into the mountains, into the subject (see \**in—into—in to*)
*like*   like a horse, like a tornado
*near*   near the window, near the top, near exhaustion
\**of*   of Wisconsin, of the same color, of my opinion, of the king
*off*   off the path, off the platform [Redundant, *off of*] off of the
path
*on*   on the road
*on account of*   on account of the weather, on account of his belief
*onto*   onto the train, onto the beach
*opposite*   opposite the house
*out*   out the window
*out of*   out of the auditorium, out of sight
*over*   over the fence, over the plains, over her head
*owing to*   owing to the emergency, owing to our inability
*past*   past the stores, past the mark, past the hour
\**per*   per day, per pound
*round*   round the Maypole, round the town
*since*   since his election, since Victorian days
*through*   through the first barrier, through accident
*throughout*   throughout the day, throughout his speech
\**till*   till morning, till the intermission
*to*   to Los Angeles, to the ocean, to Governor Smith, to the point
\**toward*   toward Fort Worth, toward dinner time, toward the
truth
*under*   under the awning, under cover, under the arch
*until*   until dusk, until two o'clock (see \**till, until, 'til*)
*unto*   [Archaic] unto death, unto the last drop
*up*   up the slope, up the scale

*upon*   upon a sure foundation, upon further investigation
*up to*   up to this point
*via*   via United Air Lines
*with*   with his fellows, with caution, with the affirmative
*within*   within bounds, within the city, within a year
*without*   without money

**3.  *Use of prepositions.***

*a*–Exact or idiomatic prepositions. A number of words are accompanied by certain prepositions, as contented *with* conditions, *in* my estimation. Some words have various meanings with different prepositions: agree *with* (a person), agree *to* (a suggestion), agree *in* (principles, qualities).

You can add indefinitely to the following list:

| | |
|---|---|
| deprive *of* pleasure | hindrance *to* advancement |
| eligible *for* membership | means *of* winning |
| fascinated *by* this glamor | pride *in* his college |
| fear *of* fire, fear *for* his safety | unconscious *of* their stares |

The customary preposition does not give much trouble with words that we use commonly, because we learn the words by hearing or seeing them in their usual constructions. Obviously it is safer to learn words as they are actually used, to learn *acquiesce in* (acquiesce in a decision) rather than just *acquiesce*. If a person uses an unidiomatic preposition, it is probably because he is not at home with the word or is confused because usage is divided on that particular locution (as *different *from* or *than* or *to*). Dictionaries give the appropriate preposition used with particular words. This book treats a few idioms that are likely to raise questions: *ability (to); *agree to, agree with; *all of; *compare—contrast; *different. (See also *Idiom and idioms.)

A special reminder is needed that when two words are used which are completed by different prepositions *both* prepositions should be used, though in Informal speech the omission of the second preposition often passes unnoticed:

The first lesson learned by the sturdy Italian boy just over from the "old country" was *obedience to* and *respect for* others besides his parents. (Not: obedience and respect *for* others)

Some people cannot reconcile their *interest in* and their *fear of* snakes.

The committee acknowledged its *interest in,* but denied its *responsibility for,* housing conditions.

When both words call for the same preposition, it need not be repeated:

The box office refused to make any *allowance* or *refund for* tickets purchased from an agent.

There are, of course, instances of *divided usage: abound *in* or *with,* hanker *after* or *for,* the necessity *of* or *for.* (See *between, among; *different; *sick.)

*b*–Prepositions bulking too large. English has a number of group prepositions (according to, in regard to, by means of) that sometimes become conspicuous. They can hardly be called wrong, but used in any noticeable numbers they tend to weigh down the style. Often a shorter preposition will do better.

In these examples, sometimes one or more of the italicized words (in brackets) can be omitted or a simple preposition (in brackets) can be substituted:

We made supper [*out*] *of* beans, fried potatoes, and steak.

Consumers Union attempts to furnish reliable information *in regard to* [*about*] all sorts of goods and services.

For politeness' sake the pronoun of the first person stands last when used [*in connection*] *with* other pronouns: "He, you, and I had better do it."

It has been said that in six months after graduation from college a man can pick up as much practical knowledge *connected with* [*of*] business administration as a nongraduate can in ten years.

... recent demonstrations *on the part of* [*by*] certain students. ...

Prepositions sometimes bulk too large in writing because we carry over to paper our tendency in speech to use double prepositions: *in back of* for *back of, outside of* for *outside, off of* for *off.* ... These are not appropriate in Formal English, which at its best makes one word do maximum duty, but in Informal English they may help give an easy tone if they do not become too noticeable. The writer should decide whether these idioms are appropriate to other traits of his style. (For further examples and discussion see the articles *as to, *of, off, *onto, and so on.)

*c*–Omission of prepositions. Spoken English shows not only a frequent piling up of prepositions but the opposite tendency too—dropping a preposition that would ordinarily be used in writing. Prepositions, especially *of,* receive so little stress that they naturally drop out entirely in rapid speech, and this same trait is now increasingly found in writers whose style is conspicuously Informal. A few examples (with the preposition usual in General English in brackets) will suggest the tendency:

The color [*of*] cloth she preferred was out of stock.

The most notable piece of equipment was an apparatus which made it possible to run the presses [*at*] almost twice their former speed.

A *couple [*of*] days later. ...

*d*–Prepositions at end of sentence. It was once fashionable for textbooks to put a stigma upon prepositions standing at the end of their constructions (What did you do it *for?*). But postponing the preposition is a characteristic English idiom, even though it runs contrary to our usual tendency to keep words of a construction close together. In fact it is so generally the normal word order that the real danger is in clumsiness from trying to avoid a preposition at the end of a clause or sentence:

Tell me what it is to which you object. [Natural: *what you object to*].

To whatever authority we may appeal, he will quibble over the method to be adopted. [Natural: *Whatever authority we may appeal to*. . . .]

Extreme cases are possible (like the boy's: "What did you bring that book for me to be read to out of for?"), but there is no reason for hesitating to let a preposition fall at the end if natural idiom and rhythm place it there. (Often the final word is not a preposition but an adverb, as in the old saw: "A preposition is a bad word to end a sentence with." Compare *Verb-adverb combinations.)

Placing the preposition at the end is such a firmly fixed habit that sometimes we use one at the beginning and end:

. . . in the lives of individuals *with* whom he had come in contact *with.*

Obviously such a sentence shows lack of revision.

(In addition to *Index* articles already referred to in this discussion, see *Parts of speech, *Function words, *Objects § 3. References: Curme, *Syntax,* pp. 566-569; Fowler, pp. 457-459 and other index entries; Fries, *AEG,* Ch. 7; Hall, pp. 213-217; M. Bertens Charnley, "The Syntax of Deferred Prepositions," *American Speech,* 1949, 24:268-277.)

**Present tense** • See *Tenses of verbs.

**principal—principle** • Associate *principal* as an adjective (the *principal* reason—the *principal* man of the town—the *principal* force involved) with other adjectives ending in *-al*: historic*al*, politic*al*, music*al*.

*Principal* as a noun is probably an abbreviation of a phrase in which it was originally an adjective: the *principal* that draws interest was once *the principal sum*; the *principal* of a school, *the principal teacher*; the *principal* in a legal action, *the principal party*; the *principals* in the cast of a play or movie, *the principal actors*. These are the only common uses of *principal* as a noun.

The noun meaning "a general and fundamental truth" (the

*principles* of science, the *principles* of government) or "a rule of conduct" (a man of high *principles,* a matter of moral *principle*) is *principle.*

### Principal parts of verbs •

Prin
    *Revision: Change the verb form to the one in good use, as given in the list below or in a dictionary.*

The principal parts of a verb are the bare form or infinitive (*ask*), the past tense form (*asked*), and the past participle (*asked*). Most English verbs are "regular"—that is, their past tense and past participle are formed by adding *-ed* to the bare form. A number, most of them descended from Old English strong verbs—verbs which formed their past tense and past participle forms by altering their root vowels—retain the older pattern (*ride, rode, ridden*). Some of these are becoming regular (*shined, weaved*), and many are made regular in speech and Nonstandard usage (*blowed, growed*).

The following list includes a number of verbs with these irregular parts or with some other question of form. A form in parentheses is decidedly less common in writing, and those labeled *NS* (Nonstandard) would not ordinarily occur in current writing. A recent dictionary should be consulted for other verbs. But usage is by no means uniform, even among speakers and writers of Standard English, and dictionaries do not record all variations.

| *Infinitive* | *Past tense* | *Past participle* |
|---|---|---|
| arise | arose | arisen |
| bear | bore | borne |
|  |  | *born (given birth to) |
| begin | began (NS: *begun*) | begun (NS: *began*) |
| bid (to offer) | bid | bid |
| bid (order) | bade | bidden, bid |
| bite | bit | bitten, bit |
| blow | blew (NS: *blowed*) | blown (NS: *blowed*) |
| break | broke | broken |
|  |  | (Inf. or NS: *broke*) |
| bring | brought (NS: *brung*) | brought (NS: *brung*) |
| *burst | burst | burst |
| catch | caught | caught |
| choose /chüz/ | chose /chōz/ | chosen |
| come | came (NS: *come*) | come |
| dig | dug (Archaic: *digged*) | dug |
| dive | dove, dived | dived, dove |
| *do | did (NS: *done*) | done |
| draw | drew (NS: *drawed*) | drawn (NS: *drawed*) |
| dream | dreamed, dreamt | dreamed, dreamt |

| *Infinitive* | *Past tense* | *Past participle* |
|---|---|---|
| drink | drank (Archaic and NS: *drunk*) | *drunk (*drank—drunken*; the latter, adjective only) |
| drive | drove | driven |
| eat | ate (Local and British: *eat* /et/; see *Divided usage) | eaten (*eat*) |
| fall | fell | fallen |
| find | found | found |
| fit | fit, fitted | fit, fitted |
| flee | fled | fled |
| fly | flew | flown |
| forget | forgot | forgotten, forgot |
| freeze | froze | frozen (NS: *froze*) |
| *get | got | got, gotten |
| give | gave (NS: *give*) | given |
| go | went | gone (NS: *went*) |
| grow | grew (NS: *growed*) | grown |
| hang | hung | hung |
| hang (to execute) | hung, *hanged | hung, hanged |
| hear | heard | heard |
| kneel | knelt, kneeled | knelt, kneeled |
| knit | knitted, knit | knitted, knit |
| know | knew (NS: *knowed*) | known |
| *lay | laid | laid |
| lead | led | led |
| lend (*loan*) | lent | lent |
| let | let | let |
| lie (see *lay) | *lay | lain |
| light | *lighted, lit | lighted, lit |
| lose | lost | lost |
| pay | *paid (of ropes: *payed*) | paid (*payed*) |
| plead | pleaded, plead, pled | pleaded, plead /pled/, pled /pled/ |
| prove | proved | *proved, proven |
| ride | rode | ridden (NS: *rode*) |
| ring | rang, rung | rung |
| rise | rose | risen |
| run | ran (NS: *run*) | run |
| say | said | said |
| see | saw (NS: *seen*) | seen |
| set | set | set |
| shine | shone, shined | shone, shined |
| show | showed | shown, showed |
| shrink | shrunk, shrank | shrunk |

| Infinitive | Past tense | Past participle |
|---|---|---|
| sing | sang, sung | sung |
| sink | sank, sunk | sunk |
| sit | sat (NS: *set*) | sat (NS: *set*) |
| slide | slid | slid (*slidden*) |
| sow | sowed | sown, sowed |
| speak | spoke | spoken |
| speed | sped, speeded | sped, speeded |
| spit | spit, spat | spit, spat |
| spring | sprang, sprung | sprung |
| stand | stood | stood |
| steal | stole | stolen |
| stink | stank, stunk | stunk |
| strive | strove (also *strived*) | striven, strived |
| sweat | sweated, sweat | sweated, sweat |
| swim | swam (NS: *swum*) | swum |
| take | took | taken |
| tear | tore | torn |
| throw | threw (NS: *throwed*) | thrown |
| tread | trod | trodden, trod |
| wake | waked, woke | waked, woke (*woken*) |
| wear | wore | worn |
| weave | wove (*weaved*) | woven, wove |
| win | won | won |
| wind /wīnd/ | wound (Nautical: *winded*) | wound /wound/ |
| wring | wrung | wrung |
| write | wrote (Archaic: *writ*) | written (NS: *wrote*; Archaic: *writ*) |

The evidence of the *Linguistic Atlas of the United States* is already providing for revision of some of these descriptions. The past participle *drank* is much more prevalent in Standard English, especially in New England, than dictionaries suggest; *shrunk* seems to be more common in the Upper Midwest as a past tense than *shrank* (see H. B. Allen, "Current English Forum," *College English*, 1957, 18:283-285); both popular and Standard usage favor *knit, laid, pled, fit,* and *sweat* as the past tense forms of *knit, lie, plead, fit,* and *sweat* (see E. Bagby Atwood, *A Survey of Verb Forms in the Eastern United States,* Ann Arbor, 1953).

(References: Fries, *AEG*, pp. 59-71; Mencken, pp. 527-528; Bryant, pp. 55, 78, 125-126, 194, 203; and recent dictionaries.)

**prior to** • *Prior to* is heavy for *before*: *Prior to (Before) coming here he had been at Stanford. Prior to* suggests legal language. *Before* is usually more appropriate in General writing.

**process, procedure, proceed** • *Process* and *procedure,* the nouns, are spelled with one *e* after the *c*; *proceed,* the verb, has two *e*'s. (The spelling situation is further confused by the verb *precede.*) The pronunciation /prō′ses/ is British rather than American, but not uncommon here. /Pros′ə sēz/ is rather affected for the plural; say /pros′es əz/.

*Proceed* means "to go," strictly in a rather formal fashion, and is best kept for movement: *We proceeded at a decent rate of speed. We proceeded to unpack* usually means no more than *We unpacked* or *Then we unpacked.*

**Profanity** • Styles change in the handling of "cuss words" and profanity. At present most writers, most editors, and most publishers are much more liberal than formerly. In college writing such words should be used only in dialog where they are spoken by a character, and you should be quite sure they are fitting and called for. Both cussing and cursing are primarily oral, matters of muscular release more than of meaning, and in print they often attract more attention to themselves than they deserve. You can't put on paper all the vulgarity proper to a vulgar person's speech; the effect will be suggested by an occasional sample. In the writing of biography, criticism, and miscellaneous informational articles there is less freedom, and double dashes and euphemistic blankety-blanks are sometimes found. Such devices ordinarily give the impression of a writer who is playing at being tough but hasn't the courage to use language he believes is really appropriate. Use the expressions the subject seriously calls for, compromising as little or as much as your temperament and circumstances demand. In material submitted to magazines, editors will make whatever alterations their policies demand. (See *Obscenity.)

**Professor** • Write:

Professor Tewksbury [or] Prof. E. W. Tewksbury [or] E. W. Tewksbury, a professor of electrical engineering

[or, as a Formal title] E. W. Tewksbury, Professor of Electrical Engineering

The colloquial *prof* is a clipped word, not an abbreviation, and if it is written should not have a period:

He said all profs were a little crazy anyway.

Strictly speaking, *professor* should be confined to names of assistant professors, associate professors, and (full) professors. When the title comes before the name (without the *of* phrase), *Professor* is used for all three ranks; when it follows the name and has the *of* phrase, the exact rank is usually indicated: *Professor A. B. Plant; A. B. Plant, Assistant Professor of Eng-*

*lish.* Applying it to instructors is sometimes a well-meant courtesy but more often carelessness. In official and business usage an *instructor* who has a Ph.D. is often addressed as *Doctor.* It would be better to address all teachers as *Mr.* or *Miss* or *Mrs.*—as many professors would prefer; but students should follow the conventions of their own campus. (See *Abbreviations § 2. For an account of the title's history in this country, see Robert L. Coard, "In Pursuit of the Word 'Professor,'" *Journal of Higher Education,* 1959, 30:237-245.)

**Progressive verb forms** • The grammatical term *progressive verb forms* is applied to verb phrases made with *to be* and the present participle: I *am asking,* he *was asking,* they *have been asking.* (See *Tenses of verbs, *Verbs.)

**Pronominal adjectives** • Several types of pronouns, used also like adjectives, are called *pronominal adjectives*:

| | | | |
|---|---|---|---|
| Interrogative: | *Which* way did he go? | | |
| Demonstrative: | *that* way | *this* book | *those* boys |
| Possessive: | *my* hat | *his* idea | *your* dog | *their* seats |
| Indefinite: | *some* people | *each* person | *all* men |

**Pronouns, types and forms** •

Pron
*Revision: Change the form of the pronoun marked to the one expected in the grammatical construction in which it stands.*

Pronouns in the English language are hard to define because traditionally this part of speech includes several groups of quite different words. They all are used in the principal syntactical functions of nouns, serving as subjects and objects, and a number have genitives. Perhaps it is enough to say that a pronoun is a word that can be replaced by a noun in a specific context. Many, like nouns, have an *-s* genitive and also a plural.

The uses of pronouns are described in *Reference of pronouns. This article lists the various types of pronouns and their forms.

**1.** *The personal pronouns.* Some of the most common grammatical problems come from the fact that separate nominative and accusative case forms survive for personal and relative pronouns though not for nouns (see *Person, *between you and me, *It's me, *who, whom §2, 3).

| | Nominative forms | Genitive forms | Accusative forms |
|---|---|---|---|
| 1st person Singular: | *I | my, mine | me |
| Plural: | we | our, ours | us |

| | | | | |
|---|---|---|---|---|
| *2nd person* | *Singular*: | you | your, yours | you |
| | *Plural*: | you | your, yours | you |
| *3d person* | *Singular*: | | | |
| | *masculine*: | he | his, his | him |
| | *feminine*: | she | her, hers | her |
| | *neuter*: | *it | its (of it) | it |
| | *either gender*: | *one | one's | one |
| | *Plural*: | they | their, theirs | them, 'em |

Archaic forms of the second person singular, *thou, thy* or *thine, thee,* are used only in religious services, by the Society of Friends (*thee* only), and occasionally in poetry.

Mine, formerly used before words beginning with a vowel (*mine eyes*), is no longer so used: *my eyes.* Under *Genitive forms,* the one before the comma is used before nouns, the one after the comma in predicative position; *its* and *one's* do not occur as predicatives in Standard English:

> The money is *mine* [*ours, yours, hers, theirs*].
> *Yours* came a whole week before *mine.*
> Rarely: Baby *mine.*

**2.** *Relative pronouns.*

| Nominative forms | Genitive forms | Accusative forms |
|---|---|---|
| *who | whose | whom |
| *that | of that | that |
| *which | of which, whose | which, whom |

*Whoever, whichever, whatever* (and archaic: *whosoever, whichsoever, whatsoever*) are less definite than the simple relatives and may have an accent of surprise, emphasis, or playfulness.

**3.** *Interrogative pronouns.* *who, *which, what; occasionally whoever, whatever

**4.** *Reflexive and intensive pronouns.* These pronouns are the personal pronouns plus the suffix *-self* or *-selves.* The Standard forms do not follow a consistent pattern; the suffix is added to *my, our, your* (genitive); *him, them* (accusative); *her, it* [*s*]. They are called *reflexive* because the action of the verb is directed toward the subject of the construction: He shaves *himself*; She bought *herself* two hats. (See *himself, herself, *myself.*)

When used as intensives, these words are usually construed as pronouns in *apposition:

> The mayor himself delivered the address.
> I can finish the job myself.

**5.** *Reciprocal pronouns.* *Each other* and *one another,* reciprocal pronouns, are used only as objects of verbs or prepositions. In Formal usage some writers keep *each other* to refer to two, *one another* for more than two. General usage has *each other* in all senses:

> They had hated each other for years.
> *Formal:* For the first time all the members really saw one another.
> *General:* For the first time all the members really saw each other.

**6.** *Numeral pronouns.* The cardinal numbers (one, two, three ...) and the ordinals (first, second, third. . .) are used as pronouns: *Three* were there; The *eighth* won.

**7.** *Demonstrative pronouns.* (See *Demonstrative adjectives and pronouns.)

*this, these *that, those (Compare *kind, sort)
the *former, the latter, the first, the second...
*such, *so (I told you so) *same

**8.** *Indefinite pronouns.* A large number of words, of greater or less indefiniteness, often function as pronouns:

| | | |
|---|---|---|
| all | everybody (see *every § 2) | nothing |
| another | everyone | *one, oneself |
| *any | everything | other |
| anybody | few | several |
| anyone | many | *some |
| anything | much | somebody |
| *both | neither | someone |
| *each | *nobody | something |
| each one | *none | *such |
| either | no one | |

**9.** *Impersonal pronouns.* See *it.

(For a discussion of questions on the uses of pronouns see *Reference of pronouns. See also *Agreement § 2, *Ambiguity § 1, *Apostrophe § 5, *Case, *Gerund § 2, *Parts of speech. References: Curme, *Parts of Speech,* Ch. 10, and *Syntax,* index references; Fries, *AEG,* index references.)

## Pronunciation •

**1.** *Pronunciation key.* The pronunciation of words is indicated in this book by respelling them with the letters and diacritical marks (with some few exceptions) used in the Thorndike-Barnhart Dictionaries, as follows:

| | |
|---|---|
| a | apple /ap′l/, fact /fakt/ |
| ā | age /āj/, say /sā/, inflate /in flāt′/ |
| ã | care /kãr/, air /ãr/ |
| ä | far /fär/, father /fä′ᴛнər/ |
| b | back /bak/, robber /rob′ər/ |
| ch | child /chīld/, question /kwes′chən/, literature / lit′ər ə chùr/ |
| d | do /dü/, did /did/ |
| e | bet /bet/, effect /ə fekt′/ |

| | |
|---|---|
| ėr | urge /ėrj/, bird /bėrd/, term /tėrm/ |
| ē | equal /ē′kwəl/, see /sē/, police /pə lēs′/ |
| f | fat /fat/, stuff /stuf/, cough /kôf/, photo /fō′tō/ |
| g | go /gō/, baggage /bag′ij/ |
| h | hotel /hō tel′/, boyhood /boi′hůd/ |
| hw | wheel /hwēl/, whether /hweᴛʜ′ər/ |
| i | if /if/, pithy /pith′ē/ |
| ī | ice /īs/, buy /bī/ |
| j | jam /jam/, edge /ej/, age /āj/ |
| k | king /king/, back /bak/, cocoa /kō′kō/ |
| l | life /līf/, silly /sil′ē/, fill /fil/ |
| m | am /am/, meet /mēt/, sample /sam′pḷ/ |
| n | note /nōt/, inner /in′ər/ |
| ng | sing /sing/, song /sông/, rank /rangk/ |
| o | rock /rok/, stop /stop/ |
| ō | open /ō′pən/, hope /hōp/, go /gō/ |
| ô | bought /bôt/, ball /bôl/, caught /kôt/, four /fôr/ |
| oi | voice /vois/, boil /boil/ |
| ou | house /hous/, out /out/, cow /kou/ |
| p | paper /pā′pər/, cap /kap/ |
| r | reach /rēch/, try /trī/ |
| s | say /sā/, listen /lis′ṇ/, yes /yes/ |
| sh | she /shē/, rush /rush/, cushion /kůsh′ən/, nation /nā′shən/ |
| t | tie /tī/, sit /sit/, kitten /kit′ṇ/ |
| th | thin /thin/, both /bōth/, bath /bath/ |
| ᴛʜ | that /ᴛʜat/, bother /boᴛʜər/, bathe /bāᴛʜ/, thee /ᴛʜē/ |
| u | cup /kup/, butter /but′ər/ |
| ů | book /bůk/, put /půt/ |
| ü | tool /tül/, rule /rül/, move /müv/ |
| ū | useful /ūs′fəl/, music /mū′zik/ |
| v | very /ver′ē/, salve /sav/ or /säv/, save /sāv/ |
| w | will /wil/, with /wiᴛʜ/ or /with/, won't /wōnt/ |
| y | young /yung/, yellow /yel′ō/ |
| z | zero /zir′ō/, breeze /brēz/ |
| zh | measure /mezh′ər/, rouge /rüzh/ |
| ə | Called schwa /shwä/, represents the indefinite vowel sound of many unstressed syllables. It is variously spelled: a in sofa /sō′fə/, e in secretary /sek′rə ter′ē/, and by the other vowels and combinations of vowels. |

/ḷ, m̩, ṇ, ṛ/ Syllabic consonants, used in unstressed syllables when no vowel sound can be distinguished: little /lit′ḷ/, wooden /wood′ṇ/. When spoken slowly these syllables have ə, and are sometimes so respelled.

The stress of syllables is represented by a ′ for a main stress and a ′ for a lighter stress, placed after the stressed syllable: /ag′rə kul′chər/.

A vowel sound in a stressed syllable will be more fully sounded than one without stress. Contrast the *o* of *below* /bi lō'/ and of *obey*—which ranges from /ō bā'/ to /ə bā'/. In unstressed syllables they tend to become the "neutral vowel" /ə/, as in the italicized vowels in *a*gain, *a*cad*e*my, dorm*i*tory, curs*o*ry, circ*u*s. (For suggestions on spelling such words see *Neutral vowel.)

An *r* following a vowel alters the vowel's sound, as in *care, sere, core, sure,* but a separate symbol is not used to represent the change (except for /ėr/ as in *term* /tėrm/): /kãr/, /sēr/, /kôr/, /shůr/. (Further details of the sounds represented by each letter of the alphabet, with examples, will be found in the articles on the separate letters, *A, *B, *C, and so on, in this *Index.* See also *Voiced, voiceless sounds.)

2. *Special points in pronunciation.*

*a*–Stress. In general, English is a rather strongly stressed (accented) language. The force of the stress varies a good deal among individual speakers. The stress of particular words (*detail, address) varies with their meaning and with their position in sentences. (See also *Noun and verb stress.)

*b*–Secondary stress. A word of three or especially of four syllables is likely to have a main and a secondary stress: *secondary* /sek'ən der'ē/, *incidental* /in'sə den't̪l̩/. One of the differences between British and American pronunciation is that we tend to keep secondary stresses in many words in which the British have but one:

*necessary*: American /nes'ə sar'ē/; British /nes'əs rē/
*dictionary*: American /dik'shən er'ē/; British /dik'shn̩ rē/

(See *American and British usage.)

*c*–Pronunciation and spelling. Words really live in their oral forms, and any guide to pronunciation must start with the spoken words, not the written. But our spelling represents, often very approximately, the sounds of words, or at least the sounds they once had.

When words are acquired from reading rather than from hearing, they are very often overpronounced, in what are known as "spelling pronunciations." *Sophomore* on most campuses is two syllables, /sof'môr/, but people who see it more than they hear it are likely to sound the middle *o* slightly /sof'ə môr/; *yearling* is /yėr'ling/ where it is regularly used, /yir'ling/ as a spelling pronunciation. Spelling pronunciation may introduce sounds that are not in the Standard pronunciation of the word (*soften* as /sôf'tən/). Sometimes these pronunciations become acceptable, usually as a minor pronunciation (*often* as /of'tən/), occasionally even forcing out the older established pronunciation (*Indian,* formerly /in'jən/). Genuine familiarity with words is shown by using the established oral rather than a spelling pronunciation.

3. *Standards of pronunciation.* Standard written English is virtually the same in all parts of the United States. But standard speech varies somewhat in different parts of our country and is basically that of the educated people of the region. It shows some regional qualities, though less than the speech of uneducated people. (See "Variations due to place," p. 5. See also *Affectation, *Divided usage.)

A person's pronunciation should be appropriate as far as possible to the situation in which he is speaking. The elaborateness of "stage" pronunciation is out of place in conversation, even in "cultivated" conversation. Too conscious attention to pronunciation will handicap the speaker and irritate the listener. Pronunciation in speaking to groups must necessarily be somewhat slower, more distinct, but fundamentally it is a refinement of the speaker's better conversational style.

The problem of a person going to live in a different part of the country is more complex. Should he drop his native speech and do as the Romans do? If he makes a specific and hasty effort to pick up the new speech, he will be almost sure to make mistakes—that is, he will confuse the two. If he can stand off the first attacks on his speechways, he will soon find that he will attract less attention. Then he will naturally acquire, bit by bit and without forcing, many of the new ways. He need not be ashamed if traces of his native speech remain.

The words to worry about are not those in everyday use so much as the new ones acquired in taking up new work or a new social status or new ideas or, in college, new subjects of study. Care should be taken to get a conventional pronunciation of these new words (*acclimate, desultory, schizophrenic* ...) as they are learned, to be at home with them from the beginning.

As Fowler puts it (p. 466), "The broad principles are: Pronounce as your neighbors do, not better." For the majority of words, your neighbors are the general public. For words in more restricted use, your neighbors are the group that uses them. Consequently there will be more local flavor in General and Informal speech, less in speaking to limited and special audiences. It is more important to avoid Nonstandard pronunciations than the regional pronunciations of educated people.

4. *Pronunciation list.* The following list is in part to raise questions of pronunciation. The pronunciations suggested should be tested by comparing them with those you hear. For most words that raise questions of pronunciation, consult a good recent dictionary.

Pronunciations of other words will be found in the articles on each letter of the alphabet, *Foreign words in English, *Spelling, *Proper names, and in various articles on particular words.

When two forms are given, no choice is implied; a distinctly less common form stands in brackets. A large number of words are spoken in two or more ways in good usage.

An asterisk before a word means that the *Index* has a separate article on that word.

abdomen /ab'də mən/,
    /ab dō'mən/
absorb /ab sôrb'/, /ab zôrb'/
absurd /ab sėrd'/, /ab zėrd'/
acclimate /ə klī'mit/,
    /ak'lə māt/
adult /ə dult'/, /ad'ult/
advertisement
    /ad vėr'tiz ment/,
    /ad vėr'tis ment/,
    /ad'vər tīz'mənt/
ally (noun) /al'ī/, /ə lī'/;
    (plural more often) /ə līz'/;
    (verb) /ə lī'/
*alma mater /al'mə mä'tər/,
    /äl'mə mä'tər/, /al'mə mā'tər/
alternate (verb) /ôl'tər nāt/,
    /al'tər nāt/; (adjective and
    noun) /ôl'tər nit/, /al'tər nit/
amateur /am'ə chər/, /am'ə tər/
apparatus /ap'ə rā'təs/,
    /ap'ə rat'əs/
applicable /ap'lə kə bḷ/,
    /ə plik'ə bḷ/
Aryan /är'ē ən/, /är'yən/
atypical /ā tip'ə kḷ/ (see *-a)
aviation /ā'vē ā'shən/,
    /av'ē ā'shən/
aye (yes) /ī/
bade /bad/, /bād/
*biography /bī og'rə fē/,
    /bi og'rə fē/
bureaucracy /byù rok'rə sē/
business /biz'nis/
chauffeur /shō'fər/, /shō fėr'/
chic /shēk/, /shik/
combatant /kəm bat'ənt/,
    /kom'bə tənt/

*contents /kon'tents/
coup /kü/
coupon /kü'pon/, /kū'pon/
coyote /kī ō'tē/, /kī'ōt/
*data /dā'tə/, /dat'ə/, /dä'tə/
debut /dā'bū/, /dā bū'/
decade /dek'ād/
desperado /des'pər ä'do/,
    /des'pər ä'dō/
diphtheria /dif thir'ē ə/,
    /dip thir'ē ə/
diphthong /dif'thông/,
    /dip'thông/, /dif'thong/,
    /dip'thong/
disputable /dis pūt'ə bḷ/,
    /dis'pyə tə bḷ/
drama /drä'mə/, /dram'ə/
economics /ē'kə nom'iks/,
    /ek'ə nom'iks/
*either /ē'ŦHər/, [Brit.]
    /ī'ŦHər/
electricity /i lek'tris'ə tē/,
    /ē'lek tris'ə tē/
Elizabethan /i liz'ə bē'thən/,
    /i liz'ə beth'ən/
err /ėr/, /är/
exquisite /eks'kwi zit/,
    /eks kwiz'it/
finance /fə nans'/, /fī nans'/,
    /fī'nans/
formidable /fôr'mə də bḷ/
fortnight /fôrt'nīt/,
    /fôrt'nit/
gibbous /gib'əs/
gladiolus /glad'ē ō'ləs/,
    /glə dī'ə ləs/
gunwale /gun'ḷ/
harass /har'əs/, /hə ras'/

heinous /hā′nəs/
human /hū′mən/
idea /ī dē′ə/
impious /im′pē əs/
indict /in dīt′/
isolate /ī′sə lāt/, /is′ə lāt/
juvenile /jü′və nḷ/, /jü′və nīl/
kimono /kə mō′nə/
laugh /laf/, /läf/
launch /lônch/, /länch/
leisure /lē′zhər/, /lezh′ər/
lever /lev′ər/, /lē′vər/
lilacs /lī′ləks/, lī′laks/
matrix /mā′triks/, /mat′riks/
menu /men′ū/, /mā′nū/
mischievous /mis′chə vəs/
news /nüz/, /nūz/
oasis /ō ā′sis/
orgy /ôr′jē/
parliament /pär′lə mənt/
patriot /pā′trē ət/,
    [Brit.] /pat′rē ət/
penalize /pē′nḷ īz/, /pen′ḷ īz/
percolator /pėr′kə lā′tər/
pianist /pē an′ist/, /pē′ə nist/
pleasure /plezh′ər/, /plā′zhər/
premier /pri mir′/, /prē′mē ər/

presentation /prez′ṇ tā′shən/,
    /prē′zən tā′shən/
process /pros′əs/, [Brit.]
    /prō′səs/
pronunciation
    /prə nun′sē ā′shən/
quay /kē/
ratio /rā′shē ō/, /rā′shō/
real /rēl/, /rē′əl/
reel /rēl/
research /ri sėrch′/,
    /rē′sėrch/
rodeo /rō′dē ō/, /rō dā′ō/
rotogravure /rō′tə grə vyùr′/,
    /rō′tə grā′vyər/
route /rüt/, /rout/
sociology /sō′sē ol′ə jē/,
    /sō′shē ol′ə jē/
strictly /strikt′li/ also /strik′li/
sumac /sü′mak/, /shü′mak/
the /ᴛHə/, /ᴛHi/; [stressed] /ᴛHē/
tomato /tə mā′tō/, /tə mä′tō/
usage /ūs′ij/, /ūz′ij/
vaudeville /vô′də vil/,
    /vōd′vil/
white /hwīt/
worsted (yarn) /wùs′tid/

(References: Kenyon and Knott; J. S. Kenyon, *American Pronunciation*, Ann Arbor, 1950; C. K. Thomas, *Phonetics of American English*, New York, 1958; *Webster's Third New International Dictionary*, especially the "Guide to Pronunciation.")

**Proofreading** • A check of copy is the last act before giving a manuscript to anyone for serious consideration. Proofreading the final copy of a paper for mechanical mistakes that may have slipped in while copying it is an important part of the work in a composition course—and one that pays dividends far beyond the mental effort required.

After copy has been set in type it must be checked for typographical and other mistakes before it is ready to be printed. A tentative print is made on long sheets known as *galley proof.* After the type has been corrected and made up into the pages which are to be finally printed, *page proofs* are taken and read for a last check.

Corrections are indicated in proof by abbreviations and symbols placed at one side of the line to be changed, with a *caret ( ∧ ) inserted at the exact point in the line where the change is to be made. Proofreader's marks are illustrated below. See publishers' stylebooks for further details.

## Proofreader's Marks

| | | | |
|---|---|---|---|
| ℒ | Delete | em/ | Insert em dash |
| ℰ | Delete and close up | en/ | Insert en dash |
| ℄ | Reverse | ⩘ | Insert semicolon |
| ⌒ | Close up | ☉ | Insert colon and en quad |
| # | Insert space | ⊙ | Insert period and en quad |
| ⌒/# | Close up and insert space | ?/ | Insert interrogation point |
| ⁋ | Paragraph | ⑦ | Query to author |
| □ | Indent 1 em | ⌒ | Use ligature |
| ⊏ | Move to left | ⓢⓟ | Spell out |
| ⊐ | Move to right | tr | Transpose |
| ⊔ | Lower | wf | Wrong font |
| ⊓ | Raise | bf | Set in **bold face type** |
| ∧ | Insert marginal addition | rom | Set in (roman) type |
| Ⅴ∧ | Space evenly | ital | Set in *italic* type |
| ✗ | Broken letter— | caps | Set in CAPITALS |
| | used in margin | sc | Set in SMALL CAPITALS |
| ⌄ | Push down space | lc | Set in lower case |
| = | Straighten line | ✗ | Lower-case letter |
| ‖ | Align type | stet | Let it stand; restore words |
| ⅄ | Insert comma | | crossed out |
| Ⅴ | Insert apostrophe | no⁋ | Run in same paragraph |
| Ⅴ | Insert quotation mark | ld in | Insert lead between lines |
| =/ | Insert hyphen | hr# | Hair space between letters |

From *A Manual of Style*, The University of Chicago Press.

**Proper adjectives** • Proper nouns used like adjectives and adjectives directly derived from proper names and still referring to the place or person are capitalized. After proper adjectives lose the reference to their origins, they become simple adjectives and are no longer capitalized:

the French language      American interests
the Indian service [but *india ink*]
a Paris (or Parisian) café [but *paris green*]
the Roman Forum [but *roman type*]

Practices of capitalizing differ radically for other languages so that students studying foreign languages should be careful to keep the English and foreign practices separated.

**Proper names** • Considerable care needs to be taken to spell and pronounce the names of people, places, companies, institutions as the people most concerned with them wish to have them spelled and pronounced. Many are rare or in some way unusual—*Thames* /temz/, *Worcester* /wûs′ter/, *San Joaquin* /san′wô kēn′/. Analogy cannot be relied on: it is *Waco* /wā′kō/, Texas, but *Saco* /sô′kō/, Maine; *Cairo* /kī′rō/ for the Egyptian city, /kā′rō/ or /ke′rō/ for the one in Illinois. In place names the recommendation to use the pronunciation current in the place is complicated because the inhabitants often do not agree. *Chicago* is/shə kô′gō/, /shə kä′gō/, and /shə ka′gō/, with other minor variants. English has tended to anglicize many foreign place names and even to prefer an alternative name for some: *Paris* /par′is/ instead of /pä rē′/; *Munich* for *München* and *Finland* for *Suomi*.

Many fairly common names occur in various forms: *Burns—Byrnes, Harvey—Hervey, Cohen—Cohn—Kohen, Mac—Mc—M′*, and so on. Special care is needed with names having silent letters or some peculiarity of spelling or phrasing: Pittsburg*h* (but Gettysburg), the John*s* Hopkins University; Pennsylvania State University and the University of Pennsylvania are different institutions.

Dictionaries and encyclopedias give the pronunciation and spelling of the names of the best-known people and places. For foreign names in current news, we can try to follow the national newscasters. They will show some variation, but they usually make an effort to find a reasonable pronunciation. Getting proper names in the right form is courtesy as well as accuracy. It is especially important to do so in all published work.

(For a discussion of capitalizing proper names, see *Capital letters § 2. See also *Course names. References: Allen W. Read, "The Basis of Correctness in the Pronunciation of Place-Names," *American Speech,* 1933, 8:42-46; *Webster's Biographical Dictionary*; *Webster's Geographical Dictionary*; W. Cabell Greet, *World Words,* New York, 1948; Thomas Lee Crowell, *NBC Handbook of Pronunciation,* 3rd ed., New York, 1964; Kenyon and Knott; recent dictionaries.)

**proposition** • The use of *proposition* as a business word for *offer, plan, proposal* has made it inappropriate in General usage, though it is common in Informal English. *"I have a proposition for you"* = *"I have a plan. . . ."*

**proved—proven** • As the past participle of *prove, proved* is much more common than *proven* and is always acceptable (He had proved . . .). But *proven* is often used (It had proven quite satisfactory), especially where the rhythm is more comfortable with two syllables or in an adjective function (a proven friend). (Reference: Bryant, pp. 165-166.)

**provided—providing** • Both are used as conjunctions: *He should be home soon provided* [or: *providing*] *the buses haven't been held up.* There is some prejudice against *providing* in this use. (See *Divided usage. Reference: Bryant, p. 166.)

**Provincialisms** • See *Localisms.

**psychology, psychiatry** • Watch the spelling of these words: *psychiatry* /sī kī′ə trē/, *psychiatrist* /sī kī′ə trist/, and *psychiatric* /sī′kē at′rik/, *psychology, psychologist, psychoanalyze,* and *psychoanalysis.*

The pronunciation of *psychiatry, psychiatrist* with short *i* in the first syllable is about as frequent as the one given above.

**public** • *Public* is a *collective noun and takes either a singular or plural construction depending on whether the writer wishes to stress the whole group or the individuals:

The *public is* invited. The *public are* invited.

Consult the libraries and you will find that the ordinary public do not read poetry.—P. B. BALLARD, *Thought and Language,* p. 250

**Punctuation, No punctuation** •

Pn,

No Pn

*Revision: Correct the error in punctuation by either inserting appropriate punctuation or deleting confusing or unnecessary punctuation. If the change to be made is not clear to you, consult the article on the particular mark.*

In "open" punctuation, typical of Informal and much General writing, there are fewer marks and lighter ones than in the "close" punctuation that characterizes Formal writing.

Details of the uses of the individual marks will be found in the articles on each:

| | | | |
|---|---|---|---|
| ' | *Apostrophe | , | *Comma |
| * | *Asterisk | — | *Dash (including the |
| { } | *Brace | | long dash ——) |
| [ ] | *Brackets | ... | *Ellipsis |
| ∧ | *Caret | ! | *Exclamation mark |
| : | *Colon | - | *Hyphen |

| .... | *Leaders | " " | *Quotation marks |
|---|---|---|---|
| ( ) | *Parentheses | ; | *Semicolon |
| . | *Period | —— | *Underlining (for |
| ? | *Question mark | | italic type) |

(See also *Division of words, *Letters, *Restrictive and non-restrictive, *Series, *Whitespace.)

**Puns** • A *pun* is a *figure of speech in which a word is used in two senses at once (*the nut that holds the wheel = automobile driver*) or in which a word is substituted for another of similar sound but different meaning (*hire education*). Reasonable punning, funny or serious, is a healthy use of language. Objection is often made to puns because of their overuse or because they involve sound and not meaning. Good puns are appropriate to Informal usage, usually giving an accent of ironic humor (as in Dorothy Parker's " a girl's best friend is her mutter") or of mild satire:

Ironically, the mansion of American education has many rooms, but the storehouse of many of its basic concepts and categories is the Attic.—WILLIAM RILEY PARKER, *PMLA*, 1964, 79 (No. 4, Pt. 2):7

But the problem of the reign in Spain is anything but plain.—*Time*, May 15, 1964, p. 47

(Compare *Homonyms.)

**purist** • A *purist* is one who believes in and tries to practice nicety of choice in the use of materials of expression. In language he is likely to fall into a rigid adherence to traditional and often inaccurate "rules." The term is therefore often used disparagingly for a person who wishes everyone to follow the rules of prescriptive grammar (*Grammar § 3) and who tries to hold words to narrower and older meanings. Dictionaries and scientific grammars are descriptive and consequently reflect the actual situation more accurately.

**Purpose** • Adverbial clauses of purpose are most commonly introduced by *so that*:

He is packing tonight *so that* he can start early in the morning.

*That* used alone is more Formal, almost archaic; and *in order that* is wordy. Informally *so* is used alone:

He is packing tonight *so* he can start early in the morning.

**Put in, put over, put across** • *Put in* is good Informal usage for *spend* as "put in time." *Put over* as "a plan, a sale," *put across* as "a scheme, an idea" are also Informal.

**Q** • This letter is unnecessary in the English alphabet. It was brought into English spelling in words borrowed from French, originally derived from Latin (*question, quarter, quit*), and later borrowings directly from Latin added to the number (*quorum, quota*). Some Old English words with the /kw/ sound (spelled *cw*) were respelled with *qu*: *quick* (from *cwic*), *queen* (from *cwen*), *quench* (from *cwencan*).

*Q* is always followed by *u* in English except in a few foreign place names (*Gulf of Aqaba*). *Qu* is ordinarily pronounced /kw/ (*quite, quill, quadrilateral*), though in a few words the French value /k/ is kept: *coquette* /kō ket'/. Final *-que* is /k/: *antique* /an tēk'/, *unique* /ū nēk'/. The French pronunciation should not be attempted in words that have been anglicized: *Quebec* /kwi bek'/, *questionnaire*.

**Question mark (?)** •

*Ques*

    *Revision: Punctuate this sentence as a question.*

**1.** The principal use of the question mark is as the end stop of a direct question:

What was the real reason?

**2.** A question mark may or may not be used after a request that is phrased as a question, depending on the Formality of the style:

*Formal*: Will you please return this at your earliest convenience?
*General*: Will you please return this at your earliest convenience.

(See also *Commands and requests.)

**3.** A question mark is not used after an indirect question:

He wanted to know what the real reason was.

(See also *Questions § 2.)

**4.** A question mark is used to show that a statement is approximate or questionable, as with uncertain dates:

Geoffrey Chaucer 1340?-1400 [or] Geoffrey Chaucer 1340 (?) -1400

**5.** A question mark in parentheses as a mildly sarcastic comment or as a label for would-be witticisms is now out of fashion and is better omitted:

In those days no fashionable (?) woman would think of going to a football game unless she looked like a giant squirrel.

**6.** When a question mark and quotation mark fall together, the question mark is outside if the quoting sentence is the question, inside if the quotation is the question:

He asked, "Did you really say that?"
Did you really say "I thought you were older than that"?

After a double question only one question mark is used.

Did she ask, "How many are coming?"

(See also *Quotation marks § 4a.)

## Questions •

1. In speech, questions are identified by word order, interrogative words, and intonation. The intonation patterns for questions are complex; some questions end with the voice rising, some with it falling. Since in writing, these patterns must all be summed up by the question mark—which does not appear until the end of the sentence—a written question is most easily identified by interrogative words and word order. It may be introduced by an interrogative word:

*Pronoun*: *Who* was that? *What* would you do in his place?
*Adjective*: *Which* way did he go? *What* book shall I read next?
*Adverb*: *Where* shall we eat? *When* will you be coming back?
*How much* is that one? *Why* didn't you say so in the first place?

A question may be indicated by inverted word order, the verb coming before its subject. In older English any verb could stand first (*Came* he yesterday?), but now this order is found only with *be, have, shall, will, can, may, must, need,* and *ought* (*Was* he there?) and in Informal, usually spoken, subjectless sentences (*Want* this one?). Ordinarily a phrasal verb is used, with the auxiliary coming before the subject to provide the inversion (*Do you think* he would go if he was asked?). A statement may be turned into a question by an inverted clause at the end (He didn't try, *did he?*).

A direct question that is parenthetically part of another sentence sometimes begins with a capital and sometimes not:

He felt a strong urge—as indeed who doesn't?—to write a really good modern novel.—NOEL COWARD, *To Step Aside,* p. 9

2. An indirect question is a question that is not quoted directly but is made a subordinate member of another sentence. An indirect question is not marked either with a question mark or with quotation marks; the tense of the verb is changed, if necessary, to fit the sentence and often a subordinating conjunction is introduced (*if, *whether):

*Direct*: "What are our plans for tomorrow?"
*Indirect*: He asked what our plans for tomorrow were.
*Direct*: He asked, "Do you really understand what you have read?"
*Indirect*: He asked us if we really understood what we had read.
He always asks us whether we understand what we have read.

3. A "leading question" is one phrased to suggest the answer desired, as *You wouldn't do that, would you?* (contrasted with *Would you do that?*).

4. Questions provide variety and, if used sparingly, may have a good stylistic effect. (See *Rhetorical questions.)

## Quotation marks (" ") •

*Quot*      *Revision: Make the quotation marks conform to conventional usage.*

1. *Methods of indicating quotations.*

   *a*–Double quotes (" ") are the usual marks. The mark before the quoted matter is the *open-quote*; the one after is the *close-quote.*

   *b*–The use of single quotes (' ') is common in England and is increasing in the United States. The single quotes are as accurate as the double and are much less spotty on the page.

   *c*–For quotations within quotations, double and single quotes are alternated. If you begin with the double marks: " ' . . . ' "; if you begin with the single: ' " . . . " '. If there are quotations within two such quotations, continue to alternate the double and single quotes.

   *d*–Indenting is used to indicate quotations, especially in factual writing involving numerous quotations of some length, as in this book. No quotation marks are used, and in print the size of type is usually reduced. Publishing houses have rules about how long a quotation must be to be reduced and indented—that it should run to at least five lines, for example, or consist of more than one complete sentence. In double spaced typewritten copy, such quotations are usually indented and single spaced; in longhand copy they are indented.

   *e*–When a long quotation which is not indented includes more than one paragraph, the marks are placed at the beginning of each paragraph of the quotation but at the end of only the last paragraph.

2. *Principal uses of quotation marks.*

   *a*–Quotation marks are used to indicate all passages taken from another writer, whether a phrase or a page or more (except when the quotation is indented). The quoted matter may stand by itself or may be worked into the constructions of the writer's own sentence:

   The most that could be said for Haig was said by Churchill: he "was unequal to the prodigious scale of events, but no one else was discerned as his equal or better." (Lloyd George, more succinctly, said he was "brilliant to the top of his army boots.")—GEOFFREY BARRA-CLOUGH, *The New York Review of Books,* May 14, 1964, p. 3

   When speeches or a short conversation are not given for their own sake but to illustrate a point, they are usually put in the body of the paragraph:

Do these instances of the beginnings of new words give us any hints in the search for those new words for which every passing month shows the urgent need? I think they do. First, simplicity and euphony—though not simplicity at all costs. Many years ago, I was chaffing an old friend about the deficiency of his native Welsh. "It's very lacking in the most ordinary scientific terms," I remarked. "For example?" "Well, what's the Welsh for *galvanometer?*" I asked. "And if it comes to that, what's the English for it?" A very proper rejoinder which, correctly interpreted, means that *gas* is preferable to *aeriform fluid,* and *drop-counter* to *stalagmometer.* All within reason, of course: does it follow, for example, that *foreword* is better than *preface?*—ALLAN FERGUSON, "The Scientist's Need for New Words," *The Listener,* Apr. 21, 1937

*b*–There are no half quotes. A sentence is either an exact quotation in quotation marks, or else it isn't and so is not quoted. A speech summarized or quoted indirectly is not marked:

*Direct quotation:* The manager told me, "I work harder in one day keeping the girls busy than they work all week."

*Indirect quotation:* The manager told me that he worked harder in one day keeping the girls busy than they worked all week. [Not: *The manager told me "That he worked harder in one day keeping the girls busy than they worked all week."*]

*c*–Some writers of fiction do not use quotation marks in the dialog of their stories, but the practice is not common, and omitting the marks is somewhat confusing.

**3.** *Miscellaneous uses of quotation marks.*

*a*–Many magazines use quotes around titles of books and periodicals, for which Formal writing uses italics:

We come upon passages that contain, all unknowing, whole futures in Nabakovian art. On one page we discover an episode that is destined to expand into a component of "Speak, Memory," on another we greet an infant revolver that will commit major execution in "Lolita," and on another we discern a suggestion of the scheme for "Pale Fire."—DONALD MALCOLM, *The New Yorker,* Apr. 25, 1964, p. 198

In academic style, which uses italics for titles of books and the names of periodicals, quotes are used for titles of written works shorter than volume length, of poems not published separately, of short stories, of magazine articles, of chapters in a book, and of contributions to a book that has more than one author. (See *References, *Titles of articles, books, etc. See also *Ships' names § 3.)

*b*–In Formal writing words that are used as words—as often in this book—rather than for their meaning are put in italics (underlined in manuscript); in General writing they would often be put in quotes:

"Capitalism" is thus a shape, a form, which speaks, commands, fights, runs away. Asked to define it, the debater on the left introduces more abstractions: "Absentee ownership," "surplus value," "class struggle," "private ownership of the means of production," "exploitation of the masses," "imperialism," "vested interests," "proletariat," "bourgeoisie," the "profit system," and many more. The great words roll.—STUART CHASE, *The Tyranny of Words*, p. 275

c—In Formal writing a word from a conspicuously different variety of speech may be put in quotation marks, but this practice is less common than formerly. In General writing there is less need for these apologetic quotes, because there is greater latitude in choice of words. If the word is appropriate, use it without apology, and if it isn't appropriate, don't use it.

Everybody told Bib what a sucker [not "sucker"] he was, but he still had confidence in the designer of the plane.

After the Yale man had said his piece, the Dartmouth frosh started to blow his horn again. [The question here is whether *said his piece, frosh,* and *blow his horn* are appropriate in the context of the paper; if they are not, quotes will not make them so or rescue the sentence.]

Common figures of speech do not need to be quoted:

After just one chorus, the trio settled to its work and was soon in orbit. [Not "in orbit"]

d—A word may be put in quotation marks to show that the writer refuses to accept its conventional sense in the context in which he has used it:

In numerous cases it is impossible to maintain on any solid grounds that one pronunciation given is "better" than another, as, for example, that one pronunciation of *swamp* is better than the others given; . . .—JOHN S. KENYON and THOMAS A. KNOTT, *A Pronouncing Dictionary of American English*, p. xxvii

e—Practice differs in writing single words that are spoken or thought:

Stephen said "Yes," so we went to work at once.
Stephen said *yes,* so we went to work at once.
Stephen said Yes, so we went to work at once.

Probably the first form is the most common.

4. *Quotation marks and other marks.*

a—When a question mark or an exclamation mark ends a quotation, it is placed inside the quotes:

"Don't go near that wire!" he shouted.
Then in a calm voice she asked, "Why didn't you say so before?"

When a question mark or exclamation mark belongs to a sentence that includes a quotation, it is placed after the quotes:

What kind of work can a man put into "the cheapest building that will last fifteen years"?—LEWIS MUMFORD, *Sticks and Stones,* p. 172

*b*–Most American publishers put commas and periods inside the close-quotes, whether they belong with the quotation or not, because the quotes help fill the small spot of white that would be left if the comma or period came outside. Some writers follow the conventions that apply to the exclamation and question marks, putting comma or period inside the quotes if it belongs with the quotation, outside if it belongs with the quoting sentence, but this usage is much less common.

Semicolons usually stand after the quotation mark.

*c*–Introductory words and stage directions are set off by a comma, or by two commas if they interrupt the quotation:

Robert said, "I should think that by now you would have learned that."

"History," it has been said, "does not repeat itself. The historians repeat one another."—MAX BEERBOHM, *Works,* p. 43

(Note that *does* is not capitalized after the interruption because it does not begin a sentence.)

When quoted phrases are closely built into the construction of a sentence, they are not set off by commas:

I hurried past the zero case with its cream molds, just barely saying "Hi!" to Danny and the girls behind it.

"I give him the book" has two equally correct passives: "He is given the book" and "The book is given to him."—E. H. STURTE-VANT, *Linguistic Change,* p. 138

A Formal introduction to a quotation is usually followed by a colon, as in the statements introducing the examples in this article.

5. *Indicating quotations in foreign languages.* The methods of indicating quotations are different for other languages. If you have occasion to quote a passage in another language which includes a quotation, you should consult a stylebook.

**R •** /r/ as in *ready, arch, arrears, car.*

The pronunciation of spelled *r* varies more from region to region than does that for any other consonant symbol—from a tongue trill in Scotland to replacement by *schwa (door* as

/dōə/) or even omission in much British as well as Eastern and Southern American speech.

The pronunciation of *r* also varies according to its position in a word. It is strongest, in all regions, before a vowel: *real, rob, cheering, fairy*. Before a consonant sound it varies, as from /bäk/ to /bärk/ for *bark*. Final *r* is most apparent in Western pronunciation, less conspicuous in the pronunciations of New England, the South, and metropolitan New York.

In Eastern and Southern speech *r* after a vowel often becomes /ə/ or disappears entirely (*farther*, /fä′ᵵнə/), except when the *r* is final and comes before a word starting with a vowel (*far away*, /fär′ ə wā′/). In areas where *r* is treated in this way, many speakers intrude an /r/ between a word ending with a vowel and one beginning with a vowel (The idea-*r* is good). In the rest of the country *r* after a vowel is altered to a special vowel which is, however, interpreted by the hearer as /r/.

In this *Index* the /r/ symbol as an indication of pronunciation is to be interpreted to mean the sort of /r/ sound the speaker is used to making. (For further details on the varieties of *r* in American pronunciation see Kenyon and Knott §§ 26, 82-85.)

**racket** • The spelling *racquet* is British. Write *tennis racket*.

*Racket* in the sense of an illegitimate way of making money, usually involving threats of violence, has made its way from slang into the General language. When used to mean a business or a particular way of making money (the baseball racket, the lumber racket), it is Informal unless used to imply illegitimate means.

**raise—rear** • *Rear* is now a Formal verb in the sense of *rearing* a child or of being *reared*. *Bring up* in this sense is current in all varieties of usage. *Raised* is General usage: *I was born and raised in Kentucky*. (Reference: Bryant, pp. 168-169.)

**rarely** • *Rarely* means "seldom" (or in archaic and Formal English, "with rare skill," as "a rarely carved panel").

*Rarely ever* (I rarely ever go), probably a telescoping of *rarely if ever*, is an established spoken idiom. (Reference: Bryant, p. 169.)

**re-** • The prefix *re-*, meaning "again," is hyphened when the form with hyphen can have a different meaning from the form without:

*reform*, to change, improve—*re-form*, to shape again
*recover*, to regain—*re-cover*, to cover again

and (rarely) for emphasis, as in *now re-seated in fair comfort,* or in Informal or humorous compounds: *re-re-married.* In other cases, there is no hyphen: *rearrange, reexamine, refine, remit.*

**-re, -er** • See *-er, -re.

**reaction** • *Reaction* has escaped from chemistry and the biological sciences to become a General word for any response of feeling or idea:

> Let me have your reaction to [Often: *on*] this.
> She reacted violently when he appeared.

Because it is used so loosely, it has tended to crowd out more appropriate or more exact words; careful users of the language therefore often avoid it.

**Reading and writing** • We read for entertainment and for instruction; inclination leads us to the first, and either inclination or necessity to the second. Besides these fundamental motives for reading, anyone interested in writing has another— reading to set a goal for his own writing. This does not mean conscious imitation of *Time* or *The New Yorker* or Walter Lippmann, Ernest Hemingway, or E. B. White. Rather it means reading with attention and occasional analysis the writers who genuinely appeal to us and allowing their work to influence ours casually and naturally.

This sort of reading influence is especially necessary in college because a student must read so much in textbooks and reference books and in the literature of earlier periods. Textbooks provide information, and the earlier literature is a necessary and valuable part of education; but the former, unfortunately, are seldom appealing, and the latter may cause the reader to lose touch with the idiom of his own time. If you are interested in writing well, you should supplement this college reading by reading as widely as you can in the better current magazines and books, fiction and nonfiction. The material you read is likely to be better than what you write, and a good background for judging your own work can come from a sensitive and critical reading of the somewhat similar work of the more important writers of your own time. The biographies of writers show that most of them probably formed their styles to a considerable extent on what they read. Though extensive reading cannot in itself make a good writer, it is the most valuable single formative influence.

In college you also have a chance to hear a great variety of spoken English, some of it well worth listening to. Although it would be a mistake to assume that good written styles are mere transcriptions of good speech, a written English which has an echo of the spoken in it is likely to be lively and interesting. Among your classmates there will be a few who talk especially well. And among your teachers there will be some who use language with remarkable skill. You will soon learn who the good talkers are; make a practice of listening to them as receptively as you can. Attentive listening is necessary in the college classroom, and if the teacher is a good talker, you will unconsciously absorb a good deal that will improve your written English. (See *Spoken and written English.)

**real—really** • *Real* is used as an adjective in Formal and General English: *a real experience, a real chore. Really* is the adverb: *a really successful party; It really went off well.*

In Nonstandard English and Informal conversation, *real* is often used adverbially: *Write real soon. It's real pretty. It went off real well.* This use is inappropriate in writing except to report conversation. (References: Pooley, pp. 161-163; Bryant, pp. 169-170.)

**realtor** • This business coinage has an advantage not possessed by most of its class, since it is much more economical than *real estate agent.* The National Association of Real Estate Boards contends that only a member of that group may call himself a *realtor.* Pronounced /rē'əl tər/.

**rear—raise** • See *raise—rear.

**reason is because** • In Formal English the construction beginning "The reason is" is usually completed by a noun or a noun clause to balance the noun *reason:*

The reason for my poor work in French was [noun:] my intense dislike of the subject.

The reason for my poor work in French was [noun clause:] that I disliked the subject intensely.

Since in speech not many noun clauses are introduced by *that,* and *because* is the connective that most obviously stresses the notion of cause, in spoken English we usually find:

The reason for my poor work in French was because I didn't like the subject.

*The reason is because* is also frequently found in writing:

In general it may be said that the reason why scholasticism was held to be an obstacle to truth was because it seemed to discourage further enquiry along experimental lines.—BASIL WILLEY, *The Seventeenth Century Background,* p. 7

Bryant writes: "*Reason . . . is because* occurs in standard usage. In formal English *reason is that* occurs somewhat more frequently, but *reason . . . is because* is a variant, which occurs more often in speech than in writing." (p. 170) Because of widespread prejudice against the construction, students should usually follow Formal usage. (References: Pooley, pp. 134-135, and *College English,* 1956, 18:110-111; F. N. Cherry, "Some Evidence in the Case of 'is because,' " *American Speech,* 1933, 8:55-60.)

**recipe—receipt** • /res′ə pē—ri sēt′/ Both words have meant "a formula, directions for making something." *Recipe* is now the more common in General English, though occasionally one or the other may be preferred by cooks, and then they are interchangeable in meaning. *Receipt* also means "a written acknowledgment for something received."

**Reciprocal pronouns** • See *each other, *Pronouns, types and forms § 5.

**reckon, guess, calculate.** See *calculate, guess, reckon.

**Redundancy** • See *Deadwood, *Repetition, *Wordiness.

**Reference of pronouns** •
*Revision: Change the pronoun marked (or revise the sentence) so that its reference will be exact and obvious and the pronoun itself will be in the conventional form.*

Ref

The syntax of a personal, relative, or demonstrative pronoun, as well as its complete meaning, often depends in part on its relation (or reference) to a previous noun in a passage, called its *antecedent.* This fact makes the accurate use of pronouns more complicated than the use of other words. Five of the personal pronouns and one of the relative pronouns—*who* —are further complicated by having a separate accusative form, as English nouns no longer do. There are some differences between speech and writing in the forms and references of pronouns, differences which become apparent when spoken practice is carried over into writing because when we read we can reexamine the phrasing at our leisure, something we cannot do when we listen. Therefore the conventions of pronoun usage as found in print should be followed in writing. A writer needs to check his pronouns in revising a paper to make sure that they are appropriate in form and in reference. Since a college student almost always knows the form that is appropriate in a given sentence, the choice of pronouns is simply a matter of care. This article runs over the main points in the use of pronouns in Standard written English.

1. *Exact and clear reference.*

*a*–If the meaning of a pronoun is completed by reference to a particular noun, the reference to this antecedent should be exact and obvious, as in the following examples:

The first hundred miles, *which* we covered before lunch, were rough, but *they* seemed to go faster than the sixty we did in the afternoon. [The noun *miles* is the antecedent of *which* and of *they*.]

All purchases for the University pass through a central purchasing office. *These* include books, trucks, building materials, food, and hundreds of other items. [*These* refers to *purchases*.]

Swimming may be more fun than calisthenics, but *it* can't give such a general development. [*It* refers to *swimming*.]

On July 3 Mr. Havermeyer asked Mr. Page to come to *his* house. [*His* refers to *Mr. Havermeyer*. Although another name has been mentioned, only a perverse reader would fail to understand the statement. *The former's* instead of *his* would be pedantic here.]

Professor Frank thought that McKinly was grateful to *him* for allowing *him* to graduate. [Actually no ambiguity is possible here and the sentence would be all right in speech and General writing.]

Confusion may arise when the pronoun seems to refer to a nearby noun to which it cannot sensibly refer or when there is no noun nearby; when it refers to a noun used subordinately in the preceding construction, perhaps to one used as a possessive or as an adjective; and when two or more pronouns are crossed so that the exact reference isn't readily clear. Usually to improve such a reference, the sentence must be revised, as in the following examples:

He isn't married and doesn't plan on *it*. [... and doesn't *plan to marry*.]

The next year he had an attack of acute appendicitis. *It* broke before the doctors had a chance to operate. [*It* cannot refer to *appendicitis* in the statement made. The second sentence should begin *His appendix broke*. Slips in reference are common when the pronoun refers back to a noun in the preceding sentence.]

A legislator should be a man who knows a little about law and government and he should know how to apply *them* to the best interests of his people. [For *them* put *his knowledge*.]

Bill provided more excitement one afternoon when he was skipping rocks across the swimming hole and cut open *a young girl's head who* was swimming under water. [... and cut open *the head of a young girl who* was swimming under water.]

To many of us the word *geology* means little in our everyday lives. Yet *it* deals with materials in use for making our homes and factories, metals of which our cars are made, and the fuel which enables us to drive them. [*It* should refer to *geology*—the science—not to *the word*. To revise, drop *the word* in the first line.]

Businessmen without regard for anyone else have exploited the mass of workers at every point, not caring whether *they* were earning a decent living wage, but only whether *they* were getting a lot of money. [The first *they* refers to *workers,* the second to *businessmen.* The sentence needs complete rewriting, but the second part could be improved somewhat by saying: . . . *not caring whether they paid a decent living wage, but only whether they were getting a lot of money.*]

Remember that clear reference is a matter of *meaning,* not just of the presence or position of certain words.

b—General English uses *which, that, this,* and sometimes *it* to refer to the idea of a previous clause. Formal usage tends to avoid this type of reference or to limit it to *this.*

*General:* Her friend was jealous of her clothes and money and had taken this way of showing it. [*It* refers to the idea in *was jealous.*]

*Formal:* Her friend was jealous of her clothes and money and had taken this way of showing her feeling.

*General:* He never seemed to realize when academic tempests were brewing, which was probably a good thing.—J. R. PARKER, *Academic Procession,* p. 86 [*Which* refers to the idea of the first clause.]

*Formal:* He never seemed to realize when academic tempests were brewing. This was probably a good thing.

*General:* From his firm grip, piercing eyes, and stern mouth I could see that he was not to be trifled with, which was well proved later. [*Which* refers to the *that*-clause.]

*Formal:* From his firm grip, piercing eyes, and stern mouth I could see that he was not to be trifled with. This was well proved later.

c—In conversation the reference of pronouns is freer than in writing. The following examples, which would probably pass unnoticed in a conversation, show one reason why, in written work, we sometimes find pronouns that seem inexact. Your written work should be read with a cold eye to find and correct inexact pronoun reference.

| *Spoken* | *Written* |
|---|---|
| Gordon's mother asked me to take him fishing because he was so interested in *it* but had never caught *one.* | Gordon's mother asked me to take him fishing because he was so interested in *it* but had never caught a *fish.* |
| Everyone likes to dance and knew he would get plenty of *it* during the party weekend. | Everyone likes to dance and knew he would get plenty of *dancing* during the party weekend. |
| In aquaplaning the ropes | The ropes should never be |

should never be wound around the wrists, because if thrown *he* would be dragged along and injured.

wound around *the planer's* wrists, because if thrown *he* would be dragged along and injured.

**2.** *Agreement of pronoun with antecedent.* Pronouns referring to specific antecedents generally agree with the antecedents in number, gender, and person.

*a*–Agreement in number. A pronoun agrees with its antecedent in number: singular antecedent, singular pronoun; plural antecedent, plural pronoun.

*Singular: Jimmy* tried to go quietly, but *he* couldn't keep from whistling.

*Plural: The boys* had tried to go quietly, but *they* couldn't keep from whistling.

In Formal American English, *each, every, everyone* are generally referred to by singular pronouns (see *every and its compounds § 1):

Almost *everyone* has some little superstitions which *he* would not violate for love or money.

In spoken English these words are treated as collectives and are found usually with a plural pronoun:

Almost *everyone* has some little superstitions which *they* would not violate for love or money.

Maugham takes *anyone* from a gigolo to a lord and develops *them* [Formal: *him*] with equal ease and finesse.

This colloquial agreement is sometimes found in print, but editors usually bring it in line with Formal usage before publication. (Reference: Russell Thomas, "Concord Based on *Meaning* versus Concord Based on *Form*: The Indefinites," *College English,* 1939, 1:38-45.)

A *collective noun is referred to by either a singular or a plural pronoun, depending upon its meaning in the sentence:

*Singular:* When a *gang* of rabbit hunters spreads out over a field, *it* doesn't lose any time.

*Plural:* When a *gang* of rabbit hunters spread out over a field, *they* don't lose any time.

Often when a pronoun does not agree with its antecedent, the antecedent should be changed rather than the pronoun:

Putting himself in the shoes of the *slave owner,* Lincoln realized that *they* had a right to feel as they did toward emancipation. [This could be made consistent by making *slave owner* plural better than by changing *they* to *he.*]

*Labor's* third and major contention is that *they* do not receive an adequate return for the services they render. [Here changing *Labor's* to *The workers'* would be more accurate than changing the pronouns to the singular.]

*b*–Agreement in person. Except in indefinite pronouns (§ 3 of this article), there is little difficulty with agreement:

First person: *I* wish Mr. Patterson had told *me* before.
Second person: *You* should have thought of that *yourself*.
Third person: *The woman* had said *she* was over twenty-one.

A relative pronoun agrees with its antecedent:

I, *who* am your nearest relative, would help you. [Because of the unusualness of the *who am*, it would not ordinarily be said or written: *I, your nearest relative....*]
He is one of those *people who* do just what *they* want to. [*They* refers to *who*, which refers to *people*.]

*c*–Form of pronouns. The form of a pronoun depends upon the construction in which it stands, not upon its antecedent. The form of a pronoun does not necessarily show its function; see the discussion of *Case and the articles there referred to (*between you and me; *It's me; *who, whom).

3. *Indefinite reference.* Often pronouns are used to refer to the readers or to people in general instead of to specifically mentioned people. English has no well-established pronoun like the German *man* or the French *on* to refer to a person in general. Our *one* has a definitely Formal and stiffish connotation. *We* and *you* seem to be slightly more personal, more expressive, and are very generally used, as in many pages in this book. This is a question of style rather than of grammar, and whether *you* or *they* (They say ...) or *we* or *one* or *people* or some other noun is used depends on its fitness in the passage.

Care should be taken to keep indefinite pronouns consistent, not shifting from *one* to *you*, for example:

When *you* have worked a day here *you* have really earned your money.
[*Or:*] When *one* has worked a day here *he* has really earned ....
[*Not:*] When *one* has worked a day here *you* have really ....

An indefinite pronoun should not be substituted for a definite personal pronoun:

For *me* there is no fun in reading unless *I* can put myself in the position of the characters and feel that *I* am really in the scene. [Not: For *me* there is no fun in reading unless *you* can put yourself in the position of the characters and feel that *you* are really in the scene.]

The indefinite pronouns (*all, any, each, everybody, few, nobody,* and so on–*Pronouns, types and forms § 8) have no expressed antecedent, so that their use involves consistency but not agreement with an antecedent.

Since English has no single pronoun to mean he-or-she, the masculine *he* is conventionally used (see *he-or-she):

The time comes to every senior when *he* [Not: *he or she*] anxiously looks forward to that eventful day.

The best way out of the difficulty is to use the plural:

The time comes to all seniors when they. . . .

**4.** *Avoiding pronouns.* Pronouns are necessary and convenient, but since they sometimes lead to inconsistent uses (that are marked by teachers and editors), some writers tend to avoid them, using a noun instead. The result is usually unidiomatic or clumsy English:

That's the reason I hesitate to picture the owner of *a grip* from the appearance of *the bag.* [Better: That's the reason I hesitate to picture the owner of *the bag* from *its* appearance.]

Arrest of *the woman* yesterday followed several days of observation of *the woman's* [Better: *her*] activities by agents of the Stores Mutual Protective Association.

Pronouns are especially useful to bind together clauses and sentences. In the following paragraph each sentence seems to be a new beginning, but with pronouns instead of *Mr. Frothingham,* the paragraph would read more smoothly:

Roland W. Frothingham died at his home on Commonwealth Avenue on Tuesday. Mr. Frothingham [He] was born in Boston in 1868 and had lived here ever since. Mr. Frothingham's [His] ancestors came from Ipswich. Mr. Frothingham [He] was educated at Harvard College.

**5.** *Omission of pronouns.* In Informal writing and in conversation, pronouns, especially *I,* are often omitted (see *I § 3), and in all varieties of English the relative pronoun is often not used in relative clauses (see *Contact clauses): *The first man (that) I met had never heard of such a street.*

(For the classes and forms of pronouns, see *Pronouns, types and forms; for further instances of their use, see the articles on particular pronouns, *I, *we, *who, whom, *himself, herself, *myself. References: All grammars treat the use of pronouns. Curme and Jespersen discuss many special uses.)

**References** • Any paper based on the writings of others should acknowledge the sources used. Not only is it common courtesy and honesty to give credit where credit is due, but it is a sign of scrupulousness to tell the source of a statement, so that a reader can judge for himself the evidence it is based on. It also allows the reader to turn to the sources for further information. College students are expected to draw their materials from various sources, but they are also expected to make a frank acknowledgment of their indebtedness to these sources. (See *Plagiarism.)

In formal academic papers—reference papers, term papers, theses, dissertations—it is conventional to give exact references in footnotes. The forms differ slightly, but the aim of all is the same—to record in some brief and consistent form the author, title, facts of publication, and exact page from which each quotation and each fact or opinion is taken. Giving these facts about sources of material is called *documentation.* The style of footnotes and bibliography suggested in this article is suitable for documentation in a college reference paper. This style follows the recommendations of the *MLA Style Sheet,* revised edition, which has been adopted by most journals in literature and history and by many university presses. In scientific papers other styles of reference are often used; these are given in *References in scientific papers. Be sure to learn from your instructor what style of documentation he wants you to follow.*

Footnotes are needed *for all direct quotations* (except well-known bits from the Bible or other literature that are used for style rather than content; for these the source is given in parentheses directly after the quotation) *and for all important statements of facts or interpretations that are summarized from written sources.* Obviously statistics, dates, descriptions of situations, scientific data, opinions, and the like that are not common knowledge and that are presented to advance the thesis of the paper need a stated source.

Although the number of sources referred to in a paper must vary with the type of subject and the kind of sources used, a typical student reference paper might average from two to five footnotes for a page of typewritten manuscript. Material from conversation, from lectures, or from any other source that a reader cannot turn to is best acknowledged in the text of the paper or in a prefatory note. The source of a diagram, map, table, or other illustration is not given in a footnote but under the illustration (see p. 8).

The reference figure is placed slightly above the line after the statement or quotation whose source is being given, usually but not always following a mark of punctuation. The notes are numbered from 1 up throughout the paper. In books they are usually numbered from 1 up on each page, but this practice is rare in college papers.

The footnotes are placed at the bottom of the page on which they belong or all together at the end on a separate sheet headed *Footnotes.* If you put them at the bottom of each page, look ahead in the rough draft to see how many footnotes will be needed on a page; put a light pencil mark where you should begin the footnote series; separate the footnote from the bottom line of the text by a triple space. The first line of each footnote is indented like a paragraph; following lines, if any, begin flush with the left margin and are single-spaced.

The footnote reference number should be slightly raised above the line as in the text; additional footnotes are separated by a double space. (For footnotes on separate sheets you may be instructed to double-space within footnotes and triple-space between them.)

1. *Form of footnotes*. The purpose of a citation footnote is to tell the reader the exact source of a statement. Uniformity is a convenience for the reader and is obligatory in scholarly papers and articles intended for publication. This section gives a pattern for use in undergraduate papers.

a—Books. The *first* reference to a book gives the author's full name (first name first), the full title copied from the title page and underlined, the place and date of publication in parentheses, the page or pages, and a period at the end of the footnote:

[1]Everett Dick, Vanguards of the Frontier (New York, 1941), p. 450.

Variations on this basic form are introduced for the following reasons, illustrated in order below: (1) more than one author, (2) an edited work, (3) a translated work, (4) a compilation by an editor, (5) an item in a collection, (6) a work in more than one volume, (7) an indication of an edition, (8) a work whose author is not known, (9) material quoted at second hand.

(1) [1]James Bradstreet Greenough and George Lyman Kittredge, Words and Their Ways in English Speech (New York, 1901), p. 185.

(2) [2]H[enry] L[ouis] Mencken, The American Language..., The Fourth Edition and the Two Supplements, abridged, with annotations and new material, by Raven I. McDavid, Jr., with the assistance of David W. Maurer (New York, 1963), p. 521, n.1.

The periods after the title show that it has not been quoted completely; the rest of it is *An Inquiry into the Development of English in the United States*. The brackets after *H* and *L* show that the full first names were not given on the title page but only the initials followed by periods. The material from "The Fourth" to "Maurer" might have been reduced to "ed. Raven I. McDavid, Jr., and David W. Maurer." After the page number "n. 1" means "[foot]note 1."

(3) [3][Thomas] Urquhart and [Peter Antony] Motteux, trans. The Works of Rabelais (London, n.d.), p. 331.

Since this is a well-known translation, the names of the translators are given first; but the note might have read "[3][François]

Rabelais, *The Works,* trans. Urquhart and Motteux (London, n.d.), p. 331."

(4) [4] Letters of Noah Webster, ed. Harry R. Warfel (New York, 1953), p. 49.

(5) [5] Wilfrid Mellers, "Music," The New Outline of Modern Knowledge, ed. Alan Pryce–Jones (London, 1956), pp. 342–365.

(6) [6] William James, The Principles of Psychology, American Science Series—Advanced Course (New York, 1890), II, 403.

Though this work is part of a series, the indication of that fact is not vital here; in other instances it may be.

(7) [7] Albert C. Baugh, A History of the English Language, 2nd ed. (New York, 1957), p. vii.

(8) [8] Britain, an Official Handbook, prepared by the Central Office of Information (London, 1962), p. 147.

(9) [9] Ludwig Wittgenstein, Philosophical Investigations (1953), pp. 65–67, quoted in Barbara M. H. Strang, Modern English Structure (New York, 1962), pp. 2–3.

Pamphlets and government bulletins are referred to in the same form as books. The items always appear in the same order (author, title, place, date, page).

For *later* references to the same book, use a short form, just enough to identify the work in the bibliography. If you have used only one work by the same man, the author's last name, followed by the page number, is sufficient:

[3] Dick, p. 128

But if you have used more than one source by the same man, you will need to cite one or two key words from the title in addition to the author's last name:

[3] Dick, Vanguards, p. 128.

b—Magazine and newspaper articles. In the *first* reference to a magazine article, give the author's name in normal order, the title of the article in quotation marks, the name of the magazine underlined, the volume in capitalized Roman numerals, the year in parentheses, and the page or pages (number only):

[4] David B. Davis, "Ten–Gallon Hero," American Quarterly, VI (1954), 114.

For magazines that number pages separately in each issue (instead of consecutively through a volume) and for newspapers, give the complete date of issue and page; the volume number may be omitted:

[5] Bernard DeVoto, "Birth of an Art," Harper's Magazine, CCVII (December 1953), 8.

A magazine article with no author given would be referred to as above, but the note would begin with the title of the article.

Reference to a newspaper story or untitled item in a magazine includes the name of the periodical underlined, the date, and the page. The column number may be given. If there are

sections paged separately, the section should also be given.
Headlines are not ordinarily given because they are often
changed from edition to edition.

[6]The New York Times, July 17, 1964, Sec. II, p. 1, col. 6.

A *later* reference to a magazine article or newspaper item
may be shortened to the author's last name, the name of the
magazine, and the page; or the periodical's name and the page:

[7]DeVoto, Harper's, p. 12.

Unsigned encyclopedia articles may be given by the title of
the article or simply by the name of the encyclopedia:

[12]"Rhetoric," Encyclopaedia Britannica (Chicago, 1964), XIX,
247.

[12]Encyclopaedia Britannica (Chicago, 1964), XIX, 247.

Unsigned publications of organizations are listed by title:

[13]American Education and International Tension (Washington,
National Education Association, 1949), p. 32.

The Latin abbreviation *ibid.* means "in the same place."
Used in a footnote, it refers to the book or article cited in
the footnote immediately preceding. *Ibid.* cannot be used if
a reference to another source intervenes. (This convention
is easy to remember if you think of *ibid.* as performing the
function fulfilled in informal listings by ditto marks; ditto
marks are never used in footnotes or bibliographies.) Though
a useful abbreviation, *ibid.* will not occur often in a good
research paper; a long succession of *ibid.*'s shows excessive
reliance on one source.

[8]Edward Everett Dale, Cow Country (Norman, Oklahoma, 1945),
p. 53.

[9]Ibid., p. 96.

c—Split note. If part of a reference is given in the text of the
paper, it need not be repeated in the footnote: if the author's
name is in the text, the footnote begins with the title; if author
and title are in the text, only the facts of publication and the
page are in the footnote. This system can be used for material
at second hand: if you give the original source in the text, cite
in the footnote the secondary source in which you found it.

d—Informational footnote. In some scholarly books, you
may find an additional fact, a statement of a different opinion,
a quotation, or a reference to other sources given in a footnote,
but in college writing it is well to use footnotes only for citations of sources; everything else belongs in the text.

e—Law cases. The following form is used to cite law cases:
the plaintiff's last name, *v.* (*versus,* meaning "against"), the de-
fendant's last name, the volume number of the reports where
the case is given, an abbreviation for the report series, the page

on which the case begins, and the year in which the decision was rendered:

16 Lochner v. New York, 198 U.S. 539 (1905).

f—Bible. Books of the Bible are not underlined. The reference form is name of the book, chapter, verse:

17 Genesis 4:16 (or 4, 16).

**2.** *Common abbreviations.* The following abbreviations are commonly used in footnotes. Although you are not likely to use them all, you should know what they mean. Those from Latin should be underlined to represent italics.

art.—article
c.—copyright
*ca.* or *c.* (*circa*)—around a given date (*ca.* 1480)
ch. or chap.—chapter; chs. or chaps.—chapters
col.—column; cols.—columns
ed.—edited by; edition (2nd ed.)
f.—following (one following page: 386 f.); ff. (more than one following page: 286 ff.) Exact references are preferable: pp. 286–287; pp. 286–291
*ibid.* (*ibidem*)—in the same place
l.—line; ll.—lines
MS.—manuscript; MSS.—manuscripts
n.—note (to refer to a footnote in a source: p. 135n.); nn.—notes
n.d.—no date of publication
n.p.—no place of publication
N.S.—new series of a periodical
O.S.—old series of a periodical
p.—page; pp.—pages
tr. or trans.—translated by
vol.—volume; vols.—volumes (the abbreviations vol. and p. are not used when figures for volume and page are given together: a reference to a volume alone would be vol. III, and a reference to a page alone would be p. 176; but if both the volume number and page number are cited, the form is either III, 176 or 3:176)

The following abbreviations were formerly in general use but are less common now:

*cf.* (*confer*)—compare (used to cite other related passages)
*et al.* (*et alii*)—and others (used for multiple authorship; English words are now more common: Maurice Frink and others)
*infra*—below (referring to something that is discussed later in the paper)
*loc. cit.* (*loco citato*)—in the place cited (referring to a passage cited in a recent footnote; not followed by a page number)

*op. cit. (opere citato)*—the work cited: Dick, *op. cit.,* p. 128;
now a shortened form of the title is more common: Dick,
*Vanguards,* p. 128

*passim*—here and there (indicating that a matter is discussed in
several places in a book or an article)

*q.v. (quod vide)*—which see (used for cross reference; now
generally replaced by "see")

*seq. (sequentes)*—following (replaced by *f.* and *ff.*)

*supra*—above (referring to something discussed earlier in the
paper)

*s.v. (sub verbo)*—under the word (used to refer to an item in an
alphabetical listing)

*vide* or *v.*—see (now replaced by the English word)

**3.** *The bibliography.* The bibliography of the sources actually
used in the preparation of a reference paper comes at the end.
It contains not all of the sources consulted but only those
which have actually furnished material. Its purpose is to enable a reader to identify the works cited in the footnotes.
Though the form of bibliographies has been pretty well standardized, you may find slight variations in punctuation and
content from one publishing house to another. The forms
recommended by the *MLA Style Sheet* for a book and for a
magazine are as follows:

> Dick, Everett. Vanguards of the Frontier. New York, 1941.
>
> Davis, David B. "Ten-Gallon Hero," American Quarterly, VI
> (1954), 111–125.

Note that authors' names are inverted and hanging indention
is used. The usual practice is to single-space each entry, double-
space between entries.

In short bibliographies all the items are run in one list,
alphabetically arranged. When no author is given, the first
important word of the title (omitting *a, an,* or *the*) is used as
the key word for alphabetizing. Very long bibliographies are
sometimes grouped by type of material: Primary Sources,
Secondary Sources; Works by an Author, Works about Him;
and so on. They should not be grouped according to type of
publication, such as books and periodicals, except in a list of
the works of a single writer.

**References in scientific papers** • Research papers in the sciences use a system of reference to sources quite different from
the system of the humanities and social sciences described in
*References. The references have the same purpose—giving the
author, title, and facts of publication of articles and books
used, to acknowledge the source of material and to make it

possible for a reader to go directly to a source if he wishes further information. The details of form vary considerably among the different scientific and technical fields and often among the books and journals within a field. If you are writing a paper on a scientific or technical subject, you will have to select among the systems given in this article (or follow your instructor's specification of which to use) or study the form of a particular journal and follow its practice. Many of these journals publish stylesheets: the *Manual for Authors* of the American Mathematical Society, for example.

**1.** *General points.*

*a*–A few scientific journals give references to sources in footnotes at the bottom of a page, but most of them, and most scientific books, use footnotes only for explanatory comments or for additional facts, as in this one from *Annual Review of Physical Chemistry* (Palo Alto, 1963), p. 145:

[3a]The lowest temperature at which super-conducting transition has been found, $0.016°K$, was reported for a $Nb_{.30}Mo_{.70}$ alloy at the St. Louis meeting of the American Physical Society (1963) by R. Blaugher, R. A. Hein, and J. W. Gibson at a post deadline paper.

Such footnotes are kept few and brief.

*b*–The reference to a source is usually given in parentheses in the text, immediately following the writer's name or following the relevant statement, as illustrated in § 2 and 3.

*c*–The references and the bibliographical entries are made as economical as possible:

Arabic numerals rather than roman are used for volumes: 24:62-63. Sometimes the volume number is printed in boldface type (**24**:62-63), indicated in manuscript by a wavy line under the figures, or in italic type (*24*:62-63), indicated by one line under the figures; but most often they are in ordinary type.

Sometimes authors' names in a bibliography are printed in capitals and small capitals: BROWNE, C. A. (Small capitals are indicated by two lines under the letters in manuscript.) But most often they are in ordinary type.

In titles usually only the first word and proper names are capitalized, and the titles of articles are not put in quotation marks. Usually the titles of periodicals or other series (bulletins, monographs) are in italics (underlined in manuscript).

Prepositions are often omitted in the titles of periodicals: *J. Nutrition, Jour. Forestry* (for *Journal of Nutrition, Journal of Forestry*).

The names of journals and other series of publications are usually abbreviated. Some common abbreviations are:

| | | | |
|---|---|---|---|
| Bull. | Bulletin | Mon. | Monograph (s) |
| J. (Jour.) | Journal | Proc. | Proceedings |

| Pub. | Publication (s) | Sci. | Science |
| Rev. | Review | ser. | series |

Abbreviations are given for commonly used words, like Am. (American), Assoc. (Association), Soc. (Society), and the names of fields (Biol., Geol.), and of well-known organizations, like IRE (Institute of Radio Engineers). The Latin abbreviation *et al.* (*et alii*, "and others") is used when a work has more than two authors, and *op. cit.* (*opere citato*, "in the work cited") occasionally for later references to a work.

*d*–In some systems the title of a periodical article is not given:

Mermin, N. D., *Ann. Phys.* (N.Y.), **81**, 421 (1962).

*e*–When the reference is to the general method described in a relatively short article or to the general conclusion of a work, specific pages are not given.

*f*–Little direct quotation is used, but when it is, the source is given between the closing quotation marks and the period ending the sentence:

. . . although it might be added that "the oldest unit of the Detroit River group, the Sylvania sandstone, is succeeded respectively by the Amherstburg dolomite, the Lucas dolomite, and the Anderson Limestone" (Ehleis, 1950, p. 1455).

*g*–Since dates are especially important in scientific work—a scientist presumably is familiar with previous work on his subject and builds upon it—they are usually given prominence by being given first or last in the facts of publication of the bibliography and are used as a key item in the reference system described in § 3.

*h*–Acknowledgment of special assistance of individuals is made either in a footnote early in the article or under a heading *Acknowledgments* just before the bibliography.

*i*–The bibliography at the end of an article may be headed *References* or *Literature cited,* but most often *Bibliography.*

*j*–In general, then, the source material used in a scientific paper is indicated by the combined reference in parentheses in the text and an entry in the bibliography. The two most common systems are given in § 2 and 3. Use one of these unless you have reason to use some of the variations indicated.

2. *References by bibliography numbers.* In this system the items of the bibliography are arranged alphabetically by author (the rare unsigned item usually under *Anonymous*) and then numbered from 1 up. The parenthetical references in the text are to these numbers in the bibliography.

Here are some sentences from an article (Robert A. Gardner and John L. Retzer, "Interpretive Soil Classification: Timber,

Range, and Watersheds," *Soil Science,* 1949, 67:151-157), with the reference numbers in parentheses. The sentences occurred in the order in which they stand, though not consecutively.

Kittredge (9) pointed out the advantages that natural forest areas offer to the study of soils, long undisturbed, in relation to forest type —advantages that cultivated soil areas cannot offer.

Veatch (15) has made extensive use of soil-forest relations in approximating areas and kinds of original forest cover in Michigan, and Roe (12) has grouped soil types of the originally forested part of the lake states. . . .

The more important relatively permanent criteria of use in the natural classification of forest soils listed by Lutz and Chandler (10) are also of importance in crop production.

The nutritive value of pasture forage as related to soils has received considerable study (1, 11), but in the main the nutritive value of range forage as related to soils is an almost untouched field (3).

The bibliography entries referred to in these sentences are given at the end of the article as follows:

(1) Browne, C. A. 1938 Some relationships of soil to plant and animal nutrition—the major elements. *U.S. Dept. Agr. Yearbook* 1938: 777-806.

(3) Cardon, P. V., *et al.* 1939 Pasture and range in livestock feeding. *U.S. Dept. Agr. Yearbook* 1939: 925-955.

(9) Kittredge, J., Jr. 1928 The use of soil surveys in forestry. *First Internatl. Cong. Soil Sci. Proc. and Papers* (1927) 4 (Comn. V): 562-565.

(10) Lutz, H. J., and Chandler, R. F., Jr. 1946 *Forest Soils.* John Wiley and Sons, Inc., New York.

(11) McMurtrey, J. E., Jr., and Robinson, W. O. 1938 Neglected soil constituents that affect plant and animal development. *U.S. Dept. Agr. Yearbook* 1938: 807-829.

(12) Roe, E. I. 1935 Forest soils—the basis of forest management. Lake States Forest Exp. Sta., Processed Rpt.

(15) Veatch, J. O. 1932 Soil maps as a basis for mapping original forest cover. *Papers Mich. Acad. Sci., Arts and Letters* (1931) 15: 267-273.

This bibliography does not use capitals or quotation marks in article titles. The year is given before the title. Only inclusive pages (for the whole item referred to) are given. This would handicap a reader who wanted to refer to the source, especially for entry 10, which is a whole book. Usually in references of this type the pages directly involved in the statement are given in the parenthetical references:

. . . in the natural classification of forest soils listed by Lutz and Chandler (10, pp. 262-266) . . . .

A variation of the numbered bibliography system is listing the sources in the bibliography in the order in which they are referred to in the text—1 for the first mentioned source, 2 for the second, and so on. This works well for quite short bibliographies but becomes a nuisance if there are many items. In this system the pages referred to are usually made part of the bibliography entry rather than being put in parentheses.

3. *Reference by author and date.* Perhaps the most widely used system gives the author and date of publication. The items of the bibliography are arranged alphabetically by author. The reference is in parentheses in the text and includes author, date of the publication, and pages when the source to be indicated is only a part of the item.

These examples are from Floyd H. Allport, *Theories of Perception and the Concept of Structure,* New York, John Wiley & Sons, 1955.

In this first example, the full data (in parentheses) stands at the end of a paragraph:

The term meaning has been further extended to apply to the experience of *insight* into one's behavior; for behavior with insight is an evidence of the existence of some manifest ego-field organization. (Koffka, 1935, pp. 175-176, 382.)

If the author's name is given in the sentence, as it frequently is, only the date and page (or chapter of a book) are given in the parentheses. If the reference is to the whole work, only the date is needed:

Hebb has presented his own account of insight and the "meaning of meaning" (1949, pp. 126-134).

The case for perceptual and cognitive learning has also been well stated by Hilgard (1948, Chapter 12).

We recall the experiment performed by Stratton (1897) and Ewert (1930).

If there is more than one item by the same writer, they are identified by the years of publication, and if there is more than one by the same writer in the same year, each is given a letter in addition to the date:

The first type, the associationistic, or S-R, theories are best represented by Hull's objective theory of behavior (1943*b*, 1951, 1952).

If the item specifically referred to is included in another work, the reference is to the latter (in the bibliography McCleary and Lazarus is not listed):

This proposition, the most challenging of all the directive-state hypotheses, was tested in its various parts by McGinnies (1949) and by McCleary and Lazarus (see Bruner and Krech, eds., 1950, pp. 171-179).

The bibliography of Allport's book is very extensive. The works referred to in the quotations just given are entered as:

Bruner, J. S., and D. Krech. 1950. *Perception and personality: a symposium*. Durham: Duke Univ. Press.

Ewert, P. H. 1930. A study of the effect of inverted retinal stimulation upon spatially coordinated behavior. *Genet. Psychol. Monogr., 7*, Nos. 3 and 4.

Hebb, D. O. 1949. *The organization of behavior*. New York: Wiley.

Hilgard, E. R. 1948. *Theories of learning*. New York: Appleton-Century-Crofts.

Hull, C. L. 1943a. The problem of intervening variables in molar behavior theory. *Psychol. Rev., 50*, 273-291.

Hull, C. L. 1943b. *Principles of behavior: an introduction to behavior theory*. New York: Appleton-Century-Crofts.

Hull, C. L. 1951. *Essentials of behavior*. New Haven: Yale Univ. Press.

Hull, C. L. 1952. *A behavior system: an introduction to behavior theory concerning the individual organism*. New Haven: Yale Univ. Press.

Koffka, W. 1935. *Principles of gestalt psychology*. New York: Harcourt.

McGinnies, E. 1949. Emotionality and perceptual defense. *Psychol. Rev., 56*, 244-251.

Stratton, G. M. 1897. Vision without inversion of the retinal image. *Psychol. Rev., 4*, 341-360; 463-481.

This bibliography shows one of the standard systems of capitalizing and of punctuating entries, with the period the usual mark between elements except that commas are used within the parts of a periodical reference.

Familiarity with the practices of their scientific field is useful for majors in the scientific and technical departments, both for reading material in the field and for writing papers in advanced courses.

**Referent** • The term, pronounced /ref'ər ənt/, is used in semantics for what a word refers to. The referent of *book* is either a particular book being discussed or a generalized notion based on our observation of various books. \*Abstract words have no specific, observable referents.

**Reflexive pronouns** • See \*myself, \*Pronouns, types and forms § 4.

**regard, regards** • Standard English uses the prepositional phrase *in regard to*; Nonstandard often uses *in regards to*. (Reference: Bryant, p. 115.)

**regardless** • *-less* is a negative ending and makes the word mean "without regard to"; prefixing an *ir-* (*irregardless) doubles the negative and makes a word which is as yet unacceptable in writing, though common in speech.

**Relative adverbs** • The group of connecting words which may be called *relative adverbs*—though they also have other functions—includes *as, after, before, that, since, until, when, whenever, where, wherever*. (For some examples of their use see *Relative clauses.)

**Relative clauses** • Because these clauses are usually introduced by a *relative pronoun (that, which, who,* etc.) or a *relative adverb (where, when, why,* etc.) without a connective (see the last adjective example below and *Contact clauses), they usually function like adjectives and are often called adjective clauses; but they may also function as nouns and adverbs in a sentence:

*Adjective function:*

The rain *that began in the morning* kept on all night.

The coach was now abused by the alumni *who two years before had worshiped him.*

The road to the left, *which looked almost impassable,* was ours.

The first place *where they camped* turned out to be impossible.

The man *I met that afternoon* has been my friend ever since. [Formal: The man *whom* I met....]

The ideas *we held in common* were few indeed. [Formal: The ideas *that* we held....]

*Noun function:*

*Whoever says so* is a liar.

He will take *what you offer him.*

He laughed at *what I said.*

*Adverb function:*

I sing *when I can.*

I go *wherever I like.*

An adjective clause stands after the noun it modifies. In the first sentence above, the clause modifies *rain*; in the second, *alumni*; in the third, *road*; the fourth, *place*; the fifth, *man*; and the sixth, *ideas*. (See *that, *who, whom, *which, *Restrictive and nonrestrictive.)

Several relative clauses in succession make for an awkward, or at least conspicuous, house-that-Jack-built sentence that should be avoided:

People *who* buy houses *that* have been built in times *which* had conspicuous traits of architecture *which* have been since abandoned often have to remodel their purchases completely.

**Relative pronouns** • One group of connecting words which introduce *relative clauses is called *relative pronouns* and includes *who (whose, whom), which (of which, whose), that, what, whatever, whoever (whomever)*, and occasionally *as*; of these, *what* and *whatever* introduce only *noun clauses.

Somebody, *who* [or: *whom*] I don't know, shouted, "Put 'em out."
The Senator, *whose* term expires next year, is already worrying about re-election.
I haven't read the same book *that* [*as*] you have.
*Whatever* I do is wrong.

*That* refers to persons or things, *who* to persons. *Which* in Standard English now refers only to animals or objects or situations, and also to collective nouns even if they refer to persons:

The army which mobilizes first has the advantage.
The Board of Directors, which met on Saturday, . . .
The Board of Directors, who are all bankers, . . .

In older English—and still in Nonstandard—*which* applies also to persons:

"Our Father which art in heaven. . . ."—*The Bible* (King James), Matt. 6:9.

(Particular points in the use of these relatives will be found in separate entries on each, especially those on *that, *which, *who, whom. See also *Subordinating conjunctions, *Restrictive and nonrestrictive.)

**remember** • In Nonstandard English the idiom is often *remember of*: *I don't remember of doing that.* In writing, the *of* is not used: *I don't remember doing it; I don't remember that at all.* Informally *disremember* means *forget.*

**Renaissance—Renascence** • *Renaissance* is the more common spelling. It is pronounced /ren'ə säns'/ or /ren'ə zäns'/, or, less commonly /ri nā'sns/; *Renascence* is usually pronounced /ri nas'sns/. The word is capitalized when it refers to the period of history, but not when it refers to a revival, as "the prewar renaissance (renascence) in poetry."

**repair, maintain, service** • See *service.

**Repetition** •
*Revision: Revise so as to remove the ineffective repetition of word, meaning, or sound.*

Rep

Repetition of word, meaning, or sound may be an effective trait of style, contributing especially to emphasis. Following

are some kinds of repetition that ordinarily require revision:
1. *Of words and phrases.* The subject of a paper or of one of
its important parts must be mentioned frequently, though pronouns and economical sentences can reduce the repetition. An
attentive reading of the following sentences should have led
the writers to revise them, removing the obvious repetitions
and other *deadwood too:

The Indian's culture was so different from the white man's
[culture] that he has done very well to change as much as he has in
such a short [period of] time.

From here on there was no trail, and if there had been it would
have been snowed under [by the snow of] the night before.

Especially conspicuous is repetition of a word used in a
different sense:

Our club is as much a fraternity as any house along the row. Our
unity and fraternity [Substitute: *brotherhood*] have brought us real
satisfaction and much success.

2. *Of meaning.* Meaning of single words or of longer groups
is often repeated in near synonyms:

. . . where he did very successful work [there].

In *many* books the setting [very often] is in some foreign country.

At eight-thirty [in the morning] you punch the time clock for the
start of the day.

New leg kicks are shown him, new arm stretches are demonstrated,
and different ways of breathing illustrated. [Rewritten: *He is shown
new leg kicks, new arm stretches, and different ways of breathing.*]

3. *Of sound.* Jingles and rhyming words are out of place in
prose and so are repetitions of unstressed syllables, especially
the *-ly* of adverbs and the endings of some abstract nouns,
like *-tion,* which are unpleasant when noticeable.

**Reports** • A *report* is essentially an orderly presentation of
data arranged for a specific purpose. In business or technical
reports the purpose may be to present the results of laboratory
or field research; to give a routine account of some activity,
process, or advance; or to recommend some action or decision
after going over the evidence upon which the recommendation
is based.

Reports vary in form, including memorandums, form reports, letter reports, and the "full" technical report. Since in
some fields the exact form of the report is rigidly specified, it
is wise in preparing such reports to follow the procedures
outlined in one of the texts listed below.

A report needs to be clear and compact, quickly understandable to the readers for whom it is intended. Since its sole aim

is presentation of data gathered for a specific purpose, it does not lend itself to amateur practice, but a student would do well to familiarize himself with the type of report likely to be used in the field he expects to work in, and if possible make a collection of reports for future guidance.

(Detailed discussions of report writing will be found in books devoted to the subject, such as the following: John Ball and Cecil B. Williams, *Report Writing,* New York, 1955; Robley Winfrey, *Technical and Business Report Preparation,* 3rd ed., Ames, Iowa, 1962; N. B. Sigband, *Effective Report Writing,* New York, 1960; J. N. Ulman and J. R. Gould, *Technical Reporting,* rev. ed., New York, 1959; B. H. Weil, ed., *The Technical Report, Its Preparation, Processing, and Use in Industry and Government,* New York, 1954.)

**Requests and commands** • See *Commands and requests.

**Research papers** • See *References.

**researcher** • *Researcher* has been added to the English vocabulary as a needed shortening for *research worker.*

**Resolutions** • An organization usually passes a resolution as a formal recommendation of action, expression of sympathy, or record of sentiment. The style is Formal and the expression arranged in a standardized formula:

WHEREAS, The experiences of the past few weeks have shown . . . ; and

WHEREAS, Our expectations of a more favorable attitude on the part of . . . ; therefore be it

RESOLVED, That this body feels it its duty to inform . . . ; and be it further

RESOLVED, That a copy of these resolutions be sent. . . .

John W. Appel, Secretary

**rest** • There are two *rest's* in English, both in good standing. *Rest,* "repose," is from Old English *rest*; *rest,* "remainder," is from French *reste.*

**Restrictive and nonrestrictive** •
*Revision: If the modifier marked is restrictive, it should not be separated from the word it modifies by a comma; if it is nonrestrictive, it should be set off by a comma or by two commas.*

*Rest*

1. *Restrictive, or close, modifiers.* A restrictive modifier defines, limits, identifies the word it refers to; that is, it provides

information essential to the meaning of the sentence. In speaking or reading aloud, there is little pause before the restrictive modifier and the voice is usually sustained, kept level. Actually the modifier becomes closely attached to, practically a part of, the element modified. If the modifier is omitted, the statement either becomes meaningless, as in the first sentence below, or else it has a quite different meaning, as in the second:

It was a quite different looking person *who walked out into the cold, frosty air a few minutes later.*

The right of the dictatorships *to decide how long this wholesale killing goes on* is unquestioned.

The italicized elements in the following sentences are restrictive and should stand as they are here, without commas:

His opponent appeared at one of the really important rallies *with a drink too much in him.*

Reform should be an application *to wider fields* of methods *with which people are already familiar* and *of which they approve.*

In many states parole boards still persist in turning loose prisoners *who should remain behind bars.*

Mr. Colman proves his versatility as an actor *when he philosophizes one minute and punches his brother on the nose the next.* He portrays a man of action *if the occasion requires* and at the same time a mild-mannered, soft-spoken individual *who gives the impression of being able to think.* He has to make important decisions *when his brother and Margo tell him that this Utopia is a lot of hooey.* Mr. Colman is the only actor I have ever seen *who can show that he is thinking.*

**2.** *Nonrestrictive, or loose, modifiers.* Modifiers which do not limit the meaning of a noun but add a descriptive detail are nonrestrictive and are set off by a comma or commas. In speaking or reading aloud, there is usually a slight pause and change in level of voice, a drop in tone, before and after a loose modifier. As a rule a nonrestrictive modifier can be omitted without altering the fundamental meaning of the statement.

The new road, *for which appropriations have been made,* will pass just north of here.

The building program includes a new building for the English department, *which now has classes all over the campus.*

Sophomores, *who were freshmen just last year,* have an exaggerated sense of their maturity.

A modifier that follows a proper noun is usually nonrestrictive, since the name itself identifies exactly the person or place mentioned:

Josie, *aged 16,* told Ma and Pa Pansky a thing or two.

Just below Poughkeepsie, *which we reached in a little over two hours,* we had another breakfast in a roadside lunch wagon.

**3.** *Optional punctuation.* Not all modifiers are clearly restrictive or nonrestrictive: there are degrees of closeness. Use of commas emphasizes a slight relationship, lack of commas suggests a closer relation. Some modifiers can be spoken or read with pause and drop in tone, or not, with some slight change in emphasis. The difference in such sentences is more of tone or movement than of meaning. The italicized modifiers in these sentences might or might not be set off by commas:

These physicians *who so vigorously oppose state medicine* have definite bases for their opinions.

They had *of course* more experience by then.

The sound of swing music reached my ears from a room on the third floor *even before I heard the tramping feet that seemed to go with it.*

In open punctuation fewer commas are used, tending to bind the parts of a sentence closer together. As a rule the safest test is reading the sentence aloud, using commas if you pause and change your tone of voice before the modifier.

(Reference: W. Paul Jones, "Punctuating Nonrestrictives," *College English,* 1948, 10:158-162.)

**Result •** Adverbial clauses of result are introduced typically by *so that, so, so . . . that, such . . . that,* and *that. So* is rather Informal, *such . . . that* and *that* likely to be Formal. The most common is *so that.*

He had been taught always to expect the worst, so that [so] he wasn't surprised.

He was so used to suffering that one more disaster made little difference.

The house was such an expense that they were giving it up.

**Reverend •** It is better form to use *Reverend* as a title only when the full name or the initials and the last name of the person to whom it refers follow; the abbreviation is used in newspaper and more or less Informal writing:

| | |
|---|---|
| Reverend James Shaw | Rev. James Shaw |
| Reverend J. T. Shaw | Rev. J. T. Shaw |

But *Reverend* before the surname alone, corresponding to *Doctor* or *Professor,* is increasingly found: *Reverend Shaw, Rev. Shaw.*

*The Reverend* before a name is rather more Formal: *the Reverend James T. Shaw, the Reverend Mr. Shaw.*

*The reverend* used instead of a clergyman's name (The reverend wasn't there) is distinctly Informal.

In the salutation of a letter, after an inside address, write *Dear Sir* or *Dear Mr. Shaw.*

**Revision** • See *Proofreading.

**Rhetoric** • *Rhetoric* is the study of the theory and practice of composition, both oral and written.

**Rhetorical questions** • *Rhetorical questions* are really statements in the form of questions, since no direct answer is expected and the writer does not intend to give one. In conversation they often carry some special accent, of accusation, for example: *Could you have done any better?*

... Why out of the first forty-six names in the Hall of Fame, have twenty-six of them from one to three relatives of national renown? Does it not argue that they probably belong to great breeds, truly noble strains of blood?—ALBERT EDWARD WIGGAM, *The New Decalogue of Science,* p. 46

**right** • *Right along, right away, right off* are Informal idioms.

In the sense of "very," *right* is a localism, in good standing in the South: *We'll be right glad to see you.*

**rise** • In referring to standing up or getting out of bed, *arise* is Formal and poetic; *rise* is Formal; *get up* is General.

**role** • In Formal usage *role* (a role in a play) is still sometimes printed with the circumflex (*rôle*) but more often without.

**Roman numerals** • See *Numbers § 3.

**round—around** • In General usage *round* and *around* are used interchangeably.

In Formal English there is some tendency to keep *around* to mean "here and there" or "in every direction" and *round* for "in a circular motion" or "in a reverse motion":

I have looked all around.     There aren't any around here.
He is going round the world.     Everyone turned round.

*Around* is Informal in the sense of "about, near":

He had around $200 in bills. Is anybody around [that is: *around here*]?

*All-round* and *all-around* are overused General adjectives (an all-round flour, an all-around athlete).

*Round* has no apostrophe.

**run** • *Run* is in good General use in the sense of "manage, operate": *He runs a hotel in Florida.*

**S** • *S* represents principally two sounds, /s/ and /z/: /s/ as in *so, sorry, biscuit, crops*; /z/ as in *easy, was, Jones.* In a few words *s* spells /sh/: *tension, sure, sugar*; and in some /zh/: *leisure, pleasure, measure.*

*S* is silent in several words, most of them from French: *aisle, debris, rendezvous, island, Arkansas, Louisville,* often in *St. Louis,* and usually in *Illinois.* (See *sh; for plurals in -*s*, *Plurals of nouns § 1, *Jones; for the genitive of words ending in -*s*, *Genitive § 1a.)

**said** • As a modifier *said* (the said person, the said idea) is legal usage; it is not used in ordinary writing.

**saint** • The abbreviation *St.* is commonly used in names of places (St. Albans, St. Louis); *Saint* is more often written out with the name of a canonized saint (Saint John, Saint Anthony of Padua). The plural of the abbreviation is SS. (SS. Peter and Paul). Occasionally the French feminine form, *Sainte,* is used (Sault Sainte Marie). The abbreviation of the feminine form is *Ste.*

**same** • *Same* is used as an adjective (the same color) and as a pronoun in such expressions as *The same happened to me once* and popularly in *I'll take the same, more of the same....*

*Same* as a pronoun is also characteristic of legal and outmoded business use—*and enclose check for same*—where better style would have *it* or *them* instead.

**Sarcasm** • Sarcasm is a quality of bitterness or reproach in a statement—ironical (that is, to be interpreted differently from the actual statement) or direct.

**say** • *Say* is the usual word for "speaking." *Talk* implies a continued "saying." *State* implies a formal "saying" and is better kept for this meaning [Not: *Mr. Owen stated that he was ready if we were*].

*Say* in the sense of "suppose," "perhaps," "for instance" is Informal: *Say they went sixteen miles.*

**scarcely** • See *Double negative § 3.

**Schoolgirl style** • A *schoolgirl style* is characterized by sentimental *counter words (*lovely, cute*), by exaggeration, and by
reliance on all sorts of mechanical forms of emphasis—exclamation marks, dashes, capitals, and one, two, and even three
underlinings. These serve as satisfying release to the writer
and may add a sort of glow to a letter, but they should not be
transferred to the printed page, and any suggestion of the style
should be avoided, except to help portray a character.

**schwa (ə)** • *Schwa* /shwä/ is the name for the neutral vowel
sound frequently occurring in unstressed syllables: *a*head,
ang*e*l, def*i*nite, *o*ccur, s*u*ggest; the symbol for it is /ə/. (See
*Neutral vowel.)

**Scientific and technical writing** • The ideal of scientific writing was expressed very early in the modern scientific movement
in Thomas Sprat's *History of the Royal Society* (1667). The
members of the Society, he said, tried:

... to return back to the primitive purity, and shortness, when men
delivered so many things, almost in an equal number of words. They
have exacted from all their members a close, naked, natural way of
speaking; positive expressions; clear senses; a native easiness: bringing all things as near the mathematical plainness as they can; and
preferring the language of artizans, countrymen, and merchants, before that of wits or scholars.

Exactness rather than grace or variety, or even emphasis, is the
goal of most scientific and scholarly writing done by members
of a profession to be read by other members. Occasionally it
attains the ideal of "delivering so many things, almost in an
equal number of words":

A stable, stainless, organic mercury compound solution of high
germicidal value, particularly in serum and other protein media.

But today Thomas Sprat would find that much scientific writing has departed far from "the language of artizans, countrymen, and merchants."

The chief reason for the *big words that seem to a layman
the most conspicuous trait of scientific writing is that scientists have discovered and named qualities and things of which
the average person is quite unaware. Their descriptions are
more detailed than people in general need. Here is a description of the *h* sound—/h/—from a book on phonetics:

The fricative /h/ occurs as the breath stream passes through the
glottis. The vocal bands obstruct the stream sufficiently to produce a
slight degree of friction. This whispered sound in therefore known
as the glottal fricative sound.—ARTHUR J. BRONSTEIN, *The Pronunciation of American English*, p. 94

Though ordinary people speak of *biliousness* and *eyestrain*, the words have no definite meaning for doctors or oculists. In contrast to the rather imprecise senses of words in General usage, scientific writers try to use words in a single specific meaning. Some scientific words are taken from the General vocabulary and given special meanings, like *magnitude* in astronomy, *force* in physics, *complex* in psychoanalysis, *dip* and *incline* in geology. But the tendency now is to build new words from Latin or more often from Greek roots and give them exact definitions: *photomicrography, bioluminescence, telesthesia.*

The sentence structure and other traits of style in scientific writing are Formal, appropriately so because its audience is specialized. The style is impersonal—completely impersonal in monographs, textbooks, and articles in the scientific journals, less so in popular treatments of scientific subjects. Three levels of scientific writing are illustrated in the following quotations. The first paragraph is a simple statement of fact:

The nature of the force exerted by a wave upon any obstacle, such as a cliff or beach, depends in part upon the type of wave and its condition at the moment of collision with the obstacle. If an unbroken oscillatory wave strikes a vertical wall or cliff the base of which reaches down to deep water, the wave is reflected back. At the instant of contact the crest of the wave rises to twice its normal height and the cliff is subjected to the hydrostatic pressure of this unusually high water column. The absence of any forward thrust of the water mass under these conditions is shown by the behavior of boats which have been observed to rise and fall with successive waves without touching the vertical wall only a few feet distant. Hagen concludes that under such circumstances débris must accumulate at the base of the wall and that therefore the prejudice against vertical sea walls and harbor walls, based on the fear of undermining by wave action, is ill-founded.—Douglas W. Johnson, *Shore Processes and Shoreline Development,* p. 57

This is part of an informative treatment of wave action, accurate and compact. It would be read, however, only by someone who was consciously looking for knowledge of the subject. The following passage is intended for a more general audience, though one limited to people with a strong interest in more than the superficial appearance of their world. The facts are presented with a minimum of technical language and made more vivid by the use of familiar comparisons ("rather like relays of messengers . . .").

These molecules move with very high speeds; in the ordinary air of an ordinary room, the average molecular speed is about 500 yards a second. This is roughly the speed of a rifle-bullet, and is rather more than the ordinary speed of sound. As we are familiar with this latter speed from everyday experience, it is easy to form some conception of molecular speeds in a gas. It is not a mere accident that molecular speeds are comparable with the speed of sound. Sound is a disturbance which one molecule passes on to another when it collides with it, rather like relays of messengers passing a message on to one another, or Greek torch-bearers handing on their lights. Between collisions the message is carried forward at exactly the speed at which the molecules travel. If these all traveled with precisely the same speed and in precisely the same direction, the sound would of course travel with just the speed of molecules. But many of them travel on oblique courses, so that although the average speed of individual molecules in ordinary air is about 500 yards a second, the net forward velocity of the sound is only about 370 yards a second.—SIR JAMES JEANS, *The Universe Around Us,* p. 101

For a still more popular audience the subject matter must be further simplified and the facts made dramatic, if possible, by being presented in action. Some technical words are used, but they seem to be incidental, even decorative, rather than fundamental as in Formal scientific writing:

We now turn to consider the frequency of sound waves. Differences of frequency are detected by the ear as differences of *pitch,* that is, of the shrillness or depth of the musical note, for every musical note corresponds to a particular frequency. The higher the note, the greater the frequency; the lower the note, the smaller the frequency.

Perhaps the easiest way to show this is to take a fine hair comb or nail file and run a stiff card along it: the more quickly the card is made to wave—that is, the more frequently the card is pulled aside and allowed to return—by the passage over the teeth, the higher the note. A better way to show it is to make use of a small wheel with teeth all around the edge: when this is kept turning at a steady measured rate, and a stiff card or thin sheet of metal held so as to touch the teeth, the frequency of the disturbance, corresponding to the pitch of the note produced, can easily be measured. The number of times a second that the wings of a humming fly or bee go up or down can be measured by matching the note of the humming with the note produced by the wheel made to turn at the right speed.— E. N. DA C. ANDRADE, *Physics for the Modern World,* p. 60

Beyond such popularizations are the sensational treatments of scientific subjects which we associate with the magazine sections of some Sunday papers. Because of the cheapness and the inaccuracy of many of these articles, scientists and scholars have tended to scorn all popularizing of their materials. But in recent years there has been an increase of reliable and interesting scientific writing for general readers as more specialists have found a challenge in seeing how much of their subject matter they can find a way of conveying to them. They are now leaving less of the work of popularizing to writers not sufficiently trained to do it accurately.

Until a person can write with authority about a specialized subject, he will most likely be doing popular or semipopular papers. Students in college can try their hand at preparing material for a somewhat limited but nonprofessional group of readers. The style of such papers would be rather Formal, and it has one real danger. The necessity for using genuine scientific words often leads to using *unnecessary* *big words. Writers in the social sciences especially have substituted unfamiliar words or *long variants for words of the General English vocabulary, as in "It is necessary to structure into a complex culture like ours a congruent hospitality to change in all institutional areas." If such writers visualized their readers, they would make more use of the General English vocabulary. P. B. Ballard puts the general principle admirably from the reader's point of view: "... when the common language fails in clearness, in dignity, or in freedom from ambiguity, it should be eked out by the language of the laboratory and of the study. Technical jargon is an evil, but a necessary evil. And necessary evils should be kept to a minimum." It is worth trying to see how much of your specialized information you can make available to an intelligent general reader.

An increasing number of jobs now depend on some competence in writing scientific or technical letters, reports, or articles. The director of research in a large corporation has this to say on the subject:

If you can't tell in written or oral English what your results are, it is impossible to get along in any industry. For instance, the laboratory worker must submit a condensed report of his experiments to his laboratory head. This man must in turn condense the reports of many workers and send a new report on to his superior. And so on, all the way up the line. If you can't put your thoughts and figures on paper in concise readable language, you're sunk.

(See *Reports, *References in scientific papers. References: Meta Emberger and Marion Hall, *Scientific Writing*, New York, 1955; W. O. Sypherd, Alvin M. Fountain, and V. E. Gibbens, *Manual of Technical Writing*, Chicago, 1957—with useful bibliography, pp. 545-553; Sam F. Trelease, *The Scientific Paper*, 2nd ed., Baltimore, 1952.)

**Seasons** • *Winter, spring, summer, fall, autumn, midsummer,* and so on are not capitalized except for stylistic emphasis, as sometimes in poetry or nature essays.

**seem** • *Seem* is often used as a counter verb (\*deadwood), making a statement needlessly qualified or distant:

The letters of Flaubert [seem to] bring us as near to the writing of *Madame Bovary* as we can come.

*Can't seem* may be "illogical," but it is a useful idiom for *be unable*: *I can't seem to learn physics.*

**self** • *Self* as a suffix forms the reflexive and intensive pronouns: *myself, yourself, himself, herself, itself, oneself, ourselves, yourselves, themselves.* These are used chiefly for emphasis (I can do that myself) or as a reflexive object (I couldn't help myself). (See \*himself, herself, \*myself.)

As a prefix, *self* is joined to the root word by a hyphen: *self-control, self-explanatory, self-made, self-respect.*

When *self* is the root word there is no hyphen: *selfhood, selfish, selfless, selfsame.*

(See also \*Hyphen § 1c.)

**semi-** • *Semi-* is a prefix meaning "half or approximately half" (*semicylindrical*), "twice within a certain period" (*semiweekly, semiannual*), or "partially, imperfectly" (*semicivilized, semiprofessional*). It is not usually hyphened except before proper names (*semi-Christian*) or words beginning with *i* (*semi-invalid*). Pronounced /sem′i/ and often /sem′ī/.

**Semicolon (;)** •

*Semi*

*Revision: Use a semicolon as the mark of separation between these sentence elements.*

A *semicolon* is used to mark a degree of separation between sentence elements considerably greater than that marked by a comma, nearly as great as that marked by a period. (The suggestion made by Bonner that we call it *semiperiod* has much to recommend it.) Although its use rather than that of another mark is largely a matter of style (§ 4), there are a few situations in which a semicolon is mandatory.

**1.** *To separate units that contain smaller elements separated by commas.* These may be items in a \*series, enumerations, figures, scores, or clauses with commas within them:

Other periodicals not entirely dissimilar were John Harris's *The English Lucian,* 1698; Ward's *Weekly Comedy,* 1699; "Sylvester Partridge's" *The Infallible Astrologer,* 1700; and the *Merry Mercury,* 1700.—GEORGE CARVER, *Periodical Essays of the Eighteenth Century,* p. xviii

Three things which a social system can provide or withhold are helpful to mental creation: first, technical training; second, liberty

to follow the creative impulse; third, at least the possibility of ultimate appreciation by some public, whether large or small.—BERTRAND
RUSSELL, *Proposed Roads to Freedom,* p. 169

**2. To separate coordinate clauses not closely related.**

*a*–Between contact clauses. A semicolon is used, especially in
somewhat Formal writing, between two *contact clauses
(clauses with no expressed connective) if the separation in
thought and structure is conspicuous. Usually the two statements could stand as separate sentences, but the writer wishes
to have them considered part of one idea. Contrasting statements are often punctuated with semicolons, as in the following examples:

Words and sentences are subjects of revision; paragraphs and whole
compositions are subjects of prevision.—BARRETT WENDELL, *English
Composition,* p. 117

Your religion does not promise you a perfect life on earth, nor
freedom from suffering; it does guarantee you the strength to bear
suffering. Your religion does not expect you to be free from sin or
mistakes in judgment; it does promise you forgiveness for your mistakes. Your religion expects you to continue making the best efforts
you can on behalf of others; it does not guarantee that you or anyone
can arrange the lives of people as he pleases.—HENRY C. LINK, *The
Return to Religion,* pp. 68-69

*b*–With heavy connectives. A semicolon is used between
clauses connected by the weightier conjunctive adverbs *(however, moreover, nevertheless, consequently* . . .). These usually
link longer clauses in a rather Formal style:

This program implies better orientation of individuals to the mani-
fold problems of adjustment; therefore, certain character traits, as
well as specific abilities, should show positive change.—*The English
Journal,* June 1937

A comma is now usually more common between clauses connected by the lighter conjunctive adverbs *(so, then* . . .). (See
*Conjunctive adverbs.)

*c*–With coordinating conjunctions. A semicolon is used between clauses connected by coordinating conjunctions *(and,
but, for, or* . . .) if the clauses are long or if the connection is
not close, if they contain commas, or if for some reason (often
for contrast) the writer wishes to show an emphatic separation
between them:

History as actuality includes all that has been said, felt, done, and
thought by human beings on this planet since humanity began its
long career; and, if Darwin is right, since the evolution of the human
organism began in the primeval dawn.—C. A. BEARD, *The Discussion
of Human Affairs,* p. 69

She already had some furniture of her own, including what she could take from Truda; and Louis could let her have some of his— yes?—G. B. STERN, *The Matriarch*, p. 199

Therefore those teachers who cannot admit that they may be wrong should not teach English composition; nor should those who never suspect that their pupils may be abler than they.—L. R. BRIGGS, *To College Teachers of English Composition*, p. 19

The semicolon is used to separate parts of the sentence which are of more importance, or which show a division more distinct, than those separated by commas; or to separate sections already separated by commas.—JOHN BENBOW, *Manuscript & Proof*, p. 89

**3.** *Semicolon and colon.* Do not use a semicolon, which is a mark of *separation* as the examples in this article show, in place of a colon (:), which is a mark of *anticipation*:

There are two principal considerations in the use of semicolons: the degree of separation to be indicated between statements and the formality of the style of the passage.

(See *Colon § 4.)

**4.** *Semicolons and other traits of style.* Except for the specific situations described in § 1, the use of semicolons is in part a stylistic matter. They are more appropriate, more necessary, in rather Formal styles and in long, aggregating sentences. They tend to slow up the reading and are consequently fewer in narrative than in exposition. In General styles commas would be used in preference, or if the distinction between the clauses is considerable, two sentences would be written. In the following passage Malcolm Cowley has chosen to rely on semicolons. Commas and periods that might have been used in a more Informal writing of the same passage are put in brackets.

College students inhabit an easy world of their own; [.] except for very rich people and certain types of childless wives they form the only American class that takes leisure for granted. Many, of course, earn their board and tuition tending furnaces, waiting on table or running back kick-offs for a touchdown; what I am about to say does not apply to them. The others—almost always the ruling clique of a big university, the students who set the tone for the rest—are supported practically without efforts of their own. They write a few begging letters;[,] perhaps they study a little harder in order to win a scholarship; [,] but usually they don't stop to think where the money comes from. Above them, the president knows the source of the hard cash that runs this great educational factory; [.] he knows that the stream of donations can be stopped by a crash in the stock market or reduced in volume by newspaper reports of a professor gone bolshevik; [.]he knows what he has to tell his trustees or the state legislators when he goes to them begging for funds. The scrubwomen in the library, the chambermaids and janitors, know how they earn their food; but the students themselves, and many of their professors, are blind to economic forces; [.] society, as the source of food and football fields and professors' salaries, is a remote abstraction.—MALCOLM COWLEY, *Exile's Return*, pp. 36-37

Students tend to use more semicolons than would be used by professional writers today in General writing. They should consider the weight of the mark in view of the general movement of their writing and make sure that the movement of the particular sentence needs the degree of separation marked by the semicolon. (Compare *Comma, *Colon. Reference: Summey, pp. 97-101.)

**Sentences** •
*Revision: Eliminate the fault in the sentence marked.*

S

The grammatical characteristics and the chief problems in writing sentences are discussed in the following articles:

| | | |
|---|---|---|
| *Agreement | *Dangling modifiers | *Reference of |
| *Clauses | *Emphasis |   pronouns |
| *Comma fault | *Fragmentary | *Shifted constructions |
| *Commands and |   sentence | *Subject and verb |
|   requests | *Fused sentence | *Subordination |
| *Conjunctions, use | *Idiom and idioms | *Tense |
| *Contact clauses | *Immediate constituent | *Wordiness |
| *Coordination | *Parallel constructions | *Word order |

**seq.** • See *Abbreviations § 2.

**Sequence of tense** • See *Tenses of verbs § 3.

**Series** • Commas are used between the items of a series of three or more short items:

The supposed contents of the physical world are *prima facie* very different from these: [four short clauses:] *molecules have no colour, atoms make no noise, electrons have no taste, and corpuscles do not even smell.*—BERTRAND RUSSELL, *Mysticism and Logic*, p. 145

There are two or three large chests, a bedstead, the inevitable cradle occupied by the latest addition to the family. The small windows are seldom curtained. There are shelves for pots and pans, spoons and forks (often wooden) , jars of gherkins, bottles of this and that, loaves of bread, sacks of flour, baskets of dried fruit.—LOUIS ADAMIC, *The Native's Return*, p. 271

Usage is divided over the insertion of a comma before the last item of such a series. A comma helps to prevent ambiguity, especially if one member is compound (tired, dirty, and black and blue). But many writers, especially in General and Informal styles, do not use the comma, particularly when the series is short:

> Ministers, teachers [,] and journalists all united against the proposal.

If the members of the series are long, or not closely connected, or if the members have commas within them, they are separated by semicolons:

> Quite a few people get credit lines in this big, handsome and heavy book: Dr. Albert Sirmay, who did the arrangements; Frederick E. Banbery, who painted the pictures; Newman Levy, who wrote an introduction to each show.—HERBERT KUPPERBERG, review of *The Rogers and Hammerstein Song Book, New York Herald Tribune Book Review*, Dec. 7, 1958

(For further examples and details see *Comma § 5, *Semicolon § 1. Reference: R. J. McCutcheon, "The Serial Comma Before 'and' and 'or,' " *American Speech*, 1940, 15:250-254.)

**service** • The verb *service* (to service a car, a refrigerator) is needed and appropriate in all varieties of English. It means more than *repair* and has a different connotation from *maintain* or *keep up*.

**set, sit** • In writing Standard English, people and things *sit* (past: *sat*) or they are *set* (past: *set*)—that is, are "placed":

> I like to sit in a hotel lobby.
> I have sat in this same seat for three semesters.
> She set the soup down with a flourish.
> The post was set three feet in the ground.

A hen, however, *sets* (on her eggs) and the sun *sets*. Though *set* replaces *sit* in the speech of many people, it is felt by most cultivated speakers to be Nonstandard.

**settle** • See *locate.

**sh** • *Sh* is a digraph for a sound which is not a combination of the sounds usually represented by *s* or *h*: *shall, shove, ash*. The *sh* sound—/sh/—is represented by various other spellings: *machine* /mə shēn′/, *tissue* /tish′ü/, *conscientious* /kon′shē en′shəs/, *ocean* /ō′shən/. Compare *zh.

**shall—will** • Future time is expressed by a number of locutions in English:

| | |
|---|---|
| I am going to ask for a raise. | There is to be a dance Friday. |
| I am asking for a raise tomorrow. | He may go next week. |

| He comes next week. | If he had the money tomorrow, |
|---|---|
| Come again. | he would pay it. |
| It's time he left. | I'll try to be on time. |
| He is sure to come tomorrow. | I shall try to be on time. |
| | I will try to be on time. |

Expressions like the first nine are probably more common than the last three, so that it is hardly accurate to say that the future is expressed only with *shall* and *will*. But since distinctions between these auxiliaries have been regarded as an important item of reputable usage, it is necessary to discuss them in more detail than they deserve. Their use has never been uniform in English, though some grammarians have attempted to insist on uniformity. The general practices in the common situations needing these words are as follows:

1. *General usage.*

*a*–Simple future. In speech and writing the prevailing use in the United States, and in many other parts of the English-speaking world, is *will* in all persons (I will ask, you will ask, he will ask . . .).

*b*–Emphatic future. In expressing determination in the future or for some special emphasis, General usage is divided. In speech the determination is expressed by stress, which may be used on either word: *I shall' go, I will' go.* There is some tendency to use *shall* in all persons as the emphatic form, because *shall* is so rare that it makes a more emphatic word than *will*: *I, you, he, she, we, you, they shall ask.* Other constructions (I have to go . . .) are also used.

*c*–Contractions. In speaking and Informal writing in which contractions are used, the future becomes *I'll, you'll, he'll,* and so on, which do not discriminate between *shall* and *will*. *Won't* is used for *will not* (formed from an obsolete *woll* and *not*) and *shan't* for *shall not,* the latter even more rare than the uncontracted form.

*d*–In questions. In asking questions *shall* is likely to be used in the first and third persons and *will* in the second, but practice is not consistent. Even here *shall* is likely to be avoided, replaced where possible by *'ll*:

Shall I go?
What shall [What'll] we do now?
What shall [What'll] he do?
Will you go?
What will [What'll] you do now?
What will [What'll] he do with it?

The significant difference between *Shall I go?* and *Will I go?* is weakened or nonexistent for most cultivated speakers of American English in *I shall go* and *I will go.*

In the negative, *won't* is much the more common:

Won't I look funny in that?
What won't he think of next?

*e–Shall* is usual in laws, resolutions, etc.:

A permanent organization shall be set up within a year.
No singer shall receive more than $700 a performance.

The Biblical *thou shalt not* would now be expressed by *you must not*.

**2.** *Formal usage.* Some writers use *shall* in the first person and *will* in the second and third persons in making the future tense, following handbook "rules" rather than usage.

| | | |
|---|---|---|
| *First person:* | I shall ask | we shall ask |
| *Second person:* | you will ask | you will ask |
| *Third person:* | he, she will ask | they will ask |

In the emphatic future, expressing determination of the speaker, Formal English theoretically reverses this use of *shall* and *will*:

| | | |
|---|---|---|
| *First person:* | I will ask | we will ask |
| *Second person:* | you shall ask | you shall ask |
| *Third person:* | he, she shall ask | they shall ask |

In asking questions a few people even use the form of *shall* or *will* in a question that the answerer would use in his reply. This usage is distinctly Formal and usually sounds unnatural:

Shall you go? [Answer: *I shall (shall not) go.*]

The efforts of purists to establish this Formal usage as General is now declining, and few editors today change copy to conform to it.

**3.** *Overuse of "shall."* The stress that schools have put on *shall* sometimes leads to an unidiomatic use:

Whether or not Congress *will* [not: *shall*] favor or pass laws against lynching is not for me to guess.

(See *should–would.)

(References: Much has been written about the use of these words. As a beginning: Curme, *Syntax,* pp. 362-371; Fries, *AEG,* pp. 150-168, a good short summary of actual usage; C. C. Fries, "The Expression of the Future," *Language,* 1927, 3:87-95; Jespersen, Chs. 25, 26 for British practice, though also illuminating for American usage; Amos L. Herold, *English Journal,* 1936, 25:670-676; Robertson, pp. 516-520; Bryant, pp. 182-183.)

**shan't** • There is only one apostrophe in the contraction of *shall not*.

**shape** • *Shape* is Informal in the sense of "manner, condition": *They were in good shape for the trip.*

**she-or-he** • See *he-or-she.

**Shifted constructions** •
*Revision: Make the constructions marked consistent
(parallel) in form.*

*Shift*

Two or more sentence elements that have the same relationship to another element in the sentence should be expressed by words in the same grammatical construction; that is, the constructions should be parallel. A specific verb form should be continued in a similar construction; a verb should be kept consistently active or passive in a sentence or passage; adjectives should be paralleled by adjectives, nouns by nouns, and so on. (The *should be* constructions in the preceding sentence are parallel.)

Shifting from one form to another may confuse or disturb a reader because it is a failure to follow established patterns of writing. Shifts should be removed in revision.

Some commonly shifted constructions are:

| *Shifted* | *Consistent* |
|---|---|
| **1.** Shift in subject | |
| The *car* starts easily, runs smoothly, and *you won't have* any trouble with it. | The *car* starts easily, runs smoothly, and *won't give you* any trouble. |
| **2.** Adjective—Noun | |
| This book seems *interesting* and *an informative piece of work.* | This book seems *interesting* and *informative.* |
| **3.** Personal—Impersonal | |
| In fact going to summer school is worse than no vacation at all, for when *you* have no vacation *you* do not think about all the things *a person* could do if *he* had one. | ... for when *you* have no vacation *you* do not think about all the things *you* could do if *you* had one. |
| **4.** Adverb—Adjective | |
| Along these walks are the cottages, many of which have stood *since the founding* [adverbial phrase], and others *more recent* [adjective]. | ... many of which have stood *since the founding,* and others of which have been built *more recently.* |

## 5. Noun—Adverb

*Associating* [noun] with these fellows and *how to adapt myself to live with them* [adverbial phrase] will be helpful to me when I am through college.

*Associating* with these fellows and *adapting* myself to live with them will be helpful to me when I am through college.

## 6. Noun—Adjective

Anyone who has *persistence* [noun] or is *desperate* [adjective] enough can get a job working on a ship.

Anyone who is *persistent* or who is *desperate* enough...

## 7. Noun—Clause

The most important factors are *time* and *temperature,* careful *control* at every point, and *the mechanical equipment must be in perfect operating condition at any time of the day or night.*

...and *mechanical equipment in perfect operating condition at any time of the day or night.*

## 8. Participle—Clause

How many times have you seen a fisherman *trying* to get to his favorite fishing spot without scaring all the fish away but instead *he sends out* messages with his rhythmical squeak-splash, squeak-splash.

...but instead *sending out* messages...

## 9. Phrase—Clause

I have heard complaints *about the plot being weak* and *that the setting was played up too much.*

...and *the setting being played up too much.*

(See also *Parallel constructions, *Tenses of verbs § 5.)

**Ships' names** • The names of ships are indicated in three ways:

**1.** In most books and generally in Formal writing they are italicized (underlined in the manuscript):

The *Caryatid,* in ballast, was steaming down the river at half-speed....—WILLIAM McFEE, *Casuals of the Sea,* p. 317

**2.** In newspapers and personal writing there is a growing tendency to regard the names of ships simply as proper names, capitalizing them but not otherwise setting them off:

The Magellan weighed anchor at 9:20 A.M. and moved slowly to her berth at Pier H, Weehawken, N.J.—*The New York Times,* Feb. 3, 1950

**3.** Occasionally ships' names are found in quotation marks:

The summer of 1926 David spent as a junior member of the American Museum Greenland Expedition. . . . on the stout little schooner "Morrissey." [Jacket of *David Goes to Greenland.* In the book *Morrissey* is italicized.]

The pronoun used in referring to a ship is usually *she.*

**Shoptalk** • *Shoptalk* is the offhand talk of people about their occupations, from medicine and law to ditchdigging and panhandling. It varies with the social class and personal taste of its users, from the talk of a garage hand to that of an automotive engineer or professor of physics. Its distinguishing feature is vocabulary. Many of the words are the necessary names for materials and processes and tools and for the people—for everything that is commonly referred to in a line of work—like *em, en, pica, pi, spreaders, platen, rule, chase,* from a printing shop. Such words are usually given in dictionaries with the name of the occupation to which they belong. Shoptalk may also include technical and scientific words, as in the conversation of interns and nurses, but it is set off from Formal technical and professional writing by the conversational tone and by the presence of the jargon of the field, sometimes called *cant,* which would not be found at the Formal level.

Shoptalk has a vigorous and often figurative vocabulary, in which words are formed with great freedom. Especially convenient are short substitutes for long technical words. (See *Abbreviations.) A *mike* may be a microphone in a radio studio, a microscope in a laboratory, a micrometer in a shop; *hypo* is a fixing bath to a photographer and a hypodermic injection in a medical context; *soup* is the name of a pourable mixture in scores of manufacturing processes. Racing has *place, show, on the nose, tipster, bookie;* unlisted securities are *cats and dogs;* football players have *skull practice;* a student pilot must *dual* for many hours before he is allowed to *solo;* a *gagman* makes up the comedian's lines; and so on.

Some of these words, like *fade-out* from the movies, are useful in discussing other subjects, and they may become a part of the General vocabulary, like *third degree.* Shoptalk is appropriate and necessary in speaking or writing about the particular occupation in which it is used, usually with some explanations required for readers who are not acquainted with it. It is often appropriate in Informal writing, but it is usually out of place in General writing, almost always in Formal writing.

(References: *American Speech* and the *Publications of the American Dialect Society* have many articles dealing with the vocabularies of particular occupations and groups.)

**should—would** •
1. *Should* and *would* are used in statements that carry some doubt or uncertainty about the statement that is being made. They are also used in polite or unemphatic requests:

They should be there by Monday. [Contrast: *They will be there by Monday.*]

Would you please shut the door on your way out? [Contrast: *Will you please....*]

In the first person both *should* and *would* are used:

I would be much obliged if you could do this.
I should be much obliged if you could do this.

Usage is so much divided on the choice between these forms that one's feeling is probably the safest guide. But it is desirable to follow one or the other usage consistently in a piece of writing.
2. *Should* as an auxiliary used with all persons expresses a mild sense of obligation, weaker than *ought*:

I should pay this bill. [Contrast: *I ought to pay this bill.*]

In indirect discourse *should* and *would* represent the future tense of direct speech, following the "sequence of tenses." (See *Tenses of verbs § 4.)

*Direct:* "I will be ready at three," Mildred said.
*Indirect:* Mildred said she would be ready at three.

*Would* has some currency in the Informal or half-humorous idiom *That would be her picture,* meaning "That is her picture, isn't it?"

**show** • *Show* is Informal or theatrical *shoptalk in the sense of "a play"; is usually humorous or Nonstandard for a dignified public performance, as of a concert; General when applied to the movies (short for *picture show*). It is Informal for "chance" (They didn't have a show of winning).

**show up** • *Show up* is Informal for "appear" (He didn't show up for two hours) and for "expose" (I showed him up, all right).

**sic** • *Sic* (Latin for *thus, so*; pronounced /sik/) in *brackets is sometimes used to mark an error in quoted matter. It shows the reader that the deviation from Standard practice was in the quoted material, and was not made by the quoter:

The letter was headed "Toledo, Ohia [*sic*], Jan. 2."

**sick, ill** • *Ill* is the more Formal, less common word. In America they mean the same. In British usage *sick* is usually restricted to mean "nauseated." In the United States *sick* in that sense is made clear by adding a phrase: *It made me sick to my stomach.* This idiom has two Standard variants: *sick at* and *sick to.* The spoken idioms *take sick* and *get sick* also occur. In the Informal *I feel sick about that,* the speaker is not referring to his health.

**Silent letters** • English spells a great many words with silent letters—that is, letters which do not represent any speech sound. A few of them are the result of mistaken analogies, like the *s* of *island,* which is there from confusion with the French *isle,* though it comes from Old English *igland* and has never had the *s* sounded. Renaissance scholars inserted a number of letters that corresponded to those in the Greek and Latin words from which the English ones derived but that had never been sounded in English: Chaucer could write *det,* but we must write *debt* because the scholars recognized the word's descent from *debitum;* and the addition of the *h* to Middle English *trone* has established a spelling pronunciation for *throne.* (See *Pronunciation § 3c.)

But most of our silent letters act, as Thomas R. Lounsbury put it, "as a sort of tombstone to mark the place where lie the unsightly remains of a dead and forgotten pronunciation"; the pronunciation has changed but the spelling hasn't, or hasn't changed enough. There they stand, those final *b*'s in *bomb, comb, climb,* the initial *g*'s and *k*'s in *gnarl, gnash, knack, knave,* the *p*'s in Greekish words like *pneumonia* and *psychology,* the *gh*'s in *through* and *night* and *caught.*

Silent letters are sometimes defended because they tend to remind us of a word's ancestry, but that fact is of use only to scholars, and there are not enough scholars of that kind to justify spelling the language for them. Besides, it's not always true: *delight* is from French *delite,* the *gh* being by analogy with *light.* Some people think these spellings have an esthetic value, that *night* has a beauty not in *nite* or that the superfluous *h* gives *ghost* a special weirdness. But this reason doesn't seem very substantial, since we learn these words from hearing them, and whatever quality *ghost* has as a word comes more from the tone in which we have heard it spoken than from the appearance of the word.

Though some of these silent letters have been dropped in the past hundred years—*apophthegm* has lost its *ph*—most of the silent letters hold firm, making spelling more difficult.

Sometimes people who are not familiar with the sound of a word are led to pronounce a silent letter, giving a "spelling pronunciation," as pronouncing *indict* /in dikt'/ instead of /in dīt'/. (See *Pronunciation § 1c. See also W. A. Craigie, *English Spelling,* pp. 36-39, 67-73.)

**similar** • The last syllable is -*lar*. Contrast *familiar*. Note the pronunciations: /sim'ə lər/, /fə mil'yər/.

**similar to** • *Similar to* is often a wordy way of saying *like*:

It was my first wreck and I hope I may never have another similar to that one [like it].

**since** • See *because, *so.

**Sino-** • See *Chinese.

**sit, set** • See *set, sit.

**situated** • *Situated* is often *deadwood:

I was staying with friends in a little town in Canada called Picton, [situated] in the province of Ontario.

**size** • As a modifier, *size* (a small size hat, king size) is in General spoken usage. In writing, it is often better omitted (a small hat). (See *-ed § 3.)

**ski** • The plural is *skis,* sometimes *ski.* The verb is *ski, skied, skiing.* The pronunciation is /skē/ (or British, following the Scandinavian, /shē/).

**Slang** • It is hard to draw a line between slang and other sorts of Informal English. Many people use the term too broadly— for almost any word not in the General vocabulary—and dictionaries have been too generous with the label, marking as "slang" many words that perhaps suggest spoken rather than written style. (Actually dictionaries include very few genuine slang expressions, because by the time they appear in their collection of quotations they have almost necessarily achieved considerable currency in print.)

The central characteristic of slang comes from the motive for its use: a desire for novelty, for vivid emphasis, for being in the know, up with the times, or a little ahead. These are essentially qualities of style, and the tone and connotation are as important as the central meaning of the words. Other varieties of language have ways of expressing the ideas of slang words, but they are often roundabout and their tone is quieter, more conventional. Young people like novelty, as do fashionable and sporty grown-ups, and comedians need it in their trade. Slang is especially common in talking about sports and amusements and all sorts of everyday activities for which the ordinary terms seem to have worn thin.

Slang words are made by natural linguistic processes. Their slang quality may lie in the intonation of a phrase *(or what have you, you and who else)*. Slang abounds in clipped words *(razz, natch, hood)*, and in compounds and derivatives of ordinary words *(screwball, sourpuss, cockeyed)*. Many are borrowed from the *shoptalk of sports and the popular arts, especially jazz *(square, cool, real gone)*. And a great many are figurative extensions of General words *(fierce* as a term of approval, *hack around, rock* for a hard guy, and the words for human stupidity, like *numb, feeble)*. To *park* a car is General English; to *park* a hat or a piece of gum is probably still slang. In the desire for novelty and emphasis one word leads to another, as *square* went to *cube*. Sound is often an important factor, as in *goof off, booboo, barf*.

Since many slang words have short lives, any discussion of slang in print is bound to be somewhat out-of-date. *Skidoo, twenty-three, vamoose, beat it, scram, hit the trail, take a powder, drag out, shag out, cut out, split* have succeeded each other almost within a generation. Words for being drunk *(soused, plastered, bombed)*, for girls *(baby, doll, chick)*, and words of approval *(tops, tough, a wow, neat, the most, cool)* and disapproval *(all wet, screwy, a fink)* change almost from year to year. Many slang words prove more permanently useful and become a part at least of the Informal vocabulary *(blind date, boy friend, go steady)*. Others have in time become General English *(ballyhoo, *highbrow, lowbrow)*.

Slang belongs primarily to familiar and rather flashy speech and comedy, to which it can give a note of freshness. This freshness wears off after some hundreds of repetitions so that the prime virtue of the words is lost. In writing, slang is less often appropriate, partly because of triteness and partly because many of the words name general impressions instead of specific ones, so that they rank with *nice* and *good*. Though occasionally used by practiced writers for special effects, slang is ordinarily out of place in Formal writing. It should not be used in General writing unless it adds a quality that is appropriate. In Informal writing it is more appropriate, especially in recounting personal experiences and for discussions of sports and campus affairs, though even with such subjects the taste of expected readers should be considered. If slang expressions are appropriate, they should be used without apology (that is, without quotation marks); if not appropriate, they should not be used. The chief objections to slang, aside from its possible conspicuousness, are to its overuse and to its use in place of more exact expressions.

Notice that many of the illustrative words in this discussion look like items in the General vocabulary. Their slangy quality

388 • slow, slowly

results from the context in which they occur. That is why few words can be labeled slang solely on the basis of their form. (See also *Abbreviations, *Shoptalk.)

**slow, slowly** • Both *slow* and *slowly* are adverbs in Standard English, each going back to an Old English adverb form (*slawe* and *slawlice,* respectively). Use whichever sounds better in the sentence. *Slow* is rather more vigorous: *Go slow.* There is, however, a rather strong prejudice against adverbial *slow.* (See *Adverbs, types and forms § 1; *Divided usage.)

**Slurred vowels** • See *Neutral vowels.

**so** • Informally, especially in speech, *so* is used as a subordinating conjunction to introduce clauses of purpose (see *Purpose):

*Informal:* He started early so he could get good seats.

*General:* He started early so that he could get good seats; ... in order to get good seats; ... to get good seats.

*So* is similarly used in clauses of result (see *Result), in which General English would usually have *so that* or change to a *since* construction:

*Informal:* I wondered what they would do with the logs, so I followed them through the woods.

*General:* Since [Because] I wondered what they would do with the logs, I followed them through the woods.

*Informal:* He is a fast reader, so he got through before I did.

*General:* Since he is a fast reader, he got through before I did.

Formal English would also use *so that* or the more exact *because* or *since* in these two constructions.

As an *intensive *so* is common in speech and is often stressed (He's *so* handsome! I was *so* excited.) and has been called the "feminine *so.*" But it is sometimes also used as an intensive in General writing: *This confinement was hard for him—he had been so active all his life.* (References: Fries, *AEG,* pp. 226-227; Russell Thomas, "The Use of *So* as an Intensifier," *College English,* 1951, 12:453-454; Bryant, pp. 190-193.)

**so ... as** • See *as ... as.

**so ... that** • Even when several words come between *so* and *that* no comma should precede *that:*

All strands of the story are so artfully and inextricably interwoven [ ] that anything but the author's desired effect is impossible.

(See *so, *Result.)

**so-called** • If you have to use *so-called,* don't duplicate the idea by putting the name of the so-called object in quotes: not *the so-called "champion,"* but *the so-called champion.* The word is rather stiff and in General writing quotation marks would often be used instead (the "champion").

*So-called* is usually hyphened when it precedes its principal word but not when it follows:

Their so-called liberal views were merely an echo of the conservative attitude. [Their "liberal" views were . . . .]
Their justice, so called, smacked of partiality.

**Social correspondence** •
1. *Informal notes.* The form and tone of Informal social notes —invitations, answers to invitations, thank you letters—are those of personal letters. (See *Letters § 1, 2.) Giving all the necessary information of time, place, and so on, being prompt in answering notes, and maintaining a tone of courtesy are more important than mechanical form. If the correspondents are not intimately acquainted, a more Formal style and more details of address may be needed than if they are intimates.
2. *Formal notes.* Formal social correspondence—announcements, invitations, answers to invitations—is impersonal and standardized. It is used for social events indicating, usually, formal dress or a gathering with distinguished guests.

For further details consult a book of etiquette.

**Solecism** • A *solecism* /sol′ə siz əm/ is a deviation from accepted practice; in language it implies an error in the use of words or constructions. The term is now distinctly Formal.

**some, and compounds with some** •
1. In written English, *some* is usually an indefinite pronoun (Some travel and some don't) or an adjective (some people, some ideas).
2. As an adverb, *some* is Informally used with comparatives (He felt some better), instead of the more Formal *somewhat.* It is also Informal when used with verbs (We talked some that afternoon).
3. The compounds *somebody, someway, somewhat, somewhere* are written as one word. *Someone* is usually one word (Someone is coming) but may be two if the *one* is stressed (Some one of them). *Someday* is written as one word or as two.
4. *Some place* is Informal for *somewhere* (I lost it some place). *Someway* and *someways* are also Informal, and *somewheres* is Nonstandard. (Compare *any, and compounds with any.)

**sooner . . . than** • After *no sooner* the preferable connective is now *than* rather than *when* or *but*:

The fly had *no sooner* hit the water *than* [not *when* or *but*] a huge trout snapped at it.

**sophomore** • Dictionaries record a three-syllable pronunciation, but recent ones note that the word is often pronounced as two syllables, /sof'môr/. The word is both noun and adjective. The adjective *sophomoric* /sof'[ə] môr'ik/ refers to supposed undesirable traits of sophomores (conceit and immaturity), as in *a sophomoric style* or *sophomoric conduct*.

**sort, kind** • See *kind, sort.

**sort of, kind of** • See *kind of, sort of.

**sort of [a], kind of [a]** • See *kind of a, sort of a.

**Sound** • See *Alliteration, *Assonance, *Homonyms, *Repetition § 3, *Style § 2b.

**species** • *Species* has the same spelling in both singular and plural; in pronunciation: /spē'shēz/, /spē'shiz/, /spē'sēz/.

*Specie* /spē'shi/, meaning money in coin, is a separate word, a collective noun without plural form.

**Spelling** •

*Sp*

*Revision: Correct the spelling of the word marked, referring to a dictionary if necessary.*

To improve spelling habits it is useful to study groups of words that have some trait in common. The following articles in this book treat such groups. Those articles marked † give the most useful rules or suggestions for mastering large groups of words.

-able, -ible (desirable, legible)
-ae-, -oe- (esthetic, ameba)
† -al ly (fatal, politically)
-ance, -ence (-ant, -ent) (attendance, existence)
Apostrophe (Bob's picture, the companies' charter)
Capital letters
† -ce, -ge (peaceable, courageous)
Contractions (didn't, he'll)
† Doubling final consonants (refer—referred)
† E § 5, silent or mute *e* (changeable, likeness)
-ed (exceptions to rule)

† -ei-, -ie- (feign, receive, achieve)
   en-, in- (encourage, inquire)
   -er, -or (debater, objector)
   -er, -re (luster, scepter)
   Foreign words in English (chauffeur, ersatz; accent marks)
† Homonymns, homophones (words pronounced alike but usually
   spelled differently: plain, plane; altar, alter)
   Hyphen (un-American, father-in-law)
   in-, un- (incapable, unedited)
   -ize, -ise (apologize, advertise)
   -le words (meddle, nickel)
† Neutral vowel (comparable, repetition)
   -or, -our (honor, Saviour)
   -ough, -augh (although, laugh)
   Plurals of nouns (beauties, birches, heroes, knives)
   Principal parts of verbs
   Pronunciation § 4
   re- (reform, re-form)
   Silent letters (debt, night)

The following list contains many words that give difficulty
in spelling. It is not exhaustive and is by no means a substitute
for a dictionary, but it can be used as the basis for improving
your spelling. Perhaps it can be most useful if you check the
particular words in it that you are not sure of and occasionally
study those to fix them better in mind. A profitable exercise
might be to have a classmate read the words for you to write
out. In the margins add others that have troubled you—in
every way possible make it *your* list.

A word preceded by * (for example, *advice*) has an article
discussing it.

A dash separating two words (*adviser—advisor*) means that
the two forms are about equally common.

A second form in brackets (*encyclopedia* [*encyclopaedia*])
means that the form in brackets is now less common than the
other.

A few words are identified by pronunciation in slashes or
definition in parentheses.

The division of words into syllables indicates how they
would be hyphened in writing and may assist in visualizing
them more accurately.

ab sence
ac a dem ic
ac cept, -ance, -able
ac cess, ac ces si ble
ac ci den tal ly
ac com mo date

ac com pa ny ing,
   ac com pa nied,
   ac com pa ni ment
ac cus tom
ache
a chieve

ac quaint, -ed, -ance
ac quired
a cross
ac tu al, -ly
ad ap ta tion
ad dress
ad o les cence
*ad vice (noun)
ad vise (verb)
ad vis er—ad vis or
*af fect (to influence)
a gainst
ag gra vate
ag gres sion, ag gres sor
air plane [aeroplane]
aisle (of a theater)
al co hol
al lege
all read y
*all right
al lu sion
*al ma ma ter
al read y
al tar (of a church)
al ter (to change)
*al though—al tho
al to geth er
*a lum nus, a lum ni,
    a lum na, a lum nae
am a teur
a nal o gous, a nal o gy
a nal y sis
an a lyze [analyse]
an es thet ic [anaesthetic]
an gel /ān'jəl/
an gle /ang'gl/
an nounc er
an nu al
an swer
anx i e ty
a pol o gy
ap pa ra tus
ap par ent
ap pear, -ance, ap pear anc es
ap pre ci ate
ap prox i mate
arc tic

ar gue, ar gu ing, ar gu ment
a roused
as cent (going up)
as sas sin
as sent (agreement)
as so ci a tion
*ath lete, ath let ics
at tacked
at tend, -ance, -ant
at ti tude
at tor ney
at trac tive
au di ence
au to bi og ra phy
aux il ia ry

bach e lor
bal ance
ba sis, bas i cal ly
bat tal ion
be gin ning
be lieve
ben e fit ed, ben e fi cial
berth (a bed)
bib li og ra phy
birth (being born)
breath /breth/
breathe /brēᴛʜ/
brid al (of a bride)
bri dle (of a horse)
bril liant
Brit ain (Great Britain)
bu reau
bu reauc ra cy
*bus, bus es—bus ses
busi ness

ca fe te ri a
cal en dar (of days)
cal i ber [calibre]
can di date
can't
can vas (sailcloth)
can vass (to go about)
cap i tal (city) , -ism
cap i tol (building)
cap tain

car bu re tor
care, -ful, -less
car goes
cas u al ties
cat e go ries
ceil ing
cen ter [centre]
cer tain ly
chal leng er
cham pagne
change a ble
chap er on [chaperone]
char ac ter is tic, char ac ter ized
chauf feur
chief, -tain
choose, choos ing (present)
chose, cho sen (past)
cig a ret—cig a rette
col lar
col le gi ate
colo nel
col or
co los sal
col umn
com e dy
com ing
com mit
com mit tee
com par a tive
com par i son
com pel, com pelled
com pet i tor
com plaint
com ple ment (to fill out)
com pli ment (to praise)
con cede
con ceive
con cer to /kən cher'tō/
con demn
con nois seur /kon'ə sėr'/
con quer or
con science
con sci en tious
con scious, -ness
con sen sus
con sist ent
con tempt i ble

con tin u ous
con trol, con trolled, con trol ling
con tro ver sy, con tro ver sial
con ven ient, con ven ience
con vert i ble
co op er a tive—co-op er a tive
 [coöperative]
corps /kôr/
corpse /kôrps/
coun cil (a group)
coun ci lor—coun cil lor
coun sel (advice)
coun sel or—coun sel lor
cour te ous, cour te sy
crept
crit i cism, crit i cize
cu ri ous, cu ri os i ty
cur ric u lar (adjective)
*cur ric u lum (noun)
cur tain
cus tom
cy lin dri cal

dair y /dãr'i/
damned
dealt
de bat er
de ceased /di sēst'/
de ceive
de cent /dē'snt/
de fend ants
def i nite, def i ni tion
de pend ent (adj. or noun)
de scend ant
de scent /di sent'/
de scribe, de scrip tion
de sert /di zėrt'/, (leave)
des ert /dez'ərt/, (waste)
de sire, de sir a bil i ty
de spair, des per ate
des sert /di zėrt'/, (of a meal)
de vel op [develope]
dex ter ous—dex trous
di a gram ma tic
di a phragm
di a ry /dī'ə rē/
die, dies, dy ing

die sel
di e ti tian [dietician]
dif fer ent
di lap i dat ed
din ing room
din ning (noise)
diph ther i a
dis ap pear ance
dis ap point ment
dis as trous
dis cre tion
dis eased /də zēzd′/
dis gust ed
dis patch [despatch]
dis si pate
dis trib u tor
dis turb ance
di vide
di vine
dom i nant
don't
dor mi to ry
dry, dri er, dri est
du al (two)
du el (fight)
dye, dyed, dye ing

ech o, ech oes
ec sta sies
ef fect
ef fi cient, ef fi cien cy
el i gi ble, el i gi bil i ty
em bar rass
em pha size, em phat ic,
  em phat ic al ly
em ploy ee, em ploy ees
  [employe, employé]
en cy clo pe di a [encyclopaedia]
en er get ic
en force
en vi ron ment
e quip ment, e quipped
es pe cial ly
es thet ic—aes thet ic
ex ag ger ate
ex am ine, ex am in ing,
  ex am i na tion

ex ceed, ex ces sive
ex cel, -lence, -lent
*ex cept (to omit)
ex cit a ble
ex er cise
ex haust ed
ex hil a rat ing
ex ist, -ence
ex pe di tion ar y
ex pense
ex pe ri ence
ex per i ment
*ex tra cur ric u lar
ex trav a gant
ex treme ly
ex u ber ance

fac ile, fa cil i ty
fair way (golf)
fal la cy
fa mil iar
fan ta sy, fan ta sies
fas ci na tion
fa vor ite
Feb ru ar y
fi an cé, fi an cée
fic ti tious
fier y
fi nal ly
fi nan cial ly
fin an cier
fli er—fly er
fore head /fôr′id/
for eign
for feit
for mal ly
for mer ly
for ty-four—for ty four
fourth
frame house
fran ti cal ly [franticly]
fra ter ni ties
*fresh man
friend, -li ness
ful fill—ful fil
fun da men tal, -ly
fur ni ture

fur ther

gauge—gage
gel a tine—gel a tin
ghost
gov ern ment
gov er nor
*grade school [graded school]
gram mar, gram mat i cal, -ly
*gray [grey]
grief
grue some [grewsome]
guar an tee, guar an teed
guard i an
guer ril la—gue ril la (fighting)
guid ance

hand i cap, hand i capped
hand ker chief
hand some
hang ar
hap pi ness
hear
here
height
he ro, he roes, her o ine
hid e ous
hin drance
hoard
hoarse (in throat)
horde
hor i zon tal
hors d'oeu vre /ôr dėrv'/
huge
hu man /hū'mən/
hu mane /hū mān'/
hu mor ous
hun gri ly
hur ried ly
hy giene
hyp no sis, hyp not ic, hyp no tize
   [hypnotise]
hy poc ri sy, hyp o crite
hys ter i cal

ig no rance, ig no rant
il log i cal

im ag ine, im ag i na tion,
   im ag i nar y
im me di ate ly
im ple ment
im promp tu, im promp tus
in ad e quate
in ces sant ly
in ci den tal ly
*in cred i ble
in de pend ence
in dict ment /in dīt'mənt/
in dis pen sa ble
in flu ence, in flu en tial
in gen ious
in gen u ous
in i ti a tion
in nu en do, in nu en does
in oc u late
in struc tor
in tel lec tu al
in tel li gent
in ter est
in tern [interne]
in ter pre tive [interpretative]
in ter rupt
in tol er ance
in ven tor—in ven ter
ir rel e vant
ir re li gious
ir re sist i ble
ir rev er ent
*its, it's
it self

ja lop y
john ny cake
jol li ty
*judg ment [judgement]

kha ki
kid nap, kid naped [kidnapped]
ki mo no, ki mo nos
kin der gar ten
kitch en ette
knowl edge

la bor, -er, -ious ly

lab o ra to ry
lat er /lā'tər/
*lat ter /lat'ər/
lau rel
lax a tive
*lead, led
leg a cy
le git i mate
lei sure ly
length, -en ing
li a ble
li ar
li brar i an
li cense
light en ing (making lighter)
*light ning (a flash)
lik a ble [likeable]
like, -ness, -ly, -li hood
li queur
liq uor
liv a ble [liveable]
live li hood
lone, -ly, -li ness
loose /lüs/
*lose /lüz/, los ing
lux u ry

mack er el
mag a zine
mag nif i cent, mag nif i cence
main tain, main te nance
man tel (the shelf)
man tle (the cloak)
man u al
man u fac tur er
mar riage
math e mat ics
mean, meant
med i cine
*me di e val [mediaeval]
me di o cre
Me di ter ra ne an
met al
met tle
mil lion aire
min i a ture
min ute

mis chief, mis chie vous
mis spelled
mold [mould]
mo not o nous
*mor al /môr'əl/, -ly
mo rale /mə ral'/
mort gage
moun tain ous
mur mur
mus cle
mus tache
mys te ri ous

*na ive—na ïve
nat u ral ly
nec es sar y, nec es sar i ly
*Ne gro, Ne groes
nei ther
nick el
niece
nine ty-ninth—nine ty ninth
no tice a ble, no tic ing
no to ri e ty
nui sance

o bey, o be di ence
o bliged
ob sta cle
*oc ca sion, -al ly
oc cur, -ring, -rence, oc curred
of fi cial
oil y
o mit, -ted, o mis sion
one self
op er ate
op po nent
op por tu ni ty
op ti mism
or gan i za tion [organisation]
or gan ize [organise]
or i gin, o rig i nal
out ra geous

*paid
pa ja ma [pyjama]
pam phlet
pan to mime

par al lel, par al leled
par lia ment
pa roled
par tic i pate
par tic u lar ly
*passed, past
pas time
ped es tal
per ceive
per form
per ma nent
per mit, per mis si ble
per se ver ance
per sist ent
per son al
per son nel
per spi ra tion
per suade, per sua sion
phase
Phil ip pines
phi los o phy
phys i cal
phy si cian
pi an o, pi an os
pick le
*pic nic, pic nicked
piece
pique /pēk/
pi qué /pi kā'/
plain
plane
planned
play wright
pleas ant
pneu mat ic
pneu mo nia
*pol i tics, pol i ti cian
pos si bil i ty
po ta to, po ta toes
prac ti ca bil i ty
*prac ti cal
prac tice [practise]
pre cede, pre ced ing
pref er ence, pre ferred
prej u dice
prep a ra tion
pres ence

prev a lent
prim i tive
*prin ci pal
prin ci ple
priv i lege
prob a ble, prob a bly
pro ce dure
pro ceed
pro fes sion
pro fes sor
pro gram [programme]
prom i nent
pro nounce, pro nun ci a tion
prop a gan da
pro pel ler
pro te in
psy cho a nal y sis,
    psy cho an a lyze
*psy chol o gy
psy cho path ic
psy cho so mat ic
pub lic ly
pump kin, punkin
pur sue, pur suit

quan ti ty
quan tum
quar an tine
quay [quai] /kē/
qui et
quite
quix ot ic
quiz, quiz zes

re al ly
re ceive
*rec i pe, re ceipt
re cip i ent
rec la ma tion
rec og ni tion
rec om mend
re-en ter
re en ter
re fer, ref er ence, re ferred
re for est a tion
rel a tive
rel e gate

rel e vant
re lieve
re li gion, re li gious
re mem ber
rem i nisce
*Ren ais sance [Re nas cence]
ren dez vous
re pel lent
rep e ti tion, rep e ti tious
re sem blance
res er voir
re sist ance
re spect ful ly
re spec tive ly
res tau rant
rev er ent
rhet o ric
rhyme [rime]
rhythm, rhyth mi cal
ri dic u lous
room mate

sac ri fice
sac ri le gious
safe ty
sal a ry
sand wich
sax o phone
scan dal ous
scar /skär/
scare /skãr/
sce nar i o
scene, sce nic
sched ule
sec re tar i al
seize
se mes ter
sen a tor
sense, sen si ble
sen tence
sep a rate, sep a ra tion
ser geant /sär'jənt/
sev er al
se vere ly, se ver i ty
shear (verb)
sheer (adj.)
shin ing

sieve
sig nif i cance
*sim i lar
sin cere ly, sin cer i ty
site (of a city)
skep ti cal [sceptical]
*ski, skis, skied, ski ing
slim y
slug gish
soc cer
sol u ble
so phis ti ca tion
*soph o more
source
speak, speech
spe cif i cal ly
spec i men, spec i mens
spec ter [spectre]
spic y, spic i ness
spon sor
stac ca to
sta tion ar y (fixed)
sta tion er y (paper)
stat ue
stat ure
stat ute
stom ach ache
sto ry [storey] (of a building)
straight
strength
stretched
stud y ing
sub stan tial
sub tle [subtile]
suc ceed, suc cess
suc cess ful, suc ces sion
suit /süt/
suite /swēt/
sul fa
sul fur—sul phur
sum ma ry, summed
su per in tend ent
su per sede
sup pose
sup press
sur prise
sus cep ti ble

sus pense
syl la ble
sym bol
sym me try, sym met ri cal
syn on y mous
syph i lis
syr up—sir up

*ta boo [tabu]
tar iff
tech nique [technic]
tem per a ment,
    tem per a men tal
tend en cy
than
*the a ter [theatre]
their
the o ry, the o ries
then
there
there fore
they're
thor ough [thoro]
though—tho
thought
thou sandths
through—thru
to, too, two
to day [to-day]
to geth er
traf fic, traf fick ing
trag e dy, trag ic
tries, tried
tru ly
Tues day
typ i cal
tyr an ny

un doubt ed ly
un nec es sar y
un prec e dent ed
un til (*till)
un u su al

use, -ful, -less, us ing
u su al ly
u ten sil

vac u um
var ies
var i ous
veg e ta bles
venge ance
ven ti late, ven ti la tion
ver ti cal
vice (evil)
view
vig i lance
vig i lan tes
vil i fy
vil lain
vise [vice] (the tool)
vis i bil i ty
vi ta min [vitamine]
vol ume

war rant
war ring
weath er
weight, -y
weird
wheth er
whis key [whisky]
whole
whol ly
whoop
who's (who is)
whose
wool en [woollen]
wool ly—wool y
write, writ ing, writ er, writ ten

yacht
yield
you're (you are)

zo ol o gy [zoölogy], zo o log i cal

(See *American and British usage, *Analogy in language,
*Apostrophe § 6, *Change in language, *Divided usage, *Pro-
nunciation § 2c. Reference: Donald W. Emery, *Variant Spelling in Modern English Dictionaries,* Champaign, 1958.)

**Split infinitive** • The word order in which an adverb comes between the *to* and the verb (The receptionist asked them *to kindly sit down*) is called a *split infinitive.*

Since the adverb modifies the verb, its natural position is next to the actual verb form, and writers of General English have never taken very seriously the puristic efforts to prohibit the construction. Changing the position of *silently* gives each of these sentences a different meaning:

He prepared silently to go along.
He prepared to go along silently.
He prepared to silently go along.

There is no point in rearranging a sentence just to avoid splitting an infinitive unless it is an awkward one. But awkward split infinitives are to be avoided:

*Awkward:* After a while I was able to, although not very accurately, distinguish the good customers from the sulky ones.

*Improved:* After a while I was able to distinguish—though not very accurately—the good customers from the sulky ones.

(See also *Latin and English § 3. References: Curme, *Syntax,* pp. 458-465; Fowler, "Split Infinitive," for overprecise distinctions; Fries, *AEG,* pp. 132, 144; W. H. Smith, "The Split Infinitive," *Anglia,* 1959, 77:257-278.)

**Spoken and written English** •
1. *Speech and writing.* Language originated as speech; the writing of it came very late in its history, some 6000 years ago. The number of significant differentiations in sound which a speaker uses is considerably larger than the number of symbols available in most established systems of writing. In English we have about forty speech sounds, four levels of pitch, four degrees of stress, and varying durations of sound and silence. (See *Intonation, *Phonemes, *Pronunciation.) To represent these elements of our speech, we have twenty-six letters, nine marks of punctuation, and a few devices like capitals and italics. As an exact representation of speech, our system of writing is obviously unsatisfactory.

The inventors of systems of writing were no doubt less concerned with transcribing every significant detail of the spoken language than with providing a reliable system of verbal communication which had permanence and could be understood visually. The fact that the heavy accent falls on the first syllable of *daily* but on the second of *today* need not be shown because the five symbols arranged in their familiar order tell the reader what word is intended; as soon as he recognizes the word, he knows where to accent it. Even with *desert,* the context will tell him whether the noun or the verb is intended and therefore whether the accent falls on the first or second syllable. Sometimes, in fact, the written forms provide more information than we really need, as a stenographer can testify from the fact that *bread* and *bred, two* and *too,* and all other homophones will look the same in shorthand and yet most will be intelligible. Although writing is never a complete transcription of speech—is no more than a good hint at exactly what might be spoken—it is a satisfactory system of communication.

Even with its limitations, writing can be a very powerful and effective medium. It is therefore legitimate to speak of the written language (or at least of the *written styles* of a language) as an entity in itself. Although *writing,* to some, suggests a weak reflection of speech, the enormous and vital prose literature of the last two or three centuries proves that such a connotation is incorrect. Most prose literature was written to be communicated through the eye, not the ear; and though oral reading often increases its effectiveness, its survival depends mainly on its capacity for communicating without the direct use of sound. What the printed material would sound like if read aloud is still important to its effect, but the actual hearing is not crucial. Many native speakers of English whose pronunciation of French is atrocious can read French prose with delight—Voltaire, for example—though they may find that even the greatest French verse—Racine or Victor Hugo—is unrewarding.

There are some instances in which the written language does better than the spoken; sometimes it makes clear what is almost impossible to communicate in speech, such as detailed instructions, which must be read repeatedly; extensive use of brief quotations, especially quotations within quotations, which can be efficiently indicated by the punctuation; some homophones which would be ambiguous in speech: *We'll halve it,* which could be mistaken for *we'll have it.*

The written language must retain a relationship to the spoken, but it should be an immediately understandable one that does not require the reader to puzzle out from inadequate transcription what would be obvious in speech. Sometimes this means the spoken language must be rephrased for writing. For instance, in *more competent men, more* might modify either *competent* or *competent men.* In speech the distinction would be shown by greater stress on *more* if it modified *competent men.* In writing, the distinction might be shown by *more men who are competent,* or if *more* modified *competent* only, by adding a modifier as in *more really competent men.*

**2.** *"Colloquial" English.* Dictionaries formerly marked words *Colloq.* to suggest that in the editors' judgment they were more common in speech than in writing. Many people took this label to mean that the dictionary frowned upon the use of these words, but even the 1934 Webster definition of *colloquial* shows that this was not true:

acceptable and appropriate in ordinary conversational context, as in intimate speech among cultivated people, in familiar letters, in informal speeches or writings but not in formal written discourse (*flabbergast; go slow; harum-scarum*). Colloquial speech may be as correct as formal speech.—By permission. From *Webster's New International Dictionary*, Second Edition, copyright 1934, 1939, 1945, 1950, by G. & C. Merriam Co.

The three expressions given as examples show that *colloquial* was not being used as a word of dispraise or even of suspicion, for though *flabbergast, go slow,* and *harum-scarum* may be more appropriate in speech than in Formal writing, they are accurate, expressive words that could be used in most General as well as Informal writing. But since a good many people continue to interpret *colloquial* as condemnatory, the label is not used in the most recent dictionaries and is used in this book only infrequently and cautiously. If a usage is more common in speech than in writing, that fact is stated; if the word or expression is in good use but would rarely be found in General or Formal writing, it is labeled Informal.

Of course there are different varieties of spoken English, from Nonstandard and even slovenly to distinctly Formal. Many educated people, especially in the professions, get most of their information from periodicals and books, so that their speech reflects the written language. Sometimes the written language may determine the spoken. Topics important in certain limited areas—especially the upper levels of scientific, scholarly, and professional fields, and in some literature—may be much more frequently written than spoken about and may almost never be discussed in ordinary speech. Here the written forms may become the norms, imitated in speech. But for the greater part of the written language, speech, somewhat condensed and made more precise, is the basis.

The closeness of the written literary English to the spoken English of the time has varied from period to period. In the nineteenth century the two were rather far apart—consider Hawthorne, and even more the rank and file of lesser writers. Since 1880 or so in England and since 1910 in the United States, there has been a closer approach of written to spoken style. Today, how closely one's written style should approximate his spoken style depends upon appropriateness; he should feel free to use words and constructions characteristic of speech when they fit naturally with other traits of his style (see *Style).

(See "Differences between speaking and writing," p. 8 and "What is good English?" p. 22.)

**Spoonerism** • A *spoonerism* is an unintentional (except for humorous effect) exchange of the initial sounds of two words, as in *a half-warmed fish* for *a half-formed wish.*

**spoonful, spoonfuls** • The Standard plurals of *spoonful, tablespoonful, teaspoonful* are *spoonfuls, tablespoonfuls, teaspoonfuls* (similarly, *basketfuls, carfuls, cupfuls, shovelfuls, tubfuls*). *Cupsful, carsful, shovelsful,* and so on are often heard, though they appear less frequently in written English.

**Squinting modifier** • See *Ambiguity § 2.

**St.** • See *street.

**St., Ste.** • See *saint.

**Staccato style** • A staccato style has—as its principal characteristic—short, emphatic sentences, often exclamations or questions, usually without expressed connectives between the statements. The words, especially verbs, are likely to be vigorous. It is effective in short passages that deserve sharp stressing but is likely to be tiresome and to lose its emphasis if it is long continued:

Hindenburg was shortening his lines. He was quitting northern France and Belgium. But he was holding the Argonne. Day by day the representatives of our G. H. Q. had shown us the map with every enemy division and reserve force marked. Hindenburg had thirty-two reserve divisions at the beginning of our Argonne drive. When November began two or three remained. What had become of an army of German reserves?—GEORGE SELDES, *You Can't Print That!* p. 35

(Compare *Telegraphic style.)

**Standard English** • See "Standard English," p. 14.

**state** • See *say.

**still** • *Still* is an adverb in the sentence *It's still raining* and a conjunction (*Conjunctive adverbs) in *I can see your point of view; still I don't agree with you.*

**strata** • *Strata* is the plural of the singular *stratum.* It is pronounced /strā'tə/ or /strat'ə/.

**street** • In many newspapers and in some Informal writing, *street* is not capitalized as part of an address. In Formal and most General writing it is capitalized (41 High Street).

The abbreviation *St.* or *st.* is not much used except to save space in newspapers, lists, or reference works.

**Stress** • See *Noun and verb stress, *Phonemes § 2a, *Pronunciation.

**Strong verbs** • See *Principal parts of verbs.

**Style** • Style has been the subject of a number of well-known aphorisms: "Proper words in proper places make the true definition of a style" (Jonathan Swift); "Style is the dress of thoughts" (Lord Chesterfield); "Style is this: to add to a given thought all the circumstances fitted to produce the whole effect that the thought ought to produce" (Stendhal); "Style is the ultimate morality of mind" (A. N. Whitehead); and, most often quoted of all, "The style is the man" (Comte de Buffon).

These are all provocative statements, and properly idealistic, but they tend to defeat profitable discussion; a student of literature or a writer needs something more explicit. Although *style* may be defined variously, it is basically the characteristics, the qualities of the language in a particular piece of discourse. (There are oral styles as well as written, but in this brief treatment only the written will be discussed.) A writer has a wide range to choose from for words, constructions, sentence patterns, and arrangement and emphasis of his material. The style is the choices he makes, consciously or unconsciously, among the options offered by the language. The formation of most noun plurals and the past tense of most verbs, the agreement of subjects and verbs, the standard word order of English are part of the structure of the language and not distinctive traits of style. But the relative length and complexity of sentences, the variations in the order of sentence elements, the use of long or short constructions, the choice and especially the connotation of words may be. The study of style is an effort to discover what qualities of the language used in a particular story, essay, or article give rise to certain of the reader's impressions of it, especially to his response to the tones that are aside from its denotation, the part of the meaning that would be largely lost in a summary or paraphrase of the passage.

1. *The study of style.* The study of style is, then, one emphasis in the study of language. It is closely related to linguistics (some books in linguistics have a term for it, usually "stylistics") and will increasingly use the methods and data of that

discipline. But the study of style is interpretive as well as descriptive; it is concerned primarily with the study of specific items of discourse rather than with the general system of the language, and it takes account of meaning and effect, matters at least currently not much explored in linguistics. The aim of the study of style is increased awareness of the qualities of language in use, viewed especially as the source of a reader's impressions.

The first step in studying a style is a natural, attentive reading, usually more than one reading. It is a good idea to make notes of the traits of language that you believe will repay further investigation and of your early impressions, perhaps describing the style as compact or diffuse, literal or allusive or figurative, flat or emphatic, direct or involved, and so on— however it strikes you as a whole.

The next step is a detailed, analytic reading of the passage. Some counting (of kinds of words, types of phrases, length and type of sentences. . .) is in order, not to accumulate figures but to gather evidence for the rightness of your first impressions (this reading may of course prove to you that your first impressions were mistaken) and to enable you to demonstrate the validity of your judgment of the style to others. (It is surprising what previously unnoticed traits will force themselves on your attention while you are concentrating almost mechanically on, perhaps, adjectives or metaphors.)

Finally, read the piece again "for its own sake" and to see the individual traits as a part of the whole. This reading should be more perceptive and more rewarding than the first. Such occasional careful studies of particular pieces should increase the fullness of your first response to others.

**2.** *Elements of style.* There are no standard categories for the study of style, but some are needed to guide observation. The headings given in this section will serve to organize most of the elements of language usually considered as traits of style. These elements can be used to begin the observation and discussion of a selection by a professional writer, but the same points can make the amateur more aware of the resources of the language that are available to him. Some of the elements will be illustrated from the three short passages on p. 407.

*a*–Thought movement. It is hard to substantiate objectively impressions such as *thin, diffuse, pithy, meaty, dense,* but they can be pretty well demonstrated by looking at the contribution made by individual sentences. The rapidity or slowness of movement, the kind of statement (simple, complex, or compound; periodic or loose . . .), the marks of continuity, the interrelations of details and generalizations vary widely among writers and contribute to the stylistic impression. The Orwell passage is closely packed with visual detail; the Thurber is more relaxed, a series of individual impressions bearing on the generalization of the first two sentences; the Conrad passage, though organized as narrative, is chiefly visual detail elaborating the narrative movement. In each case the kind of movement is allied to the purpose of the writer.

*b*-Qualities of sound. There is a question how big a part sound plays in a literature that is written primarily for silent reading. It is obviously important in verse, but it has some importance in prose literature as well. Inattention to sound is responsible for some of the shortcomings of much journalistic and "bureaucratic" prose—it is obviously not "heard" by the writer. We have to be especially cautious in discussing the *intonation: for example, an American would read aloud a passage by a British writer rather differently from the way its author would read it, and a Northerner's reading of a story by a Southern writer would be different from the writer's in some respects.

Even in reading silently we are somewhat conscious of the possible sounds, and in reading slowly we may almost form them—certainly part of our impression of a passage comes from its "sound." The important sounds are those in stressed syllables. There may be a conspicuous series of the same sound, or more often of sounds similar in some phonetic respect: voiced consonants (b, g, v, z, and so on) or unvoiced (p, k, f, s) or "stop" consonants (b, d, g, k, p, t); back vowels /ō/, /ü/, /ô/, or front vowels /ā/, /ē/, /a/; nasals or sibilants. Or there may be a marked variety (as the vowels in the last Orwell phrase are all different: /ō/, /ā/, /ī/, /u/, /a/, /ou/, /ô/, or marked contrasts in individual sounds or groups of sounds, as in the last part of the last Conrad sentence (". . . a land from which the very memory of motion had forever departed").

Three sequences of sounds are named: *alliteration, the same initial sounds (*m*emory of *m*otion), helps bind phrases together; *assonance, syllables with the same vowel but different consonant sounds (m*i*xture of c*i*nders), and consonance, syllables with the same consonants combined with different vowel and consonant sounds (Rou*nd* ma*ny* wester*n* isla*nd*s have I bee*n*).

There has been a good deal of study of prose rhythm. The older method was to scan the units of prose as verse is scanned, by dividing them into feet (iambic, dactylic, etc.). But the units of prose, actually sense units, are usually longer than a metric foot, so that dividing into feet means even less in prose than it does in verse. The sound movement in prose is essentially the intonation patterns, and the methods of linguistics—

## Passages Illustrating Points of Style

The canal path was a mixture of cinders and frozen mud, criss-crossed by the imprints of innumerable clogs, and all round, as far as the slag-heaps in the distance, stretched the "flashes"—pools of stagnant water that had seeped into the hollows caused by the subsidence of the ancient pits. It was horribly cold. The "flashes" were covered with ice the colour of raw umber, the bargemen were muffled to the eyes in sacks, the lock gates wore beards of ice. It seemed a world from which vegetation had been banished; nothing existed except smoke, shale, ice, mud, ashes and foul water.—GEORGE ORWELL, "North and South," *The Road to Wigan Pier,* p. 138

The notion that such persons ["writers of light pieces running from a thousand to two thousand words"] are gay of heart and care-free is curiously untrue. They lead, as a matter of fact, an existence of jumpiness and apprehension. They sit on the edge of the chair of Literature. In the house of Life they have the feeling that they have never taken off their overcoats. Afraid of losing themselves in the larger flight of the two-volume novel, or even of the one-volume novel, they stick to short accounts of their misadventures because they never get so deep into them but that they feel they can get out. This type of writing is not a joyous form of self-expression but the manifestation of a twitchiness at once cosmic and mundane. Authors of such pieces have, nobody knows why, a genius for getting into minor difficulties: they walk into the wrong apartments, they drink furniture polish for stomach bitters, they drive their cars into the prize tulip beds of haughty neighbors, they playfully slap gangsters, mistaking them for old school friends. To call such persons humorous, a loose-fitting and ugly word, is to miss the nature of their dilemma and the dilemma of their nature. The little wheels of their invention are set in motion by the damp hand of melancholy.—JAMES THURBER, *My Life and Hard Times,* Preface

In the stillness of the air every tree, every leaf, every bough, every tendril of creeper and every petal of minute blossoms seemed to have been bewitched into an immobility perfect and final. Nothing moved on the river but the eight paddles that rose flashing regularly, dipped together with a single splash; while the steersman swept right and left with a periodic and sudden flourish of his blade describing a glinting semi-circle above his head. The churned-up water frothed alongside with a confused murmur. And the white man's canoe, advancing upstream in the short-lived disturbance of its own making, seemed to enter the portals of a land from which the very memory of motion had forever departed.—JOSEPH CONRAD, "The Lagoon," *Tales of Unrest,* p. 187

the stresses ( ′ ^ ‵ ˘ ) and junctures (the pauses and rising and falling terminals)—can probably be developed into a workable scheme for describing it. (See *Phonemes § 2.)

Any discussion of the rhythm of prose would have to be very detailed to be accurate or helpful. Reading aloud the passages on p. 407 will give some idea of the variety in length of rhythmical units, in intensity of stresses, in position of stresses (especially at the ends of sentences and of important constructions within them), and of the general contribution of sound to the impression of styles.

***c***–Visual traits. Although the appearance to the eye is not so important for prose as for verse, there is some slight contribution to the effect of prose from such matters as length of paragraphs, use of italic type, stylistic use of capitals (*Capital letters § 10), and even from punctuation marks—close punctuation usually suggesting a slower movement than open. There is just enough effect from these matters to warrant including them in a discussion of style.

***d***–Minor points of syntax. In contemporary style the smaller elements of syntax are perhaps more important than the frame of sentences. There are some options in word forms: adverbs ending with *-ly* or without (*Adverbs, types and forms); choice between two plurals of nouns from other languages (*Plurals of nouns § 4); *comparison of adjectives and adverbs with *-er, -est* or with *more, most*; choice between two past forms of a few verbs (*Principal parts of verbs); the use or nonuse of active or *passive verbs and of *subjunctive forms. There is some variation possible in the position of adjectives (an immobility *perfect* and *final*) and more in the position of adverbial modifiers (frothed *alongside with a confused murmur*).

There are distinctly different impressions from constructions with nouns as *headwords (by the *subsidence* of the ancient *pits,* the *stillness* of the *air*) and those centered on verbs (as in Thurber's series of mishaps—*they walk . . . drink . . . drive . . . slap . . .*) and the constructions with *verbals that often have the syntax of nouns or adjectives with some of the action qualities of verbs (*mistaking* them for old school friends, *describing* a *glinting* semi-circle). A good deal has been written about the stylistic impact of the various parts of speech. People probably differ in their sensitiveness to this trait, but there are differences between styles with nouns especially prominent and those with verbs, and also differences that depend on the number and quality of modifiers (*Adjectives in use, *Adverbs in use). The Orwell passage has very few adjectives, the Conrad several emphatic ones. Pronouns and other personal words are associated with narrative, but they give ease and rapidity to exposition, as in the Thurber passage.

Numerous devices make for compactness. Most effective is the omission of words and phrases that do not contribute to meaning. Others are the use of two or more verbs with one subject instead of a repetition of the subject, the use of noun modifiers rather than prepositional phrases ("the stone house" instead of "the house of stone"), adjective clauses without the introductory pronoun or still further reduced ("ice the colour of raw umber" instead of "ice that was the colour of raw umber"), metaphors instead of similes ("the lock gates wore beards of ice" instead of "the lock gates looked as if they were wearing beards of ice").

Taken together these syntactical traits contribute to impressions of diffuseness or compactness and emphasis; to pace, a sense of slowness or rapidity; and often to the degree of Formality or Informality.

*e*–Sentences. A writer has wide latitude in how much he will put in a single sentence, of which the physical length is the external symptom. Our three passages are too short for any generalizations, but they show some range. The Orwell sentences run from 4 to 50 words, averaging 25.5; Thurber's 9 to 50, averaging 23.2; and Conrad's 9 to 42, averaging 29. Often there is contrast in arrangement, as Orwell's 4-word sentence follows one of 50, and Conrad's 9-word sentence comes between one of 42 and one of 33 words.

*f*–Words. English offers a wide range in the choice of words. They differ in the variety of English they come from, in their familiarity, in their degree of concreteness or abstractness, in their precision of meaning, and in their connotations—their tone, the associations from experience or from literature they bring to mind. The three passages show considerable range in words, from the precise words from experience of Orwell to the literary ones of Conrad.

*g*–Imagery. *Imagery (picture-forming) is a quality of words, but its importance is sufficient to warrant a separate heading. Imagery can be interpreted as roughly equivalent to concreteness. A concrete word calls up a sense impression; an abstract word ordinarily does not. But readers vary: what is an image-bearing word for one person will evoke no image at all or a very different one for another person. Much depends on the experience of the reader and on his habits of thinking.

Verbal images differ in the senses they represent (sight, sound, taste, smell, touch); sight so predominates in imagery that the use of the other senses often has unusual force. The verbal images may be simple, as in the Orwell passage, or complex, involving movement, as in the Conrad. They may be the substance of the piece, as in the Orwell and Conrad passages, or secondary, supporting an idea, as in Thurber. They differ greatly in precision, sometimes forcing an exact picture on a reader, more often allowing him considerable leeway in what image he will produce from his memory. They may be sampled, highly selective, or massed—as in a detailed description. Their connotations are usually more from the objects named than from the words, so that they may seem to be actually symbols, and often the feeling or mood associated with the objects is aroused in the reader.

*h*–Figures of speech. Figures of speech, which contribute a great deal to imagery, have always been a part of the treatment of style. The term is rather vague and certainly flexible (some of the old lists of figures of speech ran to over 280), but basically figures of speech include words and phrases that come from a context, an area of meaning, other than the subject being presented; expressions that are intensified or altered in some way; and also turns of phrase that are in some way out of the ordinary. The idea of figures of speech was originally based on the supposition that people used language basically in a literal, referential sense and that other uses were a substitution for this ordinary language—for ornament or impressiveness. We now know that all people use figures of speech freely in their everyday talk and writing—children use many figures—and that the point about metaphor and the figures is not so much their departure from literal meaning as what they contribute to the meaning. This contribution is often to the tone and the connotation, bringing into one context some quality or attitude associated with another—with a resulting freshness and emphasis.

Figures may be relatively pale—the metaphor in Orwell's "beards of ice" seems a familiar and almost literal expression, and the personification implied in the verb *wore* is so slight that it seems chiefly grammatical, allowing a more active verb than a flat *had*. Conrad's "bewitched into an immobility" and "a land from which the very memory of motion had forever departed" are more literary and allusive. The naturalness of figures is shown by Thurber's metaphors, exaggerations, allusions, and the extended metaphor or analogy of the last sentence, and even the relatively rare *chiasmus,* two constructions in which the order of keywords is reversed (the nature of their dilemma and the dilemma of their nature).

It is not necessary to be able to name all of the departures from a precise, literal use of words (most of the figures have Greek names that seem strange to us), though we should be able to identify more than metaphors and similes. The important thing is to see what they add, what associations, connotations, attitudes (many are used just for fun), and emphases the figures bring to bear on the subject being presented.

(See *Figures of speech for definitions of the most common figures—metaphor, simile, and so on. See also *Epigrams, *Imitative words and phrases, *Irony, *Negatives, *Personification, *Puns.)

3. *Generalizations about style.* The impetus to the study of style is to understand and appreciate particular items of discourse, but naturally such studies lead to generalizations, if for no other reason than to help in summarizing observations.

There are many terms for general impressions of a style (some have been mentioned earlier in this article): flexible, varied—rigid or monotonous or mannered; conventional, traditional—individual, original, fresh; tense—relaxed; simple—complex; and so on; as well as terms that emphasize separate qualities: literal—figurative; direct—involved; abstract—concrete, imagistic.

Since the earliest rhetoricians there have been efforts to classify styles in general, and in spite of various experiments in terms they come back to the polarities of the *plain,* the more literal and direct, and *heightened,* the more elaborate, using more of the devices of language, especially with emotional suggestion. In between these is a gradation, often called simply *middle* or *mixed* styles with a conversational base but showing some of the devices of more elaborate styles. The three passages on p. 407 illustrate this range: Orwell, the plain; Conrad, the heightened; and Thurber, the middle.

Since it is difficult to talk in detail about style by itself, it is natural to go to its relationships, Style and ——. There are obvious relationships between the individuality of the writer and his style, though asserting specific relationships is risky. There are some traits of style characteristic of various types of writing (fiction, science, advertising, polemic), of various subject matters (politics, religion, law), and of the literary perspectives of humor, satire, tragedy, and so on.

And finally there is the theoretical question of style and meaning, which is easier to sense than to state. Traits of language certainly affect the precision, intensity, emphasis, tone, and suggestiveness of the central message. Neglecting the style in discussing meaning may lead to misinterpretation, as neglecting the intonation of a *yes* or a *no* in a conversation may. A full and accurate understanding of the meaning of a passage depends in part on a sensitive response to the style.

4. *Style and an individual's writing.* For a practiced writer, style is not a conscious concern but a by-product of his effort to make language carry out his purpose. Most writers start under the influence of some other writer and may even intentionally imitate him for a time. But better is a good deal of varied reading that will show the possibilities of the language. You

will unconsciously pick up traits that suit your material, your purposes, and your temperament. Occasional rereading and reading aloud from a writer whose work you would like yours to resemble in some way may help. But nothing can take the place of your own experiments and your own purposeful writing. Your style will develop as you improve in effective completion of your own writing projects.

(Some articles treating aspects of style, in addition to those starred in context, include: \*Colon § 4; \*Conjunction § 2, 3; \*Fundamentals § 4; \*Jargon § 1; \*literary; \*Originality § 2; \*Scientific and technical writing; \*Semicolon § 4; \*Subjunctives; \*Telegraphic style; \*Usage. The following references will provide a guide to a fairly full study of style: Paul F. Baum, *The Other Harmony of Prose,* Durham, 1952—the best starting point for a consideration of prose rhythm; Bonamy Dobrée, *Modern Prose Style,* Oxford, 1934—discussion of passages of prose grouped by subject matter; Edith Rickert, *New Methods for the Study of Literature,* Chicago, 1927—a program of detailed analysis; George Saintsbury, *A History of English Prose Rhythm,* London, 1922—comments on various aspects of the style of past periods; R. A. Sayce, *Style in French Prose,* Oxford, 1953—a topical discussion with various suggested devices; Norton R. Tempest, *The Rhythm of English Prose,* Cambridge, 1930—the analysis of rhythm by metrical feet; Stephen Ullmann, *Style in the French Novel,* Cambridge, 1957—an application of linguistics to style; Richard M. Weaver, *The Ethics of Rhetoric,* Chicago, 1953—stylistic qualities of the parts of speech; W. K. Wimsatt, Jr., *The Prose Style of Samuel Johnson,* New Haven, 1941—one of the more detailed studies of the style of an individual writer.)

**Stylebooks** • For editors and printers *style* means the method of handling various mechanical matters such as capital letters, punctuation, forms of plurals, division of words, details of typography. Since usage is divided on many of these points, a publisher chooses what form will be used in his publications. Most newspapers, magazines, and publishing houses have stylebooks—documents ranging from a single page to an elaborate volume containing the particular rules to be followed in preparing copy for specific publications. They often show arbitrary choices, to attain a consistency that most publishers feel is desirable. One factor in recent changes in practices in writing and printing has been the decision of some of the book publishers to let authors' copy stand nearly as written, so long as it is consistent.

Most newspaper stylebooks are not generally available, though that of *The New York Times,* revised 1962, is for sale.

The University of Chicago Press *Manual of Style,* eleventh edition (Chicago, 1949), is the most influential stylebook among book publishers. The *United States Government Printing Office Style Manual* (Washington, D.C., 1953) is one of the best stylebooks.

### Subject and verb •

1. *As sentence elements.* The backbone of the typical English sentence is a subject and a verb. The subject names the starting point of the statement, and the verb advances the statement. The subject is the noun or substantive in most intimate relation to the verb. Except in inverted sentence order the subject stands before the verb, and its position there is the main grammatical device we have to identify it as the subject, just as the position of the object after the verb identifies it. In the sentence *The submarine sank the cruiser* we know that the submarine and not the cruiser did the sinking because *submarine* is in the subject position in the sentence.

2. *Agreement of subject and verb.* When the verb form permits it, a verb shows agreement with its subject in number and person. This usually means with the grammatical number of the subject. But since, except for the verb *be,* our verbs have only one form for both numbers and for all persons except an -*s* in the third singular present (and the *modal auxiliaries lack this -*s*), relatively few problems in agreement can arise. Users of English can rely very little on formal indications of relation between subject and verb; therefore lack of agreement in form seldom causes ambiguity, though it may be felt by the hearer or reader to be a serious mistake: *I is,* for example, is entirely intelligible but it is also certainly Nonstandard.

*Singular: I am* more tired than usual. *A chair was placed* in the corner. *This job takes* four weeks. *The job took* four weeks.

*Plural: We are* more tired than usual. *Three chairs were placed* along the wall. *These jobs take* four weeks. *The jobs took* four weeks.

The problems that arise in the agreement of subject and verb come either from a construction in which the grammatical number of the subject is uncertain or is blurred by other words, or from the meaning of the subject as the basis for agreement rather than its grammatical form.

*a*–Collective nouns. Agreement according to meaning is seen most clearly in collective nouns, which take either a singular or plural verb, depending upon whether the speaker or writer is emphasizing the group as a whole or the individuals of which it is composed. In writing, the verbs and pronouns of a given sentence should be all plural or all singular in referring back to a collective subject.

Emphasizing the unit: The class *is* the largest in six years.

Emphasizing the individuals: The class *are* by no means all intellectual giants, but *they* have done very well. [More likely: *The students in this class . . . .*]

(For further examples and discussion see *Collective nouns.)

*b*–Compound subjects. Ordinarily a compound subject has a plural verb:

Alice and Francis *were* the first to arrive.

The text of the poem and the commentary *make* good reading.

When the two elements of a compound subject refer to the same person or thing, the verb is singular:

The best teacher and the best scholar here *is* Professor Babcock.

The spirit and accomplishment of these men *speaks* for itself.

The verb is often singular when a compound subject follows:

There *is* both health and wealth in this way of life.

For the winner there *was* a large cash prize and weeks of glory.

When a second part of the subject is connected with the first by *with, together with, as well as,* the agreement varies. In Formal English such a construction is kept singular. In General English a plural is often found if the expression is equivalent to a compound subject:

The rudder is the only essential control in taxiing, and this together with a regulative speed *keeps* the plane going in a relatively straight line.

The winner with the four runners-up *were* given a reception. [To make this more Formal, the *with* should be changed to *and,* rather than the *were* to *was.*]

He is not a good speaker, since his hesitating manner with long "uh's" interspersed in the address *make* [Formal: *makes*] him hard to listen to.

Subjects connected by *or* or *either . . . or* take a singular verb if both are singular, a plural verb if both are plural or if the one nearer the verb is plural, and often a plural verb if the idea is felt to be plural (especially in questions, where the verb precedes); similarly with *neither . . . nor,* with the plural more common:

A novel or a biography *is* to be read outside of class.

Novels or biographies *were* the same to him.

A novel or five short stories *were* to be read.

Either a dentist or a doctor *is* to treat such cases.

*Do* Tim or any of the others want to come?

Since neither chemistry nor physics *were* [more Formal: *was*] required, most students had no basic physical science.

When the two elements of the subject are pronouns in different persons, the verb is usually plural:

You and I *are* sure to go, anyway.
Either you or he *are* likely to go. [*Is* is possible here to emphasize the singleness of choice.]
Neither you nor I *are* fit for that job.

In questions the plural is common:

*Are* [or: *Is*] Fred or Harry in?

*c*–Plural modifier of singular subject. When a rather long plural modifier of a singular subject comes between it and the verb, Formal and General English usually have a singular verb, but Informal often has a plural verb:

This *group* of essays *is* [not: *are*] concerned with problems in sociology and philosophy as they are related to biology.
The *form* of your bibliography and footnotes *is* not standard.
To a beginner on the organ the *array* of stops and pistons, couplers, and pedals *seems* [Informal: *seem*] at first quite bewildering.
Two thousand dollars' *worth* of pictures *were* [Formal: *was*] destroyed.

*d*–Relative pronouns. A relative pronoun referring to a singular noun has a singular verb (The person *who takes* enough pains can do it) and one referring to a plural noun has a plural verb (The people *who take* pains win in the long run). In idioms like *This is one of the most discouraging things that has come out of the situation,* Formal usage requires *that have come,* since the antecedent of *that* is *things;* Informal often and General occasionally have *that has come,* because the central idea (of *one*) is singular.

*Formal:* Jeffrey is one of those moderns *who are* making *their* money talk.
*Informal and, less often, General:* Jeffrey is one of those moderns *who is* making *his* money talk.

(See *one of those who.)

*e*–Subject and complement of different number. The verb agrees with the subject:

A day's work is four trips.      Four trips make a day's work.

*f*–Plural subject with singular meaning. When the idea conveyed by a plural subject is singular in intent, the verb is usually singular: *Five years is a long time.*

(References: Curme, *Syntax,* Ch. 4; Fries, *AEG,* pp. 188-190, 249-250, and index references; Pooley, pp. 78-88.)
3. *Punctuation between subject and verb.* Since the subject and verb are part of one construction, they should not normally be separated by a comma:

Another example of what can happen [ ] is furnished by the experience of two young women who were staying at the hotel.

However, a comma may be used to prevent misreading:

Let those who will, rear lion cubs; I'd plump for a baby giraffe, not more than seven feet tall.—MARTHA GELLHORN, "Animals Running Free," *Atlantic,* Feb. 1966, p. 70

(See *Comma § 8.)

**Subject of a gerund** • See *Gerund § 2.

**Subject of an infinitive** • See *Infinitives § 5.

**Subject of a sentence** • See *Adjectives, types and forms § 6; *Agreement § 1; *Compound subject; *Gerund § 1; *Infinitives § 4; *Shifted constructions; *Subject and verb.

**Subjective case** • See *Nominative case.

**Subjunctives** • It is not necessary to use the Latin grammar subjunctive mood in describing English verbs. It is probably inaccurate to do so for two reasons: very few forms can be surely identified as "subjunctives," hardly enough to furnish a paradigm; and the use of the few identifiable forms is so irregular that no definite syntactical criteria can be stated to define it.

This article presents some facts about the nontypical subject-verb agreement traditionally called the subjunctive.

**1.** *Form of subjunctives.*

*a*–Simple subjunctive. In current English the form called subjunctive is identifiable only in certain forms of *be* (I, you, he . . . *be*; I, he . . . *were*); in forms made with *be* (he *were asking*); and in the third person singular of most verbs (*he ask* instead of *he asks*; *he have* instead of *he has*).

*b*–Subjunctive with auxiliaries. Some grammarians include as subjunctives all the locutions that can be used in expressing ideas that may also be, or have at some time been, expressed by the subjunctive, or the forms that could be used in translating subjunctives found in other languages. Under this system several auxiliaries—*may, might, should, would, let, have to,* and others—become subjunctives. This broad interpretation makes consideration of the subjunctive more complicated than is necessary, since the meaning and connotation of such constructions come from the meaning of the auxiliary or from adverbs.

For that reason, in the following discussion only the simple subjunctive—that is, a verb form differing from the one ordinarily expected—is considered.

**2.** *Uses of the subjunctive.* Because of the paucity of forms, English makes much less use of the mood than most of the modern European languages do. There are a number of idioms in which the subjunctive may be used in English, especially in Formal English, though it is almost always possible to use other verb forms. It is fairly common in wishes, conditions, qualified or doubtful statements, and in *that*-clauses and after expressions like *It is necessary.* The following examples illustrate typical uses of the subjunctive and give alternative idioms that would be more common.

*a–*Formulas. The subjunctive is found in numerous formulas, locutions surviving from a time when the subjunctive was used freely. Most of these are no longer common idioms; that is, we do not make other sentences on the pattern of *Far be it from me.* . . .

| Suffice it to say | Heaven forbid | Heaven help us | Be it said |
| If I were you | God bless you | Be that as it may | As it were |

Many mild oaths have this form: *Confound it; Psychology be hanged.*

Some of these formulas are used in all levels of the language; some, like *Come what may,* are rather Formal, and the oaths are chiefly Informal.

*b–*In *that*-clauses. The subjunctive is mandatory in idioms for recommendations, resolutions, demands, and so on. These idioms are usually in a Formal context. Note the following examples:

*Formal:* We recommend that the Commissioner *designate* for this use the land formerly belonging to Mr. Brewster.

*Formal:* I ask that the interested citizen *watch* closely the movements of these troops.

*General:* I ask the interested citizen to watch the movement of these troops closely.

*Formal:* . . . the order that he *be* dropped

*General:* . . . the order to drop him

*Formal:*It is necessary that every member *inform* himself of these rules.

*General:* It is necessary for every member to inform himself of these rules. It is necessary that every member should inform himself of these rules. Every member must [should] inform himself of these rules.

*c–*In conditions. The subjunctive may be used in *if*-clauses when there is doubt of fulfillment of the condition, or when the condition is "contrary-to-fact"—impossible or not believed by the writer:

If one good *were* really as good as another, no good would be any good.—Irwin Edman, *Four Ways of Philosophy,* p. 80

The meaning here does not require the less common *were*, since the contrary-to-factness is conveyed by the use of a past form (either *was* or *were*) with a present or future meaning. Edman's idea would certainly be as clear if he had written "If one good was as good as another, no good would be any good," but the tone would be a little different.

In fact, few writers make such a distinction and a large proportion of the "subjunctives" found are in "simple" conditions:

*Formal*: If the subject of a verb *be* [More usual *is*] impersonal, the verb itself may be called impersonal.—ARTHUR G. KENNEDY, *Current English*, p. 296

The fellow who worked next to him in the plant had been turned off, and Jim could not help wondering if that *were* [More usual: *was*] a sign that some of the rest of them would be discharged, too.— ERSKINE CALDWELL, *Kneel to the Rising Sun*, p. 129

(See *as if, as though, and *Conditions.)

In all of these constructions a speaker or writer has a choice between the "subjunctive" and a regular form of the verb (which may be an "auxiliary") or an infinitive. Charles C. Fries found that in both Standard and Nonstandard English the subjunctive was used rather seldom, in considerably less than one fifth of the locutions in which it might be. Actually "subjunctives" are a trait of style rather than of grammar and are used by writers, consciously or unconsciously, to set their language a little apart from everyday usage rather than for basic meaning. The school insistence on the *were* form has even led to its use in statements of fact. (Reference: William M. Ryan, "Pseudo-Subjunctive 'Were,' " *American Speech*, 1961, 36:48-53, and 1962, 37:114-122.)

Students in foreign language courses should remember that very few French, Latin, and German subjunctives can be satisfactorily translated by an English subjunctive. They should try to find the natural idiomatic way of expressing the idea that is idiomatically expressed by the subjunctive in the language they are translating.

(References: The point of view presented in this article will be found in general in Fowler, article "Subjunctives"; Fries, *AEG*, pp. 103-107; Hall, pp. 311-314; Jespersen, Ch. 27; Marckwardt and Walcott, pp. 30, 37, 88, 89; Pooley, pp. 55-59; Thyra J. Bevier, "American Use of the Subjunctive," *American Speech*, 1931, 6:207-215. A different point of view will be found in Curme, *Syntax*, Ch. 20; C. A. Lloyd, "Is the Subjunctive Dying?" *The English Journal*, 1937, 26:369-373; Charles D. Cannon, "The Subjunctive Mood in English," *American Speech*, 1959, 34:11-19.)

**Submitting manuscript** • The conventions for submitting a manuscript for publication depend a good deal on its destination. Increasingly, publishers specify in style sheets how the material should be submitted.

In general the manuscript should be carefully typed, double spaced, on good paper (see *Typewritten copy). Generous margins should be left for editorial operations. Plenty of space, half a page or so, should be left around the title. A carbon copy should be kept for reference.

The writer's name and address may be put in the upper left-hand corner of the first page. The approximate length in words may be put in the upper right-hand corner. Additional facts, such as an account of sources of material or suggestions for illustrations, may be given in an accompanying letter.

Mail in a roomy envelope. Photographs or drawings should be clearly labeled and carefully packed between stiff cardboard.

Enclose an envelope large enough to hold the manuscript as it is folded, addressed to yourself, and carrying sufficient postage for its return.

**Subordinate clauses** • See *Clauses, *Commas § 2.

**Subordinating conjunctions** • The most common subordinating conjunctions—words that connect subordinate clauses with the main clauses of sentences—are:

| | | | |
|---|---|---|---|
| after | *because | since | unless |
| *although | before | *so | *when |
| *as | how | *so that | *where |
| *as if | *if | though | *while |
| as long as | in order that | *till | why |

The relative pronouns (*who, which, that, what*) function also as subordinating conjunctions. (See also *for.)

**Subordination** •
*Revision: Correct the faulty subordination.*

*Sub*

Subordinate sentence elements may be single words, phrases, or clauses that expand other elements in the sentence; but the term "faulty subordination" applies specifically to the handling of dependent clauses. Dependent clauses are introduced by the connectives listed in *subordinating conjunctions or by relative pronouns. The clauses are used in the grammatical functions of nouns, adjectives, and adverbs. Three types of faulty subordination are commonly distinguished:

**1.** "Tandem" or excessive subordination is the piling up of one dependent clause after another, each modifying an element in the preceding clause. The weakness is in style, not grammar:

*Tandem:* For his teachers, he had carefully selected those who taught classes that had a slant that was specifically directed toward students who intended to go into business.

*Revised:* For his teachers, he had carefully selected those who slanted their courses toward students intending to go into business [or: *toward future businessmen*].

**2.** "Thwarted" subordination occurs when *and* or *but* is added to a dependent clause that is already connected with the independent clause by its subordinating conjunction or relative pronoun. It is a grammatical lapse most commonly found in the form of *and which* and *but which* (see *which § 4):

*Thwarted:* In the first semester of the course we used three textbooks, and which were continued for the second semester.

*Revised:* In the first semester of the course we used three textbooks, which were continued for the second semester.

(Compare the appropriate use of a coordinating conjunction to join two dependent clauses that are parallel: "Tolerance is a virtue [which] all of us praise but [which] few of us practice.")

**3.** "Upside-down" or inverted subordination is not a blunder in style or in grammar but a failure to use subordination in such a way as to make the relationship between statements sensible and logical. It is therefore harder to discuss in isolated sentences, for often it is only the context that determines when subordination is "upside-down." In one writing situation, "Pearl Harbor was attacked when Roosevelt was President" would be satisfactory; in another, "When Pearl Harbor was attacked, Roosevelt was President" might be much better. Without a context, we cannot make a choice as to which statement should be put in the independent clause and which in the dependent clause. But the nature of the statements may make the choice apparent. It is hard to think of a context in which this sentence would not sound odd or absurd: "When I was in class, President Kennedy was assassinated." The relationship of dependent to independent clause needs to be changed; the revision might be "I was in class when the news of President Kennedy's assassination reached the campus." Ordinarily, upside-down subordination is corrected by simply turning the dependent clause into an independent clause and vice versa, but as this example shows, some rewriting will often produce better results than mechanically reversing the clauses. (See *Coordination.)

**Substantive** • *Substantive* is a term that includes nouns and pronouns and other words or groups of words used in the functions of a noun.

**such** • As an *intensive, such* is somewhat Informal (It was such a hot day; such energetic people). In Formal and most General writing the construction would usually be completed by a *that* or an *as* clause (It was *such* a hot day *that* the tar melted; I have never seen *such* energetic people *as* they are). (Reference: Russell Thomas, "*Such* as an Intensive," *College English,* 1954, 15:236-238; Bryant, pp. 199-201.)

Idiomatic constructions with *such* are:

There was such a crowd *that* [not: *so that*] we couldn't even get to the door.

The invitation is extended to such nonmembers *as* are interested. [*As* here is a relative pronoun. The General construction would be: *The invitation is extended to all nonmembers who are interested.*]

A good lecturer? There's no such thing. [*No such a thing* is questionable.]

The following constructions with *such* are possible but not very common and seem somewhat stiff:

His condition was such that he could not be moved. [More usual: *His condition would not allow him to be moved.*]

Psychologists could probably find various reasons why it is regarded as such. [. . . why it is so regarded.]

**such as** • As a coordinating conjunction, introducing examples, *such as* has a comma before but not after:

He was interested in all sorts of outlandish subjects, such as palmistry, numerology, and phrenology.

(See *such, *namely and other introductory words.)

**such . . . that** • See *such, *Result.

**Suffix** • An element that can be placed after a word or root to make a new word of different meaning or function is called a *suffix*: *-ize* (*criticize*), *-ish* (*foolish*), *-ful* (*playful*), *-th* (*warmth*). (See *Adjectives, types and forms § 1; *-ce, -ge; *Origin of words § 3a.)

**Suggestion** • Making use of the associations, the connotations of words, is called *suggestion.* The words *liberty, immemorial, mystical, butcher, homey,* and thousands of others have acquired associations from their past use that may call to a listener's or reader's mind some feeling or attitude that goes beyond their original core of meaning. Relying on suggestion to substitute for statement is risky as well as lazy, for there is no guarantee the reader will make the association the writer intends; but a responsible use of suggestion can add richness and depth without sacrificing accuracy.

**Sunday school** • Capitalize only the *Sunday* except in names of particular Sunday schools:

Sunday school　　　　　　　the Methodist Sunday School

**Superlative degree** • See *Comparison of adjectives and adverbs § 2.

**sure** • *Sure* in Standard written English is primarily an adjective (sure footing; as sure as fate; Are you sure?). As an adverb, *sure* instead of *surely*—equivalent to *certainly* or *yes*—is Informal (Sure, I'm coming; That's sure fine of you) and would not ordinarily be written.

**swim** • The principal parts are *swim, swam* or rarely *swum, swum. He swam half a mile* is the written form rather than *He swum half a mile.*

**Syllabication** • See *Division of words, *Monosyllables.

**Syllogism** • See *Logic.

**Syntax** • *Syntax* means the relationship between the words or word groups in a sentence. (Many articles in this book discuss points of syntax, as, for example, *Adjectives in use, *Style § 2d, *Subject and verb, *Verbs § 3, *Word order.)

**T** • /t/ as in *type, quote, attach, Thomas.*
　*-ed* is pronounced /t/ after the sound /f/, /k/, /p/, or /s/ in the same syllable: *laughed, fixed, confessed, tipped, picked*; *t* is silent in *Christmas, listen, thistle, mortgage, mustn't,* and many other words, and in ordinary speech it is absorbed by the *d* in word groups like sit down /si doun′/; *ti* is pronounced /ch/ in such words as *question,* and /sh/ in such words as *nation, notion.*
　The *t* sound /t/ is produced exactly like the *d* sound /d/ except that the vocal cords do not sound; /t/ is called a voiceless consonant. (Compare *D.) Double *t* usually is pronounced like single *t*: *latter, later.* In much of the United States *t* (and *tt*) between vowels is voiced and not clearly distinguishable from *d*: compare the pronunciations of *writer* and *rider* by

those in your community. (Reference: Donald J. Sharf, "Distinctiveness of 'Voiced T' Words," *American Speech*, 1960, 35: 105-109.)

**taboo—tabu** • *Taboo* /tə bü′/ is more generally used than *tabu*, except in anthropology. The plural is *taboos*; the past tense of the verb, *tabooed*.

**Taboo in language** • A number of words not used in certain circles—many of them not even appearing in dictionaries—are said to be *tabooed*. Communication in the subjects to which they belong is often carried on by accepted substitutes. (See *Euphemisms, *Obscenity. References: Jespersen, *Language,* p. 239; Edwin R. Hunter and E. Gaines, "Verbal Taboo in a College Community," *American Speech*, 1938, 13:97-107.)

**Tabulations** • Series of facts can often be more clearly presented in a table systematically arranged in convenient and meaningful columns. (See examples of tabulations in *Tenses of verbs § 2.)

Occasionally in the body of a paper it is convenient to arrange a series of parallel statements in a numbered tabulated form. The device should not be overworked, but it is a good way of securing emphasis by display:

The English textbook of the future, to sum up, must recognize the social nature of language, and English in particular, by

1. acknowledging that language is the tool of the social group,

2. granting that utility is the only valid basis for the creation or perpetuity of a language form,

3. pointing out the part each individual speaker plays in the retardation or acceleration of change,

4. regarding the written language in its proper light as the secondary and partial representation of the real language.—ROBERT C. POOLEY, *Grammar and Usage in Textbooks on English,* p. 151

(Reference: University of Chicago Press, *Manual of Style,* pp. 158-172.)

**talk** • See *say.

**Tandem subordination** • See *Subordination § 1.

**teach—learn** • See *learn—teach.

**technic** • *Technic* /tek′nik/ is a variant form of *technique.* It is also used, especially in the plural (*technics*), for *technology.*

**Technical writing** • See *Scientific and technical writing.

**Telegraphic style** • "Telegraphic style" refers to writing in which many *function words (especially articles and connectives) are omitted. It suggests also compact constructions and vigorous words. It is not appropriate in ordinary writing but is used in some reference works to save space and in newspaper headlines for vigor: *Gang Flees Cops; Find Loot—Ditch Guns, Stolen Cash Near River.* (Compare *Staccato style.)

**Tenses of verbs** •

*Tense*

*Revision: Make the tense of this verb conventional in form (§ 2) or consistent with others in the passage (§ 4 and 5).*

**1.** *Tense and time.* In grammar a tense is a distinctive form or phrase of a verb (*ask, asked, have asked*). The traditional names of the tenses are mainly words indicating time (*past, present, future*); it is therefore assumed that the function of tense is to show time and that the time shown is that suggested by the name of the tense. Both assumptions are only partly true. In *He was here, He is here,* and *He will be here,* the tenses of *be* are respectively past, present, future; the times indicated are also past, present, and future; and the function of the verb is primarily to show time. But in *When did you say you were going home?* only one tense, the past, is used; but two times, past and future, are indicated. And in *Art is long but life is fleeting,* though the tense is present, the time is of little consequence. (In the Latin form of the aphorism no verb is used—*Ars longa, vita brevis.*)

In English most sentences require a *finite verb, and the verb necessarily occurs in a tense form. But the indication of time in the sentence may be supplied by an adverb, or the adverb may modify the time suggested by the verb. In *He plays well,* the verb, despite its present tense form, does not declare that his playing is good only at the present moment; we infer, rather, that it is good at all times. But in *He plays tomorrow* the adverb restricts the time to the future, though the tense is still present. In *I've got two letters from him already, I've got time now,* and *I've got two exams tomorrow,* the tense is the same—perfect—but the times are respectively past, present, and future.

The tense names in English should be considered, then, as convenient but rather arbitrary terms used to identify verb forms and phrases, the actual function of the verb in each sentence being finally determined by other elements in the construction.

**2.** *Tense forms.* It is customary to distinguish six tenses in English, corresponding in name to the six in Latin. Of these only the present and the past can be single words (*ask, asked*). Like the other four tenses, they also occur as phrases (*is asking, was asking,* progressive; *does ask, did ask,* emphatic). The following table presents forms most commonly associated with time distinctions along with their traditional names:

| | | ACTIVE | PASSIVE |
|---|---|---|---|
| PRESENT TENSE | | he asks | he is asked |
| | | he is asking | he is being |
| | | he does ask | asked |
| PAST TENSES | *Past perfect* (Past of some time in the past) | he had asked | he had been |
| | | he had been asking | asked |
| | *Past* (A time in the past not extending to the present) | he asked | he was asked |
| | | he was asking | he was being |
| | | he did ask | asked |
| | *Perfect* (Past, extending to the present) | he has asked | he has been |
| | | he has been asking | asked |
| FUTURE TENSES | *Future* (Future, extending from the present) | he will ask | he will be |
| | | he will be asking | asked |
| | | he is going to ask | |
| | *Future perfect* (Past from some future time) | he will have asked | he will have been asked |
| | | he will have been asking | |

"Strong verbs" show a change of vowel in the past tense instead of the *-ed* ending (*he begins, he began; he rides, he rode*) and also in the past participle, often with the ending *-en* (*he has begun; he has ridden*). (See *Principal parts of verbs. References: Curme, *Parts of Speech,* pp. 241-333; Fries, *AEG,* pp. 59-71, 128-198; Mencken, pp. 235-247, 525-542; Jespersen, Chs. 23-26; Leah Dennis, "The Progressive Tense: Frequency of Its Use in English," *PMLA,* 1940, 55:855-865.)

**3.** *Special tense functions.*

*a*–The "progressive phrases" (*is asking, was asking, has been asking* . . .) tend to emphasize the actual activity and are increasingly being used in English.

*b*–The present tense is used to make a statement that is generally true, without reference to time:

Oil *floats* on water.

The Captain reminded the ladies that the equator *is* an imaginary line.

*c*–Participles and infinitives express time in relation to that of the main verb. The present infinitive expresses the same time as the main verb or, often with an adverb, a time in the future:

Our team is playing *to win*.     I hope *to go abroad* next summer.

A perfect infinitive expresses action prior to that of the main verb:

I am sorry *to have disappointed* you.

A present participle generally refers to the time of the main verb:

*Rounding* a turn in the road, he came suddenly in full view of the lake.

*d*–The present tense with an adverb may show future time: *He leaves tomorrow.*

4. *Sequence of tenses.* When the verb of a main clause is in the past or past perfect tense, the verb in a dependent clause is also past:

Frank knew that the Statlers were visiting us.

Frank knew that the Statlers would visit us the following week.

The old man wondered whether the train had arrived.

I have never seen Slim when he *hadn't* [or: *didn't have*; not *hasn't*] a wad of tobacco in his mouth.

A present infinitive is, however, usual after a past verb:

I thought you would have liked *to ride* [not: *to have ridden*] in their car.

They intended *to stop* [not: *to have stopped*] only an hour in the village.

The perfect infinitive is used chiefly to indicate action previous to the time of the main verb: *She is sorry to have started the gossip.*

5. *Consistent use of tenses.* It confuses a reader to find tenses shifted without definite reason, as in this paragraph:

I *sit* down at my desk early with intentions of spending the next four hours studying. Before many minutes *passed,* I *hear* a great deal of noise down on the floor below me; a water fight *is* in progress. Study *was forgotten* for half an hour, for it *was* quite impossible to concentrate on Spanish in the midst of all this commotion. After things *quiet* down I *begin* studying again, but I *have* hardly *started* when a magazine salesman *comes* into the room, hoping to snare a large sale. After arguing with him for several minutes I finally *got* rid of him.

Shifts of this sort should be carefully avoided.

In single sentences the inconsistency usually comes from carelessness, especially from forgetting the form of the first of two parallel verbs:

Last fall in the Brown game I saw Bill Geyer hit so hard that he was knocked five feet in the air and then *land* [for *landed*] on his head. [The writer forgot the tense of *was knocked*.]

(Reference: Curme, *Syntax*, Ch. 18.)

**textbook** • Now usually written as one word, it is often shortened simply to *text*.

**th** • *Th* spells a single voiceless sound /th/ as in *path* /path/, *think* /thingk/, and a single voiced sound /ᴛʜ/ as in *paths* /paᴛʜz/, *the* /ᴛʜə, ᴛʜi, ᴛʜē/, *bathe* /bāᴛʜ/. *Th* is silent in *isthmus* and pronounced /t/ in *Thomas*, *Thames*, and *thyme*. (See \*ye=the.) In some proper names the older *t* sound /t/ has been partly or completely replaced by /th/ on the basis of the spelling: *Theodore* and *Arthur*—always /th/ (but *Ted* and *Art*); *Anthony*—/th/ and /t/ (but *Tony*).

**than** •
1. *Conjunction. Than* as a conjunction introduces the second member of a comparison in which one thing or situation is greater than the other:

Their house was bigger than ours.
Nobody was more aware of the need for action than he was.

*Than* is the idiom after *no sooner*:

He had no sooner opened the door than the flames flared up.

(For other idioms, see \*Comparison of adjectives and adverbs.)
2. *Preposition. Than* is often a preposition. Since the clause with *than* is usually verbless (*than he, than I*), *than* here seems to be a preposition rather than a conjunction and frequently in Informal usage, especially in speech, is followed by an accusative:

*Formal and General*: You are certainly faster than I.
*Informal*: You are certainly faster than him.

In the Formal *than whom, than* functions as a preposition:

We admire the power of Jack Kramer, than whom there is no greater tennis player.

(References: Jespersen, p. 133; Pooley, pp. 166-170.)

**3.** *Confusion with "then."* *Then* is often carelessly written for *than.* (See \*then—than.)

(See \*different. Reference: Dwight L. Bolinger, "Analogical Correlatives of 'Than,'" *American Speech,* 1946, 21:199-202.)

**that** •

**1.** *Conjunction.*

*a–That* should usually be repeated with each of a series of parallel dependent clauses:

Rejecting scientific fatalism, he is convinced that society is not a machine or a biological organism, that the person exists apart from his actuarial status, that he has opportunities to make decisions, that artists and intellectuals influence even mass culture, that behaviorists have not accurately denoted the terms of our lives.—WYLIE SYPHER, "The Uses of Yes and No," *Book Week,* Feb. 6, 1966, p. 15

*b–That* should not be repeated within a single clause:

Many people seem to think that if an article is advertised by a joker they like or an athlete they admire [not: *that*] it is a good product to buy.

*That* is usually needed for clarity in the second of two parallel clauses:

I had hoped that the book would be finished by June and that it would be published by January [*that it* could be omitted, changing the clause-pattern of the sentence, but if *it* is kept, *that* should be kept too—not *and it would be*].

**2.** *Relative pronoun. That* refers to persons or things, *who* usually to persons, *which* usually to things:

The number of men *that* [or: *who*] fell within the age limits of the draft was 3,500,000.

He solved in five minutes a problem *that* [or: *which*] I had struggled with for five hours.

*Which* usually introduces clauses that are nonrestrictive; *that* more often introduces clauses that are restrictive but may also introduce nonrestrictive clauses:

The book *that she selected for her report* [restrictive] was the longest on the list.

The privilege of free speech, *which we hold so dear* [nonrestrictive], is now endangered. [*That* is also possible here.]

**3.** *Clauses without "that."* Clauses are often made without the introductory *that.* These constructions are not elliptical (for *that* is not "omitted" or to be "understood") but are a commonly used shorter idiom. They are Standard usage in both speech and writing:

He said he would go. [Or: He said that he would go.]
I remembered my mother's birthday fell on March 10. [Or: I remembered that my mother's birthday fell on March 10.]
The first man he met turned out to be Alexander. [Or: The first man that he met turned out to be Alexander.]

The *that* is necessary when the clause comes first (That one could be punished for such a thing had not occurred to him); in appositive clauses after such nouns as *wish, belief, desire* (My hope that he would finish today was not fulfilled); and with anticipatory *it* (It is not true that I promised to pay the whole sum at once), though in short constructions, especially in speech, it is not needed (It isn't true he likes me better than he does you). (See *Contact clauses. References: Curme, *Syntax,* index references; Jespersen, pp. 350-351.)

**4. *That which.*** *That which* is Formal and rather archaic for *what:*

He had no clear idea of *what* [not: *that which*] he was trying to say.

**5. *Referring to an idea.*** *That* (or *this*) is used to refer to the whole idea of a preceding statement when the reference is clear:

While I was studying, he sometimes turned on the radio. That was annoying, but I didn't object.

If the *that* refers to an idea suggested but not contained in a particular word, the sentence should be revised to make the reference clear:

*Vague reference:* My uncle is a doctor, and that is the profession I intend to enter.

*Exact:* My uncle's profession is medicine and that is going to be mine too.

(Reference: Bryant, pp. 172-174.)

**6. *"That" as an adverb.*** Adverbial *that* is General English in such constructions as *I didn't go that far.* It is sometimes used in constructions like *I'm that hungry I could eat shoe leather,* but *so* would be more common.

**7. *Demonstrative pronoun and adjective:***

I like that.     I like that book.

In this function *that* has a plural, *those.* The use of *them* as the adjective plural is Nonstandard (them books).

**8. *That there chair*** is Nonstandard, though *that chair over there* is Standard in speech, about the only way it could occur. (Reference: Bryant, pp. 213-214.)

**that, so . . . that, such . . . that •** See *Result.

**that is** • *That is* introduces a statement the equivalent of, or the explanation of, what precedes. It is a Formal connective and is best kept to introduce series or complete statements. In such a use it is usually preceded by a semicolon and followed by a comma:

The men worked continuously for three whole weeks to complete the dam on time; that is, they worked twenty-four hours a day in three shifts, seven days a week.

In briefer constructions a comma would be more usual, and the *that is* would not be used:

*Formal*: They used the safest explosive for the purpose, that is, dynamite.

*General*: They used the safest explosive for the purpose, dynamite.

(Compare *namely and other introductory words.)

**the** •
1. Repetition of the article before the various nouns of a series emphasizes their distinctness:

The color, *the* fragrance, and *the* beautiful patterns of these flowers make them universal favorites.

The color, fragrance, and pattern of these flowers are distinctive.

2. In the idiom *the . . . the,* the second *the* is a survival of the Old English instrumental case form of *the* and functions adverbially.

Usage is divided over the punctuation. In Formal writing a comma is frequently used between the phrases, in General usage not:

*General*: The greater one's economic insecurity the greater the tendency to sacrifice spiritual independence.—STUART CHASE, "The Luxury of Integrity," *The Nemesis of American Business*

*Formal*: The greater one's economic insecurity, the greater the tendency to sacrifice spiritual independence.

3. Sometimes a possessive pronoun is used where *the* would be more idiomatic:

We stopped to see *the* [rather than *our*] first unusual sight.

4. Keep *the* with the name of our country: *the United States*.
5. *The* is given minimum stress in speech, with the pronunciation /ᴛʜə/ before consonants, /ᴛʜi/ before vowels. In rare instances where *the* has demonstrative force and is emphasized, it is pronounced /ᴛʜē/:

He is *the* man for the job.

**theater, theatre** • Both spellings are used, the second especially in names established some time ago. (See *-er, -re.)

**their •** *Their* is the genitive of *they. Theirs* is the emphatic or absolute form: *This table is exactly like theirs.*

Informally *their* is often used to refer to the collective indefinite pronouns (*anybody, anyone, everybody, everyone*), though these are singular in form:

*Informal and sometimes General*: Everybody finally found their hats and coats.

*General and Formal*: Everybody finally found his hat and coat.

(See *every and its compounds.)

**them •** *Them* as a demonstrative is Nonstandard: *These, those books* (not *them books*). (Reference: Bryant, p. 215.)

**then •** *Then* is an adverb of time, frequently used as a connective (conjunctive adverb). Often the connection between clauses is made closer by using *and* with the *then*:

The next three hours we spent in sightseeing; *then* we settled down to the business of being delegates to a convention.

He ate a good meal, *and then* he took a nap before starting home again.

**then—than •** *Then* is an adverb of time, *than* a conjunction in clauses of comparison:

*Then* the whole crowd went to Louie's.

I think *The Big Sky* was better *than* any other novel I read last year.

Although etymologically *then* and *than* come from the same source, they must now be carefully distinguished in writing.

**then too •** *Then too* is overused as a connective in amateur writing:

A reader enjoys a fast moving story; then too he may enjoy something that will set him thinking.

[Better:] A reader enjoys a fast moving story, but he may also enjoy something that will set him thinking.

*Then too* is an especially mechanical connective when used between paragraphs.

**there is, there are •**
**1.** *There* is a lesser, preparatory, or anticipatory subject, used with the real subject following the verb. *There is* is usually followed by a singular subject (though often, especially in speech, by a plural), *there are* by a plural:

There is a size for every need.

There are several ways in which this can be done.

A singular verb (there *is*, there *was*) followed by a plural subject is common, and the choice between a singular or plural verb is pretty much a matter of taste when the first element of the compound subject is singular:

> There is too much starch and fat in the food we eat.
> There was both affection and pride in her message.

(References: Fries, *AEG*, p. 56; David S. Berkeley, "Agreement of Subject and Verb in Anticipatory Clauses," *American Speech*, 1953, 28:92-96; Robert J. Geist, "Current English Forum," *College English*, 1952, 14:115-116; 1954, 16:188-189.)
2. Frequent use of these impersonal constructions results in a loss of emphasis:

> There was a vague feeling of discontent evident in everyone's manner.
> *Direct*: A vague feeling of discontent was evident in everyone's manner.
> There are a good many college students who are easily discouraged.
> *Direct*: A good many college students are easily discouraged.

(See *it.)

**therefore** • The conjunctive adverb *therefore* is a rather heavy connective. It should be—but is often not—used sparingly in ordinary writing:

> *Formal*: My experiences in preparatory school had been very unpleasant; therefore I was surprised to find college students and college teachers so agreeable.
> *General*: My experiences in preparatory school had been so unpleasant that I was surprised to find college students and college teachers so agreeable.

**therein** • *Therein* is archaic or Formal for *in it, in that respect.*

**they** • *They* is often used as a pronoun of indefinite reference (They say...); though it occurs in all varieties of English, a more compact construction is usually preferable in writing:

> They have had no serious accidents at the crossing for over two years. [More compact: *There have been no serious accidents....*]

(Reference: Bryant, pp. 211-212.)

**thing** • *Thing* is often *deadwood in writing:

> The other thing that I have in mind is going to France.
> *Improved*: I am also thinking of going to France.
> The first thing you do is to get a few small twigs burning.
> *Improved*: First you get a few small twigs burning.

An even more superfluous expression is: *The thing of it is that* . . . .

**this •**
1. *This,* like *that,* is regularly used to refer to the idea of a preceding clause or sentence:

He had always had his own way at home, and this made him a poor roommate.

The company trains its salesmen in its own school. *This* [More Formally: *This practice*] assures it a group of men with the same sales methods.

(Reference: Paul Roberts, "Pronominal 'This': A Quantitative Analysis," *American Speech,* 1952, 27:171-178; Bryant, pp. 172-174.)
2. *This* is used Informally as a sort of intensified definite article: *This old man went into this restaurant.* Such a use is ordinarily out of place in writing.
3. *This here chair* is Nonstandard, though *this chair over here* is Standard in speech, about the only way it could occur. (Reference: Bryant, p. 213.)

**thou •** *Thou, thy, thine, thee* are archaic pronouns for the second person, now used in Standard English only in the Formal language of church services. Amateur poets should avoid them except in archaic contexts. Although they correspond grammatically to the second person pronouns of various European languages, and as late as the seventeenth century had much the same force that the pronoun now has in those languages, they preserve none of that connotative force and should not ordinarily be used in making translations.

**though •** Colloquially *though* is used as a word of qualification or hesitation: "I didn't think he would do it, though." This use is less common in writing. If used, *though* would normally be set off by a comma or commas.

(For use as a conjunction see *although, though.)

**Thwarted subordination •** See *Subordination § 2.

**Tilde •** The *tilde* is a mark (∼) placed over a letter, as in the Spanish *cañon,* represented in English by *ny* (*canyon*).

**till, until, 'til •** These three words are not different in meaning. Since *'til* in speech sounds the same as *till* and looks slightly odd on paper, it is rarely used now. Use *till* or *until* according to the stress or the feel of the phrase you want.

*Until* is most often used at the beginning of sentences or clauses:

Until he went to college, he never had thought of his speech.

He had never thought of his speech *till* [or: *until*] he went to college.

**Time** • In subordinate clauses the various time relationships are indicated by the conjunctions *after, *as, as long as, as often as, as soon as, before, since, *till, until, when, whenever, *while.* (See also *Tenses of verbs, *Centuries, *Dates, *Hours.)

**Titles of articles, books, etc.** •
1. *Formal usage.* In most college writing, in most books, and in some periodicals, the titles of books and the names of magazines and newspapers are put in italics (indicated in manuscript by underlining). Capitals are used for the first word, for all nouns, pronouns, verbs, adjectives, and adverbs, and for prepositions that stand last or that contain more than five letters:

| | |
|---|---|
| *No Place to Hide* | *You Can't Take It with You* |
| *Wit and Its Relation to the Unconscious* | *Parts of Speech and Accidence* |
| *The New Yorker* | *The Kansas City Star* |

Often the *the* of magazine and newspaper titles is not regarded as a part of the title and so is not capitalized. In some periodicals the name of the city in a newspaper name is not italicized (the Milwaukee *Sentinel*). Usage is divided on this point. If the name of the city is not part of the name of the newspaper, it would not, of course, be italicized: the London *Times*.

If the official title of a work does not follow these conventions, references to it may use the exact title or standardize it (as, *The Story of a Novel,* which was printed as *the story of a NOVEL*). Library catalogs and some long bibliographies do not use italics and capitalize only first words and proper nouns or adjectives.

Titles of short stories and magazine articles are put in quotation marks when they are used with or near titles of books or names of periodicals. They are often italicized when used without reference to their means of publication, especially in discussion of them as works of literature. Usage is divided on the titles of poems, but academic writing tends to use italics for the titles of separately published poems. In less formal style, the titles of short poems are quoted.

The words *Preface* and *Introduction* are not italicized or quoted, but chapter titles are put in quotation marks. (See

*Chapters, *Quotation marks § 3a. Reference: University of Chicago Press *Manual of Style,* index references.)

**2.** *Informal usage.* In many magazines (*The New Republic, The Saturday Evening Post,* for example) and in most newspapers, titles of books and names of periodicals are treated as proper names, capitalized but not quoted or italicized.

In Formal papers for college courses and in theses Formal usage should be followed; in other college papers either style may be used, as the instructor prefers.

**3.** *Typed copy.* In typed copy that is not going to be printed it is simpler to write titles all in capitals (to save backing up and underlining). This is the common form in publishers' letters. (See *References.)

**Titles of persons** • *The New York Times Style Book* recommends using *Mr., Mrs.,* or *Miss* for persons of every nationality unless a special title seems called for. (See *Abbreviation § 2, *Mr., *Mrs., *Professor, *Reverend. For fuller accounts see the "Forms of Address" sections in *Webster's Seventh New Collegiate Dictionary* and *Webster's New World Dictionary.*)

**Titles of papers** • Since titles help stir the reader's interest, a striking and easily remembered title is an advantage. But strained titles are often ludicrous, and if no good title comes to mind, it is better just to name the subject of the paper as exactly as possible in a few words and let it go at that. As a rule, titles that give no clue to the subject, such as *The Moving Finger Writes* or *The Greeks Had a Name for It,* are better avoided. Don't postpone writing a paper (or handing one in) to hunt for a clever title. In published work the title is often made by the editor rather than by the writer.

The title is considered a separate part of the paper, and the first sentence should not refer to it by a pronoun. Leave a blank line between the title and the beginning of the text.

**to** •

**1.** The confusion of *to* and *too* in writing is conspicuously careless and one of the small matters to be watched in revision of papers.

**2.** It is generally understood that in expressions like *pages 56 to 89* the last numbered unit is included. Hours are an exception, as in *1 to 3 p.m. Up to* or *till* excludes the last unit.

**today** •

**1.** *Today* (like *tonight* and *tomorrow*) is rarely hyphened.

**2.** *Today, of today* are often *deadwood, adding nothing to the meaning of a statement already placed in the present:

Economic conditions [of today] are more unsettled than they have been for two generations.

**too** • When *too* in the sense of *also* comes within a construction, it is usually set off by commas, but in Informal writing it usually is not when it comes at the end:

"I, too, have become a philosopher," she said sadly.—IRWIN EDMAN, *Philosopher's Holiday*, p. 74

I'm going too. [More Formal: I'm going, too.]

**toward—towards** • These words are identical in meaning, and the choice of one or the other is a matter of taste. The first is the more frequent. (Reference: Bryant, p. 220.)

**Transition** •

*Trans*     *Revision: Make the transition between these sentences (or paragraphs) clear and smooth.*

Amateur writing frequently suffers from a lack of transitions —words or phrases or sentences that show the relation between one statement and another, one paragraph and another, one part of the paper and another. When a sentence or paragraph stands as an isolated unit (as if nothing had preceded it and nothing was to follow it), the reader is bound to be puzzled about its relevance. A lack of transition between one paragraph and another is sometimes a sign of faulty organization, sometimes simply neglect on the part of the writer to provide a signpost that will show the reader where he has been or where he is going. A lack of transition between sentences usually indicates that the writer has not thought through carefully the relationship between consecutive statements.

The most familiar of the transitions that indicate relationships and knit a piece of prose together are connectives and adverbs—*and, but, still, yet, for, because, then, though, while, in order that, first, second, however, moreover, therefore, for example.* Choosing the right one for the relationship to be expressed is rarely a problem, once the need for a transition is recognized; but overuse of the heavier connectives (*however, nevertheless, consequently*) can weigh down the style and make it sound artificial and contrived. Less obtrusive transitions can be made by repeating a key word from sentence to sentence, by using a synonym or a pronoun to echo or pick up the key word, and by binding sentences or parts of sentences together through parallel structures. Whether the transitions are overt or subtle, they are the chief means of making a piece of writing coherent. (See *Coherence.)

**Transitive and intransitive verbs** • These are syntactical terms borrowed from Latin grammar to describe whether a verb does or does not take an object in a particular construction. Because a verb which takes an object can usually be put into a passive construction (He was given a book) and one that does not cannot (He slept calmly), it might be assumed that all transitive verbs can be passive and no intransitive ones can. But *It cost a dollar* can't be made passive nor *Her clothes became her.* And verbs like *laugh, look, sleep,* intransitives when used alone, occur in passive constructions: *He was laughed at. She was looked at. The bed was slept in.* A verb is transitive when it is used with an object to complete its meaning: *They fought the whole gang. He was given a book.* A verb is intransitive when it does not have an object: *The choir will sing. The hymn was sung by the choir. They hid in the tall grass.* Many verbs are used in both constructions, often with different meanings: *He wrote two books* (transitive). *She cannot write* (intransitive). Dictionaries note whether a verb is typically used transitively or intransitively, and in what senses. *Lie* and *sit* are intransitive, *\*lay* and *\*set* are transitive. *Linking verbs (be, become, taste . . .)* are regarded as intransitive. (References: Curme, *Parts of Speech,* Ch. 4; Jespersen, *Modern English Grammar,* III:16.)

**Transpire** • Long objected to in the sense of *happen* or *occur* because of its etymology (*trans,* "across"; *spirare,* "breathe"), *transpire* is frequently used Informally to mean *happen* and is understood by many people in no other sense.

**Transpose** • A change in the order of sentences or paragraphs in copy can be shown by using numbers in the margin opposite the elements to be changed, or by circling the material to be shifted and drawing arrows.

The transposition of letters is shown by a curved line:

Conne⌐t⌐c⌐icut     rec⌐i⌐e⌐ve

**Triads** • Parallel series of three units are so common in writing, especially in Formal writing, that they form a definite trait of style. Such a series is called a triad:

> To delight in war is a merit in the soldier, a dangerous quality in the captain, and a positive crime in the statesman.—GEORGE SANTAYANA, *Reason in Society,* p. 84

> The Prince possessed a handsome, florid face, a splendid, if slightly plump, figure, and first-class legs, of which he was inordinately proud.—J. H. PLUMB, "An Oriental Palace for an English King," *Horizon,* Nov. 1962, p. 22

**Trite •**

Trite

*Revision: Replace the trite expression with one that is simpler and fresher.*

Trite words are usually worn out figures of speech or phrases: *the picture of health, the order of the day, reign supreme, from the face of the earth, crack of dawn, acid test.* What was once fresh and striking has become stale and hackneyed from being used again and again. This passage compresses a great number of such expressions into small space:

The Blushing Bride

I suppose it is natural that I should have been asked to step into the breach on this happy day, if only because I have had the privilege of knowing Geraldine since she was so high. . . . Onlookers see most of the game, you know, and it is easy to be wise after the event, but I thought I could see which way the wind was blowing last August.

They say marriages are made in Heaven, well, be that as it may, these two look as happy as the day is long. It was a great pleasure to me to see Hubert give away his one ewe lamb to such a regular chip off the old block as our friend here. Like father like son, they say, and I think his father deserves a pat on the back. As for Geraldine, bless her, she is a real Trojan, and has been a tower of strength to her dear mother, who doesn't look a day older than when I first set eyes on her, far longer ago than either of us cares to remember.

At moments like this, when family ties are stronger than ever, these young things should remember how much they owe to their parents.

One last word, I must not fail to remind Geraldine that the way to a man's heart is his stomach, and to warn Bertrand that the hand that rocks the cradle rules the world.

Now, I mustn't take up any more of your valuable time, I feel sure you will all join me in drinking the health of the happy couple, and wishing that all their troubles may be little ones.—GEORGINA COLERIDGE, *I Know What I Like,* p. 41

The author dedicates her book as follows:

Because I know which side my bread is buttered, this *magnum opus* is dedicated to my better half, the master of the house who wears the trousers, and who has proved conclusively that two heads are better than one.—p. 5

(See *Adjectives in use, *Figures of speech.)

**trousers, pants •** See *pants, trousers.

**Type •** Typography is a complex technical field, but many people make a hobby of it, and most writers have some curiosity about it. Here are a few of the fundamental facts:

1. *Type faces.* There are many different type faces, each with its characteristic appearance. They may differ in thickness of line in the letters, in length of ascenders and descenders (as in *h* or *y*), in wideness of letters, in serifs (thin or smaller lines used to finish off a main stroke of a letter, as at the top and bottom of *M*), and in other features. Every type face is made in many standard sizes and style variations. Some popular faces for book and periodical use are set here in 10 point size:

| | |
|---|---|
| This type face is Caslon. | This type face is Bodoni. |
| This type face is Garamond. | This type face is Granjon. |
| This type face is Times Roman. | |

This book is set in the following type faces and sizes:

The text is set in 10 point Baskerville Roman.

The quotations are set in 9 point Baskerville Roman.

The footnotes are set in 6 point Bulmer Roman.

**The entry words are set in 10 point Baskerville Roman bold.**

*The subheads are set in 10 point Baskerville italic.*

2. *Type style variations.* A given face and size of type is available in several standard variations of style:

| *Name and example* | *Abbreviation* | *Indicated in manuscript by:* |
|---|---|---|
| ROMAN CAPITALS | Caps. | Three lines underneath |
| roman lower case | l. c. | Unmarked manuscript |
| ROMAN SMALL CAPITALS | s. c. | Two lines underneath |
| *ITALIC CAPITALS* | Ital. Caps. | One line underneath and labeled "all caps" |
| *italic lower case* | ital. | One line underneath |
| **BOLD FACE CAPITALS** | b. f. caps | Wavy line underneath and labeled "all caps" |
| **bold face lower case** | b. f. | Wavy line underneath |

3. *Type measurement.* Type is measured in *points,* a point equaling .0138 or approximately 1/72 of an inch. A square unit of type of any size is an *em.* Space is usually measured in *pica* (12 point) *ems* (1/6 of an inch). Type ranges in size from 4 to 144 points, but the most generally used sizes are those from 6 to 72 points.

This line is set in 6 point type.

This line is set in 10 point type.

## This line is set in 14 point type.

(See *Proofreading. References: The University of Chicago Press *Manual of Style* contains much information about type, as do other stylebooks and books on journalism, advertising, and typography.)

**-type** • This is an overused suffix: *handsome-type man.* (Compare *-wise.*)

**type of** • The idiom *type of* is being shortened colloquially by omitting the *of*: *this type letter.* Although the construction is beginning to appear in print, General usage should still be followed: *this type of letter* (but not: this type of *a* letter). (Reference: Bryant, pp. 221-222.)

**Typewritten copy** • Manuscript for a printer, business letters and reports, and impersonal writing should be typed. Whenever possible, college papers should be typed. In the United States we are so accustomed to typescript (which is so much more legible than most handwriting) that it can be used in a good deal of personal correspondence. Since there is a convention that longhand shows added courtesy, *social correspondence should usually be handwritten.

In general, typewritten copy follows the customs of good manuscript, but some points need special emphasis. Use only one side of the sheet, leave wide margins (especially at the right side, since letters cannot be compressed as in longhand), keep type clean, and change ribbons regularly. Ordinarily use a black ribbon.

Regular manuscript should be double spaced. Personal writing may be single spaced, and for economy single space is generally used in business writing. If single spaced, the lines should be kept fairly short to make the reading easier. Full, crowded pages are forbidding reading. In typing first drafts, leave plenty of space for revision, perhaps using triple space between lines and extra space between paragraphs.

In single-spaced typing, use double space between paragraphs. For double-spaced typing, make a triple space between paragraphs only if you wish an open appearance or special emphasis on the paragraphs. Indent paragraph first lines from five to eight spaces.

Long quotations may be indicated in double spaced copy by indenting the number of spaces used for paragraphs and single spacing the quoted matter. No quotation marks are used with this style.

The standard typewriter keyboard has no symbol for the figure 1. Use the small *l* (not capital *I*). For a dash use two hyphens not spaced away from the words on each side. Leave a space after all other punctuation marks except at the end of sentences, where two should be used.

Transposed letters should be erased and retyped or corrected by the proofreader's symbol. (See *Transpose.*) Strikeovers are often hard to read. A few mistakes can be corrected in ink, but if there are so many that the page will look messy it should be retyped.

(To type ! and [ ], see *Exclamation mark, *Brackets. See also *Proofreading; some of the marks and symbols can be used to make corrections on typescript.)

# U •

1. There are two "long *u*" sounds: /ü/ as in *rule* /rül/, *blew* /blü/, *shoe* /shü/, *true* /trü/, *juice* /jüs/, *move* /müv/, *lose* /lüz/, *booby* /bü′bē/, *hoodoo* /hü′dü/; and /ū/, a diphthong beginning with a /y/ sound and ending with /ü/ as in *use* /ūs/ or /ūz/, also spelled as in *few, cute, beauty, you, hue, nuisance, neuter, view, yew, yule, ewe*.

After *t, d, n, s, st* usage is divided between these two sounds: *tune* /tūn, tün/, *duty* /dū′ti, dü′ti/, *news* /nūz, nüz/, *stew* /stū, stü/. In such words the /ü/ sound is frequent and is increasingly used by educated speakers in spite of widespread prejudice against it. (See Kenyon and Knott § 109 and their entries on particular words of this type.)

2. There are two "short *u*" sounds: /u/ as in *cup* /kup/, *fun* /fun/, *under* /un′dər/, *son* /sun/, *love* /luv/, *come* /kum/, *trouble* /trub′əl/, *does* /duz/, *other* /uᴛʜ′ər/, *blood* /blud/; and /ù/ as in *full* /fùl/, *pull* /pùl/, *wood* /wùd/, *woman* /wùm′ən/, *wolf* /wùlf/, *should* /shùd/.

3. *U* as in *burn* and *curl* is represented by ė /bėrn, kėrl/.

An unpronounced *u* is sometimes spelled after *g*, as in *guest*, usually in words from French to show the "hard" value of *g*.

The letter *u* is one form of a Latin letter of which the other form is *v*; only within the last few hundred years have the two been consistently differentiated in English.

**Umlaut** • In some German words, the vowels *a, o*, and *u* are *umlauted* (*ä, ö, ü*). On a typewriter the symbol can be made with the quotation mark. To omit it in German words is to misspell them; *ä, ü*, and *ö* are quite different from *a, o*, and *u*.

**Underlining** •
*Revision: In longhand and typewritten copy underline words and passages to correspond to the conventions of using italic type.*  *Und*

These conventions are of great importance in Formal manuscript and in material to be printed. Newspapers have generally abandoned italic type, but most magazines and books use it, and in academic writing—course papers, articles in the learned journals, monographs, dissertations, reference books—rather strict conventions are still followed.

Underlining is used:

1. *To indicate titles of books and periodicals.* The complete title should be underlined; usage is divided on whether the underscoring should be broken between words or whether it may be continuous:

I like <u>Barbary</u> <u>Shore</u> the best [<u>Barbary Shore</u>].
He took <u>Time</u> and <u>The</u> <u>Reader's</u> <u>Digest</u> [or: and <u>The Reader's Digest</u>].

(For details of this use see *Titles of articles, books, etc., and *References. Compare *Ships' names. Reference: The University of Chicago Press, *A Manual of Style,* pp. 46-54.)

2. *For emphasis.* Words that would be heavily stressed if spoken may be underlined:

He was <u>the</u> man that night.

Any word a writer wishes to emphasize may be underlined (italicized in print), but this is a rather mechanical form of emphasis and loses its force if overused. Whole sentences, except in textbooks and manuals, are better not underlined, since there are usually more intelligent ways of securing emphasis. As Fowler (p. 305) put it: "To italicize whole sentences or large parts of them as a guarantee that some portion of what one has written is really worth attending to is a miserable confession that the rest is negligible." (See *Emphasis § 7, *Schoolgirl style.)

3. *To mark words and locutions considered not for their meaning but as words.* This is a common use of underlining (italicizing) in this and all books on language:

If we take such a sentence as *I am hungry,* neither a grammarian nor a logician would have any difficulty in pointing out the predicate, though one would say that it was *am hungry* and the other that it was simply *hungry.*—P. B. BALLARD, *Thought and Language,* p. 88

4. *To mark foreign words.*

But good clothes were a *sine qua non.*

(See *Foreign words in English.)

**Understatement** • See *Negatives § 1.

**unique** • In strict Formal usage *unique* means "single, sole, unequaled," and consequently is not compared. In General usage, like so many other words of absolute meaning, it has become somewhat extended, and as an emphatic *rare,* it is sometimes found compared with *more* or *most:*

. . . the more unique his nature, the more peculiarly his own will be the colouring of his language.—OTTO JESPERSEN, *Mankind, Nation and Individual from a Linguistic Point of View,* p. 204

(See \*Comparison of adjectives and adverbs § 4.)

**United States** • We live in *the* United States. The temptation to drop *the* is greatest when *United States* is forced to do duty as an adjective: *Europe needs the money from United States imports.* In such a case it is better to use *American* or *imports of the United States.* (See \*American.)

**Unity** • Gross disregard of unity—including material that is quite unrelated to a paragraph or to a paper or that distracts from its main point—is exasperatingly apparent to a reader. Genuine unity is to be judged in the light of the writer's purpose. The test of unity is found not in any general principles that can be applied in every situation but in appropriateness to the writer's view of his material and his consistent carrying out of his purpose. Even so, the reader must always be considered; he cannot be expected to discern a unity that exists in the writer's mind but fails to show up in his paper.

**unquote** • Used orally, *unquote* indicates the end of a quotation, *quote* to begin it. Do not use it in writing.

**until, 'til, till** • See \*till, until, 'til.

**up** • *Up* is a member of many typical \*verb-adverb combinations in general use (*give up, grow up, sit up, use up*). Because they have developed meanings which are not the sum of the meanings of their parts, they are usually entered separately in dictionaries and they behave like independent verbs, including the possibility of being used as passives. *Up* is also an intensive in a number of other combinations to which it contributes no new element of meaning (*divide up, fill up, raise up, join up*). The latter usage is appropriate in General writing but is usually avoided in Formal.

**up to** • See \*to.

**Upside-down subordination** • See \*Subordination § 3.

**-us, -ous** • See \*-ous, -us.

**Usage** • The view presented in this book is that there are three emphases in the study of current English—on linguistics, on style, and on usage. The same materials are studied and the methods have much in common, but there are characteristic differences in the three emphases, particularly in purposes. *Linguists* are chiefly concerned with the objective observation and analysis of the language—primarily of the spoken language —in order to discover and describe its system or "structure." Students of *style* examine specific examples of language—in our culture especially of written literature—primarily to find the qualities of language that produce an effect on a listener or a reader. Students of *usage* observe specific items in the language —both spoken and written—primarily to ascertain their currency and appropriateness in speech and writing of various sorts.

Some would regard style and usage simply as divisions of linguistics, but while linguistics furnishes much of the data and methods of the other two, and will do so increasingly, style and usage involve some consideration of social attitudes and responses usually not the concern of linguistics. An analysis made by a linguist will usually be more detailed than a student of usage requires, and often more detailed even than a student of style needs. Though linguists recognize the importance of sensitivity to qualities of style and of judging the appropriateness of usage, they seldom consider these their primary concern and feel that preoccupation with such questions may interfere with their descriptive and analytical purpose. Although all people working with current English need a good deal of the same basic training, some division of labor, based on a recognition of the different purposes of the three emphases, will work not only for simplicity but for efficiency.

1. *The varying emphases of usage, style, and linguistics.* Though all three approaches start with the facts of usage, with ways in which the various units are actually used in the language, the emphasis of linguistics is on systematic description, of style on aesthetic judgment, and of usage on socially significant details. In the linguistic approach, the concern is with all the units, from the smallest to the largest, or at least all that seem to fit into a describable structure. In the stylistic approach, the concern is with the units which offer linguistic choices. And in the usage approach, the concern is with the units which have socially significant variants.

Linguistics deals with every detail of the sound system (see *Phonemes) of the language, of word forms, and of sentences. It does the best it can with the meanings of words. Since writing is a secondary and incomplete manifestation of language, linguistics gives it only incidental attention.

Stylistics is less concerned with word forms than with the choice of words and their arrangement in phrases and sentences. It is also concerned with the sounds of the language when they produce effects such as rhyme, *alliteration, onomatapoeia (see *Imitative words and phrases), etc.

Usage study investigates socially significant variations in the units of the language itself and in the transcription of it, units which may extend in size from the smallest to the largest. For variation in individual phonemes, see *A §5, 6, *T, *U, *wh; see also Kenyon and Knott, pp. xxxviii-xlv. In the pronunciation of individual words, there are hundreds of examples of *divided usage; some of the variants are Standard (see *Pronunciation § 4), some are not (*municipal* as /mū'ni si'pəl/, *piano* as/pī a'nə/, etc.). The same is true for word forms (see, for example, the past tense and past participial forms under *Principal parts of verbs; some of these variants are unlabeled, hence Standard, some are labeled *NS*, Nonstandard). Many English constructions, made up of words which in themselves are entirely acceptable in Standard, arrange those words in combinations which are Nonstandard: *We was, He don't have no time, being as, used to could,* etc. And Nonstandard uses a great many words in senses which are unacceptable in Standard. Sometimes the inappropriate usage results from confusion of words of similar sound—*formally, formerly; ingenious, ingenuous; notorious, notable; respectively, respectfully* (for extreme examples, see *Malapropisms). One of the functions of dictionary definitions is to discriminate Standard senses of words from Nonstandard ones. It is not surprising that two dictionaries sometimes report different findings.

Usage study is also much concerned with the conventions of writing. Correctness in spelling is entirely a matter of conforming to the prevailing usage in Standard printed material, and much the same is true for capitalization and punctuation. Many errors in writing exist solely because of failure to follow Standard usage in spelling, punctuation, and capitalization, as in the following sentence, where the numbered items deviate from Standard written (though not spoken) usage:

Mary and [1] jane were under the [2] allusion [3], that [4] there father had [5] dyed.

**2. *The study of usage.*** The study of usage helps us to decide what to say or write in a particular situation. Questions usually arise either from lack of knowledge of what people say or write in a particular variety of English or from uncertainty because of differing practices. Since we are usually less at home in writing than in speaking, the questions often relate to written usage.

The study of usage is based on an accumulation of specific instances and depends on wide observation of what people say and write in various situations to provide a basis for judging the standing of particular words, forms, and constructions. No one person can cover thoroughly this vast field, though he can amass a considerable body of data. Since many people make special studies of individual points and present them in articles—in *American Speech, College English, Word Study,* and other periodicals—a good deal of reliable information accumulates. Four important books on usage are worth studying for their method, data, and conclusions:

Albert H. Marckwardt and Fred G. Walcott in *Facts About Current English Usage* (1938) present not so much a record of actual usage as of attitudes toward it. They include the results of the Leonard questionnaire to editors, teachers, and businessmen asking their judgment of a number of proscribed items and add the record of scholarly studies of those items. They give recommendations based on this material.

C. C. Fries' *American English Grammar* (1940) presents systematically the language found in a large group of letters and considers it in relation to the education and social position of the writers. The study made clear that educated writers of Standard English show more variation in usage than was commonly thought.

George Summey's *American Punctuation* (revised 1949) discusses the practices in punctuation he discovered from studying a large body of printed material. Although he found considerable range, he reported practices that could be followed safely by individual writers.

Margaret M. Bryant's *Current American Usage* (1962) is the most recent reliable compilation of evidence on American usage. It contains about 240 entries and is based on hundreds of individual studies.

As a result of these and other usage studies we now have a more accurate picture of what educated users of English say and, more especially, write. Such studies, presenting not a "liberal" but simply a more accurate picture of the language in use, have done a good deal to limit the puristic tendencies of textbooks on grammar and usage.

But recording usage by itself is not enough, partly because there is variation in the matters that are likely to raise questions. Relative frequency of occurrence is an important fact, but it gives only the range of usage. Evaluation of the data and further study are needed. Dictionaries record what their files show on particular words and phrases and give "usage labels" for many, designating them as colloquial or slang or restricted to some occupation. Such books are useful but may not adequately present actual cultivated practice. The *style-books of publishers, such as the *United States Government Printing Office Style Manual* or the Associated Press *Stylebook,* give the choices their publishers have made for printed matter and should be taken into account. The history of a word or construction, in the *Oxford English Dictionary* or a history of the language, is often instructive (*\*shall—will, \*don't*), because such histories reveal that a good many of the more puristic strictures on usage are of relatively recent origin. Another source of information is the explicit or incidental comments by writers, defending their own preferences or lamenting those of others.

People's attitudes toward usages—which sometimes are not consistent with their own usage—need to be taken into account. Though *\*disinterested* is widely used in the sense of "uninterested" and is so recorded in dictionaries, many people object to it; the same is true of *\*like* as a conjunction, the construction "the *\*reason* is because," and many others. Actual use of *shall* and *will* has not materially changed in recent years, but the attitudes toward the usage have. In fact, most questions are concerned not with differences between Standard and Nonstandard English (*we was,* the *\*double negative) but with matters of *\*divided usage within Standard English. A student of usage, then, has not only to observe widely what is said and written but also to note the attitudes of people toward particular items.

And finally he has to use his judgment, based on his accumulated data. Judgments will vary somewhat, depending on the range of the individual's information and to a certain extent on his preferences in language. The best safeguard against avoidable bias is awareness of some principles of selection. (Principles of appropriateness are presented in more detail on pp. 22-31. See also *\*American and British usage, \*Divided usage, \*Mixed usage.*)

**used to** • Although the spelling *use to* comes closer than *used to* in representing what we say, the *d* is required in writing: *used to.* (See *\*-ed.*) The negative constructions *didn't use to, used not to,* etc., are common in speech but are rarely found in print. (Reference: Bryant, pp. 68-69.)

**utilize** • *Utilize* means specifically "put to use"; *use* (verb) is often preferable.

**V** • /v/ as in *very* /ver′ē/, *vivid* /viv′id/, *save* /sāv/; also spelled *ph* in *Stephen* /stē′vən/; and *f* in *of* /ov/. The letter is a variant of *u* (see *\*U*).

**Verb-adverb combinations** • In *I looked up at the top of the tree,* the verb *look* is used in its ordinary sense and is modified by the adverb *up.* In *I looked up the word in the dictionary, looked up* is a verb meaning "investigated," a meaning not explained by a literal use of the two words. Similarly a man may *break out* (literally) of jail, or *break out* with measles; he can *look after* a departing car, or *look after* the children. In each of these pairs of expressions, the first has a verb modified by an adverb in its ordinary meaning, and the second is really a different verb, with a meaning of its own, composed of two elements. These have become a single word, the parts of which can sometimes have more than one position in a sentence. Compare "I *looked up* the word in a dictionary" and "I *looked* the word *up* in a dictionary."

There are hundreds of such verb-adverb combinations in use, most of them one-syllable verbs with adverbs like *about, around, at, by, down, for, in, out, through, to, up, with.* They are widely used in General English and often give an emphatic rhythm differing from the more Formal *investigate (look into), sacrifice (give up), surrender (give up).* This pattern is now the most active way of forming new verbs in English. When the combinations develop meanings beyond what their elements imply, they are separately entered in dictionaries. (See \*Prepositions § 3b.)

**Verb forms** • See \*Verbs § 3.

**Verb stress** • See \*Noun and verb stress.

**verbal, oral** • See \*oral, verbal.

**Verbals** • The parts of a verb that function as nouns or adjectives are called *verbals. Gerunds* (or verbal nouns) are used in the function of nouns (though they may, like verbs, have a subject or object), *participles* in the function of adjectives, and *infinitives* in the functions of adjectives or nouns:

*Gerunds: Swimming* is better exercise than *rowing. Having been invited* pleased him enormously.

*Infinitives:* His only ambition was *to pass.* It was too good *to last. To have asked* for more would have wrecked the whole conference. He had plenty of money *to spend.*

*Participles:* He reached the float, *swimming* as easily as he had before he had been hurt. *Asked* to take a part, he refused at first but finally accepted. *Having been invited,* he began to make plans.

(For the various uses of verbals see \*Gerund, \*Infinitives, \*Participles.)

# Verbs •

**1.** *Verbs as a part of speech.* If we exclude *be* and the modals, all verbs can be identified by their capacity of adding to the base form (*ask, sing, tear*) the suffix *-ing*, the suffix *-s* (when the verb has as its subject a singular noun or the pronouns *he, she, it*), and the suffix *-ed* or the equivalent (but *have+s=has; have + ed = had*). *Ask,* for example, has the forms *ask, asks, asking, asked.* Some verbs use other formal devices as the equivalent of the *-ed—sing, sings, singing, sang, sung; tear, tears, tearing, tore, torn;* and *hit, hits, hitting, hit. Be* has eight forms (*be, am, is, are, was, were, being, been*); *can, may, must,* and other \*modal auxiliaries have only one or two forms. We recognize verbs by their form and sentence position even when we don't know their meaning. In *I am sure that his words will coruscate,* we know that *am, will,* and *coruscate* are verbs—*am* and *will* because we have already learned their forms, functions, and meanings, and *coruscate* because it depends on *will,* even if we have no notion of its meaning. As suggested in the first sentence of this paragraph, verbs fall into two classes, a closed one (no new ones are added) whose function is primarily grammatical, and an open one (new ones are constantly added) whose \*lexical meaning is important. In *He got hurt, got* performs the grammatical function of showing past tense and passive voice and *hurt* carries the lexical meaning.

**2.** *Typical function.* The syntactical function of verbs is typically to form the predicate of a clause or sentence—that is, to join with a subject, and perhaps an object, to form a single construction. For convenience we are using *verb* instead of some more specific word like *predicator* to indicate this function as well as to indicate the part of speech.

**3.** *Details of verb forms.* The following articles give details of the principal characteristics of verbs:

| | |
|---|---|
| \*Auxiliary verb | \*Phrasal verb |
| \*Commands and requests | \*Principal parts of verbs |
| \*Gerund | \*Progressive verb forms |
| \*Infinitives | \*Subjunctives |
| \*Linking verbs | \*Tenses of verbs |
| \*Modal auxiliaries | \*Transitive and intransitive verbs |
| \*Mood | \*Verbals |
| \*Participles | \*Voice |

**4.** *Syntax of verbs.* Besides articles on numerous particular verbs (such as \*ain't, \*be, \*do, \*can—may, \*get, \*need, \*shall—will), the following articles are especially concerned with the use of verbs in speaking and writing:

| | |
|---|---|
| \*Absolute constructions | \*Clauses |
| \*Agreement | \*Collective nouns |

| | |
|---|---|
| *Commands and requests | *Participles |
| *Conditions | *Passive verbs |
| *Dangling modifiers | *Predicate adjective |
| *Finite verbs | *Split infinitive |
| *Fragmentary sentence | *Subject and verb |
| *Function words | *Subjunctives |
| *Gerund | *Tenses of verbs |
| *Infinitives | *Verb-adverb combinations |
| *Objects | *Voice |

(References: Fries, Curme, Jespersen, and all grammars treat verbs; see especially Fries, *AEG*, Ch. 8, and Fries, *Structure*, Chs. 5-7.)

**Vernacular** • *Vernacular* as applied to English formerly referred to the native, spoken language—as opposed to the literary languages of Latin or Norman French. It now usually means Nonstandard and perhaps Informal English, the native homely, spoken language as contrasted with Formal or literary English, usually with the implication that, though inelegant, the vernacular has more vitality and force.

**Verse** • See *Capital letters § 3, *Poetry.

**Verse form** • The form of a line of verse is described by telling the arrangement of the stressed syllables (the kind of "foot"), the length of the line (the number of feet), and many other qualities of movement or variation from the typical movement that it shows. This article presents the vocabulary and an outline of the facts necessary for describing verse form.

*The feet:* *The length of lines:*

| | |
|---|---|
| *Iambic*   ∪ − (An iamb) | *Dimeter:* Two feet |
| *Trochaic*  − ∪ (A trochee) | *Trimeter:* Three feet |
| *Anapestic*  ∪∪ − (An anapest) | *Tetrameter:* Four feet |
| *Dactylic*  − ∪ ∪ (A dactyl) | *Pentameter:* Five feet |
| *Spondaic*  − − (A spondee) | *Hexameter:* Six feet |

*Other facts:*

A line is *end-stopped* if its end corresponds with a distinct sense of pause, either the end of a sentence or of a major sentence element; it is *run-on* when the construction is carried over the end of the line.

*Alexandrine*: A line containing six iambic feet

*Anacrusis*: An extra unstressed syllable at the beginning of a line

*Catalexis*: The dropping of the final unstressed syllable

*Feminine ending*: An extra unstressed syllable at the end

*Refrain*: A line repeated, typically at the end of each stanza of a poem

A *cesura* (*caesura*) is a rhythmic pause within a line.

Two successive lines rhyming are a *couplet*.

A four-line stanza is a *quatrain,* which may have any rhyme scheme: *abab, abba*; an iambic tetrameter quatrain rhyming *abcb* is the *ballad stanza.*

More complex stanza forms (sonnet, ode, ballade, and so on) are described in books on literature and poetry.

*Blank verse* is unrhymed iambic pentameter. *Free verse* is verse of varied length lines with a flexible movement, usually unrhymed.

*Examples of scansion*:

Iambic pentameter (feminine ending):

Ă thing ŏf beauty is ă joy forevĕr

Anapestic tetrameter:

Thĕre ărĕ brains, thŏugh thĕy mouldĕr, thăt dream iñ thĕ tomb

Trochaic tetrameter (catalectic), a couplet:

Souls ŏf poets dead ănd gone,

What Elysium have ye known,

These examples show that scansion tells the typical physical characteristics of verse but does not define the rhythm, which is far more important. For the more important qualities of poetry, such as imagery, tone, color, rhythm (not to mention meaning), see books on poetry and literature.

**very •**

1. *"Very" as an intensive. Very* is so much used that its intensive force is slight. A writer should make sure that it really adds to the meaning of his phrase.

The *Emporia Gazette* once described its war upon *very* this way:

"If you feel you must write 'very,' write 'damn.' " So when the urge for emphasis is on him, the reporter writes "It was a damn fine victory. I am damn tired but damn well—and damn excited." Then, because it is the Emporia (Kan.) Gazette, the copy desk deletes the profanity and the quotation reads: "It was a fine victory. I am tired but well—and excited." That's how the Gazette attains its restrained, simple, and forceful style. Very simple.

2. *"Very" and past participles.* In Formal English many people will not use *very* with a past participle (He was very ex-

cited), because *very,* now used primarily as an intensive, supposedly marks only a high degree of a *quality,* as in *very happy,* and the verb function of the participle denotes an action rather than a quality. The Formal locution would be: He was *very much* excited.

This distinction, since it is based purely on arbitrary grammatical reasoning, is too insubstantial for users of General English, who use *very* to modify such participles without any qualms (I shall be very pleased to come; We shall be very delighted to have you).

When the President and the trustees finally decided to allow the Psychology Department to sponsor a clinic, Dr. Bonham was very elated.—JAMES REID PARKER, *Academic Procession,* p. 13

**viewpoint** • *Viewpoint* is a natural and economical substitute for *point of view.* It is not stigmatized in the dictionaries.

Before we condemn him for affectation and distortion we must realize his viewpoint.—E. M. FORSTER, *Aspects of the Novel,* p. 182

**viz.** • *Viz.* is the abbreviation of the Latin *videlicet* /və del'ə- sit/, which means "to wit, namely." *Viz.* exists only in the language of rather Formal documents or reference works. It is usually read "namely." (See *namely and other introductory words.)

**Vocabulary** • See *Words.

**Voice** •
*1. Definition and forms. Voice* is a term borrowed from the grammars of the classical languages where it usually differentiates distinctive endings on verbs. In English the term *passive voice* refers to constructions made with the past participle and some form of the verb *be* (*was killed*); all other forms are *active.*

|  | Active | Passive |
|---|---|---|
| *Present:* | he (is asking) asks | he is asked (is being asked) |
| *Future:* | he will ask | he will be asked |
| *Perfect:* | he has asked | he has been asked |
| *Infinitives:* | to ask, to have asked | to be asked, to have been asked |
| *Participles:* | asking, having asked | being asked, asked |

*Get* and *become* are also used, especially in Informal English:

If he should get elected, we'd be lost.
Our house is getting painted.
They had become separated from their guide.

The traditional definition in terms of meaning is often a

useful guide in identifying active and passive verbs. When the subject of a verb is the doer of the action or is in the condition named by its verb, the verb is said to be in the active voice:

The congregation *sang* "Abide with Me."
They *will go* swimming.                 Our side *had been winning.*
Jimmy's father *gave* him a car.       We *rested* an hour.

When the subject of a verb receives the action, the verb is said to be in the passive voice:

"Abide with Me" *was sung* by the congregation.
Jimmy *was given* a car by his father.
The pit *was dug* fully eight feet deep.
They *had been caught.*

These different expressions of the verb give considerable flexibility in sentence word order. They allow the speaker or writer to emphasize by position the thing that is most important to him:

The *house* was finished by the crew in record time.
The *crew* finished the house in record time.

Or, more often, they merely allow the speaker to approach the statement from the viewpoint of his thinking about it (the *house* or the *crew,* for example, in the sentences above). The construction in English is more important as a matter of style than of grammar and is one of the devices that make it possible for one's expression to come close to his process of thought.

**2.** *Use of active verbs.* Active verbs are more common than passive because we are accustomed to the actor-action-goal pattern of expression. In the text of the preceding paragraph, for example, the seven finite verbs (*give, allow, is, allow, is, is, make*) and the three infinitives (*to emphasize, to approach, to come*) are active.

**3.** *Use of passive verbs.* Passive verbs may occur less frequently, but they have several important uses. (The frequency of the passive construction in Standard writing appears to run from a high of 13 percent in expository writing to as low as one percent in narrative. See Margaret M. Bryant, "The Passive Construction," *College English,* 1960, 21:230.)

The object, the goal, may be more important, in the writer's mind, than the doer:

The bill *was passed* without opposition.
The well *was drilled* in solid rock.
Our house *was painted* last year.

In indefinite statements the passive is often used when the actors may not be known or are not to be named in the statement:

Much *has been written* on both sides.
Many records *have been set* in past Olympics.

The passive allows various degrees of emphasis by placing the name of the act or of the doer at the end:

Our house *is being painted.* (Active: They *are painting* our house.)

Our house *was painted* by Joe Mead and his brother. (Active: Joe Mead and his brother *painted* our house.)

"Abide with Me" was sung by the choir [that is, not by the congregation].

Sometimes the passive shows a change in the relation between subject and verb (though the shift should not be made within a sentence unless the action is continuous):

We *drove* [active] there and *were taken out* [passive] in a dory.

(For discussion of the object of a passive verb, see *Objects § 1b.)

4. *Overuse of the passive.* (For the objectionable use of passive verbs when active would be more effective, see *Passive verbs.)

(References: Curme, *Syntax,* pp. 102-103; Fries, *AEG,* pp. 188-193; Jespersen, Ch. 12.)

**Voiced, voiceless sounds** • In voiced sounds the vocal cords vibrate, as in the vowels and *b, d, g, v, z* /zh/, and *th* /ᴛʜ/; *p, t, k, f, s, sh,* and *th* /th/ are the voiceless sounds corresponding to these voiced consonants. In addition there are the voiced consonants *m, n, ng, w, y, r* and the voiceless *h*; some phoneticians would add *j* (voiced) and *ch* (voiceless), though others consider these as combinations of /d/ plus /zh/ and /t/ plus /sh/.

Some nouns and verbs are distinguished by voicing of the consonant in the verb: *use* (noun, /ūs/—verb, /ūz/), *proof—prove* (noun, /prüf/—verb, /prüv/), *grief—grieve* (/grēf/—/grēv/).

A few spelling errors seem to be caused by a confusion between voicing and non-voicing, as *significance* /-kəns/ often appears as *signifigance* /-gəns/.

**Vowels** • See *Neutral vowel, *Pronunciation, *schwa.

**Vulgate English** • See *Nonstandard English.

**W** • /w/ as in *wild* /wīld/, *twinkle* /twing'kḷ/; also spelled as in *quick* /kwik/, *choir* /kwīr/. *W* is silent in *write* /rīt/, *two* /tü/, *sword* /sôrd/, and other words, and spoken though not spelled in *one* /wun/, *once* /wuns/.

The letter, as the name indicates, is two *u*'s—formerly written vv—together.

**wake** • English is oversupplied with verbs for waking from sleep (intransitive) and waking someone else from sleep (transitive); all are used in each function:

*awake* (*awaked, awaked* or *awoke, awoke*). Rather Formal; more commonly used intransitively (I *awoke*).

*awaken* (*awakened, awakened*). Formal.

*wake* (*waked* or *woke, waked* or *woke* [*woken*]). More widely used than the preceding.

*waken* (*wakened, wakened*). Less common than *wake*.

The usual solution is the *verb-adverb combination *wake up* (*waked* or *woke up*):

She waked up [woke up] at eleven. She waked [woke] me up at six.

**want** • The General idiom with *want* has an infinitive:

*General*: I want you to get all you can from the year's work.

*Local*: I want for you to get all you can from the year's work.

*Local*: I want that you should get all you can from the year's work.

*Want* is Informal for *ought, had better*: *You want to review all the notes if you're going to pass his exam.*

In the sense of *lack* or *need*, *want* is Formal and suggests British usage: *The letter, though clear, wants correcting.*

*Want in, want out* without a complementary verb (The dog wants out) seems to be of Scotch rather than German origin and is widely heard in the United States. (See Albert H. Marckwardt, "*Want* with Ellipsis of Verbs of Action," *American Speech*, 1948, 23:3-9.) *Want off* is common in the speech of some areas. (Reference: Bryant, pp. 224-225.)

**way, ways** • *Way* is Informally used for *away* (way over across the valley). *Way* is used in a number of General and Informal idioms (*in a bad way, out our way*, I don't see how she can act *the way* she does).

*Ways* is often used in speech for *way* in expressions like *a little ways down the road.*

**we** •

1. *Indefinite "we."* *We* is frequently used as an indefinite pronoun in expressions like *We find, We sometimes feel*, to avoid passive and impersonal constructions. (See *Reference of pronouns § 3.)

2. *Editorial "we."* In editorial columns and in some other regular departments of periodicals, like "The Talk of the Town" in *The New Yorker*, the writer refers to himself as *we*, which leads to the curious form *ourself*. In some instances the *we* refers to an editorial board that determines the opinions expressed but more often it is a convention. It is less used than formerly.

The usage has passed into Informal writing, especially of a light tone. Used merely to avoid *I, we* is usually conspicuous and to be avoided. (See *I § 2.)

3. *Parental "we."* *We* is used Informally in softened requests, especially to children (We won't lose our mittens, will we?). This is a more effective use than the nurse's "How are we feeling this morning?"—sometimes called the "medical *we*."

**well—good** • See *good—well.

**wh** • *wh* is the English spelling for the sound /hw/: *what* /hwot/ or /hwut/, *when* /hwen/, *wheel* /hwēl/, *whether* /hweᴛʜ'ər/, *why* /hwī/. In *who* /hü/, *whole* /hōl/, *whoop* /hüp/, *wholly* /hōl'ē/, and so on, *wh* represents /h/.

**when** • Most handbooks warn against statements like "Welding is when two pieces of metal are heated and made into one." The reason given is that it is illogical or ungrammatical to equate an "adverbial clause" with a noun. Even the reasoning is fallacious because a clause cannot be classified solely by its introductory word, and in any case usage studies show that *when* (and *where*) clauses are frequently used (1) in noun constructions, as in "Do you have any way of knowing *when she will come?*" in which the *when* clause is the object of *knowing*, and (2) as adjective modifiers, as in "There comes a time *when a man has to be careful of his diet*," in which the clause modifies *time*.

The objection to the construction is stylistic rather than grammatical and comes from the overuse of *when* clauses in amateurish definitions: *Communism is when all property is owned by all the people together or by the state.* The more Formal pattern would be: *Communism is a system in which all property is owned by all the people together or by the state.*

The construction, then, is to be used with caution rather than shunned altogether. (References: Fries, *AEG,* pp. 233-234; Marckwardt and Walcott, p. 115; Russell Thomas, *College English,* 1949, 10:406-408. Compare *reason is because.)

**when, as, and if** • Securities are advertised "when, as, and if issued," and the phrase *when and if* or *if and when* is used in talking about goods whose future is uncertain. It should not be used when the matter is certain, and is generally inappropriate in all nonbusiness contexts.

**whence** • See *where.

**where** • *Where* clauses are frequently used to modify nouns, most commonly when some notion of place is involved:

*General:* This is the place where the trucks stop.
*General:* He wants a job where he will be with people.
*More Formal:* He wants a job in which he will be with people.

*Where* clauses in definitions are subject to the same objections that *when* clauses (see *when) are—that is, they frequently sound amateurish:

*Amateurish:* Etching is where you cut lines in a copper plate and then print from them.
*General:* Etching is the process of cutting lines in a copper plate and then printing from it.

English once had *whither,* "place to which"; *whence,* "place from which." They are now rarely used, and *where* has taken their place with help from other words—always with *from* to replace *whence*; often with *to* for *whither.* This pattern of *where* plus a preposition has been completed in Nonstandard: *"Where* is he *at?"* The construction also crops up in Informal speech but not in General or Formal writing. (References: Fries, *AEG,* pp. 234-235; Marckwardt and Walcott, p. 115.)

**whether** • *Whether* is used in indirect questions: *He asked whether you could come.*

In statements *whether* is used with *or* to indicate two alternatives: *They have never decided whether he committed suicide or was murdered.*

In Formal usage *or not* is frequently used with *whether* to indicate a second alternative when it is simply the negative of the one stated (They have never decided whether or not he was murdered). But in General usage *or not* is frequently omitted (They have never decided whether he was murdered), and should not be used if it will make an awkward statement, as it often will.

*General:* Whether or not this was the best plan, they went ahead. [Or: *Whether this was the best plan or not, they went ahead.*]
*General:* It is a sorry state when pupils don't know whether or not to believe their teachers.
*Clumsy:* It is a sorry state when pupils don't know whether to believe their teachers or not [Omit the *or not*].

(Reference: Fries, *AEG,* pp. 207, 217. See \*if § 2, \*Conditions.)

**which •**
1. *Which* refers to things and to groups of people regarded impersonally (The legislature which passed the act . . .). It is no longer used in Standard English to refer to a person or persons.
2. *Which* (like *that* and *this*) frequently has as its antecedent the idea of a phrase or clause:

> Relative pronouns are as troublesome to the inexpert but conscientious writer as they are useful to everyone, *which* is saying much.
> —H. W. FOWLER, *A Dictionary of Modern English Usage,* p. 709

As with other uses of pronouns, the reference should be clear. (See *which* in *Webster's Third New International Dictionary;* Bryant, pp. 172-174; and James A. Drake, "How 'Which' Is Used in America Today," *American Speech,* 1960, 35:275-279. Compare \*this.)
3. *Whose* is often used as the genitive of *which,* instead of the more cumbersome *of which*:

> This story of the life of General Custer is *Boots and Saddles,* whose author is the General's wife.

4. *And* and *but* are carelessly used to join a *which* clause, which is subordinate, to a main statement.

> *Inaccurate*: He got the contract to install new copper work on the Post Office, and which will require 4500 pounds of lead-coated copper.
>
> *Accurate*: He got the contract to install new copper work on the Post Office, which will require 4500 pounds of lead-coated copper.

**while •** *While* most exactly is a connective of time:

> While the rest were studying, he was playing cards.

*While* also means *though* or *but,* but rather weakly:

> Magazines, newspapers, and scientific books became my chief interest, *while* [More exact: *but*] poems were still a torture to me.

*While* is occasionally used for *and*:

> The second number was an acrobatic exhibition, *while* [Better: *and*] the third was a lady trapeze artist.

*Awhile* is an adverb, written as one word: *Awhile ago.* In phrases in which *while* is a noun, the *a* should be written separate: *In a while; After a while.* (Reference: Fries, *AEG,* pp. 236-237.)

**Whitespace •** Whitespace has the function of a punctuation mark m display matter. It has now taken the place of commas and periods at the ends of lines in envelope addresses, in letter headings, in titles of books and articles, in outlines, in lines that are spaced off in advertisements, posters, etc., in matter set in tables or columns. No punctuation marks are used at the ends of lines in Formal social notes. In indented quotations whitespace has displaced the quote marks. These various uses have helped relieve the spottiness of correspondence and many printed pages.

**whither** • See *where.

**who—whom** •
1. *Antecedent of "who."* Who refers to people, to personified objects (a ship, a country), and occasionally to animals:

Diogenes Checkpoints says what is needed is a list of horses who should be out of training.—AUDAX MINOR, *The New Yorker*, Aug. 27, 1938.

*Whose* is commonly used as the genitive of *which* rather than *of which*. (Reference: Hall, pp. 320-327. See *which § 3.)
2. *"Who" versus "whom."* In 1928 the *Oxford English Dictionary* said *whom* was "no longer current in natural colloquial speech." The struggle to make writing conform to grammatical rules of case is consequently difficult and full of problems. *Whom* consistently occurs only when it immediately follows a preposition as object (I don't know to whom I should go). But since the preposition often comes last in the expression, in General usage we find *who* (I don't know who I should go to). The most important reason for the development of this usage is that we no longer depend on the form to indicate the case function (except genitive). None of the other relative pronouns show case function by form, nor do the nouns (again, except genitives); the personal pronouns are too few to keep us sensitive to case forms, and two of them (*you, it*) lack an accusative form. Three other factors combine to make this *who* construction usual: (1) the position before the verb—the "subject-territory," (2) the infrequent use of *whom* in speech, and (3) our habit of not using relative pronouns in the object function to introduce clauses (I know the man [whom] you mean).

Formal usage generally keeps the accusative form when the pronoun is used as an object:

*Formal*: Whom [object of *introduce*] do you introduce to whom [object of the immediately preceding *to*]?
*General*: Who do you introduce to whom?
*Formal*: No matter whom [object of *meets*] one meets, the first thing one mentions is the weather.

*General*: No matter who you meet, the first thing you mention is the weather.

Which you use, then, depends on the variety and tone of the particular piece of writing. In Formal and academic writing and in much General writing, *whom* is what usually gets printed in the object function; in Informal narratives and personal writing, *who* is usually appropriate when the pronoun is used as an object. The unfortunate effect of the excessive attention given to these forms is that when used as an object either one now calls attention to itself in print. Another result is that *whom* is occasionally found in subject function: The man *whom* I know was guilty was exonerated. The same problems affect *whoever*. (References: Fries, *AEG*, pp. 88-96, 237; Pooley, pp. 72-77, 221; all other descriptive grammarians.)

3. *"Who" separated from verb.* When *who* is the subject of a verb separated from it by other words, care should be taken to keep the subject form:

He made a list of all the writers who [subject of *were*] he thought were important in the period.

This construction is troublesome, probably because the speaker recognizes that *he thought* restricts *who were important*; he may make an unconscious transformation of *writers he thought were important* into *he thought them important* and turn *them* into *whom* [*whom he thought*].

4. *The number of the verb.* A verb with *who* as its subject has the number of the antecedent of the *who*:

I'm one of the few people who don't [antecedent *people*] like to read many books.

I'm one who doesn't [antecedent *one*] like to read books.

Informally there is a strong tendency to make the verb of the *who* clause agree with the principal subject, which would give *doesn't* in the first sentence above. This is avoided in careful writing. (See *one of those who.)

**whose** • See *which.

**-wise** • This suffix has long had a limited currency in forming adverbs from nouns (*edgewise, lengthwise, slantwise*). Recently it has greatly increased in use, especially in an abstract rather than a spatial sense: *average-wise, budget-wise, legislation-wise, tax-wise.* (It is usually hyphened in these new formations.)

This use of *-wise* occurs chiefly in commercial, journalistic, and political contexts; it carries the connotation of jargon as well as of faddish overuse and hence is inappropriate to college writing in spite of some advantages in economy (*economy-wise*).

**with** • There is a temptation to use *with* when another preposition or a different construction would be more accurate:

Our outfit was composed of two platoons *with* [Better: *of*] 43 men each.

I'll never forget the farmer who, not seeing the wave, tried to get his few cows to safety and was washed away *with* [Better: *by*] the water.

Americans believe in freedom, but with Germans it is different [Or: *but Germans are different*].

**without** • Nonstandard for *unless*.

I won't go without you do.

**woman** • *Woman* is the singular form, *women* the plural. Notice that in the spelling only one letter is altered from singular to plural; in the pronunciation, both syllables have changed vowels. (See also *man, woman.)

**Wordiness** •
*Revision: Compress this passage by replacing the wordy expressions with more compact and exact ones.*                 Wdy

The use of unnecessary words in conveying one's ideas results in flabby writing. The commonest types of wordiness are:

1. *Circumlocution*—the use of several words instead of one exact word:

destroyed by fire often means *burned up* or *burned down*
come in contact with usually means *meet* or *know*
the necessary funds usually means no more than *the money*
in this day and age means *today*
the sort of metal they use for plating the shiny parts of automobiles might mean *chromium*

2. *Long function words*—function phrases that might be replaced by one or by fewer words:

During the time that [*while*] she was in Los Angeles she had at least six different jobs.

(See *Function words § 2.)

3. *Deadwood*—words which add nothing to the meaning:

The cars are neat and graceful [in appearance].
In the majority of cases they do not. [For: *The majority do not.*]
It was the first time [in my life] I had seen Niagara Falls.

The home of my boyfriend was in a town called Hillsdale. [For: *My boyfriend's home was in Hillsdale.*]

**4.** *Formless, fuzzy writing:*

| *Wordy* | *Revised* |
|---|---|
| It has some of the best ski trails in the country and as far as the other cold weather sports are concerned, they have them too, along with one of the most fashionable hotels in the country. | They have a very fashionable hotel, all the cold weather sports, and some of the best ski trails in the country. |

(See \*case, \*Deadwood, \*Passive verbs, \*seem, \*there is, there are.)

**Word order •**

WO

> *Revision: Change the order of words or other elements so that the meaning is clearer, or the sentence is more natural or more effective.*

The order of words and of other locutions in a sentence is the most important device of English grammar to show the relations of words in sentences. It plays a large part in style, especially emphasis. The work done in many languages by inflections (endings) is in English performed largely by \*function words (prepositions, auxiliary verbs, and so on—whose function is made clear by their position) and by the word order. Since we pick up the standard word order as we learn to talk, it offers little difficulty. We use the subject-verb-object order of clauses and sentences; we put adjectives before their nouns and relative clauses after their nouns and in general put modifiers near the words modified.

This article is intended to bring the fact of word order to your attention rather than to cover its enormous number of details.

**1.** *Position changed for emphasis.* As a rule an element taken out of its usual position receives increased emphasis, as when the object is put before both subject and verb:

*Object first:* That book I read when I was sixteen. (Instead of: *I read that book when I was sixteen.*)

*Predicate adjective first:* Lucky are the ones who register early. (Instead of: *The ones who register early are lucky.*)

**2.** *Interrupted constructions.* When a word or words interrupt a construction, the effect is usually unhappy unless the interrupting word deserves special emphasis:

*Between subject and verb*: Newspaper headlines in these trying and confused times are continually intensifying the fears of the American people. [More natural: In these trying and confused times newspaper headlines are. . . .]
*Between verb and adverb*: He played quietly, efficiently on. He took a pack from his pocket and she took one thoughtfully out. (More·natural: He played on, quietly, efficiently. He took a pack from his pocket and she took one out thoughtfully [or: and she thoughtfully took one out].)

(See *Split infinitive.)

**3.** *Misleading word order.* English usually has a modifier close to the word modified and care must be taken that modifiers separated from their main words do not mislead the reader.

| *Misleading* | *Improved* |
|---|---|
| I wish to order one of the machines which I saw advertised in *The Saturday Evening Post* sent to the above address. | I wish to order sent to the above address one of the machines which I saw advertised in *The Saturday Evening Post.* |
| Her uncle, King Leopold, was even unable to influence her. | Even her uncle, King Leopold, was unable to influence her. |
| This success in villages will probably be duplicated in the cities as time goes on at an accelerated rate. | As time goes on, this success in villages will probably be duplicated at an accelerated rate in cities. |
| Until recently the chains have been able to get special prices on the goods they buy from producers with little opposition. | Until recently the chains have been able to get with little opposition special prices on the goods they buy from producers. |

(See *Ambiguity § 2. References: Margaret M. Bryant, *College English*, 1944, 5:434-438; Fries, *AEG*, Ch. 10; Curme, *Syntax*, Ch. 17; C. Alphonso Smith, *Studies in English Syntax*, Boston, 1906, Ch. 2.)

**Words** • The framework for the treatment of words and word usage in this book is provided by the opening section, "The varieties of English," pp. 2-31. Many specific words that are likely to raise problems have articles of their own (for instance, *contact, *drunk, *hope, *however, *notorious). Articles containing general discussions about words and their uses include:

| | |
|---|---|
| *Abstract and concrete words | *Antonym |
| | *Compound words |

*Concrete words
*Context
*Contractions
*Counter words
*Division of words
*Double negative
*Ellipsis
*Euphemisms
*Foreign words
   in English
*Function words
*Gobbledygook
*Group-words
*Headword
*Homonyms
*Hyphen
*Idiom and idioms

*Linguistics
*Localisms
*Meaning
*namely and other
   introductory words
*Origin of words
*Phrases
*Pronunciation
*Repetition
*Shoptalk
*Slang
*Spelling
*Style
*Suggestion
*Underlining
*Usage
*Wordiness

**worthwhile** • *Worthwhile* is now usually written as one word, occasionally hyphened, rarely as two words.

**would—should** • See *should—would.

**would have, would of** • See *have § 3.

**writ large** • The phrase is "bookish" (see *literary).

**Written English** • See *Spoken and written English. See also *Experiments in written English, *Factual and imaginative writing, *Style.

**Wrong word** •

WW    *Revision: Replace the word marked with one that says what you mean.*

No word is right or wrong in itself. As used here, "wrong word" means that the word does not convey a meaning that makes sense in the context. In this sentence, *comprehensibility* does not make sense: *What he said showed real comprehensibility of the problems in Asia.* The writer probably meant *comprehension.* Errors like this occur when the writer is attempting to use a vocabulary in which he is not at home, when he confuses words of similar sound, or when he simply writes too hurriedly and fails to proofread his work before turning it in. (See *Carelessness.)

**X** • is an unnecessary letter in English. It spells several sounds transcribed phoneticaly as /ks/ as in *fox* /foks/, *exclusive* /eks klü′siv/, *exceed* /ik sēd′/; /gz/ as in *exist* /ig zist′/, *exhibit* /ig zib′it/; /ksh/ as in *luxury* /luk′shə rē/; /gzh/ as in *luxurious* /lug zhŭr′ē əs/ or /luk shŭr′i əs/; /z/ as in *xylophone, Xantippe, Xavier* (not /eks zā′viər/). In British usage *ct* is sometimes spelled *x* as in *inflexion*; and in this country *cks* is spelled *x* for the baseball teams *White Sox* and *Red Sox*.

A correction symbol indicating a careless mistake. (See *Carelessness.)     X

**Xmas** • *Xmas* is an Informal word seen chiefly in advertising; it is pronounced like *Christmas,* for which it stands. The *X* is from the initial letter of the Greek spelling of *Christ.*

**X-ray** • *X-ray* is hyphened as a verb and noun; also printed *X ray* as a noun. It is usually capitalized, though as a verb it is sometimes not.

**Y** • /y/ as in *yes* /yes/, *beyond* /bi yond′/. *Y* also spells /ī/ and /ē/, as in *sky* /skī/, *bloody* /blud′ē/.

A final *y* following a consonant is changed to *i* before a suffix beginning with a vowel except *i*: *duty—dutiable, try—tries, body—bodies, bodied*; but *play—played, playing, playable, fly—flying*.

**ye = the** • In Old English the sound of *th* in *thin* was repre-
sented by the letter thorn, **þ** . In early printing the letter *y,* which in the type fonts of the time looked most like the thorn, was used to represent it. Consequently we find *ye* (*the*), *yat* (*that*), *yem* (*them*) in early books, and even oftener find the forms in manuscript down to about 1800.

This *y* then represents *th* and is pronounced like *th*. Its use in recent faking of antiquity has not changed this fact: *Ye Olde Coffee Shoppe* is just *The Old Coffee Shop* and should presumably be so pronounced, though there is no telling what pronunciation the proprietor intended.

**ye = you** • *Ye,* originally the nominative plural and then also the nominative singular of the second person pronoun (now *you*), survived for a long time in poetry and other literature with a tendency to be archaic (sermons, florid oratory). It is now obsolete in writing, though the unstressed pronunciation of *you* ("whad ya think?") is probably much like what *ye* used to represent.

**yes** • *Yes* and *no* are labeled *adverbs* in dictionaries. They may modify a sentence (Yes, you're right) or may have the value of a coordinate clause (No; but you should have told me) or may stand as complete sentences. ("Do you really intend to go with him?" "Yes.")

*Yes* and *no* have variants in speech, where there are innumerable substitutes, from *ye-us* to *yop* and the "colloquial nasals," for which there are no satisfactory spellings (*uh-huh, huh-uh, humph, eh,* etc.), not to mention the current slang affirmatives and the longer lived ones like *OK. (See *sure.)

**yet** • *Yet* is an adverb (The books haven't come yet); it is also used as a *coordinating conjunction, equivalent to *but*:

His speech was almost unintelligible, yet for some unknown reason I enjoyed it.

**you** • *You* is used as a pronoun of indefinite reference (It's a good book, if you like detective stories) in General writing. Formal English would more often use *one,* though the prejudice against *you* is declining. (See *one, *they.)

When *you* is used in an Informal approach to readers or to an audience, it sometimes may be unintentionally personal (or even insulting) or seem to indicate an invidious distinction between writer and reader (Take, for instance, *your* [better: *our* or *one's*] family problems). In speech the indefinite *you* is distinguished from the personal *you* by the reduced stress on it.

**you all** • In Southern American *you all,* contracted to *y'all,* is frequently used as the plural of *you,* as in some other regions *you folks* is used. It is also used when addressing one person regarded as one of a group, usually a family. It is sometimes asserted that *you all* is also used as a singular, addressing one. (See *American Speech,* especially volumes 2 and 4.)

There are at least three current locutions that attempt to remedy the lack of distinction between second person singular and plural in English: *youse, you'uns,* and *you all.* Only *you all* has achieved respectability. (References: Mencken, pp. 543, 545-549; George P. Wilson, "You All," *Georgia Review,* 1960, 14:38-54.)

**your—you're** • In revision, check for careless confusion in the transcription of these words. *Your* is a possessive pronoun (your books); *you're* is a subject and verb (You're all right).

**youth** • *Youth* is overused in the sense of "young people" and suggests a ministerial style.

**you was, you is** • *You was* and *you is* are Nonstandard.

**youngster, child, kid** • See *kid.

**Z** • /z/ as in *Zion* /zī'ən/, *buzz* /buz/, *busy* /biz'ē/, *shoes* /shüz/. The sound is also spelled *s* as in *desire, x* as in *anxiety, ss* as in *scissors*.

**zh** • The phonetic symbol representing the sound in *rouge* /rüzh/, *measure* /mezh'ər/, and so on. (See *G § 3.)

**&** • See *Ampersand.

A "correction symbol" expressing approval of the idea or style. ✓

# Symbols for marking papers

To the student: These revision symbols cover the common errors in composition. When you find one marked on your paper, look up the page where the error is discussed and make the suggested revision. A ring around words or phrases in your paper indicates that there are *Index* articles for them which you should consult.

Id   Expression marked is not *idiomatic*, 213

Inf  Word or passage is too *Informal* for subject or style of the paper, 225

*lc*   Use a *lower case* ("small") letter here, 252

Local   Replace *localism* with word or expression in General use, 242

Logic   Reëxamine and revise the *logical* relationship that is expressed or implied, 249

Mng   Replace word, phrase, or sentence with one that conveys the *meaning* you intend, 255

MS   Revise *manuscript* form, 254

NS   Change *Nonstandard* word, form, or idiom to one in Standard usage, 266

Num   Mistake in use of *numbers*, 269

Org   Improve the *organization* of your paper and/or correct the form of your outline, 279

¶, No¶   Change *paragraphing*, either by making new paragraph, or by joining present paragraph to preceding one, 289

P.Adj   Follow linking verb with a *predicate adjective*, 313

Par   *Paragraph* unsatisfactory, 289

Paral   Make elements *parallel* in form, 290

Pass   Change the *passive* verb or verbs to active, 298

Pn, No Pn   Mistake in *punctuation*, 334

Prep   Change *preposition* so that it is more exact or idiomatic, less conspicuous, or less Informal, 314

Prin   (*Principal parts of verbs*) Change verb form to one in good use, 320

Pron   Change form of the *pronoun* marked, 324

Ques   *Question mark* needed, 336

Quot   Mistake in use of *quotation marks*, 338

Ref   Change pronoun marked so that its *reference* will be exact and obvious and the pronoun itself will be in the conventional form, 345

Rep   Revise to remove ineffective *repetition* of word, meaning, or sound, 363

Rest   Revise punctuation of modifier by deleting commas if it is *restrictive*, inserting commas if it is *nonrestrictive*, 365

S   Correct the fault in the *sentence* marked, 377

Semi   *Semicolon* needed here, 374

Shift   (*Shifted constructions*) Make the marked constructions consistent, 381

Sp   Mistake in *spelling*, 390

Sub   Revise the faulty *subordination*, 419

Tense   Revise *tense* of verb, 424

Trans   Make the *transition* clear and smooth, 436

Trite   Replace *trite* expression with one that is simpler or fresher, 438

Und   *Underline* to indicate italics, 441

Wdy   Replace *wordy* expressions with more compact and exact ones, 461

WO   Change *word order* for clarity, naturalness, emphasis, or effectiveness, 462

WW   Replace this *wrong word* with one that says what you mean, 464

X   *Careless* mistake, 465

✓   Good—not just competent—in thought or style or both

# Acknowledgments

The authors gratefully acknowledge the kindness of authors and publishers in giving permission to reproduce their materials in *An Index to English*. Where the territory rights are divided among various publishers, the acknowledgment states what permission was granted. An unqualified acknowledgment indicates that world permission was granted.

Appleton-Century-Crofts: selections from *American English Grammar* by Charles Carpenter Fries, copyright 1940. The National Council of Teachers of English and Charles C. Fries; reprinted by permission of Appleton-Century-Crofts.

Brandt & Brandt: selection from *John Brown's Body* by Stephen Vincent Benét, published by Farrar & Rinehart, Inc.; copyright 1927, 1928 by Stephen Vincent Benét.

Cambridge University Press: selection from *The Universe Around Us* by Sir James Jeans.

Jonathan Cape, Ltd.: British Empire except Canada for selection from *Green Hills of Africa* by Ernest Hemingway.

Malcolm Cowley: selection from *Exile's Return* by Malcolm Cowley.

Curtis Brown Ltd.: selection from "The Blushing Bride" in *I Know What I Like* by Georgina Coleridge, copyright 1959 by Chatto & Windus Ltd.; copyright 1963 by Georgina Coleridge; reprinted by permission of the author. World exclusive of the United States and Canada for selection from *Hard Lines* by Ogden Nash; copyright 1931 by Ogden Nash, reprinted by permission of Little, Brown and Company and the author.

J. M. Dent & Sons Ltd.: selection from "The Lagoon" in *Tales of Unrest* by Joseph Conrad, copyright 1898, 1920 by Doubleday & Company, Inc.

Duell, Sloan & Pearce, Inc.: selection from *Virgin Spain* by Waldo Frank, copyright 1926, 1942 by Waldo Frank.

Faber and Faber, Ltd.: world exclusive of the United States for selection from "Gerontion" by T. S. Eliot.

Allan Ferguson: selection from "The Scientist's Need for New Words" by Allan Ferguson in *The Listener*, April 21, 1937.

C. C. Fries: selections from *What Is Good English?* by C. C. Fries.

Harcourt, Brace & World, Inc.: selections from *Poems 1923-1954* by E. E. Cummings, 1954; reprinted by permission of the publishers, Harcourt, Brace & World, Inc.; *The Road to Wigan Pier* by George Orwell.

George G. Harrap & Co., Ltd.: selection by E. N. da C. Andrade from *Physics for the Modern World;* additional credit to Barnes and Noble, Inc.

Holt, Rinehart & Winston, Inc.: from "On Looking Up by Chance at the Constellations" from *Complete Poems of Robert Frost,* copyright 1928 by Holt, Rinehart & Winston, Inc.; copyright renewed © 1956 by Robert Frost; reprinted by permission of Holt, Rinehart & Winston, Inc.

Alfred A. Knopf, Inc.: selection from *Poems* by Rex Warner.

Little, Brown and Company: United States and Canada for selection from *Hard Lines* by Ogden Nash, copyright 1931 by Ogden Nash; reprinted by permission of Little, Brown and Company and the author. Selection from *Teacher in America* by Jacques Barzun.

McGraw-Hill Book Company: selection from *Propaganda and the News* by Will Irwin, copyright 1936; courtesy of McGraw-Hill Book Company, New York.

New American Library of World Literature, Inc. (Mentor Books): selection from *Christopher Columbus, Mariner* by Samuel Eliot Morison.

*The New Yorker:* selection from article by Meyer Berger, November 26, 1938.

Oxford University Press, Inc.: selections from *American English* by Albert H. Marckwardt; *The Uses of the Past* by Herbert J. Muller.

Prentice-Hall, Inc.: selection reprinted with permission of Prentice-Hall, Inc., from *The Open Self* by Charles Morris, © 1958 by Prentice-Hall, Inc., Englewood Cliffs, New Jersey; published by Prentice-Hall, Inc.

Charles Scribner's Sons: selection from "Haircut" in *Roundup* by Ring Lardner. World exclusive of the British Empire for selection from *Green Hills of Africa* by Ernest Hemingway.

*Soil Science:* selection from "Interpretive Soil Classification: Timber, Range, and Watershed" by Robert A. Gardner and John L. Retzer, 1949; published by The Williams and Wilkins Co.

*The Times Literary Supplement:* selection from "The Language of Scholarship"; reprinted by permission from *The Times Literary Supplement,* August 17, 1956, The Times Publishing Company, Limited.

United Feature Syndicate: selection from "Candle Is Remarkable Invention" by Inez Robb, printed in Seattle *Post-Intelligencer,* February 6, 1954.

University of Chicago Press: "Proofreader's Marks" reprinted from *A Manual of Style,* 11th ed. copyright 1949 by permission of The University of Chicago.

Vanguard Press, Inc.: selection from *Representative Opinions of Mr. Justice Holmes,* edited by Alfred Lief.

The Viking Press, Inc.: selection from "The Squirt and the Monkey" in *Triple Jeopardy* by Rex Stout, copyright 1957.

John Wiley & Sons, Inc.: selections reprinted by permission from *Shore Processes and Shoreline Development* by Douglas W. Johnson and from *Theories of Perception and the Concept of Structure* by Floyd H. Allport, published by John Wiley & Sons, Inc.

Yale University Press: selection from *Sweden: The Middle Way* by Marquis W. Childs.